THE ROUTLEDGE HANDBOOK OF GLOBAL PUBLIC POLICY AND ADMINISTRATION

The Routledge Handbook of Global Public Policy and Administration is a comprehensive leading-edge guide for students, scholars and practitioners of public policy and administration. Public policy and administration are key aspects of modern societies that affect the daily lives of all citizens. This handbook examines current trends and reforms in public policy and administration, such as financial regulation, risk management, public health, e-government and many others at the local, national and international levels. The two themes of the book are that public policy and administration have acquired an important global aspect, and that a critical role for government is the regulation of capital.

The handbook is organized into three thematic sections – Contemporary Challenges, Policy and Administration Responses and Forging a Resilient Public Administration – to allow readers to quickly access knowledge and improve their understanding of topics. The opening chapter, introductions to sections and extensive glossary aid readers to most effectively learn from the book. Each chapter of the book provides a balanced overview of current knowledge, identifying issues and discussing relevant debates. The book is written by authors from Europe, Asia, North and South America, Africa and Australia.

Thomas R. Klassen is Professor in the School of Public Policy and Administration, and in the Department of Political Science, at York University, Toronto, Canada. He has written widely on public policy topics.

Denita Cepiku is Professor of Public Management in the Department of Management and Law at the University of Rome "Tor Vergata", Italy. She is a board member of the International Research Society for Public Management and Chair of the Public and Non-Profit special interest group of the European Academy of Management. Her research interests are in the areas of network management and strategic performance management in the public sector.

T. J. Lah is Professor in the Department of Public Administration at Yonsei University, South Korea. His major research interests lie in public management, sustainability and environmental policy.

THE ROUTLEDGE HANDBOOK OF GLOBAL PUBLIC POLICY AND ADMINISTRATION

Edited by Thomas R. Klassen, Denita Cepiku and T. J. Lah

Routledge
Taylor & Francis Group

LONDON AND NEW YORK

First published 2017 by Routledge

2 Park Square, Milton Park, Abingdon, Oxfordshire OX14 4RN

52 Vanderbilt Avenue, New York, NY 10017

Routledge is an imprint of the Taylor & Francis Group, an informa business

First issued in paperback 2019

British Library Cataloguing in Publication Data
A catalogue record for this book is available from the British Library

Library of Congress Cataloging in Publication Data
Names: Klassen, Thomas Richard, 1957- editor. | Cepiku, Denita, editor. | Lah, T. J.
Title: The Routledge handbook of global public policy and administration / edited by Thomas R. Klassen, Denita Cepiku and T.J. Lah.
Other titles: Handbook of global public policy and administration
Description: Abingdon, Oxon ; New York, NY : Routledge, 2017. | Includes bibliographical references and index.
Identifiers: LCCN 2016013658| ISBN 9781138845220 (hardback) | ISBN 9781315710020 (ebook)
Subjects: LCSH: Public administration. | Political planning. | Globalization--Political aspects.
Classification: LCC JF1351 .R59 2017 | DDC 320.6--dc23
LC record available at https://lccn.loc.gov/2016013658

ISBN: 978-1-138-84522-0 (hbk)
ISBN: 978-0-367-35263-9 (pbk)

Typeset in Bembo
by Saxon Graphics Ltd, Derby

To our families

This work was supported by a National Research Foundation of Korea grant funded by the Korean Government (NRF-2014S1A3A2044630).

CONTENTS

Contents

FIGURES

TABLES

CONTRIBUTORS

John Alford is Professor of Public Sector Management at the Melbourne Business School, University of Melbourne. His research focuses on strategic management in the public sector, contracting and partnering, tackling wicked problems, and client–organization relationships.

Stephen J. Bailey is Emeritus Professor in Public Sector Economics at Glasgow Caledonian University, Scotland. He has published widely on topics dealing with public finance, as well as having undertaken work for government departments and international organizations.

Tony Bovaird is Emeritus Professor of Public Management and Governance at the University of Birmingham, United Kingdom, and Director of Governance International. His research interests include strategic management of public services, performance management in public agencies, and the evaluation of governance reforms. He is co-editor of *Public Management and Governance* (Routledge, 3rd edition, 2015).

Denita Cepiku is Professor of Public Management in the Department of Management and Law at the University of Rome "Tor Vergata", Italy. She is a board member of the International Research Society for Public Management and Chair of the Public and Non-Profit special interest group of the European Academy of Management. Her research interests are in the areas of network management and strategic performance management in the public sector.

Peter T. Y. Cheung is Associate Professor in the Department of Politics and Public Administration at the University of Hong Kong. His research focuses on the relations between Beijing and the Hong Kong Special Administrative Region, and the management of cross-boundary issues in south China.

Yoon Jik Cho is Associate Professor in the Department of Public Administration at Yonsei University, South Korea. His research areas are public management, organizational behavior, human resource management, and non-profit management.

Alexander Dawoody is Associate Professor and Director of the Master of Public Administration program at Marywood University, United States. His research interests include complexity and systems studies, Middle Eastern studies, foreign policy and national security studies. He is the Founding President of the Association for Middle Eastern Public Policy and Administration as well as the founder of two sections on complexity and Middle Eastern studies at the American Society for Public Administration.

Fatih Demiroz is Assistant Professor in the Department of Political Science at Sam Houston State University, United States. His research interests are inter-organizational networks, governance, and emergency management and homeland security.

Giulia Di Pierro is Senior Officer in the Department of Technical Cooperation at the European Bank for Reconstruction and Development. She has a Bachelor degree in Economics, a Master of Science degree in Business Administration and a postgraduate degree in International Public Procurement Management. Her main research interests include European Union and public procurement.

Marianna Elmi holds a PhD in Public Management and Governance at the University of Rome "Tor Vergata", where she is part of a research group on network management. Her main research interests are on network governance, especially in the context of natural and cultural heritage, protected areas and sustainable tourism.

Sarah-Sophie Flemig is an Early Career Fellow in Service Management in the University of Edinburgh Business School, Scotland. Her research interests centre on the intersection between law and political science, public policy, and innovation and change.

Masa Higo is Professor of Sociology and Social Gerontology at Kyushu University, Japan. His research focuses on the roles of population aging and economic globalization in creating and reproducing risks and inequalities in later life.

Alessandro Hinna is Professor in the Department of Management and Law at the University of Rome "Tor Vergata". He is Chair of the Organization Behaviour special interest group of the European Academy of Management, and editor of Studies in Public and Non-Profit Governance (Book Series), for Emerald Group Publishing Limited. His research interests include organization design, human resources management, and public management.

Graeme Hodge is Professor in the Faculty of Law at Monash University, Australia. He publishes on the privatisation of public sector enterprise, outsourcing/contracting-out government services, public–private partnerships and performance measurement and strategy in the public sector.

Michael Howlett is Professor in the Department of Political Science at Simon Fraser University, Canada, and in the Lee Kuan Yew School of Public Policy at the National University of Singapore. He specializes in public policy analysis, political economy, and resource and environmental policy.

Owen E. Hughes is Dean of Students and Professor at the Royal Melbourne Institute of Technology, Australia. He has published widely in management, public management, public policy and Australian politics.

Yijia Jing is a professor in public administration at the School of International Relations and Public Affairs at Fudan University, China. He is editor-in-chief of the *Fudan Public Administration Review*, associate editor of the *Public Administration Review*, and co-editor of the *International Public Management Journal*. He is the founding co-editor of the Palgrave book series, *Governing China in the 21st Century*.

Paul Joyce is an Associate at the Institute of Local Government Studies, University of Birmingham, UK, an Affiliated Researcher in the Department of Public Management at the Solvay Brussels School of Economics and Management, Belgium, and Visiting Professor at Leeds Beckett University, UK. His research interests include leadership, strategic management and modernization of the public sector.

Claire Kaiser is a Research Fellow at the Center of Competence for Public Management at the University of Bern, Switzerland. In 2013, she was a Visiting PhD Researcher at Queen Mary University of London.

Naim Kapucu is Professor in the School of Public Administration at the University of Central Florida, United States. His research interests include collaborative public management, network leadership and governance, and emergency and crisis management.

Thomas R. Klassen is Professor in the School of Public Policy and Administration, and in the Department of Political Science, at York University, Canada. He has written widely on public policy topics.

T. J. Lah is Professor in the Department of Public Administration at Yonsei University, South Korea. His major research interests lie in public management, sustainability and environmental policy.

Jenny M. Lewis is Professor of Public Policy at the University of Melbourne and an Australian Research Council Future Fellow from 2013 to 2016. She has published widely on policy influence, governance and the policy process and is currently working on the debate surrounding performance measurement.

Cheol Liu is Assistant Professor at the KDI School of Public Policy and Management in South Korea. His research interests are the fiscal health of governments, the impact of corruption on economic, political and administrative variables, and reforms in the public budgeting process.

Heather McKeen–Edwards is Associate Professor in the Department of Politics and International Studies at Bishop's University in Quebec, Canada. Her research interests revolve around global political economy and financial services policy and regulation.

Eduardo Missoni is Adjunct Professor at the Department of Policy Analysis and Public Management at Bocconi University, and at the Department of Sociology of the Milano-Bicocca University, in Milan, Italy, and at the Geneva School of Diplomacy, Switzerland. His research activities include the management of international institutions and non-profit organizations, as well as global-health-related management and policy-making. The academic activity is based on his decades-long experience as an adviser to the Italian Ministry of Foreign Affairs, a UNICEF officer, and a medical volunteer in international development cooperation.

M. Jae Moon is Underwood Distinguished Professor of Public Administration at Yonsei University, South Korea. He is an elected Fellow of the National Academy of Public Administration and International Director of the American Society for Public Administration, and he also chairs the Section of Korean Public Administration. His research interests include e-government, public management, information technology and development administration.

Riccardo Mussari is Professor in the Department of Business and Law at the University of Siena, Italy. His research interests are in public sector management and accounting, program evaluation and performance measurement.

Oliver Neumann is a doctoral researcher in business administration in the Center of Competence for Public Management at the University of Bern, Switzerland, where his interests include employee motivation, person–job fit, prospect theory, and big data and statistical modelling. He received his bachelor's degree from the University of Mannheim, Germany, and completed his master's degree at the University of Konstanz, Germany, and at York University in Toronto, Canada.

Edoardo Ongaro is a Professor of International Public Services Management at Northumbria University in the United Kingdom. He is currently serving as the President of the European Group for Public Administration and editor of *Public Policy and Administration*. His research is focused on the comparative analysis of public management reform, encompassing both national and supranational polities.

Stephen Osborne is Professor of International Public Management and Director of the Centre for Service Excellence in the University of Edinburgh Business School, Scotland. His research interests include public management reform, third sector management, services management, public policy, innovation and change.

Joshua L. Osowski is a doctoral student at the School of Public Affairs and Administration, Rutgers University–Newark. He also works for the New Jersey State Park Service and is the Superintendent of Stokes State Forest.

Sanjay K. Pandey is Professor of Public Policy and Public Administration at the George Washington University, United States. His research focuses on public management and deals with questions central to leading and managing public organizations.

Alketa Peci is Professor at the Brazilian School of Public and Business Administration. Her research interests include regulation, public sector reforms, organizational theory, social fields and discourse analysis.

Gustavo Piga is Professor of Economics at the University of Rome "Tor Vergata", where he chairs the International Master's in Public Procurement Management. He has published extensively on public procurement, macroeconomics and public debt management.

Barry Quirk is the Chief Executive of the London Borough of Lewisham, United Kingdom. He specializes in urban change and social policy in London, and is an advisor to many cities and counties across the UK on effective corporate governance and management arrangements.

M. Ramesh is Professor at the Lee Kuan Yew School of Public Policy in the National University of Singapore. He specializes in research on public policy and governance in Asia with a particular focus on social policy.

Adrian Ritz is Professor of Public Management at the University of Bern, Switzerland. His main research areas are in the field of public management, leadership, motivation and human resources management, administrative reforms, evaluation and performance management.

Ian Roberge is an Associate Professor of Political Science at Glendon College, York University in Toronto, Ontario. He specializes in public administration and public policy, and, among other topics, conducts research on financial services sector policy and regulation.

Carina Schmitt is an Associate Professor at the Research Center on Inequality and Social Policy at the University of Bremen in Germany. She was previously a John F. Kennedy Memorial Fellow at Harvard University. Her research interests are in comparative political economy and comparative welfare states.

Robert P. Shepherd is Associate Professor in the School of Public Policy and Administration at Carleton University, in Ottawa, Canada. His research interests lie mainly in the areas of public management, program evaluation, ethics and public service reform, mainly in Westminster countries. He is currently interested in comparative approaches to lobbying regulation, whistleblowing and managing public service ethics programs.

Reto Steiner is Professor at the Center of Competence for Public Management at University of Bern, Switzerland. His main areas of research are organizational design and change, local and regional governance, public corporate governance, and public management.

Christopher Stoney is Associate Professor in the School of Public Policy and Administration at Carleton University, Canada. His current research includes public–private partnerships, transparency and accountability, and citizen engagement.

Christopher Tapscott is Professor in the School of Government at the University of Western Cape, South Africa. His current research focus is on the local state and on the political and administrative challenges in the delivery of public services in countries of the global South.

Lori Turnbull is Associate Professor in the Department of Political Science at Dalhousie University, Canada. Her major areas of research are parliamentary governance, political ethics, elections, electoral systems and public engagement.

Wouter Vandenabeele is Assistant Professor in Human Resources Management at Utrecht University, the Netherlands. His field of expertise is human resource management in the public sector.

ACKNOWLEDGEMENTS

This work represents the efforts of many individuals, foremost the 43 distinguished scholars, teachers, researchers, practitioners and experts from around the world who wrote the chapters that comprise this handbook. We are most grateful for their enthusiasm and willingness to share their knowledge, expertise and insights. Indeed, we estimate that as a group, the authors have approximately one thousand years of know-how and wisdom in their respective fields, which is showcased in the book you now hold in your hands or see on your screen.

We are also most grateful for the support we received from Yongling Lam, Commissioning Editor at Routledge, and her assistants Aletheia Heah and Samantha Phua. Their advice and assistance was crucial in bringing this book to print, as was their positive attitude when obstacles arose. We thank Daniel Bourner and Alaina Christensen, production editors at Taylor & Francis, and their team, especially Katia Houghton who expertly copyedited the volume, for their wonderful job in shaping the beautiful final product. The Routledge graphic designers are to be commended on the cover image which perfectly captures the global theme of this book. Finally, we thank Terry Clague, senior publisher at Taylor & Francis, for suggesting that the focus of this book be explicitly global.

We are also indebted to our research assistants who supported us at different stages of this project. Haneul Choi, an MA student in the Department of Public Administration at Yonsei University (in South Korea), played an important role in the early stages of the preparation of this volume. Do Yun Kim, a doctoral student in the same department, was instrumental in formatting the chapters and ensuring the style guide was correctly applied to the manuscript.

We are thankful to Yonsei University and York University (in Canada) for providing funding that allowed us to organize an international symposium in August 2014 in Seoul. This event was an opportunity for some of the contributors from Africa, Asia, Europe and North America to meet and to help shape the final product. We acknowledge the helpful comments on the contents of the handbook from Professors Teresita Cruz-del Rosario, Filippo Giordano and John Walsh at the symposium.

Generous funding was also received from the SSK International Regimes and State Capacities team to allow the last phases of the project to be completed. In that regard we thank Professor M. Jae Moon and his team. We are grateful to Professor Greg Sharzer, from the School of Global Communication at Kyung Hee University in South Korea, who expertly copy-edited many of the chapters in this volume. We also acknowledge the generous financial assistance from the Faculty of Liberal Arts and Professional Studies at York University that helped at different stages of the writing and production process.

The anonymous reviewers – who have on two separate occasions reviewed the manuscript and provided valuable suggestions and critique – strengthened the final work. Reviewers, especially anonymous ones, have a critical role in scholarly publications, but are rarely accorded sufficient recognition. As such, we do want them to know that the time they invested resulted in a clearer and improved final product.

The co-editors also thank their respective departments and institutions, and especially the colleagues within those for providing the necessary resources and support to undertake their role in this project. Klassen received financial support from the Faculty of Liberal Arts & Professional Studies at York University via its Grants for International Collaboration. He is also thankful to his colleagues in the School of Public Policy and Administration at York University who inspired his interest in the teaching of public policy and administration. Lastly, Klassen is deeply indebted to the Department of Public Administration at Yonsei University who hosted him as Visiting Professor during 2014–2016.

Cepiku is thankful to Professor Marco Meneguzzo for arousing, a long time ago, her curiosity and interest about public management and public administration issues, and to her fellow researchers at the University of Rome Tor Vergata for having shared the journey.

Lah is thankful to his co-editors Denita Cepiku and Thomas Klassen, who initiated and led the project. It was a great pleasure for him to work with punctual and humble colleagues.

August 2016
Toronto, Canada
Rome, Italy
Seoul, South Korea

1

PUBLIC POLICY AND ADMINISTRATION IN AN ERA OF GLOBALIZATION

Thomas R. Klassen, Denita Cepiku, and T. J. Lah

Introduction

Among the most dreaded questions that anyone interested, or engaged, in public policy and administration can be asked is: "What is public policy?" and "What is public administration?" One answer is that public policy and administration is what government does and how it does it. This is indeed a good initial definition that encompasses the amazing variety of activities involved in public policy and administration.

To understand the vast and complex actions of government, two approaches have developed: public policy and public administration. The first – public policy – focuses on setting goals and objectives. The second – public administration – is the implementation of the policy. Consider when you decide to travel with your family or friends. First you will investigate the places you might visit, the money you have (your budget), the time available for travel, transportation options and so forth. This is analogous to policy. Then you will implement or carry out the travel plans that you've made; the equivalent of administration.

As the above analogy suggests, and as you might have experienced in your own life in making plans, "policy-making is not … simply a matter of problem-solving, of taking some common goal and seeking the 'best' or most cost effective 'solution.' It is rather a matter of choice in which resources are limited and in which goals and objectives differ and cannot easily be weighed against each other" (Simeon 1976: 550).

Public administration is the implementation or execution of policy. This involves the organization of human, financial and other resources to attain the goal(s) established by a policy (Lane 1994). This too is far from simple because one policy may conflict with another (provide more services to the public, but spend less); resources may be limited; time frames may be unreasonable; or objectives may be impossible (eliminate poverty).

The distinction between public policy and administration is not often clear, but that is not a problem. Some authors use public policy to encompass implementation as well, while others use public administration to also include planning and setting objectives. What is important is that public policy and administration are distinct from the political realm; that is, from political/legislative decisions. Referring back to the analogy of taking a trip, the legislative branch is the equivalent of your parents (or perhaps your spouse, or employer) who have the power to approve, or reject, what you've planned.

Those responsible for planning and the implementation of public programs are (in a democratic form of government) answerable to, and follow the direction of, elected legislators and politicians. Thus politicians ultimately decide. This is sometimes referred to as the *legislative branch* of government, which is separate from the *executive branch* of government that has responsibility for planning and implementation of decisions reached by the legislative branch. In this book, therefore, little will be found on presidents, premiers, prime ministers, chancellors, cabinet members, senators, legislators, councilors, parliaments, political parties, elections and so forth. Of course, politicians rely extensively on the advice of public administrators in passing laws and making regulations, a topic analyzed in Chapter 24 of this handbook. Moreover, politicians rely completely on public administrators to execute decisions by delivering programs and services.

History and importance

Public policy and administration are fundamental components of modern societies, and important and flourishing areas of scientific study. Indeed, civilization is founded on the ability of small groups of people – namely rulers – to make decisions and to have these implemented. This in one sense is the hallmark of public policy and administration. When the first urban civilizations arose 5,000 years ago in Mesopotamia, in what is now Iraq, a defining feature was that the larger scale of public administration allowed a substantial number of people to be impacted by decisions made by a small ruling elite. Many of these decisions dealt with religious matters, warfare and trade, but they also included urban planning, agricultural techniques, science and art.

As urban civilization sprang up in other parts of the world, large-scale government became even more important. For example, consider the building of the pyramids, the rules and regulations that were needed to run the Roman Empire, build the magnificent temples of Angkor Wat in Cambodia, or the administration of the city of Teotihuacan, in modern-day Mexico, with over 100,000 residents almost two thousand years ago.

Three significant changes have occurred over the past two centuries with respect to public policy and administration: (1) the rise of representative systems of governments; (2) a dramatic increase in the scope and scale of government; and (3) the application of the scientific method to matters relating to public policy and administration. First, the rise of representative democracies gave citizens more say in the decisions made by rulers; that is, politicians.

Second, the past century has seen the rise of the welfare state; that is, the government taking a larger role for the health and well-being of citizens. Thus, to various degrees public education, health care and income security for the old and injured came into existence. This has occurred gradually at different rates and times, and indeed continues to occur today in parts of the world. However, in nearly all parts of the world today, the government plays the central, or key, role in providing not only education, health care and some level of income security to large swathes of the population, but also other services such as roads, garbage disposal and much else. In addition, the government has taken a critical role in regulating activities, from airplane flights, the consumption of alcohol and cigarettes, banking and various other behaviors and activities which traditionally were left to the "invisible hand" since they were regarded as entirely private undertakings.

The expansion of the role of government resulted in a much larger scale of organization. After all, services like education, public health and temporary income for those unable to work, as well as regulating behavior, require large and complex organizations or departments. Many of these organizations are structured in a hierarchical and bureaucratic manner, able to deliver the same service across an entire country. Indeed a defining feature of modern public policy and administration is that it transpires within the realm of large, complex bureaucratic organizations (Weber 1947).

The explosion in the role of the government resulted in a large numbers of people (excluding those in the military) gaining employment with government departments and agencies. In some nations these are chosen largely through formal examinations, while in other nations entry to public policy and administration professions is through other routes, such as specialized educational programs.

Public policy and administration employees take many forms, including advisors and communication specialists who work on a daily basis with presidents, prime ministers and other legislators. At the other end of the spectrum are the numerous frontline service staff, sometimes called street-level bureaucrats, who interact with citizens on a daily basis. These public or civil servants process applications for passports or drivers' licenses, teach students in public schools, or collect refuse from streets (Lipsky 1980). In between is a whole range of people that includes everyone paid from money spent by the government.

The final trend is that like other endeavors, public policy and administration became a subject of study for scientists and scholars. One of the first scholars in the English-speaking world to study public policy and administration was Woodrow Wilson (1856–1924), who went on to become president of the United States of America. His concern and that of many who followed him was how to make the activities of government more efficient (Wilson 1887).

Of course, public policy and administration have been a concern for rulers for millennia. In seeking policy advice, rulers and politicians over the millennia have turned to magic, religion, oracles (such the Oracle of Delphi in ancient Greece). Empires, the Egyptian, Roman and many others, were distinguished, and indeed the result of, powerful and effective administrative arrangements. Individuals such as Thomas Cromwell (1485–1540) are remembered today for their work to institute laws and administrative procedures, conducting censuses and other activities. In some cases, this work resulted in dramatic social and economic transformations in the decades and centuries that followed. Writings such as those of Niccolò Machiavelli (1469–1527) deal with public policy topics – such as how rulers/politicians can achieve specific goals – that continue to be relevant.

Modern scientists quickly discovered that public administration and policy are fiendishly difficult to study, and to do so requires the application of several scholarly disciplines, including political science, economics and accounting, psychology, law, sociology and others. Since the 1970s there has been an upsurge in public management studies focusing on the organization and coordination of (limited) resources and activities in order to achieve efficiency, effectiveness and value for money. The continued relevance of management principles and theories for public administrations will largely depend on the ability to make the field of studies context-specific and politically relevant.

The global aspect of policy and administration

Public policy and administration/management is of relevance to the lives of individuals regardless of place of residence. Most citizens interact with frontline public administrators on a regular basis, and the provision of public services impacts citizens every day. Public policy decisions often have far-ranging impacts on individuals, families, communities, regions, nations and the global environment. As such, arguably the scholarly study of these areas is more important than ever.

This book provides a global and comprehensive perspective for those interested in the scholarly study of public policy and administration, as well as for practitioners who wish to understand the latest developments. A theme that runs through this book is that to understand and to make public policy and implement it via public administration requires greater attention than has often been given in the past to the regional, national and global contexts. In other words, a defining feature of public policy and administration is that for the first time in history there is a global component.

In addition to the three developments discussed above – the rise of representative government, the welfare state and the scholarly study of public policy and administration – we suggest that a fourth major trend has begun; namely, the influence of globalization on public policy and administration.

The words global and globalization are much used these days. We use global in this book to mean two things. First, that no country, region or group of scholars has a monopoly on excellence, innovation or knowledge in public policy and administration. As a consequence, the chapters that follow focus much more than other reference books on public policy and administration developments in non-Western countries, including Latin America, Africa and Asia. Indeed, the chapters are written by experts based in, or writing about, every major region of the world. Contained in this handbook are answers and suggestions on motivating public officials, causes and cures for corruption, reacting to emergencies and more … much more.

The second meaning of global in this book refers to the nature of public policy problems. There are more aspects of public policy and administration than ever that are global, in the sense that no one nation or government can reasonably effect change, such as the environment, public health, terrorism, financial regulation and others. As a result, this book includes chapters on public policy and administration topics that have recently become high profile in generating debates such as risk governance and social innovation, global health, and public procurement, and e-government and social media.

Most obvious is the role of global governance institutions in shaping the policies pursued by nations: the International Monetary Fund (IMF), the World Bank, the United Nations and organizations affiliated with it (such as the World Health Organization), the World Trade Organization (WTO) and many others. International agencies such as the Organisation for Economic Co-operation and Development (OECD) seek to help and influence governments tackle the economic, social and governance challenges of a globalized economy.

For example, the 2007–2008 financial crisis and its aftermath have highlighted the magnitude of state institutions and regulatory bodies in the context of an increasingly globalized economic system. Public health crises in the form of outbreaks of infectious diseases also illustrate how public policy and administration often has a global component. Globalization, itself, has increased the interconnection among governments, and heightened the understanding that in many policy fields government actions in one nation have impacts elsewhere. Moreover, there has been a shift – as explained in several chapters – in that government often needs to act in concert with other groups in society to implement policy.

Readers

Scholars and researchers have responded to the increased importance and complexity of public policy and administration by publishing books and articles in a range of both well-established and newly developed journals, as well as in many other ways. They have documented how in the past several decades the role of government has been modified in response to political, economic, social and technological developments. In this book we have collected the most current and cutting-edge topics that anyone – whether student, researcher or practitioner – would need an introduction to.

The audience of this book includes students, scholars and practitioners of public policy and administration. Our foremost aim in editing this volume is to aid students in the many undergraduate and graduate programs throughout the world, as well as students in related disciplines such as political science. As we've suggested above, public policy and administration problems and topics are fascinating to study, and often involve a variety of tools from economics, political science and other fields of study.

For students beginning or in the middle of their studies, we invite you to use this book as a way to engage with a specific topic or group of related topics, or as a way to gain an overview of public policy and administration as whole. For more senior students as well as researchers and scholars we hope the book is a way to help you keep "on top" of the latest developments. For practitioners, this is a reference book to turn to when faced with new or recurring challenges in serving citizens or clients. For all three groups of readers we trust the book will serve as a seminal reference work, highlighting key issues and debates, while also opening the door to further exploration and resources.

The chapters in this volume are written by authors based in all regions of the world. The authors comprise leading global experts in their respective subject areas. Most are senior contributors with decades of experience studying, and in some cases, making or implementing policy, while others are emerging scholars in the field with a record of publication. We are grateful that they have shared their knowledge.

Organization of this book

The volume is organized into three parts, each with a brief introduction written by the editors. Each section contains a mix of chapters, some focused on broad topics, and some that are primarily case studies. At the end of the book is a glossary providing definitions of key words.

The first part – "Contemporary challenges of public policy and administration: a global perspective" – is an exploration of some of the key challenges faced by public policy makers and administrators, as well as an analysis of the state of the discipline. This part introduces central ideas and debates that assist students to appreciate the core aspects of policy and administration, as well as guiding those already employed by government to situate their day-to-day work. For practitioners of public policy and administration, we hope this book will expose you to new ideas and perspectives that can apply to the challenges you face.

The first part focuses on the how public administration increasingly – in all regions of the world – involves the regulation of capitalism. That is, we are living in an era of regulatory capitalism in which one of the central objectives of government is to place limits, or impose rules, on the operation of free enterprise or capitalism.

The second part – "Cross-sector and cross-level policy and administration responses" – examines some of the chief responses to public policy and administration challenges of the 21st century, especially those posed by regulatory capitalism. The major responses which are analyzed in this part are collaborative governance, citizen co-production and citizen engagement. This part also explores specific governance issues such as risk governance, governance changes and federalism in the context of a variety of policy domains: emergency and crisis management, regulatory reform, global health and global cultural heritage policies.

The final part – "Forging a resilient public administration" – looks to the future by considering how a robust and innovative public administration can be crafted to meet the needs of the 21st century. Investigated in this section are both longstanding challenges and more recent conundrums: risk management, leadership, strategic management and long-term thinking, performance management, program evaluation, public budgeting, policy capacity, motivation, public procurement and e-government.

Running through the three parts are the two themes that bind this volume together. First, as discussed above, there is the increasingly global dimension of public policy and administration. Second is that increasingly a central role of public policy and administration is the regulation of capitalism: the creation of rules to ensure the proper operation of private enterprise.

Terminology

As is the case in many fields, from sports to medicine, there are specific words and terms that have come into use with respect to public policy and administration. These can be frustrating for persons "not in the know" and those being exposed to public policy and administration for the first time.

State is a word often used to mean the same as government. However, the two have distinct meanings. A state is a territory (usually a country) that has a large group of people with a shared history, language and culture. Government, on the other hand, refers to the group of bodies (legislators, departments, courts and more) that make decisions (laws) in a state and implement and enforce these. Many modern nations have a head of state (such as a monarch or president) who seeks to exemplify the characteristics of the state, and a separate head of government (such as a prime minister) who is responsible for implementation of laws. The head of a government, and indeed the group (or party) in power, can change without having any impact on the state. Some nations – notably the United States – have a combined head of state and government (the president). The key distinction to remember is that the state is broader and more abstract than government.

Another way to think of the state is to consider the stages of history of human civilization. Until 5,000 years ago all humans on the planet lived in bands (a few dozen people), or in tribes (a few hundred people), or in chiefdoms (a few thousand people). As noted at the start of this chapter, some 5,000 years ago in Mesopotamia, the state arose as a political, economic and social way to live and unite people. As recently as 500 years ago, "Less than 20 percent of the world's land area was marked off by boundaries run by [politicians,] bureaucrats and governed by laws" (Diamond 1999: 255). Today, other than Antarctica, the planet it divided into complex societies that have centralized power structures composed of millions of people: states. Although some people in the more remote parts of the world continue to live in bands, tribes or chiefdoms, they are ultimately still bound by the state within which they reside.

Governance is a word that is found in many chapters that follow. It refers to the interactions between the state and other parts of society: families, businesses, religious organizations and many more. In particular, the word highlights that the state acts – in implementing programs – not solely on its own but also by working with and coordinating other parts of society (Pierre and Peters 2000; Kooiman 1993).

New public management, sometimes shortened to NPM, is also a term found in the pages that follow. The NPM arose in the late 1970s and early 1980s, when citizens in many industrialized nations grew disillusioned with the inability of governments to solve longstanding social problems: unemployment, poverty and inequality. One result of this disenchantment was that politicians and public administrators introduced more cost-efficient and effective ways of delivering programs by restructuring agencies, streamlining and simplify processes and decentralizing decision-making (Denhardt and Denhardt 2009). A landmark book – *Reinventing Government: How the Entrepreneurial Spirit is Transforming the Public Sector* by Osborne and Gaebler

(1992) – popularized the notion that public administration needs to be more streamlined, flexible and responsive. Some proponents of NMP explicitly argue that public administrators must adopt the practices of the private sector; that is, government should be run like a private sector business.

More recently, *public management* has moved from a set of uncritically imported tools and techniques from the private sector, to an approach that can contribute to protecting and enhancing the public interest. Thus public management involves focusing more on results, rather than procedures, and placing priority on the quality of public services provided to citizens. Finally, public management also highlights the role of collaboration between public administrators, individual citizens and other groups.

To help readers, this handbook includes a glossary with definitions of key terms. If you're in doubt while reading a chapter, or just need to clarify the meaning of a word or terminology, refer to the glossary at the end of the book. You might even review the glossary first, before plunging into the chapters.

Happy reading!

References

Denhardt, R. B. and J. V. Denhardt. 2009. *Public Administration: An Action Orientation*. Belmont, CA: Thomson Wadsworth.

Diamond, J. 1999. *Guns, Germs, and Steel: The Fates of Human Societies*. New York: W. W. Norton.

Kaboolian, L. 1998. "The New Public Management: Challenging the Boundaries of the Management vs. Administration Debate," *Public Administration Review*. 58, 3: 189–193.

Kooiman, J. 1993. *Modern Governance: New Government–Society Interactions*. London: Sage.

Lane, F. S. 1994. *Current Issues in Public Administration*. New York: St. Martin's Press.

Lipsky, M. 1980. *Street-Level Bureaucracy*. New York: Russell Sage Foundation.

Osborne, D. and T. Gaebler. 1992. *Reinventing Government: How the Entrepreneurial Spirit is Transforming the Public Sector*. Reading, MA: Addison-Wesley.

Pierre, J. and B. Guy Peters. 2000. *Governance, Politics and the State*. London: Macmillan.

Simeon, R. 1976. "Studying Public Policy," *Canadian Journal of Political Science*. 9, 4: 548–580.

Weber, M. 1947. *The Theory of Social and Economic Organization*. Translated by A. M. Henderson and T. Parsons. London: Collier Macmillan.

Wilson, W. 1887. "The Study of Administration," *Political Science Quarterly*. 2: 2: 197–222.

PART I

Contemporary challenges of public policy and administration

A global perspective

Introduction

This first part of the handbook highlights key challenges of contemporary public policy and administration. In particular, how for the first time in history there is an explicit and prominent global dimension to both the study and understanding of policy and administration, and to its practice. The part introduces key ideas and debates that will help students understand the fascinating world of policy and administration, and guide practitioners in government around the world in their daily work.

Graeme Hodge from Australia, in Chapter 2, "Public policy and administration in an era of regulatory capitalism", proposes that a defining feature of current public policy and administration is regulation. Indeed, Professor Hodge argues that the world has entered the age of regulatory capitalism and that this forms an overarching theme for public policy and administration scholars. This theme is taken up in the chapters that follow in this part, as well as chapters in the second and third parts of the book.

Chapter 2 makes clear that regulation exists to increase trust; whether it is in the arenas of food safety, the exchange of money, product labelling, property laws, or the rights and responsibilities of individual people or corporate entities. Regulation is one of the key features of civilization, with some of its elements – taxes, trade treaties and a regulated money supply – found as far back as the Babylonian cities of more than 5,000 years ago. There is a range of regulatory tools, from "hard" (laws passed by legislators and backed by enforceable sanctions) to "soft" (such as industry codes of practice).

Professor Hodge makes clear that in the 21st century regulation is fundamentally different in scope, importance and impact, at the national and global levels, from that of earlier eras. For instance, regulation involves many more actors than just the government, especially civil society and business organizations.

The chapter concludes that in an era of regulatory capitalism, the major debates will move beyond those that traditionally have been at the forefront: deregulation, privatization and small versus big government. Rather, debates will focus on the role of government, and how government is to be part of a larger set of overlapping regulatory webs in which public administrators compete with others to influence the behavior of citizens.

In his chapter Professor Hodge includes brief case studies on privatization, and financial market regulation. These two topics are explored in more depth in other chapters in this part, with Chapter 3 analyzing privatization in developed and developing nations, while Chapter 12 studies the regulation of finance. Most other chapters in this book return to themes raised by Professor Hodge, either by studying aspects regulation, or by using regulatory capitalism as a conceptual lens through which to view public administration and policy.

Chapter 3, "Public policy and administration in an era of privatization", by Carina Schmitt from Germany, follows directly from Chapter 2 in analyzing the privatization of state-owned enterprises during the past three decades. As Professor Schmitt writes, privatization is not a phenomenon found only in rich democracies, but rather is as widespread in low- and middle income nations.

In comparing privatization in developed and developing countries, Professor Schmitt finds both similarities and differences. One similarity is that some sectors such as telecommunications and energy have been popular targets for privatization activities in almost all countries. A further common feature is that the greatest share of privatization revenues came from a small number of transactions. She also finds that nations follow international trends and emulate privatization policies of neighboring countries or important trading partners.

The findings of the chapter show that, in regard to privatization, developing countries face greater pressure from international bodies such as the International Monetary Fund and the World Bank. Lastly, she notes the influence of past decisions and institutions in shaping the timing and extent, thus linking with Chapter 11, which explicitly analyzes how past policy choices constrain and influence future ones.

Chapter 4, "Public policy and administration in an era of austerity: rethinking local public services", written by Stephen J. Bailey from Scotland, analyzes the legacy of public sector debt incurred by governments over many decades of spending more than they were able to finance with their tax revenues. Professor Bailey notes that many nations face prolonged public sector austerity due to the accumulated debt. He then turns his gaze to local or municipal governments, which usually provide the services that affect citizens on a daily basis (from waste disposal, parks, road maintenance and much more). His chapter argues, in reference to Europe, but by extension to other parts of the world, that local governments must reform service delivery models. These reforms do not necessarily mean service withdrawal and privatization, but rather public administrators adopting innovate service delivery models fit for the 21st century within increasingly pluralistic social needs.

Municipalities will increasingly have to procure innovation and add social and public value by engaging a wider range of stakeholders in the co-design, co-production and co-governance of public services. The topic of new means to deliver services raised by Professor Bailey is taken up in numerous chapters in Part II of this book, which examines policy and administrative responses to global problems. For instance, collaborative government is the focus of Chapter 13, while co-production is the focus of Chapter 14.

T. J. Lah from South Korea and Yijia Jing and Peter T. Y. Cheung from China, in their chapter "Public policy and administration in an era of expansion: China, South Korea and Hong Kong", review how public policy and administration is practiced in these three East Asian jurisdictions. They find that over the past four to five decades the three jurisdictions have broadly similar experiences in administrative restructuring in that privatization, outsourcing, downsizing and reorganization have been extensive. This is finding is in keeping with the regulatory lens that Professor Hodge introduced in Chapter 2, and the findings of Chapter 3 on privatization.

Professors Lah, Jing and Cheung also uncover another common trend: in all three jurisdictions there was a strengthening of the role of civil society and public involvement in the policy-making process. This too fits with Chapters 2 and 4, which argue that currently there is movement in many nations to extend the roles of civil society groups, private organizations and citizens in policy-making and the delivery of government programs and services.

Chapter 5 also makes clear that in East Asia, and by extension in other parts of the world, there has been significant transformation of the role of government. In China, for example, new policies and programs for social welfare, social insurance and health care were developed, or significantly expanded, within the space of a decade. At the same time, in China, South Korea and elsewhere, government administrators have had to adjust to expanding social freedoms, citizens' rights and a much more global economy. Later chapters in this book take up how effectively policy-makers and administrators have adapted to these new conditions.

Chapter 6, authored by Alexander Dawoody from the United States, entitled "Revolution, terrorism, and governance in the Middle East", reviews the linkages between governance, revolution and terrorism in that region of the world. Professor Dawoody notes that the Middle East is the origin of many features of modern administration, such as writing, libraries/records, standing military forces and others, and that the first governments and public administrators (as we would recognize them) arose in that region.

The chapter analyzes the major obstacles to reforming governance structures in the Middle East including the rise of failed states, and the role of tribal and religious schisms. Professor Dawoody examines how revolutions represent the demand by large segments of the population for sound governance, better lives and a more secure future. Revolutions in the form of mass protests, demonstrations, labor strikes and peaceful gatherings arise in the absence of democratic channels and viable opposition political movements. Widespread terrorism, that is, the use of violence to impose narrow ideology on a majority, can also occur in situations where political and administrative governance fails to operate along democratic channels.

The chapter concludes by observing that democratic reforms in the region, whether imported by outsiders (as in Afghanistan and Iraq) or through revolutionary movements, face substantial barriers. Responding to these impediments, whether in the Middle East or elsewhere, is one the major challenges of contemporary politics, public policy and administration.

In Chapter 7, "Participate or be punished: administrative responses to protest", Christopher Tapscott from South Africa, employs a case study to take readers into and behind citizens' demands for basic socio-economic rights and services. Unlike Chapter 6, which examined mass-based protests that sought to change the political order, Professor Tapscott spotlights smaller-scale protests in which participants seek greater access to specific government services. His chapter extends the discussion of citizen participation raised in Chapter 4, and illustrates some of the limits, or at least challenges, of engaging citizens in reforming local public services.

Professor Tapscott makes explicit that while protests are recognized as a legitimate form of citizen action, they are not recognized as a valid form of interaction between citizens and government. Thus, protesters cease to be rights-bearing citizens and instead are viewed by government officials as adversaries. In examining one local government in South Africa, the chapter finds that although peaceful protest action is permitted by municipal legislation, groups wishing to demonstrate must formally apply to the local governments, which may set stringent conditions or refuse permission. When protests do occur, these are usually referred to disaster management units and the police, as there is little interest on the part of local administrative officials to address the reasons that caused the protests.

As the chapter explains, the failure by public administrators to recognize, validate and address minor protest fuels frustration and gives rise to more protests, some of which can involve violence. Thus, because the original legitimate protest action is either ignored or is dispersed by the police, protesters become angry and sometimes violent, which reinforces state stereotypes of their behavior. Professor Tapscott concludes the chapter by noting that peaceful protest is no longer an aberration, but rather has become an entrenched form of citizen participation. Consequently, governments, especially at the local level, need more formalized structures and procedures to respond to the demands of protesters, including understanding the factors which give rise to protest.

Cheol Liu from South Korea uses Chapter 8, "Public corruption: causes, consequences, and cures", to analyze officials using their public offices for personal gain, through behavior like nepotism, favoritism, bribery and the misuse of authority and power. Public corruption is not restricted to any one nation or region, and indeed has been a feature of public policy and administration through the ages. As Professor Liu explains, one of the major causes or prerequisites for corruption is the discretionary power that public officials have; that is, the ability or room to decide when to apply, revise or enforce regulations. For example, consider a police or law enforcement officer (a public administrator, in other words) and the discretion she or he has to issue a warning, or fine, or to take other action in a specific case such as an automobile driver exceeding the posted speed limit.

Following on from Chapter 2 on the increasing importance of regulation, and from Chapter 3 on privatization, Professor Liu notes that regulatory activities provide particular scope for public administrators to engage in corruption. Moreover, periods of rapid privatization can increase the discretion of public officials and incentives to enrich themselves, or unfairly compete in the privatization processes.

The second part of the chapter examines the three main strategies to decrease corruption. The first is to strengthen laws and their enforcement to increase the costs and risks to public administrators of engaging in corrupt practices. The second strategy is providing public officials with sufficient incentives and compensation, such as wages, bonuses and performance pay, for them not to engage in corruption. The last strategy is to reduce the discretionary power of public officials, for example by increasing transparency, so as to diminish opportunities for corruption.

Chapter 9, by Yoon Jik Cho from South Korea, entitled "Trust in public organizations", continues with a theme raised in Chapter 2: how to ensure and increase trust. Trust is essential in the interaction of public administrators (and politicians) with citizens, but also within public sector organizations. Professor Cho's focuses on interpersonal trust within organizations, and discusses why trust matters and how it works in the context of public organizations.

Trust is a key element in all organizations but, as Professor Cho explains, even more so in public administration where it is used to motivate individuals, increase performance of employees, reduce uncertainly, facilitate innovation and much more. Chapter 9 links directly with Chapter 8 in that a high level of trust is critical in reducing corruption. For example, an organization whose members have trust among themselves (and with their clients) will exhibit altruistic behaviors in that individuals will assist others without expecting a reward for doing so. More generally, when the trust level is high, employees are more likely to follow organizational rules and procedures.

The chapter concludes by reminding us that, as with many other characteristics, too high a level of trust may have negative consequences. For instance, under very high levels of trust, organizational members are so closely connected that they may hesitate to raise problems (whistle blowing, for example), or become reluctant to accept external criticism against their organization.

In Chapter 10, "Global aging: understanding its challenges", Masa Higo from Japan explores one of the defining features of public policy and administration of the 21st century: namely, rapid population growth that has impacted developed nations, and will have even greater impact on developing nations. Professor Higo, living in a nation where one of every four people is 65 and older, provides an overview of the rapid demographic shifts that are found in every region of the world.

The chapter makes clear that while population aging is a global trend, it progresses differently by region, at least in the timing and speed of the increase in the population's share of older people. For instance, in many developing countries, population aging is taking place at a much faster rate than was the case for developed countries. As a consequence, in the coming decades, global aging will involve greater risks in later life for people in many developing countries, while public administrators will struggle to provide adequate health care and income security.

Professor Higo illustrates how global aging, and the policy decisions of individual nations, has started a global labor market for a long-term care workforce. That is, many developed (and richer) nations currently face shortages of long-term care workers to aid their elderly population, and have implemented immigration policies to attract health care workers such as nurses' aides from other parts of the world. Thus, governments of some developing (and poorer) countries – notably the Philippines – have encouraged their younger workers, women in particular, to migrate to developed countries as long-term care workers for older people.

Professor Higo concludes with the need to formulate global-scale policies in response to the growing risks of securing socio-economic resources for supporting older people. He notes that although some international organizations, such as the United Nations, have sought to address these issues, much more effort is required for collective – that is global – policy, governance and programs that aim to protect the well-being and survival of older people in both developed and developing countries.

In Chapter 11, "Public policy and administration: tradition, history and reforms", Edoardo Ongaro reviews the influence of past decisions and policy choices on administration and public policy. His starting point is that past choices about the structure and processes of government – for example, whether universities are public or private in a country – have long-term term effects. That is, there is path dependency, in that once a decision has been made and implemented, further decisions must generally conform to the pattern or path that the earlier decision, or policy choice, set into motion.

Professor Ongaro begins by analyzing why past choices about the structure and processes of government cause present effects. He then goes on to explain how – notwithstanding the constraints of the past – dramatic change does occur in public policy and public administration. Such abrupt or radical change can arise from a number of sources: external shocks or the accumulation of a series of small changes that ultimately lead to a fundamental change.

The second part of the chapter turns explicitly to explaining changes that occur to public administration (rather than policy). In this regard, the chapter presents two models. The first model places contextual influences at the core, such as the relationship between politicians and senior public servants. The second model uses the concept of administrative tradition, a set of basic traits that characterize the public administration of clusters of countries, as the key in explaining reforms. The chapter concludes by analyzing the extent to which two models can be applied globally; that is, beyond mainly Western European or Anglo-American nations.

Chapter 12, by Ian Roberge and Heather McKeen-Edwards from Canada, "Decentered policymaking and regulatory finance", completes this section of the handbook by analyzing the regulation of financial markets and institutions. The chapter links directly to Chapter 2 (which proposed that regulating capitalism has become a key – if not the central – role of government) by examining regulation, re-regulation, deregulation, non-regulation and self-regulation in the financial sector. Professors Roberge and McKeen-Edwards focus on the 2007–2008 global financial crises and aftermath to reveal the complexity of policy-making.

The chapter begins by outlining the two major justifications for financial regulation; that is, for the government making rules for banks, investment, insurance and other financial industries. First, that an effective financial system is central to the health of the overall economy; second, that supervision and regulation prevent or minimize market breakdown, which could have spillover effects on the larger economy.

As explained in the chapter, regulation of the financial services is characterized by complexity, fragmentation, interdependencies and the rejection of a clear public/private dichotomy. Each of these is analyzed in the chapter; for example, the fast-pace of change and innovation in technology, products and services. The chapter also notes that although financial services are to some extent globalized, they are also fragmented in that there is no single financial services sector, but rather a collection of industries: banking, investment and insurance.

In tracing global financial supervision and regulation during the past six decades, Roberge and McKeen-Edwards deduce that without government intervention, the global financial crises of 2007–2008 likely would have been much worse. However, they also conclude that new and innovative forms of regulation are required to prepare for the next crises. However, the authors remain skeptical – in part because of the constraints of past policies that professor Ongaro reviewed in Chapter 11 – that new forms of regulation in fact will be implemented.

Thus, the chapter and section conclude with a return to the theme of Chapter 2; namely, that the defining feature of contemporary public policy and administration is the regulation of capitalism, but that it remains uncertain whether public officials have the tools, knowledge and scope to introduce the kind of innovative regulation and service delivery that are demanded by civil society and other groups.

2

PUBLIC POLICY AND ADMINISTRATION IN AN ERA OF REGULATORY CAPITALISM

Graeme Hodge

Introduction

Public administration and public policy have proud, long pedigrees. Our shared history of both (Lynn 2005; Parsons 1995) reveals cutting-edge developments in understanding bureaucracy and its administration as an effective organisational machine for both public and private purposes, as well as the subsequent advances in new public management (NPM), notions of post-NPM government (Halligan 2009), and networked arrangements amidst the complexity of today's governance systems (Klijn 2008). Past decades have been littered with public policy initiatives which have been successful if we look at education, pension plans, disease control and economic growth, as well as unsuccessful, from our experience in drug control, paedophilia and internet bullying. Importantly, many areas of public policy, such as privatisation for example, have also seen high expectations and political promises dashed under the weight of more limited real-world reform outcomes.

But is governing today really that different from governing in past eras? The past few decades have been marked by loud calls for better regulation and reduced regulatory burdens on business. Our post-Global Financial Crisis (GFC) environment has certainly seen much chatter about how governments should more strongly regulate the financial sector. Yet these pressures exist alongside continuing calls for deregulation. The tensions in this opposing rhetoric are palpable. At the same time, commentators have implored us to rethink the state, reinvent it, commercialise it, join it up and have it act more as a partner through better networked capability. Commentators have also told us that we were increasingly in the grip of the audit society (Power 1999), the evaluative state, the welfare state and, more recently, the regulatory state. Meanwhile, commodity and financial market engines have provided spectacular growth and rising wealth for many, and some began almost worshipping the apparent wealth-generating powers of markets. Post-GFC, however, we now know that bigger forces were at work and that harder lessons needed to be acknowledged about the behaviour of less than perfectly rational consumers in markets as well as governing markets that were themselves imperfect. Getting governments and policy tools, such as markets, to serve the needs of citizens continues to be a profound challenge today.

This chapter suggests that we have entered the age of regulatory capitalism and that this forms an overarching theme for public policy and administration scholars. The chapter begins by exploring the nature of regulation, and what can be learned from the cross-disciplinary contestation on this issue. We then examine the lenses of regulatory capitalism and regulatory governance, and look closely at how such lenses fit into contemporary questions facing governments. Overall, the chapter argues that a regulatory lens is a different and productive way to slice the public administration and public policy cake. Subsequently, it is suggested that broader notions of regulation help interpret many public policy topics, and help in reconsidering the role of government. Four brief case examples are discussed; privatisation, public–private partnerships (PPPs), financial market regulation and regulating the water sector. The chapter then reflects on how the success of contemporary government depends on better understanding regulation at the levels of policy and of governance, before making conclusions. So, what is regulation and how might it be reconceptualised?

Changing notions of regulation

At its heart, regulation exists to increase trust, whether oriented towards food safety, the exchange of money, product labelling, property laws, or the rights and responsibilities of individual people or corporate entities. Parker and Braithwaite (2003) note regulation through taxes as probably being 5,300 years old and older than state law itself. Braithwaite and Drahos (2000) comment that Babylon had a legally regulated money economy in the third millenium BC, that trade treaties with Rome existed in 509 BC and that early Roman civil law had food laws looking at weights and measures, economic loss, labelling and fraud.

The idea of regulation has been heavily contested and rethought over the past three decades, however, with profound implications. There are a wide variety of different concepts and definitions of regulation. Two ideological extreme vantage points are possible: at one end, regulation might be characterised as 'a dirty word representing the heavy hand of authoritarian governments and the creeping body of rules that constrain human or national liberties'; and at the other, it can be viewed as 'a public good, a tool to control profit-hungry capitalists and to govern social and ecological risks' (Levi-Faur 2010, p. 4). Some have viewed regulation only with reference to the work of governments, whilst others have gone beyond this. Moreover, as Levi-Faur (2010) points out, disciplines have traditionally viewed regulation differently: with law scholars emphasising legal instruments; sociologists emphasising other forms of control; economists viewing regulation as a tool used only when necessary to deal with market failures; and with public administration scholars emphasising the authority of the state and its formal regulatory organisations.

Our fundamental conceptions of regulation have ranged from, at the one end, seeing regulation as a strict legal concept in which laws and regulations are determined through the legislative processes of Parliament, through to a more fluid behavioural concept in which regulation is seen as a focused attempt at controlling the behaviour of others. Contemporary regulation is now viewed as covering multiple disciplines, as decentralised and as crossing all sectors. So industry and civil society both regulate, as too does government. The traditional narrow 'command and control' concept of regulation has thus been broadened to include instruments and activities that extend well beyond the law. According to Black (2002, p. 26), for example, regulation is more than just rules. It is: 'the sustained and focused attempt to alter the behaviour of others according to defined standards or purposes with the intention of producing a broadly identified outcome or outcomes'.

This broader notion of regulation has led to several important insights for public policy and governance debates. First, the modern conception of regulation encompasses a wide range of actions in terms of regulatory mechanisms and tools. These range from government acts and regulations through to codes, guidelines, standards, contracts, grants, economic incentives, information usage, markets, licenses and accreditation schemes. There is a multitude of regulatory tools and techniques now at our disposal, with black letter law being just one of these options. Moreover, if our conception of regulation has been broadened to one where regulation involves sustained attempts to alter behaviour according to standards for an outcome, then the role of regulation involves far more than simply those people employed in formal regulatory agencies. As Levi-Faur (2010: 10) put it, 'while only few of us are acting as professional regulators, most, if not all of us, act as regulators in some capacity'. The point being made here is fundamental: if our aim is to change behaviour in a sustained way, we are regulating.

Second, not only is there a wide range of activities that can be regarded as regulatory, there are several different rationales as to why behaviour may change. Looking at how governments regulate, for instance, Freiberg (2010) lists six different pure modes. Each mode typically has dozens of different tools within it. These are shown in Figure 2.1. He explains that states may act through economic tools (such as through making markets, or by influencing markets via taxing, quotas or pricing); through transactional tools (where governments influence behaviour through contract or grant conditions for minimum wages, for example); through authorising tools (of registration, licensing, permission, accreditation or litigation); through informational tools (such as product labelling or disclosing interest rates for example); through structural tools (of physical design, or processes such as our pay as you go tax arrangements); or through the more traditional and familiar legal tools (where laws, rules and regulations are made). What is clear here is that there are a range of regulatory tools available to the government and that traditional command and control instruments, where government acts as a legislature, constitute only one of these tools. Importantly too, regulation activities may be either positive (so that particular behaviours are encouraged through incentives) or negative (where behaviours are discouraged through disincentives).

Third, under Black's (2002) broader conception of regulation, regulation is not only made within government, but also within business and within civil society. Indeed, whilst business is not able to enact legislation, it is able to adopt many of the other tools shown in Figure 2.1. So, when business initiates just-in-time contracts, when it implements compliance systems, and when it signs contracts full of conditions aimed at influencing the behaviour of other firms or customers (in addition to precisely specifying products to be supplied), it is in one sense, regulating. Likewise, regulatory activities are undertaken in civil society when we insist on eating halal foods, use the Forest Stewardship Council to accredit products or drink coffee accredited as being produced under fair trade conditions. Regulation is undertaken in all three sectors.

The fourth insight is that the locus of regulation may be from inside government, through independent institutions or through hybrid mechanisms.[1] It may also occur through co-regulation, self-regulation or even meta-regulation, where one regulatory body oversees others (as occurs with accreditation bodies for the professions, for example) who themselves do the detailed oversight. The last two decades have certainly seen the rise of the independent regulator, as noted by Gilardi et al. (2006). They found that the number of independent regulators across 48 countries increased through the 1990s by two-and-a-half times the increase over the previous three decades. Whilst regulatory agencies were not, strictly speaking, a new feature of modern systems of governance, they became a highly popular form of governing throughout the 1990s (Levi-Faur 2010: 15). Not only was it a global phenomenon, but it was also observed across both economic sectors (including utilities such as electricity or telecommunications reforms, or

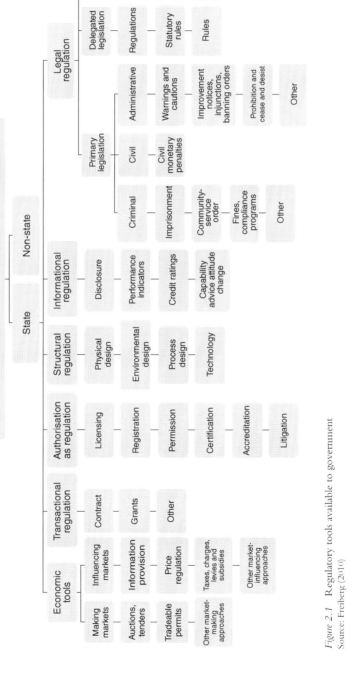

Figure 2.1 Regulatory tools available to government
Source: Freiberg (2010)

through more general competition reform) and social sectors (such as food safety, pharmaceuticals, media or the environment). This is shown in Figure 2.2.

As our fifth insight, we have come to understand that regulation has not simply been the result of privatising essential public services. It has represented a more fundamental reordering of societal priorities and power. As Majone (1999) put it, regulation has essentially been recognised as a distinctive mode of policy-making and become an alternative mode of public control. This is a powerful insight. Others have pushed this notion further, suggesting that the regulatory role of government was not only an important one, but a role that was increasing (Braithwaite et al. 2007). They have noted that the work of governments broadly included three functions – providing, distributing and regulating – and observed that, whilst the government's role in directly providing services was currently decreasing (through, for example, outsourcing and privatisation), and their role in distributing (or redistributing) wealth will continue through time, the government's role in regulating is increasing in myriad ways. Indeed, regulation had become a policy preference of government.

The sixth insight is that regulatory activity of public matters, despite being increasingly technological and professionalised, remains an inherently political activity. Whether governments choose to regulate directly through, for example, legislation, independent institutions, monitoring and reporting regimes, markets or the employment of incentives or contracts, the choice of mechanism and the content comprising the regulatory fabric are political decisions. Moreover, regulation is preceded by policy choices in the face of public interest debates and discussion. Such choices involve, by definition, conflicts in values. Indeed, as Van de Walle (2009) rightly states, government by its nature 'is constantly dangling in an uneasy equilibrium between competing values'. There is rarely one single 'best approach' in organising regulatory regimes to benefit citizens. Even a straightforward-sounding task to regulate the 'risks of harm' involves conflicts in values because the concept of risk itself is culturally and historically contingent. In order to understand risk, scientific calculus of actuarial risk needs to be complemented by dimensions that include the disruption of established socio-cultural patterns and valued beliefs along with political risks and threats to political power or survival (Haines et al. 2007).

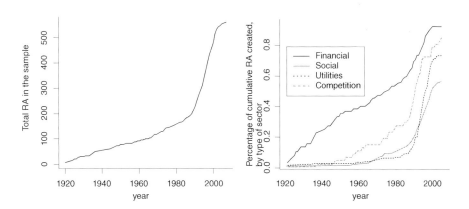

Figure 2.2   Cumulative annual creation of regulatory agencies (RA) across 48 countries and 16 sectors over 88 years (1920–2007)
Source: Jordana et al. (2009)

Seventh, many useful models exist to help interpret regulatory actions. The regulatory pyramid idea (Ayres and Braithwaite 1992) has proved particularly useful. Now in use internationally, this framework is also known as the enforcement pyramid. It suggests that regulation in practice includes a range of possible actions from hard law through to soft law. The notion underpinning this framework is that the behaviour of the regulator depends to a degree on the behaviour of the regulatee, and that, in the first instance, the philosophy of the effective and responsive regulator is to initially encourage compliance and try the least cost measure. If these measures do not work, then regulatory actions taken by the regulator are escalated upwards, so that increasingly punitive and increasingly legal methods are adopted to ensure compliance. The implication of this is that much regulatory time is spent on establishing systems of compliance for 'normal behaviour' (through licensing and accreditation schemes, for example), and on measuring and monitoring, as well as in regulatory conversations, assessing and reporting, as opposed to formal court proceedings. And many of these activities are inherently cross-disciplinary rather than belonging to one specific group. Regulation has quietly become a cross-disciplinary professional pursuit.

In essence then, today's conceptions of regulation are more expansive than in the past. Regulatory scholars are most interested in how behaviour is influenced and ordered. This regulatory lens acknowledges that one of the crucial functions of law is to prevent poor behaviour and encourage desirable behaviours. But importantly, no matter which regime of regulation we analyse, from food safety or smoking to teaching in universities, the actual role of law in altering behaviour is usually modest. As Colin Scott put it, 'the behaviour of those regulated in those regimes is shaped only partly by legal rules, but also by other forms of control' (Scott 2008). Regulatory scholars, therefore, tend to look 'outside the court room' and observe attempts to control, order or influence the behaviour of others. They understand that law also functions to facilitate private arrangements and government functions, settle disputes, and in addition expresses our shared values (Raz 1979: 176). They tend not to focus on legal doctrine and the text of legislative instruments, but instead debate how regulatory systems can be best designed, what tools and mechanisms work most effectively in responding to particular circumstances, and the degree to which citizens and other stakeholders see regimes as having legitimacy and credibility (Bartle and Vass 2007; Black 2008).

All of this means that a richer and more sophisticated discourse around issues of public policy and governing is needed.

The age of regulatory capitalism

So, what are the implications of rethinking regulation for discussions concerning governance and public policy? At the level of governing, one crucial argument has been that the very notion of the state as the centre of regulation is a misconception. For a start, the three sectors (state, market and civil) potentially regulate each other as well as themselves, as we hinted earlier. Businesses regulate other businesses (through contractual standards for food manufacturing or processing throughout the world, for example), and parts of government regulate other parts of government. NGOs accredit codes of conduct to assure clean or ethical business practices. International accounting bodies regulate through reporting standards. ISO develops standards that underpin law which supports trade and economic flows. And so on. Regulation, in a sense, has been decentered (Black 2001). Additionally, auditors and ombudsmen ought to be viewed as part of the growing web of scrutiny, influence and governance oversight. We inhabit a world in which our governing (and regulating) structures themselves are inherently networked and interlinked (Klijn 2008). Trust has grown, sometimes through commercial values and sometimes through democratic values.

How might modern governance systems be conceptualised and characterised? The era of 'the regulatory state' (Majone 1999) seems to be a popular and convincing label capturing the essence of changes in governing capitalist economies (Jordana and Levi-Faur 2004: 8). But it is also perhaps a misnomer. On the one hand, the term regulatory state 'suggests [that] modern states are placing more emphasis on the use of authority, rules and standard-setting, partially displacing an earlier emphasis on public ownership, public subsidies, and directly provided services. The expanding part of modern government, the argument goes, is regulation' (Jordana and Levi-Faur 2004, p. 8). But this argument is also a state-centric view in a world in which we really need to look well beyond the state to multiple overlapping webs of influence (Grabosky 1995).[2] So regulatory regimes are complex and overlapping, with governments being only one of the influential players. This view is also accompanied by some warnings: that multiple forms of control are employed in governing capitalist economies with several modes often co-existing; that the state does not operate as the sole source of regulatory control in any event; and that the regulatory state probably has a certain multi-levelness to it both within one country as well as internationally (Levi-Faur 2010). Having said this, public policy analysts well recognise the major elements characterising the regulatory state:

- bureaucratic functions of regulation are separated from service delivery;
- regulatory functions are separated from policy-making (and therefore are placed at arm's length from their political masters); and
- regulation and rule making emerge as a distinct stage in the policy-making process, and therefore, a distinct profession and administrative identity (Levi-Faur 2010, pp. 18–19).

Allied to this 'regulatory state' idea is the concept of 'regulatory governance'. Minogue and Carino (2006) argue that 'regulatory governance is now fully accepted as a significant part of the literature on regulation'. To them, it is an attempt to go beyond formal rules governing today's public and private relationship to a 'broader framework of state–market relations, and drawing on disciplinary contributions that range across economics, law, politics, and public policy and management' (Minogue and Carino 2006: 4). This regulatory governance perspective looks inside the policy process and 'behind the institutional façade to grasp the "real world" of public action', as Minogue and Carino nicely put it.

Even more broadly stated again has been the suggestion that we live in an age of 'regulatory capitalism'. Braithwaite (2008: xi) explains that whilst many people saw the state running fewer things and regulating more, some analysts started talking about the regulatory state. He continues that:

> then it was recognized that many other organizational actors beyond the state were also doing a lot more regulating of other organizations than in the past, so some analysts … spoke of a regulatory society. Along came David Levi-Faur and Jacint Jordana to point out that capitalist markets had become more vibrant at the same time as regulation of markets had become more earnest.

Not only did they coin the phrase regulatory capitalism, but they also produced a large body of data showing that privatised markets and regulatory institutions had expanded beyond the West to around the world, and that markets themselves had been used as a regulatory mechanism of choice. To Braithwaite's mind, then, we therefore saw not only 'freer markets, more rules' (Vogel 1996), but 'more capitalism, more regulation'; a proliferation of new technologies of regulation; increased delegation to business and professional self-regulation and to civil society, to international networks of experts, and to increased regulation of the state by the state (particularly for competition).

More formally, Levi-Faur (2010) describes regulatory capitalism as:

- the growth in scope, importance and impact of regulation at the national and global levels;
- the growing investments of political, economic and social actors in regulation in general and regulatory strategies in particular; and
- the emergence, extension and consolidation of hybrid forms of regulation which shape diverse and more complex forms of regulatory regime.

To him, the idea of regulatory capitalism took regulatory thinking beyond national boundaries and beyond formal state-centred rule-making. It denoted a world where regulation was increasingly also a hybrid of different systems of control, where statist–civil regulation evolved, where national regulation expanded with international and global regulation, where private regulation expanded with public regulation, and where voluntary regulation existed with coercive regimes. So not only were we dealing with the growth of the regulatory state, but also the growth in the number of civil and business actors that invested in regulation and their own business-to-business regulatory institutions and instruments.

The notion of regulatory capitalism as a way of framing modern governance systems has been a challenge to traditional social science disciplines. Braithwaite (2008), for example, argues that these ideas oppose traditional scholarship 'preoccupied with geographically bounded political systems, legal systems and cultures'. Morgan and Yeung (2007) likewise observe that broader notions of regulation challenge those in the legal profession, and we might add traditional public administration bureaucrats as well. They posited three challenges. First, our assumption that the state is the primary locus for articulating community goals, compared with the social influence of multiple non-state, civil society and business organisations. Second, the assumption of hierarchy – that the state has final authority, compared with multiple sites of governance operating in overlapping ways rather than simply vertically. And thirdly, the assumption of centrality of rules – or, in other words, commands as the primary mode of shaping behaviour, compared to the real limitations of legal rules and potential for alternatives such as economic incentives to steer business, moral suasion, by shaming, and architecture.

The regulatory capitalism lens is thus a fresh conceptual lens through which to view the world of public action. And it has implications for interpreting our world. Braithwaite, for example, tackles the oft-told story, of the triumph of neoliberalism at the end of the twentieth century. To him, this widely believed view on the far left and the far right is nothing short of a 'fairytale'. Neoliberalism (defined as 'a program for destroying collective structures which may impede the pure market logic') and its Hayekian prescriptions of small government, privatisation and deregulation did not occur. Government typically got bigger in terms of spending power and employment numbers and was not hollowed out, the state was still seen as vital to long-term economic growth prospects, and changes from state ownership to private led to more regulation, not less. Likewise, the cousin of neoliberalism, the 'Washington Consensus', stalled after disastrous privatisations in jurisdictions such as Russia, and the 'Washington Consensus' became the 'Washington Consensus plus good governance and the rule of law'. To Braithwaite, then, regulatory capitalism triumphed, whilst neoliberalism lost the war for the hearts and minds of the world's policy-makers. Interestingly, despite the fact that the era of regulatory capitalism had arrived rather than the alternative neoliberal prescription, those on the right still could not use the dirty word 'regulation'.

Contemporary public policy and administration: four case studies

Despite the observation that regulation barely rates a mention in the index of many public policy handbooks, the notion of regulatory capitalism adds a sensible lens through which to view public policy. Four different theatres of public policy will now illustrate this: utility privatisation, public infrastructure delivery through public–private partnerships, the water sector and financial markets.

Utility privatisation

The field of privatisation has seen many lessons from public policy scholars (Hodge 2000; Parker 2004; OECD 2009). Although generalisations are risky, three decades of research after worldwide divestitures suggests several themes: the breadth of the privatisation phenomenon; the multiplicity of political objectives posed by governments globally; the loud ideological and almost religious fervour often accompanying privatisation transactions; the mixed empirical evidence on entity performance gains; and the recurring theme of deepening inequality in outcomes. Perhaps the bigger research lessons from the perspective of regulatory capitalism, however, have been threefold. First, the overwhelming observation has been that strong regulation mattered more than ownership, despite the obsession of advisors, economists and finance market actors with the ownership issue. In other words, governing with integrity mattered most, and getting the regulatory regime right itself was a crucial defining upfront task. We learnt that markets did not exist naturally – they required clear legal and regulatory structures to enable their very existence. Capable independent regulators had to be established and competition laws strengthened. Likewise, essential service excellence did not naturally evolve without strong regulatory standards, incentives and monitoring. Empirically, regulation was a stronger influence on better performance than changing ownership.[3]

Having said this, though, our second lesson was that the regulation of essential services (i.e. utilities) such as electricity water and communications services was traditionally achieved through public sector ownership. In other words, ownership was the regulatory technique employed historically. This contrasts with the regulatory techniques now applied to such privatised services, including the use of markets, the establishment of independent regulatory bodies to oversee service quality, cost structures and governance matters, as well as a potentially greater recourse to the courts as well. So regulation in terms of steering and influencing the behaviour of essential service providers has always existed, but our regulatory technique has changed.

On the broader matter of public versus private interests, too, the third regulatory lesson of the past few decades is that, if we see the world in terms of simply a private versus public battle, a bigger point is missed – it is really the fabric and effectiveness of balanced regulatory arrangements that matter most. Regulatory capitalism essentially takes for granted a strong government and a strong private sector, with each interdependent on the other, rather than one dominating. As Mintzberg (1996, p. 75) argued decades ago, the so called triumph of capitalism over communism in the 1980s was not so much a triumph of the free market idea over government, but "the triumph of balance". Or as Simon said in 1997, 'a strong democratic society needs a dispersal of power, not one dominated by private business interests (to run government), or powerful governments (to corrupt democratic processes)'. There are myriad different versions of capitalism, but there is also no doubt that philosophically we have moved from 'public versus private' to 'public and private'.

Infrastructure delivery through public–private partnerships

To some, infrastructure PPPs are the ultimate NPM tool, maximising private sector involvement through performance-oriented contracts. But after almost three decades, PPPs remain as controversial as they are popular. Public policy based lessons to date are many including the contested definition of PPP, the power of the rhetorical 'partnership' label, the wide range of objectives adopted to justify PPPs, the inherently political as well as complex technical nature of these arrangements, the breadth of differing contract types and financial arrangements that occur in practice, the mixed performance measured for private finance initiative (PFI) type PPPs including value-for-money (VfM), along with the clear political success of many PPP types and our continued desire to get the best of both sectors.

Using a regulatory frame, however, some additional lessons are possible. First, how the government governs (or regulates) the project throughout its long life is crucial. Second, we need to understand that the contract itself performs as a regulatory tool. Both of these issues deserve a comment. On the first matter, and much like its privatisation cousin, there is a serious governing role required in initially assessing the relative need and planning for infrastructure, developing and signing long-term infrastructure contracts (LTICs), in overseeing and monitoring the performance promises made, and in establishing formal institutional arrangements to steer medium and long-term governing decisions where any decision-making discretion occurs. For example, when the facility needs to be upgraded, when ownership changes or refinancing occurs, when contracts are found to be incomplete, when new unpredictable risks appear or when the public's expectations or democratic demands change, the government's role is to work for the public interest and negotiate new arrangements. There are often acute tensions between the commercial and business expectations accompanying such LTICs on the one hand, and the democratic expectations of citizens on the other, especially when a dozen or more different future governments are likely to be elected over a contract term of say 30 or 40 years. The Toronto Highway 407 Express Toll Route in Canada exemplifies this. Here, toll increases from Macquarie Bank were proposed contrary to the democratic expectations of both citizens and a newly elected government in early 2004, but they were arguably in line with the signed legal contract (Torrance 2008). In the case of Australia's East–West Project, an incumbent government signed a $17 billion contract two weeks prior to the caretaker period and immediately prior to a state election. The opposition party campaigned that it would rip up the contract, and was then elected. The contract was eventually renegotiated, but the exercise was painful and it was high profile.

In both cases, citizens felt a direct tension between democratic values on the one hand, and commercial values on the other, given the signed, legally valid contract. They were left pondering the question 'who governs' when governments sign private-contract-law-based PPP contracts? We know that this question has a simple answer – ultimately, the signed private contract largely governs (Hodge 2002). But clearly there is a tension here between the government's responsibility to properly regulate the LTIC project in the public interest throughout its life on the one hand, and the fact that the private contract itself already acts as the major regulatory tool on the other. Little wonder that some commentators view LTICs as being an illegitimate child of the PPP family and governance as the biggest challenge for PPPs (Hodge 2006; Skelcher 2010). This is particularly the case when 'the governance of PPPs has predominantly been used to remove them from public scrutiny and informed debate, justified on the grounds of commercial confidentiality or managerial discretion', as Skelcher (2010, p. 303) says. So, whilst complex and technocratic LTIC arrangements may have served governments well in delivering infrastructure projects, they are still seen by citizens as lacking democratic legitimacy.

The water sector

Our thoughts now turn towards regulating the water sector. This sector has a long history, often sprinkled with public policy controversies (Hodge 2007). The provision of clean water alongside the adequate management of sewerage nonetheless rate as perhaps one of the most effective professional interventions in history in terms of saving lives. In the shadow of this achievement, and with most OECD countries regulating the supply of water through public utilities (Hodge 2007), this sector has equally been criticised as being rather conservative in terms of its willingness to experiment with innovations and reforms. In recent times we have heard calls for cities to become more 'water sensitive', more 'resilient' and more 'liveable'. Perhaps the apparent conservatism of the sector is understandable when we consider the progressively increasing demands being placed on it by the community and by the water professionals themselves. Brown et al. (2009) argue that over the past century cities have been progressively transitioning from water systems focused initially on water supply, to also incorporating drainage control, sewerage management and waterway environmental health, towards systems that represent a broader philosophy that accounts for the overall water cycle and more sophisticated water-sensitive urban forms along with a wide range of water-sensitive urban practices. The cumulative aim has been a more liveable city.

Innovation in this sector, such as encouraging the re-use of water from roof tops or private land for drinking purposes, is desirable. But how might such innovation evolve? Industry professionals continue to be concerned that regulation hinders innovative practices. If we go through the process of defining the various regulatory webs influencing the water sector, five extensive and overlapping regulatory regimes are uncovered: the water resource regulation system; the service delivery and price regulation system; the built environment regulation system; the environmental health regulation system and the public health regulation system. So, from a regulatory perspective, the first lesson here is that the 'regulatory space', as Hancher and Moran (1989) labelled it, for governing urban water is complex. A multitude of interrelated and overlapping regulatory webs exist.

If we then further look carefully at the public health regulation system for drinking water, it is evident that potable water is regulated by a specific legislative regime, but this regime assumes that the water supplied comes only from the publicly owned water corporation. There are no current specific legally binding regulatory requirements for the re-use of other water sources, such as stormwater re-use schemes. Neither is there any clarity at present from the perspective of government policy on whether stormwater, specifically, can be re-used as drinking water. Some water professionals have gone so far as to say that this space was unregulated. Strictly speaking, however, and this is our second lesson from the water sector, no space is truly unregulated. Whilst no specific regulatory regime exists in this case, the general law of negligence imposes a duty of care on those operating stormwater harvesting and re-use regimes not to cause reasonably foreseeable damage to other people (McCallum 2014). In other words, the background law provides a 'regulatory safety net' under which activities are governed, at least in theory.

The third lesson here is that innovative activities for new supplies of drinking water can and do occur in the midst of this complex regulatory space. But such advances are usually modest and are being made at a measured pace. In this way, high levels of citizen–public water agency trust are being maintained even in the absence of a specific regulatory regime controlling the re-use of runoff water (McCallum 2014). In other words, on top of our extensive formal water regulation regimes, the water and health professionals themselves regulate each other's activities in the absence of explicit rules covering the new innovative activity, in order to maintain high public trust. This socio-professional control, as well as a preference for political risk aversion, in the water sector was strongly influential.

Financial market regulation post global financial crisis

In the historical sense, financial upheavals such as the global financial credit crisis of 2008–2009 are not new. But 'this one was truly different, stunning in its breadth, speed and dramatic consequences' (Jain and Jordan 2009, p. 416). The American dream became a global nightmare, as Legg and Harris (2009, p. 350) put it. They chart the 'largest global shock since the Great Depression, inflicting heavy damage on markets and institutions at the core of the financial system'; the emergence of 'sub-prime' mortgages in the United States and its 'low-doc' loans; how defaulting loans then led to the collapse of Lehman Brothers and the spiral of others that followed. And few countries escaped the contagion.

It is difficult to separate out lessons from the perspective of public policy as distinct from regulatory lessons because financial regulation itself is a complex, power-dependent and technocratic art. But there is little doubt that two factors were central. Jain and Jordan (2009) suggest:

- complexity (where financial engineers baffled their boards and financial products became "incomprehensible gibberish");[4]
- ideology and denial (where both 'foolish and irresponsible lending practices' and the slow reactions of the United States Federal Reserve and United States Treasury exacerbated the crisis rather than ameliorated it).[5]

On the surface, it appears that financial institutions clearly failed to disclose essential information to investors and shareholders (Kirby 2010). But more deeply, the intellectual foundation was the efficient market hypothesis, or as Soros (1998) coined it a decade earlier, 'market fundamentalism'. Unquestioned faith in the idea of market equilibrium alone driving social progress blinded us to crucial instabilities and the likely chain reaction and meltdown about to unfold. Colourful policy rhetoric after the event saw some commentators quickly blaming poor government policy and ineffective regulators, whilst others saw the GFC as an example of the complete failure of the capitalist model altogether.

Has this rhetoric and failure to learn lessons from history continued today? Yes. Current discussions around the Eurozone crisis likewise fail to acknowledge these conditions as not unique, with the United States having experienced a similar crisis following the financial panic of 1837.[6] The lessons of history are clear here. First, the social trust systems that underpinned financial markets and economies are fragile. Second, the idea of privatising the profits from transactions and socialising the losses during financial crises is a well-worn historical position, if we learn from the 1839 American and British financiers who floated this idea at the time. Third, the social effects of the economic crisis were, in the words of Roberts (2010: 200), 'profound and sometimes unexpected'. Civil order became difficult to maintain, 'elections became especially violent' and a mass movement of workers felt disenfranchised and powerless. Little wonder that many voters 'resented measures that rewarded foreign and domestic bankers who had played such a large role in triggering the crisis'. All this would be simply academic if not for the eerie parallels between these historical observations from 1837–1848 and the past decade of global regulatory reforms.

Historical parallels aside, what are the primary regulatory themes which have emerged from the aftermath of the GFC? There are several. First, legal rules are important, and continually improving these is necessary. But they are also insufficient. Much of the regulatory environment is less formal, in the hands of global peer organisations such as the credit rating agencies, or even self-enforced through professional regimes and cultures. Such arrangements can nonetheless be powerful in their influence. Corporate reputation, for instance, can be an effective target for regulatory influence and it may be worthwhile promoting new tools of transparency including innovative uses of naming and shaming. Second, large webs of internationally connected regulatory bodies exist, including credit rating agencies and banking oversight bodies as well as markets themselves. Our debates should rightly continue to question the effectiveness of these schemes, but much of this apparatus is outside the direct authority of the state. Third, in this context, the state clearly competes with others for regulatory attention and indeed for regulatory influence. Fourth, the state continues to play an important role, but it is only one part of a much bigger regulatory world. Indeed, the business sector and private firms themselves may be just as influential as governments when it comes to regulation. For example, Deloittes (2014) studied the red tape burden imposed by Australian governments and reported that the risk and compliance procedures imposed by businesses on themselves resulted in far higher compliance costs than government red tape.

Governing and policy change amidst regulatory capitalism

What does all this mean for the task of governing? Modern governments are increasingly subject to a growing hard legislative governing structure as more legislation is passed. In addition, a crowded set of soft regulatory influences, including new transparency, oversight and accountability mechanisms, also applies. Moreover, this oversight and accountability space itself is being more strongly contested over time. A further significant issue nowadays is risk. Beck's philosophical comment three decades ago (Beck 1986, 1992) was that modernisation processes have generated today's 'risk society'. Put another way, the basic orientation of modern society and its organisation 'had shifted away from material production toward coping with risks' (Todd 2015). As a consequence, we are now for the first time in history more preoccupied with the future than the past (Giddens 1999). Our political desire to continue regulating our way towards solutions to public policy problems as we simultaneously accept calls for regulatory reform and lower regulatory burdens suggests an intense degree of ambiguity and confusion in our polity.

Indeed, we could go further. Bernard Crick said in his seminal 1962 book *In Defence of Politics*, that we lived in a time of 'brittle cynicism about the activities of politicians'. Exactly half a century later Matthew Flinders' book (*Defending Politics: Why Democracy Matters in the 21st Century*), repeated this observation in 2012. He observed that there is strong support for the notion that democracy is now in crisis and that a Parliamentary decline has occurred. Our poor assessment of democracy is in one way surprising. As Mullin (2012) commented, citizens in many countries 'see no connection between the great social gains of the 20th century – pensions, free secondary education and health care, sick pay, redundancy pay, the minimum wage, protection from unfair dismissal – and the political process that brought them about'. So, how is it, Mullin asks, that in an age when citizens are so demonstrably better off materially as well as better educated, we have 'managed to manufacture such stunning levels of ignorance, stupidity and indifference'?

Flinders' assessment of this decline in trust is rather provocative. He suggests that 'the nature of political rule has altered in ways that have generally made the business of government more difficult' (Flinders 2014, p. 3). Importantly, he comments that an increasing gap seems to exist between citizens and what they expect of governments on the one hand, and political leaders and what they are able to achieve on the other. To Flinders, it is this expectations gap that explains much of our disappointment in democracy. Citizens assume the past age of abundance will continue and provide an ever-increasing standard of living, at the same time as the electorate possesses both a growing sense of entitlement yet a diminishing sense of responsibility. This leaves political leaders with a difficult task – to reduce the size of the expectations gap, and remind us that continuing abundance may not occur. This is a message we are unlikely to want to hear. Of course there are other explanatory factors as well as the unrealistic expectations of voters: political leaders, for example, who consistently shoot themselves in the foot through Parliamentary expense scandals or else the discovery of conflicts of interest that risk corrupting democratic processes and certainly destroy trust; as well as a voracious 24-hour news cycle demanded by a 'feral and destructive media'.[7] Despite all this, Flinders nevertheless remains optimistic and sees politics as a 'great and civilising human activity', albeit that it inherently remains muddled and messy looking. So, is democracy really in crisis? Perhaps our personal assessment of this, learning from Flinders' ideas, depends on what we expect of democracy and how realistic (or unrealistic) our expectations are.

Recalling the major themes of this chapter, however, there is little doubt that the world of public policy and public administration will change. If Flinders' thesis is right, governments will in fact be more constrained than they have ever been historically, and this will make the task of governing anew and changing policy directions more tricky than ever. Future policy discourse will of course continue to be contested in terms of framing and reframing, and will include loud rhetoric, claims and counter-claims, and self-interested calls for public action. Future discourse will also see continued debates contesting assumptions as to what motivates human behaviours.[8] Strong multidisciplinary inquiries into human behaviour have indeed occurred throughout the past half-century, and contrast with the recent trumpet blowing from fields such as behavioural economics. After all, defining and pursuing the public interest is the central purpose of government.

Importantly, too, future arguments will increasingly revolve around issues of regulatory effectiveness and regulatory legitimacy (Hodge 2006; Levi-Faur 2010). On the first point, fresh questions around the effectiveness of all regulatory tools will occur. We have long known that law as a regulatory tool, for example, has both strengths and weaknesses. It is backed by enforceable sanctions, is democratic and is widely regarded by citizens as 'legitimate', but it is also slow, costly and rigid. Soft regulatory tools such as industry codes of practice also have positives, such as intricate knowledge of the domain, flexibility in development, agility in application and low cost, whilst its downsides include the uncertainty around the effectiveness of enforcement activity, and its potential to be regarded as 'illegitimate' given its corporate nature. Whatever our personal beliefs here, solid debate on the effectiveness of regulatory tools across all economic and social arenas is a welcome focus. An increasingly important aspect of this effectiveness debate is the issue of 'systemic effectiveness' versus 'individual effectiveness'. Clearly, nationalising a state-owned entity with the objective of stabilising the banking or financial system as a whole is different to issues of individual corporate efficiency or a dash by the government for cash.[9] Likewise, policies directed towards ensuring systems of energy provision or telecommunications services become more resilient if the onset of climate change impacts is different to the resilience of individual facilities or corporate entities. Measures encouraging system stabilisation and resilience will be at the heart of the public interest in future as well as traditional issues of individual merit. Notwithstanding this, we ought to still be asking 'who is paying for what, here?', 'who is getting what from the immediate transactions?', and 'who is getting what in the longer term as a result of these measures?'. We also ought be wary of being part of ritualistic regulation or ritualistic compliance, and always ask in which areas regulation is most energetic and effective. These priority questions will require transparency and clarity not seen to date.

The second point concerning legitimacy is also a welcome focus for future public policy debates. Many of our increasingly technocratic regulatory tools and market structures rightly face the obvious question of democratic legitimacy. Whether it is the complex rules governing electricity markets, the technocracy of food regulation and labelling (at the government's door, or for halal food or fair trade coffee), the use of private contracts for public purpose, or any one of many other sectors, the ultimate test for civilised governance is one of legitimate common regulatory regimes acting in the public interest.

New uses of tools such as transparency may need to be trialled, even knowing that these may challenge our previous assumptions as to what is public and what is private. Interesting tensions occur here. From a perspective of democratic legitimacy, even if business practices are 'legal', that does not mean they are fair or socially legitimate. The returns made by private investors on projects built for public purpose are a case in point. Are such returns a private matter or a legitimate public matter? And in any event, the question of complexity in modern public systems is often not an issue of itself, but an issue of how complexity is handled in the polity. Today's financial system, which Cioffi (2011, p. 644) characterises as 'dangerously unstable and destructively extractive', often reveals serious public interest questions of secrecy and disclosure for governments, including access to information under complex contractual arrangements. In this light, the practice of appealing to 'commercial-in-confidence' to shield reforming governments from disclosing contract information results in the public viewing such arrangements as little more than a 'figleaf' behind which governments hide. Transparency in the media is another interesting point, because whilst Flinders criticised the power and role of the media, the media itself represents an enormously powerful and useful accountability tool, and one which is democratically crucial.[10]

Conclusions

The notion of regulation in its broadest form has something important to offer today's world of public policy and administration. Acknowledging our entry into an era of regulatory capitalism, this chapter concludes that we have an alternative lens into government that helps move policy discussions beyond old debates of deregulation, privatisation and small versus big government. The question 'what is the role of government?' will of course remain crucial to ongoing policy and governance debates. But the government''s role will need to be recognised as part of a larger set of overlapping regulatory webs, complexity will continue to rise, and governments will continue to compete with others to influence citizen behaviour. In addition, future governments may well be more constrained and face an increasing gap between what citizens expect of them and what it is realistically possible for them to deliver.

Public policy-making will therefore face difficult choices ahead, and policy-making will become trickier with citizens being more educated and becoming better informed. Public servants, analysts and administrators will thus need to renew their efforts to make clear whose interests are behind new policy initiatives and whose interests underlie the framing of both policy 'problems' and comments currently in the public arena. Fresh debates will need to be increasingly informed by discussions around the effectiveness of a much broader range of regulatory tools than has been acknowledged to date. And the democratic legitimacy of both current regulatory assumptions as well as new proposals to solve wicked problems will require careful scrutiny.

Public policy analysts and public administrators will need to be prepared to challenge the existing boundaries between public and private and test old assumptions as to conflicts of interest as we debate the role of transparency, moving forward. And whilst we will clearly continue to ask 'who is giving what?' and 'who is getting what?' through public policy reforms, there is little doubt that strong contestation will continue on just what constitutes effective regulation and what responses may be proportionate to the harms.

Notes

1 Levi-Faur (2010) observes that regulation may be 'first party' (where self-regulation occurs), 'two party' (where one party regulates another) or 'third party' (where there are three actors: the regulator, a middle party who regulates through say auditing or certifying compliance, and the regulatee). He theorises that with the three sectors (state, market or civil) potentially acting as either a regulator, a regulatee, or a 'third party', there are some 27 (i.e. 3^3) different forms of third-party regulation technically possible.

2 Indeed Grabosky (1995, p. 529) goes further, suggesting that 'it is perhaps more useful nowadays to regard a regulatory system as consisting of layered webs of regulatory influence, of which conventional activities of regulatory agencies constitute but a few strands'.

3 The early analysis of British Telecom data in the United Kingdom by Hodge (2000) suggested that regulatory arrangements were some 3.4 times more influential than changing ownership. Likewise, analysis of contracting out data showed that competition drove cost reductions more powerfully than whether the contracts were undertaken by public sector business units or private sector companies.

4 Jain and Jordan (2009, p. 417) cite Buchheit (2008) and give the example of 'a Cayman Islands special purpose bankruptcy-proof vehicle borrows money from qualified institutional buyers in order to acquire a credit-linked note issued by a Luxembourg entity, guaranteed by a Jersey financing subsidiary of a Cyprus corporation that in turn hedges the risk with a credit default swap written by an Irish entity'.

5 Jain and Jordan (2009) indeed argue that the US Federal Reserve and the US Treasury 'were a main driver of the chaos' when they finally did intervene against their overwhelming faith in the market to self-steer.

6 This is an extraordinarily interesting story. Roberts (2010, p. 197) relates how between 1837 and 1848, the US saw the 'bursting of an asset bubble, followed by a banking collapse, followed next by a depression and defaults by eight of the country's twenty six state governments'. Indeed, 1837 saw the United States struck with a 'paralysis of private credit'. This series of events led to extraordinary political turmoil and undermined the stability of the federal system itself. The subsequent restoration of political and economic order was 'a long and painful process, as enraged voters confronted the costs of inaction and [eventually] accepted new constraints on democratic processes' (Roberts 2010, p. 196).

7 Mullin (2012) cites 'a fickle electorate, the triumph of the market over collective values and over the public interest in general [and] rampant consumerism' as also underpinning our poor assessment of democracy.

8 Centuries of literature have dealt with human behaviour and the human condition. Herb Simon's writings in economics, including his thoughts on 'bounded rationality', go back over five decades. Michel Foucault analysed how humans regulated and governed themselves psychologically through power, knowledge and social control over a similar period. And the commercial advertising industry has likewise been well aware of our human frailties and imperfections in order to boost sales over the past half-century (Jones et al. 2013).

9 History again reminds us that the issue of systemic rescue is not entirely new. A complete banking crash was avoided in the instance of the South Sea Company bubble in 1720 only because of government assistance in stabilizing the banks.

10 Studies such as McMillan and Zoido (2004) suggest that the role played by a free media is surprisingly strong compared to traditional mechanisms such as ministerial responsibility, or even the judiciary. Their study examined the corrupt regime of Peru, which in the 1990s had a full set of democratic institutions. The secret police chief Montesinos, however, systematically undermined them all with bribes. They quantified the bribes paid out. Surprisingly, Montesinos paid a television channel owner about a hundred times what he paid a judge or a politician. Indeed, one single television channel's

bribe was five times larger than the total of the opposition politicians' bribes. Their conclusion was that the strongest check on the government's power was the news media.

References

Ayres, I. and Braithwaite, J. 1992. *Responsive Regulation: Transcending the Deregulation Debate*. New York: Oxford University Press.

Bartle, I. and Vass, P. 2007. "Self-regulation within the Regulatory State: Towards a New Regulatory Paradigm?" *Public Administration* 85 (4): 885–905.

Beck, U. 1992. *Risk Society, Towards a New Modernity*. London: Sage Publications.

Beck, U. 1986. *Risikogesellschaft. Auf dem Weg in eine andere Moderne*. Frankfurt a.M.: Suhrkamp.

Black, J. 2008. "Constructing and Contesting Legitimacy and Accountability in Polycentric Regulatory Regimes," *Regulation & Governance* 2 (2): 137–164.

Black, J. 2002. "Critical Reflections on Regulation." *Australian Journal of Legal Philosophy* 27 (1): 1–27.

Black, J. 2001. "Decentring Regulation: Understanding the Role of Regulation and Self-Regulation in a 'Post-Regulatory' World." *Current Legal Problems* 54 (1): 103–146.

Braithwaite, J. 2008. *Regulatory Capitalism – How It Works, Ideas for Making It Work Better*. Cheltenham: Edward Elgar.

Braithwaite, J., Coglianese, C., and Levi-Faur, D. 2007. "Can Regulation and Governance Make a Difference?" *Regulation & Governance* 1 (1): 1–7.

Braithwaite, J., and Drahos, P. 2000. *Global Business Regulation*. Cambridge: Cambridge University Press.

Brown, R., Keath, N., and Wong, T. 2009. "Urban Water Management in Cities: Historical, Current and Future Regimes." *Water Science & Technology*, 59 (5): 847–855.

Buchheit, L. 2008. "Did We Make Things Too Complicated?" *International Financial Law Review* 27 (24).

Cioffi, J. W. 2011. "After the Fall: Regulatory Lessons from the Global Financial Crisis." In *Handbook on the Politics of Regulation*, edited by Levi-Faur. D., 642–661. Cheltenham: Edward Elgar.

Crick, B. 1962. *In Defence of Politics*. Chicago: University of Chicago Press.

Deloittes. 2014. "Get Out of Your Own Way: Unleashing Productivity." *Deloittes, Building the Lucky Country Series*. October 29. www2.deloitte.com/au/en/pages/building-lucky-country/articles/get-out-of-your-own-way.html.

Flinders, M. 2014. "Explaining Democratic Disaffection: Closing the Expectations Gap, Commentary." *Governance: An International Journal of Policy, Administration, and Institutions* 27 (1): 1–8.

Flinders, M. 2012. *Defending Politics: Why Democracy Matters in the 21st Century*. Oxford: Oxford University Press.

Freiberg, A. 2010. *The Tools of Regulation*. Leichhardt: Federation Press.

Giddens, A. 1999. "Risk and Responsibility." *Modern Law Review* 62 (1): 1–10.

Gilardi, F., Jordana, J., and Levi-Faur, D. 2006. "Regulation in the Age of Globalization: The Diffusion of Regulatory Agencies across Europe and Latin America." In *Privatization and Market Development: Global Movements in Public Policy Ideas*, edited by Hodge, G. A. Cheltenham: Edward Elgar.

Grabosky, P. N. 1995. "Using Non-governmental Resources to Foster Regulatory Compliance." *Governance* 8 (4): 527–550.

Haines, F., Sutton, A. and Platania-Phung, C. 2007. "It's All About Risk, Isn't It? Science, politics, public opinion and regulatory reform." *Flinders Journal of Law Reform* 10: 435.

Halligan, J. 2009. "New Public Management in the Hybrid State," paper presented at the panel, Administrative Reforms Today: From NPM Models to Neo-Weberian Bureaucratization? Paper presented at IPSA's 21st World Congress, Santiago, July 12–16.

Hancher, L. and Moran, M. 1989. "Organising Regulatory Space." In *Capitalism, Culture and Economic Regulation*, edited by Hancher, L. and Moran, M. Oxford: Clarendon Press.

Hodge, G. A. 2007. "The Regulation of Public Services in OECD Countries: An Overview of Water, Waste Management and Public Transport." Paper presented at OECD Group on Regulatory Policy, June.

Hodge, G. A. 2006. "Public–Private Partnerships and Legitimacy." *University of New South Wales Law Journal* 29 (3): 318–327.

Hodge, G. A. 2002. "Who Steers the State When Governments Sign Public–Private Partnerships?" *Journal of Contemporary Issues in Business and Government* 8 (1): 5–18.

Hodge, G. A. 2000. *Privatization: An International Review of Performance* (Theoretical Lenses on Public Policy Series). Boulder: Westview Press.

Jain, A. and Jordan, C. 2009. "Diversity and Resilience: Lessons from the Financial Crisis." *University of New South Wales Law Journal* 32 (2): 416.

Jones, R., Pykkett, J., and Whitehead, M. 2013.*Changing Behaviours: On the Rise of the Psychological State.* Cheltenham: Edward Elgar.

Jordana, J. and Levi-Faur, D. 2004. "The Politics of Regulation in the Age of Governance." In *The Politics of Regulation: Institutions and Regulatory Reforms for the Age of Governance*, edited by Jordana, J. and Levi-Faur, D. Cheltenham: Edward Elgar.

Jordana, J., Levi-Faur, D., and Fernándezi Marín, X. 2009. "The Global Diffusion of Regulatory Agencies: Channels of Transfer and Stages of Diffusion." Working Paper No. 2009/28, Institut Barcelona d'Estudis Internacionals.

Kirby, M. 2010 "Bankruptcy and Insolvency: Change, Policy and the Vital Role of Integrity and Probity." Paper presented to the Insolvency Practitioners' Association of Australia, Adelaide, May 19.

Klijn, E. 2008. "Governance and Governance Networks in Europe: An Assessment of Ten Years of Research on the Theme." *Public Management Review* 10 (4): 505–525.

Legg, M. and Harris, J. 2009. "How the American Dream Became a Global Nightmare: An Analysis of the Causes of the Global Financial Crisis." *University of New South Wales Law Journal* 32: 350.

Levi-Faur, D. 2010. "Regulation and Regulatory Governance." Jerusalem Papers in Regulation & Governance, Working Paper No. 1, February.

Lynn, L.E. 2005. "Public Management: A Concise History of the Field." In *The Oxford Handbook of Public Management*, edited by Ewan Ferlie, Laurence E. Lynn Jr., and Christopher Pollitt, 27–50.

Majone, G. 1999. "Regulation in Comparative Perspective." *Journal of Comparative Policy Analysis: Research and Practice* 1 (3): 309–324.

McCallum, T. 2014. *Better Regulatory Frameworks for Water Sensitive Cities, Kalkallo: A Case Study in Technological Innovation amidst Complex Regulation.* Melbourne: Cooperative Research Centre for Water Sensitive Cities.

McMillan, J. and Zoido, P. 2004."How to Subvert Democracy: Montesinos in Peru." *Journal of Economic Perspectives* 18 (4): 69.

Minogue, M., and Carino, L. 2006. "Introduction: Regulatory Governance in Developing Countries." In *Regulatory Governance in Developing Countries*, edited by Minogue, M., and Carino, L. Cheltenham: Edward Elgar.

Mintzberg, H. 1996. "Managing Government, Governing Management." *Harvard Business Review* 74 (3): 75–84.

Morgan, B., and Yeung, K. 2007. *An Introduction to Law and Regulation: Text and Materials.* Cambridge: Cambridge University Press.

Mullin, C. 2012."Review: Defending Politics – Why Democracy Matters in the 21st Century by Matthew Flinders." *NewStatesman*, May 16. Accessed 29 Feb 2015. www.newstatesman.com/culture/culture/2012/05/review-defending-politics-why-democracy-matters-21st-century-matthew-flinder.

OECD. 2009."Privatisation in the 21st Century: Recent Experiences of OECD Countries." Report on Good Practices, Paris, January.

Parker, C., and Braithwaite, J. 2003."Regulation." In *The Oxford Handbook of Legal Studies* edited by Tushnet, M. and Cane, P., 119–145. Oxford: Oxford University Press.

Parker, D. 2004. "Editorial: Lessons from Privatisation." *Economic Affairs.* 24 (3): 2–8.

Parsons, W. 1995. *Public Policy: An Introduction to the Theory and Practice of Policy Analysis.* Cheltenham: Edward Elgar.

Power, M. 1999. *The Audit Society: Rituals of Verification.* 2nd ed. Oxford: Oxford University Press.

Raz, J. 1979. "The Functions of Law." In *The Authority of Law: Essays on Law and Morality*, edited by Raz, J., 163–179. Oxford: Clarendon Press.

Roberts, A. 2010. "An Ungovernable Anarchy: The United States' Response to Depression and Default, 1837–1848." *Intereconomics* 45 (4): 196–202.

Scott, C. 2008. "Regulating Everything." UCD Geary Institute Discussion Paper Series. Dublin: Geary Institute.

Simon, H. A. 1997. "Keynote Address." Presented to the American Society for Public Administration Annual Conference, Pittsburgh, July.

Skelcher, C. 2010. "Governing Partnerships." In *International Handbook on Public–Private Partnerships*, edited by Hodge, G. A., Greve, C., and Boardman, A. E. Cheltenham: Edward Elgar.

Soros, G. 1998. The Crisis of Global Capitalism: Open Society Endangered. New York: PublicAffairs.

Todd, M. 2015. "The Author of *Risk Society*: Ulrich Beck, 1944–2015." January 7. Available at: www.socialsciencespace.com/2015/01/the-author-of-risk-society-ulrich-beck-1944-2015/.

Torrance, M. 2008. "Forging Glocal Governance? Urban Infrastructures as Networked Financial Products." *International Journal of Urban and Regional Research* 32 (1): 1–21.

Van de Walle, S. 2009. "International Comparisons of Public Sector Performance: How to Move Ahead?" *Public Management Review* 11 (1): 39–56.

Vogel. S. K. 1996. *Freer Markets, More Rules: Regulatory Reform in Advanced Industrial Countries*. New York: Cornell University Press.

3

PUBLIC POLICY AND ADMINISTRATION IN AN ERA OF PRIVATIZATION

Carina Schmitt

Introduction

Public enterprises, especially public utilities, played an important role in economic and social policy particularly during the first three decades after the Second World War. With the rise of the neoliberal paradigm in the 1980s, state involvement in economic affairs was challenged and the privatization of state-owned firms moved to the top of national political agendas. Almost all countries around the globe privatized public enterprises. While privatization in rich democracies has been extensively studied, we know less about privatization and its determinants in developing countries. Do the pathways of privatization differ between rich democracies and low- and middle-income countries? Which similarities and differences can be identified when comparing privatization trajectories in developed and developing countries? Were the same forces driving the retreat of the state or do the determinants of privatization differ between the OECD world and beyond?

This chapter answers these questions by describing privatization pathways in rich democracies in a first step, followed by a brief discussion of the results on the driving factors of privatization processes provided by the empirical literature. The subsequent section addresses the privatization trends in developing countries and highlights region-, period- and sector-specific differences. Furthermore, the factors discussed in the literature to push privatization policies in developing countries are presented. The next section summarizes the main similarities and differences between rich democracies and developing countries with respect to the pathways and determinants of privatization. A final section concludes.

Privatization pathways

Privatization has been a very popular instrument within rich democracies from the beginning of the 1980s onwards. Figure 3.1 illustrates the average development of public entrepreneurship in 20 OECD countries from 1980 until 2007. The y-axis indicates the value added by public enterprises (SOEs) owned by the central government in relation to the GDP. The x-axis refers to the time line.[1]

When looking at the general trend in the last 30 years, the figure clearly shows that the state retreated from entrepreneurial activities in nearly all countries over the past decades.

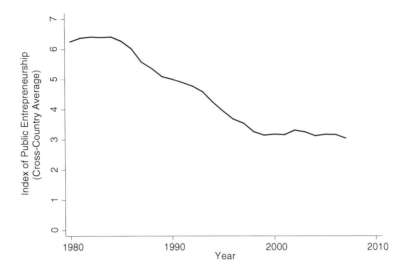

Figure 3.1   The average level of public entrepreneurship in 20 countries

Governments throughout the OECD world launched comprehensive privatization programs and divested public enterprises to the private sector. On average, the turnover of public enterprises amounted to 6.3 per cent of GDP in 1980, whereas the respective share was only 3.0 per cent in 2007.

Despite the common downside trend, there are remarkable differences in privatization intensity across countries (see Table 3.1). First, the involvement of the state in the national economy in 1980 looked quite different when comparing OECD countries. While Canada (2.4 per cent of GDP) and Australia (3.6 per cent) had comparatively low starting values of public entrepreneurship at the national level in 1980, Ireland's initial value of public entrepreneurship was 13.6 per cent, and Great Britain had a value of 7.6 per cent of GDP in 1980, indicating that many big companies were publicly owned in the post-war period. The initial size of the state-owned enterprise sector of these countries is comparable to France with its well-known state interventionist tradition. The Southern European and most of the Scandinavian countries range in between. Germany is also an interesting case as the initial size of the public enterprise sector was rather small and similar to that in Canada and Australia. Rather surprisingly, countries with a large public enterprise sector in 1980 did not necessarily privatize the most. For example, all English-speaking countries launched comprehensive privatization programs even though the public involvement in the economy differed widely in 1980. An extremely marked decline of public entrepreneurship can be observed in the United Kingdom. The value added by British SOEs of almost 8 per cent of GDP in 1980 is today close to zero. Countries in Southern Europe such as Spain and Portugal also relied strongly on privatization. In both countries the involvement of the state in the economy declined by about 85 per cent. However, not all countries divested themselves of public enterprises on such a grand scale. Particularly in Scandinavia, the rollback of the state was only moderate and in countries such as Norway and Sweden the state is today even more involved in the national economy than in the 1980s. Norway is an extreme case as the value added by SOEs rose from 6.8 per cent of the GDP in 1980 to 13.4 per cent in 2007. This is an increase of almost 100 per cent. However, this development is mainly driven by a few big oil companies that significantly raised their turnover during the 1990s. For example, in companies such as Norsk Hydro the state was still the majority stakeholder in 2007. Between the extreme examples of the United Kingdom on the one hand and Norway on the other we find countries such as Switzerland and Denmark, where governments privatized only to a moderate extent. Table 3.1 summarizes the starting values in 1980 and the end values in 2007 as well as the changes over time.

A breakdown by sector reveals similarities as well as differences across countries. In terms of the industrial sector, the notion about what is considered as a strategic sector and where the state should intervene differed widely between nations. For example, while the French state was and still is highly engaged in the aerospace industry, the Austrian government was heavily involved in basic and heavy industry. Public utilities such as railway services, electricity and water supply as well as telecommunication services, in turn, were publicly controlled in almost all rich democracies for strategic and political reasons. Yet the rise of the neoliberal paradigm and technological change even challenged the public service provision in these network-based industries. Figure 3.2 shows the privatization trajectories in three main public utility sectors operated at the national level: the telecommunications, the postal and the railway sectors. The horizontal line displays the time axis and the vertical axis the cumulative number of countries that have begun the divestment of shares.

Table 3.1 Value added by public enterprise in relation to the GDP

	Start Value 1980	End Value 2007	Change 1980–2007 (%)	Mean 1980–2007	SD 1980–2007
Australia	3.55	0.48	−86.48	2.42	1.04
Austria	7.75	3.03	−60.90	6.22	2.09
Belgium	4.70	1.92	−59.15	3.51	1.13
Canada	2.41	.55	−77.18	1.45	.85
Denmark	4.38	2.74	−37.44	3.41	.79
Finland	8.63	6.93	−19.70	7.67	1.36
France	9.55	5.38	−43.66	8.32	1.99
Germany	3.21	1.41	−56.07	2.32	.73
Greece	5.21	1.28	−75.43	2.90	1.30
Italy	6.45	2.17	−66.36	4.58	2.00
Ireland	13.71	1.83	−86.65	6.30	3.74
Japan	4.30	1.20	−72.09	2.75	.90
Netherlands	7.83	2.20	−71.90	4.61	2.34
New Zealand	7.63	3.78	−50.46	3.95	2.37
Norway	6.82	13.36	95.89	11.66	1.62
Portugal	5.57	.90	−83.84	2.82	1.70
Spain	5.24	.71	−86.45	2.61	1.70
Sweden	6.10	7.89	29.34	6.36	1.36
Switzerland	4.35	2.74	−37.01	4.23	1.01
UK	7.65	.44	−94.25	2.45	2.53
Sample	6.25	3.05	−51.20	4.53	1.63

Notes: REST Database, SD = standard deviation

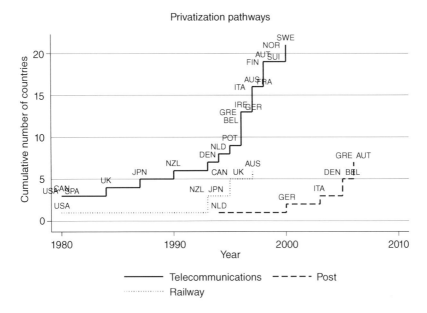

Figure 3.2   Privatization trajectories in public utilities

The figure shows that the telecommunications sector is by far the sector where privatization has advanced the most. Common law countries, such as Great Britain und New Zealand, privatized their national telecommunications providers very early while countries such as the German-speaking nations did not start the material privatization process until 1996. By 2000, the divesture of enterprises had begun in all 21 OECD countries, and by now, some states have retreated completely from service delivery by divesting all public shares. In contrast, railway and postal service providers have been privatized to a much lesser extent and the divesture of SOEs operating in these sectors also began later. Precisely, only seven out of 21 countries have divested public shares in the postal sector and only the Netherlands entirely sold its former postal provider. In the railway sector, the extent of material privatization is similarly low but the selling off started earlier. English-speaking countries have been among the first countries that sold their railway operators. Some countries, such as the UK and New Zealand, have at least partly revoked their privatization decision. However, in most countries the railway operator is still fully owned by the government (Schmitt 2013).

Overall, we can summarize that countries differed highly in the size of public enterprises on the eve of privatization. From the 1980s onwards almost all developed countries launched major privatization programs. However, there is more heterogeneity than expected. While the state has almost completely withdrawn from public enterprises in Anglo-Saxon countries, governments remained highly involved in entrepreneurial activities or even expanded their role in Northern Europe. Continental Europe falls in between. Furthermore, there are sector-specific trends. For example, the state typically has retreated from the industrial sector as well as from telecommunications and power services while remaining involved in the railway and postal sector.

Explaining privatization trends

International comparative studies emphasized domestic and external factors as being relevant for the timing and the extent of privatization processes. With regard to domestic factors, Boix (1997) finds in one of the first international comparative studies for a sample of OECD countries that right-wing parties are more inclined to privatize than left-wing parties. This result is supported by a recent study analyzing the effects of partisan differences on privatization in times of globalization for 20 rich democracies (Obinger et al. 2014). Regarding institutional effects on privatization, Zohlnhöfer and Obinger (2006) find for a sample of 14 European and 21 OECD countries that institutional pluralism hampers privatization. Furthermore, Schmitt and Obinger (2011) show that particularly constitutional provisions regarding privatization are decisive constraints for governments when planning the divesture of major public enterprises. One further factor that has been identified by empirical studies to be highly relevant for privatization decisions is the financial pressure. Empty public coffers or the budgetary constraints that arose from the Maastricht Treaty clearly pushed governments to divest SOEs. Privatization has been one central instrument to mitigate budgetary crises without the political costs related to alternative unpopular measures such as cutting social expenditure or increasing taxes (Zohlnhöfer and Obinger 2006; Belke et al. 2007; Obinger et al. 2014). However, privatization is not always and necessarily an effective instrument to raise revenues. For example, before privatizing public enterprises in Eastern Germany after reunification, the German government expected revenues amounting to 300 billion EUR. The reality was a loss of 100 billion EUR, since most of the nationally owned companies have not been found attractive by private investors.

Some studies examine the influence of Europeanization on privatization policies. In a sample of 20 OECD countries between 1970 and 2000, Schneider and Häge (2008) find that European integration accelerated the reduction of public involvement in the infrastructure sectors in the EU member states. In contrast, Thatcher (2004) states that governments have used European policy to justify and legitimate change rather than change itself being fueled by EU policy-making. Schmitt (2012) find that the influence of the European Union differs by sector. While the privatization in telecommunication services is a global trend, the postal and railway sectors are highly influenced by regulations at the European level. Furthermore, studies have analyzed the impact of globalization on privatization and mainly come to the conclusion that the pressure to implement privatization policies is higher in open-market than in closed economies (e.g. Obinger et al. 2014).

In recent years, scholars have begun to consider policy diffusion when analyzing privatization processes. Research on privatization focusing on policy diffusion concludes that privatization has "diffused rather than [been] reproduced independently as a discrete event in each country and sector" (Levi-Faur 2005: 28). There is strong empirical evidence that governments emulate the strategies adopted by trading partners and neighboring countries (Fink 2011; Schmitt 2011, 2014).

Overall, privatization in rich democracies is shaped by the political partisanship of political actors. Left-wing governments have more reluctantly privatized than their conservative counterparts. Moreover, there is strong evidence that a restrictive policy-specific institutional environment effectively decelerates privatization processes. Furthermore, privatization is fueled by empty public coffers. Governments faced with high public debt used privatization to encounter fiscal pressure. Regarding inter- and supranational factors, economic globalization and the European integration process seem to put pressure on governments to reduce the public intrusion in economic affairs. And lastly, privatization is not only a national phenomenon. Countries privatize when economically related countries and closely located countries do so.

Privatization pathways beyond the OECD

Privatization pathways

Privatizations are not only a phenomenon in rich democracies but have been also launched in developing countries. Figure 3.3 shows the privatization trends in more than 70 low- and middle-income countries from 1988 to 2008.[2] The bars represent the annual number of privatization transactions (left y-axis) while the solid line displays the annual sum of proceeds from privatization transactions across countries from 1990 onwards in million USD (right y-axis).

The figure clearly indicates that major privatizations in developing countries in terms of revenues took place in the late 1990s and in the second half of the past decade. Privatization proceeds in 1997, for example, reached around 65 billion USD and in 2007 about 130 billion USD, compared to 13 billion USD in 1990 and 16 billion USD in 2001. Interestingly, this does not necessarily correspond with the number of privatization transactions, which was the highest in 1998 with 1,796 privatization transactions, whereas the number of privatization events in the 2000s was on the level of the early 1990s. This surprising evidence becomes clear when looking at the size of single transactions. In the second half of the past decade, particularly China and Russia divested huge energy companies and financial service providers. For example, in 2007 China privatized Shenhua Energy CO and PetroChina Co Ltd for around 18 billion USD. In the same year, Russia divested Vneshtorgbank and Sberbank, two big banks, for 17 billion USD. Together, China and the Russian federation account for 100 billion USD of all privatization revenues in 2007. Hence, even though the number of transactions was comparatively low in the early 2000s the revenues per transaction clearly have increased over time.

Apart from this general pattern, privatization differed strongly across countries and over time. Figure 3.4 shows the revenues from privatization separated by region and period. It can be observed that the lion's share of privatizations over the whole period took place in Asia. This

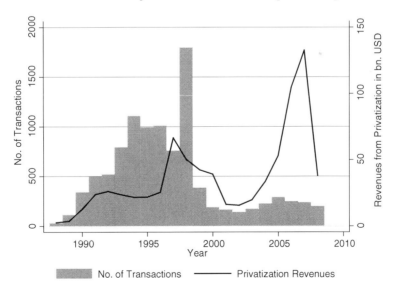

Figure 3.3   Revenues from privatization transactions in developing countries

finding is driven particularly by China but also by the Russian federation. Even though China only privatized 7.4 of the average annual GDP[3] between 2000 and 2008 and therefore only ranks in place 17 regarding this indicator in the sample, the absolute value of revenues in this period is enormous, equalling 171.5 billion USD. China is therefore clearly on the top with regard to privatization revenues in the 2000s.

In European middle-income countries, the revenues from privatization only marginally exceed those in the Americas. Obviously, the lowest efforts toward privatization occurred in African countries, where many companies are still in public hands. "In Algeria, for example 65 percent of all value-added is still produced by public enterprises, and 90 percent of all banking is state owned and operated" (Nellis 2006: 9).

When looking at the period-specific developments in the different regions, it turns out that most of the revenues have been generated in in the first decade of this millennium rather than in the last decade of the past century. This is most obvious in Asia. However, also in the European middle-income countries, the privatization revenues in the 2000s are more than 100 per cent higher than in the 1990s. For example, the privatization revenues of Bulgaria and Serbia from 2000 to 2008 range between 14 and 16 per cent of the average annual GDP. In Romania, the divesture of SNP Petrom (2004), the Romanian gas transmission company (2007) and the Banca Comerciala Romania, brought 9 billion USD. Only in the American region were privatization revenues higher in the 1990s, when Latin American countries in particular launched huge privatization programs. For example, while Argentina privatized around 20 per cent of the annual national GDP (e.g. divesture of Yacimientos Petroliferos Fiscales for 18.5 billion USD), the amount of privatization dropped to 0.1 per cent in the period from 2000 to 2008.

There are not only region-specific but also sector-specific differences. Table 3.2 summarizes the number of privatization events as well as the average revenues raised per transaction differentiated by sector. It shows that most of the privatization transactions have taken place in the manufacturing sector. The number of transactions in this segment is larger than in all other

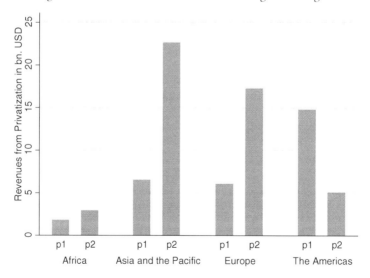

Figure 3.4 Revenues from privatization by region and period
Notes: p1 =period from 1988 until 2000, p2 = period from 2000 until 2008

Table 3.2 Sector-specific privatization transactions

Sector	No. of Transactions	Revenue per Transaction (Mean)	Maximum
Energy	290	399.64	15,400
Financial	650	286.74	22,041
Infrastructure	1419	219.94	6,550
Manufact. and Services	3600	30.25	4,800

Notes: Revenues per Transactions in million USD

sectors put together. Manufacturing is followed by the infrastructural, the financial and the energy sector. However, when comparing the average revenues per transaction, it becomes obvious that even though most of the privatization events took place in manufacturing, it is not the most attractive sector for private investors. The average divesture in the energy sector brought almost 400 million USD into the public coffers, in comparison to only 30 million USD in the manufacturing sector.

However, the picture becomes slightly different when looking at the overall revenues per sector and period. It is shown that most of the revenues come from the privatization of public enterprises operating in the infrastructure sector even though the average privatization in infrastructure yields less than in the energy and financial sectors. Within infrastructure, telecommunications and energy companies account for the lion's share of privatizations (Parker and Kirkpatrick 2005). The revenues are the largest in both periods at a comparable level. In contrast, revenues from divesting banks and other financial services are only high in the second period, namely from 2000 until 2008. It is quite surprising that the revenues from selling off energy companies in both periods together are lower than in the infrastructure in one period and are comparable to those in the manufacturing sector. This clearly is a result of the comparable low number of transactions which is about 12 times lower than in the manufacturing sector. The lowest revenues come from privatizations in the primary sector.

Explaining the privatization trend

Which factors drive the privatization pathways in developing countries? Empirical studies typically do not exclusively explain privatization trends in developing countries. Most of the studies that include developing countries are based on a broad country sample also comprising developed countries. Furthermore, while Latin American countries are often included in these samples, the divesture of public enterprises on the African continent is far less analyzed. However, the results of these studies help to identify the factors driving privatization across the world. As in the case of studies focusing on developed countries, studies analyzing a larger sample of countries emphasize that domestic as well as international factors have been shaping privatization pathways.

For two large samples of 34 and 49 countries, Bortolotti et al. (2003) highlight the importance of the economic situation for privatization. They state that slow economic growth encourages the state's retreat from entrepreneurial activities and that the liquidity of stock markets and government credibility is associated with high privatization proceeds. Regarding the influence of partisan politics, the evidence does not support the (strong) influence of partisan variables on privatization (e.g. Henisz et al. 2005). One reason for this result might be that particularly in developing countries, parties often do not cluster along the left–right divide. Strong empirical

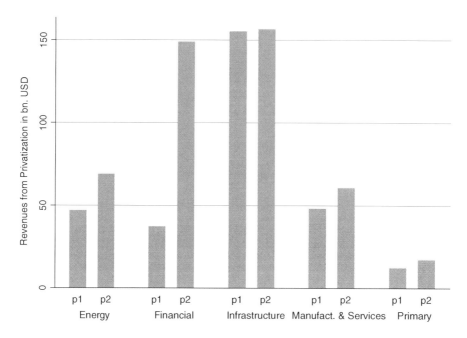

Figure 3.5 Privatization revenues by sector
Notes: p1 =period from 1988 until 2000, p2 = period from 2000 until 2008

evidence is given for the influence of the domestic economic and political environment. Functioning economic and political institutions increase the likelihood of privatizations as well the amount of privatization revenues. For example, when market-supporting institutions are underdeveloped, the preconditions for privatization are non-existent. Effective market supporting institutions are typically lacking in the poor African regions (Ramamurti 1999). Moreover, Bortolotti et al. (2003) find in their study that the legal protection of private investors strongly increases the incentives for privatizing public enterprises. "Privatisation requires suitable political and legal institutions to be set in motion" (Bortolotti et al. 2003: 331). This is supported by Chong et al. (2010), who find for a sample of 308 privatization processes around the world for the period form 1982 until 2000 that institutions effectively regulating political processes are highly important for privatization activities. One further crucial factor is the budgetary situation of a country. Ramamurti (1992) finds for a global sample of developing countries that financial pressure fosters the privatization of public enterprises, and this view is supported by Kogut and Macpherson (2010).

Apart from these domestic factors, international organizations have been identified as being important driving forces for privatization. Brune et al. (2004) examine a sample of 96 countries that have received support from the IMF and emphasize the relevance of the IMF for privatization activities. Ramamurti (1992) has also observed that a high dependence on the World Bank fosters privatization. Henisz et al. (2005) find for 71 countries and territories between 1977 and 1999 that countries succumb to international coercive pressure from the IMF and the World Bank.

In recent years more and more studies have analyzed the role of diffusion for privatization. In line with Levi-Faur (2003), Meseguer (2004, 2009) shows that privatization efforts in Latin

American countries are a result of diffusion processes and the emulation of regional experiences. Using a sample of 92 countries, Kogut and Macpherson (2008) show that the spread of American-trained economists in think tanks fosters the diffusion of privatization.

Overall, economic and political institutions are decisive constraints for privatizations and determine whether the divesture of public enterprises is an attractive tool for policy-makers. Given favorable institutional preconditions and pro-market ideological orientations of the relevant policy-makers, privatization has been regarded as a possible policy instrument for raising revenues and to fill empty public coffers. Furthermore, international organizations such as the World Bank and the IMF are important promoters for launching privatization programs as a strategy to increase firm efficiency and productivity. In line with Doyle (2010), it can be concluded that international organizations rather explain the decision to privatize whereas the cross-national differences in privatization revenues are shaped by different domestic political and economic situation across countries.

Privatization across the world: comparing rich democracies and developing countries

Privatization pathways

Privatization has been a common phenomenon in almost all countries around the globe. When comparing the privatization pathways between rich democracies and developing countries, similarities and differences can be identified. One similarity is that some sectors, such as telecommunications and energy, have been popular targets for privatization activities in almost all countries. While the privatization of public enterprises operating in the manufacturing sector did not realize high revenues, telecommunications and energy providers as well as financial operators are the family silver and highly attractive for private investors. This holds for nearly all countries around the globe. A further common feature is that the lion's share of privatization revenues came from the single transaction of specific companies; the above-mentioned divestures of a few large financial and energy providers in China and the Russian federation, but also single transactions in developed countries such as the privatization of Deutsche Telekom are cases in point.

However, the timing of privatization differs between high-income and developing countries. While the wave of privatization swept through the OECD world mainly in the late 1980s and early 1990s, the peak of privatization in developing countries was in the late 1990s with regard to privatization events, and in the first half of the past decade with regard to privatization revenues. Furthermore, even though revenues from privatization in developing countries increased significantly in the last decade, the total amount is much smaller than in rich democracies. For example, 952 billion USD of privatization revenues were raised in 25 European countries in the period from 1988 to 2008 in comparison with 773 billion USD in more than 70 developing countries in the same period.

Explaining privatization trends

In terms of the driving factors, we can observe that some account for privatization around the world while others seem to be more relevant in specific regions. There is a consensus that political institutions constrain the possibilities for launching privatization programs. However, in developing countries important institutions are the protection of private investors, the rule of law and effective market-supporting regulations. In rich democracies, these institutions are typically more or less existent. Therefore, the timing of privatization rather than the decision per se is influenced by institutions, for example by the constitutional provisions for privatization (Schmitt and Obinger 2011). Apart from the national political and economic institutional arrangement, the budgetary situation is an important factor in privatization around the globe.

In terms of the influence of international factors, one factor that has influenced privatization processes all over the globe is policy diffusion. Countries follow international trends and emulate the privatization policies of neighboring countries or important trading partners. However, rich democracies and developing countries differ in terms of the relevance of single diffusion mechanisms. While in rich democracies competition and trade relations, and therefore horizontal interdependencies, are of particular relevance, in developing countries more coercive forms of policy diffusion arising from the pressure of international factors such as the IMF and the World Bank are highly prominent.

Overall, a comparison of determinants of privatization between developing countries and rich democracies suggests that differences can be found in the importance of specific explanatory factors rather than in completely different logics and motives driving the privatization process. Only one factor, namely the pressure from international organizations such as the IMF and World Bank, is almost exclusively present in developing countries, whereas in European countries, the European Union puts pressure on governments for privatization and liberalization.

Conclusion

Privatization has swept the world in recent decades. It is one of the most salient policy developments across the globe. This chapter has summarized the general privatization trends in high-income and developing countries. It has shown that privatization in rich democracies is very similar around the world. Differences exist in terms of timing, size and the importance of single causes of privatization.

This chapter has mainly analyzed the period from 1988 until 2008, and therefore ends at the peak of the financial crisis. Interestingly, developed and developing countries have reacted differently to the financial and economic crisis. While government interventions to rescue, for example, financial operators, mainly occurred in developed countries, this phenomenon in developing countries is limited to a few cases such as the Parex Bank in Latvia or the Alliance Bank in Kazakhstan (Kikeri and Perault 2010: 4). One reason might be that developing countries, in contrast to rich democracies, did not have the capacity to intervene in the economy when confronted with consequences of the crisis such as decreasing revenues and higher expenditures. Which reaction has been more effective in countering the crisis has to be answered by future research.

Notes

1   For details regarding measurement see Schuster et al. (2013).
2   See http://data.worldbank.org/data-catalog/privatization-database for details on the database.
3   The sum of privatization revenues in relation to the average annual GDP.

References

Belke, A., F. Baumgärtner, F. Schneider, and R. Setzer. 2007. "The Different Extent of Privatization Proceeds in OECD-countries: A Preliminary Explanation Using a Public-Choice Approach." *Finanzarchiv* 63 (2): 211–243.

Boix, C. 1997. "Privatizing the Public Business Sector in the Eighties: Economic Performance, Partisan Responses and Divided Governments." *British Journal of Political Science* 27 (4): 473–496.

Bortolotti, B., M. Fantini, and D. Siniscalco. 2003. "Privatisation around the World: Evidence from Panel Data." *Journal of Public Economics* 88 (1): 305–332.

Brune, N., G. Garrett, and B. Kogut. 2004. "The Privatizations by Shares in the World Economy: Credible Ideologies and International Financial Institutions." *IMF Staff Papers* 54: 195–219.

Chong, A., J. Guillen, and A. Riano. 2010. "Political and Institutional Environment and Privatization Prices." *Public Choice* 142 (1–2): 91–110.

Doyle, D. 2010. "Politics and Privatization: Exogenous Pressures, Domestic Incentives and State Divesture in Latin America." *Journal of Public Policy* 30 (3): 291–320.

Fink, S. 2011. "A Contagious Concept: Explaining the Spread of Privatization in the Telecommunications Sector." *Governance* 24 (1): 111–139.

Henisz, W. J., B. A. Zelner, and M. F. Guillén. 2005. "The Worldwide Diffusion of Market-Oriented Infrastructure Reform, 1977–1999." *American Sociological Review* 70 (6): 871–897.

Kikeri, S., and M. Perault. 2010. *Privatization Trends*. Washington, DC: World Bank.

Kogut, B. and J. M. Macpherson. 2010. "The Mobility of Economists and the Diffusion of Policy Ideas: The Influence of Economics on National Policies." *Research Policy* 40 (1): 1307–1320.

Levi-Faur, D. 2005. "The Global Diffusion of Regulatory Capitalism." *Annals of the American Political and Social Science* 598 (1): 12–32.

Levi-Faur, D. 2003. "The Politics of Liberalisation: Privatisation and Regulation-for-Competition in Europe's and Latin America's Telecoms and Electricity Industries." *European Journal of Political Research* 42 (5): 705–740.

Meseguer, C. 2009. *Learning, Policy Making, and Market Reforms*. Cambridge: Cambridge University Press.

Meseguer, C. 2004. "What Role for Learning? The Diffusion of Privatisation in OECD and Latin American Countries." *Journal of Public Policy* 24 (3): 299–325.

Nellis, J. 2006. "Privatization. A Summary Assessment." In *Development*, edited by C. F. G. Working Paper No. 87.

Obinger, H., C. Schmitt, and R. Zohlnhöfer. 2014. "Partisan Politics and Privatization in OECD Countries." *Comparative Political Studies* 47: 1294–1323.

Parker, D. and C. Kirkpatrick. 2005. "Privatisation in Developing Countries: A Review of Evidence and Policy Lessons." *Journal of Development Studies* 41 (4): 513–541.

Ramamurti, R. 1999. "Why Haven't Developing Countries Privatized Deeper and Faster." *World Development* 27 (1): 137–155.

Ramamurti, R. 1992. "Why Are Developing Countries Privatizing?" *Journal of International Business Studies* 23 (2): 225–249.

Schmitt, C. 2014. "The Diffusion of Privatization in Europe: Political Affinity or Economic Competition." *Public Administration* 92 (3): 615–635.

Schmitt, C. 2013. "The Janus Face of Europeanisation: Explaining Cross Sector Differences in Public Utilities." *West European Politics* 36 (3): 547–563.

Schmitt, C. 2011. "What Drives the Diffusion of Privatization Policy? Evidence from the Telecommunications Sector." *Journal of Public Policy* 31 (1): 95–117.

Schmitt, C. and H. Obinger. 2011. "Constitutional Barriers and the Privatization of Public Utilities in Rich Democracies." *World Political Science Review* 7 (1).

Schneider, V. and F. M. Häge. 2008. "Europeanization and the Retreat of the State." *Journal of European Public Policy* 15 (1): 1–19.

Schuster, P., C. Schmitt, and S. Traub. 2013. "The Retreat of the State from Entrepreneurial Activities: A Convergence Analysis of the Entrepreneurial State, 1980–2007." *European Journal of Political Economy* 32: 95–112.

Thatcher, M. 2004. "Winners and Losers in Europeanisation: Reforming the National Regulation of Telecommunications." *West European Politics* 27 (2): 284–309.

Zohlnhöfer, R. and H. Obinger. 2006. "Selling Off the 'Family Silver': The Politics of Privatization." *World Political Science Review* 2 (1): 29–52.

4

PUBLIC POLICY AND ADMINISTRATION IN AN ERA OF AUSTERITY

Rethinking local public services

Stephen J. Bailey

Introduction

There is increasing recognition of the need to make public services and welfare systems sustainable over the long term. International organisations such as the International Monetary Fund (IMF), the Organisation for Economic Co-operation and Development (OECD), the World Bank and the International Bank for Reconstruction and Development have recently advised many countries not only to cut their public spending but also to restructure their economies by investing in economic growth to increase the sustainability of public sector welfare programmes.

Chapters 2 and 3 deal with the second measure in their analyses of economic restructuring in OECD countries, including deregulation (Chapter 2) and privatisation of public sector activities, sometimes under the auspices of the World Bank and the IMF (Chapter 3). This chapter focuses on the first measure, detailing and analysing the ongoing public sector austerity.

It considers both supply-side and demand-side initiatives to secure sustainable public finances, the latter having been largely ignored in the ongoing austerity-driven policy debates of most European Union (EU) countries. In fact, there is considerable scope to reduce the demand for public (and especially municipal) services to contribute to the increasing sustainability of public finances. The contribution of those measures is insufficiently recognised as policymakers focus on reducing the levels (i.e. supply) of local public services in order to reduce public spending.

The focus of this chapter is on local government austerity measures within the EU, where a 'Fiscal Compact' has been adopted by the Eurozone countries and those intending to adopt the euro single currency. The Compact defines budget rules whose aim is the containment of EU member states' general government deficits (i.e. borrowing) and debts. It imposes a 'debt brake' on all 25 of the 27 EU countries' governments that signed it in 2013. They are committed to progressively reducing their gross public sector debt by one-twentieth of the difference between the current level of debt as a proportion of national output measured by Gross Domestic Product (GDP) and the 60 per cent Maastricht limit. This debt brake requires their budgets to be reduced year after year for the foreseeable future, the more so if GDP growth remains low.

The rationale for austerity budgets

Levels of debt are indicative of a government's ability to repay the money it has borrowed. Assuming, *ceteris paribus*, the higher that debt as a proportion of GDP the greater the risk of it not being repaid because, ultimately, tax revenues will not be sufficient to repay the original sum borrowed and the interest on it. This is especially the case where debt exceeds 100 per cent of GDP and is on a rising trend.

Official Eurostat data shows gross government debt for the euro group of countries rose from 66.2 per cent of GDP in 2008 to 90.9 per cent in 2014. Some countries' public debt was below the 60 per cent limit but clearly, given the 90.9 average figure, most exceeded it, debt being particularly high in Ireland (117 per cent), Portugal (122 per cent), Italy (126 per cent) and Greece (158 per cent).

To avoid default, those governments must reduce their deficits and debts by imposing austerity budgets across the public sector. Governments will still have to reduce their spending even if they do default because they will almost certainly no longer be able to raise more loans from international and domestic financial markets to finance spending on public services and social security benefits. In this default scenario, they will become unable to control austerity as it becomes driven by financial markets, rather than by the Fiscal Compact programme.

Assuming, *ceteris paribus*, this will lead to a fall in the value of the euro against other currencies because the demand for euros falls as overseas investors stop buying EU governments' bonds, in turn, this devaluation of the euro will drive up the rate of inflation as the prices of imports rise in terms of euros, thereby reducing the real purchasing power of incomes and so creating austerity.

It may, however, be thought that the crisis in the public finances will soon be over and that austerity is therefore not necessary. First, the global financial crisis (the '2007–2009 credit crunch') led some governments to bail out their banks, rescuing them from bankruptcy by using public money to buy their shares (Bailey et al. 2009). Second, the economic crisis caused by the credit crunch led to rising expenditures on unemployment-related social security payments simultaneously with falling tax revenues as incomes, consumer spending and consequently profits fell during recession. Once the banks have returned to commercial viability, those governments may be able to repay the money they borrowed by selling at a profit the bank shares they bought to rescue the banks, and economic recession may soon turn to recovery. So is the Fiscal Compact's programme of prolonged austerity really necessary?

The answer is that even if the financial and economic crises are fully reversed, it would be mistaken to believe that the public sector austerity will soon be over. This is because there have been five decades of increasingly unsustainable public finances, the remedy for which requires the multifaceted causes of 'structural gaps' in the public finances (spending persistently greater than revenues over many years) to be resolved, namely the financial, political, institutional, economic and cultural causes of 'black holes' in the public finances (Bailey et al. 2014a).

Five decades of increasingly unsustainable public finances

Even before the 2007–2009 credit crunch, time-series analysis of international public finance data made clear that 'public finance appears to be becoming increasingly unsustainable' (Bailey 2004: 204) in most developed countries and that 'ultimately, corrective action will be required. This may involve radical cuts in public expenditures as well as sharp increases in taxation' (ibid.: 180).

That analysis demonstrated the relatively high levels of public finance as proportions of national income in almost all developed countries within the OECD. Since the 1960s the average growth of spending on public services in those 34 or so countries only kept up with the growth in GDP. However, from the 1980s, those countries' relatively high percentages of public spending as percentages of GDP were increasingly due to current (rather than capital) expenditures and especially social security transfers, most notably in EU countries, as made clear in Figures 4.1 to 4.3.

Compared with the OECD averages, EU governments have long had relatively high levels of final consumption spending on goods and services (Figure 4.1), average levels of capital spending (Figure 4.2) and much higher welfare payments, especially the Eurozone (Figure 4.3). EU countries' social security transfers (i.e. welfare payments) were below the OECD average before the mid-1970s but above it thereafter with a rising trend (Bailey et al. 2014a).

The rising proportions of the value of GDP accounted for by current expenditure, and especially on state pensions and other forms of income support in EU member states, were increasingly financed by public sector borrowing, tax revenues being increasingly and persistently less than current expenditures and so leading to increasing public sector debt as proportions of GDP (Bailey et al. 2014a).

In previous years, rapid economic growth yielded growing tax revenues as incomes, profits and expenditures on which taxes are levied increased. Moreover, moderate to high inflation reduced the real value of public sector debt (Bailey 2004). However, as both economic growth and inflation fell from the late 2000s, the warnings in the above quotations became much more prescient and prophetic.

There is now a huge legacy of public sector debt caused by governments increasingly spending more than they are able to fully finance with their tax revenues, and increasingly because of their relatively generous income-support programmes, this being especially the case in Eurozone countries. On average, those countries also spend relatively high percentages of GDP on health, education and other social services.

This long-term trend is the ultimate cause of the Eurozone sovereign debt crisis, not the financial and economic crises beginning in the late 2000s which, together, acted as triggers for

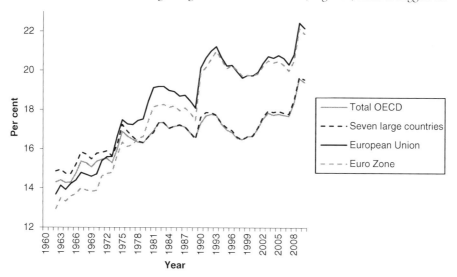

Figure 4.1 Government final consumption as a percentage of GDP: OECD vs. EU and large economies

Source: Author's depiction of data in OECD (2011a)

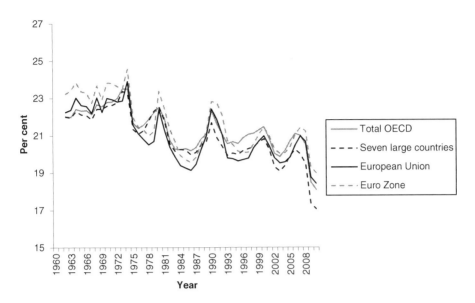

Figure 4.2 Government capital expenditure as a percentage of GDP: OECD vs. EU and large economies
Source: Author's depiction of data in OECD (2011a)

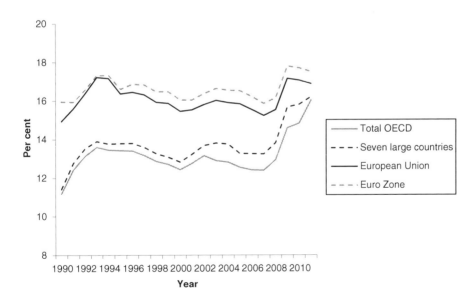

Figure 4.3 Social benefits other than social transfers in kind as a percentage of GDP: OECD vs. EU and large economies
Source: Author's depiction of data in OECD (2011a)

the inevitable public debt crisis. Those countries already had such excessive national debt levels and budget deficits that foreign lenders became increasingly reluctant to lend governments money to refinance public debt, at least not without unsustainably high and increasing interest rates on government bonds.

As a consequence of the high debt-to-GDP ratios noted above, it became virtually impossible for Portugal, Ireland, Greece and Spain (referred to as the PIGS countries) to borrow in order to refinance their debts and deficits in 2010 and thereafter. They were bailed out by the so-called Troika (meaning 'group of three') of the European Commission (EC), the IMF and the European Central Bank (ECB) so that they avoided defaulting on their debts.

The Troika only bailed out those countries whose public finance crisis was so severe as not to be capable of being resolved domestically. Those Troika-funded bailouts were made conditional upon the governments of the PIGS countries implementing stringent public sector austerity measures. Put simply, those countries lost control of how austerity is managed within their own public finances, a group of auditors from this triumvirate of international lenders carrying out regular checks to see if the bailed-out countries are fulfilling the conditions of their bailout agreements. These conditions typically include cuts in state pensions and in pay for, and employment of, public sector workers and structural reforms in their economies, including privatisation of state property and making it easier for firms to hire and fire employees. These measures are intended to make the PIGS countries more competitive on European and world markets.

Figures 4.1 to 4.3 make clear why these and other austerity measures are being introduced more generally across the EU, including reduced eligibility for state pensions and other welfare payments. The alternative is to close the 'black holes' in public finances by raising tax revenues (by increasing the rates and bases of existing taxes and introducing new taxes), but that would make EU member states' exports less competitive on increasingly globalised markets at the very time it is necessary to promote economic growth in countries with weak economies.

Any further borrowing should be used to fund capital expenditures on economic infrastructure capable of promoting sustainable and self-reinforcing growth of GDP over the longer term rather than current expenditures on services and social security. This is what is required if countries are to restructure their economies.

This pro-growth strategy has also to accommodate the relentless growth in demand for public services at a time of heavily constrained government budgets that may not even keep up with inflation. Raising the retirement age, constraining the growth of other welfare payments, reform and merger of government departments and municipalities, and maybe reducing their responsibilities are options being implemented or considered in many countries.

However, it is questionable whether these changes will be sufficient to reverse public sector borrowing so that budgetary surpluses can be achieved with which to reduce public sector debt and/or finance supply-side measures to improve national productivity. In particular, the number of people of pensionable age will continue to grow in most countries and conventional municipal austerity measures will not be sufficient.

Conventional municipal austerity measures

The alternative austerity measures are depicted in Table 4.1. Short-term 'quick wins' are crude knee-jerk management approaches, relatively easy to justify pragmatically, but they only buy time to deal with austerity budgets. They take no account of organisational strategy, priorities and political sensitivities. They can cause essential services to fail to achieve key organisational objectives. They are temporary measures and are neither sufficient nor sustainable.

Table 4.1 Categorizing austerity measures

Short-term "quick wins"	• "salami slicing" cuts to all service budgets
	• freeze vacant posts and do not renew temporary posts
	• reduce opening hours (e.g. for libraries, museums and galleries)
	• pay freezes for public sector workers
	• postpone spending on repairs and maintenance
	• cut capital expenditures
Medium-term measures	• provide only statutory (not discretionary) services
	• voluntary and/or compulsory redundancies and early retirements
	• public sector pay limits
	• bulk purchasing across the public sector to reduce input costs
	• contracting out public services
	• joining up top management structures to reduce manager numbers
	• sharing back-office services (finance, legal, etc.)
Long-term measures	• integrate front-line services (e.g. social and medical care of elderly people)
	• merge municipalities to achieve economies of scale
	• reform public sector workers' pensions to reduce their costs
	• adopt new service technologies in health and social care, education, etc.
	• develop self-service for digitised information and advisory/support services
	• move from crisis management to prevention by early intervention for health, education and social care

Source: Author's summary of the academic literature referenced herein

Medium-term measures are more considered approaches to manage austerity budgets but voluntary redundancy and early retirement compensation deals may result in imbalanced staffing structures (especially loss of key skills and service capabilities). Planned compulsory redundancies can help avoid such problems but still create additional compensation costs. Sharing managers and back office services can reduce costs at corporate level but economies of scale arising from the merger of municipalities are limited.

More strategic long-term measures include moving out of service silos to integrate services (such as social and medical care of elderly people) or otherwise promote better horizontal collaboration across services to eliminate duplication and work better together, pooling budgets for services and places (e.g. a neighbourhood). Such restructuring of services and service providers may achieve economies of scope as well as of scale.

Although the specific measures adopted have varied from country to country, the overall approach to managing austerity has been broadly similar throughout the EU, governments initially focusing on the short-term measures listed in Table 4.1 because they believed the crisis would soon be over (Kickert 2012; Kickert et al. 2013). The more radical medium-term austerity measures in Table 4.1 were not introduced until the severity and longevity of the problem was recognised. In general, the savings ('fiscal consolidation') pursued by austerity measures are greatest the greater the sizes of public sector deficits and debt, all measured as percentages of GDP (OECD 2011b, 2012).

The pragmatic supply-side approaches to austerity listed in Table 4.1 face many problems, particularly resistance from bureaucrats and service workers afraid of losing budgets and jobs, and from existing service users who wish to retain existing levels and methods of provision. Moreover, they do not address growing service demands, instead focusing on reducing budgetary costs. Increased social risks may arise because of the disproportionately negative effects of service cuts for young adults, people with disabilities and/or long-term illness, women, homeless people, elderly people, single parents and ethnic minorities heavily reliant upon public services (TUC 2010; Callen et al. 2011; Stephenson and Harrison 2011; Taylor-Robinson and Gosling 2011; CEU 2012; Hastings et al. 2012; Oxfam 2012; WEF 2012; Asenova et al. 2013).

These cost-cutting measures take place within the direct-provider model of service provision and so may not be an effective or sustainable solution to austerity budgets facing increasing demands. This model must increasingly ration availability of, and access to, services via longer waiting times (e.g. for health services) and stricter eligibility criteria (e.g. for social care of elderly) and so exacerbate the social risks just identified. There is already evidence that withdrawing services and social security from such vulnerable and disadvantaged groups may substantially increase social risks, for example as child protection services are withdrawn and as young adults face unemployment rates twice the average rate (McCormick and Harrop 2011; ONS 2012).

Municipalities must therefore seek to manage and mitigate those social risks by rethinking the way services are provided and used, the objective being to reduce their costs whilst increasing their outcome effectiveness. This means much more than 'rolling back the frontiers of the state' by adopting neoliberal policies promoting deregulation (see Chapter 2) and privatising state-owned enterprises (SOEs) and municipal assets and liberalising municipal service provision via contracting out to private sector firms (see Chapter 3). Receipts arising from the sale of SOEs are finite, and outsourcing the provision of public services to the private sector to secure potential cost savings is rather limited in utilising much the same service model and even those limited potential savings are not always achieved (Bailey et al. 2011). Transformative municipal austerity measures are also required.

Transformative municipal austerity measures

To put the public finances on a sustainable footing it is necessary to consider more collectivist alternatives to the traditional direct-provider municipal service model and to the enabling model under which public services can be provided not only directly but also by private and voluntary (charity) sector contractors.

Under both models municipalities are geared up to supply services rather than manage demand for them and are continually under pressure to achieve cost reductions via the cost-containment measures listed in Table 4.1. Depending on those measures means that they remain locked into their institutionally constrained mindsets and their departments remain locked into 'service silos'. Instead, they need to seek transformative change by 'thinking out of the box' in terms of both supply-side and demand-side measures.

Very much bigger potential cost savings can be achieved by managing demand for services whereby municipalities encourage behavioural changes on the part of service users and citizens and their communities. This can be implemented by development of personal budgets for social care of elderly people and community budgets for street cleaning, parks maintenance, recycling and the other measures listed in Table 4.2.

In the UK, for example, municipalities should recognise that they face tough times (Audit Commission 2011), that the austerity era is here to stay (CIPFA 2012), that they cannot realistically 'weather the storm' (Wallace et al. 2013) or 'game' the cuts (Manning 2013). Instead, they will have to manage a significant and sustained adjustment in public sector funding (Solace 2009) by progressively transforming their model of service provision from direct provider, through enabling and empowering to a catalytic model in order to change behaviours of both service users and service providers (Keohane 2011).

This devolution of decision-making can make services more effective by incentivising individuals and communities to make best use of their municipally allocated budgets by changing

Table 4.2 Alternatives to direct provider model

Transform the model of service provision via direct-provider → enabling → empowering → catalytic role	
Procure innovation and added value by making use of external skills available in:	• private sector and social enterprises via not-for-profit strategic alliances • communities via community budgets for neighbourhoods • households via proactive engagement in schooling, health, child and social care, etc.
Transfer assets to mutual and collective organisations and cooperatives	• to provide their own services (e.g. leisure and recreation)
Focus on 'smart' municipalities 'leading from behind' using networks and service platforms to create additionality	• by improving social productivity and social and public value creation – not just service output productivity • by adopting the 'learning organisation' model to promote corporate and community learning for increasingly diverse populations
Evolve from statist to civic entities engaging proactively with all stakeholders	
More enterprising leadership style fostering	• more engaged citizens • civic enterprise • smarter working • preventative and re-ablement services • co-producing solutions with (not for/to) stakeholders • recognising their assets and capabilities

Source: Author's summary of the academic literature referenced herein

their behaviours and the ways in which they use services so as to reduce costs and be innovative in the co-design and co-production of services with municipalities and with other organisations such as micro-social enterprises and neighbourhood associations.

This approach within the public and voluntary (third) sectors is 'the other side of the coin' of regulatory capitalism in the private sector whereby development of a multifaceted web of governance aims to change (steer) not only the behaviour of profit-seeking companies in the private sector but also that of citizens interacting with their public, private and voluntary sector providers of public services in order to improve service outcomes.

Chapter 2 refers to this as the move away from a predominant focus on 'command and control' by governments and towards development of non-state, civil society and business organisations operating through overlapping non-hierarchical multiple sites of governance utilising incentives and moral suasion to steer (nudge) the behaviours of organisations and citizens.

If they do not change their model of service provision in such ways, municipalities will become increasingly preoccupied with cost savings, paying less attention to securing cost-effective outcomes and so becoming a tool of austerity, this being a particularly bleak outlook for local public services. Instead, it is better to manage and reduce service demand, not by rationing and cost shifting but instead by building resilience of communities by helping supportive social and community networks to stimulate community-led innovation.

This change in municipalities' modus operandi empowers communities so that they can make provision of public services by themselves much more cheaply and effectively than their local governments. In this method of working, municipalities 'lead from behind' to act as catalysts to help communities improve their own wellbeing by building on their skills and capabilities. Municipalities can help them by transferring ownership of their physical assets to neighbourhoods ('locked in' to prevent their sale) so that such civic enterprise is not blocked by high up-front costs, for example community houses, parks and other sports and leisure facilities which communities then manage day-to-day, making use of volunteers where possible.

Unless there is transformative change, during the prolonged austerity, municipalities will have to increasingly ration services, for example by imposing more restrictive eligibility criteria for social care of frail elderly people. This may only shift costs to other parts of the public sector, for example from social care of frail elderly people in their own homes to their care in hospital accident and emergency units. Worse, it may lead to higher costs by disrupting services and so reducing their effectiveness, and because crisis management is generally more expensive than preventative action.

To avoid this scenario, municipalities need a change of mindset from supplying local public services to reducing demand for them. They must foresee and reduce otherwise rising future dependency by focusing on early intervention to reduce demand, working with the community to build resilience and personal responsibility via strength-based approaches, for example for social care (Fox 2013). This will also require public sector risk managers to recognise the social risks created by austerity and become proactively engaged in the management of austerity programmes (Asenova et al. 2014, 2015). This is referred to in Chapter 2 as being more preoccupied with the future rather than the past.

They will have to utilise a 'Nudge Agenda' to encourage people to reduce smoking, consumption of alcohol and junk foods and to take more exercise to improve their physical and mental wellbeing and so reduce future demand on public services. Such catalytic municipal services can strengthen supportive social and community networks. Additionally, municipalities can seek to promote strategic change in their areas through 'place-shaping' for community wellbeing and by developing the 'Big Society' for social/societal wellbeing. This requires municipalities to formulate public policies with all stakeholders in the voluntary, community and faith sectors, many of which already provide preventative services independently of local governments. Municipalities will also have to engage with the public about spending reductions required by the austerity measures and to make clear the cost and value of services to stimulate new thinking and formulation of new policies for community-led innovation in local services

Instead of 'doing more with less' it is a question of 'doing things differently' because although there is scope to improve service productivity to do so is difficult and slow (Bailey et al. 2014b). Otherwise municipalities are likely to become residualised providers of increasingly rationed services, sharing out the misery of austerity as more and more growing demand remains unmet. Instead, 'doing things differently' has much more potential to improve social productivity via multi-stakeholder partnerships (strategic alliances) and networks for service co-production and co-governance to help communities help themselves by changing the modus operandi of municipalities.

A more optimistic vision is that municipalities have to be more proactive 'place shapers', abandoning the traditional 'one-size-fits-all' model of public services which leads to a mismatch between service provision and what citizens ultimately want and need and which, in turn, leads to service costs being unnecessarily high. Instead, municipalities must rethink new whole-systems approaches, focusing on improving outcomes, reforming their delivery through service integration, collaboration, partnerships, strategic alliances and commissioning. Clearly, merging small municipalities into larger ones is only a very small part of the much more holistic reform to structure, functions, financing and especially methods of working that is required for the municipal sector.

Transformational rethinking is also required, 'Smart Cities' not only utilising inter-organisational collaboration and outsourcing but also developing public–third sector partnerships (non-profit models), mutual organisations, etc. to promote community and individual wellbeing. This method of working is distinct from being a direct provider of services and seeks to improve productivity in terms of outcomes as distinct from outputs. This modus operandi has potential to secure more public value co-creation than cost reduction but can save costs nonetheless.

Conclusions

Many countries face prolonged public sector austerity due to weak or negative economic growth and the need to deal with persistent public sector deficits and debt. They cannot afford to wait for spontaneous economic recovery and the ensuing extra tax revenues, tempting though that may be for politicians reluctant to take unpopular decisions. Other countries must begin to act now in order to mitigate financial and social risks so as to protect the wellbeing of their citizens. The bailed out EU member states left it much too late and so much more drastic action is required by the Troika's austerity programme than might otherwise have been necessary. This has severely reduced the wellbeing of their populations and condemned them to years if not decades of cuts in their welfare states.

It has been made clear that municipalities need to develop a new multi-stakeholder governance model of service provision (strategic alliances) with or without austerity so that they develop non-statist service models as social needs and solutions evolve. Austerity is therefore an opportunity to rethink services, their objectives and service models, moving from top-down municipal models to bottom-up deinstitutionalised structures giving up control to communities by changing municipal functions, financing and modus operandi.

This is not neoliberal governments 'getting out of the way' through service withdrawal and privatisation. Instead, it is based on developing new non-statist community service models made innovative, catalytic, resilient, and fit for the 21st century within increasingly pluralistic social needs and solutions. Municipalities will increasingly have to procure innovation and add social and public value by engaging a wider range of stakeholders involved in co-design, co-production and co-governance of public services.

Much more strategically, municipalities will ultimately have to redefine the relationship between the citizen and state, so that individuals, families and communities begin to do more for themselves while the state does less as they learn by doing and become more confident in their own abilities and capacities to promote their wellbeing and resilience.

Reducing public spending requires strategic thinking about both economic and societal restructuring. Local governments must become learning organisations as they pilot-test new models of service provision, using whichever model is appropriate for a specific service at that point in time but recognising that societies, institutions and local economies evolve as new capabilities are developed.

Clearly, there is no 'magic bullet' solution or quick fix to the inevitably prolonged austerity and the real difficulty is in escaping the prevailing municipal culture of the paternalistic technocratic direct-provider supply-oriented model of local government in most countries, not least those in the EU.

References

Asenova, D., McCann, C., and Bailey, S. J. 2015. "Managing Municipal Austerity: Mitigation of Social Risks." *Local Government Studies* 41 (1): 1–19. Accessed 3 June 2016. http://dx.doi.org/10.1080/03003930.2014.919268.

Asenova, D., Bailey, S. J., and McCann, C. 2014. "Public Sector Risk Managers and Spending Cuts: Mitigating Risks." *Journal of Risk Research* 41 (1). Accessed 3 June 2016. http://dx.doi.org/10.1080/13669877.2014.910683.

Asenova, D., Bailey S. J., and McCann, C. 2013. "Managing the Social Risks of Public Expenditure Cuts in Scotland." Joseph Rowntree Foundation. Accessed 3 June 2016. www.jrf.org.uk/publications/public-spending-cuts-scotland.

Audit Commission. 2011. "Tough Times." Councils' Responses to a Challenging Financial Climate. London: Audit Commission.

Bailey, S. J., Valkama P., and Salonen, S. 2014a. "The EU's Public Finance Crisis: Causes, Consequences and Cure." *Public Money and Management* 34 (2): 83–90.

Bailey, S. J., Anttiroiko, A. V., and Valkama, P. 2014b. "Application of Baumol's Cost Disease to Public Sector Services: Conceptual, Theoretical and Empirical Falsities." *Public Management Review*, advance online publication. http://dx.doi.org/10.1080/14719037.2014.958092.

Bailey, S. J., Valkama, P., and Anttiroiko, A. V. 2011. "Failure of Risk Governance in Public Sector ICT-based Innovations: Analysis and Synthesis." *Journal of Risk and Governance* 2 (3): 159–172.

Bailey S. J., Asenova D., and Beck, M. 2009. "UK Public Private Partnerships and the Credit Crunch: A Case Of Risk Contagion?" *Journal of Risk and Governance* 1 (3): 1–11.

Bailey, S. J. 2004. *Strategic Public Finance*. Basingstoke: Palgrave Macmillan.

Callan, T., Leventi, C., Levy, H., Matsaganis, M., Paulus, A., and Sutherland, H. 2011. "The Distributional Effects of Austerity Measures: A Comparison of Six EU Countries." EUROMOD Working Paper Series No. EM6/11, Colchester: University of Essex.

CEU. 2012. "The Social Impact of the Economic Crisis and Ongoing Fiscal Consolidation." Third Report of the Social Protection Committee (2011), Brussels: Council of the European Union.

CIPFA. 2012. "The Long Downturn." London Chartered Institute of Public Finance and Accountancy. Accessed 3 June 2016. www.cipfa.org/Policy-and-Guidance/Reports/The-Long-Downturn.

Fox, A. 2013. *The New Social Care: Strength-based Approaches*. London: RSA.

Hastings A., Bramley, G., Bailey, N., and Watkins, D. 2012. *Serving Deprived Communities in Recession*. York: Joseph Rowntree Foundation.

Keohane, N. 2011. *Changing Behaviours*. London: New Local Government Network.

Kickert, W., Randma-Liiv, T., and Savi, R. 2013. "Politics of Fiscal Consolidation in Europe: A Comparative Analysis." Working Paper COCOPS. Accessed 3 June 206. http://itemsweb.esade.edu/idgp/IRAS%20fiscal%20consolidation%20in%20Europe%20conclusions%20december%202013.pdf.

Kickert, W. 2012. "State Responses to the Fiscal Crisis in Britain, Germany and the Netherlands." *Public Management Review* 14 (3): 299–309.

Manning, J. 2013. "Gaming the Cuts." London: New Local Government Network.

McCormick, J., and Harrop, A. 2011. "Devolution's Impact on Low-income People and Places." York: Joseph Rowntree Foundation. Accessed 3 June 2016. www.jrf.org.uk/report/devolutions-impact-low-income-people-and-places.

OECD. 2012. "Restoring Public Finances, 2012 Update." Special Issue of the *OECD Journal on Budgeting*.

OECD. 2011a. "Historical Statistics, Revenue Statistics 1965–2010." Tax Statistics and iLibrary Paris: Organisation for Economic Co-operation and Development.

OECD. 2011b. "Restoring Public Finances." Special Issue of the *OECD Journal on Budgeting*.

ONS. 2012. "Characteristics of Young Unemployed People." London: Office for National Statistics.

Oxfam. 2012. "The Perfect Storm: Economic Stagnation, the Rising Cost of Living, Public Spending Cuts, and the Impact on UK Poverty." Oxfam Briefing Paper, June. Oxford: Oxfam.

Stephenson, M. A., and Harrison, J. 2011. "Unravelling Equality? A Human Rights and Equality Impact Assessment of the Public Spending Cuts on Women in Coventry." Coventry Women's Voices and the Centre for Human Rights in Practice. School of Law, University of Warwick.

Solace. 2009. "After the Downturn – Managing a Significant and Sustained Adjustment in Public Sector Funding." Society of Local Authority Chief Executives.Accessed 3 June 2016. www.solace.org.uk/library_documents/After_the_Downturn.pdf.

Taylor-Robinson, D. and Gosling, R. 2011. "Local Authority Budget Cuts and Health Inequalities." *British Medical Journal*, 342: 1487.

TUC. 2010. "The Gender Impact of the Cuts." A TUC Cuts Briefing. Trades Union Congress.

Walker, N. 2002. "The Idea of Constitutional Pluralism." *Modern Law Review* 65 (3): 317–359.

Wallace, J., Mathias, M., and Brotchie, J. 2013. "Weathering the Storm? A Look at Small Countries' Public Services in Times of Austerity." Dunfermline: Carnegie UK Trust.

WEF. 2012. "Global Risks 2012." Insight Report. Geneva: World Economic Forum.

5

PUBLIC POLICY AND ADMINISTRATION IN AN ERA OF EXPANSION

China, South Korea and Hong Kong

T. J. Lah, Yijia Jing, and Peter T. Y. Cheung

Introduction

The modern form of public administration (PA) studies began in America (Mosher 1975). Although there were also a few early studies in Europe and England (Lynn 2005: 38) that influenced the establishment of the profession of public administration in the US, the American influence on the development of public administration in developing countries was dominant. However, the practice of public administration and policy exists in various forms in each country, since the social characteristics and political contexts of each nation define the way government works (Riggs 1964). This chapter deals with the developments of governmental policy phases and practices in China, South Korea and Hong Kong. It describes the historical developments of each jurisdiction and its unique administrative and policy characteristics.

China

General introduction

China has a long history of civilization and administration. It has a territory of 960 million square kilometres and the mainland population reached 1.35 billion by the end of 2012. Since the second half of the 20th century, China has accelerated its industrialization and modernization. It successfully changed from a planned to a market economy. Its national GDP became the second largest in the world in 2010. As the world's biggest and fastest-developing society, China's public policy and administration are facing unprecedented opportunities and challenges.

The historical development of public administration and policy in China

1978–1991: introducing public administration
Post-1978 reform brought China's long administrative history into its public administration stage (Jing 2010). Along with the shift of the ruling Chinese Communist Party (CCP) from a revolutionary to a pragmatic strategy, the government's top priorities changed to performance, especially economic performance. Economic growth, investment, employment and international

trade became the government's major goals. Scientific management and regular PA institutions were introduced. Beginning in the 1980s, normal procedures for the recruitment, training, promotion and retirement of civil servants were established. In 1988, the Ministry of Personnel was established. The State Civil Servant Examination gradually replaced a labor allocation system for staffing government agencies. Local governments gained increasing autonomy to deal with local economic and social issues.

1992–2001: market-oriented reforms

In 1992 the CCP's 14th National Congress formally decided to build China's socialist market economy. This led to China's entry into the World Trade Organization (WTO) in 2001. Administrative reforms during this period focused on the government's adaptation to and facilitation of an emerging market economy. Most state-owned enterprises (SOEs) were privatized, while large SOEs were incorporated. The government continued to shed its micro-economic management functions and regulations, endeavouring to establish new markets, market rules and property rights protection. Macro-economic fiscal management was strengthened: for example, the 1994 tax-assignment and the 1998 Central Bank reforms tried to build a national market. In 1993, the Provisional Regulations for State Civil Servants were enacted as a milestone for China's building a modern civil service.

2002–2011: further globalization and social protection

China's entry into the WTO forced further domestic reforms. Administrative reforms, rule changes, and adjustments to industrial policies and economic regulations all deepened China's economic engagement with the world system. Nominal GDP and fiscal revenues grew at annual rates of 16 per cent and 21 per cent during these ten years. China became the world's second largest economy and trading country. Structural reforms, such as super-ministry reforms, were introduced to facilitate policy coordination. Meanwhile, cumulated problems in social, environmental and other areas attracted policy attention and resource inputs. Harmonious society, inclusive development, and balanced development were officially proposed. Since 2002, social welfare, social insurance and public service systems were developed. Government social expenditures increased quickly. In 2005, a Civil Service Law was enacted, signalling a dual emphasis on rational management of the bureaucracy and its political loyalty to the Party (Chan 2007).

2012– : modernization of state governance system and capacities

The turnover of leadership in 2012 created new momentum for China's public administration. At this stage, incremental reform, or the philosophy of "touch the stone to cross the river" faced increasing difficulties. Pragmatic and trial-and-error methods of handling problems were not sufficient. Systematic institutional reforms and the comprehensive enhancement of public sector management were expected. In 2013 the CCP had an important conference in Beijing and decided to push forward the modernization of state governance system and capacities, setting institutional foundations for effective responses to challenging issues like corruption, social polarization, rural poverty, environmental degradation and the middle-income trap. The unprecedented anti-corruption movement led by President Jinping Xi was intended to bring the self-seeking and economy-driven bureaucracy back into law-abidance and fairer public services.

The characteristics of public policy and administration in China

Government structure

Historically, China had a centralized administrative regime and has maintained a unitary system of government. The command-and-control chain links five levels of government: central, provincial, municipal, county, and finally rural township and urban street governments. Below that, mass autonomous organizations – Villagers' Committees and Urban Residents' Committees – implement government policies. By the end of 2013, the numbers of the four levels of local governments and the mass autonomous organizations were 34 provinces, 333 municipalities, 2,853 counties, 40,497 local governments and 683,000 mass organizations.[1] Since the late 1970s, reforms decentralized intergovernmental relations, delegating and devolving functions downward.

The organizational system of Chinese public administration has three parts. The core comprises governmental agencies like the Ministries of Finance and Education. In 2008, the State Council directed 27 ministries and commissions, 16 bureaus, four offices and 14 public service units. Beyond that are the administrative agencies of the Court, the People's Congress, the People's Political Consultative Conference, the CCP and eight Democratic Parties, the Youth League, the trade unions, the Women's Union and a few other organizations. Employees of these agencies are civil servants subject to civil service laws. The periphery of the public administration system is composed of public service units that are sponsored and led by the first two kinds of agencies. In 2011, the latter employed 7.02 million and 880,000 civil servants, while public service units had 25–30 million employees.

Reform path

Reform became orthodox rhetoric in the late 1970s and its strong symbolic values have been deeply incorporated into the political culture. Announcing a major reform helps the government display legitimacy and effective leadership. Major administrative reforms were launched in 1982, 1988, 1993, 1998, 2003, 2008 and 2013, years when new governments were elected. Reorganization, downsizing and market facilitation were major themes of these reforms (Ngok and Zhu 2007).

Reforms are incremental in nature. Least resistance and Pareto improvement were expected when designing reform packages. Reforms often start tentatively from local areas, and may become formal and national policies after successful experiences are summarized and recognized by the central government. The vitality of incremental reform in China has largely been due to the fast-growing economy, which created new opportunities and solutions and thus avoided zero-sum games. However, continuous reliance on incremental reforms is getting more difficult. Further reforms have to touch on issues of redistribution, as economic polarization reaches unprecedented levels and causes a social backlash. As President Xi said in an interview, "China's reforms have got into deep-water areas, easy and win–win reforms were done, and the reforms before us are all bones instead of meat."[2]

State–market–society relations

Marketization has been a major tool for the Chinese government to reshape state–market relation. Reforms in the 1980s and 1990s aimed at building basic market institutions and introducing real market players. Governments gradually reduced direct economic participation and intervention by shrinking SOEs and through deregulation. Foreign-funded enterprises and private enterprises prospered. While the non-state economy accounted for the majority of China's urban employment and industrial outputs, China's economic dependence on international markets also rose dramatically. Nonetheless, the government still plays a much stronger and wider role in economic management compared to many other transitional and developing countries. State-owned enterprises, fiscal and financial policies and industrial policies, as well as direct administrative interventions, are major instruments to manage a state-steered market economy. In theory and in practice, a laissez-faire market economy is not an appropriate model for China.

State–society relations have experienced vast changes as economic marketization has brought about fundamental changes to the social structure. Major changes include expanding social freedoms, citizen rights, and social services and welfare. Meanwhile, civil association attained legitimation. China's social organization policy has been shifting from a control focus to an empowerment focus, albeit not decisively (Jing 2015). The state has realized it needs social organizations for service delivery and collaborative governance purposes. As China has been in a major process of transition, state–society relations will be hybrid and complex, encompassing the full spectrum of rivalry, supplementary and complementary relationships (Young 2000).

Policy system

Policy-making in China has been adapting to vast socioeconomic and technical changes. An increasingly modernized and diverse society makes public policies more important as their consequences are getting more difficult to predict, evaluate and control. Although the CCP continues to be the political centre of the country's political, ideological and organizational leadership, policy-making and implementation have been getting more rational, evidence-based, participative, and transparent. Governments have made serious efforts to improve due process, collective decision-making, policy analysis, implementation, performance measurement, and accountability. New policy instruments such as contracts, grants and subsidies, vouchers, loan guarantees, tax expenditures, and public–private partnerships are widely used. The adoption of these policy instruments led to the engagement of various non-state actors in the process of policy implementation. While policy-making and implementation still suffer from inadequate intergovernmental and interagency coordination, ICT, big data techniques, and new decision-support instruments create a potential for scientific decision-making advocated for by the Chinese government. Besides an obvious pursuit of efficiency and effectiveness, the policy process in China is fundamentally conditioned by its political system and values.

South Korea

General introduction

Established on August 15, 1948, the Republic of Korea (ROK) is located at the southern part of the Korean Peninsula and neighboured by China to the west and Japan to the east. With an area of approximately ten thousand square kilometres and a population of 51.14 million in 2013, South Korea ranks 109th in the world in terms of land area and is the 14th most populated country. The national GDP of South Korea is the 13th largest in the world. In this free democratic polity, the President is elected by the direct vote of the people for a five-year term. The country has 17 regional local governments and 227 basic local governments. As an open-market capitalist economy, the country has turned from being impoverished to an economic powerhouse that aims to be the financial hub of northeast Asia.

The historical development of public administration and policy in South Korea

The 1950s and 1960s: the foundation of the Republic and the establishment of economic infrastructure

The UN recognized the ROK as the only legitimate government on the Korean Peninsula. On the northern part of the Peninsula, however, the Democratic People's Republic of Korea (DPRK) was established as a Communist country under the auspices of the Soviet Union. The ideological confrontation between the two entities led to the Korean War. After the all-out three-year long war ended in 1953, the peninsula was divided and left with few natural resources and destroyed industrial facilities. South Korea was among the world's poorest countries until the 1960s.

The first President, Rhee Syngman, was forced out of office by popular pressure in 1960 after rigging an election, and the political situation became unstable. General Park Chung-hee carried out a coup d'état that eventually led him to become President in 1963. Park established a five-year economic development plan to modernize the country. As reflected by the phrase "the Miracle on the Han River," the country's economy grew tremendously based on an export-oriented policy. The Saemaeul Undong (New Community Movement) greatly contributed to the improvement of living conditions in general.

The 1970s and 1980s: continued economic growth despite political turmoil

President Park extended his term by declaring martial law and announcing the Yusin (Revitalization Reform) in 1972. The 18 years of his dictatorship finally came to an end when Park was assassinated in 1979. However, Singunbu, a group of army officers led by General Chun Doo-hwan, seized power and delayed the onset of democracy. The country made steady economic growth throughout this period. From 1962 to 1981, the average growth rate was 8.45 per cent (Kang, Lee, and Choi 2008: 181). Roh Tae-woo, the successor to President Chun, announced direct elections for the position of President. The Roh administration improved diplomatic relations with Communist countries such as China and the Soviet Union.

The 1990s and 2000s: the beginning of the democratic state

Two life-long fighters for democracy were elected to presidential office in the 1990s. Kim Young-sam fought against corruption and increased transparency. High-ranking public officials were required to register all their assets. The use of false names was banned from all financial transactions. The newly enacted local autonomy system allowed residents to elect their administrative leaders.

Kim Dae-jung's administration had to deal with the foreign exchange crisis inherited from the Kim Yong-sam government. The economic downturn hit the country hard. Kim Dae-jung is best remembered by the "Sunshine policy" toward North Korea, in which the two Koreas established a collaborative economic partnership led by the private sector.

Roh Moo-hyun, the political successor to Kim Dae-jung, was inaugurated as President in 2003. The Roh administration concentrated on three objectives: the realization of democracy with the participation of the people, balanced social development, and the construction of peaceful and prosperous relationships with Northeast Asian countries (Korean Culture and Information Service 2015: 220). Kim and Roh's terms were criticized due to economic slowdown. Although the nation was governed democratically, a variety of social conflicts began to emerge.

New developments since the late 2000s: governmental reform to serve people better

The administration of Lee Myung-bak attempted to make the government work more efficiently by reforming administrative regulations, targeting public enterprises, and reducing its size through privatization. Massive development projects started under the name of a "Green Growth policy," but received more criticism than praise since it focused narrowly on economic growth (Lah 2013). The GDP growth rate during Lee's term was a record low 3 per cent.

In 2012, Park Geun-hye was inaugurated as the country's first female president. The Park government has had to deal with a variety of hardships, including the sour relationship with North Korea, an ongoing economic depression, and conflicts between ideologically polarized social groups. The Park administration is currently pursuing governmental reform, namely "Government 3.0." The goal is to regain the public's trust by achieving transparent, competent and service-oriented government through more openness. The reform aims to provide customized services for individual citizens and support for job creation and a creative economy by opening and sharing public information as well as removing barriers from government operations (MSPA 2014).

The characteristics of public policy and administration in South Korea

A strong administration system and delayed democratization

South Korea is the only country that has transformed from an Overseas Development Aid recipient to a donor. The country made great economic strides in a relatively short time period, and many developing countries see its development path as a model. Two strengths, well-educated human resources and a government-led development system, help explain the country's extraordinary success. Scarcity of natural resources has caused the nation to focus on developing its human resources and emphasize the importance of education. The compulsory education system requires all Koreans to finish middle school. The government supports all families with infants by providing allowances until children are five years old. Almost 80 per cent of high school graduates go to college. This strategy has helped South Korea achieve rapid economic growth.

The country also needed a strong government system to remove the legacies of the Japanese colonial period and quickly improve the economy. Since public positions are traditionally regarded as prestigious, and since most public jobs guarantee life-long employment, competent elite groups have wanted to fill these positions, and they have become even more popular in the unstable job market. South Korea relied heavily on a powerful government filled with elite bureaucrats. This model created hugely successful economic development (Ahn and Jung 2007), but came at the cost of an undemocratic policy-making framework (Ha et al. 2009). Government traditionally possesses relatively stronger decision-making power than other social sectors. The checks and balances of the legislature, the media, and the public have been relatively weak in South Korea. This may have come from the dictatorial years, but it can also be attributed to the close connection between social elite groups. The lack of a consensus-building process let the government freely push forward its agenda as it wanted. This government domination of the public policy-making process continued at least until the late 1980s. Economic success was only possible based on a secretive, top-down-style policy-making process (Lah 2010). However, rapid development resulted in neglect of democratic values such as human rights, equity and fairness, transparency, and most of all public trust and respect for government.

With ten years' experiences of two progressive presidents, however, society gained momentum for more democratic development. Since the 2000s, many kinds of public participation have been used, including citizen referendums, citizen recall, citizen litigation, a citizen budget system, and citizen participation in the trial system (Lah 2010). The democracy in Korea, however, came at the cost of social conflicts. NGOs strengthened their activities and the media freely criticized governmental policies. It became very hard to find a consensus-based solution to national projects such as the Sapaesan Tunnel Project, naval base construction in Jeju, a Free Trade Agreement with the US, and the Four Rivers restoration project. The Park Geun-hye government created the Presidential Committee for National Cohesion to deal with social conflicts. South Korea needs more experience in order to balance democracy and social stability.

New Public Management and Performance Management

Following the global trend called New Public Management (NPM), a performance management system was introduced in the early 2000s to create a mission-driven, incentive-based, decentralized senior civil service and top-down budgeting system. Performance management in South Korea has four different managerial dimensions: organization, human resources, finance, and evaluation (Lee and Moon 2010). The team-based structure and executive agency system are examples of organizational reforms. Human Resource Management (HRM) reforms include a more open and competitive civil service, performance agreements, performance-based pay, individual performance evaluation, and decentralization. A top-down budgeting system and total wage system characterize financial management. Programs are evaluated annually and the results are directly linked to the increase or decrease of the programs' budget allocation the next year. The government may have become more competitive through performance management, but its emphasis on competition makes collaboration between actors and organizations difficult. The success of performance management in South Korea depends on how to effectively overcome this conflict.

The use of IT and e-government

South Korea is well known for its cutting-edge information technology and top-notch e-government (see Chapter 33 in this volume for an in-depth analysis). Comprehensiveness, fragmentation, and orientation toward citizen services and operational efficiency, as well as building new systems rather than changing existing ones, characterize Korean e-government (Choi 2010). It has fundamentally changed the way government works (Kim 2005). In the mid-1990s, with the advance of information technology (IT) and the democratization of society, a networked system was created. With the Framework Act on Informatization Promotion, the government started to devise ways to use IT for improving the efficiency of public administration, including estate registration processes, patent filing, military services operations, and so on. E-government also increased transparency and helped decrease corruption. In the 2000s, the government began to provide citizen–oriented services online and accept ideas from the public. The relationship between e-government and democracy is already a virtuous circle. More IT has brought more transparency and vice versa. The current e-government represents the overall policy orientation of South Korea. The Park administration claims to be a more open government by sharing information publicly, breaking down barriers between ministries and setting up a "creative economy" by sharing previously confidential governmental data with the public. The government plans to collect public opinions on major policies and projects and seek cooperation with the private sector through online, direct democracy (MSPA 2014).

Hong Kong

General introduction

After 155 years of British colonialism, Hong Kong was established as a Special Administrative Region (SAR) of the People's Republic of China in July 1997. The SAR operates separate economic, political, administrative and legal systems under the Basic Law and the policy of "One Country, Two Systems" laid down by Chinese leader Deng Xiaoping. With only 1,104 square kilometers, Hong Kong is home to more than seven million people, among the highest population density in the world. Benefiting from China's reform and opening up since 1978, Hong Kong has transformed itself from a manufacturing into a service economy. Already a global financial and business center, Hong Kong is not only the world's eighth largest trading economy and sixth largest stock market, but also a premier gateway for trade and investment in Mainland China (HKSAR Government 2013).

Historical development of public policy and administration in Hong Kong

The colonial era

Public administration in colonial Hong Kong was characterized by the building of a meritocratic bureaucracy under the rule of law and the British administrative tradition (Lee 2011). The colonial bureaucracy was established mainly to maintain law and order and hence to facilitate British business interests, rather than to serve the local people, so the public sector in Hong Kong remained small before the end of World War II. Only after the 1967 riots instigated by leftists did the highly authoritarian colonial regime launch more social policies to alleviate massive social discontent. During the 1970s, the philosophy of the colonial government moved from laissez-faire to a more proactive "positive non-interventionism" (Cheung 2010), so it could intervene selectively, especially in education and housing. Through the "administrative absorption of politics," appointing businesspeople and professionals to advisory and statutory bodies, the colonial government co-opted the emerging middle class and local business elites. The highly centralized structure of the bureaucracy was reorganized and policy functions were delegated to six policy branches and two resource branches in the Government Secretariat, according to the recommendations of the 1973 McKinsey Report. This division into policy-making branches (later called bureaus) and departments for execution has remained the framework of the Hong Kong government ever since. Public administration was considered "administratively pragmatic, economically conservative and fiscally limited" (Cheung 2010).

The transition to Chinese rule from the mid-1980s

The 1984 Sino-British Joint Declaration was overshadowed by a confidence crisis about Hong Kong's future. Full democratization did not happen during this transition but, beginning in the mid-1980s, direct elections at the district level were introduced to incorporate community views. More social programs were also launched. Concerns about the cost and quality of services in the public sector prompted the introduction of NPM reforms. Nonetheless, the 1989 political crisis in Mainland China shook the confidence of Hong Kong citizens during the transition to Chinese sovereignty.

The post-1997 period

Under the Basic Law, the political system kept the key elements of the colonial government intact, but the political and policy contexts have experienced profound changes since 1997. The Chief Executive (CE) replaced the Governor as the head of government. The Accountability System for Principal Officials was introduced in 2002 to enhance the CE's power over the bureaucracy and to recruit non-civil servants into the top echelons. Each bureau would be headed by a politically appointed Secretary accountable to the CE. The number of bureaus dropped from 16 to 11 to facilitate better allocation of resources and closer coordination of policy portfolios. A further reorganization of the Government Secretariat in 2007 increased the number of bureaus to 12. Nonetheless, since 2002, about half of these ministers have still come from the civil service. The need for economic restructuring after the 1997 Asian financial crisis compelled further administrative changes. For instance, Hong Kong witnessed a downsizing of the civil service from 184,639 in 1997 to 153,477 in 2008 and 170,404 in early 2014 through efficiency drives, voluntary retirement, and an open recruitment freeze (Scott 2010; Civil Service Bureau 2014).

Growing social inequality, ageing population, and popular demands expedited the modification of the government's non-interventionist stance. Public expenditure increased from HK$194.4 billion in 1997–1998 to HK$421.0 billion in 2014–2015, representing a growth of 4.7 per cent per annum. Education, social welfare, and health are the key expenditures, contributing about 57 per cent of total recurring expenditures in 2014–2015. Revenue increased from HK$281 billion in 1997–1998 to HK$430 billion in 2014–2015, representing a growth of 2.5 per cent per annum (Working Group on Long-Term Fiscal Planning 2014).

NPM measures such as corporatization, outsourcing, and privatization expanded after 1997. The Asian financial crisis and the ensuing economic depression led to unprecedented budgetary deficits and the acceleration of private sector involvement in delivering public service. Increasing challenges from opposition groups and social expectations, coupled with external economic pressures, have compelled the government to take a more assertive role in socioeconomic development, even though its capacity to command public trust and deliver service eroded after 1997.

Key challenges of public policy and administration in Hong Kong since 1997

The political executive and executive–legislative relations

The formal powers of the executive are extensive. The CE, however, lacks a clear popular mandate, as he was elected by an election committee composed of 1,200 from the elites. Without political party support under the current system, he has to rely upon pro-establishment legislators to pass laws, but such support cannot be taken for granted. After 1997, the Legislative Council (LegCo) has evolved into the main opposition to the executive. The Basic Law constrains the power of LegCo to propose policy alternatives or amendments that challenge the government's policy agenda, and the separate vote-counting mechanism requires separate majorities in both the geographical and functional constituencies for passing any motion, bill, or amendment introduced by individual legislators. Pro-government forces regularly constitute the majority in the functional constituencies, but not in the geographic constituency of LegCo. The government cannot assume unanimous support from pro-establishment parties for unpopular proposals when they find it politically expedient to oppose the government. The prospect of reaching a broad-based agreement is often difficult, and tortuous bargaining between the government and the LegCo is routine. The legislature, which is constituted by a proportional representation electoral system, cannot serve as an effective mechanism in aggregating societal interests. Policy agenda setting has also been increasingly shaped by politics outside the legislature, as social movements have often mobilized strong opposition to challenge the government.

The bureaucracy and the public sector

The policy secretaries are accountable to the CE but they dictate priorities within their portfolios, so coordination between them has weakened, in sharp contrast to the pre-2002 system dominated by the administrative elites with a stronger esprit de corps. In the absence of a popular mandate and effective leadership, amid a period of economic fluctuation, growing social demands increasingly expose the legitimacy deficit of the government. The politically appointed secretaries have been noted for their lacklustre performance, further weakening the morale of the civil service and the performance legitimacy of the regime. In short, the policy capacity of the post-1997 government has weakened in a highly turbulent economic and political environment.

The role of citizen participation

In order to legitimize policies in a quasi-democratic polity, mechanisms for public participation established in the colonial period, such as district and advisory bodies and public consultation exercises, were retained after 1997. However, they have been challenged by an increasingly vocal civil society, especially since 2003 when it mobilized against the national security legislation. The government was compelled to adopt more participatory public engagement mechanisms in areas such as heritage preservation and urban planning, but the utilization of such mechanisms varied widely across policy areas (Cheung 2011). Judicial review has been regularly used by critics to delay the policy process, and filibustering tactics have also been employed by opposition legislators.

A wave of new social movements, featuring youth participation and digital activism using social media for mobilization, has emerged, as reflected most aptly in the Occupy protests fighting for universal suffrage in late 2014. Increasing protests and demonstrations revealed the inadequacy of existing participatory channels, the rise of local identity and the legitimacy deficit of the quasi-democratic regime amidst closer socioeconomic interactions between Hong Kong and Mainland China. To conclude, public administration in Hong Kong has been facing important challenges since 1997 because the existing regime lacks sufficient popular support to drive policy consensus and to deliver better public service to satisfy a demanding population.

Conclusion

In pursuit of better public administration and policy, more commonalities than differences are found in the three unique jurisdictions China, South Korea, and Hong Kong. All three governments underwent a period of modernization, characterized by rapid economic development and a struggle for democracy. A similar path was found in the introduction of modern public administration structure and policy procedures, which can be summarized as a more efficient government. In particular, China and South Korea are remarkable in their rapid economic development in the late 20th century. Large-scale governmental policy developments were seen as essentially instrumental to the repositioning of the state to be more market-oriented.

The pursuit of efficiency and better performance was echoed by the government reforms in all three jurisdictions. The reform efforts were not always fully successful but nevertheless made meaningful improvements. The reforms often took the form of administrative restructuring.

Privatization, outsourcing, downsizing, and reorganization proposed by the NPM movement were manifested in the three jurisdictions and even fueled by the financial crisis in the late 1990s. The new reform efforts also emphasized the role of the non-governmental sector by empowering civil society and encouraging public involvement in the policy-making process. Although government still has a very strong power and capacity, it has become more responsive to the demands of civil society. Governments in the three jurisdictions have become keen to be perceived as more democratic, especially on matters such as transparency and public collaboration.

Globalization, which first affected and was brought about through the market, has also affected public administration. As such, the reforms to public administration in the three jurisdictions over the past couple of decades conform to the global norms such as NPM and the new emphasis on the collaboration of diverse social players. As such, these three jurisdictions follow many of the themes outlined in the preceding three chapters: the increased complexity of public administration and the ascent of new means to include more stakeholders. Of course, the particular path of reforms balanced domestic circumstances with broader global trends. Challenges still remain for each government. China is calling for more systematic coordination between government entities. Civil unrest within an omnipresent democracy is one of the most significant challenges for Korea. In Hong Kong, the performance and accountability of the government is currently in question due to the absence of effective political leadership and fully developed democracy.

Notes

1   Data from www.mca.gov.cn/article/zwgk/mzyw/201406/20140600654488.shtml. Local governments have very different forms: for example, the 34 provinces include four Directly-Supervised Municipalities, 23 Provinces (including Taiwan), five Minority Autonomous Regions, and two Special Administrative Districts (Hong Kong and Macao).
2   Interview with Jinping Xi on Feb 10, 2014. Retrieved from http://cpc.people.com.cn/pinglun/n/2014/0212/c241220-24335444.html.

References

Ahn, B. Y. and M. Jung. 2007. "Democracy, equity, and administration: looking for the theoretical and empirical implications for Korean public administration research." *Korean Public Administration Review* 41 (3): 1–40.

Chan, H. S. 2007. "Civil Service Law in the PRC: A Return to Cadre Personnel Management." *Public Administration Review* 67 (3): 383–398.

Cheung, B. L. A. 2010. "In Search of Trust and Legitimacy: The Political Trajectory of Hong Kong as Part of China." *International Public Management Review* 11 (2): 38–63.

Cheung, P. T. 2011. "Civic Engagement in the Policy Process in Hong Kong: Change and Continuity." *Public Administration and Development* 31 (2): 113–121.

Choi, H. S. 2010. "E-government in South Korea." In *Public Administration in East Asia: Mainland China, Japan, South Korea, and Taiwan*, edited by E. M. Berman, M. J. Moon, and H. Choi. Boca Raton, FL: CRC Press.

Civil Service Bureau. 2015. "Annually-Updated Civil Service Personnel Statistics." Accessed 04/06/2016 from www.csb.gov.hk/english/stat/annually/547.html.

Ha, Y. S., J. H. Joo, Ma. A. Kang, T. J. Lah, and J. H. Jang. 2009. "Social Conflicts and Policy-Making in Korea: Interpretation of Policy Failures through a Public Discourse Perspective." *International Review of Administrative Sciences* 75 (4): 649–664.

Hong Kong SAR Government. 2013. "Hong Kong 2013." Accessed 04/06/2016 from www.yearbook.gov.hk/2013/en/index.html.

Jing, Y. 2015. "Between Control and Empowerment: Governmental Strategies of Nonprofit Development in China." *Asian Studies Review*, 39 (4): 589–608.

Jing, Y. 2010. "History and Context of Chinese Public Administration." In *Public Administration in East Asia: Mainland China, Japan, South Korea and Taiwan*, edited by E. M. Berman, M. J. Moon, and H. Choi, 33–53. Boca Raton, FL: CRC Press.

Kang, K., Y. Lee, and S. Choi. 2008. "Policy decision system in the rapid growth period in Korea: The Economic Planning Board and Policy Implementation Institutions." Sejong: Korea Development Institute.

Kim, S. 2005. "Towards a New Paradigm of e-Government from Bureaucracy Model to Governance Model." In *Building e-Governance: Challenges and Opportunities for Democracy, Administration and Law*, edited by P. S. Kim, and W. Jho, 103–119. Korea: International Institute of Administrative Sciences, Belgium & National Computerization Agency.

Korean Culture and Information Service. 2015. *Facts about Korea.* Sejong: Korean Culture and Information Service.

Lah, T. J. 2013. "The Four Major Rivers Project in South Korea: Disguise of Green Growth Policy?" Paper presented at London Symposium.

Lah, T. J. 2010. "Public Policy Processes and Citizen Participation in South Korea." In *Public Administration in East Asia: Mainland China, Japan, South Korea, and Taiwan*, edited by E. M. Berman, M.J. Moon, and H. Choi. Boca Raton, FL: CRC Press.

Lee, C. K. and M. J. Moon. 2010. "Performance Management Reforms in South Korea." In *Public Administration in East Asia: Mainland China, Japan, South Korea, and Taiwan*, edited by E. M. Berman, M. J. Moon, and H. Choi. Boca Raton, FL: CRC Press.

Lee, Eliza W. Y. 2011. "History and Context of Public Administration in Hong Kong." In *Public Administration in Southeast Asia: Thailand, Philippines Malaysia, Hong Kong and Macao*, edited by E. M. Berman, 239–253. Boca Raton, FL: CRC Press.

Ministry of Security and Public Administration. 2014. "2014 Action Plan for Government 3.0." South Korea: MSPA.

Lynn Jr., L. E. 2005. "Public Management: A Concise History of the Field." In *The Oxford Handbook of Public Management*, edited by Ewan Ferlie et al., 27–50. Oxford: Oxford University Press.

Mosher, Frederick C. 1975. *American Public Administration: Past, Present, Future.* Birmingham: University of Alabama Press.

Ngok, K. and Zhu. G. 2007. "Marketization, Globalization and Administrative Reform in China: A Zigzag Road to a Promising Future." *International Review of Administrative Sciences* 73 (2): 217–233.

Riggs, F. 1964. *Administration in Developing Countries: The Theory of Prismatic Society.* Boston: Houghton Mifflin.

Scott, I. 2010. *The Public Sector in Hong Kong.* Hong Kong: Hong Kong University Press.

Working Group on Long-Term Fiscal Planning. 2014. Report of the Working Group on Long-Term Fiscal Planning. March 3. Accessed 04/06/2016 from www.fstb.gov.hk/tb/en/docs/3_wg_report_executive_summary.pdf.

Young, D. R. 2000. "Alternative Models of Government–Nonprofit Sector Relations: Theoretical and International Perspectives." *Nonprofit and Voluntary Sector Quarterly* 29 (1): 149–172.

6

REVOLUTION, TERRORISM, AND GOVERNANCE IN THE MIDDLE EAST

Alexander Dawoody

Introduction

Twentieth-century governance and public administration in the Middle East has been significantly impacted by the creation of most Middle Eastern nation-states by colonial powers after World War I, most notably France and Great Britain (Sorenson 2013). The inorganic nature of this creation provided an environment for injustice to be institutionalized and for marginalization and alienation of the public to become the norm. Although similar processes occurred in other parts of the world, including in Africa and Asia, in the Middle East its consequences have been particularly severe. Some observers suggest that some of the origins of the region's current failed states are a result of the nature of their birth (Lynch 2013).

Three movements emerged immediately after the creation of the modern Middle East, each attempting to deal with problems inherited from the inorganic nature of the region's creation: nationalism, socialism, and Political Islam. Nationalism arose from a new class whose leaders were educated abroad or exposed to national ideologies of the Western bourgeoisie. This class, later, also came to include members of the military from poorer classes that seized political power via military coups (Dawoody 2014).

Overall, the nationalist movement formed political organizations espousing patriarchal nationalistic ideologies and policies of economic protectionism. Puritanism became the hallmark of this movement in many nations, institutionalized as the cult of "Great Leader". Dictatorships with initial considerable popular support eventually became unpopular because of their inability to resolve social problems through civic institutions, competent public administration, and sound economic development.

A second movement grew parallel with nationalism, espousing socialist ideology and challenging the first movement for control of public policy and political power. Although the Cold War gave some momentum to the movement, the collapse of the Soviet Union resulted in its demise. Today this movement is nothing but nostalgia and the recital of outdated political dogma.

The third movement arose largely from Political Islam, which developed during the aftermath of the collapse of the Ottoman Caliphate in the early years of the twentieth century. The objective of the movement was a return to, or adoption of, the Islamic Caliphate and

Sharia-based governance as a model for a modern state. The third movement – partly because it was opposed, sometimes violently, by the other two movements – involved considerable grassroots development. The Iranian Revolution of 1979 that resulted in the overthrow of a nationalist "great leader" is the most enduring example. In some cases, the movement's violent manifestations took precedence, resulting in groups and organizations that vary only in their range of tactical application of violence (Lewis 2004).

Ironically, parts of the region that we call the Middle East were some 3,500 years ago the places where the art and science of administration were developed, specifically by the scribes of Mesopotamia. Public administration became a viable tool for the foundation of the first state in history, known as Akkad. Administration was also the main element responsible for the creation of writing, an instrument that early Mesopotamian scribes needed in order to record offerings to the temples (Van De Mieroop 1999).

The powerful empires of the ancient Middle East, such as the Persian, Assyrian, Babylonian, Umayyad, and Abbasid powers, had sophisticated administrations, universities, libraries, hospitals, cities, irrigation systems, and militaries. Although their governance was marred by socio-political conflicts and often manipulated for the benefits of the ruling oligarchies at the expense of vast sectors of the population, their public policies and administrations were responsible for transforming the region into a center of achievements in philosophy, science, music, poetry, and the arts for many centuries (Leick 2003).

After the sack of Baghdad by the Mongols in 1258 and the destruction of most of the administrative systems of the Abbasid state, the Middle East entered a period of turmoil that to some extent continues to the present (Kennedy 2006). For example, hydrocarbon resources (oil and gas) have produced massive wealth for a few in the past 70 years, while also creating a poor and heavily dependent, non-productive swathe of the population that lacks basic needs (Ross 2013).

Governance in the Middle East today, with the exception of very few nations, is a mix of authoritarian and pseudo-democratic systems. The ruling oligarchies' decades-old practice of manipulating governmental apparatus in order to siphon public resources and tighten their grip on power has led to high levels of corruption and nepotism, a lack of transparency and accountability, and censorship, as well as an extensive and oppressive police state (Dawoody 2013).

Causes of upheaval in the Middle East

The chapter now turns to the unique challenges to reforming governance structures in the Middle East. In particular, four factors are analyzed: (1) the role of political elites and opposition groups; (2) the role of foreign involvement, especially that of the United States; (3) the rise of failed states; and (4) the role of tribalism and religious schisms.

Elites and opposition

The modern Middle East and the new countries that were brought to existence in the aftermath of the Sykes–Picot Agreement of 1916 (Fromkin 2009) have usually been governed by isolated oligarchies, military juntas, and tribal chieftains that cared primarily about solidifying their position in power and enriching their lot (Khoury and Kostiner 1991). The governmental apparatus acted as a tool of oppression creating massive, dysfunctional bureaucracies feeding on corruption, a police state, censorship, and nepotism, rather than serving the public interest. In such an atmosphere all forms of opposition were silenced and freedom of expression, gathering and organization were met with political torture, imprisonment, and summary executions (Lesch and Haas 2012).

Internal and external enemies were created in order to justify the continuous imposition of laws suspending individual rights and prolonging the tenure of political leaders and parties by decree, in the complete absence of participatory processes. Ideological indoctrination was imposed in each aspect of daily life in order to normalize this abnormal trend. In many nations, the central ideology gradually shifted from nationalism to socialism to Political Islam (Dawoody 2014). To enforce obedience, the state and religion became interchangeable, persuading citizens that an opposition to the status quo was an opposition to religious teachings and thus God's will.

The relative absence of political debates in the Middle East and the domination of repetitive, mundane and unthinking forms of schooling (perpetuated by the Madrasa system) reinforced by governmental propaganda machines have produced a class of citizens who are disfranchised but have few alternatives to express their grievances. This is compounded by the migration of highly educated individuals and families from the Middle East to the West for economic, social, personal, and political reasons.

The absence of a viable political opposition that can lead public movements and demand political reforms has created a vacuum that in some cases has been filled by Political Islam and its extremist wings. Mosques are employed as a connective nexus to support an anti-establishment movement logistically, ideologically, and politically (Bokhari and Senzai 2013). This role of mosques has been long-standing through centuries of political oppression and tyrannical forms of governance.

After the Arab Spring of 2013 and the collapse of reactionary and tyrannical regimes in Tunisia, Libya, Egypt, and Yemen, the environment was right for the emergence of democratic and representative governments. However, due to the absence of viable civic institutions, democratic opposition movements, and democratic traditions, these countries fell prey to Political Islam (Bradley 2012). Within a short time, these leaders were ejected from power and governance once again either returned to the rule by the old guard (as in Tunisia), the military (as in Egypt), or descended into chaos (as in Libya and Yemen). Terrorist groups saw in Libya and Yemen a perfect swamp for growth, engaging the old guard that returned to power in Egypt and Tunisia in almost a daily confrontation (mostly in Egypt, since the Muslim Brotherhood has the support of many poor and disenfranchised citizens).

In Syria, however, the Arab Spring took a different turn from the paths that had emerged in Tunisia, Egypt, Libya, and Yemen. Although the popular uprising against the Assad regime remained peaceful for the first six months, the movement lacked international backing, as was the case elsewhere (Hokayem 2013). When offenses by the Assad regime escalated, including the use of chemical weapons against civilian population, the peaceful movement turned to armed struggle by defected Syrian soldiers calling themselves the "Free Syrian Army" (US Government 2014). Jihadist groups seized the vacuum created by the West's reluctance to support the Free Syrian Army in order to pour into Syria and utilize the situation for their advantage (Erlich and Chomsky 2014).

With Iran, Iraq, Russia, and Hezbollah of Lebanon backing Assad both militarily and financially, the rich Arab oil countries such as Qatar, Saudi Arabia, and Kuwait backed those fighting against Assad (Hokayem 2013). As the violence escalated and nearly 120,000 Syrians were killed and another two million became refugees, Syria became a no-man's land. The capital city of Damascus and a narrow strip around it remained under Assad's regime while the rest of the country was divided by fighting Jihadists. Groups such as Al Nusra, Islamic State of Iraq and Syria (ISIS) and others emerged, espousing the most reactionary and violent doctrines (US Government 2014).

In 2014 the Syrian civil war spilled into Iraq, capitalizing on the weakness of the Iraqi army and the despised sectarian policies of its corrupt and incompetent government (Cockburn 2015). Supported by the local Sunni population, who had suffered since 2003 under the Shiite-dominated government in Iraq, the Jihadist groups in Syria (namely ISIS) were able to build alliances with Saddam's former military officers and easily capture the provinces of Mosul, Salahhdin, and Anbar (Weiss and Hassan 2015). Soon after, ISIS announced the rebirth of the Islamic Caliphate and began its terror campaign against the Iraqi Yazidis and Christians, destroying their homes, cities, and villages, killing men and raping women. It was only when ISIS fighters turned their attention to the Kurdish region that the West, headed by the United States, decided to intervene through an air campaign in order to stop ISIS's advances (Cockburn 2015).

Foreign involvement

Post World War II, with the discovery of oil and the withdrawal of old colonial powers, the United States became the major power broker in the Middle East and sought to advance its economic and political interests, especially in the oil-rich areas of the region.

Security and order became the mantra of the US and its client states in the region, at the expense of democratization and individual freedoms (Migdal 2014). The result was that the US supported tyrannical and reactionary regimes in the Middle East and on occasions directly interfered, either militarily or through covert intelligence operations, to support these regimes. The most obvious examples of this include the orchestration of the 1953 coup in Iran against a democratically elected government, as well as US military intervention to support the oil sheikhs of Kuwait and Saudi Arabia, and providing financial resources for the dictatorships of Egypt.

The priority of the US to protect oil supplies meant that Saddam Hussein and his Ba'ath regime in Iraq enjoyed unwavering US military, financial, and political support when his actions were beneficial to US interests, especially during the Iran–Iraq War of 1980–1988 (Hahn 2005).

When Hussein gassed Kurdish minorities in 1988, killing more than 5,000 civilians with mustard gas, the US treated his actions as an internal matter. Only later, when Hussein occupied Kuwait's oil fields and thus threatened US economic interests, did the Kurdish massacre suddenly surface in American politics, and he was denounced for committing genocide and harboring weapons of mass destruction (Charountaki 2010).

The two Gulf Wars, led by the US against the Ba'ath regime in Iraq in 1991 and 2003, and the devastating United Nations-imposed sanctions on Iraq from 1991 to 2003, resulted in more than three million deaths in Iraq, the destruction of the infrastructure, and high levels of malnutrition, poverty, unemployment, and institutionalized sectarian violence (Ismael and Ismael 2015). Today Iraq is a model for a failed state ridden with terrorist bombs, kidnapping, beheading, corruption, and a dysfunctional governmental system (Al-Ali 2014). Components of Iraq's ethnic and religious communities are fighting one another for control of power and resources: Sunnis against Shiites, Muslims against Christians, and Arabs against Kurds (Rayburn 2014). When governance is incapacitated to such an extent as it is in Iraq, the environment becomes ripe for terrorist groups such as ISIS to capitalize on and manipulate the situation to its advantage.

Failed states

Poor governance, sometimes further compounded by foreign intervention, creates ineffective policies that result in political crisis, stagnation, and some forms of lawlessness and disorder. For the most part, these crises are manageable and can be placed under control through repressive and undemocratic measures, such as military dictatorships. However, the Middle East is saturated with failed states that in some cases aided the growth and spread of terrorism. Examples of these failed states are Libya, Iraq, Syria, Somalia, Yemen, Lebanon, and Afghanistan.

In Libya, after four decades of Qaddafi's tyrannical regime, NATO's military intervention in the aftermath of the Arab Spring in 2013, and then its quick withdrawal without helping Libyans build a strong government, left the nation without internal peace and order (Engelbrekt and Mohlin 2013). Today, the government in Libya is nothing but a few individuals who are hiding in hotels while the country is torn between Jihadist terrorist groups. The latter are supported by Qatar and Turkey, who use them to force their own Islamist-driven political agenda on the entire region.

In Iraq, the occupation of the country by the US in 2003 resulted in the dismantling of the state and its administrative apparatus, the institutionalization of quotas and sectarianism in the new Iraqi Constitution, and as a result the alienation of the country's Sunni community. The disempowered Sunnis saw in Islamist terrorist groups a perfect vehicle to force their demands and return to power. Iraq today is torn between ethnic and sectarian violence, with a third of its land controlled by terrorist organizations (Ismael and Ismael 2015). The central government is powerless, decapitated by corruption, political opportunism, incompetence, and non-government militia (Al-Ali 2014). Ordinary Iraqi citizens are trapped between a government that represents the narrow views of Shiite militia and terrorist groups that want to use terror to return Iraq to the seventh century.

Syria is now geographically partitioned into several distinct regions. The capital city of Damascus and the Alawites strip near the Mediterranean Sea are under the Assad regime control. Dara and most of southern Syria is under Free Syrian Army control. Most of the western region is under Al-Qaeda and Al-Nusra control. Aleppo, northern Syria, Ar-Raqqah, and part of the eastern region are under ISIS control. Northeastern Syria is under Kurdish control (mainly PPK fighters who identify Turkey as their arch enemy). With nearly 120,000 Syrian civilians killed, two million refugees in Jordan, Lebanon, Iraq, and Turkey, and nearly 20,000 foreign Jihadists making their way to Syria through Turkish borders, often with the knowledge and permission of the Turkish authorities, Syria today is a failed state and considered the most dangerous place on earth. It is a hub that breeds terrorism and a magnet to continually attract future recruits.

Somalia has been a failed state since the collapse of Mohammad Siad Barre's government in 1991, due to tribal and military conflicts and the agony of civil war that lasted until 2006. It was during this civil war that the world became aware of the famine caused by drought that was devastating the Somalian population. Warlords were hijacking international aid packages in order to solidify their power and control over the population (Fergusson 2013). The US military attempt to guard these relief efforts resulted in the disastrous downing of a Black Hawk helicopter in 1993, and the killing and parading of the bodies of its pilots in the capital city Mogadishu (Clarke and Herbst 1997). In 2012, a weak government was formed to restate the state's control and authority over a land that disintegrated into three states, Somalia, Somali Land, and Putland, and a population terrorized by pirates known as Al-Shabab (Hansen 2013), an offshoot of Al-Qaeda which recently affirmed its allegiance to ISIS.

Yemen, long ruled by its strong military man Ali Abdullah Salih, was forcibly united in 1990 after eight years of civil war between its northern and southern parts (Brehony 2013) and became the fourth country in the Middle East to witness the Arab Spring in 2011 after Tunisia, Egypt, and Libya (Lynch 2013). Demonstrations continued to be peaceful despite a military crackdown by Salih's regime. Eventually, after mediation by Saudi Arabia, Salih agreed to step down in 2012 and hand power to his Vice President Abd Rabbuh Mansur Hadi (Rabi 2015). The government of Hadi, however, collapsed under pressure from a Shiite tribal group known as Al-Houthies (Salmoni and Loidolt 2010). Today, Yemen is one of the strongholds of Al-Qaeda, and with the Al-Houthy tribe in power, the failed state has paved the way for organized terrorist groups (namely Al-Qaeda, since Yemen was the birthplace of its founder, Osama bin Laden) to wreak havoc on regional and world security, including maritime travel in the straits of Aden in the Red Sea.

Although better functioning than other failed states in the region, Lebanon nevertheless is a failed state and a hub for the largest legitimized terrorist organization in the Middle East: Hezbollah. Not only does Hezbollah paralyze the Lebanese state, it is the Lebanese state (Worrall and Clubb 2015). No one is elected and placed in power, including the country's ceremonial Christian President, the Sunni Prime Minister, or the Shiite head of Parliament, without Hezbollah approval. Hezbollah has its own military, institutions, members of cabinet, and members of Parliament and it dictates the country's domestic and foreign policy. Because of such paralysis, Lebanon is a de facto failed state (Levitt 2013). Lebanon's proximity to Syria had always made it a target for Syria's state-sponsored terrorism, including the assassination of its leaders, such as the assassination of Lebanese Prime Minister Rafiq Hariri in 2005 by Syrian intelligence and Hezbollah operatives. Today, Hezbollah is fully engaged (including sending armed men) in defending the Assad regime in Syria, making Lebanon and Lebanese–Syrian borders an open arena for conflicts and violence.

In the case of Afghanistan, the US used the Soviet invasion in 1979 as a recruiting ground for Islamist Jihadists to fight the Soviets in the name of God and freedom. Once defeated, the Soviets withdrew from Afghanistan in 1989, along with the US, leaving the Jihadists to fight among themselves for control of the country (Coll 2004). The civil war continued until 1996, when an Afghani terrorist group named the Taliban, trained and armed by Pakistan, took power and established one of the most reactionary, misogynist, and repressive regimes in modern history (Tanner 2009). The Taliban hosted Osama Bin Laden and his Al-Qaeda network. After September 11, 2001 and when they refused to surrender Osama Bin Laden to the United States, the Taliban were driven out of power by the US military and Afghanistan came under US military control (Tucker-Jones 2014).

Although the United States allowed elections to be held for president and an independent government to be formed, the US-protected Afghani government lacks any real existence outside the capital city of Kabul. Hence, the President of Afghanistan is best called the mayor of Kabul. Most of the countryside is back under Taliban control. This situation makes Afghanistan yet another failed state and a safe haven for terrorist groups such as Taliban and Al-Qaeda.

Tribalism and religious schisms

A final feature of governance in the Middle East is the continuous domination of tribalism and religious schisms (Kamrava 1998). When individualism is crushed or undermined and decisions are made by tribal chieftains, group interests become more important than individual rights. If the state cannot broker the interests of different tribes – when government, for example, is dominated by other tribes and thus has to respond to the dominant tribes' interests – the disaffected parties invite terrorist groups to advance their objectives. For example, this is what is taking place in parts of Iraq today. When the Shiite-dominated government in Baghdad systemically excluded Sunni tribes from sharing power, these tribes invited terrorists such as ISIS to force its demands. Only when these tribes realize that such an alliance with these terrorist groups may limit their autonomy do they then turn against their allies and expel them.

Tribalism reinforces sectarian divides in the Middle East, especially among Sunnis and Shiites. The division between the Sunnis and Shiites in Islam is not recent but rather dates back to the early years of Islam, particularity after the Prophet Muhammad's death when the Caliphate passed to his friend and father-in-law instead of his cousin, Ali. For the bulk of history, Muslims largely restricted the division to religious rituals (Hazleton, 2010). Recently, however, terrorist groups such as Al-Qaeda and ISIS, as well as Shiite militia, have been using this divide for political reasons in order to gain complete power at the expense of others.

Conclusion

Today in the Middle East, two major paths have emerged in efforts to make governance more representative, transparent, accountable, and effective. The first is led by civic society groups advocating a change in governance to make it more democratic and better engaged in building a prosperous civil society. This group is largely unorganized and spontaneous, exemplified by events labelled by the Western media as the Arab Spring. Unfortunately, due to the newness and disorganized nature of the movement, it is easily manipulated by traditional power brokers and entrenched groups. The second path is followed by groups that yearn for a change in governance that returns to, or builds on, the sixth-century Islamic Caliphate and the constitutionalization of Sharia Law. Some groups advocating such a foundation of governance sometimes resort to terrorist acts.

When analyzing changes in governance in the Middle East, it is imperative to differentiate between revolution and terrorism. Although both may share some causality (such as a rejection of the existing order), they differ in regard to legitimacy. Revolution signifies the demand by large segments of the population for sound governance, better lives, and a better future. In the absence of democratic channels and viable opposition political movements, revolutions in the form of mass protests, demonstrations, labor strikes, and peaceful gatherings such as the Arab Spring are both necessary and required in order to ensure legitimate governance. If tyrannical governmental apparatus responds to these mass protests with violence, as was the case in Syria in 2011, then citizens have the right to fight oppression and defend their homes and families and pursue their demands. This is emphasized, for example, by the US Constitution, which legitimizes arming a popular militia when government no longer democratically represents the will of the public.

In the case of terrorism, however, there is less justification for violence. The main reason for this is that terrorism does not represent the free will of the people but rather uses violence to impose a narrow ideology on the majority. Terrorism ends the legitimacy of the state and replaces it with a savage Hobbesian lawless society where only the strong survive at the expense of security, freedom, and rights.

The region's recent experiments with democracy, whether top-down like the one imported by outsiders into Iraq or Afghanistan, or through internal strife like the Arab Spring, have largely failed to bring sustained change to governance structures. This chapter points to four barriers to sustained reform.

First, the absence of civic institutions at grassroots levels and the powerful conservative elite groups seek to maintain the status quo. Second, foreign involvement, especially the role of the US, supports governance structures that meet its objectives. Third, the existence of failed states, which require extraordinary efforts to establish robust governance systems, spread terrorism in the Middle East, particularly terrorism associated with Political Islam. Lastly, longstanding tribal and political schisms impose limits on the governance structures of modern states, along with tribal and cultural traditions that emphasize collectivism at the expense of individualism.

References

Ali, Ayaan Hirsi. 2008. *The Caged Virgin: An Emancipation Proclamation for Women and Islam*. New York: Atria Books.

Al-Ali, Zaid. 2014. *The Struggle for Iraq's Future: How Corruption, Incompetence and Sectarianism Have Undermined Democracy*. New Haven, CT: Yale University Press.

Bradley, John R. 2012. *After the Arab Spring: How Islamists Hijacked The Middle East Revolts*. New York: Palgrave Macmillan.

Brehony, Noel. 2013. *Yemen Divided: The Story of a Failed State in South Arabia*. London: I. B. Tauris.

Bokhari, Kamran and Farid Senzai. 2013. *Political Islam in the Age of Democratization*. New York: Palgrave Macmillan.

Charountaki, Marianna. 2010. *The Kurds and US Foreign Policy: International Relations in the Middle East since 1945*. London and New York: Routledge.

Clarke, Walter S. and Jeffrey Herbst. 1997. *Learning from Somalia: The Lessons of Armed Humanitarian Intervention*. Boulder, CO: Westview Press.

Cockburn, Patrick. 2015. *The Rise of Islamic State: ISIS and the New Sunni Revolution*. London and New York: Verso.

Coll, Steve. 2014. *Ghost Wars: The Secret History of the CIA, Afghanistan, and Bin Laden, from the Soviet Invasion to September 10, 2001*. New York: Penguin Books.

Dalacoura, Katerina. 2011. *Islamist Terrorism and Democracy in the Middle East*. New York: Cambridge University Press.

Dawoody, Alexander. 2014. *Public Administration and Policy in the Middle East*. New York: Springer.

Dawoody, Alexander. 2013. "The Middle East and Learning from BRIC." *Innovation Journal*. 18(1): 1–11.

Dawoody, Alexander. 2012. "Teaching Public Policy in a Global Context." In *Globalization*, edited by Hector Cuadra-Montiel, 275–290. Rijeka, Croatia: In-Tech Publications.

Engelbrekt, Kjell and Marcus Mohlin. 2013. *The NATO Intervention in Libya: Lessons Learned from the Campaign*. London and New York: Routledge.

Erlich, Reese and Noam Chomsky. 2014. *Inside Syria: The Backstory of Their Civil War and What the World Can Expect*. Amherst, NY: Prometheus Books.

Fergusson, James. 2013. *The World's Most Dangerous Place: Inside the Outlaw State of Somalia*. Boston: Da Capo Press.

Fromkin, David. 2009. *A Peace to End All Peace: The Fall of the Ottoman Empire and the Creation of the Modern Middle East*. New York: Holt Paperbacks.

Hahn, Peter L. 2005. *Crisis and Crossfire: The United States and the Middle East since 1945*. Washington, DC: Potomac Books.

Hansen, Stig Jarle. 2013. *Al-Shabaab in Somalia: The History and Ideology of a Militant Islamist Group*. Oxford and New York: Oxford University Press.

Hazleton, Lesley. 2010. *After the Prophet: The Epic Story of the Shia–Sunni Split in Islam*. New York: Anchor.

Hokayem, Emile. 2013. *Syria's Uprising and the Fracturing of the Levant*. London and New York: Routledge.

Kamrava, Mehran. 1998. *Democracy in the Balance: Culture and Society in the Middle East*. New York and London: CQ Press.

Kennedy, Hugh. 2006. *When Baghdad Ruled the Muslim World: The Rise and Fall of Islam's Greatest Dynasty*. Cambridge, MA: Da Capo Press.

Khoury, Philip S. and J. Kostiner. 1991. *Tribes and State Formation in the Middle East*. Oakland, CA: University of California Press.

Ismael, Tareq Y. and Jacqueline S. Ismael. 2015. *Iraq in the Twenty-First Century: Regime Change and the Making of a Failed State*. New York: Durham Modern Middle East and Islamic World Series.

Lappin, Yaakov. 2010. *Virtual Caliphate: Exposing the Islamist State on the Internet*. Washington, DC: Potomac Books.

Leick, Gwendolyn. 2003. *Mesopotamia: The Invention of the City*. New York: Penguin Books.

Lesch, David W. and Mark L. Haas. 2012. *The Arab Spring: Change and Resistance in the Middle East*. Boulder, CO: Westview.

Lewis, Bernard. 2004. *The Crisis of Islam: Holy War and Unholy Terror*. New York: Random House.

Lewis, I.M. 2003. *A Modern History of the Somali: Nation and State in the Horn of Africa*. Athens, OH: Ohio University Press.

Levitt, Matthew. 2013. *Hezbollah: The Global Footprint of Lebanon's Party of God*. Washington, DC: Georgetown University Press.

Lynch, Marc. 2013. *The Arab Uprising: The Unfinished Revolutions of the New Middle East*. New York: Public Affairs.

Migdal, Joel S. 2014. *Shifting Sands: The United States in the Middle East*. New York: Columbia University Press.

Rabi, Uzi. 2015. *Yemen: Revolution, Civil War and Unification*. London: I. B. Tauris.

Rayburn, Joel. 2014. *Iraq after America: Strongmen, Sectarians, Resistance*. Stanford, CA: Hoover Institution Press.

Ross, Michael L. 2013. *The Oil Curse: How Petroleum Wealth Shapes the Development of Nations*. Princeton, NJ: Princeton University Press.

Salmoni, Barak A. and Bryce Loidolt. 2010. *Regime and Periphery in Northern Yemen: The Huthi Phenomenon*. Santa Monica, CA: RAND Corporation.

Saunders, Doug. 2012. *The Myth of the Muslim Tide: Do Immigrants Threaten the West?* New York: Vintage.

Sorenson, David. 2013. *An Introduction to the Modern Middle East: History, Religion, Political Economy, Politics*. Boulder, CO: Westview.

Tanner, Stephen. 2009. *Afghanistan: A Military History from Alexander the Great to the War against the Taliban*. Philadelphia: Da Capo Press.

Tucker-Jones, Anthony. 2014. *The Afghan War: Operation Enduring Freedom 2001–2014*. Barnsley, UK: Pen and Sword Military.

US Government. 2014. *The Resurgence of Al-Qaeda in Syria and Iraq – AQIM, Ansar al-Sharia, Al Nusrah Front, ISIS, Islamic Front, Aleppo, Alawites, Sunni, AQAP, Assad, Al-Shabaab, Salafist*. New York: Progressive Management.

Van De Mieroop, Marc. 1999. *The Ancient Mesopotamian City*. New York: Oxford University Press.

Weiss, Michael and Hassan Hassan. 2015. *ISIS: Inside the Army of Terror*. New York: Regan Arts.

Worrall, James and Gordon Clubb. 2015. *Hezbollah: From Islamic Resistance to Government*. Westport, CT: Praeger.

7

PARTICIPATE OR BE PUNISHED

Administrative responses to protest

Christopher Tapscott

Introduction

Over the course of the past three decades citizen participation in the formulation and implementation of state policy has been portrayed as integral to the notion of good governance, however amorphously defined this concept might be. The literature is replete with debates on the prospects for participatory and deliberative democracy and co-production as ways of strengthening the state–civil society interface (Fung and Wright 2003; Cornwall and Coelho 2007). By far the bulk of this writing has focused on the design of effective participatory systems and processes, on the dangers of elite capture, and on state co-optation amongst other issues (Hickey and Mohan 2009). Where attention has focused on forms of state–civil society engagement which fall outside of the participatory domain, namely protest action, this has been addressed in the extensive social movement literature which has examined the multiple ways in which different social groups mobilise to actualise their rights. However, despite the proliferation of protest, particularly, but not exclusively, in emerging democracies in the global South, little attention has been paid by public administration theorists to the ways in which states respond administratively to this form of engagement and whether state officials pay any heed to the demands put before them.

In recent years there has been considerable international focus on the mass-based protests which have brought about the downfall of ruling regimes in various parts of the world. Yet, leaving aside the revolutionary protest movements that led to the Arab Spring and to upheavals in Syria, Iraq, Ukraine, and elsewhere, other forms of protest which relate more to citizens' demands for basic socio-economic rights than a desire to change the political order are both widespread and growing, especially in countries in the global South. Whether in Brazil, India, or South Africa protest action has increasingly become a common medium through which disempowered citizens engage with the state. Reflective of this, in an analysis of 843 protests occurring in 84 countries (comprising 90 per cent of the world's population) during the period from 2006 to 2013, Ortiz et al. recorded a steady increase in the overall numbers of protests every year (Ortiz et al. 2013).[1] The study found that in aggregate, the main reason why people around the world were protesting (58 per cent of total protests) was a perceived lack of economic justice (Ortiz et al. 2013: 14). The perceived lack of economic justice related to popular outrage at policy failures, the lack of equitable development, the demand for jobs and better working and living conditions together with demands for public sector reforms amongst others (ibid.: 16) Significantly, the single most prevalent protest issue (26 per cent of all protests counted) related to the demand for 'real democracy', which was understood as a call for direct participation in decision making affecting the daily lives of the population and for access to the benefits promised by democracy. It was further found that protests for real democracy were not confined to any political regime or income group (ibid.: 22).

Although some studies link the recent upsurge in protest action to the austerity measures introduced following the 2008 global financial crash, Ortiz et al. assert that popular grievances extend well beyond the short term. "It is instead", they maintain, "a measure of people's growing awareness that policy making has not prioritised them – even when it has claimed to do so … Many of the world's protest arise when the majority of people feel left out, and when neither the middle classes nor the poor find public services adequate for their needs" (Ortiz et al. 2013: 19). Such protests are invariably directed not towards the attainment of first-order democratic rights (such as the right to vote, to free association, or to freedom of speech) but rather towards the actualisation of rights already recognised in legislation and policy. In a seeming paradox, such protests also frequently occur in new democracies in a context where legislation and policy exist to facilitate citizen participation and, formalistically at least, to encourage their input in state decision making. In practice, as has been documented in the literature (Cooke and Kothari 2001; Cleaver 2001), it is frustration with the shortcomings of these very systems of participatory democracy and their failure to deliver positive outcomes for the poor which is giving rise to protest action.

There are, of course, multiple types of protest and equally numerous factors which give rise to these forms of collective action. A significant proportion inevitably comes about as a consequence of dissatisfaction with political leaders and the perceived failure of their policies. It is also certain that some of these protests are intended to supplant prevailing leadership structures and/or to bring about regime change. Such protests typically do not open themselves up to any form of negotiated settlement and some are intentionally confrontational and latently violent. It is equally certain, however, that there is a range of protest action which is not intended to be either disruptive or violent but which is genuinely seeking some form of engagement with and redress by the state. It is this form of protest, and the responses of state officials to it, that form the focus of this chapter.

Notwithstanding the fact that protest, and particularly peaceful protest, has become a commonplace in state–civil society interactions in countries throughout the world, there is little evidence that it is recognised by state officials as a legitimate form of engagement or that the concerns raised through this process are taken into consideration or addressed. This is despite the fact that the right to freedom of association and to peaceful protest is enshrined in the constitutions of most, if not all, democratic states. Implicit in the right to protest is the understanding that citizens are entitled to express their dissent and to hold the state to account.

The consensual model of participation

Whilst the essentially adversarial nature of multi-party politics is seen as integral to the workings of democratic systems and is formally accommodated in the practices of state legislatures, no such latent tensions are recognised in state–civil society relations which tend to be viewed in an idealised a-political way. This is because participatory democracy, along with the participatory processes which are assumed to emanate from this concept, is premised on the belief that the relations between citizens and the state should be essentially harmonious. In terms of this consensual model, the parties involved are expected to accept and apply the same rules of engagement notwithstanding the fact that these typically have never been mutually negotiated nor are they the outcome of contestation through which the parameters for interaction have been agreed to in some form of compact. These rules of engagement, consequently, are seldom, if ever, based on equal power relations. Beyond the rhetoric of policy, the practicalities of engagement are shaped by state officials who set out the parameters for state–civil society interaction and prescribe under what conditions they should take place. In this context, the consensual model makes little provision for dissenting views and the balance of power is always vested in the state. Whether or not, as some critics maintain, this power asymmetry in inherent in neo-liberal governance systems and forms part of their hegemonic design, the net effect is official intolerance of any citizen interaction that falls outside these parameters.

Whilst participatory policies invariably include prescriptions on how the views of citizens must be heard and taken into consideration, this provision appears not to extend to citizens who take part in protest action. This disconnect between rights formalised in constitutions and their exercise in protest activity appears to be missed by state officials and the police in particular. In large part this is due to the fact that protest action, whilst tacitly recognised as a legitimate form of social/political mobilisation, is not recognised as a valid form of interaction between the state and civil society. Protesters, as a matter of course, cease to be rights-bearing citizens and instead are viewed as adversaries. In that respect, the official notion of participation denies the latent tension which exists in the relationship between the state and its citizens. In part, this might be ascribed to an unwillingness on the part of officials to engage with citizens on anything other than their own terms. Those who step outside of the formally created spaces for participation (Cornwall 2009), and create their own platforms for engagement with the state, stand to lose their legitimacy. However, as indicated, numerous studies have pointed to the fact that this form of engagement with the state is the product of frustration and anger at the repeated failure of formal participatory structures to deliver favourable outcomes. It is also evident that protest action is only one of several modes of interaction adopted by protestors, and it is often a last resort once other measures have been exhausted.

States characteristically display little reflexivity and seldom systematically assess the factors which might have led to protest action and, instead, resort to shorthand caricatures of the motives of those so engaged. Labelling a protest as 'politically motivated' is a typical conceit intended to de-legitimise the concerns raised by protesters and to suggest that their demands fall outside accepted ways of holding the state to account. Yet state–civil society interactions are, by their nature, decidedly political and whilst it would be naïve to ignore the fact that political parties and movements contesting for power do, in certain circumstances, mobilise their supporters to confront the state, it is also true that many local protest organisers shun party politics precisely because it can divert attention from their core grievances.

It is also certain that the very process of mobilising for protest serves a multiplicity of objectives, particularly for the disempowered and voiceless. Over and above the fact that it provides a platform for the public airing of grievances, it also serves to establish forms of solidarity and collective identity (Corrigall-Brown 2012) that are not possible in participatory processes. This, as the literature reveals, is because participatory systems often serve to exclude the more marginalised segments of society. In this context, the refusal of permission to protest is viewed as confrontational both because it is dismissive of what are perceived to be legitimate grievances and because it is decidedly disempowering. In that regard, official responses to collective action are generally out of touch with the socio-cultural and socio-political realities of the times and the changing nature of state–civil society relations. As a consequence, their anticipation of and response to protest are frequently slow and ill informed.

The actions of the state, thus, are frequently both the cause and the effect of the escalation of protest activity. People protest in the first instance as a consequence of dissatisfaction with the performance of the state and its lack of accountability. Thereafter, they protest further when the state fails to take seriously the demands that they have raised or to respond in a satisfactory manner. This occurs especially, as indicated, in cases where protest is reduced to a law and order issue devoid of any social or political legitimacy. However, as experiences from many parts of the world have illustrated, the involvement of police in protests invariably leads to confrontation and violence (Global Justice Clinic 2012; Arriola 2013). As Mitra points out in the context of popular mobilisation in rural India, "One of the critical determinants of the form and intensity of protest is state responsiveness … the more unyielding the state, the more radicalised collective protest gets, whereas through the accommodation of some strategic demands, the state can enhance its legitimacy and take the wind out of the sail of revolution" (Mitra 2002: 213).

The section which follows looks at state, and particular local state, responses to protest action in post-Apartheid South Africa where, in a seeming paradox, there has been an escalation of social mobilisation notwithstanding the existence of a comprehensive legislative framework and a plethora of policies which compel all tiers of government to ensure effective citizen involvement in official decision making.

The paradox of participation and protest: a case study from Cape Town, South Africa

With the advent of democracy in 1994, the incoming African National Congress government placed considerable emphasis on the need for citizen participation and especially at the local level where legislation explicitly instructs municipalities to "establish appropriate mechanisms, processes and procedures to enable the local community to participate in the affairs of the municipality" (Republic of South Africa 2000: section 17.2). However, despite these measures over the course of the past decade there has been an unprecedented upsurge in social mobilisation at the local level in what have come to be known as service delivery protests. According to a report by the South African Police Service, during the year 2012/13 the police had to respond to a total of 13,575 'crowd-related' incidents, 14 per cent of which were violent and 86 per cent were peaceful, an average of 32 'peaceful' and five 'violent' incidents a day (South African Police Service 2013: 26; Burger 2014). Significantly, however, while peaceful incidents increased by 47 per cent in the three years from 2009/10 (7,913 incidents), incidence of violent protests increased by 92 per cent (994) in the same period (Burger 2014).

There is agreement in the literature that while frustration with the slow pace of service delivery and job creation are the proximate stimuli for protest actions, a variety of reinforcing factors has given rise to this state of affairs and serves to inhibit the substantive participation of the poor in democratic institutions and processes (Bond 2000; Daniel et al. 2005; Tapscott 2008). Faced with the reality that the state has been slow in responding to demands raised through formal institutional channels, disaffected citizens and the organizations that represent them have increasingly sought alternative means to express their grievances. The majority of these protests have been directed against local governments. The triggers for protest are multiple and context specific; nevertheless, a number of trends are discernible. The most often reported reason relates to concerns that municipalities are failing to provide such basic services as public housing, water and sanitation to poor communities. A second relates to an inability on the part of dissatisfied citizens to determine whom they might hold to account for the failings of the state. In the context of a complex system of inter-governmental relations where responsibilities for the delivery of services are shared concurrently by all three tiers of government (national, provincial, and local) ordinary citizens are often unsure where ultimate responsibility for administrative shortcomings is to be located. A third reason relates to the failure of the participatory structures in place to bring about any meaningful change in the lives of poor people.

The City of Cape Town, which has also experienced repeated protest action, has in place a formalised system for the promotion of public participation in municipal decision making. This includes a public engagement policy, which sets out the principles for public participation in the development and amendment of by-laws and policies and in the preparation of Integrated Development Plans (IDP), and a Public Participation Unit, which facilitates these processes. The stated purpose of the engagement policy is "to help people to understand and encourage them to contribute to the decision-making processes of the Municipality", and to that end, it is asserted that "(e)veryone will have the opportunity to influence how the Council functions through effective and meaningful public engagement processes, leading to more relevant policies in the governance of the City" (City of Cape Town 2009). However, the vast majority of the participation exercises embarked upon by the Public Participation Unit deal with uncontentious issues (such as street naming and parking regulations), which are unlikely to raise the ire of the poor or the public in general nor are they likely to lead to protest action.

Amongst the varied reasons why the City's participation process is failing in its intent to satisfactorily involve the public is the fact that the reach of existing systems is extremely limited and the proactive measures taken to contact citizens reach only a fraction of the population in any one year. This is evident in the process of drawing up an IDP which the municipality is mandated to produce in consultation with its citizens. Consultation in the drawing up of the 2012–2017 IDP was proclaimed to have involved "the most extensive public participation process undertaken by the city … (whereby) (c)itizens across the metro were canvassed through numerous mediums, from public meetings, to newspaper inserts, to information brochures, to websites and to social media" (City of Cape Town 2012: 9). The singular ineffectiveness of this process, however, is apparent in the fact that 91 per cent of those interviewed in the City's 2011 Customer Satisfaction Survey had never heard of the IDP (City of Cape Town 2011: 57).

In contrast to the range of mechanisms in place to promote citizen participation, limited or no provision is made to accommodate opinions advanced by the population outside of these formalised structures, and particularly those raised through protest action. Despite the assertion in the Constitution that "Everyone has the right, peacefully and unarmed, to assemble, to demonstrate, to picket and to present petitions" as well as the right to freedom of association (Republic of South Africa 1996: sections 17 and 18), municipalities have no formal mechanisms for dealing with protest action, and other than in ensuring that law and order is maintained.

Peaceful protest action is permitted in municipal and provincial legislation but this is a highly formalised process which generally serves to disempower those taking part. Groups wishing to demonstrate must formally apply to the municipality, which may set stringent conditions or refuse permission. In the case of the latter, this measure is seen as disrespectful and highly confrontational. Mass protest was a key instrument deployed in the struggle against Apartheid, and it remains strong in collective memory as a means to bring about change in state policy and practice. To that extent it has both symbolic and practical content in that it serves as a means for mobilising communities towards collective action. Most problematically, however, there appears to be little interest on the part of municipal officials to understand the reasons why a segment of the population has mobilised, to assess the validity of the demands being made, or to determine what ameliorative measures might be introduced to alleviate further action. In contrast to participation, which has a dedicated unit and an array of formal support systems, protest has no such structures and is typically referred to the disaster management unit and the police.

A failure to address minor protest inevitably fuels frustration and over time this gives rise to more violent forms of interaction with the state. To that extent, state responses to protest action become self-fulfilling. Following this sequence, legitimate protest action is either ignored or is dispersed by the police, protesters become angry and sometimes violent and this reinforces state stereotypes of their behaviour. However, recognition of the fact that the resolution of protest action should be addressed at an administrative level rather than as a law and order issue is evident in a report of the South African Police Service itself, which states that in order "to mitigate the proliferation of public incidents, it is critical for the parties involved in wage disputes and service delivery complaints to establish means to resolve matters in order for the aggrieved parties to avoid escalating their dissatisfaction to the streets and encountering the police" (South African Police Service 2013: 26).

Evidence of the self-fulfilling nature of citizen confrontation of the state can be seen in the case of people living in the Joe Slovo informal settlement in the township of Langa, who were scheduled to be moved to the periphery of Cape Town to make way for the construction of a formal housing development; this was despite the fact that some residents had lived in the area for more than a decade and had some entitlement to be there (Tapscott 2011). Following an initial series of removals the residents of Joe Slovo resolved to fight any further evictions. This resistance in the first instance entailed approaching the municipal ward councillor to assist them in securing access to low cost housing in the area. When this proved unsuccessful, they delivered a memorandum to the Provincial Minister for Housing, requesting his assistance. Despite vague promises this intervention also amounted to nothing. This was followed with a march on parliament, wherein the community's leaders delivered a strongly worded memorandum to the national Minister of Housing demanding that they be consulted on the future development of their informal settlement. Over and above the demand for genuine participation in planning processes that affected their lives, the memorandum expressed the community's anger that they were being forcibly removed from the area. When the Minister refused to meet the marchers and sent an assistant to receive their memorandum, a decision was taken to escalate the protest and shortly thereafter the community blockaded the N2 arterial highway to Cape Town International airport. The police were called and, in a stand-off, rubber bullets were fired, people were injured, and others were arrested.

The Department of Housing laid the blame for this confrontation squarely on the Joe Slovo leadership and its outright rejection of their demands was also accompanied by explicit threats against those seeking to resist relocation, including their removal from the municipal housing waiting list: "The police and National Prosecuting Authority have been encouraged to maintain law and order by bringing charges against the perpetrators. Government will use all legal instruments at its disposal to ensure the development of Joe Slovo proceeds without further hindrance" (Department of Housing 2007). Shortly thereafter a court order was issued to forcibly evict the residents of Joe Slovo. In response, with the assistance of the Legal Resources Centre (LRC) at the University of Cape Town, which offered its services as a Friend of the Court, responding papers were prepared and the matter was referred to the Constitutional Court on the grounds that the eviction contravened elements of the Bill of Rights and other legal provisions. Although the Constitutional Court ruled against the Joe Slovo community and authorised their removal from Langa, the political momentum and public sympathy with their cause was such that the government ultimately acceded to their demands to remain.

The case study of the Joe Slovo informal settlement provides an example of the progression of citizen engagement with the state from peaceful lobbying of the local, provincial, and national political representatives, to protest marches and, subsequently, to disruption of public order and confrontation with the police. It is clear that the path of confrontation which they ultimately adopted was precipitated by the fact that they believed that they had exhausted all formal channels for expressing their grievances and that more direct action was the only option open to them.

Conclusion

The determinants of the protest actions that have swept the globe in recent decades, as intimated, are varied and complex, and they are shaped by local, national, and international factors. Whilst a significant proportion of these are addressed to political leaders and poor governance, it is also evident that the way in which state officials, and particularly those of the local state, interact with citizens is a contributory factor. In the first instance, as discussed, the failure of formal participatory structures either to engage with citizens in an effective manner or to deliver favourable welfare outcomes has prompted people to seek more direct forms of engagement with the state. The failure of these formal spaces for participation is aggravated by the fact that disgruntled citizens are unsure whom in the government hierarchy to hold to account and to whom to direct their concerns. It is further evident that when protests do take place state officials do not see them as a legitimate form of citizen engagement and they are either ignored or suppressed. In this context the potential for more violent forms of protest increases significantly. At a broader level, however, the protest may be viewed as part of a process of actualising rights and of deepening of democracy both in established and newly democratised states.

Whilst the form and extent of protest action might be contextually determined, there are similar patterns in the way in which states respond to the demands raised by their citizenry. What this suggests is that there are similar official understandings of protest actions in countries across the globe and these generally fail to recognise the legitimacy of this form of state–civil society interaction. This in contrast to the provision which is made for citizen engagement in formalised participatory structures. These are supported by legislation and policy and, in many instances, by designated officials and systems and processes specifically designed to facilitate citizen participation. The response to protest, as indicated, is invariably adversarial. There are no specialist units in place to assess the legitimacy of protesters' demands and to assess whether they might feasibly be met, and no formalised channels to engage with the protest leaders in an attempt to resolve contentious issues. The response is to reduce what might be legitimate grievances to a law and order issue. Whilst this approach serves to diffuse the immediate threat of disorder, it generally does little to address the root causes of citizen dissatisfaction and can lead to an escalating spiral of confrontation and potentially violent social unrest.

What appears to be called for is a wider recognition, both in the literature and in official understandings, of the reality that peaceful protest is no longer an aberration, that it has become a well-established form of citizen participation, and that it needs to be addressed in both a more interactive and pro-active fashion. This also suggests the need for more formalised state structures, particularly at the local level, to examine the legitimacy of protesters' demands and the manner in which they might be addressed. It also calls for the training of officials both to understand the factors that are giving rise to protest, and to mediate their influence should they occur.

Note

1   Whilst the study of protest events is not without critics (both on grounds of definition and in terms of the manner in which events are recorded) the findings of Ortiz et al. reflect similar trends to those recorded by the International Labour Organisation (2013), Economist Intelligence Unit (2012) and others.

References

Arriola, L. 2013. "Protesting and Policing in a Multiethnic Authoritarian State, Evidence from Ethiopia." *Comparative Politics* 45 (2): 147–168.

Bond, P. 2000. *Elite Transition: From Apartheid to Neoliberalism in South Africa.* Pluto Press.

Burger, J. 2014. "Politicians, Not the Police, Must Solve Public Dissatisfaction in South Africa." *ISS Today*, December 5. Accessed 06/06/2016, www.issafrica.org/iss-today/politicians-not-the-police-must-solve-public-dissatisfaction-in-south-africa. City of Cape Town Community Satisfaction Survey. 2011. TNS Research Services 2011.

City of Cape Town. 2009. "Public Engagement Policy." Approved By Council: March 30.

Cleaver, F. 2011. "Institutions, Agency and the Limitations of Participatory Approaches to Development." In *Participation. The New Tyranny?* edited by Cooke, B. and Kothari, U. Zed Books.

Cooke, B. and Kothari, U. 2001. *Participation: The New Tyranny?* Zed Books.

Cornwall, A. 2009. "Spaces for Transformation? Reflections on Issues of Power and Difference in Participation in Development." In *Participation from Tyranny to Transformation?* Edited by Hickey, S. and Mohan, G. Zed Books.

Cornwall A. and Coelho, V. 2007. *Spaces for Change: The Politics of Citizen Participation in New Democratic Arenas.* Zed Books.

Corrigall-Brown, C. 2012. *Patterns of Protest: Trajectories of Participation in Social Movements.* Stanford University Press.

Daniel, J. Southall, R., and Lurchman, J. 2005. *State of the Nation 2004–2005.* Human Sciences Research Council.

Department of Housing. 2007. "Department of Housing Issues a Stern Warning against Violent Protesters in Joe Slovo Informal Settlement." Department of Housing. September. Accessed 06/06/2016, www.gov.za/housing-condemns-violent-protests-joe-slovo-informal-settlement-n2-gateway-pilot-project.

Economist Intelligence Unit. 2013. "Rebels without a Cause. What the Upsurge in Protest Movements Means for Global Politics." Economist Intelligence Unit.

Fung, A. and Wright, E. 2003. *Deepening Democracy: Institutional Innovations in Empowered Participatory Governance.* Verso.

Global Justice Clinic and the Walter Leitner International Human Rights Clinic. 2012. *Suppressing Protest: Human Rights Violations in the US Response to the Occupy Wall Street.* Protest and Assembly Rights Project.

Hickey, S. and Mohan, G. 2009. *Participation from Tyranny to Transformation?* Zed Books.

International Labour Organisation. 2013. "World of Work Report 2013: Repairing the Economic and Social Fabric." Geneva.

Mitra. S. 2002. *Power, Protest and Participation: Local Elites and Development in India.* Routledge.

Ortiz, S., Burke, S., Berrada, M., and Cortés, H. 2013. "World Protests 2006–2013." Initiative for Policy Dialogue and Friedrich-Ebert-Stiftung.

Republic of South Africa. 1996. "The Constitution of the Republic of South Africa Act 108 of 1996." Typeface Media.

Republic of South Africa. 2000. "Municipal Systems Act (Act 32 of 2000)." Government Printer.

South African Police Service, Annual Report 2012/13 (SAPS Strategic Management 2013).

Tapscott, C. 2011. "Citizen Leadership in Cape Town, South Africa: A Tale of Three Communities." In *Citizen Leadership: Deepening Democratic Accountability in India, Brazil and South Africa*, edited by Jha, V., Vaishnava, B., and Bandyopadhyay, K. Academic Foundation.

Tapscott, C. 2008. "The Challenges of Deepening Democracy in Post-Apartheid South Africa." In *Foundations for Local Governance: Decentralisation in Comparative Perspective*, edited by Saito, F. Springer.

8

PUBLIC CORRUPTION

Causes, consequences and cures

Cheol Liu

Introduction: a quagmire of defining corruption

After realizing that international development requires good governance, the study of corruption has come of age. Policy makers often fail to introduce optimal policies, not only because they do not know what the best policy should be, but also because they would distort public policies for their private interests. Thus, combating corruption can be a means of developing optimal policies (Jain 2001).

A study on corruption should start by defining corruption because its definition determines the model and measurement of the study. Corruption is a deviation from the activities expected from Max Weber's ideal type of rational-legal bureaucracy. A long debate has concluded that corruption refers to an act in which the power of public office is used for personal gain and the rules of the game are violated. The range of definitions varies widely. Broad terms include diverse elements of clientelism, nepotism, patronage appointment, favoritism, and the misuse of authority and power, such as the "misuse of public power" and "moral decay." Strict terms limit corruption to a deviation from formal rules regulating public officials' behaviors, such as bribery (Andvig et al. 2001).

Lancaster and Montinola (1997) classify the definitions of corruption into six categories:

1   Within a public interest-centered definition, corruption is public officials' behavior deviating from the public interest.
2   In the public office-centered definition, corruption implies public officials' behavior deviating from legal norms.
3   In the norm-based definition, corruption includes public officials' behaviors deviating not only from written rules but also from moral norms sanctioned by the public.
4   Patrimonialism means "a form of domination with an administrative apparatus whose members are recruited from personal dependents of the ruler."
5   According to the market-oriented definition, a corrupt public servant regards his public office as his private business.
6   Finally, corruption is defined as "the perversion of agency relationships" among players in democracy. Under an ideal principal–agent relationship, the agent acts on behalf of the

principal in exchange for some form of compensation. Any behavior deviating from this ideal agency relationship is recognized as corruption.

There is a general consensus that there is currently a lack of a complete and comprehensive definition of corruption. It is impossible to develop a universal list of corrupt practices covering all societies because perceptions, cultures, and formal rules related to corruption vary across societies. It is also impossible to find a consistent definition of corruption even within a society because rules and ideas regarding corrupt behavior change over time. The term "definitional quagmire" expresses the difficulty of finding a single definition and further effort to find a complete and universal definition of corruption appears futile. The literature suggests that researchers focusing on corruption had better simply choose the most useful definition "appropriate for their particular concern and disciplinary taste" rather than getting bogged down in a quagmire of searching for a perfect definition of corruption (Collier 1999; Kaufmann 1998; Lancaster and Montinola 1997).

Causes of corruption

Three key determinants of corruption are discretionary power, economic rent, and (the lack of) deterrents to corruption. First, a public official must have a certain degree of discretionary power with which he or she is able to make, change, or administer regulations. Second, this discretionary power must be related to a certain amount of economic rent. Third, it is assumed that the official's potential corruption will rarely be detected and/or will be punished lightly.

Discretionary power

Corruption takes place when public officials as agents of the public misuse their discretionary power. By assuming that the agents are motivated to enhance their private interests at the cost of the principal, the literature describes the relationship between public officials' discretionary power and corruption from a number of perspectives.

First, regulations give discretionary power to those who are able to implement them. A more regulated and controlled economy provides agents with stronger discretionary power compared to a competitive market economy (Rose-Ackerman 1978). A greater degree of discretion afforded to public officials through regulation results in a higher burden on businesses, which makes them move to the unofficial economy (Johnson et al. 1997). Bliss and Di Tella (1997) show that a corrupt agent with discretionary power is able to maximize profit by converting a competitive market to a monopoly.

Second, corruption may take place in the process of liberalization, privatization, and economic reforms as officials' discretion increases over such a period. Strong involvement on the part of a government is required to introduce liberalization, which enhances officials' discretionary power and opportunities for corruption (Weyland 1998; Heywood 1997). An official may also enjoy "control rights" in the course of privatization. As an example, market-oriented reforms in China provided local officials and cadres with new discretionary power and created incentives to enrich themselves (Johnston and Hao 1995).

Value of economic rent

Braguinsky (1996) argues that the single most important prerequisite of corruption is the presence of rents. Expecting greater rent, a property owner will attempt to evade regulation or to provide officials holding discretion with a larger bribe. Corruption is more serious in countries pursuing industrial policies more actively because they transfer economic rent more often to firms in favored sectors. There is a strong positive relationship between "the size and scope of the public sector" (government expenditure) and corruption (Goel and Nelson 1998; Ades and Di Tella 1997; Scully 1991).

A lack of deterrents to corruption

A public official engages in corruption if the expected gain is greater than the expected loss. Deterrents to corruption increase the expected loss, which is related to the probability of being detected, prosecuted, and punished. Deterrents are also related to income, political institutions, economic variables, and the moral value of society.

The probability of being caught and the extent of punishment on being caught work jointly as deterrents: The higher the probability of being caught, the lower corruption; the greater the penalty, the lower corruption; the stronger enforcement, the lower corruption (Sosa 2004; Goel and Rich 1989; Becker 1968). Corruption is also significantly affected by the openness, accessibility, independence, and effectiveness of the legal system (Jain 2001; Johnson et al. 1997).

There is a negative relationship between public wages and corruption. An official with a lower salary is tempted to supplement his income by taking bribes. An official with a higher salary is more reluctant to engage in corruption because the expected loss from corruption is higher when malfeasance is detected (Andvig et al. 2001).

A number of political institutions may work as deterrents to corruption. Voting is a representative method of expelling corrupt officials. The probability that a corrupt official will be revealed is much higher in a more democratized society because the populace is more participatory in monitoring and disclosing public figures' activities. The freedom of the press induces journalists and interest groups to expose the misuse of office (Paldam 1999; Diamond and Plattner 1993). Decentralization can be used as an alternative means of deterring corruption (Fisman and Gatti 2002; Goldsmith 1999; Klitgaard 1988). However, it should be noted that some empirical studies provide contradictory evidence related to the effects of political institutions on corruption (Treisman 2000; Manor 1999; Wilson 1989; Banfield 1975).

The literature finds a negative association between economic openness, trade, liberalization, and corruption. Economic development improves the level of education, literacy, and arm's length relationships in a society. Social stigma concerning corruption is substantial and longstanding in more economically developed societies (Baksi et al. 2009; Wei 2000; Ades and Di Tella 1999; Ekpo 1979).

A different rate of corruption is also attributed to differences in moral, historical, and cultural traditions between countries. An activity considered corrupt in one society can be accepted as normal in another. A "lack of trust" among citizens is a key cultural factor incubating corruption. Greater ethnic diversity weakens trust among people but generates higher competition for government-created rent, which leads to greater corruption (Treisman 2000).

Consequences of corruption

Studies of the consequences of corruption may overlap with those of the causes of corruption because most economic and political variables affected by corruption simultaneously influence corruption. In view of this, researchers should not compare a situation with corruption against an "ideal political and economic result." It makes more sense to compare it against "what would have happened without corruption" (Johnson et al. 1997).

Grease the wheels vs. sand in the machine

Corruption may have a positive effect on procedural efficiency and political integration. Bribery "greases the wheels" of rigid bureaucracy and improves it by cutting redundant red tape. Money also serves as political "cement," integrating multiple interests and groups into a political party (Liu and Mikesell 2014; Nye 1967). However, some studies provide contradictory findings. Corrupt officials will find multiple ways to create bribe-inducing delays by increasing regulations and red tape; in such cases, corruption acts like "sand in the machine" (Gupta et al. 1998; Kaufmann 1998; Tanzi 1998).

Micro- and macro-economic consequences

Public corruption has a negative effect on various economic variables in general. It reduces the amount of capital investment (Brunetti and Weder 1998; Brunetti et al. 1998; Elliott 1997; Mauro 1995, 1997; Knack and Keefer 1995). Corrupt officials make inefficient decisions on public procurement projects. They award projects to those who provide bribes, not to those who provide the best quality service (Celentani and Ganuza 2000; Hellman et al. 2000; Rose-Ackerman 1997). Corruption damages private firms' business activities, output per worker, productivity, and economic growth as a whole (Leite and Weidmann 2002; Hall and Jones 1999; Johnson et al. 1997; Kaufmann et al. 1999; Mauro 1995). The share of the unofficial and underground economy is greater in a more corrupt country. The level of income inequality and poverty becomes worse because of corruption (Jain 2001; Rose-Ackerman 1999; Gupta et al. 1998; Tanzi and Davoodi 1997; Mauro 1995).

The literature notes the seriousness of governments' budgetary corruption. This leads to inefficient and ineffective resource allocation. First, budgetary corruption makes public spending wasteful. Corrupt governments are likely to launch unnecessary and unproductive public projects. Public services and purchases tend to become over-estimated in a more corrupt country. Public resources can be given to "ghost employees" and wasted on the private interests of a few corrupt officials (Tanzi 1998; Motza 1983). Second, public corruption distorts the resource allocation of a government because of corrupt officials' rent-seeking behavior. Rent-seeking behavior pervades in items with greater rent, higher secrecy, and lower competitiveness. A government with a higher level of corruption is likely to spend more on sectors such as defense, infrastructure, the military, energy, and housing, at the cost of spending on education, welfare, health, and social protection (Baraldi 2008; Delavallade 2006; Gupta et al. 1998; Mauro 1998; Shleifer and Vishny 1993). A recent US cross-state study has found that more corrupt states waste substantial public resources. Moreover, corruption distorts state governments' resource allocations in favor of "bribe-generating" and "more-lucrative" sectors, such as construction, capital, highways, borrowing, and total wages and salaries, while it reduces spending on education, public welfare, health, and hospitals, which are 'less lucrative' for corrupt officials (Liu and Mikesell 2014).

The effects of public corruption on international macro-economic variables are also substantial. A country with a higher level of corruption faces difficulty attracting foreign direct investment (FDI). Corruption has a harmful impact on the volume of trade because international agents escape from a market contaminated by corruption. A nation with a higher level of corruption is likely to have a higher loan-to-FDI ratio and face difficulty borrowing from international financial markets, which leads it to fall into a currency crisis (Lambsdorff 1998; Wei 1997, 2000).

Political and social consequences

Nye (1967) is a pioneer in the study of the effect of corruption on political development. Most political science studies on corruption describe a negative influence of corruption on a number of political and institutional variables. These include democracy, the legitimacy of the government, freedom of press, campaign funds, decentralization, political stability, interest groups, civil society, citizens' confidence and trust, public participation, electoral turnout, government quality, and governance. Corruption has a negative effect on social variables such as distrust and civic culture, deteriorates "good" social capital, generates a set of "dark networks," and undermines the foundation of rule of law (Themudo 2014; Linde and Erlingsson 2013; Villoria et al. 2013; Holmberg et al. 2009; Rothstein and Teorell 2008; Fisman and Gatti 2002; Rose-Ackerman 1999).

Public managerial and administrative consequences

Public administration scholars agree that it is one of the fundamental objectives of public administration to reduce public corruption (Perry 2015; Themudo 2014). Corruption has a negative impact on financial management, budget report transparency, information management, administrative performance, and the legitimacy of government administration (Ongaro 2011; Bastida and Benito 2007; Rocheleau 1999; Gould and Amaro-Reyes 1983). Graycar and Villa (2011) find that public employees' petty corruption has a deleterious effect on governance capacity and the administrative practices of a city government. They conclude that a loss of governance capacity due to public corruption is more than a monetary loss. Compared to the other disciplines above, there remains room for further study on the impact of corruption on public management and administrative variables.

Cures for corruption

One of the most important issues regarding corruption is how to curb it. The search for an effective cure for corruption should start from understanding and controlling the major determinants of corruption. The cures for corruption suggested by the existing literature are classified into three perspectives, namely, the lawyer's approach, the businessman's approach, and the economist's approach (Andvig et al. 2001; Ades and Di Tella 1997; Rose-Ackerman 1997). Similarly, the Organization for Economic Co-operation and Development notes two general approaches to improve ethical conduct in the public sector: compliance-based or integrity-based ethics management. The one focuses on strict compliance with formal procedures and rules. The other emphasizes incentives and encourages good behavior of public servants, based on aspirations (OECD 2000).

Lawyer's approach: penalties and monitoring

The lawyer's approach stems from the seminal work of Becker (1968) and focuses on strengthening laws and their enforcement to increase the costs and risks of engagement in corruption. Two dimensions of this approach are penalties and monitoring. First, effective penalties should be tied to the marginal benefit of payoffs received from corruption. A penalty includes both the probability of detection and punishment, and the level of punishment upon conviction. The expected penalty should increase as the extent of corruption becomes higher. Both those who pay and those who receive bribes should be punished. Second, monitoring means collecting information about officials' activities and prosecuting any dishonest behaviors detected. This provides public officials with incentives against corruption (Ades and Di Tella 1997; Rose-Ackerman 1997).

The effectiveness of internal control systems will be promoted by some external institutions such as an independent and honest judiciary, investigative agencies, anti-corruption commissions, auditing bodies, and an ombudsman. Whistle-blowers and watchdog groups should be protected and a free press should be guaranteed. The active role of non-governmental organizations and the public should be encouraged. The case of Hong Kong illustrates that some drastic measures are sometimes required to make anti-corruption campaigns effective. The Prevention of Bribery Ordinance of Hong Kong stipulates that those accused of corruption should prove their innocence. The Independent Commission Against Corruption (ICAC) of Hong Kong is allowed to search and seize without a legal warrant. Hong Kong ranks very low in international corruption indices (Tanzi 1998; Ades and Di Tella 1997).

Businessman's approach: providing incentives not to engage in corruption

The businessman's approach would "buy out" corruption by giving officials sufficient incentives and compensation for them not to engage in corruption. The incentive mechanism includes wages, bonuses, commission, and performance pay. The most common formal incentive proposal is to pay very high fixed wages to public officials who may otherwise commit malfeasance. Some informal incentives are also applicable, such as career concerns and reputation.

The effectiveness of wages in deterring corruption is not clear. It is argued that inadequate wages are a prime cause of bureaucratic corruption and higher wages increase the value of remaining in a job, which reduces the possibility of a public official shirking. An "efficiency wage" scheme allows a manager to pay employees more than a market-clearing wage to increase their productivity or efficiency. Besley and McLaren (1993) find that this solves the moral hazard problem and deters bribery. The "fair wage–effort hypothesis" develops the discussion on the effect of pay on corruption in the civil service. It assumes that public workers are willing to forego opportunities for corruption if they receive wages that meet the subsistence level or are "fair" (Akerlof and Yellen 1990). However, the "shirking model" suggests that wages have no influence on corruption if the expected income from corruption is very high. It has been found that a rather large wage increase is required to remove corruption solely by raising wages. Some officials engage in corruption even under the risk of losing their jobs when income from bribery is very large. Therefore, to deter corruption, it is necessary to raise wages to a very high level, which implies that the wage policies suggested may not be very practical (Van Rijckeghem and Weder 2001; Gould and Amaro-Reyes 1983). Chand and Moene (1999) find an incentive system works better when both wages and bonus schemes are introduced together.

There are other incentive schemes such as pay for performance, competitive salaries, internal promotion, career stability, and meritocratic recruitment. However their effect on reducing corruption is not clear either. The main reason for this is that the effectiveness of the schemes depends on multiple institutional factors of an organization. These factors include the precise range of instruments available for providing incentives, the extent of discretion available to bureaucrats, the relevant dimensions of bureaucratic performance, team work, and equity within the bureaucracy, and the external legal and political environment (Rauch and Evans 2000; Mookherjee 1997).

Economist's approach: reducing discretionary power and rent

The economist's approach is also called a market approach, focused on reducing the range and value of transactions that might be exploited by corrupt officials. When the discretionary power of public officials is weakened, the opportunities for corruption will be reduced. Deregulation and the streamlining of unnecessary laws aim to reduce public officials' discretion. Transparent and simple rules also weaken officials' discretion by making administrative processes public and open. The introduction of market-based user charge schemes in the area of environmental protection is often designed to limit regulators' discretion (Rose-Ackerman 1997). Another way to reduce discretion is to increase competition among public officials, which dampens their monopolistic power and allows clients to obtain public services from multiple sources (Ades and Di Tella 1997; Shleifer and Vishny 1993). Transparency and the "free flow of information" to control public corruption are also important. It has been found that the lack of fiscal transparency of East Asian countries has undermined trust in them, heightened their funding costs, and resulted in financial crises as a consequence (Kaufmann 1998).

The three approaches above are not exclusive. To be effective, reform to curb corruption should utilize all of them together. In addition, the importance of commitment from top leadership cannot be overemphasized in fighting corruption. Reforms should not be incidental or short term. The literature notes the importance of sustainable corruption controls (Galtung 1998).

Conclusion

What is missing in the existing corruption literature? Compared to studies on the consequences of corruption, systemic studies on the cures for corruption are lacking, although the principal objective of corruption study is to search for optimal policies to curb corruption. In addition, there remains room for efforts by public management students to investigate the effect of corruption on public administration and management variables. Future corruption studies should explore cases in developed countries because the existing literature deals mainly with cases in developing countries. Public resource allocation looks to be one of the sectors most vulnerable to public corruption. Closer attention is required in this area, in particular the fiscal resource allocation of governments. There is an urgent need to search for rigorous research methods which would help researchers overcome the fundamental problems of empirical study in the field of corruption, such as endogeneity occurring because of omitted variables that are correlated with corruption and errors simultaneously and reverse causality. Such measures would enhance the trustworthiness of empirical corruption studies.

References

Ades, A. and Di Tella, R. 1999. "Rents, Competition, and Corruption." *American Economic Review* 89: 982–993.

Ades, A. and Di Tella, R. 1997. "National Champions and Corruption: Some Unpleasant Interventionist Arithmetic." *Economic Journal,* 1074: 1023–1042.

Akerlof, G. A. and Yellen, J. L. 1990. "The Fair Wage Effort Hypothesis and Unemployment." *Quarterly Journal of Economics* 105 (2): 255–283.

Andvig, J. C., Fjeldstad, O. H., Amundsen, I., Sissener, T., and Søreide, T. 2001. *Corruption: A Review of Contemporary Research.* Bergen: Chr. Michelsen Institute.

Baksi, S., Bose, P., and Pandey, M. 2009. "The Impact of Liberalization on Bureaucratic Corruption." *Journal of Economic Behavior and Organization* 72 (1): 214–224.

Baraldi, L. 2008. "Effects of Electoral Rules, Political Competition and Corruption on the Size and Composition of Government Consumption Spending: An Italian Regional Analysis." *B.E. Journal of Economic Analysis and Policy* 8 (1): 1–37.

Banfield, E. 1975. "Corruption as a Feature of Governmental Organization." *Journal of Law and Economics* 18 (3): 587–605.

Bastida, F., and Benito, B. 2007. "Central Government Budget Practices and Transparency: An International Comparison." *Public Administration* 85 (3): 667–716.

Becker, G. 1968. "Crime and Punishment: An Economic Approach." *Journal of Political Economy* 76 (2): 169–217.

Besley, T. and McLaren, J. 1993. "Taxes and Bribery: The Role of Wage Incentives." *Economic Journal* 103 (416): 119–141.

Bliss, C., and Di Tella, R. 1997. "Does Competition Kill Corruption?" *Journal of Political Economy* 105 (5): 1001–1023.

Braguinsky, S. 1996. "Corruption and Schumpeterian Growth in Different Economic Environments." *Contemporary Economic Policy* 14 (3): 14–25.

Brunetti, A., Kisunko, G., and Weder, B. 1998. "Credibility of Rules and Economic Growth: Evidence from a Worldwide Survey of the Private Sector." *World Bank Economic Review* 12 (3): 353–384.

Brunetti, A., and Weder, B. 1998. "Investment and Institutional Uncertainty: A Comparative Study of Different Uncertainty Measures." *Review of World Economics* 134 (3): 513–533.

Celentani, M. and Ganuza, J. J. 2000. "Corruption and Competition in Procurement." *Technical Report*, Department of Economics, Universitat Pompeu Fabra.

Chand, S. K. and Moene, K. O. 1999. "Controlling Fiscal Corruption." *World Development* 27 (7): 1129–1140.

Collier, M. W. 2002. "Explaining Corruption: an Institutional Choice Approach." *Crime, Law and Social Change* 38 (1): 1–32.

Delavallade, C. 2006. "Corruption and Distribution of Public Spending in Developing Countries." *Journal of Economics and Finance* 30 (2): 222–239.

Diamond, L. and Plattner, M. F. 1993. *The Global Resurgence of Democracy.* Baltimore, MD: Johns Hopkins University Press.

Ekpo, M. U. 1979. *Bureaucratic Corruption in Sub-Saharan Africa: Toward a Search for Causes and Consequences.* Washington, DC: University Press of America Inc.

Elliott, K. A. 1997. "Corruption as an International Policy Problem: Overview and Recommendations." In *Corruption and the Global Economy,* edited by Elliott, K. A. 175–233. Washington, DC: Institute for International Economics.

Fisman, R. and Gatti, R. 2002. "Decentralization and Corruption: Evidence across Countries." *Journal of Public Economics* 83 (3): 325–345.

Galtung, F. 1998. "Criteria for Sustainable Corruption Control." *European Journal of Development Research* 10 (1): 105–128.

Goel, R. K. and Nelson, M. A. 1998. "Corruption and Government Size: A Disaggregated Analysis." *Public Choice* 97 (1): 107–120.

Goel, R. K. and Rich, D. P. 1989. "On the Economic Incentives for Taking Bribes." *Public Choice* 61 (3): 269–275.

Goldsmith, A. 1999. "Slapping the Grasping Hand: Correlates of Political Corruption in Emerging Markets." *American Journal of Economics and Sociology* 58 (4): 865–883.

Gould, D. J. and Amaro-Reyes, J. A. 1983. "The Effects of Corruption on Administrative Performance: Illustrations from Developing Countries." *Working Papers Number 580 Management And Development Series Number 7.* Washington, DC: World Bank.

Graycar, A. and Villa, D. 2011. "The Loss of Governance Capacity through Corruption." *Governance: An International Journal of Policy Administration and Institutions* 24 (3): 419–438.

Gupta, S., Davoodi, H., and Alonso-Terme, R. 1998. "Does Corruption Affect Income Inequality and Poverty?" *Working Paper no. 98/76.* International Monetary Fund.

Hall, R. E. and Jones, C. I. 1999. "Why Do Some Countries Produce So Much More Output per Worker than Others?" *Quarterly Journal of Economics* 114 (1): 83–116.

Hellman, J. S., Jones, G., Kaufmann, D., and Schankerman, M. 2000. "Measuring Governance, Corruption and State Capture." *Policy Research Working Paper no. 2312.* Washington, DC: World Bank.

Heywood, P. 1997. "Political Corruption: Problems and Perspectives." *Political Studies* 45 (3): 417–435.

Holmberg, S., Rothstein, B., and Nasiritousi, N. 2009. "Quality of Government: What You Get." *Annual Review of Political Science* 12: 135–161.

Jain, A. K. 2001. "Corruption: A Review." *Journal of Economics Surveys* 15 (1): 71–121.

Johnson, S., Kaufmann, D., Shleifer, A., and Goldman, M. I. 1997. "The Unofficial Economy in Transition." *Brookings Papers on Economic Activity*, 159–239.

Johnston, M. and Hao, Y. 1995. "China's Surge of Corruption." *Journal of Democracy* 6 (4): 80–94.

Kaufmann, D. 1998. "Challenges in the Next Stage of Anticorruption." *Technical Report*. World Bank.

Kaufmann, D., Kraay, A., and Zoido-Lobaton, P. 1999. "Governance Matters." *Policy Research Working Paper no. 2196*. World Bank.

Klitgaard, R. 1988. *Controlling Corruption*. Berkeley: University of California Press.

Knack, S. and Keefer, P. 1995. "Institutions and Economic Performance: Cross-Country Tests Using Alternative Institutional Measures." *Economics and Politics* 7(3): 207–227.

Lambsdorff, J. G. 1998. "An Empirical Investigation of Bribery in International Trade." *European Journal of Development Research* 10 (1): 40–59.

Lancaster, T. D. and Montinola, G. R. 1997. "Toward a Methodology for the Comparative Study of Political Corruption." *Crime, Law and Social Change* 27 (3): 185–206.

Leite, C. and Weidmann, J. 2002. *Does Mother Nature Corrupt? Natural Resources, Corruption, and Economic Growth*. Washington, DC: International Monetary Fund.

Linde, J. and Erlingsson, G. O. 2013. "The Eroding Effect of Corruption on System Support in Sweden." *Governance* 26 (4): 585–603.

Liu, C. and Mikesell, J. L. 2014. "The Impact of Public Officials' Corruption on the Size and Allocation of U.S. State Spending." *Public Administration Review* 74 (3): 346–359.

Manor, J. 1999. *The Political Economy of Democratic Decentralization*. Washington, DC: World Bank.

Mauro, P. 1998. "Corruption and the Composition of Government Expenditure." *Journal of Public Economics* 69 (2): 263–279.

Mauro, P. 1997. "Why Worry about Corruption?" *Economic Issues no. 6*. International Monetary Fund.

Mauro, P. 1995. "Corruption and Growth." *Quarterly Journal of Economics* 110 (3): 681–712.

Mookherjee, D. 1997. "Incentive Reforms in Developing Country Bureaucracies: Lessons from Tax Administrations." *Technical Report*. Washington, DC: World Bank.

Motza, M. 1983. "Corruption and Budgeting." In *Handbook on Public Budgeting and Financial Management*, edited by Rabin, J. and Lynch, T. D., 509–537. New York: Marcel Dekker.

Nye, J. S. 1967. "Corruption and Political Development: A Cost–Benefit Analysis." *The American Political Science Review* 61 (2): 417–427.

OECD. 2000. *Trust in Government: Ethics Measures in OECD Countries*. Paris: OECD.

Ongaro, E. 2011. "The Role of Politics and Institutions in the Italian Administrative Reform Trajectory." *Public Administration* 89 (3): 738–755.

Paldam, M. 1999. "The Big Pattern of Corruption: Economics, Culture and the Seesaw Dynamics." *Working Paper No. 1999–11*. Department of Economics, University of Aarhus.

Perry, J. L. 2015. "Revisiting the Core of Our Good Government Ethos." *Public Administration Review* 75 (2): 186–187.

Rauch, J. E. and Evans, P. B. 2000. "Bureaucratic Structure and Bureaucratic Performance in Less Developed Countries." *Journal of Public Economics* 75 (1): 49–71.

Rocheleau, B. 1999. "Prescriptions for Public-Sector Information Management: A Review, Analysis, and Critique." *American Review of Public Administration* 30 (4): 414–435.

Rose-Ackerman, S. 1999. *Corruption and Government: Causes, Consequences, and Reform*. Cambridge: Cambridge University Press.

Rose-Ackerman, S. 1997. "The Pursuit of Absolute Integrity: How Corruption Control Makes Government Ineffective." *Journal of Policy Analysis and Management* 16 (4): 661–664.

Rose-Ackerman, S. 1978. *Corruption: A Study in Political Economy*. New York, NY: Academic Press.

Rothstein, B. and Teorell, J. 2008. "What is Quality of Government? A Theory of Impartial Government Institutions." *Governance: An International Journal of Policy, Administration, and Institutions* 21 (2): 165–190.

Scully, G. W. 1991. "Rent-seeking in U.S. Government Budgets, 1900–88." *Public Choice* 70: 99–106.

Shleifer, A. and Vishny, R. 1993. "Corruption." *Quarterly Journal of Economics* 108 (3): 599–617.

Sosa, L. A. 2004. "Wages and Other Determinants of Corruption." *Review of Development Economics* 8 (4): 597–605.

Tanzi, V. 1998. "Corruption and the Budget: Problems and Solutions." In *Economics of Corruption*, edited by Jain, A. K., 111–128. Norwell, MA: Kluwer Academic.

Tanzi, V., and Davoodi, H. R. 1997. "Corruption, Public Investment, and Growth." *Working Paper no. 97/139.* International Monetary Fund.

Themudo, N. S. 2014. "Government Size, Nonprofit Sector Strength, and Corruption: A Cross-National Examination." *The American Review of Public Administration* 44 (3): 309–323.

Treisman, D. 2000. "The Causes of Corruption: a Cross-National Study." *Journal of Public Economics* 76: 399–457.

Van Rijckeghem, C. and Weder, B. 2001. "Bureaucratic Corruption and the Rate of Temptation: Do Wages in the Civil Service Affect Corruption, and by How Much?" *Journal of Development Economics* 65 (2): 307–331.

Villoria, M., Van Ryzin, G. G., and Lavena, C. F. 2013. "Social and Political Consequences of Administrative Corruption: A Study of Public Perceptions in Spain." *Public Administration Review* 73 (1): 85–94.

Wei, S. J. 2000. "Natural Openness and Good Government." *Policy Research Working Papers.* World Bank.

Wei, S. J. 1997. "How Taxing Is Corruption on International Investors?" *Working Paper no. 6030.* National Bureau of Economic Research.

Weyland, K. 1998. "The Politics of Corruption in Latin America." *Journal of Democracy* 9: 108–121.

Wilson, J. 1989. *Political Corruption: A Handbook.* New Brunswick/London: Transaction Publishers.

9

TRUST IN PUBLIC ORGANIZATIONS

Yoon Jik Cho

Introduction

Trust matters. It can be divided roughly into two types, institutional and interpersonal trust, each with their own values. From a macro- or meso-perspective, the former works as a valuable political resource. Citizens' trust in government is a representative example of it. When a government conducts any policy, citizens' trust works as a powerful driver for successful policy implementation. On the contrary, without trust in its political leaders, a government will have difficulty finding momentum to initiate new policies. For example, in South Korea, a recent presidential administration faced public distrust in its early period because of its policy toward US beef imports, which became one factor that frustrated other items on its policy agenda. When citizens' trust in government is high, compliance to public policies increases. Scholz and Lubell (1998) found that people are more willing to pay taxes without resistance when they trust the government. On the other hand, with micro-perspective, interpersonal trust concerns interpersonal relationships within organizations. It works as a valuable managerial resource. It is expected to decrease transaction costs and the necessity of monitoring while increasing job satisfaction, information sharing, and performance (Dirks and Ferrin 2001; Creed and Miles 1996; Culbert and McDonough 1986). A lack of trust brings negative outcomes such as low commitment, low motivation, and cynicism (Carnevale and Wechsler 1992).

This chapter focuses on interpersonal trust within organizations, and discusses why trust matters and how it works in the public organizational context. Building trust may be even more necessary in the public sector than in the private sector, because it may supplement managerial authority and discretion. Reviews of public–private comparisons commonly report that public-sector leaders have less authority over their subordinates as a result of institutional constraints coming from excessive rules and regulations (Ingraham, Sowa, and Moynihan 2004; Rainey and Bozeman 2000; Perry and Porter 1982). This assertion is supported by the reports from the Volcker Commissions in the United States in 1989 and 2003, which called for a deregulation of personnel systems to free public managers from excessive constraints. Their low level of discretion is related to their lack of capacity to reward or punish subordinates. Because of difficulties in tying rewards to performance, public leaders face greater challenges in motivating employees than do their private-sector counterparts (Rainey and Bozeman 2000; National

Commission on the Public Service 1989; National Commission on the State and Local Service 1993; Perry and Porter 1982). Even within those constraints, however, one can still observe public leaders who successfully motivate their subordinates. Their common characteristic is their competence in building trust with their followers (Rainey and Thompson 2006; Riccucci 1995; Doig and Hargrove 1987). Accordingly, trust may work as a more valuable resource within public organizations and it is worthwhile to investigate how to engender it.

This chapter reviews the role of interpersonal trust in public organizations. First, it defines trust, and illustrates its effects. The section explains theories supporting the positive effects and expected outcomes of trust. It also explains how trust works by modifying Cho and Ringquist's (2011) heuristic model. They sought to integrate trust and management literature to understand the role of trust within organizations. The revised framework considers trustworthiness as an antecedent of trust, suggesting that managerial attention should focus on the factors developing and maintaining trust. Finally, this chapter considers Mayer et al.'s (1995) synthesis of the factors of trustworthiness, finding three factors, including ability, benevolence, and integrity, with the potential to build trust.

What is trust?

Definition

Scholars in various disciplines emphasized different foci in defining trust, including belief (Levi 1998), expectation (Golembiewski and McConkie 1975), willingness to be vulnerable (Mayer et al. 1995; Zand 1972), attitude (Griffin 1967), and rational assessment (Hardin 2006). Scholars such as Farris, Senner, and Butterfield (1973: 145) emphasize personal characteristics by explaining that trust is "a personality trait of people interacting with the peripheral environment of an organization." Similarly, Lieberman (1981) and Good (1988) insist that trust depends on factors such as trustee behavior, competence, and integrity. Other scholars focus on expectations shaped by external actors or environments. Rotter (1967: 651), for example, defines trust as "an expectancy held by an individual or a group that the word, promise, verbal or written statement of another individual or group can be relied upon."

After reviewing numerous definitions of trust, Rousseau et al. (1998) conclude that most scholars investigating interpersonal trust commonly emphasize its psychological aspect. They define trust as "a psychological state comprising the intention to accept vulnerability based upon positive expectations of the intentions or behavior of another" (Rousseau et al. 1998: 395). The Mayer et al. (1995: 712) definition is also widely adopted in trust research: "the willingness of a party to be vulnerable to the actions of another party based on the expectation that the other party will perform a particular action important to the trustor, irrespective of the ability to monitor or control that other party." In sum, trust is a psychological state of willingly taking some risks based on positive expectation of outcomes.

Types of trust and expected outcomes

Rousseau et al. (1998) insist that trust depends on factors such as trustee behavior, competence, and integrity. Other scholars focus on expectations shaped by external actors or environments. Rotter (1967: 651) provides three forms of trust: calculative, relational, and institutional. Calculative trust resembles economic exchange in that trust emerges when a trustor perceives that a trustee performs an action in order to benefit. On the other hand, relational trust is based on repeated interactions between the trustee and trustor. Relational trust differs from calculative because it has emotional elements. Intimate reciprocity is formed based on frequent and long-term interactions (McAllister 1995). However, both of them can be categorized as interpersonal trust because, regardless of different motivations, the object of trust is a person. In contrast, institutional trust resides in certain institutions: for example, citizens' trust in government.

The trend of trust research can be classified by these forms of trust. One can roughly divide trust research into two streams: one focusing on institutional trust and the other dealing with interpersonal trust. Many political science studies employ the former approach by considering trust in institutional settings (Cho 2008). Scholars demonstrate that, by effectively managing stakeholder groups and policy recipients, trust helps successful policy implementation (Lubell 2004; Scholz and Lubell 1998). For example, in the regression analysis, after controlling citizens' perception of punishment risks, citizens' trust in government and each other decrease non-compliance with tax laws (Scholz and Lubell 1998). Similarly, Habibov (2014) demonstrated that people with a high level of institutional trust have more positive attitudes toward welfare expenditure. Another study found that citizens with high levels of institutional trust are more likely to participate in local government activities including municipal meetings and participatory budget meetings (Mendoza-Botelho 2013).

The interpersonal approach is adopted by management studies, which deal with trust as an internal organizational resource. Numerous studies demonstrate the value of interpersonal trust within organizations. As a lubricant of organizational functioning, trust increases job satisfaction, commitment, and individual and organizational performance (Dirks and Ferrin 2002; Culbert and McDonough 1986; Bennis and Nanus 1985; Zand 1972). A lack of trust, in contrast, leads to negative workplace outcomes, including low commitment, low motivation, and cynicism (Carnevale and Wechsler 1992; Kanter and Mirvis 1989).

Effects of trust

Theoretical support

One can find several theories supporting the positive effect of trust. From managerial perspective, trust in higher authority is commonly investigated in that managers play a major role in motivating members of organizations. For example, Dirks (2000) emphasizes that trust in leadership makes a team willing to accept a leader's activities, goals, and decisions, and work hard to achieve them. If we focus on that type of trust, leadership theories can serve as a theoretical ground to explain the effect of trust.

Leader-member exchange (LMX) theory seems to be the most relevant theory to explain the effects of trust in higher authorities. The theory adopts the transactional framework between leader and subordinate, but addresses both the material and psychological benefits of transactions (Duchon, Green, and Taber 1986). It argues that interactions between leaders and followers have a significant influence on organizational effectiveness (Graen and Uhl-Bien 1995; Bass 1990). In a high-quality LMX, where trust is a representative indicator of LMX quality, leaders and organizations have more committed subordinates with less turnover and better performance (Graen and Uhl-Bien 1995; Deluga 1994; Liden and Graen 1980). Based on this reasoning, LMX theory can serve as a theoretical foundation explaining the positive effects of trust in higher authorities.

Besides the LMX theory, many scholars value trust as the core of effective leadership (Zand 1997; Hogan, Curphy, and Hogan 1994; Fairholm 1994; Bass 1990). One current trend of leadership research emphasizes the inspirational aspect of leaders (Robbins and Judge 2008). Such theories, including transformational and charismatic leadership, treat trust as an important attribute for effective leadership (Kirkpatrick and Locke 1996; Podsakoff et al. 1990). Dirks and

Ferrin (2002) distinguish two theoretical perspectives on trust in leadership: relationship-based perspective and character-based perspective. The former focuses on the nature of the leader–follower relationship, whereas the latter focuses on the perception of the leader's character and how it influences a follower's sense of vulnerability in a hierarchical relationship (Dirks and Ferrin 2002). Although the expected causal mechanisms are different, both perspectives anticipate positive effects of trust in higher authorities.

Besides leadership theories, scholars from different disciplines also nominate trust as a valuable managerial resource. For example, Zand (1972) assumes that high levels of trust decrease social uncertainty, which facilitates information sharing among group members. This enhanced information sharing is assumed to increase problem-solving capacity. The assumption is demonstrated by his experiment, in which high-trust groups showed a better problem-solving ability than low-trust groups.

In discussing the second generation model of rational choice, Ostrom (1998) places reciprocity, reputation, and trust at the core of the model. During social dilemma situations such as free rider problem, cooperative behaviors are explained by three reinforcing factors: trust that individuals have in others, investment of others in their own reputations of trustworthiness, and the probability that participants will reciprocate (Ostrom 1998: 12). This model implies that trust is at the core of cooperation. Although cooperation can emerge solely from a control mechanism within organizations (Cook, Hardin, and Levi 2007), trust still plays a substantial role in its creation.

Scholars of transaction cost theory argue that trust reduces transaction costs by decreasing opportunistic behaviors, which in turn saves monitoring and negotiation costs (Zaheer, McEvily, and Perrone 1997; Cummings and Bromiley 1996; Creed and Miles 1996; Zaheer and Venkatraman 1995; Williamson 1993; North 1990). The reduced costs then lead to more flexibility and better performance. One can expect these benefits in intra- as well as inter-organizational settings. Within organizations, trust helps supervisors effectively manage subordinates with minimal supervision. In organizational networks with high levels of trust, the related organizations increase the effectiveness of collaboration by saving on the costs of negotiating with and monitoring each other.

Finally, scholars from various disciplines provide theoretical reasoning expecting the positive influence of trust. Although the underlying reasons are different, they seem to agree that trust works as a valuable resource within organizations.

How trust works

Then, how does trust work within organizations and reveal its expected effects? To explain that, this chapter modifies Cho and Ringquist (2011)'s heuristic model of trust, which integrates trust and management research streams. From a trust research perspective, one can think of how trust plays roles within organizations. Kramer (1999) provides three routes through which trust affects performance: decreasing transaction costs, facilitating altruistic behaviors, and increasing voluntary deference. First, as scholars of transaction cost theory argue, trust relieves transaction costs within organizations and the saved resources can be utilized to enhance performance. Second, trust expedites altruistic behaviors, such as organizational citizenship behavior (OCB). By helping others without expecting extra pay or rewards, OCB enhances cooperation, communication, and collective goods within organizations. These positive outcomes are expected to bring better organizational performance. Finally, trust contributes to performance by increasing voluntary compliance. When the trust level is high, employees are more likely to follow organizational rules and procedures (Kramer and Tyler 1996). Accordingly, without much effort, management can obtain employee agreement with its policies.

On the other hand, from management research, one can think of the role of management in enhancing performance. Numerous studies have demonstrated that management matters for enhancing performance. The various roles of management can be classified into three categories: managing the external environment, cultivating a positive organizational culture, and managing internal resources (Cho and Ringquist 2011). Related to the concept of "managing upward" (Moore 1995), cultivating a favorable external political environment is sometimes critical to better performance. Establishing networks with external actors may help an organization obtain some useful resources. Cultivating organizational culture is also a key role of management. As a social glue, an organizational culture strengthens the unity of organizational members by guiding appropriate behaviors and norms, while it also engenders commitment to an organization that goes beyond individual self-interest (Robbins and Judge 2007). Finally, managing internal resources effectively is critical for performance. Efficient allocation of resources has been traditional role of management. Management is also responsible for establishing fair treatment of personnel in various aspects of human resource management. All these managerial efforts will pay off through increased employee motivation and organizational performance.

The heuristic model in Figure 9.1 takes the features of the above discussion and integrates them into a single framework. In addition, it assumes managerial trustworthiness as the antecedent of trust. The basic logic is that managerial trustworthiness builds interpersonal trust within organizations, which has positive influence in both direct and indirect ways, nurturing the positive behavior of organizational members. The direct effect of interpersonal trust – such as reduced monitoring and greater rule adherence – is presented by Avenue 1. Trust indirectly affects organizational outcomes by elevating the effectiveness of managerial practices. In other words, while each type of managerial effort – managing the external environment, cultivating an organizational culture, and managing internal resources – directly contributes to improving organizational performance, such effects are further escalated when interpersonal trust level is high. Regarding managing external environments, interpersonal trust increases the effectiveness of managing external environments by helping managers to focus on those activities. As stated, with a high level of trust, managers do not need to pay lots of attention to their subordinates. Organizational rules and procedures are observed closely, and subordinates conduct their roles without much external control or supervision. Resources and effort usually spent on internal management can be redirected to conduct external managerial activities.

This moderating effect of trust is presented by Avenue 2. Interpersonal trust also enhances the effectiveness of managerial activities in cultivating organizational cultures. By facilitating altruistic behaviors, trust helps to nurture cooperative cultures. For example, by engaging in various types of OCBs, employees may help absent or busy co-workers. They are also willing to help newly hired employees by conducting informal job training and work extra hours without expecting additional pay or rewards. All of those activities will enhance the effectiveness of managerial effort to cultivate a cooperative culture. In other words, efforts to strengthen social bonding show better outcomes when conducted within high levels of interpersonal trust. The route is presented by Avenue 3.

Finally, Avenue 4 indicates the indirect effect of trust in advancing the effectiveness of internal resource management. As stated, because trust increases one's willingness to accept organizational rules and procedures, the internal management process will operate more smoothly when trust level is high. That is, the overall level of trust and complaints or opposition to managerial decisions are negatively associated, and the effectiveness of internal management will upsurge under conditions of high levels of trust. As a result, one can summarize the ways in which trust affects organizational outcomes in terms of four routes, one direct and three indirect. Each route can be investigated further.

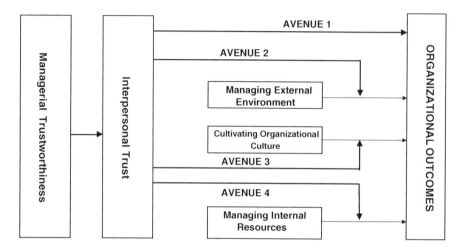

Figure 9.1 Heuristic model of trust
Source: Modified from Cho and Ringquist (2011)'s framework

Trustworthiness and trust

Trustworthiness as antecedent of trust

If one believes that trust matters for organizational effectiveness, the next logical question is, "How do we build trust?" Drawing on Figure 9.1, this chapter finds the answer in the concept of managerial trustworthiness. Trustworthiness, being an antecedent of trust, means "worthy of trust or confidence; reliable" (Oxford English Dictionary 1989). One can find empirical support that trustworthiness leads to trust (e.g., Davis et al. 2000). Thus, based on the concept and empirical evidence, trustworthiness is a necessary condition for trusting someone.

Differentiating trust from trustworthiness is not always easy. In some contexts, an evaluation of someone's trustworthiness becomes trust in him or her (Hardin 2002). However, one cannot ignore the distinction. Trust focuses on a trustor's psychological state, which indicates that he or she is willing to take risks for a trustee regardless of whether monitoring or control are present. But trustworthiness focuses on the characteristics of a trustee: for example, whether the trustee is reliable or behaves in a trustworthy manner. The fact that a trustee is trustworthy is conceptually distinct from whether a trustor is willing to take risks for him or her.

Just as many scholars have emphasized the importance of trust as a managerial resource, they have also identified elements of trustworthiness as antecedents of trust. Based on interviews with 84 managers, Butler (1991: 648) summarized ten conditions of trust: availability, competence, consistency, discreetness, fairness, integrity, loyalty, openness, promise fulfillment, and receptivity. Other elements, such as trustworthy intentions (Cook and Wall 1980), value congruence (Sitkin and Roth 1993), and personal attraction (Griffin 1967), are also nominated as antecedents of trust.

After reviewing relevant studies, Mayer et al. (1995) synthesized these elements into three core antecedents of trust: ability, benevolence, and integrity. Ability means a trustee's competence in a given role within an organization. From a rational perspective, ability is the basis on which to build trust because, in a trusting relationship, a trustor expects a trustee to do something. In many cases, the phrase "A trusts B" means that "A trusts B to do C" (Hardin 2006). The implication is that B has enough competence to do C. In other words, if B does not have the ability to do C in the first place, trust cannot be generated. While ability is critical, it is not enough to be considered trustworthy. An affective element, benevolence, also constitutes trustworthiness. Benevolence is "the extent to which a trustee is believed to want to do good to the trustor, aside from an egocentric profit motive" (Mayer et al. 1995: 718). It means that a trustee has a positive personal attachment to a trustor. When a trustee pays attention to a trustor's personal well-being, the trustor is more likely to show his or her vulnerability. Integrity is a broad concept encompassing many issues, such as "the consistency of the trustee's past actions, credible communications about the trustee from other parties, belief that the trustee has a strong sense of justice, and the extent to which the trustee's actions are congruent with his or her words" (p. 719). The importance of integrity is well known from organizational justice literature. Fair treatment by leadership largely forms the subordinates' perception of how much risk one can take in a relationship with a leader, which is related to the level of trust.

Theoretical support for trustworthiness

Social exchange theory provides a good explanation of the effect of trustworthiness on the building of trust (Aryee, Budhwar, and Chen 2002; Whitener et al. 1998). Social exchange means the "voluntary actions of individuals that are motivated by the returns they are expected to bring ... from others" (Blau 1964, p. 91). As it includes both material and psychological benefits, social exchange differs from a purely economic exchange (Whitener et al. 1998; Yukl 1994). In social exchange, there is no specified obligation for the action and the expected benefits are rarely specified in advance (Aryee et al. 2002; Blau 1964). Such social exchanges are frequent in the workplace, and trust is built based on repeated exchanges among individuals within organizations (Aryee et al. 2002; Blau 1964). A minimum level of trust is required to initiate an exchange, and supervisors commonly become the initiators of trust building (Gould-Williams and Davies 2005; Eisenberger, Fasolo, and Davis-Lamastro 1990). They begin social exchanges by showing their trustworthiness, which gives subordinates a reason to trust them. Through reciprocity, trust is developed and maintained among organizational members.

Conclusion

This chapter has reviewed the definition of trust, the expected outcomes of trust, how trust works, and trustworthiness as an antecedent of trust. The role of trust is influential and critical to enhance organizational effectiveness. More attention from top management to this valuable resource is required. Scholars may want to examine various direct and indirect effects of trust, and Figure 9.1 can serve as a guide. Simultaneously, it is important to pay some attention to negative side of trust as well, as it sometimes brings negative outcomes. For example, under high levels of trust, organizational members are very closely connected, which may make them hesitant to raise opposition as well as reluctant to accept external criticism toward their organization. This is the so-called groupthink problem which negatively affects organizations. Thus, efforts to explore roles of trust and establish comprehensive understanding of it should continue.

In addition, attention needs to be paid to trustworthiness factors. While this chapter introduced the factors of perceived trustworthiness identified by Mayer et al. (1995), it is likely that other new factors may be found as contexts change. There may be some factors unique and distinctive to the public sector context. Consequently, there are practical benefits and guidance to be obtained by researching trust and trustworthiness.

References

Aryee, S., P. S. Budhwar, and Z. X. Chen. 2002. "Trust as a Mediator of the Relationship between Organizational Justice and Work Outcomes: Test of a Social Exchange Model." *Journal of Organizational Behavior* 23(3): 267–85.

Bass, B. M. 1990. *Bass and Stogdill's Handbook of Leadership*. 3d ed. New York: Free Press.

Bennis, W. G. and B. Nanus. 1985. *Leaders: The Strategy for Taking Charge*. New York: Harper & Row.

Blau, Peter M. 1964. *Exchange and Power in Social Life*. New York: Wiley.

Butler, John K. 1991. "Toward Understanding and Measuring Conditions of Trust: Evolution of a Conditions of Trust Inventory." *Journal of Management* 17(3): 643–63.

Carnevale, David G. and Barton Wechsler. 1992. "Trust in the Public Sector: Individual and Organizational Determinants." *Administration and Society* 23(4): 471–94.

Cho, Y. 2008. *Trust in Managerial Leadership within Federal Agencies: Antecedents, Outcomes, and Contextual Factors* (Doctoral dissertation). Indiana University, Bloomington, IN.

Cho, Y. and E. J. Ringquist. 2011. "Managerial Trustworthiness and Organizational Outcomes" *Journal of Public Administration Research and Theory* 21(1): 53–86.

Cook, K. S., R. Hardin, and M. Levi. 2007. *Cooperation without Trust?* New York: Russell Sage.

Cook, J. and T. Wall. 1980. "New Work Attitude Measures of Trust, Organizational Commitment, and Personal Need Nonfulfillment." *Journal of Occupational Psychology* 53: 39–52.

Creed, W. E. and R. E. Miles. 1996. "Trust in Organizations: A Conceptual Framework Linking Organizational Forms, Managerial Philosophies, and the Opportunity Costs of Controls." In *Trust in Organizations: Frontiers of Theory and Research*, edited by R. M. Kramer and T. R. Tyler, 16–38. Thousand Oaks, CA: Sage.

Culbert, S. A. and J. J. McDonough. 1986. "The Politics of Trust and Organizational Empowerment." *Public Administration Quarterly* 10(2): 171–88.

Cummings, L. L. and P. Bromiley. 1996. "The Organizational Trust Inventory (OTI): Development and Validation." In *Trust in Organizations: Frontiers of Theory and Research*, edited by R. M. Kramer and T. R. Tyler, 302–30. Thousand Oaks, CA: Sage.

Davis, J. H., F. D. Schoorman, R. C. Mayer, and H. H. Tan. 2000. "The Trusted General manager and Business Unit Performance: Empirical Evidence of a Competitive Advantage." *Strategic Management Journal* 21(5): 563–76.

Deluga, Ronald J. 1994. "Supervisor Trust Building, Leader-Member Exchange and Organizational Citizenship Behavior." *Journal of Occupational and Organizational Psychology* 67: 315–26.

Dirks, K. T. 2000. Trust in Leadership and Team Performance: Evidence from NCAA Basketball. *Journal of Applied Psychology* 85(6): 1004–12.

Dirks, Kurt T. and Donald L. Ferrin. 2002. "Trust in Leadership: Meta-Analytic Findings and Implications for Research and Practice." *Journal of Applied Psychology* 87(4): 611–28.

Dirks, Kurt T. and Donald L. Ferrin. 2001. "The Role of Trust in Organizational Settings." *Organization Science* 12(4): 450–67.

Doig, Jameson W. and Erwin C. Hargrove. 1987. *Leadership and Innovation*. Baltimore: Johns Hopkins University Press.

Duchon, D., S. G. Green, and T. D. Taber. 1986. "Vertical Dyad Linkage: A Longitudinal Assessment of Antecedents, Measures, and Consequences." *Journal of Applied Psychology* 71(1): 56–60.

Eisenberger, R., P. Fasolo, and V. Davis-Lamastro. 1990. "Perceived Organizational Support and Employee Diligence, Commitment and Innovation." *Journal of Applied Psychology* 75(1): 51–59.

Fairholm, Gilbert. W. 1994. *Leadership and the Culture of Trust*. Westport, CT: Praeger.

Fairholm, M. R. 2004. "Different Perspectives on the Practice of Leadership." *Public Administration Review* 64(5): 577–90.

Farris, G., Senner, E., and D. Butterfield. 1973. "Trust, Culture, and Organizational Behavior." *Industrial Relations* 12(2): 144–57.

Golembiewski, R. T. and M. L. McConkie. 1975. "The Centrality of Interpersonal Trust in Group Process." In *Theories of Group Processes*, edited by C. L. Cooper, 131–85. New York: John Wiley.

Good, D. 1998. "Individuals, Interpersonal Relations, and Trust." In *Trust: Making and Breaking Cooperative Relations*, edited by D. G. Gambetta, 131–185. New York: Blackwell.

Gould-Williams, Julian, and Fiona Davies. 2005. "Using Social Exchange Theory to Predict the Effects of HRM Practice on Employee Outcomes: An Analysis of Public Sector Workers." *Public Management Review* 7(1): 1–24.

Graen, G. B. and M. Uhl-Bien. 1995. "Development of Leader-Member Exchange (LMX) Theory of Leadership over 25 Years: Applying a Multi-Level Multi-Domain Perspective." *Leadership Quarterly* 6(2): 219–47.

Griffin, K. 1967. "The Contribution of Studies of Source Credibility to a Theory of Interpersonal Trust in the Communication Department." *Psychological Bulletin* 68(2): 104–20.

Habibov, N. 2014. "Individual and Country-Level Institutional Trust and Public Attitude to Welfare Expenditure in 24 Transitional Countries." *Journal of Sociology & Social Welfare* 41(4): 23–48.

Hardin, R. 2006. *Trust.* Malden, MA: Polity Press.

Hardin, R. 2002. *Trust and Trustworthiness.* New York: Russell Sage Foundation.

Hogan, R., Curphy, G., and Hogan, J. 1994. "What We Know about Leadership: Effectiveness and Personality." *American Psychologist* 49: 493–504.

Ingraham, Patricia W., Jessica E. Sowa, and Donald P. Moynihan. 2004. "Linking Dimensions of Public Sector Leadership to Performance." In *Art of Governance*, edited by Patricia W. Ingraham and Laurence E. Lynn, 152–70. Washington, DC: Georgetown University Press.

Kanter, D. L. and P. H. Mirvis. 1989. *The Cynical Americans: Living and Working in an Age of Discontent and Disillusion.* San Francisco: Jossey-Bass.

Kirkpatrick, S. A. and E. A. Locke. 1996. "Direct and Indirect Effects of Three Core Charismatic Leadership Components on Performance and Attitudes." *Journal of Applied Psychology* 81(1): 36–51.

Kramer, R. M. 1999. "Trust and Distrust in Organizations: Emerging Perspectives, Enduring Questions." *Annual Review of Psychology* 50: 569–98.

Kramer, R. and T. Tyler. 1996. *Trust in Organizations: Frontiers of Theory and Research.* Thousand Oaks, CA: Sage.

Levi, M. 1998. "A State of Trust." In *Trust and Governance*, edited by A. Braithwaite and M. Levi, 77–101. New York: Russell Sage.

Liden, R. C. and G. Graen. 1980. "Generalizability of the Vertical Dyad Linkage Model of Leadership." *Academy of Management Journal* 23(3): 451–65.

Lieberman, J. K. (1981). *The Litigious Society.* New York: Basic Books.

Lubell, M. 2004. *Social and Institutional Trust in a Policy Context.* Manuscript submitted for publication.

Mayer, Roger C., James H. Davis, and David Schoorman. 1995. "An Integrative Model of Organizational Trust." *Academy of Management Review* 20(3): 709–34.

McAllister, D. 1995. "Affect- and cognition-based trust as foundations for interpersonal cooperation in organizations." *Academy of Management Journal* 38(1): 24–59.

Mendoza-Botelho, M. 2013. "Social Capital and Institutional Trust: Evidence from Bolivia's Popular Participation Decentralization Reforms." *Journal of Development Studies* 49(9), 1219–37.

Moore, M. H. 1995. *Creating Public Value: Strategic Management in Government.* Cambridge, MA: Harvard University Press.

National Commission on the Public Service. 2003. *Urgent Business for America: Revitalizing the Federal Government for the 21st Century.* Washington, DC: Brookings Institution.

National Commission on the Public Service. 1989. *Leadership for America: Rebuilding the Public Service.* Lexington, MA: Lexington Books.

National Commission on the State and Local Public Service. 1993. *Hard Truths/Tough Choices: An Agenda for State and Local Reform.* New York: Nelson A. Rockefeller Institute of Government.

North, D. C. 1990. *Institutions, Institutional Change, and Economic Performance.* Cambridge, UK: Cambridge University Press.

Ostrom, E. 1998. "A Behavioral Approach to the Rational Choice Theory of Collective Action: Presidential address. American Political Science Association, 1997." *American Political Science Review* 92(1): 1–22.

Oxford English Dictionary. 1989. 2d ed. http://dictionary.oed.com/ (accessed May 20, 2007).

Perry, James L. and Lyman W. Porter. 1982. "Factors Affecting the Context for Motivation in the Public Sector." *Academy of Management Review* 7(1): 89–98.

Podsakoff, P. M., S. B. MacKenzie, R. Moorman, and R. Fetter. 1990. "Transformational Leader Behaviors and Their Effects on Followers' Trust in Leader, Satisfaction, and Organizational Citizenship Behaviors." *Leadership Quarterly* 1(2): 107–42.

Rainey, Hal G. and Barry Bozeman. 2000. "Comparing Public and Private Organizations: Empirical Research and the Power of the a priori." *Journal of Public Administration Research and Theory* 10(2): 447–69.

Rainey, Hal G. and James Thompson. 2006. "Leadership and the Transformation of a Major Institution: Charles Rossotti and the Internal Revenue Service." *Public Administration Review* 66(4): 596–604.

Riccucci, Norma M. 1995. "'Execucrats,' Politics, and Public Policy: What Are the Ingredients for Successful Performance in the Federal Government?" *Public Administration Review* 55(3): 19–230.

Robbins, S. P. and T. A. Judge. 2007. *Organizational Behavior.* Upper Saddle River, NJ: Pearson Prentice Hall.

Rotter, J. B. 1967. A new scale for the measurement of interpersonal trust. *Journal of Personality* 35: 651–65.

Rousseau, Denis M., Sim B. Sitkin, Ronald S. Burt, and Colin Camerer. 1998. "Introduction to Special Topic Forum: Not So Different after All: A Cross-Discipline View of Trust." *Academy of Management Review* 23(3): 393–404.

Scholz, John T. and Mark Lubell. 1998. "Trust and Taxpaying: Testing the Heuristic Approach to Collective Action." *American Journal of Political Science* 42(2): 398–417.

Sitkin, Sim B., and N. L. Roth. 1993. "Explaining the Limited Effectiveness of Legalistic "Remedies" for Trust/Distrust." *Organization Science* 4(3): 367–92.

Whitener, E. M., S. E. Brodt, M. A. Korsgaard, and J. M. Werner. 1998. "Managers as Initiators of Trust: An Exchange Relationship Framework for Understanding Managerial Trustworthy Behavior." *Academy of Management Review* 23(3): 513–30.

Williamson, O. 1993. "Calculativeness, Trust and Economic Organization." *Journal of Law & Economics*, 36: 453–486.

Yukl, G. 1994. *Leadership in Organizations.* 3rd ed. Englewood Cliffs, NJ: Prentice-Hall.

Zaheer, A., B. McEvily, and V. Perrone. 1997. "Does Trust Matter? Exploring the Effects of Interorganizational and Interpersonal Trust on Performance." *Organization Science* 9(2): 141–59.

Zaheer, A. and N. Venkatraman. 1995. "Relational Governance as an Interorganizational Strategy: An Empirical Test of the Role of Trust in Economic Exchange." *Strategic Management Journal* 16(5): 373–92.

Zand, Dale E. 1997. *The Leadership Triad: Knowledge, Trust, and Power.* New York: Oxford University Press.

Zand, Dale E. 1972. "Trust and Managerial Problem Solving." *Administrative Science Quarterly* 17(2): 229–39.

10

GLOBAL AGING

Understanding its challenges

Masa Higo

Introduction

Population aging refers to an increase in the relative portion of older people as a share of the total population in a given region. The world population is aging and will continue growing older, even at an accelerated pace, over the coming decades. As "clearly one of the most significant demographic trends of the twenty-first century" (United Nations 2012a, p. 3), global aging – population aging worldwide – stands out as a key demographic environmental factor affecting the lives of citizens around the world, those in later life in particular, throughout the twenty-first century (Uhlenberg 2009).

The trend of population aging is in part the outcome of positive human achievements. It has resulted partly from the advancement of medical knowledge, the development of welfare programs for the aged, and the wide availability of those societal efforts around the world (World Health Organization [WHO] 2012). Population aging is, therefore, an achievement of modern society's commitment and ability to help its citizens to live longer and more healthily than have previous generations. However, this demographic shift has also posed unprecedented challenges for most countries around the world. Contributing to increasing the economic and social burdens of intergenerational dependency, this demographic shift has already strained, and will continue to undercut, existing economic resources, social institutions, and cultural legacies that have long supported older people (Higo and Williamson 2011). The trend of global aging thus suggests growing risks in later life in countries around the world, particularly in securing socio-economic resources necessary for the wellbeing of older people in coming decades.

Population aging has reshaped existing age-related public policies and governance across countries (Chen and Liu 2009). As a worldwide demographic shift, furthermore, global aging has significant implications for future policymaking not only at the national level but also on a global scale. Most countries face the common burden of adequately providing for their older populations. However, the impact of this global demographic shift is not uniform; it unevenly distributes risks in later life between economically developed and developing countries. While most of today's developed countries have already experienced some level of population aging, the majority of today's developing countries are either currently aging or will begin aging in the decade ahead at a much faster speed than what the developed countries experienced (Higo and

Khan 2014). This chapter suggests that global aging will distribute greater risks in later life for those living in today's developing countries of the world, particularly for vulnerable populations such as destitute elderly, unmarried older women and widows, and those who lack minimum financial or social support.

This chapter highlights three areas of uneven distribution of risks in later life between today's developed and developing countries. In coming decades many of today's developing countries will likely contend with greater risks in later life in (1) mitigating the burden of disease in epidemiological transition; (2) protecting financial security in retirement; and (3) securing a long-term care workforce. The overarching goal of this chapter is to call for a formulation of effective global-scale policies in order to help protect the wellbeing and survival of citizens in later life, particularly for those in today's developing countries. The remainder of this chapter is structured as follows. First, it provides an overview of the trends of global aging. Next, it introduces the different processes of population aging between today's developed and developing countries. Then the chapter discusses in detail the three areas in which today's developing countries will likely face greater risks in later life. Finally, the chapter concludes by summarizing the main discussions.

Global aging: an overview of the demographic trend

On a global scale, the rate of population aging in the twenty-first century will be without historic parallel. Throughout recorded history, young children (below the age of five) have always outnumbered older people (aged 65 or older). Between the years of 2015 and 2020, however, older people are projected to outnumber young children for the first time. In 2015, the number of young children and that of older people are projected to be about 666 million and 604 million, respectively. By 2020, however, the corresponding numbers will be about 668 million and 716 million, respectively. By 2050, the gap is projected to further increase to about 684 million and 1.49 billion, respectively.

The trend of global aging is also measured by the share of those aged 65 or older as a percentage of the world total population. Worldwide, in 2000 this age group accounted for 6.9 percent of the total population, and this figure is projected to increase to 10.3 percent by 2025 and to 15.6 percent by 2050 (United Nations 2015).

One of the main demographic factors that directly contributes to population aging is a decline in mortality rates at all age levels, a demographic shift which translates into an increase in life expectancy at birth: the number of years a newborn infant is expected to live after birth (WHO 2012). Globally, the average life expectancy, including both men and women, increased from 46.9 years for the 1950–1955 birth cohort to 67.1 for the 2000–2005 birth cohort. The figure is projected to further increase to 72.8 years for the 2025–2030 birth cohort and to 75.9 for the 2045–2050 birth cohort (United Nations 2012b). In combination with the decline in mortality rates, a decrease in childbirth rates is also contributing to population aging (Lloyd-Sherlock 2010). Roughly speaking, since the 1950s, the world population has experienced an overall decrease in childbirth rates. Between the years 1950 and 1955, worldwide, the total fertility rate – average number of children born to each woman over the course of her lifetime – was about 4.97. This figure decreased substantially to 2.59 by 2000 to 2005. The rate is currently projected to continue decreasing, reaching 2.37 between the years 2025 and 2030 and 2.24 between 2045 and 2050 (United Nations 2015).

Developed and developing countries: two worlds of an aging globe

While population aging is a global trend, it progresses differently by region, at least in the timing and speed of the increase in the population's share of older people. To clarify these differences, this chapter adopts what the United Nations (2015) refers to as the more developed and less developed regions. The former consists of countries in Europe and North America, Australia, New Zealand, and Japan, and the latter includes all the rest of the world, including the so-called emerging economies: China, India, Brazil, Mexico, and those countries that are economically underdeveloped or devastated such as those in sub-Saharan Africa. The remainder of this chapter refer to these regional categories as developed and developing countries, respectively.

In many developed countries, in Europe in particular, population aging began slowly during the late nineteenth century, partly because childbirth rates entered a phase of sustained decline and life expectancies at birth began to gradually increase (Rowland 2009). According to the United Nations (2015) projection, by the end of 2015, the shares of the population aged 65 and older out of the total will be the highest for Japan (26.4 percent), followed by Italy (21.7 percent), Germany (21.4 percent), Greece (20.2 percent), and Sweden (20.0 percent). However, the number and proportion of older people have also been growing in today's developing countries. By the end of 2015 there will be more people aged 65 and over living in China alone (132.5 million) than in all of Europe (128.8 million). As Figure 10.1 illustrates, as of 2010, some 62.4 percent of the world's population aged 65 and over lived in the developing countries – an estimated 331.1 million people. This figure is projected to increase to 682.5 million by 2030: about a 73 percent increase. By 2050, almost 1.2 billion of the expected 1.5 billion people aged 65 or older are projected to live in today's developing countries.

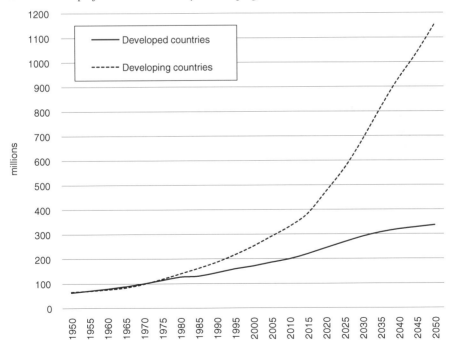

Figure 10.1 Developed vs. developing countries of the world – population aged 65 and older, 1950–2050

Source: United Nations (2015)

In many developing countries, population aging is taking place at a much faster rate than is the case for developed countries. Figure 10.2 shows when population aging occurred (or will occur) and how fast it proceeded (or will proceed) for some selected countries in developed and developing countries, respectively. For instance, it took 115 years (from 1865 to 1980) for France's population aged 65 and over to increase from seven percent to 14 percent of the country's total population. To make the same demographic shift took Sweden 85 years (from 1890 to 1975), Australia 73 years (from 1938 to 2011), and Canada 65 years (from 1944 to 2009). It will have taken the United States 69 years (from 1944 to 2013). In contrast, what follows illustrates how much more rapidly the population aging will proceed in developing countries: Singapore will take 19 years (2000–2009), Brazil 21 years (2011–2032), Thailand 22 years (2002–2024), Colombia 25 years (2017–2032), China 26 years (2000–2026), and Chile 37 years (1988–2025). Generally, developing countries are projected to go through similar increases in the proportion of elderly but much more rapidly. This projection suggests that, unlike in developed countries, many developing countries' policies, economies, cultural norms, and family structures will have much less time to make necessary adjustments to such rapid growing of the population.

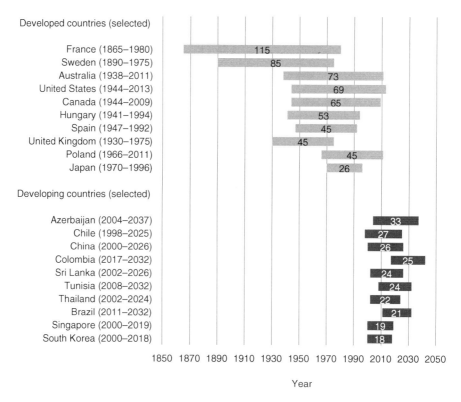

Figure 10.2 Developed vs. developing countries – number of years taken or expected for percent of population aged 65 years or older to increase from 7% to 14%
Source: Higo and Khan (2014); Kinsella and Phillips (2005)

110

Greater risks for developing countries in mitigating the burden of disease in epidemiological transition

In the coming decades, global aging will distribute greater risks in later life for many of today's developing countries. The first unequal distribution of risk is the public burden of disease. The world is currently experiencing an epidemiological transition, which refers to changes in leading causes of death in a given population (WHO 2008). Worldwide, the leading causes of death are shifting from acute and infectious diseases, including HIV/AIDS, pneumonia, influenza, and leprosy among others, to chronic and non-communicable diseases such as cerebral-vascular disease, cancers, and ischemic heart disease, which are characteristics of old age (Agyei-Mensah and Aikins 2010). While populations have come to live longer than previous generations, the number of deaths due to chronic and non-communicable diseases has been rapidly increasing and will continue rising over the next decades (World Economic Forum 2011). In 2004, the worldwide number of deaths from cardiovascular diseases and cancers – typical non-communicable diseases – was about 19 million, and that figure is projected to jump to more than 40 million by 2030. Overall, chronic and non-communicable diseases are projected to account for about three-quarters of all deaths worldwide in 2030 (WHO 2009).

This epidemiological transition takes on major importance in connection with both global aging and any given country's stage of economic development. Shifts in the leading diseases often posit challenges for allocating scarce economic resources for medical care and government interventions such as public expenditures on healthcare for citizens (Crystal and Siegel 2009). In many countries today, healthcare costs are rapidly rising; in some countries the growth rates of public healthcare expenditures are projected to exceed the national economic growth rates in the decade ahead (WHO 2012).

To date, developed and developing countries have encountered significantly different paths in undergoing this epidemiological transition. In many countries in Europe and North America, the epidemiological transition began approximately in the late eighteenth century, the time around which childbirth rates in this region began to slowly decline (WHO 2009). By contrast, in most of today's developing countries the epidemiological transition did not begin until well into the twentieth century but has been taking place at a much faster pace than in most developed countries since then (Crystal and Siegel 2009).

The *burden of disease* is a measure of the region-specific economic burden caused by diseases in a baseline year and is calculated by combining years of life lost due to premature mortality and time lived in less than full health (WHO 2008). The burden of non-communicable diseases has already been a major problem in most developed countries. In the near coming decades, the same burden is projected to increase rapidly in many of today's developing countries as well. In 2004, the share of the total burden of disease attributed to non-communicable diseases was about 85 percent for the developed countries and about 44 percent for the developing ones. By 2030, these figures are projected to increase to about 89 percent and 54 percent, respectively (WHO 2008).

The challenges of the burden of diseases, in the context of the epidemiological transition, will likely be much greater for developing countries. While chronic and non-communicable diseases are currently imposing a growing burden on an increasing number of developing countries, many of these countries have limited economic resources to provide their citizens with formal healthcare (Nuscheler and Roeder 2013). Simultaneously, certain infectious diseases including HIV/AIDS, tuberculosis, and malaria, to name a few, will likely remain a devastating health issue. According to the WHO's (2008) estimate, while the burden attributed to infectious diseases in the developed countries is estimated to be only about three percent by

2030, the figure for the developing countries is projected to remain very high: around 32 percent. Therefore, many of these countries will likely contend with a double burden of disease: a condition in which high rates of infectious diseases including HIV/AIDS will persist in combination with increasing rates of non-communicable diseases associated with old age (Aboderin 2011).

Greater risks for developing countries in protecting financial security in retirement

The second area of greater risks in later life for developing countries is related to protecting financial security in retirement. Population aging has raised the debate over the sustainability of existing public old-age pension schemes in many countries (Klassen 2013; Organization for Economic Co-operation and Development [OECD] 2013). While global aging will likely expose many older workers to high levels of individual financial security risks in retirement, these risks will most likely be greater in developing countries.

Public old-age pension programs were developed first in developed countries and have later become common in many developing countries as well. These programs have come to play an increasingly important role in providing sources of financial security for retirees and their families in many developed countries, particularly since the mid–1950s. By 2000, public old-age pension programs covered more than 90 percent of workers in OECD-affiliated countries (OECD 2009). Most of these programs are based on the pay-as-you-go defined benefit model. This is based on an intergenerational contract by which, for the most part, pension benefits are not pre-funded, and revenues from the current working population's payroll taxes are used to finance the benefits of current retirees. Benefits are based primarily on some measure of a worker's average or final wage and the number of years the worker has contributed, rather than being contingent upon fluctuations in financial markets (Williamson 2011). From the early 1950s through the 1980s, retirement was gradually institutionalized in most developed countries as the availability of relatively generous pension benefits for many retirees became a foundational source for financial security in later life (Orenstein 2008).

In the midst of global aging, however, worldwide the number of pensioners relative to contributors is increasing. Many countries around the world are therefore facing insufficient government resources to provide all workers with promised amounts of pension benefits. This demographic shift has called the sustainability of the conventional, pay-as-you-go defined benefit model into serious question (Williamson 2011). Today, many developed and developing countries have begun considering and in some cases implementing market-oriented, partial-privatization schemes as a way to reform their existing public pension programs.

In recent years the introduction of a defined contribution scheme to conventional programs has received a great deal of attention (Williamson, Price, and Shen 2012). This alternative scheme is a form of partial privatization of the responsibility for individuals' financial security in retirement; it promises that a specified amount of premiums will be contributed each month, but no promise is made with respect to the amount of the actual pension benefits that will be paid based on those contributions. Each covered worker creates an individual account with the funding based on their own contributions. Each worker's contribution is often supplemented by contributions from his or her employer via payroll taxes and the earnings or losses on those assets over the years when they are invested by private sector money management organizations – such as banks and trust funds – in financial markets (Williamson 2011).

Promising less governmental support for securing financial security in later life, the introduction of a defined contribution scheme aims partly to shift much of the risk to individual workers (Orenstein 2008). To date, more than 20 developing countries – including Chile and many others in Latin America and Eastern Europe – have already introduced funded individual accounts for defined contribution schemes, thereby partially privatizing their existing public pension schemes (Williamson, Price, and Shen 2012).

According to the United Nations (2012), by 2004, public old-age pension programs had been established in 167 countries. These programs, however, typically cover a much smaller fraction of workers in developing countries relative to those in developed countries. For instance, it is not uncommon for less than 10 percent of the total workforce to be covered by the pension programs in developing countries; in Thailand, the Philippines, and Malaysia, public pension coverage is restricted to certain categories of workers, such as public sector employees and military personnel. Nearly one-third of African countries that currently offer public pension benefits have a life expectancy lower than the statutory pensionable age both for men and women (Orenstein 2008).

While the projected future costs of such narrowly applied public pension programs are a major concern, many developing countries must first also contend with the pressure to seek ways to finance their strategic development plans, particularly those linked to infrastructure, security, education, and public health (United Nations 2012a). Moreover, the new defined contribution schemes make financial security in retirement depend on a number of factors that involve different forms of risk, including: what forms of financial assets a worker is able to save, how those savings are invested, fees assessed for managing these assets, and fluctuations in financial markets, to name a few (Williamson, Price, and Shen 2012). This shift toward greater pension privatization may therefore generate greater risks in protecting financial security in retirement, particularly for low-wage workers and their families and single widows in developing countries.

Greater risks for developing countries in securing a long-term care workforce

Global aging will likely generate greater risks for developing countries in securing a workforce for long-term elderly care. Over the past few decades, the demand for a long-term care workforce has been steadily increasing in many countries, and home and community based long-term care workers directly serving the frail and disabled elderly have been in particularly high demand (O'Brien and Gostin 2011).

Since the mid–1980s, an increasing number of developed countries, including Canada, the United Kingdom, and the United States, have promoted aging-in-place for elderly care. This shifts the site of long-term care services for the elderly from institutions such as hospitals, palliative care facilities, and nursing homes to the patients' own homes and communities (Kenner 2008). The promotion of aging-in-place has raised the demand for long-term care services to service local environments. In addition, the ever-increasing financial cost of direct long-term care in institutional settings has also contributed to the increasing demand for home and community-based direct long-term care services (Black 2008).

Over the past two decades, an increasing number of both developed and developing countries have been developing a global labor market for a long-term care workforce (Browne and Braun 2008). Many developed countries are major importers and consumers of this workforce. This is due partly to declining childbirth rates, increasing divorce rates, and increasing female employment in multiple labor sectors, such that many developed countries are currently facing shortages of long-term care workers for their already increasing elderly population. A number of developing countries have gradually been integrated into the global labor market as providers of this healthcare workforce (Nuscheler and Roeder 2013).

Over the past three decades, the governments of these countries have encouraged their younger workers, and women in particular, to migrate to developed countries as long-term care workers (Browne and Braun 2008). Since the mid-1990s, for instance, the Philippine government has supported the education, training, and export of many Filipinas, mainly as long-term care workers including nurse aides (Luts and Palenga-Möllenbeck 2012). One of the main reasons behind this initiative is the financial benefits from money remitted by these workers back to their families (Ball 2008).

The rise of this global labor market for a long-term care workforce is referred to by some as "global care drain": a global shift in which the direct long-term care workforce is drawn from developing countries to developed ones (Luts and Palenga-Möllenbeck 2012). The transnational migration of these workers has steadily increased over the past few decades; in the United States, for instance, where foreign-born workers accounted for only five percent of the total long-term care workforce in 1980, the figure had increased to about 17 percent by 2010 (Cremer and Roeder 2013).

To date, many of the exporting developing countries have economically benefited from participating in this global labor market (Luts and Palenga-Möllenbeck 2012). However, the more thoroughly these countries are integrated into the global labor market, the more likely it is that they will likely contend with shortages in the long-term care workforce in their own countries. According to a WHO (2008) projection, over the next two decades the need for healthcare for the aged in some developing countries will increase by as much as 400 percent. Even now, a significant portion of developing countries do not have enough laborers for long-term care. Also as noted by the WHO (2008), the ratio of health workers to the total population, also referred to as the health worker density, needs to be at least 2.5 workers per 1,000 people in a given population. Among 192 countries worldwide, 76 countries do not reach this minimum rate, and 45 of these are in sub-Saharan Africa. Generally, developing countries are about to experience population aging and at a more abrupt pace than did most developed countries. Worldwide, the majority of older people will soon be in today's developing countries, where, consequently, an unprecedented level of demand for a direct long-term care workforce will emerge even as that very workforce has been drained away to developed countries.

Conclusion

This chapter emphasizes that a formulation of global-scale policies is needed in response to the growing risks of securing socio-economic resources for supporting older people. Global aging is a key demographic environmental factor that significantly affects the wellbeing of citizens in later life. The need for global-scale policies stems from the tendency of global aging not only to challenge most countries but also to unevenly distribute risks in later life between developed and developing countries. In coming decades, developing countries will contend with greater risks in later life relative to developed countries; many of those countries are not only newcomers to the challenges of population aging, but are also experiencing this demographic change more abruptly, while simultaneously being continually pressured to develop their economic and social infrastructures for citizens of all ages.

This chapter has focused on three specific areas in which such global inequalities will likely be most pronounced in the coming decades. First, developing countries will likely face a double burden of disease in epidemiological transition: while still combating persistent acute and infectious diseases, many of these countries will be burdened with allocating public resources to reduce increasingly prevalent diseases characteristic of old age such as chronic and non-communicable diseases. Second, many of today's developing countries will be drawn into a global trend of pension privatization, while even now their public pension programs offer relatively limited protection for workers and their families.

Third, but not least, many developing countries will contend with severer shortages in the long-term care workforce for their elderly populations as an increasing number of those countries become subject to the global care drain. It is worth noting that among developing countries, certain vulnerable groups would be particularly at risk, including: the disabled; those who are socially marginalized; and economically vulnerable elderly women such as widows, those never married and those without adult children. In some countries, risks in later life will be greater for those women who are responsible for the care of their grandchildren due to the death of their adult children, often linked to diseases such as HIV/AIDS.

The world population is aging in part because citizens in most countries have come to live longer and in better health than previous generations. Arguably, this positive human achievement is due partly to societal commitment and public effort – often through orchestrated endeavors beyond national borders – to provide for the elderly. By a similar token, the twenty-first century demographics call for developing collective and solidaristic efforts to pursue collective measures across the world, in order to address the growing risks in later life that citizens will face today and in the future. Over the past decades, a few international NGOs and programs – including, but not limited to, HelpAge International and United Nations Population Fund (UNFPA) – have been organized, aiming at least in part to address these issues. More efforts, nonetheless, are necessary to generate more effective and sustainable impacts. Rather than leaving each country responsible for addressing these risks for their own citizens alone, decision makers around the world may need to formulate new policies, governances, and programs that aim to protect the wellbeing and survival of older people in both developed and developing countries around the world.

References

Aboderin, I. (2011). "Global ageing: perspectives from Sub Saharan Africa." In *Handbook of Social Gerontology*, edited by Dannefer, D. and Phillipson, C., 405–419. Thousand Oaks, CA: Sage Publications.

Agyei-Mensah, S., and Aikins, A. (2010). "Epidemiological transition and the double burden of disease in Accra, Ghana." *Journal of Urban Health* 87 (5): 879–897.

Ball, R. E. (2008). "Globalized labor markets and the trade of Filipino nurses: implications for international regulatory governance." In *The International Migration of Health Workers*, edited by Connell, J., 30–46. New York: Routledge.

Black, K. (2008). "Health and aging-in-place: implications for community practice." *Journal of Community Practice* 16 (1): 79–95.

Browne, C. V. and K. L. Braun. 2008. "Globalization, women's migration, and the long-term-care workforce." *Gerontologist* 48 (1): 16–24.

Chang, W. C. (2012). "Family ties, living arrangement, and marital satisfaction." *Journal of Happiness Studies* 14 (1): 215–233.

Chen, F. and Liu, G. (2009). "Population aging in China." In *International Handbook of Population Aging*, edited by Uhlenberg, P., 157–172. New York: Springer.

Cremer, H. and Roeder, K. (2013). "Long-term care policy, myopia and redistribution." *Journal of Public Economics* 108: 33–43.

Crystal, S. and Siegel, M. J. (2009). "Health care policy and the demography of aging in cross-national perspective." In *International Handbook of Population Aging*, edited by Uhlenberg, P., 607–630. New York: Springer.

Higo, M. and Khan, H. T. A. (2014). "Global population aging: unequal distribution of risks in later life between developed and developing countries." *Global Social Policy*. doi: 10.1177/1468018114543157.

Higo, M. and Williamson, J. B. (2011). "Global aging." In *Handbook of Sociology of Aging*, edited by Settersten, R. A., and Angel, J. L., 91–112. New York: Springer.

Kenner, A. M. (2008). "Securing the elderly body: dementia, surveillance, and the politics of 'aging in place.'" *Survelliance & Society* 5 (3): 252–269.

Klassen, T. R. (2013). *Retirement in Canada*. Oxford: Oxford University Press.

Lloyd-Sherlock, P. (2010). *Population aging and international development: From generalization to evidence*. New York: Polity Press.

Luts, H. and Palenga-Möllenbeck, E. (2012). "Care workers, care drain, and care chains: reflections on care, migration, and citizenship." *Social Politics* 19 (1): 15–37.

Nuscheler, R. and Roeder, K. (2013). "The political economy of long-term care." *European Economic Review* 62: 154–173.

O'Brien, P., and Gostin, L. O. (2011). "Health workers shortages and global justice." *Milbank Memorial Fund*. Retrieved from www.integration.samhsa.gov/workforce/Workforce,_resources.pdf.

Orenstein, M. A. (2008). *Privatizing pensions: The transnational campaign for social security reform*. Princeton, NJ: Princeton University Press 2008.

OECD. (2009). *Pensions at a glance 2009: Retirement-income systems in OECD countries*. Paris: OECD Publications.

OECD. (2013). *Pensions at a glance 2013: OECD and G20 indicators*. Paris: OECD Publications.

Rowland, D. T. (2009). "Global population aging: history and prospects." In *International Handbook of Population Aging*, edited by Uhlenberg, P., 37–65. New York: Springer.

Uhlenberg, P. (2009). "Introduction." In *International Handbook of Population Aging*, edited by Uhlenberg, P., 1–4. New York: Springer.

United Nations. (2012a). *Ageing in the twenty-first century: A celebration and a challenge*. UNFPA and Help Age International.

United Nations. (2012b). *World population prospects: The 2012 revision*. Retrieved from www.un.org/esa/population/publications/worldaging19502050/.

United Nations. (2015). *World population prospects: The 2015 revision*. Retrieved from https://esa.un.org/unpd/wpp/Publications/Files/Key_Findings_WPP_2015.pdf.

Williamson, J. B. (2011). "The future of retirement security." In *Handbook of Aging and the Social Sciences*, edited by Binstock, R. H. and George, L. K., 7th ed, 281–294. Millbrae, CA: Academic Press.

Williamson, J. B., Price, M., and Shen, C. (2012). "Pension policy in China, Singapore, and South Korea: An assessment of the potential value of the notional defined contribution model." *Journal of Aging Studies* 26 (1): 79–89.

World Economic Forum. (2015). *The global economic burden of non-communicable diseases*. Retrieved from www3.weforum.org/docs/WEF_Harvard_HE_GlobalEconomicBurdenNonCommunicableDiseases_2011.pdf. Accessed 06/06/2016.

World Health Organization. (2012). *Good health adds life to years: Global brief for world health day 2012*. Geneva: World Health Organization.

World Health Organization. (2009). *Global health risks: Mortality and burden of disease attributable to selected major risks*. Retrieved from www.who.int/healthinfo/global_burden_disease/GlobalHealthRisks_report_full.pdf.

World Health Organization. (2008). *Global burden of disease: The 2004 update*. Retrieved from www.who.int/healthinfo/global_burden_disease/GBD_report_2004update_full.pdf. Accessed 06/06/2016.

11

PUBLIC POLICY AND ADMINISTRATION

Tradition, history and reforms

Edoardo Ongaro

Introduction

This chapter addresses the issue of how to interpret the influence of the past on contemporary public administration and public policies. Historical Institutionalism (HI) is the chosen theory of reference for explaining tradition and the influence of the past – or, put differently, for explaining the influence of context as the consolidation of past choices and events on present choices and events (Pollitt 2013; Pollitt and Dan 2011).

Context is a notion that denotes more than the consolidation of past choices in contemporary institutions, as it is also composed of contemporaneous higher-level events: for example, the fiscal crisis occurred in certain euro-zone countries over 2010–2015 became part of the context of fiscal and administrative policies in those countries. Contemporaneous events combine with pre-existing structures, processes and institutions to affect the dynamics of public policy. However, institutions stemming from past events are a crucial part of the context, and that set of contextual influences is the subject of the present chapter.

We at first examine the question of causality: why do past choices about the structure and processes of government cause present effects? What is the causal foundation of path dependency? Then we discuss the conditions under which non-incremental change – gradual, radical, and transformative – may occur in HI, and the levels of applicability of this theoretical perspective. Subsequently, we focus on the domain of administrative reforms and review models rooted in HI that try to explain administrative change. This chapter concludes with a foray into the complex issues of the generalizability of predictions when making attempts to explain and theorise phenomena within an HI perspective.

Foundations of causality in historical institutionalism

The preliminary, and in a sense foundational, question to be addressed is that of causality in HI: why do past choices about the structure and processes of government cause present effects? What is the causal foundation of path dependency? One approach is to adopt a logic of appropriateness perspective (e.g. March 1999) and consider that institutions shape what is considered appropriate by decision-makers, hence constraining the boundaries of what is considered to be feasible or opportune. This approach has its roots in the cognate theoretical strand of normative new institutionalism (Peters 2005), which sees pre-existing institutions as shapers of judgements about what is appropriate behaviour: in this perspective decisions are taken by matching the specific circumstances with general patterns of appropriate behaviour. The logic of appropriateness provides at least a partial explanation for why past decisions that have shaped institutions, which in turn shape what is deemed to be "appropriate behaviour" have an influence on present decision-making. Framed this way, however, HI tends to be subsumed under the strand of normative new institutionalism, and its distinctive focus on past choices may be blurred or lost.

Another theoretical perspective for explaining path dependency is more akin to rational choice new institutionalism but can be distinguished from it for its specific use of the notion of increasing returns. Its emphasis on the role of institutions, however, places it firmly within the neo-institutionalist stream and distances it from rational choice modelling or behavioural public administration.

The starting point of this approach for explaining causality in HI is the consideration that the estimation and evaluation of the consequences of decisions is centre-stage in decision-making, but decision-makers do not make their decisions in a vacuum. Rather, institutions shape the opportunity structure within which decisions are made. This approach borrows from the discipline of economics the conceptual tool of increasing returns in order to account for path dependence:

> In an increasing returns process, the probability of further steps along the same path increases with each move down the path. This is because the relative benefits of the current activity compared with other possible options increase over time. To put it a different way, the costs of exit – of switching to some previously plausible alternative – rise.
>
> *(Pierson 2000a: 252, emphasis in original)*

Increasing returns is then a departure from equilibrium analyses (often based on decreasing rather than increasing economic returns), which point to a single optimal outcome. Conversely, increasing returns is a theoretical perspective for accounts of political and policy processes that assume the long-term survival of a plurality of arrangements in political systems. Path dependency is grounded in the consideration that "not just [...] institutional arrangements may make a reversal of course difficult. Individual and organizational adaptations to previous arrangements may also make reversal unattractive" (Pierson 2000b: 491). As a consequence, initial institutional decisions, even suboptimal ones, can become self-reinforcing over time: they can last over long time frames, even if they contain dysfunctional elements (which, it should be added, is not necessarily the case).

A logic of increasing returns combined with a logic of appropriateness, we argue, may thus provide an explanation for the influence of past choices on present public policy processes. The influence is in the direction of persistency and stability, so questions about the possibility for change to occur arise: how is change, other than a marginal or at most an incremental one, attainable under an HI perspective? It is to this question that we now turn.

Change in historical institutionalism: mechanisms and types

Can change occur in an HI perspective? If so, what kind of change is possible beyond a marginal or incremental one? And how does change unfold in such a perspective?

HI has been interpreted as a theory leading to consider political systems in general, and hence administrative systems and public policies, as either very stable (though dysfunctionally so) or subject to change only through rupture mode. Here, the collapse of an equilibrium leads to its replacement by another equilibrium, which tends to last a relatively long time due either to the self-reinforcing mechanisms of increasing marginal returns, or to the reinforcing of behaviours shaped by a logic of appropriateness. In the words:

> In the absence of analytic tools to characterize and explain modes of gradual change, much of the institutionalist literature relies – explicitly or implicitly – on a strong punctuated equilibrium model that draws an overly sharp distinction between long periods of institutional stasis periodically interrupted by some sort of exogenous shock that opens things up, allowing for more or less radical reorganization.
>
> *(Streeck and Thelen 2005: 1)*

Conversely, Streeck and Thelen (2005) argue about a third option between stability and perpetuation, on the one hand, and breakdown of the system and replacement by another one, on the other hand. They identify mechanisms whereby gradual transformation – incremental change with transformative results – may occur. Previous choices do affect the paths that can later be taken but do not impede change (Thelen 1992, 2003; Thelen and Steinmo 1992; Steinmo, Thelen, and Longstreth 1992). Streeck and Thelen identify a number of mechanisms enabling gradual transformation: layering, conversion, displacement, drift, exhaustion. Layering is the creation of new policy or institutions without eliminating the old, allowing the former to serve new purposes at least partly bypassing the influence of previous institutions. Conversion is the internally driven adaptation of institutions, whereby "existing institutions are redirected to new purposes, driving changes in the role they perform and/or the functions they serve", Thelen 2003: 226). Displacement is the discovery and activation of alternative institutional forms that did exist before but were considered deviant. Drift is the gradual and sometimes unplanned adaptation of institutions, while exhaustion occurs as the institution gradually loses its purpose and, though formally still in place, ultimately breaks down.

They represent mechanisms – often operating in combination – whereby change may occur within path dependency in a gradual way but ultimately leading to profound transformation of the system or policy, a process substantially different from change occurred through abrupt, transformation at critical points of system breakdown. They also explain why political and policy changes may be relatively frequent across polities and jurisdictions, even in the presence of sustained continuity accounted for by path dependency.

Two further mechanisms may lead to more radical change, yet they originate in small internal changes rather than in system breakdown caused by an external shock. They are accumulation, in which the accruing of a series of small changes can ultimately lead to a large radical change, and threshold, where slow incremental change reaches a critical threshold beyond which radical change suddenly occurs.

Summing up, HI is a theoretical perspective to explain both continuity and change in public policy and public administration, provided the analysis of the mechanisms that are at work is carried out. The repertoire of mechanisms recalled above is far from exhaustive yet may provide a good entry point for analysis.

HI is a way to account for the influence of history and tradition on continuity, as well as change in public policy and administration, which can be applied at different levels. First, at the level of political systems or subsystems at a large, encompassing level: for example, the political institutions of a state, polity or jurisdiction, or significant portions of it. Second, to substantive public policy domains: for example, the environmental policy, health policy, social security policy, etc.

Third, to the public sector and its reform, both of the general configuration of public administration and of the systems employed for managing it, government-wide reforms of public management systems have been conceptualized by authors as a distinctive policy in its own right: the public management policy is a specific policy whose target is not a category of final users of public services, but rather the management processes of public administration itself (Barzelay 2001). Fourth, to individual public services organizations and their organizational behaviour an application of HI lies in explaining the contextual conditions under which strategy forms in public services organizations which in turn is part of the answer to the question of why and under what conditions public services organizations form a strategy at all (Ferlie and Ongaro 2015). Fifth, to sub-units of the public sector (e.g. an office or bureau) or even the behaviour of individuals (at this level, institutionalism and institutional analysis most benefit from being combined with "behavioural" public administration).

In the remainder of this chapter we focus on how, in the perspective of HI, tradition and past choices affect public sector reform at the level of public management systems, or more broadly at the level of the general configuration of public administration.

Comparative studies (Pollitt and Bouckaert 2011) have in fact shown that tradition and past choices affect how countries respond to global pressures to reform. The doctrines of the New Public Management (NPM) (Barzelay 2001; Hood 1991) have, mainly over the 1990s, propagated and shaped the global discourse of public sector reform, yet countries have responded very differently to such reform pressures. Some, like Australia, New Zealand or the United Kingdom, have embraced them, and in important respects are still saturated with such ideas (Ferlie et al. 1996), while others, such as France, have only limitedly, if at all, introduced such doctrines (Bezes 2010). An explanation for such striking differences lies in the receptivity of different jurisdictions to NPM doctrines. In turn, this difference in receptivity may be explained by considering how history and the past have shaped the systems – that is, from the perspective of HI.

We introduce two widely cited models elaborated by academic authorities to examine ways in which the theoretical perspective of HI may be employed to explain continuity and change in the configuration of the public sector and its management as well as enduring differences across jurisdictions. We conclude the chapter by briefly discussing the extent to which models drawing on HI can be generalizable in their scope and remit, or whether they remain idiosyncratic to specific configurations and settings.

Focus: Two models for explaining administrative change rooted in HI

Pollitt and Bouckaert (2011) present a framework for the analysis of contextual influences that singles out five contextual dimensions for their influence on the dynamics of public management reforms. First, the vertical and horizontal dispersion of authority within the polity under consideration. Second, the dominant administrative culture, that is, the beliefs and expectations held by the staff about what is normal and acceptable; the administrative culture tends to fall into either of two categories: the "Public Interest" culture of governance, typical of most Anglo-Saxon countries, whereby public organizations receive legitimacy through the effectiveness and usefulness of what they deliver to the public; and the "Rechtsstaat" culture of governance, widely spread, for example, across most of continental Europe, in which the law is at the core of administrative action and legitimacy. Third, the configuration of the relationships between executive politicians and senior public servants. Fourth, the nature of executive government, and notably whether it is majoritarian – minimal-winning coalition governing – or larger and more composite in its parliamentary bases. Fifth, the sources of policy advice in matters of administrative reform: whether the bureaucracy is also a major provider of advice to reformers, or conversely external sources, like multi-national consultancies, have ease of access to the government in matters of public management reform and play an influential role in it.

Subsequent studies have applied the model developed by Pollitt and Bouckaert (2000) to other jurisdictions and further elaborated on it. For example, in the study of Southern European countries (Ongaro 2009; Ongaro 2011; Kickert 2011), additional dimensions such as clientelism and the geographical provenance of the civil service (whether it is polarized or evenly distributed across the country) have proved useful for a better understanding of the dynamics of administrative reforms.

Each of these dimensions potentially affects the contents and/or the process of administrative reform, though in combination with other contingent factors, and not in a mechanistic way (Pollitt and Bouckaert 2011). Thus, for example, a public interest culture may facilitate the diffusion of tools like performance contracts that link the performance of public agencies to some kind of monetary reward resembling or imitating the functioning of markets. This tool understands public services legitimacy as being driven by the notions of results and delivery, which are more akin to this type of culture of governance than to a Rechtsstaat conception.

Shifting from influences on the contents of reforms to the process of reforming, it has been argued that majoritarian governments may facilitate radical and broad-scope public management reforms, and speed them up, as the government can more easily get parliamentary backing, and a limited number of key decision-makers tend to have a say in the reform process; indeed a few can "call the shots", something that is more unlikely to happen in non-majoritarian systems. Majoritarian government enables radical change and an intense pace of reforms, at least at the policy decision level, whilst implementation may turn out to be even more challenging, if consensus has not previously been created and facilitating conditions not set up.

Pollitt and Bouckaert (2011) work out a framework for analyzing such lines of influence based on the study of 12 countries plus the special case of a supranational institution like the European Commission, adding important qualifications and caveats. The academic debate stemming from this prominent contribution has led to more nuances being identified by later works and the model being further qualified. For example, in another work I argue that the application of this framework to a supranational institution like the European Commission would require introducing the notion of compound institutional systems as a further qualification of the vertical dispersion of authority (Ongaro 2013).

The key question is: how wide is the scope of application of this model? Can it be applied to all polities and jurisdictions across the world or is it mainly meaningful only for the western world, or perhaps just a subset of it? All 12 countries examined by Pollitt and Bouckaert (2011) in their comparative study belong either to Western Europe or Scandinavia, or to the Anglosphere (Australia, Canada, New Zealand and the US), while for example the whole of Latin America, which can well be included as part of the western world, is not covered by the study.

The second model we introduce is proposed by Martin Painter and Guy Peters (2010). This model is wider in its ambition and encompasses most administrative systems across the world. It is grounded in the idea of administrative tradition, a set of basic traits that characterize the public administration of clusters of countries.

Administrative tradition is "a historically based set of values, structures and relationships with other institutions that defines the nature of appropriate public administration within society" (Peters 2008). For example, a number of countries have been influenced by and adopted institutions of the French public sector and they still display similar traits in their administrative systems. Notwithstanding the differences that their respective histories have brought about, they may be characterized as belonging to the "Napoleonic" administrative tradition (Ongaro 2009, 2010). Notably, these countries are located in the south of Europe: Greece, Italy, Portugal and Spain – though the influence of this tradition may also be found in Africa and Latin America.

Painter and Peters (2010: 13–14) have identified and outlined certain distinctive traits of a number of such clusters, intended to form major families or groups, based on a range of geographical, historical and cultural considerations: Anglo-American; Napoleonic; Germanic; Scandinavian; Latin American; Post-colonial South Asian and African; Confucian (East Asian); Soviet/Post-Soviet; and Islamic.

Alongside these, hybrids and transplants can be added, like the Netherlands, Hong Kong, or Japan, where the Meiji Revolution brought certain basic traits of both the Napoleonic and the Germanic administrative traditions into an East Asian system.

The usefulness of the notion of an administrative tradition lies in the possibility it creates to provide key entry points for analysis. In the words of the authors:

> The ability to hold some variables constant and to highlight significant differences based on a rigorous classification of different traditions provides a key entry point to comparative analysis of a variety of phenomena, such as administrative reform and policy capacity. To some extent traditions fulfil the same function as a model such as Weber's model of bureaucracy. We can compare real world cases against the model of the tradition, e.g. is the United States really an Anglo-American system, or something quite distinctive? On the other hand, we can attempt to collect as much information as we can about the individual systems and attempt to develop the models of the traditions from that empirical data.
>
> *(Painter and Peters 2010)*

Four basic variables are used to characterize a tradition. First is the conception of the state and its fundamental relation to society. The main distinction is between organic conceptions of the state, whereby the state is assumed to be linked from its inception with society, and hence almost a given, and contractarian conceptions of the state, whereby the state is conceived of as a human construct, malleable by the parties to the contract. Second is the relationship of the bureaucracy with political institutions. Such a dimension encompasses a range of profiles, from the politicization of careers within the bureaucracy, to how much the bureaucracy itself becomes a general-purpose elite for the state, to the extent to which careers in the civil service are distinct from both political careers and private sector careers, or whether they are interconnected. Third is the relative importance attached to law vs. management. Fourth is the nature of accountability in the public sector: either relying upon the law or upon political actors, especially parliaments, as the primary mechanism to enforce accountability.

The Painter and Peters model is grander in its scope and remit; it is, however, shorter on drawing specific implications about the alleged effects of contextual dimensions on administrative reforms, which brings us back to the key question of how far we can go in terms of scope or domain of applicability of models rooted in HI when the drawing of causal explanations, rather than mapping and interpreting, is the ultimate goal.

Both these models are terms of reference in the study of administrative reforms, and both have strong roots in HI and can then be considered as exemplars of an application of an HI perspective to the study of public administration (though it should promptly be recognized that they draw from a range of theoretical sources and cannot be ascribed only to an HI perspective). Questioning the scope of applicability of such models is thus a good entry point to address the issue of how generalizable are explanations of policy and administrative change rooted in HI. It is to this big question, which here we can only briefly introduce and discuss, that we turn in the conclusion of the chapter.

Can contextual knowledge be global?

What do these models of analysis by leading scholars in the field tell us? What analyses of causal influences can be derived of general applicability? And hence, what can be stated about the question of whether theoretical perspectives rooted in HI are generalizable in their scope and remit or rather idiosyncratic to specific configurations and settings? Put differently, can "contextual knowledge" (HI being a theoretical perspective that emphazises context-dependent explanations) be global, or is this very idea inherently contradictory (Ongaro and Van Thiel 2017)?

We should immediately state that our aim here is more to raise a question we consider to be important and pertinent, rather than attempt to provide an answer, however tentative. We discuss the applicability of the two models in order to engage with this major issue, and hopefully leave the reader with the appetite to move on along this important line of reflection and study.

We at first discuss briefly the application of the Pollitt and Bouckaert model outside of the "West", mainly Western European or Anglo-American countries, making special reference to its potential application to the "East" (meaning mainly Eastern Asia). Expanding case studies across the continents would lead to further refinements of the discussion presented here.

A first point is that the Pollitt and Bouckaert model is elaborated based on the study of exclusively liberal-democratic political systems. Does it require re-elaboration for application to non-liberal-democratic systems? This question raises big defining issues around democracy that go beyond the scope of this chapter, including whether democracy is a matter of grade – more or less democratic – or quality – either a political system is democratic or it is not. Yet, the question deserves at least some tentative discussion, especially considering the apparent consolidation of the so-called new authoritarianism. As Hensengerth puts the matter (referring also to Krastev 2011), across the world a number of regimes have defied the so-called third wave of democratization, that is, the assumption that countries move from authoritarianism to democracy. A number of countries have remained authoritarian, at times combining this basic character with some limited openings. Yet, this has not systematically led to grey and dull top-down countries – rather, some authoritarian countries have exhibited surprising vibrancy in social and economic development and have developed flexible governance structures that allows them to accommodate social and economic change, including capitalist reforms and a diversification of society.

The framework suggested by Pollitt and Bouckaert looks quite resilient even to such major shifts: most dimensions of context, as modelled by the authors, tend to look applicable also to non-democratic regimes. Along a number of contextual dimensions, such country cases will tend to be polarized (for example, the dispersion of authority will tend to be limited, then along that dimension authoritarian countries will tend to cluster with countries with altogether different democratic credentials, and yet with a similarly limited vertical and horizontal dispersion of power). The one contextual dimension that may require significant adaptation is the nature of executive government, which will tend to exceed also the "harsh majoritarian" – but fully democratic – countries; yet conventions of governing, when it comes to the specific field of administrative reforms, may not be so different: authoritarian regimes may too require consensus – though from different institutions than the elected parliament – which may make them similar in this regard to democratic governments. Indeed, any depiction of authoritarian regimes as centralized decision-making systems may be misleading when it comes to matters of administrative reform.

Most dimensions of the Pollitt and Bouckaert framework may require being revisited, yet at face value seem to travel well from west to east and beyond. Concerning the culture of governance, the basic distinction of Rechtsstaat versus the Public Interest culture of governance may require being revisited, though, following Pierre, it may be stated, with obvious caveats, that such a basic distinction may be widely applicable, and that there may be a limited number of systems in the world which do not fall more or less squarely into either of these two basic models (Pierre 1995).

The distinction between internal and external sources of administrative policy advice seems to travel quite well. The vertical dispersion of authority does too, although important qualifications are required. For example, in countries like China or Vietnam, it is necessary to explore how the one-party system that mirrors the state structure frames both the process and the content of public sector reforms.

Other dimensions of analysis employed in the Pollitt and Bouckaert model would probably require more extensive re-working to be applicable in a non-western context, notably the civil service systems and their interconnections with political careers, particularly the politicization of the civil service and clientelism. For example, it is to be weighed in the heavy role of the "organization department" of the single party ruling the country vis-à-vis the decision-making powers of tenured bureaucrats in the state administration; similarly, the modalities of stakeholders involvement in policy processes will require adaptation beyond the conventional categories (pluralism vs. corporatism) adopted when studying western countries. Such categories would necessitate in-depth adaptation, yet in their very basic conception they seem to maintain their explanatory power for first approximation modelling purposes.

The administrative tradition model as proposed by Painter and Peters has been elaborated through a multiplicity of contributions from scholars whose expertise and knowledge of the administrative system collectively encompasses different geographical areas. Since its inception, this model was intended as more global in scope, in fact aiming to detect the traits of bureaucratic systems across the world by detaching it from the variable features of political systems. It also explicitly encompasses Confucian and Islamic legacies in public administration, which were not touched in the Pollitt and Bouckaert study. Yet in many respects, the administrative tradition model is more descriptive than the Pollitt and Bouckaert model: it describes and interprets similarities and dissimilarities in public administration across the world and argues for the existence and enduring significance of administrative "families" or clusters of countries. It does not, however, make strong predictions concerning implications for reforming public administrations, or for the conditions of delivering public services.

Summing up, models rooted in HI Can be expanded or adapted and provide useful entry points for interpreting the dynamics of administrative reform across a plurality of administrative systems. Further analysis will then be required on a case-by-case basis concerning what mechanisms are at work, and hence what causal explanations and, ideally, predictions for continuity and change in the administrative systems may be made.

This suggests that research on the influence of the past on administration and public policy is an area of continued interest for furthering our knowledge of the contemporary dynamics of this very important side of public life.

References

Barzelay, M. 2001. *The New Public Management*. Berkeley and Los Angeles: University of California Press.

Bezes, P. 2010. "Explaining the French Administrative Reform Trajectory through Institutions and their Legacies." In *Tradition and Public Administration*, edited by Painter, M. and Peters, B. Guy. New York: Palgrave Macmillan.

Ferlie, E., Ashburner, L., Fitzgerald, L., and Pettigrew, A. 1996 *The New Public Management in Action*. Oxford: Oxford University Press.

Ferlie, E., and Ongaro, E. 2015. *Strategic Management in Public Services Organisations: Concepts, Schools and Contemporary Issues*. Abingdon, UK: Routledge.

Hensengerth, O. 2015 "Multi-Level Governance of Hydropower in China? The Problem of Transplanting a Western Concept into the Chinese Governance Context." In *Multi-Level Governance: The Missing Linkages*, edited by Ongaro, E., 295–320. Bingley: Emerald.

Hood, C. 1991. "A Public Management for All Seasons?" *Public Administration* 69 (1): 3–19.

Kickert, W. 2011. "Distinctiveness of administrative reform in Greece, Italy, Portugal and Spain. Common characteristics of context, administrations and reforms." *Public Administration* 89 (3): 801–818.

Krastev, I. 2011. "Paradoxes of the New Authoritarianism." *Journal of Democracy* 22 (2): 5–16.

March, J. G. 1999. *The Pursuit of Organizational Intelligence*. Oxford: Blackwell.

Ongaro, E. 2013. "The administrative reform trajectory of the European Commission in comparative perspective: Historical New Institutionalism in compound systems." *Public Policy and Administration* 28 (4): 346–363

Ongaro, E. 2011. "The role of politics and institutions in the Italian administrative reform trajectory." *Public Administration* 89 (3): 738–755.

Ongaro, E. 2010. "The Napoleonic administrative tradition and public management reform in France, Greece, Italy, Portugal, Spain." In *Tradition and Public Administration*, edited by Painter, M. and Peters, B. Guy. Basingstoke: Palgrave Macmillan.

Ongaro, E. 2009. *Public Management Reform and Modernization: Trajectories of Administrative Change in Italy and France, Greece, Portugal, Spain*. Cheltenham, UK and Northampton, MA: Edward Elgar.

Ongaro, E. and S. Van Thiel (2017). "Introduction" In *Palgrave Handbook of Public Administration and Management in Europe*, edited by Ongaro, E. and Thiel, S. V. Basingstoke/London: Palgrave.

Painter, M. and Peters, B. Guy. 2010. *Tradition and Public Administration*. London: Palgrave MacMillan.

Peters, B. Guy 2008. "The Napoleonic tradition." *International Journal of Public Sector Management*, Special Issue on "Public management reform in countries in the Napoleonic administrative tradition: France, Greece, Italy, Portugal, Spain" 21 (2): 118–132.

Peters, B. Guy. 2005. *Institutional Theory in Political Science: The New Institutionalism*. 2nd ed. London and New York: Continuum.

Pierre, J. 1995. *Bureaucracy in the Modern State: An Introduction to Comparative Public Administration*. Aldershot: Edward Elgar.

Pierson, P. 2000a. "Increasing returns, path dependence, and the study of politics." *American Political Science Review* 94 (2): 251–267.

Pierson, P. 2000b. "The limits of design: Explaining institutional origins and change." *Governance: An International Journal of Policy and Administration* 13 (4): 475–499.

Pollitt, C. 2014. "Some inconvenient truths for the Anglo-sphere." *Keynote speech* at the 2014 annual conference of the International Institute of Administrative Sciences, Ifrane, Morocco, June 13–16.

Pollitt, C. 2013. *Context in Public Policy and Management: The Missing Link?* Cheltenham, UK and Northampton, MA: Edward Elgar.

Pollitt, C. and Bouckaert, G. 2011. *Public Management Reform: A Comparative Analysis*. 3rd ed. Oxford: Oxford University Press.Pollitt, C. and Dan, S. 2011 "The impacts of the New Public Management in Europe: A meta analysis." FP7 Project Coordinating for Cohesion in the Public Sector of the Future (COCOPS), Work Package 1, Deliverable 1.1.

Steinmo, S., Thelen, K., and Lonstreth, F. (eds). 1992. *Structuring Politics: Historical Institutionalism in Comparative Analysis*. Cambridge: Cambridge University Press.

Streeck, W. and Thelen, K. 2005. "Introduction: Institutional change in advanced political economies." In *Beyond Continuity: Institutional Change in Advanced Political Economies*, edited by Streeck, W. and Thelen, K. Oxford: Oxford University Press.

Thelen, K. 2003. "How institutions evolve. Insights from comparative historical analysis." In *Comparative Historical Analysis in the Social Sciences*, edited by Mahoney, J. and Rueschmeijer, D., 208–240. Cambridge: Cambridge University Press.

Thelen, K. 1999. "Historical institutionalism in comparative politics." *Annual Review Political Science* 2 (1): 369–404.

Thelen, K., and Steinmo, S. 1992. "Historical institutionalism in comparative politics." In *Structuring Politics: Historical Institutionalism in Comparative Analysis*, edited by Steinmo, S., Thelen, K., and Lonstreth, F. Cambridge: Cambridge University Press.

12

DECENTRED POLICYMAKING AND REGULATORY FINANCE

Ian Roberge and Heather McKeen-Edwards

Introduction

Policymakers, private sector and non-governmental actors alike concur that the creation of an effective, efficient, stable and secure financial services sector is essential for a prosperous economy. There remain, however, disagreements on the best way by which to attain this broad policy objective of a thriving yet safe financial system. Policy preferences range from those that prefer pro-active state intervention and regulation to those that favor free market mechanisms, and minimal regulation … and everything in between. The 2007–8 financial crisis highlighted again this substantive division in preferences. The crisis, just as importantly, also showed the major cost of policy failure in this field.

This chapter provides an overview of the key elements of financial services policymaking. How is policy in the financial services sector made? What are the key drivers of reform post the 2007–8 financial crisis? In this chapter, we argue that policymaking in the financial services sector results from the interplay between efforts to create more effective regulation and efforts to liberalize markets. To be more precise, policymaking in finance reflects oscillating processes of regulation and re-regulation, de-regulation, and non-regulation, evidenced in practices of self-regulation. Despite popular and often repeated claims that finance has been deregulated, or is unregulated, the reality is much more nuanced and complex. The trend pre-global financial crisis 2007–8 favored liberalization, yet it was far from universal or linear. Governments, including that of the United-States, continued to impose, even in the heyday of the Washington consensus, various regulatory obligations. Structurally, financial services sector policymaking takes place in a decentred space (Andenas and Chiu 2014; Black 2002) spread across levels of political authority, and between public and private sector actors. However, national governments, operating in a globalized environment, have remained the pillars of finance policymaking; there remain important policy variations across states. In this complex environment recent reform proposals have tended to result in marginal – at least, for now – changes as opposed to a radical restructuring of financial supervision and regulation (Moschella and Tsingou 2012).

This chapter extensively refers to the global financial crisis of 2007–8, which can be seen as a critical juncture. We do not, however, provide a detailed account of the crisis, and its lessons (for a complete analysis of the crisis, please see Blinder 2013). It is equally important to note that we use finance as a generic term, covering the whole of financial services sector industries. Due to space constraints, however, we largely focus on policies relating to banking and investment, and we only mention in passing insurance and other financial industries.

Why states regulate

There are two main justifications for financial regulation, and for considering this topic in a global public policy handbook. The first reason, as referred to above, is that an effective financial system, including banking, investment, and insurance industries, is central to the health of the overall economy. Finance's basic role is to facilitate the distribution of limited resources within the economy and it provides the means by which capital through investment can support economic activity. More broadly, Zysman (1983) long ago identified a typology that denotes how countries tend to finance their economic activity through either bank-based lending (e.g. France) or securities markets (e.g. United States). The 'varieties of capitalism' approach (Hall and Soskice 2001) also suggests important differences in economic structures across states based largely on institutional legacies, and incremental changes over time. The approach distinguishes between liberal market economies, represented by most English speaking countries, and the more tightly regulated European, Scandinavian, or Asian countries. Put simply, the way finance works, and the way it is supervised and regulated is central to the proper functioning of the economy.

The second related reason for financial services sector policy, supervision and regulation is to prevent market breakdown, so as to minimize the impact of policy failure or crisis in the financial system and potential spillover effects into the larger economy. It may be argued that new information technologies and new synthetic financial products – financial products that depend on other investments, instead of directly supporting an economic activity – have, to an extent, decoupled the financial services sector from what is, at times, called the 'real economy'. However, the economic costs of this most recent financial crisis were still far ranging in geographic and economic scope – the world saw 'the biggest drop in global trade since the 1930s' (Warwick Commission 2009: 9). There are many explanations and causes for the 2007–8 crisis; what is fairly clear is that it emanated from a problem in the US sub-prime mortgage market, a smallish subsection of the larger financial sector, demonstrating the impacts that even a relatively small subcategory of financial activities can have on the global economy. The European Commission, for example, has argued that, 'A safer, sounder, more transparent and more responsible financial system, working for the economy and society as a whole and able to finance the real economy, is a precondition for sustainable growth' (2010: 2).

To avoid market breakdown, the government intervenes to minimize the risks posed by the financial sector, particularly chances of systemic risk, credit risk, and market risk. Systemic risk refers to the concern that the failure of a 'too big to fail' institution, or of many institutions, can have a contagious effect across the whole of the financial services sector, within and across states with serious impact on the 'real economy'. Credit risk refers to the possibility that a firm becomes insolvent and may not be able to meet its financial implications. Market risk refers to the possibility of actor misconduct. Governments and regulators have put various measures in place to protect investors and consumers, who may not always be market savvy. Credit and market risk can lead to systemic risk, though they do not have to. Traditionally, regulators have sought to address most of these risks through micro-prudential supervision – particularly making sure that firms are solvent – and, to a much lesser extent macro-prudential supervision – the overall state of the sector. After the 2007–8 global financial crisis, governments have become much more interested and concerned with strengthening macro-prudential supervision (Baker

2013). Financial crises are bound to happen; moreover, they are happening with increasing frequency. Governments intervene, therefore, to minimize the likelihood of an occurrence and most importantly to contain a crisis.

How states regulate

The public debate on financial services sector policy has often oversimplified a more complex and multi-faceted process to a government versus liberalization dichotomy. In this framing, liberalization is achieved through processes of de-regulation, i.e. the freeing of financial actors and markets to pursue the most efficient, and generally global, financial system. Regulation, in turn, serves to contain potential negative impacts when markets falter, though pro-market advocates usually see it as stifling market innovation and growth. However, the story is clearly more multi-faceted. As we will show below, processes of regulation and reregulation, deregulation and non-regulation overlap in the policy realm throughout history. While a general trend can be identified at a specific point in time, the actual policy environment is one where there is interplay between coexisting efforts to ensure effective controls and efforts to liberalize segments of the market.

The most useful way by which to think of financial services sector policymaking is as decentred (Andenas and Chiu 2014; Black 2002). Decentred policymaking is characterized by complexity, fragmentation, interdependencies, ungovernability, and the rejection of a clear public/private dichotomy.

Complexity refers to the nature of problems that must be dealt with. Fragmentation refers to the fragmentation of knowledge, resources and capacity for control in the regulatory space. Interdependencies refers to the dynamics between the participants in the regulatory space, co-producing and co-enforcing norms of governance. Ungovernability refers to the autonomy and unpredictability of actor behavior in the regulatory space, which will pose challenges to assumptions made by regulatory authorities. In a decentred landscape, there is, some argue, no public-private distinctions as all participants contribute to and influence governance (Andenas and Chiu 2014: 74).

We detail each component below.

The financial services sector is a complex field characterized by fast-pace change and innovation, particularly with the rise of scientific finance (for a more complete discussion, see De Goede 2001). For instance, the 2007–8 financial crisis helped reveal that senior managers may not have always understood the way their own firms operated, or the products they were peddling. Few, if any individuals at all, have a complete view and understanding of financial markets.

The financial services sector is also said to be globalized, and though to an extent this is true, it is also quite fragmented. For instance, there is no single financial services sector, but rather a collection of industries – banking, investment and insurance – and even within each industry, there are important distinctions between commercial and investment banks, stock markets, over-the-counter activities, clearing and settlements, insurance and re-insurance, etc. Financial firms offer different products and services based on their size and whether they compete within local, national or international markets. The financial services sector does not have a single interest per se. Private sector actors often disagree among themselves when speaking to a specific policy proposal, given that changes are likely to advantage and disadvantage different aspects and actors in finance simultaneously. Governments – finance or treasury departments and regulators – must work to make sense of this disaggregated, but interconnected, whole.

The three remaining components of decentred policymaking are the existence of interdependencies in the regulatory space, the ungovernability of the sector, and the public/

private dichotomy. Networked governance, which includes regulators and representative bodies, industry actors and others, best exemplifies interdependencies. There are a range of public–private governance arrangements from traditional lobbying to regulatory partnerships to the more nefarious regulatory capture and regulatory arbitrage, where firms shop around between and across regulators, taking advantage of gaps in the financial services sector infrastructure within a state; regulatory capture and arbitrage appear to have happened frequently in the lead-up to the 2007–8 financial crisis in the United States. Interdependencies help blur the public/private dichotomy. The rise of private authority in finance, through a sheer belief in the power of markets to self-regulate, is now well documented (Cutler, Haufler, and Porter 1999). The 2007–8 crisis only partially shook this belief system; Helleiner (2014), for instance, shows how the emerging regulatory regime for over-the-counter trading – previously unregulated – directly relies on private sector actors. As for ungovernability, the global and interconnected nature of the sector, among other variables, makes this sector hard to govern. The number of financial crises, as we noted previously, has increased substantially following the end of Bretton Woods, and the lapse time in between crisis appears ever shorter. The crisis cycle is well known, but we remain susceptible to it – this time is rarely, if ever, different (Reinhart and Rogoff 2009). What has emerged is a polycentric regulatory regime that presents interesting challenges for legitimacy and accountability (Black 2008).

Financial services policy is still largely national, though is also influenced by interactions across the national and international levels. National governments are under pressure from various domestic – and, at times international – lobby groups, and policy often results from existing country-specific institutional arrangements. As such, there remain important policy variations across states. Lavelle (2013) points out that financial policy in the United States is generated from the interaction over time between various public and private sector actors. There are circumstances, though, when policy emerges from a two-level game type process between actors at the national and international levels. In her examination of the Volker Rule – which refers to the possibility for an investment bank to play the market with its own money – Lavelle (2013) shows how international actors attempted to influence domestic policy. Singer (2004), among others, also highlights the importance of national governments when it comes to interpreting and implementing voluntary transnational level standards. Policymaking in finance is generally national, but the level of analysis stretches across levels of authority from the local all the way to the international.

Global finance

This section considers the overlapping processes of regulation and re-regulation, deregulation and non-regulation that have taken place in global financial supervision and regulation over time. The analysis also further supports the idea that policymaking in finance is decentred.

The mid-1900s, particularly under the guise of the Bretton Woods System, was a period of capital control and regulation. Bretton Woods, among other characteristics, served to provide stability on financial markets because of its fixed exchange rates practices and its use of the American dollar, still pegged to gold, as the reserve currency. The United States announced in 1971 that it would no longer convert dollars into gold, the definitive end of convertibility, signaling at the same time the end of the Bretton Woods System (for a complete discussion of the Bretton Woods System, see, among many, Best 2005). The pressures for financial liberalization, though, predated the end of Bretton Woods. The creation of the euro–dollar and subsequently euro-currencies markets – trading using a currency outside of its original jurisdiction – in London in 1957 signals the growth of de-territorialized and unregulated finance. The euro-currencies markets provided the opportunity for the rise of offshore finance, which has become a major component of the global financial system (for a more complete discussion, see Palan 2006). Offshore finance – constructed on the concept of state sovereignty and supportive of deregulated and unregulated finance – is now generally perceived as the ultimate symbol of globalized, fragmented and ungovernable finance.

After Bretton Woods, market pressure favoring liberalized capital flows, deregulation in the banking sectors and other neo-liberal policies began in earnest. The reducing or removing of government controls, particularly in the securities markets, became a dominant trend in financial regulation until the turn of the century, and arguably up to the global financial crisis. These efforts toward deregulation of financial services and markets have also been combined with a tendency to avoid creating regulation in areas that were unregulated. There may be a tendency to present these trends as driven by market actors outside of the power and influence of states. The financial system that emerged, however, was not necessarily beyond the power of states; rather, the relaxation of capital controls and efforts to relax regulations that limited financial actors from particular activities or areas, including ensuring separation between banking and securities markets, could be argued to have reflected distinct political preferences (Helleiner 1994).

Moreover, a new international financial infrastructure and new regulation did emerge during this period, alongside the trends of deregulation and non-regulation. The creation of a voluntary standard to harmonize capital adequacy for banks – capital adequacy is the amount of capital a bank, or another financial institution must hold in their reserves at any point in time – Basel I (1988) and Basel II (2004), is a good example. Most studies of Basel I tend to agree that it is an outcome of the interaction between different states seeking to achieve international financial stability while at the same time considering issues of international competition in banking and the need to minimize the competitive implications of the capital requirement (Wood 2005; Simmons 2001). There are other examples including the construction of a full-blown regime to address money laundering and terrorist financing from the 1980s onward, whereas prior nothing of the kind existed (Sica 2000). The interplay between regulation, re-regulation, deregulation and non-regulation on the whole created during this period a less restrictive regulatory environment.

The 2007–8 global financial crisis led to a short-lived crisis of legitimacy for the neo-liberal paradigm (Helleiner 2010; Nesvetailova and Palan 2010). The policy window for substantive policy change, however, closed quickly. Instead, 'across the system, as they had done after every other crisis since the 1970s, leading states acknowledged their preference for not abandoning the policy trade-offs and global architecture permissive of large-scale capital movements' (Pauly 2009). What emerged was a mixed range of reforms, some with the potential to become important and others quite minimal (Pomerleano 2010). There has been, however, an apparent shift in the relative weight of the long-running push and pull between increased governmental regulation and decentralized regulation of markets toward the former. This is evidenced by the quick adoption and implementation of Basel III, various Financial Stability Board initiatives, and attempts to regulate previously unregulated activities. Most states and jurisdictions, including the United States and Europe, with a few exceptions, also undertook important reforms of their national financial services sector. The exact nature of this shift and its impact is yet to be fully determined or felt; the crisis left scars and remains fresh enough in people's mind to incite, at the very least, the appearance of action.

The United States

The United States remains at the center of the global financial system and New York is still the world's largest financial center. We focus on the United States both because of its central role in global finance, but also because it is the starting point for the 2007–8 global financial crisis.

American financial regulation before the global crisis of the early twenty-first century can be split into two eras. The first appeared after the stock market crash of 1929 and the resulting Great Depression. During this period, the United States' regulatory infrastructure and its principal regulations were put into place. Financial services policymaking aimed on creating regulatory structures that would limit the overlap of banking and securities markets. The Glass–Steagall Act of 1933 is the signature legislation of this period. The Act forced banks to choose between the more traditional roles of a deposit-taking commercial bank or becoming an investment bank, creating a division that attempted to keep the commercial banking sector used by average citizens safe from the more speculative, and less stable, activities of securities markets and investment.

The second period started in the 1970s and 1980s when pressure from banks was mounting on the federal government to remove regulatory barriers to bank activities. The passing of the Financial Services Modernization Act (also known as the Gramm–Leach–Bliley Act) in 1999 repealed the Glass-Steagall imposed barriers between commercial banking services and investment operations for banks. It also 'repealed the parts of the Bank Holding Company Act of 1956 that separated commercial banking from the insurance business' (Barth, Brumbaugh, and Wilcox 2000: 190). The Gramm–Leach–Bliley Act amplified and exacerbated the general trend toward financial deregulation discussed earlier by facilitating the expansion of large financial firms into multiple areas of activity, creating in turn the tangled web of overlapping liabilities that would become prominent during the 2007–8 sub-prime crisis.

Though there was a trend toward less government regulation of the market between the 1970s and the 2000s, it is important to highlight that there were also some moves to expand the regulatory reach prior to the global financial crisis. Three initiatives in the early years of the new millennium are worth highlighting. First, the Uniting and Strengthening America by Providing Appropriate Tools Required to Intercept and Obstruct Terrorism Act – more commonly referred to as the USA Patriot Act – was quickly adopted in the weeks that followed the terrorist attacks of September 11, 2001. The Act imposed many obligations on financial firms to help deter money laundering and terrorist financing. In this regard, the Act built on earlier international and domestic efforts to address the, more or less, recently created threats associated with illicit finance. Second, the government adopted the Sarbanes–Oxley Act in 2002 to respond to problems of fraudulent accounting, which came to light during the Enron scandal. Both the Patriot Act and the Sarbanes–Oxley Act imposed significant costs on the industry. Third, credit rating agencies like Standard and Poors and Moodys received extensive coverage because of the facilitation role they played during the global financial crisis. The unregulated nature of the industry has often been noted (Sinclair 2005). While it is true that these bodies were poorly regulated, it is also worthwhile noting that limited regulations were first introduced in the US as early as 2006.

The 2007–8 financial crisis highlighted a range of problems with financial services sector policy, supervision and regulation in the US. The failure to properly regulate, coupled with the political choices in some cases not to regulate, is a central component in the build-up of the sub-prime mortgage bubble. The neo-liberal preferences for self-correcting markets and minimalist regulation, shared by regulators and private sector actors alike, helps to explain the policy failure, why it was difficult to act and intervene, and the breadth and depth of the crisis.

Unsurprisingly, after the crisis the United States moved to reform its financial regulatory system. The Dodd–Frank Wall Street Reform and Consumer Protection Act adopted in 2010 represents a comprehensive financial reform effort. The Act aimed 'to promote the financial stability of the United States by improving accountability and transparency in the financial system, to end 'too big to fail', to protect the American taxpayer by ending bailouts, to protect consumers from abusive financial services practices, and for other purposes' (United States 2010: 2).

Yet even in this new era of financial regulation, American policymaking in this sector is undoubtedly still decentred. The policy field is complex; many of the synthetic products at the heart of the 2007–8 crisis were invented and popularized by American financial institutions. The policy field is fragmented. It is important to remember that much finance in the United States is regulated at the sub-national level by State governments. There are five major banks in the United States – JPMorgan Chase, Bank of America, Citigroup, Wells Fargo, and Goldman Sachs – but there are thousands of state-regulated banks across the country. The financial services sector remains ungovernable despite the rather imposing supervisory and regulatory infrastructure. It is also highly networked. At the federal level alone, the infrastructure is centered around the Federal Reserve System, the Treasury Department, the Federal Deposit Insurance Corporation, and the Office of the Comptroller of the Currency (the Office of Thrift Supervision was amalgamated with the Comptroller of the Currency in 2011) and, the Securities and Exchange Commission; regulators have, in fact, often appeared in competition with each other. The governance arrangements and the relationships between governments, regulators and private firms – interdependencies and the blurred public/private dichotomy – have also drawn a lot of attention coming out of the crisis. Johnson and Kwak (2010) have described the close connection between public sector and private sector individuals.

Whether the American financial system, at the time of writing, is safer than it was prior to the 2007–8 financial crisis is still difficult to say. There came a very short policy window following the crisis that allowed for the adoption of the Dodd–Frank Act. The real issue is not whether the Dodd-Frank Act goes too far or does not go far enough, but whether the right measures were adopted and implemented to minimize the risk, and contain the effects, of a future crisis.

Conclusion

Throughout this chapter, we have endeavored to provide an overview of policymaking in the financial services sector. We have argued that financial services policymaking is the result of the interplay between regulation and efforts to liberalize markets. This has resulted in a mix of regulation and reregulation, deregulation, and non-regulation (often under the guise of self-regulation). We have suggested, as well, that policymaking in finance takes place in a decentred space.

During the 2007–8 financial crisis, policymakers, the press and observers often suggested that a fundamental change in financial policy was needed, that the time was right for a paradigm shift in the relationship between the state and the market. Barely a few years after the crisis, it is clear that such a paradigm shift has not occurred. The trend favors greater government intervention, but it is not definitive and is reversible, especially the further we move away from the 2007–8 crisis. How ready are governments around the world for the next crisis? How safe are financial markets and are they safer now than they were pre-2007? Without government intervention, the global financial crisis of 2007–8 likely would have been much worse. Governments, however, often prepare for the last crisis and lack the necessary foresight to organize for the one that is forthcoming. Maybe it is time, before it is too late, to consider anew the state–market relationship.

References

Andenas, M. and Chiu, I. H. Y. 2014. *The Foundations and Future of Financial Regulation: Governance for Responsibility*. Abingdon: Routledge.

Baker, A. 2013. "The New Political Economy of the Macroprudential Ideational Shift." *New Political Economy* 18 (1): 112–139.

Barth, J. R., Brumbaugh, D. R., and Wilcox, J. A. 2000. "The Repeal of Glass–Steagall and the Advent of Broad Banking." *Journal of Economic Perspectives* 14 (2): 191–204.

Best, J. 2005. *The Limits of Transparency: Ambiguity and the History of International Finance*. Ithaca, NY: Cornell University Press.

Black, J. 2008. "Constructing and Contesting Legitimacy and Accountability in Polycentric Regulatory Regimes." *Regulation & Governance* 2 (2): 137–164.

Black, J. 2002. "Critical Reflections on Regulation." *Australian Journal of Legal Philosophy* 27 (1): 1–35.

Blinder, A. S. 2013. *After the Music Stopped: The Financial Crisis, the Response and the Work Ahead*. New York: Penguin Press.

Cutler, A. C., Haufler, V., and Porter, T. 1999. *Private Authority and International Affairs*. Albany: State University of New York Press.

De Goede, M. 2001, "Discourses of Scientific Finance and the Failure of Long-Term Capital Management." *New Political Economy* 6 (2):149–170.

European Commission. 2010. *Regulating Financial Services for Sustainable Growth*. Brussels. http://ec.europa.eu/internal_market/finances/docs/general/com2010_en.pdf.

Hall, P. A. and Soskice, D. 2001. *Varieties of Capitalism. The Institutional Foundations of Comparative Advantage*. Oxford: Oxford University Press.

Helleiner, E. 2014. "Out from the Shadows: Governing Over-the-Counter Derivatives after the 2007–2008 Financial Crisis." In *The Return of the Public in Global Governance*, edited by Best, J. and Gheciu, A., 70–94. Cambridge: Cambridge University Press.

Helleiner, E. 2010 "A Bretton Woods Moment? The 2007–08 Crisis and the Future of Global Finance." *International Affairs* 86 (3): 619–636.

Helleiner, E. 1994. *States and the Re-emergence of Global Finance*. Ithaca, NY: Cornell University Press.

Johnson, S. and Kwak, J. 2010. *Thirteen Bankers: The Wall St. Takeover and the Next Financial Meltdown*. New York: Pantheon Books.

Lavelle, K. C. 2013. *Money and Banks in the American Political System*. Cambridge: Cambridge University Press.

Moschella, M. and Tsingou, E. 2012. *Great Expectations, Slow Transformations: Incremental Change in Post-Crisis Regulation*. ECPR Press.

Nesvetailova, A. and Palan, R. 2010. "The End of Liberal Finance? The Changing Paradigm of Global Financial Governance." *Millennium – Journal of International Studies* 38 (3): 797–825.

Palan, R. 2006. *The Offshore World: Sovereign Markets, Virtual Places, and Nomad Millionaires*. Ithaca, NY: Cornell University Press.

Pauly, L. W. 2009. "The Old and the New Politics of International Financial Stability." *Journal of Common Market Studies* 47 (5): 955–975.

Pomerleano, M. 2010. "Waiting for Godot: The Elusive Quest for a Financial Stability Framework." *International Economic Bulletin*, Carnegie Endowment for International Peace, June.

Reinhart, C. M. and Rogoff. K. 2009. *This Time is Different: Eight Centuries of Financial Folly*. Princeton, NJ: Princeton University Press.

Sica, V. 2000. "Cleaning the Laundry: States and the Monitoring of the Financial System." *Millennium – Journal of International Studies* 29 (1): 47–72.

Simmons, B. 2001. "The International Politics of Harmonization: The Case of Capital Market Regulation." *International Organization* 55 (3): 589–620.

Sinclair, T. J. 2005. *The New Masters of Capital: American Bond Rating Agencies and the Politics of Creditworthiness*. Ithaca, NY: Cornell University Press.

Singer, D. A. 2004. "Capital Rules: The Domestic Politics of International Regulatory Harmonization." *International Organization* 58 (3): 531–565.

United States. 2010. *Dodd–Frank Wall Street Reform and Consumer Protection Act*. Public Law 111–203, July 21. www.gpo.gov/fdsys/pkg/PLAW-111publ203/pdf/PLAW-111publ203.pdf. Accessed 06/06/2016.

Warwick Commission. 2009. *The Warwick Commission on International Financial Reform: In Praise of Unlevel Playing Fields*. Coventry: University of Warwick.

Wood, D. 2005. *Governing Global Banking: The Basel Committee and the Politics of Financial Globalization.* Aldershot: Ashgate.

Zysman, J. 1983. *Governments, Markets and Growth: Financial Systems and the Politics of Industrial Change.* Ithaca: Cornell University Press.

PART II

Cross-sector and cross-level policy and administration responses

Introduction

This section of the handbook deals with public administration issues that cross sectors and policy areas. The first three chapters address how to effectively respond to public problems that government cannot solve on its own. Collaborative governance, co-production and citizen engagement are suggested as alternatives to the traditional governing modes in dealing with the inter-dependent and wicked problems that governments frequently face. The middle chapters of this section analyze specific governance issues such as risk governance, governance changes and federalism. The discussion of governance is then expanded in the final chapters of this section and linked to a variety of policy domains: emergency and crisis management, regulatory reform, global health and global cultural heritage policies.

In Chapter 13, "Collaborative governance", Denita Cepiku from Italy argues that a collaboration-based approach is the most effective mode to solve complex and interdependent public problems. As an alternative to hierarchy and competition, collaborative governance includes inter-institutional networks, public–private partnerships, joined-up government and co-production.

After defining collaborative governance, the chapter explains through three different theoretical bases why organizations work together. A series of interesting cases show how collaboration can contribute to the solving of public problems. The later part of the chapter explains how to cope with management challenges. Professor Cepiku argues that since the collaborative approach is not without limits, public managers should pay careful attention to institutional design choices and process management, leadership and performance management of collaborative arrangements.

While Chapter 13 is a broad review of interdependent collaborative approaches, Chapter 14 focuses more explicitly on co-production as one form of collaboration. In his chapter, titled "Citizen co-production of public services: meanings, processes, antecedents and consequences", John Alford from Australia explores important facets of co-production. Drawing mainly on theory-building or case analysis, Professor Alford addresses two key questions about co-production: when should it be utilized and how can it be elicited?

In addressing the first question, the author explains that replacing the old one-size-fits-all approach, a contingent approach now prevails with regard to the utilization of co-production.

The contingent approach makes clear that whether the benefits of utilizing co-production outweigh the associated costs depends on the situation. And the answer, in turn, depends on the nature of the service, the context, staff capabilities and the degree of inter-dependency between the actors. The chapter also identifies multiple drivers of co-production: the motivations and capacities of the co-producer; perceptions of service itself; and satisfaction with the government's communication, consultation and overall performance.

In Chapter 15, Reto Steiner and Claire Kaiser from Switzerland note that public participation is an essential aspect of the democratic way of governing. Based on an extensive analysis of international democratic theory and participation literature, the chapter titled "Democracy and citizens' engagement" provides an overview of the relationship between democracy and citizen engagement. This chapter fits with the preceding two chapters by sharing the same theme – that is the role of citizens – but takes an explicitly international perspective.

The authors note a decrease in optimism about democracy despite the increased number of democratic systems worldwide. The chapter classifies political participation into two contrasting camps. In the "old" democracies, the idea of citizens' engagement is seen as generally positive resulting in few harms; whereas the "new" democracies have a variety of concerns with regard to effectiveness of democratic processes and structures. The authors make it clear that more citizen participation is not always, or necessarily, better. For example, despite many advantages, citizens' engagement in the public affairs can at times entail serious risks and may not produce better outcomes than decisions made by politicians or administrators. Furthermore, heightened citizen participation does not directly solve problems like poverty, crime and others. Thus, the authors conclude that citizen engagement should not be understood as a panacea.

Chapter 16, "The public policy context for risk governance and social innovation", explains that to achieve successful innovation in public policy, public managers have to pay due attention to the associated risks. Noting that the current literature does not adequately discuss the nexus between risk and social innovation in public policy, Sarah-Sophie Flemig and Stephen Osborne from the United Kingdom introduce two key propositions and suggest a holistic framework of risk management and social innovation in public policy.

The first proposition is: risk management approaches should distinguish between risk and uncertainty. Known risks can encourage innovation in public policy by providing the opportunity to find new ways of thinking, but may also function as barriers to innovation. Uncertainty, on the other hand, cannot be known ex ante but may provide a jolt to spur innovation. The second proposition suggests that risk management should differentiate between hard management such as regulation and rules and soft management such as delegation of risk management, communication and deliberation. From an overview of past studies Flemig and Osborne reveal that risk management is closely related to blame avoidance, and policy-makers are prone to "playing safe". The authors conclude that to bring about innovation in public policy and programs it is essential to skillfully manage risks.

Jenny M. Lewis of Australia takes on the question of how governance has changed in different policy sectors and nations. Chapter 17, "Governance change across policy sectors and nations", shows how theoretical arguments can be integrated with empirical case studies. Professor Lewis first proposes a framework for analyzing governance change, and then applies this framework to policy domains by examining health policy in Australia and the Netherlands with a comparative lens.

The proposed framework has three dimensions: institutions, politics and ideation. First, as historical and sociological features of the state, national health insurance can be seen as an institution. Second, since politics is the power relation between state and non-state actors, the relationship between the state and the medical profession is a political variable. Finally, ideation is defined as the dominant ideas underpinning a policy sector, with foundational models of health and illness paramount in this regard. The comparison of recent reforms in governance of health policy in Australia and the Netherlands reveals contrasting results. The chapter demonstrates how existing institutions, different political systems, and societal traditions shape governance change. Professor Lewis concludes by noting that the three concepts may also be useful to understanding governance changes in other policy areas.

The discussion of governance in Chapter 18, "Devolution and federalism", takes on a different, but central, dimension of public policy and administration: intergovernmental relations. Public managers today find themselves in the situation where many issues cannot be tackled without coordination and negotiation between different levels of government in a nation. Owen E. Hughes of Australia reminds us that in decentralized governance, found in many nations including the US, Canada, Russia, China, Australia, Brazil and others, no single level of government has sole jurisdiction over a policy issue or field. Even in nations with more centralized forms of government, such as France, there is tension between the national level and the local level. The chapter explains that the formal kind of federalism where there is a clear division of power between governments is no longer realistic.

Professor Hughes provides three approaches to conceptualize federalism: coordinate, cooperative or organic. He then outlines the positive aspects of the federal system of government under which most of the world's population lives, as well as its limitations. For example, federalism can enhance consensus as national and sub-national governments must reach agreement, but also simultaneously stimulate conflicts between the two levels of government. The result, as the author explains, is that managers in government are often involved in what may well be difficult processes across the levels of government, where they are required to come up with solutions for which they often have no formal authority.

Through a case study, Fatih Demiroz and Naim Kapucu of the US illustrate that disaster management, arguably a key role of the state, is by its very nature a collaborative endeavor. Chapter 19, titled "Emergency and crisis management: the Soma mine accident case, Turkey", shows that collaborative arrangements are required to effectively respond to emergency situations. The central question in this chapter is how governance can succeed when stakeholders hold conflicting views about policy objectives. By taking on a tragic mining accident that happened in 2014 in Turkey in which hundreds of miners were trapped and killed, the authors describe what role collaborative public management plays and, in turn, what role leadership plays in the accident.

The authors make clear that a national or organizational leader's communication skills are a critical factor in emergency management, and this holds true in collaborative governance as well. The reader will learn in this chapter how a leader's timely and effective communication with media and public reduces social costs in emergency situations. Four main components of communication are identified: tell the truth; send a complete message; provide timely information; and work hard to resolve problems and let the public know of such efforts.

Chapter 20, "Regulatory reform and the better regulation agenda: traveling from center to periphery", written by Alketa Peci of Brazil, studies the processes and outcomes of regulatory reforms and the recent development of better regulation in Latin America, with a focus on Brazil. Professor Peci sees two forces playing major roles in shaping the regulatory reforms in the region: pressure from international sources upon Latin America, and domestic forces that support more effective regulation.

In studying international forces, the chapter reveals how economic liberalization and international organizations such as the Organisation for Economic Co-operation and Development (OECD) or World Bank have been central to the diffusion of regulatory reforms in Latin America. However, Professor Peci reveals that domestic factors have also been decisive in influencing regulatory diffusion in the region. In this regard, she focuses on two key processes of regulatory reforms: (1) the adoption of independent or semi–autonomous regulatory agencies, and (2) the adoption of a better regulation agenda. The chapter concludes that the success of regulatory reform in Latin America, and especially in Brazil, Chile and Mexico, is in part due to strong professional bureaucracies that have pursued innovation, resisted political pressure and gained legitimacy.

In Chapter 21, "Global health", Eduardo Missoni from Italy describes the complex governance system of global health, in which a balance of power is critical yet hard to achieve due to many actors who influence policies. After providing a historical review of global health policies, the author identifies the main actors involved in public health at the global level. His analysis includes the "leadership and authority" agencies such as the World Health Organization, the World Bank, and other UN system entities, and the World Trade Organization, transnational companies, and transnational hybrid organizations, and shows how their actions interweave and influence the formation of global health policies.

Although Professor Missoni does not deny the contribution the international institutions made to fill the global health governance gap, he makes clear that due to their powerful influence, effective regulation and normative actions both at global and national levels are not likely to function properly, and as a result, the governance system fails to fulfill its mission. He concludes by calling for an enhanced governance framework for global health.

Chapter 22, "Global cultural heritage policies and their management: the case of Italian UNESCO World Heritage Sites", written by Marianna Elmi and Alessandro Hinna from Italy, analyzes the execution of global cultural policies from a multilevel network perspective. The chapter identifies the main actors, describes the processes and points out the management strategies used in implementing World Heritage policies.

The authors see the implementation of UNESCO World Heritage policy as a multi-level process since it has three dimensions: the presence of multiple organizations; the collaborative nature of the interaction of actors; and the establishment of a coordinating body and coordination strategies. The complex characteristics make a single simple solution impossible and entail managerial challenges.

By adopting a case study of Italian UNESCO World Heritage Sites, the chapter shows that the policy implemented through network structures can result in a lack of cooperation between actors and may fail to produce expected results. The authors argue the policies can only succeed with the contribution of all related organizations and institutions, including the sharing of resources, tasks, and responsibilities.

13

COLLABORATIVE GOVERNANCE

Denita Cepiku

Introduction

The need for public managers to work across organizations and societal sectors is not new although the number and scale of complex problems, their global nature and interdependency has escalated in the past two decades (Huxham 2000). Simultaneously, there has been a change in government roles, as they become more demanding but also more indirect. The collaboration-based public administration approach to decision-making and service delivery is also considered a reaction to the institutional fragmentation and contraposition created by previous public sector reforms such as the New Public Management.

Similarly, evidence of collaborative governance can be found decades afore but it has multiplied since the mid-1990s (Friend et al. 1974). Achieving environmental sustainability, reducing poverty, alleviating global health problems, homeland and urban security, improving quality of life of the elderly, social inclusion of immigrants, urban renewal, territorial development, recovery from drug addiction, emergency management, raising school standards, improving community wellbeing, reducing youth unemployment, cannot be solved by any single organization, be it public, non-profit, business, or civil society association. Attempts to reduce fragmentation include inter-institutional networks, public–private partnerships, joined up government (horizontal coordination and integration between departments and agencies within government), and users' engagement through co-production.

While policy makers and public managers now feel confident that collaboration is the most effective answer to such problems, less attention is paid to what it requires to function properly and achieve its aims. Management mechanisms and systems are reasonably expected to change in collaborative settings compared to how they work in traditional organizations.

The chapter provides an integrated framework for understanding collaborative governance, regardless of the specific forms (networks, co-production, public–private partnerships) or labels (coordination, cooperation, collaboration, collaborative public management, collaborative governance, civic engagement) it may assume (O'Leary and Vij 2012). Competencies required by public managers who engage in hybrid modes of service provision are identified and recommendations for policy makers drawn.

The central thesis of the chapter is the imperative of going beyond the early years' euphoria, adopting what Alford and Hughes (2008) call public value pragmatism: this means abandoning the cult of collaboration considered a panacea and addressing the managerial challenges of collaborative, non-hierarchical environments.

Defining collaborative governance

Collaborative governance theory draws on a variety of disciplines such as political science, public administration, urban affairs, social welfare, public management, and organizational/sociological research (Keast et al. 2014). Collaborative governance can be defined by considering the two words that compose it. The term *governance* is loaded with ambiguity and several definitions, normative and positive, can be found in the literature (Cepiku 2013; Frederickson 2005). In this chapter, a neutral definition has been chosen, which allows the meaning to be carried by the word collaboration rather than governance. Thus, governance refers to "government's ability to make and enforce rules and to deliver services" (Fukuyama 2013: 350).

Collaboration is a relationship "intended to increase public value by [...] working together rather than separately" (Bardach 1998: 8; Huxham 1996). It "is based on the value of reciprocity and can include the public" (Agranoff and McGuire 2003: 4). It is part of a continuum that goes from: (1) cooperation, which is short term, informal and limited to sharing information, to (2) coordination, in which organizations remain separate but contribute to a specific, agreed program of action, and to (3) collaboration: long-term, risky, needing system changes and based on strong linkages with a commitment to common missions and part of a total picture (Mandell and Keast 2008).

Alternatives to collaboration are hierarchy and competition, both practiced in the public sector and well known under the headings of Weberianism and New Public Management. Different from hierarchy and competition, collaboration is voluntary; partners can step out at any time if they are not satisfied or aware of the value achieved through it (Hill and Lynn 2003: 65).

Collaborative governance is, thus, a hybrid mode of decision making and service provision in which a public agency deliberately and directly engages non-state entities in a formal, consensual, and collective decision-making process to manage programs, and to solve problems that cannot be easily or at all solved by single organizations (Ansell and Gash 2007: 544; Agranoff and McGuire 2003). This definition belies the reality of numerous collaborative forms, each entailing specific management issues (Huxham 2000: 341).

Collaboration can be institutional or individual; in other terms, it can take place mainly among organizations or among people. This distinction, though helpful to categorize empirical evidence, is fine line: collaboration among institutions is always carried out by people interactions; on the other hand, individual collaboration has a short life if it is not embedded in an institutional framework.

Why collaborate? Rationale and drivers to collaboration

Organizations and people work together to achieve collaborative advantage, i.e. something that could not be realized by acting alone (Huxham 1996). Bretschneider et al. (2012) identify three different approaches to understand incentives to collaborate: (1) theories of organizational behavior; (2) public value theory; and (3) the availability of performance information. Organization theories refer mainly to resource dependency theory, according to which individual organizations do not have all the resources they need to achieve their goals (Pfeffer and Salancik 1978). Public value theory is more recent. Public managers are willing to give away some of their autonomy if they feel that public value will be more easily and effectively created through a joint collaborative effort. Finally, performance information can be a motivator for the sharing or reallocation of resources among organizations.

Two recurring concepts in collaborative governance theory are wicked problems and interdependency. Wicked problems are unstructured as causes and effects are difficult to identify and continuously evolving. They cross multiple policy domains, levels of government and jurisdictions and, consequently, several stakeholders, each bringing in different views, priorities, values, cultural and political backgrounds and championing alternative solutions (Weber and Khademian 2008). If not managed, this multiplicity easily translates in conflict.

Interdependency is created when no single actor, public or private, has all knowledge, information, or power required to solve complex, dynamic and diversified problems. No actor has sufficient overview to make the application of the needed instrument effective or sufficient action potential to dominate unilaterally in a particular governing model (Kooiman 1993: 4). Collaborative arrangements are established when there is a wicked problem and the multiple actors involved are aware of the interdependency and recognize a certain value of working with others (Mandell 2010; Kickert et al. 1997: 6). Since collaboration is voluntary, collaborative interactions to exchange resources and negotiate shared purposes, are rooted in trust and regulated by shared rules, instead of sovereign authority.

At an individual level, citizens are motivated by different reasons to collaborate with public sector professionals (Alford 2014). These include both material self-interest and intrinsic rewards such as satisfying the need to feel competent and self-determining sociality (sense of belonging). The way in which these motivations affect the willingness of people to collaborate or co-produce depends on personal features, on the kind and salience of the service provided, on transaction costs that make voice more relevant than exit, and ease of involvement, among others.

Box 13.1 Killing two birds with one stone: administrative barter in Italian cities

The global economic and financial crisis has a scissor effect on local governments, due to decreased tax revenues and increased demand for social services. Indeed, some cities are able to collect no more than half of the taxes due. A higher demand for welfare services leaves fewer resources available for services such as the maintenance of schools, parks and green urban areas.

The Italian government has envisaged a possible solution with a law approved in November 2014 (nr. 164), the so-called administrative barter (*baratto amministrativo*), which gives citizens the possibility to pay lower taxes if they are willing to contribute to the maintenance, improvement and embellishment of their territory. It is interesting to note that citizens are not merely executors of local government projects but make their own project proposals on urban regeneration. Moreover, priority is given to projects submitted through civil society associations rather than individually.

It is still too early to assess the effects of the law on the spread of individual and collective co-production practices. Some local governments have already turned down this possibility, as the amount of unpaid taxes is too large to give away. Others have adopted detailed regulations that enable the active participation of citizens and their associations to urban management policies.

Box 13.2 NASA taps citizen-scientists to find novel ways to use earth science dataset

NASA is well known as an innovator that employs some of the smartest people alive. The agency has recently announced two related Earth science challenges designed to take ideas from a much large source: the public.

The challenges give citizens a chance to provide NASA with new ways to make use of the extensive datasets its Earth science satellites capture, much of which are available to the public through the Open NASA Earth Exchange, or OpenNEX. OpenNEX is a data, supercomputing and knowledge platform hosted on the Amazon Web Services cloud, where academics, developers and users can search through a massive collection of climate and Earth science datasets. NASA already collects the data, but the public could help the agency better figure out to do with it.

The challenges come in two phases. The first is the ideation stage, which will offer as much as $10,000 in awards for ideas that lead to "novel uses of the datasets." The second aspect is the builder phase that will build off the ideas generated during the ideation stage and will offer between $30,000 and $50,000 in awards for the development of applications or algorithms that promote climate resilience using OpenNEX datasets.

The OpenNEX challenges also address policy mandates on big data, open data and climate data from the Obama administration, but bringing innovation from outside the agency is likely where its biggest efforts will lie.

Speaking at the Amazon Web Services symposium in Washington, DC, [...] Tsengar Lee, program manager in the Earth Science Division of the Science Mission Directorate at NASA Headquarters, said building the data simply isn't enough: "The agency wants to maximize its uses. The expectation was if you build the data, they will come, but that was not the case," Lee said.

Source: Extract from www.nextgov.com/technology-news/2014/06/
nasa-announces-earth-science-challenges/87280/, May 5 2015.

One of the main motivations of public agencies to collaborate with citizens and civil service organizations in delivering public services is achieving strong user and citizen engagement per se (OECD 2011: 48). For instance, collaboration with citizens in designing and delivering healthcare services has been proven to improve implementation processes and strengthen compliance.

Other determinants include governance drivers, such as low administrative capacity of public sector, and logistical drivers, deriving from the intrinsic nature of the specific public service (Bovaird 2007; Joshi and Moore 2004: 855). For instance, monitoring the quality of lake water or parks or urban streets can be far more effective and less expensive if communities and residents are involved (OECD 2011).

Modes of collaborative governance: networks and co-production

Several forms and modes of collaborative governance exist. Two main arrangements are inter-institutional networks and co-production.

Networks are relatively stable patterns of social relations among interdependent actors, which take shape around policy problems and programs and that are being formed, reproduced and changed by an ecology of games between these actors (Kickert et al. 1997). They include multiple organizations, tied by some form of structural interdependence in which one unit is not the subordinate of others by virtue of its formal position (O'Toole 1997: 45). They are often viewed as pooled authority systems that are based more on expertise than on position (Agranoff 2003: 11). Milward and Provan (2006: 11) distinguish among service implementation, information diffusion, problem solving, and community capacity building networks.

A second form of collaborative governance is co-production, first studied in the late 1970s (Parks et al. 1981; Ostrom et al. 1978; see chapter 14 in this handbook). Co-production can be defined as "the mix of activities that both public service agents and citizens contribute to the provision of public services. The former are involved as professionals, or 'regular producers', while 'citizen production' is based on voluntary efforts by individuals and groups to enhance the quality and/or quantity of the services they use" (Parks et al. 1981). Co-production transforms the relationship between service users and providers, enabling the user to take more control and ownership. It contributes to aligning results with citizens' aspirations and needs and can lead to better outcomes and make better use of resources, thereby reducing the need for expensive services.

Another interesting form of co-production is user innovation, which encompasses an understanding of key user needs and their systematic involvement in the innovation process (Wise and Høgenhaven 2008). The organization makes use of assets from other organizations and individuals to discover, develop and implement ideas within and outside its boundaries (Eggers and Singh 2009: 98; Bommert 2010). Benefits include improved awareness of social problems, more effective practices based on broad citizen experience, and increased trust between government and citizens. Key conditions that enable user innovation are found at different levels: public policies and country traditions of stakeholder involvement at the macro level; legal and institutional conditions at for participatory governance in specific policy fields at the meso level, power resource asymmetries, incentives and past experiences at the organizational level (Sørensen and Torfing 2011: 860). User innovation has an impact on organizational structures and behaviors and requires a focus on expertise rather than on position (Meijer 2014: 213).

Box 13.3 Patient innovation

User innovation can be feasible and rewarding even in a highly professionalized area such as healthcare. Patients can become experts in their own conditions and are the only people who are present at all stages during the provision of care: from diagnosis to recovery (Rathert et al. 2011). Especially in chronic and rare diseases, users or patients know things that many professionals may not know and their engagement can make a service more effective by the extent to which they go along with its requirements (users as critical success factors; self-management of long-term conditions; Bovaird 2007). Moreover, supporting user innovation is key to implementing innovative ways of addressing such diseases at reasonable costs (Von Hippel et al. 2011).

The increasing availability of medical information on the internet and stronger patient communities are some of the drivers to more active patients.

Recent evidence from rare diseases has highlighted the necessity of professional support to complement patients' lack of expert knowledge. The combination of a service-oriented working climate and an efficient cooperation and mindset of healthcare professionals to motivate and support patient innovation has the potential to foster patients' innovative stimuli (Henrike and Schultz 2013).

> Public managers must revisit their outlook on the roles that they and the public should play in public services. The ways in which organizational cultures mediate patients' empowerment matters. Patients make a transition from simple users and choosers to makers and shapers of health services (Cornwall and Gaventa 2000).

Cross-sector collaboration and community engagement are relevant and equally spread at local and global levels. They are increasingly being adopted in global development strategies, including the post-2015 Development Agenda that will follow the United Nations' Millennium Development Goals.[1]

Especially in developing countries, they tend to be initiated by international institutions or philanthropic organizations or even self-organized communities rather than by public agencies (Cepiku and Giordano 2014).

Box 13.4 Tigray: a community-based network to fight malaria

Malaria is an entirely preventable and treatable mosquito-borne illness that accounted for 207 million cases and 627.000 deaths in 2012. Remedies include insecticidal nets and artemisinin-based combination therapies. Health costs of malaria stand for 40 per cent of public health expenditures and 30–50 per cent of inpatient hospital admissions (WHO 2013).

Despite steep increases in global malaria financing since 2003, people continue to die. The "unclearly defined potpourri" of corporate giving, philanthropic and CSR projects, although may do good for a while, lacks effectiveness in the longer-term. Low access to health structures, inadequate diagnosis, low provider compliance and patient adherence to therapy, bring down the impact of treatment from a 98 per cent of clinical efficacy of the drugs to a 37 per cent real effectiveness.

The Tigray project, named after the Ethiopian region in which it was implemented, sheds some light on how collaborative governance can dramatically improve the impact of traditional intervention strategies, be they State-centered or philanthropic.

From 2005 to 2009, a global public–private network was created including as partners Novartis Italia, the Italian Ministry of Health, the WHO, the Tigray Health Bureau, and two local hospitals. It made use of community health workers (CHWs) to provide diagnosis and treatment of malaria. CHWs are subsistence farmers, members of the communities where they work, supported by the health system, and who have shorter training than professional workers.

During the project, 98 health workers were trained in malaria diagnosis and treatment, including 33 CHWs. With a limited US$569.901 investment, they treated 130.000 people in their villages, approximately 58 per cent of all suspected and confirmed cases of malaria.

The collaboration-based strategy led to a 40 per cent reduction in malaria deaths compared to the traditional hospital-based approach. Caseload for health structures was reduced of one fourth and proper diagnosis saved US$1,41 per patient examined. Services provided by CHWs were assessed as more appropriate to health needs than those of clinic-based services, less expensive, and able to foster self-reliance and local participation

Columbia University, has estimated that financing needs of 1 million CHWs in Africa would be US$2,3 billion per year, 0.005 per cent of donor GDP. This collaborative approach among international institutions and donors, local authorities and recipient communities is considered the most effective and less expensive to achieve the health-related Millennium Development Goals (Earth Institute 2011).

Source: Adapted from Cepiku 2014.

Management challenges in coping with collaborative governance

Collaborative governance is not immune to failure, just as market and hierarchy. Still, there are policy issues that can only be satisfactorily solved through collaboration. Critical aspects of collaboration are varied commitment to common goals and different perspectives of the actors involved on the nature of the problem, the desired solution or the best organizational arrangements, culture clash, power issues, loss of autonomy, coordination fatigue and commitment of time and costs, lack of incentives to cooperate and blockades to collective action, potential for reduced accountability by participants and closeness, few rewards for role in the collaborative setting as compared to role in organizations, absence of important actors, poorly deployed resources, erroneous task integration, among others (Kenis and Provan, 2009: 444; Mandell and Keast, 2008; Kickert et al. 1997: 9, 167; Provan and Milward 1995). Well-known trade-offs and tensions intrinsic to collaborative governance include efficiency versus inclusiveness and equity, internal versus external legitimacy, and flexibility versus stability. For instance, in community collaborations there is a risk of less vocal citizens or those "willing but unable" to participate (OECD 2011). Co-production may be accessible only to specific social groups, thus worsening the gap between advantaged and disadvantaged social classes (Brandsen and Helderman 2012; Bovaird and Downe 2008).

Although most of these issues can be successfully addressed through effective management, collaborative governance remains a more complex approach and must be adopted only if the problem at hand is not satisfactorily solved by more traditional approaches. Moreover, often there is excessive focus on formally creating collaborative forms such as networks and community partnerships rather than developing systems and structures for managing them and steering competencies.

Managing a public–private partnership, a network or a co-production project is public management in situation of interdependencies. It consists in mutually adjusting the behavior of actors with different objectives and ambitions; coordinating strategies of actors with different goals and preferences with regard to a certain problem; initiating and facilitating interaction processes; creating and changing institutional arrangements for better coordination (Kickert et al. 1997: 10, 43–4; Friend et al. 1974).

Collaborative public management includes designing the most appropriate institutional form, developing management mechanisms, including performance management systems, and ensuring an effective leadership.

Institutional design

Just as there are design choices for organizations, there are design choices for collaborative arrangements and these affect the way collaborative agendas are formed and implemented and have consequences for what can actually be achieved (Kenis and Provan, 2009; Cross et al.

2002; Huxham and Vangen 2000; Provan and Milward 1995; Baker and Faulkner 1993). Defining the institutional design of collaboration includes designating the lead organization, influencing formal policy (division of resources and actor positions), defining the rules of entry and, thus, the boundaries of collaboration, influencing values, norms and perceptions (mass information campaigns, social engineering, collective learning processes).

With reference to networks, three ideal types of institutional forms have been identified: self-governance networks; lead-organizational networks; administrative-organization networks (Kenis and Provan 2009; Provan and Milward 1995). The main point for public managers is that the most appropriate institutional design form must be chosen and then implemented and this is critical for the sustainability of collaboration as it evolves.

At an early stage of collaboration and when only a few actors are involved, it may be appropriate to operate as a self-governed network where decisions are taken on the basis of unanimous consensus. This form, however, may prove inefficient with frequent meetings and difficulty in reaching consensus, but the partners do not fear a loss of control. In a lead organization network, one member bears the responsibility for network management. It has a clear direction and is efficient, but the domination by the lead organization may produce lack of commitment by the partners. A crisis of leadership may force the collaborative form to evolve towards a network administrative organization network, in which there is a distinct administrative entity set up to manage the network. It may be both efficient and sustainable, but hierarchy may be perceived and operational costs borne by the members.

Process management

During process management, the organizational structure (roles, rules, positions and resource division) is considered as given. Collaborative interaction process management includes a range of functions from activating collaboration, to arranging and facilitating interaction, brokerage, mediation and arbitration, and legitimacy building.

Identifying, motivating and activating the parties necessary for tackling a particular problem may require an analysis of previous strategies (Kickert et al. 1997). Once the collaborative arrangement has been put in place, mechanisms able to arrange interaction, manage accountability and avoid free rider behavior and premature pulling out are needed. This may require signing a formal agreement and defining, in advance, conflict-regulating mechanisms. Activities of a procedural nature such as ensuring that meeting places and times are agreed upon, notes and minutes are kept, and monitoring the quality of the dialogue are important to facilitate collaborative interaction (Milward and Provan 2006: 18). Brokerage consists in matching problems, solutions and actors.

Mediation and arbitration are carried out when conflict exists and the interaction process finds itself at an impasse. They consist in ensuring that relations are maintained, exploring standpoints, confronting the parties with the perceptions and interests of the "outside world".

Building and maintaining legitimacy of the collaborative governance strategy is particularly critical, also due to its voluntary nature (Milward and Provan 2006: 19). An effective performance management and communication system and the wise use of early achievements can support this task.

Collaborative leadership

One key feature of collaborative arrangements is that there is no hierarchical authority, no formal subordination, and interaction is based on expertise, trust and legitimacy. For a long time, this has translated into the wrong belief that collaborative governance is leaderless (Lipnack and Stamps 1994). On the contrary, leadership is imperative to overcome the several critical aspects and trade-offs that characterize collaborative governance.

This lacuna has exacerbated by a prevailing Weberian approach in leadership studies consisting in a priori locating the leader by office and assuming that whatever functions she/he performs are leadership functions (Lemaire and Provan 2010: 10; Weber 1947). While inappropriate in many traditional organizations, this approach is close to impracticable when it comes to collaborative settings. Traditional leadership theories that assume a leader–follower relationship fail to grasp the very meaning of collaboration (Ospina and Foldy 2010; Vangen and Huxham 2003; Huxham and Vangen, 2000). Even if one partner is more powerful than another, it still lacks hierarchical authority to impose goals, strategies or timeframes over other collaborating partners (Morse 2010). In collaborative settings, leaders need to count on other factors such as positive past experiences, suitable incentives for sharing authority, political consensus and the ability to instill trust (Eglene et al. 2007: 95).

More recently, a bottom-up approach, inspired by the works of Chester Barnard (1938), has emerged, which, first, identifies the key leadership behaviors and functions, and then looks at who exhibits certain behaviors (i.e. performs the executive functions). This approach is in line with what is called distributed or shared leadership (Crosby and Bryson 2010; Bryson and Crosby 1992). Defining leadership by functions, rather than by formal position, allows finding multiple leaders throughout the collaborative arrangement (Lemaire and Provan 2010). Reconceptualizing leadership as a team-level construct shifts the focus from personal traits to steering processes and leadership behaviors. A model by Van Wart (2004, 2008), commonly used in the literature, includes three kinds of behavior: task-oriented, people-oriented and organization-oriented. This model is shown in Table 13.1.

Leadership of collaborative arrangements has been variously labeled as integrative public leadership, collaborative leadership, network leadership, and inter-organizational leadership (Sun and Anderson 2012). The steering role is taken on by "people willing to invest their resources in return for future policies in their favour" (Kingdon 1984: 214). Motives may range from self-interest to genuine concern, including the possibility for an organization to stabilize its environment by building alliances and networks. Leadership in collaborative settings is crucial in matching governing mechanisms to context appropriately and should complement structure (Crosby and Bryson 2010: 224; Martin et al. 2008: 770). Leaders in collaborative settings

> initiate discussions or joint projects that help others recognize public problems, their stake in those problems, and opportunities to resolve them. The challenge for such leaders is to integrate the interests and actions of multiple stakeholders by appealing to shared goals and structuring deliberative processes by which the stake holders can devise joint, flexible strategies to pursue those goals.
>
> *(Page 2010: 247)*

The legitimacy to lead in collaborative settings is generally conferred on those who can "make things happen" (Sun and Anderson 2012; Morse 2010; Huxham and Vangen 2000). It is particularly those participants who have the skills to activate potential partners in a selective way who increase their influence on the collaborative decision-making process. This can lead to situations in which an actor with a relatively small amount of resources wields more influence than an actor who has many resources but lacks the necessary skills. A smart manager will understand that dealing with the network structure will give them a very powerful instrument with which to increase their influence in the collaborative decision-making process (Klijn and Teisman, in Kickert et al. 1997).

Reticulist skills include the ability to assess who should be involved in the interaction and which information should be given to them, the ability to negotiate and mediate, to distinguish among different target groups and adapt approaches to them, have a certain amount of technical expertise and "tactical and strategic" know-how. The ability to retain an independent position and the legitimacy are also important.

Managers involved in collaborative projects need to identify leadership functions that are needed to complement the organizational structure, rough out how these are ensured and who has the most appropriate skills in the network to cover them.

Table 13.1 Leadership behavior categories

Behavior categories	Description	Examples
Task-oriented	Express a concern for accomplishing the goals of the collaborative arrangement and are aimed at defining and organizing group activities. The primary concern is high efficiency in the use of resources and reliability of operations, products and services.	• Agenda framing. • Taking charge when emergencies arise. • Making sure individual roles are understood. • Scheduling the work to be done. • Asking to follow standard rules and regulations. • Keeping work moving at a rapid pace. • Assigning to particular tasks. • Selecting performance measures.
People-oriented	Reflect a concern for the welfare of the participants and a desire to foster good interpersonal relations among members. The primary objective is to ensure commitment and high levels of trust and cooperation.	• Treating all as equals. • Freely sharing information and providing the system of communication. • Looking out for the personal welfare. • Creating trust. • Brainstorming. • Sharing leadership role. • Inspiring enthusiasm and managing commitment. • Maintaining a closely knit between single partners and the collaborative arrangement. • Permitting participants to set their own pace. • Settling conflicts when they occur.
Organizational-oriented	The primary objective is to introduce major innovative improvements and adapt to external changes.	• Encouraging support from superiors. • Identifying resources. • Encouraging support from stakeholders. • Establishing a shared vision. • Establishing partners' commitment to joint mission. • Publicizing goals and accomplishments. • Influencing values and norms. • Changing the collaborative institutional structure.

Source: based on Van Wart (2004, 2008), Silvia and McGuire (2010), Milward and Provan (2006)

Managing performance of collaborative arrangements

The voluntary nature of collaborative arrangements makes measurement and use of performance information even more relevant, especially when these are community-based and composed of both public and private actors. A key part of management tasks of collaborative arrangements includes understanding the most relevant performance dimensions, as perceived by the different constituencies, and the determinants that influence performance.

Performance of collaborative arrangements, including effectiveness, needs to be analyzed at multiple levels. According to a conceptual framework originated in the seminal article of Provan and Milward (1995) and further developed in the literature (Cepiku 2014; Klijn et al. 2010), performance of collaborative settings includes: (1) intermediate outcomes in terms of quality of collaboration management; (2) outcomes produced for the benefit of each partner (or organizational-level performance); (3) outcomes achieved for the community at large. Figure 13.1 illustrates this framework.

The quality of collaboration can be assessed by measuring: conflict resolution; the extent to which the collaborative process has encountered stagnations or deadlocks; the productive use and reconciliation of differences in perspectives; and the frequency of interactions between actors (Klijn et al. 2010). Administrative efficiency, inclusiveness of decision-making, stability and flexibility of rules and of the organizational form, and satisfaction of the participants with network management are other criteria useful for assessing the quality of interaction (Mandell and Keast 2008).

The outcomes of the collaboration at the single-partner level refer to the satisfaction of each member with both the management of the interaction and the results coming from collaboration (Crosby and Bryson, 2010: 226).

The outcomes at the environmental level refer to the overall benefits for the community that go beyond partner-increased wellbeing. Beside the direct benefits to the users of the service or the beneficiaries of the policy, positive and negative externalities must be considered such as costs to the community, the social capital created and public perceptions that problems are being solved (Provan and Milward 1995). Collaboration could be a means for achieving broader

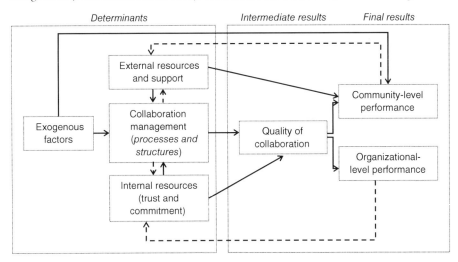

Figure 13.1 Performance dimensions and determinants in collaborative arrangements

effects such as enhanced social capital through cohesive communities, shared values, which are the basis for active citizenship, and generation of mutual trust. It can be a means for the strengthening or revitalization of democracy, contributing to the development of a new relationship between citizens and the State based on trust, ethical standards, and accountability (Alford 2014; Cahn and Gray 2012; Pestoff 2006; Ostrom et al. 1978). Particular attention must be paid to negative and unforeseen effects in terms of equity and external accountability and to longer-term impact.

Finally, exogenous and endogenous determinants of collaborative performance are necessary for interpreting performance. Exogenous elements include those characteristics over which collaboration managers or partners do not have full control: system stability, resource munificence and cohesion, goal consensus among partners prior to collaboration, competing institutional logics and complementarity of partners, their number and geographical location, trust and previous collaboration history, external legitimation (support from public opinion, community and other stakeholders at inception), purpose of the collaborative arrangement, nature of tasks and severity of the problem, environmental shocks, and number and kind of constituencies, among others (Kenis and Provan 2009; Provan and Milward 1995). The presence and relative relevance of these elements changes from case to case and from one policy sector to another. The context in which collaboration takes place is a relevant determinant of both the quality of interaction and the final outcome produced for the partners and the community.

Endogenous factors, on the other hand, can be instrumentally managed by the collaborative leaders and include the organizational structure, the management processes and the leadership style, assumed to be primary determinants of success and failure (McGuire and Agranoff 2007: 23).

While the majority of the literature on collaboration is quite positive, collaborative governance does not always pursue the public good. Some authors have adopted a more holistic view and focused on dark networks developed around international drug, terror, diamond and weapons trade (Raab and Milward 2003). Conflicts of interest and trade-offs between short- and long-term aims are common in public–private collaborative governance. Performance management systems should be carefully designed to support dialogue, interaction and strategic choice among different strategic policy options and governance arrangements.

Box 13.5 Large-scale partnerships with the private sector undermine Africans' land rights, drive inequality and damage the environment

Government policies and almost US$6 billion in aid money in support of large partnerships with the private sector to fight poverty and food insecurity are risking Africans' land rights, worsening inequality and damaging the environment.

With growing global demand for natural resources, donors and African governments are looking to capitalize on increasing interest from the private sector in African land. Mega-public–private partnerships (PPP) "growth corridor" projects in Tanzania, Burkina Faso, Malawi, Ghana and Mozambique illustrate this trend.

"After decades of underinvestment, governments in Africa are turning to partnerships with donor aid agencies and large companies or investors to develop the agriculture sector. This offers the allure of capital, technology and foreign exchange, but the downside risks of this approach are huge – particularly for the land rights of local communities in the investment areas," says Robin Willoughby, Oxfam's Policy Adviser on Agriculture and Food Security.

According to Oxfam, long-term development goals have been sacrificed in order to quickly establish mega public–private partnerships, as companies are offered land, tax and trade incentives to enter these schemes. Due to weak land tenure found in many African countries, these land subsidies and transfers are likely to undermine local communities' land rights. This model also threatens to worsen inequality in African countries, which is already severe across the continent, and damage the environment through the introduction of plantation agriculture.

Rather than prioritizing partnerships between governments and donors with large private sector players, Oxfam is calling for the tried and tested investment to deliver benefits for almost 600 million Africans working in agriculture. This involves public sector investment in smallholder farmers, local markets and regional markets, and strong regulation to ensure that private sector investment can 'do no harm' and benefit millions of smallholder producers living in rural areas.

Source: Extracted from www.oxfam.org/en/pressroom/pressreleases/2014-08-26/giant-partnerships-
threaten-small-farms-africa-xxx, September 1, 2014.

Performance information affects partners' willingness to collaborate with others and can be used to strengthen commitment and to inform them on the convenience of the collaborative arrangement as compared with other organizational forms (Bretschneider et al. 2012; McGuire and Agranoff 2007: 21).

Policy and operational implications

Several implications originate from the analysis of collaborative governance carried out in this chapter. First and foremost, collaborative governance arrangements are far more complex and difficult to manage than traditional hierarchical organizations, and the likelihood of disappointing outcomes is high (Huxham 2000; Bardach 1998). When desired outcomes can be achieved only through collaboration, public managers must equip themselves with the necessary skills and tools.

Second, this sensibility at the managerial level must go hand in hand with an adaptation of public sector policies to support collaboration. Risk is higher in collaborative settings. If public policies do not acknowledge this, risk adverse behavior may prevent managers from adopting innovative solutions to wicked problems (Osborne and Brown 2010). Lack of collaboration is not the consequence of the stupidity or intransigence of public managers but highlights their ability to comprehend and respond to a myriad of incentives from hierarchical superiors, legislative overseers, and self-appointed accountability holders (Behn 2010: 435).

Too often, networks and co-production are launched as exceptional projects isolated from the rest of the organization. This approach makes them an exit strategy to capacity deficiencies and puts at risk their own sustainability. Instead, integrated planning and management is recommended.

Context – what we called exogenous determinants of performance – matters. Therefore, the launch of large-scale collaboration initiatives should be preceded by interventions aimed at strengthening community ties and inter-institutional collaboration. This also means that collaboration is generally not free but requires resources and investment for its full potential to be realized.

Note

1 Since the 1980s, private foreign investment in developing countries has risen 15-fold; and since 2000, private capital has accounted for 80 per cent of all capital flowing to these countries. Cf. www.brookings.edu/research/reports/2014/04/private-sector-post-2015-agenda.

References

Agranoff, R. and M. McGuire. 2004. *Collaborative Public Management: New Strategies for Local Governments.* Washington, DC: Georgetown University Press.

Alford, J. 2014. "The Multiple Facets of Co-Production: Building on the Work of Elinor Ostrom." *Public Management Review* 16 (3): 299–316.

Alford, J. and O. Hughes. 2008. "Public value pragmatism as the next phase of public management." *American Review of Public Administration.* Online publication. doi:10.1177/0275074008314203.

Ansell, C. and A. Gash. 2008. "Collaborative governance in theory and practice." *Journal of Public Administration Research and Theory* 18 (4): 543–571.

Baker W. E. and R. R. Faulkner. 1993. "The social organization of conspiracy: Illegal networks in the heavy electrical equipment industry." *American Sociological Review* 58 (6): 837–860.

Bardach, E. 1998. *Getting Agencies to Work Together: The Practice and Theory of Managerial Craftsmanship.* Washington, DC: Brookings Institution Press.

Barnard, C. I. 1938. *The Functions of the Executive.* Cambridge, MA: Harvard University Press.

Behn, R. D. 2010. "Collaborating for performance: or can there exist such a thing as CollaborationStat?" *International Public Management Journal* 13 (4): 429–470.

Bommert, B. 2010. "Collaborative innovation in the public sector." *International Public Management Review* 11 (1): 15–33.

Bovaird, T. 2007. "Beyond engagement and participation: user and community coproduction of public services." *Public Administration Review* 67 (5): 846–860.

Bovaird, T. and J. Downe. 2008. "Innovation in public engagement and co-production of services." Policy Paper to Department of Communities and Local Government. Cardiff: Cardiff Business School.

Brandsen, T. and J. Helderman. 2012. "The conditions for successful co-production in housing: a case study of German housing cooperatives." In *New Public Governance, The Third Sector and Co-Production*, edited by Pestoff, V. T. Brandsen, B. Verschuere. New York: Routledge.

Bretschneider, B., Y. Choi, T. Nabatchi, and R. O'Leary. 2012. "Does public value matter for collaboration? Evidence from an experimental analysis." Paper presented at the Creating Public Value Conference, University of Minnesota, September 20–22.

Bryson, J. M. and B. C. Crosby. 1992. *Leadership for the Common Good: Tackling Public Problems in a Shared-Power World.* San Francisco: Jossey-Bass.

Cahn, E., and C. Gray. 2012. "Co-production from a normative perspective." In *New Public Governance, the Third Sector and Co-Production*, edited by Pestoff, V., T. Brandsen, and B. Verschuere. New York: Routledge.

Cepiku, D. 2014. "Network performance: toward a dynamic multidimensional model". In *Network Theory in the Public Sector: Building New Theoretical Frameworks*, edited by Keast, R., M. P. Mandell, and R. Agranoff. New York: Routledge.

Cepiku, D. 2013. "Unraveling the Concept of Public Governance: A Literature Review of Different Traditions." In *Conceptualizing and Researching Governance in Public and Non-Profit Organizations. Studies in Public and Non-Profit Governance*, edited by Gnan, L., A. Hinna, F. Monteduro, 3–32. Emerald Group Publishing.

Cepiku, D. and F. Giordano. 2014. "Co-production in developing countries: insights from the community health workers experience." *Public Management Review* 16 (3): 317–340.

Cornwall, A. and J. Gaventa. 2001. "Bridging the gap: citizenship, participation and accountability." *PLA notes* 40 (2001): 32–35.

Crosby B. C. and J. M. Bryson. 2010. "Integrative leadership and the creation and maintenance of cross-sector collaborations." *Leadership Quarterly* 21 (2): 211–230.

Cross R., A. Parker., and S. Borgatti. 2002. *A Bird's-Eye View: Using Social Network Analysis to Improve Knowledge Creation and Sharing.* Somers, NY: IBM Corporation.

Earth Institute. 2011. *One Million Community Health Workers: Technical Task Force Report.* New York: Columbia University.

Eggers, W. D. and K. S. Singh. 2009. *The Public Innovator's Playbook: Nurturing Bold Ideas in Government.* Washington, DC: Deloitte Research and Ash Institute for Democratic Governance at the Harvard Kennedy School of Government.

Eglene, O., S. S. Dawes, and C. A. Schneider. 2007. "Authority and leadership patterns in public sector knowledge networks." *American Review of Public Administration* 37 (1): 91–113.

Frederickson, H. G. 2005. "Whatever happened to public administration? Governance, governance everywhere." In *Oxford Handbook of Public Management*, edited by Ferlie, E., L. Lynn, and C. Pollitt, 281–304. Oxford, UK: Oxford University Press.

Friend J. K., J. M. Power, and C. J. L. Yewlett. 1974. *Public Planning: The Inter-Corporate Dimension.* London: Travistock Publications.

Fukuyama, F. 2013. "What is governance?" *Governance* 26 (3): 347–368.

Henrike, H. W. and C. Schultz. 2014. "The impact of health care professionals' service orientation on patients' innovative behavior." *Health Care Management Review* 39 (4): 329–339.

Hill, C., and L. Lynn. 2003. "Producing human services: why do agencies collaborate?" *Public Management Review* 5 (1): 63–81.

Huxham, C. 2000. "The challenge of collaborative governance." *Public Management* 2 (3): 337–358.

Huxham, C. 1996. *Creating Collaborative Advantage.* Sage.

Huxham, C. and S. Vangen. 2000. "Leadership in the shaping and implementation of collaboration agendas: How things happen in a (not quite) joined-up world." *Academy of Management Journal* 43 (6): 1159–1175.

Joshi, A. and M. Moore. 2014. "Institutionalised co-production: unorthodox public service delivery in challenging environments." *Journal of Development Studies* 40 (4): 31–49.

Keast, R., M. P. Mandell, and R. Agranoff. 2014. *Network Theory in the Public Sector: Building new Theoretical Frameworks.* New York: Routledge.

Kenis P. and K. G. Provan. 2009. "Towards an exogenous theory of public network performance." *Public Administration* 87 (3): 440–456.

Kickert, W. J. M., E. H. Klijn, and J. F. M. Koppenjan. 1997. *Managing Complex Networks, Strategies for the Public Sector.* London: Sage.

Kingdon, J. W. 1984. *Agendas, Alternatives and Public Policies.* Boston, MA: Little Brown.

Klijn, E. H., A. J. Steijn, and J. Edelenbos. 2010. "The impact of network management strategies on the outcomes in governance networks." *Public Administration* 88 (4): 1063–1082.

Kooiman, J. 1993. *Modern Governance: New Government–Society Interactions.* London: Sage.

Lemaire, R. H. and K. G. Provan. 2010. "The functions of network executives: multifaceted leadership in a publicly funded child and youth health network." Paper presented at the APPAM Research Conference, Boston, November 4–6.

Lipnack, J. and J. Stamps. 1994. *The Age of the Network: Organizing Principles for the 21st Century.* Harmondsworth: Omneo.

Mandell, M. P. 2010. "Learning the three 'R's' of networks Roles, Rules and Responsibilities." Lecture at the University of Lugano, October 2010.

Mandell, M. P. and R. Keast. 2008. "Evaluating the effectiveness of interorganizational relations through networks." *Public Management Review* 10 (6): 715–731.

Martin, G. P., G. Currie, and R. Finn. 2008. "Leadership, service reform and public-service networks: the case of cancer-genetics pilots in the English NHS." *JPART* 19 (4): 769–794.

McGuire, M. and R. Agranoff. 2007. "Answering the big questions, asking the bigger questions: expanding the public network management empirical research agenda." paper presented at the 9th Public Management Research Conference, Tucson, October 25–27.

Meijer, A. J. 2014. "From hero-innovators to distributed heroism: an in-depth analysis of the role of individuals in public sector innovation." *Public Management Review* 16 (2): 199–216.

Milward, H. B. and K. G. Provan. 2006. *A Manager's Guide to Choosing and Using Collaborative Networks.* Washington, DC: IBM Center for the Business of Government.

Morse, R. S. 2010. "Integrative public leadership: Catalyzing collaboration to create public value." *The Leadership Quarterly* 21 (2): 231–245.

O'Leary, R. and N. Vij. 2012. "Collaborative public management: where have we been and where are we going?" *The American Review of Public Administration.* Online publication. doi: 10.1177/0275074012445780.

O'Toole, L. J. 1997. "Treating networks seriously: practical and research-based agendas in public administration." *Public Administration Review* 57 (1): 45–52.

OECD. 2011. *Together for Better Public Services: Partnering with Citizens and Civil Society.* Paris: OECD.

Osborne, S. P. and L. Brown. 2011. "Innovation, public policy and public services delivery in the UK. The word that would be king?" *Public Administration* 89 (4): 1335–1350.

Ospina, S. and E. Foldy. 2010. "Building bridges from the margins: the work of leadership in social change organizations." *Leadership Quarterly* 21 (2): 292–307.

Ostrom, E., R. B. Parks, G. P. Whitaker, and S. L. Percy. 1978. "The public service production process: a framework for analyzing police services." *Policy Studies Journal* 7 (s1): 381–381

Page, S. 2010. "Integrative leadership for collaborative governance: civic engagement in Seattle." *Leadership Quarterly* 21 (2): 246–263.

Parks, R. B., P. C. Baker, L. Kiser, R. Oakerson, E. Ostrom, et al. 1981. "Consumers as co-producers of public services: some economic and institutional considerations." *Policy Studies Journal* 9 (7): 1001–1011.

Pestoff, V. 2006. "Citizens as co-producers of welfare services: preschool services in eight European countries." *Public Management Review* 8 (4): 503–520.

Pfeffer, J. S. and G. R. Salancik. 1978. *The external control of organizations: A resource dependence perspective.* New York: Harper & Row.

Provan, K. G. and H. B. Milward. 1995. "A preliminary theory of network effectiveness: a comparative study of four community mental health systems." *Administrative Science Quarterly* 40 (1):1–33.

Raab, J. and H. B. Milward. 2003. "Dark networks as problems." *Journal of Public Administration Research and Theory* 13 (4): 413–439.

Rathert, C., N. Huddleston, and Y. Pak. 2011. "Acute care patients discuss the patient role in patient safety." *Health Care Management Review* 36 (2): 134–144.

Silvia, C. and M. McGuire. 2010. "Leading public sector networks: An empirical examination of integrative leadership behaviours." *The Leadership Quarterly* 21 (2): 264–277.

Sørensen, E. and J. Torfing. 2011. "Enhancing collaborative innovation in the public sector." *Administration & Society* 43 (8): 842–868.

Sun, P. Y. and M. H. Anderson. 2012. "Civic capacity: building on transformational leadership to explain successful integrative public leadership." *Leadership Quarterly* 23 (3): 309–323.

Vangen, S. and Huxham, C. (2003). "Enacting leadership for collaborative advantage: dilemmas of ideology and pragmatism in the activities of partnership managers." *British Journal of Management* 14: S61–S76

Van Wart, M. 2008. *Leadership in Public Organizations: An Introduction.* Armonk, New York: M.E. Sharpe.

Van Wart, M. 2004. "A comprehensive model of organizational leadership: the leadership action cycle." *International Journal of Organization Theory and Behavior* 6 (4): 173–208.

Von Hippel, E. A., S. Ogawa, and J. P. de Jong. 2011. "The age of the consumer-innovator." *MIT Sloan Management Review* 53 (1): 27–35.

Weber, M. 1947. "The types of authority and imperative co-ordination." In *The Theory of Social and Economic Organization,* edited by Parsons, A. M. and T. Parsons. New York: The Free Press.

Weber, E. P. and A. M. Khademian. 2008. "Wicked problems, knowledge challenges, and collaborative capacity builders in network settings." *Public Administration Review* 68 (2): 334–349.

Wise, E. and C. Høgenhaven. 2008. "User-Driven Innovation-Context and Cases in the Nordic Region." *Innovation Policy,* June.

WHO. 2013. *World malaria report 2013.* Geneva: WHO.

14

CITIZEN CO-PRODUCTION OF PUBLIC SERVICES

Meanings, processes, antecedents and consequences

John Alford

Introduction

When we visit a doctor, we usually assume – if we give it any thought at all – that we are receiving a service. For a fee, the doctor brings her expertise to bear on your ailment, identifying its likely cause and prescribing medicine or other treatment to alleviate and hopefully cure it. In this and in many other fields, the assumption is that services are delivered by staff inside the organisation to consumers.

But complicating this picture is the fact that the consumer often not only receives the service but also contributes to its production. This is co-production, now the subject of a considerable body of public administration scholarship, especially by clients but also by other actors. This notion emerged first in a short flurry of interest in the early 1980s, then re-emerged on a broader and more sustained basis from the 2000s (Verschuere et al. 2012; Alford 2009; Bovaird 2007).

This chapter surveys co-production of public services, mainly by citizens and clients. It explores the meaning of co-production and how we conceive of those who co-produce. Then, after consideration of the products and processes of co-production, the chapter addresses two key issues: (1) when should it be utilised? and (2) how can it be elicited?

The chapter draws mainly on theory-building or case analysis, since the co-production research has offered very little in the way of quantitative empirical evidence. Now, however, a major study has provided the most substantial survey research evidence thus far, covering five EU countries (Czech Republic, Denmark, France, Germany and UK) with a sample of 1,000 in each. This chapter will draw on that study, as the only large-sample, multi-country random empirical research in this field to date (Bovaird et al. 2015; Parrado et al. 2013; Loeffler et al. 2008).

What is co-production?

'Co-production' has a number of meanings. In essence, it is about government agencies involving members of the public in the 'execution of public policy as well as its formulation' (Whitaker 1980: 241); it was founded on the idea that not only the consumption but also the production of public services can require the participation of those who consume them.

One important dimension along which types of co-production vary is in the range of actors who play a co-production role. Originally, the focus was the role of consumers of public services in their production. As Parks et al. put it, 'coproduction involves the mixing of the productive efforts of regular and consumer producers' (1981: 1002).

But over time, the conception broadened beyond consumers to include citizens more generally: 'By co-production, I mean the process through which inputs used to produce a good or service are contributed by individuals who are not "in" the same organisation' (Ostrom 1996, 1073). This encompasses not only the consumers of a service, but also those individuals who voluntarily contribute to co-production even though they don't receive any private value from the organisation (for example, citizens who help with meal-deliveries for 'Meals on Wheels'). These citizen volunteers (or 'individual volunteers') are not the same as voluntary/third sector organisations, which may employ their workers, but they do help create public as well as private value.

At the same time, both European traditions of civil society engagement and emerging American antipathy to big government gave impetus to more collective forms of co-production, embracing a spectrum of types of contributors to productive activity – not only individuals but organisations. These definitions could also validly be seen as co-production, but more usually they are characterised as 'collaboration' or 'partnership', which are dealt with in later chapters in this handbook.

Here we will focus mainly on the simplest form, where clients are the main co-producers, not because it is the 'correct' term but simply because they occupy a similar role to 'customers' at the organisation's 'business end', but without the latter's private-sector connotations. However, we also take into account the citizenry in their role as volunteers as well as consumers of collective value.

Whatever the type, it cannot be seen as co-production without two fundamental characteristics, illustrated in Table 14.1, adapted from Bovaird (2007). The vertical axis shows the actors' roles, while the horizontal axis refers to who does the work.

First, co-production must entail external actors performing some of the actual work instead of (or in addition to) deliberating about whether or how to do it. This is at odds with commentators who envisage co-production as a consultative arrangement; it is about production rather than governance or deliberation. Second, the prefix 'co-' adds the element of jointness to the work, which is shared by the organisation with external parties, such as other organisations or individuals. In the public sector, then, co-production is where a government organisation and one or more external actors jointly create something of value, as shown in cell 5 of Table 14.1.

While these fundamentals are broadly accepted, some other aspects deserve clarification. One is how we see the 'products' of co-production. For it to be worth managerial attention, it

Table 14.1 Basic types of involvement and performer

	Performed by		
Type of involvement	Government organization alone	Government organization and external party	External party alone
Governance (deciding what to do)	1 Government decision	2 Joint decision	3 Private decision
Production (doing it)	4 Production by govt organization	5 Co-production	6 Private production/ self service

must lead to results which are valuable in some way to the public at large, not only to the individuals in question – i.e. they should on balance contribute to the common good or 'public value'. Usually this entails the provision of private value as well, but the creation of some public value is the justification for devoting public resources to it (Moore 1995).

Another aspect is to acknowledge that the line between 'governance' and 'production' is porous, and that there are some activities which fall somewhere between the two: planning, design and management – as shown in Table 14.2.

A further aspect is whether co-production refers only to joint activity (i.e. cell 5 in Table 14.1). Some writers include cell 6 (private production/self-service) to the extent that it contributes to public value, even though external parties appear to be acting alone (Sharp 1980). But in some of these cases, the government agency, even though it does not join directly in the production, nevertheless influences the citizen/client activity. Drivers slowing down at a road intersection roundabout – which reduces the chances of accidents occurring – may be seen as producing value on their own. But if they have been prompted to do so by the presence of the roundabout, government has helped bring about the outcome (safer driving at intersections) even though none of its public servants are present at the locations in question. This is the phenomenon known as 'nudge', wherein policy outcomes are generated by structuring people's contexts so that they are gently reminded or warned to behave in a particular way, rather than coerced to do so (Thaler and Sunstein 2008). So we include an (additional) cell 10 in Table 14.2, described as 'nudged' private production or self-service.

Also important is how relational (rather than transactional) the interaction is: that is, the extent to which it is based on frequent dealings, agreed purposes, information sharing and trust, with accompanying social bonds. Some writers criticise as too narrowly transactional the application of the term to relatively routine activities such as writing postcodes on mail, or completing and lodging tax returns (e.g. Boyle and Harris 2009). But this critique confuses the social relationship with the operational one. The issue is not whether the participants have developed close social relationships, but rather about whether any value emanates from a given interaction by citizens with government organisations, in which case it is by definition co-production – whether it is narrowly transactional or multi-dimensionally relational. Co-production should not be seen as one or the other, but rather as embracing both (Alford 2009).

A still further issue is whether only voluntary activity by clients or citizens should be seen as co-production, or it can also be described as such if there is coercion. Some scholars insist on

Table 14.2 Elaborated types of involvement and performer

	Performed by		
Type of involvement	*Government organization alone*	*Government organization and external party*	*External party alone*
Governance (deciding what to do)	1 Government decision	2 Joint decision	3 Private decision
Planning/ design	1 Government management, planning or design	2 Joint management, planning or design	3 Private management, planning or design
Production (doing it)	4 Production by government organization	5 Co-production 10 'Nudged' private production/self service	6 Private production/ self service

the primacy of the voluntary model: 'If citizens act in accordance with public service goals because they fear reprisals for their refusal, …. their actions do not constitute co-operation. Co-operation is voluntary' (Whitaker 1980: 243).

It is true that voluntarism is the animating spirit of co-production, but this does not rule out compliance measures as partial ways to enlist contributions of time and effort by citizens. The regulation literature tells us that most compliance programmes contain an element of consent or voluntarism (Ayres and Braithwaite 2002) – for example, a drug addict placed under a court order to undertake a rehabilitation programme – and it is often hard to delineate the two. Here we take the view that co-production is essentially voluntary, but it can play a role in compliance.

Finally, focusing on citizens and clients requires defining these terms, to which we now briefly turn.

Who is the co-producer?

One of the ways public management reform over the last three decades has sought to make the public sector more like the private one is by substituting the notion of public as 'customers' for the historical conception in public administration that they are citizens (Clarke et al. 2007; Osborne and Gaebler 1992). Scholars have reacted critically, arguing inter alia that it doesn't capture the collective nature of the value consumed by the citizenry; that many of the people whom government serves, such as welfare recipients, pay no money directly to service providing organisations; and that some members of the public, such as prisoners, are obliged to receive the 'service' whether they like it or not. All of these factors negate the notion of the customer transaction as a voluntary economic exchange. Instead, the exchange is social rather than economic – an exchange of behaviours rather than of products and services for money. This social exchange, in which clients receive tangible or intangible 'gifts' in the sense used by Titmuss (1970) and other scholars (Ekeh 1974; Levi-Strauss 1969), offers its own possibilities for eliciting co-productive contributions.

Unfortunately, the issue has tended to slide into a somewhat sterile debate as to whether members of the public are citizens or customers (Barrett 2009; Clarke et al. 2007; Fountain 2001). However, a more integrated conception is emerging: that they are both citizens and customers – indeed they have multiple aspects, as citizens first and foremost, but also some, whom we will call clients, as paying customers, beneficiaries or obligatees. These are roles rather than categories, so that any one individual (for example, a public school pupil) might simultaneously be a citizen receiving public value, a beneficiary receiving the private value of an education without paying any money directly for it, and an obligatee subject to the school rules and liable to punishment for breaching them.

Two other roles also need consideration:

1 What we will call the 'citizen volunteer' or 'individual volunteer'. This is where co-productive effort is contributed by individuals who do not receive goods or services in the same way as clients, but do it typically for reasons such as moral norms or social encouragement.
2 'Collective' co-producers, where citizens organise themselves as a group to contribute. Two important issues here are: whether the production is individual or collective; and whether the consumption is of private value or public value.

Thus the public servant may have to deal with members of the public in different incarnations at the same time – providing public value to the citizenry and private value to clients. We can therefore define *co-production* as any active behaviour by any client of a government agency which is: prompted by some action or contribution of the agency; at least partly voluntary; and either intentionally or unintentionally creates some public value. In this context: *client* co-production is co-production by clients; *citizen* co-production is co-production by individuals who do not receive private value for their contributions; and *collective* co-production is carried out by self-organised groups.

These are not the only types of co-producer, but others are dealt with elsewhere in this handbook. The multi-country research mentioned above casts some light on the issues of individual vs collective co-production and private vs public value.

The products and processes of co-production

Co-production necessarily entails the participating individuals or organisations contributing inputs to the operation of a government organisation's program or service, in order to achieve valuable outcomes. But the research to date has not offered a systematic way of understanding the different types of inputs, nor of comprehending the points in the 'production process' at which these resources enter these processes.

Consider a child protection service (CPS) situated in a government department and employing mainly social workers, whose mandated outcome is to ensure that children are safe from (physical or sexual) abuse. From the point of view of the government, achieving this purpose requires certain tasks to be performed (Figure 14.1). First, children at risk need to be notified to the CPS. Second, the seriousness and likelihood of the risk has to be ascertained. Third, a decision will have to be made as to what should happen to the child. Among possible options are: (1) that the child could be removed from the family home and placed in a state institution or foster care.; or that s/he could remain with the family while the CPS works with the parent(s) to change their behaviour in a manner conducive to better parenting. Fourth, there needs to be ongoing monitoring to ensure that these tasks continue to be performed at a reasonable standard.

Following that, the CPS can perform the tasks of assessing the risk (with some reliance on interested parties to disclose the truth) and of assigning the child either back to its family under supervision, or to foster or institutional care. It is noteworthy that in cases where the child is returned to its family, important and sometimes difficult co-productive work has to be carried out by those who are, along with the child, also clients of the organisation: the parents. For instance, if the father (or stepfather) is unemployed and inclined to a quick temper or excessive alcohol, then he may need to undertake a rehabilitation programme for his alcoholism, attend an anger management course, and be provided with job training or job search assistance.

Of course, this situation is much more complicated than suggested by the production line in Figure 14.1; it contains feedback loops, multiple causation, and hard-to-measure cause-and-effect relationships. But what is interesting about this analysis is that although it initially puts

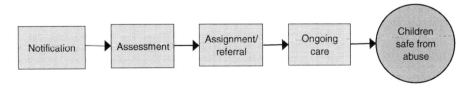

Figure 14.1 Simple 'process logic' for child protection service

forward a simple set of activities as seen from the perspective of the government organisation, it provides a scaffold that enables consideration of co-production possibilities. Table 14.3 sets out the specific contributions of various external parties at different points in the process. It shows first that various actors in the family's environment provide information about children at risk, something they are more inclined to do because the CPS and other agencies adopt various ways of encouraging people to do so: 'consciousness-raising' publicity material; 'hotlines' for notifications; refuges and other transitional avenues out of threat. Also important is that the same people are willing to provide information about child abuse offences truthfully, which they are more likely to do if they are reassured that it will be acted on and they will be protected from retribution. Perhaps most importantly, the parents change their own behaviour, in many cases through programmes, but also in some cases with the support of extended family. And if all else fails, there are state-sponsored facilities to domicile the children out of harm's way. This is often less desirable but sometimes unavoidable.

Underlying these elements of the process are two more general questions (Loeffler et al. 2008). One is whether the co-production is individual or collective. The other is whether the products delivered are consumed individually or collectively (i.e. do they constitute private or public value?)

The EU study found that, with some important exceptions, the incidence of individual and private production and consumption seems to prevail over the collective and public forms. It provided a list of 15 co-productive behaviours – five each from public/neighbourhood safety, the environment and health – and asked respondents to indicate how often they performed them. It revealed two clear findings. One is that individual co-production is much more common than collective co-production: the most performed activities don't require interaction with other people (recycling, locking doors and windows, exercising). By contrast, the least performed activities involve group participation, liaising proactively with authorities (e.g. asking for advice on property protection) and 'face-threatening' activities (telling people on the street what to do).

The other clear finding is that the most-performed activities are mainly devoted to producing private value – for instance, the personal benefits gained by saving on electricity costs or exercising more. Recycling is an exception, but its popularity can be explained by the efforts authorities have put in to making it easier in various ways. Also commonly performed are activities involving reciprocity (e.g. neighbours keeping an eye on each other's properties). By contrast, most of the least-performed activities produce largely public value, with a smaller component of private value (Parrado et al. 2013; Loeffler et al. 2008).

Thus, the forms and outcomes of co-production seem contrary to commonsense understandings, which would most likely assume co-production to involve communities and groups within them.

Table 14.3 Contributions of co-producers of child protection services, by stage of process

Stage	External co-producer(s)	Specific contributions of external co-producers
Notification	Neighbours, extended family, teachers, doctors, police	Information
Assessment	As above in some cases	Accuracy and truthfulness of information
Assignment/referral	Courts	
Ongoing care	Parents, extended family. State institutions	Behavioural self-change. Care if all else fails.

When should co-production be utilised?

'One size fits all' reforms have bedevilled the public sector since at least the 1960s, from the handing over to business of many government functions under NPM to the more recent interest in network governance. Partly this 'one-size-fits-all' mentality derived from reformers' ideological predilection for market solutions (Alford and O'Flynn 2012; Boston 1996; Osborne and Gaebler 1992; Pollitt 1990), partly it was facilitated by the system-wide nature of reforms, which were mainly introduced on a 'whole-of-government' basis (Pollitt and Bouckaert 2000). Indeed, when co-production enjoyed a brief period of popularity in the early 1980s (after which it languished until the 2000s), it was governments' preferences for market solutions that pushed co-production to the margins.

Now, however, a more contingent approach is increasingly prevalent across most types of public services, including co-production. Instead of saying 'Everything should involve co-production with clients' or 'Everything should be done in-house by our own staff and delivered to clients', it is now increasingly recognised that 'It all depends'. What it depends on is whether the benefits outweigh the costs – which is in turn shaped by factors such as the nature of the service, the context, or staff capabilities.

Addressing these benefits and costs first requires analysis of the degree of inter-dependency between the actors in question. One possibility is where the work of the organisation is inter-dependent with that of the clients – for example when unemployed people need the assistance of a public employment agency to find vacancies and refer them to possible employers, while the agency depends on the clients to make themselves job-ready and persuade employers to hire them. Here the issue for the organisation is not whether to utilise co-production but how better to do it. This challenges the idea that co-production is a kind of 'optional extra' that it would be nice to have. Where the organisation and the clients have an inter-dependent relationship, co-production is embedded in the service, so the parties have no choice but to acknowledge its presence, and indeed to make it function more efficiently and effectively.

If, on the other hand, there is a relatively low level of inter-dependency between them, then client co-production is basically a substitute for in-house production by the organisation's staff. In this situation, the organisation should weigh up the benefits and costs of each, much as it would when determining whether to contract out to the private sector. In the early work of Ostrom and her colleagues on this issue, they argued that the key consideration was the marginal costs (for all intents and purposes, the relative 'wage' rates of internal workers and external co-producers) (Parks et al. 1981: 1003). However, recent studies indicate that probably a more important criterion is the relative capabilities of the internal and external workers, which vary from case to case (Alford 2009). In some situations, citizen co-producers may constitute well-meaning but bumbling amateurs, whereas in others they may have a real edge in knowledge of or legitimacy with a particular community or constituency.

Thus, the relative weight of what we might call the service costs and benefits will vary according to the situation. But there are also two other types of benefits and costs to consider in this substitution scenario (see Alford and O'Flynn 2012). One is the relationship costs and benefits, i.e. those concerning the dealings with the other party to make the arrangement work. The costs might involve those to do with: choosing which citizens are to be engaged in the task (or given more encouragement to do so); specifying (and promulgating) what work is required; ascertaining whether it is being done; and incentivising them to do it. A benefit in this respect from a more collaborative client relationship might be a greater sense of social connection with the other party.

The remaining types of benefits and costs are those relating to the strategic positioning and core competences of the organisation as a whole, i.e. where the particular co-production initiative affects some aspect of the organisation other than the service in question. On the plus side, these effects could include: more coherent and widely accepted strategies; distributing risks; or enhanced reputation. On the minus side, they can include impacts on underlying values or diminished reputation. Taking these three factors together, it may be that a child protection service determines that placing a child in the care of its extended family offers the best net service benefits, but on the other hand finds that the costs of monitoring, and of reputational loss by the CPS, outweigh those benefits.

In summary, whether to enlist co-production by clients depends in the first instance on whether their work is inter-dependent with that of the organisation, in which case it is unavoidable. If it is not inter-dependent, but rather a potential substitute for it, then the relative benefits and costs – service, relationship and strategic – of each alternative must be weighed up.

Thus, the theory suggests that co-production is perhaps a more significant phenomenon than we might expect at first glance. This is implicit in the structural reality that co-production can be either inter-dependent with or a substitute for the work of the organisation's internal staff. But the available empirical data indicate that this assertion should be modified. In the EU study (Bovaird et al. 2015), the researchers compiled an index of individual co-production, and another of collective co-production, each a composite picture of people's propensity to co-produce. They found that on average 62.4 per cent of people were willing to take part in individual co-production, whereas only 35.5 per cent were willing to engage in collective co-production – findings consistent with those cited above about the propensity to co-produce different types of activities.

Eliciting co-production

The question of what makes clients and other external parties co-produce public services is probably the most studied area in the co-production literature (see Bovaird et al. 2015; Verschuere et al. 2012; Alford 2009), although much of it, as with other co-production aspects, is focused on theory-building rather than quantitative empirical research. However, the EU research provides some insight (Bovaird et al. 2015).

The theoretical consensus is that people's propensity to co-produce is motivated by multiple factors: the motivations and capacities of the co-producer; perceptions of the service itself; and satisfaction with the government's communication, consultation and overall performance. On the first of these, the public administration and wider social science literature point to a variety of motivations as major drivers. These include: a desire to avoid sanctions, economic self-interest, and various non-material incentives such as intrinsic rewards, social connection and moral values (Thomas 2012; Verschuere et al. 2012; Clary et al. 1996, 1998; Rosentraub and Sharp 1981; Wilson 1973). Co-production is also encouraged by facilitators that make it easier to do, such as task-simplification or information and training (Thomas 2012; Verschuere et al. 2012). These two sets of factors – willingness to co-produce and ability to do so – have been the central focus of case analysis and theorising about people's propensity to co-produce (Verschuere et al. 2012; Alford 2002, 2009). No single factor accounts for this phenomenon; rather it is the specific mix of them that is important in each situation.

One way that some of the research encapsulates aspects of motivation and facilitation in a single construct is to focus on citizen self-efficacy, that is, 'the feeling that individual political action does have, or can have, an impact upon the political process' (Campbell, Gurin, and Miller 1954: 187). The EU study found this to be one of the two major factors associated with willingness to undertake individual coproduction, with a regression weight of 0.22, while the other factor was age (0.24). Other lesser factors were: female respondents (0.13) are more inclined; and satisfaction with government information (0.11) also prompts individual co-production. On the other hand, those supporting individual co-production had a negative satisfaction rate (–0.10) with the performance of government overall. By contrast, the only substantial driver of collective co-production was efficacy (0.28).

Thus efficacy, with its basis in sense of competency and also intrinsic and social motivations, seems to be of signal importance. A further layer of understanding may come from the emergence recently of behavioural economics (Kahneman 2011) as well as the related and increasingly popular notion of 'nudge' (Thaler and Sunstein 2008). If people's propensity to co-produce (or indeed take any action) is largely a function of their willingness and ability to do so, then the way in which motivators and facilitators are framed will affect their actions in important ways.

Conclusions

Co-production seems to be here to stay. Governments around the world are designing and implementing service reform measures that owe a lot to co-production ideas, and research in the field is approaching maturity, with a bedrock of theory, likely to be fuelled by the emergence of more empirical research.

This will have implications for important aspects of our social, economic and political life. By activating citizens to engage more with the work of the public sector, it has the potential to increase popular trust in government and help develop social capital (Fledderus et al. 2014). As a corollary, it may enhance the political influence of ordinary citizens, as well as improve the workings of public services. On the other hand, each of these potential consequences could be negated or over-shadowed by shortcomings in political systems, service capabilities or unsustainability.

In the public sector itself, the spread of co-production will amend the role of public servants and their managers consistently with other governmental reforms: in addition to or even instead of their task of delivering services, they will partly have the job of inducing citizens and clients to contribute to service delivery. Given that these actors are external to the organisation, and therefore outside public managers' command authority, this task will call for the ability to influence, encourage and negotiate rather than to give orders – which in itself may be an additional benefit of co-production. Thus changes in the roles of members of the public may also generate change in the public service, for which it will need to develop increasing capability.

References

Alford, J. 2009. *Engaging Public Sector Clients: From Service Delivery to Co-Production.* London: Palgrave.

Alford, J. 2002. "Defining the client in the public sector: A social exchange perspective." *Public Administration Review* 62 (3): 337–346.

Alford, J. and J. O'Flynn. 2012. *Rethinking Public Service Delivery: Managing with External Providers.* Basingstoke: Palgrave Macmillan.

Ayres, I. and J. Braithwaite. 2002. *Responsive Regulation: Transcending the Deregulation Debate.* New York: Oxford University Press.

Barrett, P. 2009. "Customers versus citizens – does the language matter?" *Public Money & Management* 29 (2): 81–83.

Boston, J. 1996. "Origins and destinations: New Zealand's model of public management and the international transfer of ideas." In *Reshaping the State: New Zealand's Bureaucratic Revolution*, edited by J. Boston, J. Martin, J. Pallot, and P. Walsh. Auckland: Oxford University Press.

Bovaird, T. 2007. "Beyond engagement and participation: user and community coproduction of public services." *Public Administration Review* 67 (5): 846–860.

Bovaird, T., G. van Ryzin, E. Loeffler, and S. Parrado. 2015. "Activating citizens to participate in collective co-production of public services." *Journal of Social Policy* 44 (1): 1–23.

Boyle, D. and M. Harris. 2009. *The Challenge of Co-Production: How Equal Partnerships between Professionals and the Public Are Crucial to Improving Public Services.* London: NESTA.

Campbell, A., G. Gurin, and W. Miller. 1954. *The Voter Decides.* Evanston: Row, Peterson & Co.

Clarke, J., J. Newman, N. Smith, E. Vidler, and L. Westmarland. 2007. *Creating Citizen-Consumers: Changing Publics and Changing Public Services.* London: Sage.

Clary, E., M. Snyder, and A. Stukas. 1996. "Volunteers' motivations: Findings from a national survey." *Nonprofit and Voluntary Sector Quarterly* 25 (4): 485–505.

Clary, E., M. Snyder, R. Ridge, J. Copeland, A. Stukas, et al. 1998. "Understanding and assessing the motivations of volunteers: A functional approach." *Journal of Personality and Social Psychology* 74 (6): 1516–1530.

Ekeh, P. 1974. *Social Exchange Theory: The Two Traditions.* Cambridge, MA: Harvard University Press.

Fledderus, J., T. Brandsen, and M. Honingh. 2014. "Restoring trust through the coproduction of public services: A theoretical elaboration." *Public Management Review* 16 (3): 424–443.

Fountain, J. 2001. "Paradoxes of public sector customer service." *Governance* 14 (1): 55–73.

Kahneman, D. 2011. *Thinking, Fast and Slow.* London: Penguin Books.

Levi-Strauss, C. 1969. *The Elementary Structure of Kinship.* Boston: Beacon Press.

Loeffler, E., S. Parrado, T. Bovaird, and G. Van Ryzin. 2008. *"If You Want to Go Fast, Walk Alone. If You Want to Go Far, Walk Together": Citizens and the Co-production of Public Services.* Paris: French Ministry of the Treasury, Public Accounts and Civil Service, on behalf of the Presidency of the EU.

Moore, M. 1995. *Creating Public Value: Strategic Management in Government.* Cambridge, MA: Harvard University Press.

Osborne, D. and T. Gaebler. 1992. *Reinventing Government: How the Entrepreneurial Spirit is Transforming the Public Sector.* New York: Plume.

Ostrom, E. 1996. "Crossing the Great Divide: Coproduction, Synergy, and Development." *World Development* 24 (6): 1073–1087.

Parks, R., P. Baker, L. Kiser, R. Oakerson, E. Ostrom, et al. 1981. "Consumers as Coproducers of Public Services: Some Economic and Institutional Considerations." *Policy Studies Journal* 9 (7): 1001–1011.

Parrado, S., G. Van Ryzin, T. Bovaird, and E. Loeffler. 2013. "Correlates of Co-Production: Evidence from a Five-Nation Survey of Citizens." *International Public Management Journal* 16(1):85–112.

Pollitt, C. 1990. *Managerialism and the Public Services: The Anglo-American Experience.* Oxford: Oxford University Press.

Pollitt, C. and G. Bouckaert. 2000. *Public Management Reform: A Comparative Analysis.* Oxford: Oxford University Press.

Rosentraub, M. and E. Sharp. 1981. "Consumers as producers of social services: coproduction and the level of social services." *Southern Review of Public Administration* 4: 502–539.

Sharp, E. 1980. "Towards a New Understanding of Urban Services and Citizen Participation: The Co-production Concept", *Midwest Review of Public Administration* 14 (2): 105–118.

Thaler, R. and C. Sunstein. 2008. *Nudge: Improving Decisions about Health, Wealth, and Happiness.* New Haven: Yale University Press.

Thomas, J. 2012. "Citizen, customer, partner: Rethinking the place of the public in public management." *Public Administration Review* 73 (6): 786–796.

Titmuss, R. 1970. *The Gift Relationship: From Human Blood to Social Policy.* London: Allen and Unwin.

van Eijk, C., and T. Steen. 2014. "Why people co-produce: Analysing citizens' perceptions on co-planning engagement in health care services." *Public Management Review* 16 (3): 358–382.

Verschuere, B., T. Brandsen, and V. Pestoff. 2012. "Co-Production: The State of the Art in Research and the Future Agenda." *Voluntas* 23 (4): 1083–1101.

Whitaker, G. 1980. "Co-Production: Citizen Participation in Service Delivery." *Public Administration Review* 40: 240–246.

Wilson, J. 1973. *Political Organization.* New York: Basic Books.

15

DEMOCRACY AND CITIZENS' ENGAGEMENT

Reto Steiner and Claire Kaiser

Introduction

Citizens' expectations regarding public services have risen, and governments around the world face demands to become more citizen-oriented. Citizen engagement is a means of involving citizens in decision making regarding public policies and administration. This development is at least partly rooted in the New Public Management discourse, and governments have increasingly aligned their service provisions with citizens' demands.

Two examples illustrate the types of projects in which citizen engagement has been an important issue. Stuttgart 21 is a railway and urban development project in Southern Germany involving the renewal of the Stuttgart main station. The project has been controversial for years. The local council rejected a petition for a referendum (Bürgerbegehren) against the project in 2007. After the official decision was made to undertake the project, there were protests in which thousands of citizens were involved and that culminated in riots with the police in 2010. Ensuing mediation talks between proponents and opponents resulted in a compromise proposal; a referendum held in 2011 backed the project, and implementation of the project was subsequently begun.

In another example, Singapore faces huge challenges in urban planning due to its high population density. After a long history of top-down urban planning, Singapore is experimenting with different methods of encouraging the participation of its citizens in the planning process (Soh and Yuen 2006). In 2008, the Urban Redevelopment Authority (URA) published its draft Master Plan for public consultation to guide Singapore's land-use development over the medium term using GIS. More than 200,000 people visited the website, and many provided feedback on its urban planning proposals.

These examples highlight the relevance of citizen engagement in the political process globally. They also show that political cultures and processes vary from country to country. As a result, fundamental questions about the relation between the development of democracy and the use of citizen engagement as well as the relationship between democracy and public management are raised. More practical questions relate to the level and the phase of the political process at which citizen engagement is appropriate. Finally, last but not least, governments must address what the opportunities and risks of increased citizen engagement are.

Based on an extensive analysis of the international democratic theory and participation literature, this chapter provides an overview of the state and the development of democracy and citizen engagement from a global perspective. The chapter is structured as follows. Following the definition of the terms 'democracy' and 'citizen engagement', an analytic framework including democracy theory and public management is developed in the subsequent section. The next section examines the democratic governance of a state and its development from a global perspective, while the following explains the relationship between democracy and public management. The chapter then focuses on the development and state of political participation. We examine the possible process of citizen engagement, and highlight the advantages and disadvantages of citizen engagement. In the final section, we draw the main conclusions from the chapter.

Defining 'democracy' and 'citizen engagement'

The manner in which democracy is implemented in countries around the world differs considerably in the same way that democracy has been variously defined by scholars throughout history (Deleon 2007). Aristotle (350 BC, new edition 1987) understood democracy as the 'rule of the poor in their own interests', whereas Schumpeter (1943) defined it as 'that institutional arrangement for arriving at political decisions in which individuals acquire the power to decide by means of a competitive struggle for the people's vote'.

Regarding representative democracy, Schmitter and Karl (1991: 76) posit that '[m]odern political democracy is a system of governance in which rulers are held accountable for their actions in the public realm by citizens, acting indirectly through the competition and cooperation of their elected representatives.' Emphasizing participation, Cohen (1971: 7) defines democracy as 'that system of community government in which [...] the members of a community participate, or may participate, directly or indirectly, in the making of decisions that affect them'.

A distinction is made between indirect and direct democracy. In an indirect democracy – or a representative democracy – the people themselves do not rule but instead elect representatives to rule (Sartori 1992: 122). Direct democracy may be understood as people's rights, the exercise of such rights or single-item referenda put to a popular vote (Linder 2005: 242). The entire political decision-making system – including government, parliament and citizens – is typically referred to as semi-direct democracy. These different understandings of democracy share the notion that the people should be the basis of government and that they should have some means of influencing the political decision-making process (Deleon 2007). The democratic style of decision making contrasts with the autocratic decision-making style, in which one individual decides without consulting others (Denhardt and Baker 2007).

Certain key political institutions are required for democratic governance. Dahl (2005) names six requirements for a democratic country. First, citizens elect officials under a system of representation. Second, the electoral system guarantees free, fair and frequent elections. Third, citizens enjoy freedom of expression without threat of punishment. Fourth, citizens must have access to a wide variety of information and to alternative sources of information, i.e. a free and independent media. Fifth, citizens must have the right to form organizations or associations, such as political parties and interest associations. Finally, citizenship must be inclusive (Dahl 2005: 188 et seq.).

A common understanding of democracy therefore also implies participation by citizens (Parry, Moyser, and Day 1992). There have been many attempts to define political participation: 'Political participation refers to those activities by private citizens that are more or less directly aimed at influencing the selection of government personnel and/or the actions they take'

(Verba and Nie 1987: 2). An alternative formulation focuses on 'actions by ordinary citizens directed toward influencing some political outcome' (Brady 1999: 737).

These and similar definitions have certain essential elements in common. First, they refer to people in their role as citizens and not as politicians or civil servants. Second, participation requires active engagement by citizens, which means that being interested in politics is not the same as being a 'participant'. Third, participation is a rather broad term, involving the entire political system and not only single phases in the decision-making process (van Deth 2003: 170 et seq.). As a rule, political participation is voluntary. It may occur at different levels in the political system. In addition to the national, state and communal levels, it may also occur at a transnational level, such as the European Union (Andersen and Wichard 2003). The institutional framework and openness of the political system determines the degree to which citizens may be involved in the political process (Lowndes et al. 2006: 539). Thus, the terms 'participation' and 'citizen engagement' may be used synonymously.

Analytical framework

Citizen engagement is a concept frequently discussed in the context of participatory democracy theory, as input legitimacy may increase with citizen involvement. The underlying framework for this article depicted in Figure 15.1 therefore embeds the spectrum of citizen engagement (adapted from Sheedy 2008 and IAP2 2015) in the discussion about participatory democracy.

Proponents of theoretical approaches to participatory democracy – such as Rousseau – emphasize the connections and interactions between an individual and governmental authorities and institutions (Pateman 1970: 103). Normative postulates of participatory democracy theory include, for example, that citizen participation is central to democracy (Verba and Nie 1987) and that as many citizens as possible should participate in as much governance as possible (Bertelsmann Stiftung 2004: 20 et seqq.). Some researchers argue in favor of an enlarged circle of participants. They plead for equal opportunities for disadvantaged social groups, such as full political rights for women, adolescents and foreigners. The legitimacy of the political system might be enhanced under this view by maximizing citizen engagement (Kohout 2002: 53). Participatory democracy theory has been criticized for its (overly) optimistic conception of the human being and for overestimating the competency of citizens (Bertelsmann Stiftung 2004: 21).

What is required for citizens to be truly empowered? Public managers can involve citizens along a wide spectrum, with varying levels of public impact. The possible spectrum of citizen engagement ranges from merely informing or consulting citizens to involving them, collaborating with them or truly empowering them and even reimbursing them for participating in the policy- and decision-making processes (Berry, Portney, and Thomson 1989). The level of public impact increases along this line. Informing citizens means providing the public with objective information to understand problems, alternatives and solutions. Consulting citizens entails obtaining feedback from citizens regarding a particular issue. Involving citizens means working with the public throughout the process and thereby ensuring that their concerns are considered. Collaborating means involving citizens in every aspect of the decision-making process, and empowering them by placing the final decision in their hands. Some argue that the first two stages do not qualify as citizen engagement because there is no two-way flow of information between the government and its citizens (Sheedy 2008; IAP2 2015).

This framework is an alternative to the so-called 'ladder of citizen participation', a more differentiated, classical model of participatory democracy theory developed by Arnstein (1969), in which eight steps on a ladder represent different levels of citizen participation. At the lowest level, citizens have no or only slight levels of participation. At the highest level, citizens assume

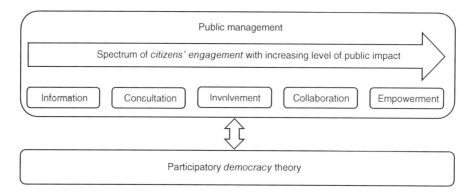

Figure 15.1   Analytical framework of democracy and citizen engagement

active and engaged participatory roles. The different intensities of participation range from 'manipulation' and 'therapy' as instruments of 'non-participation' to 'informing', 'consultation' and 'placation' as symbolic participation acts, to 'partnership', 'delegated power' and 'citizen control' as ways in which citizens can influence public administration (Kersting et al. 2008: 15 et seq.; Callahan 2007: 1138). Notably, citizen participation is not limited to politics but extends to involvement in the economic and social spheres, such as in the private sector or in nonprofit organizations (Deleon 2007). In particular, the concept of co-production, which involves citizens in the delivery of public services (Berry, Portney, and Thomson 1989; Bovaird 2007), is described by John Alford in Chapter 14, "Citizen co-production of public services", of this volume.

Development of 'old' and 'new' democracies in a global perspective

Against the background of different social conditions and paths of development regarding the democratic system and participation issues, it makes sense to distinguish between 'old' and 'new' democracies. In the West today, democracy is almost taken for granted. Among scholars, however, there has been skepticism regarding democracy as a concept. The rationality of its inner logic has been questioned (Arrow 1951), and/or it has been denoted as ideological or utopian (Dunn 1979). In developing countries, in particular, democracy has also been criticized for being 'too messy, uncontrolled and prone to manipulation and abuse to provide the stability and continuity needed for sustained social and economic reform' (UNDP 2002: v). Advocates of democratic systems, however, argue that debates on policies promote economic growth and the meeting of social needs (UNDP 2002: v).

Although democratic theory has been scrutinized in the past, interest in it has recently increased mainly because of the rising number of democracies worldwide, such as in sub-Saharan Africa, Asia, Latin America, the former Soviet Union and the Arab states (Shapiro 2003; UNDP 2002). Since the 1980s, over 80 countries have moved toward more democratic systems, and 140 of the nearly 200 countries in the world hold multiparty elections. However, there is currently less optimism about democracy than there was in the last two decades of the twentieth century. It has become clear that 'effective democratic governance is not yet a reality' (UNDP 2002: v). Only 80 countries are fully democratic. Several countries that had taken steps toward democracy have returned to more authoritarian rule (such as Pakistan and Zimbabwe). Some countries remain in a system between democracy and authoritarianism in which politics are dysfunctional and political freedom is limited, whereas other countries have become breeding grounds for violent conflict and extremism (UNDP 2002: 1). Thus, democracy cannot just be 'imported' into a country but is instead shaped based on a country's history and circumstances (UNDP 2002: 4).

There have been different understandings of what constitutes a 'democracy' not only among different countries but also throughout the centuries. Democratic institutions did not emerge simultaneously. The first democratic constitution was established in Athens circa 500 BC (see, for example, Kagan 1991). In the 'old' democracies, the right to elect the legislature was introduced early, i.e. in the thirteenth century in Britain and in the seventeenth and eighteenth centuries in the United States. One of the main differences between current and earlier democracies involves the notion of universal suffrage. For a long time, political engagement was restricted to a minority of male adults. Women gained the right to vote only after the Second World War in a number of otherwise highly democratic countries, such as Belgium, France and Switzerland (Dahl 2005), the latter being one of the most distinct examples of (semi-)direct democracy.

The nature of democracy and its possibilities also varies between different levels of government, i.e. national or local (Deleon 2007). As a result of their size, local governments often have more methods at their disposal to involve citizens than regional or national governments (Peters 1996: 58).

The relationship between public management and democracy

The relationship between democracy and bureaucracy has been a frequent subject of discussion in the literature (Denhardt and Baker 2007; Rouban 2012). The main question typically relates to the legitimacy of public management, i.e. that democratic theory implies that the people are the basis of legitimate power and that there should be a connection between administrators' activities and citizens' preferences (Deleon 2007). Some scholars argue that an administrative body that is not organized democratically is not consistent with the ideas of a democratic society (Cleveland 1920) and that 'a democratic state must be [...] democratically administered' (Levitan 1943: 359). Denhardt (1993) even argues that in a democratic country, a public organization should be an example of a democratically organized workplace. This 'workplace democracy' entails that democratic practices – such as debates, voting and inclusion in decision making – should be applied in the workplace context. The governance literature identifies hierarchies, markets and networks (for the latter, see Chapter 13 by Cepiku on "Collaborative governance" in this volume) as strategies involving coordination between public management and the political system (Deleon 2007; Newman 2001).

There is extensive research on how public management can be democratized, including a selection of various means of achieving this objective (Deleon 2007). Thus, a 'representative bureaucracy' indicates that the composition of the citizenry (with respect to class, ethnicity, gender, etc.) should be reflected in the public staff (Bradbury and Kellough 2011). Such an arrangement entails equal opportunities and implies that policies and actions represent the public interest. As minorities become represented in the political and administrative system, their issues may be more present on the political agenda, but it is also possible that representatives who do not belong to a minority may nonetheless act on behalf of disadvantaged groups (Deleon 2007). A bottom-up approach involves 'street-level bureaucracy' that focuses on the front-line workforce that interacts directly with the clients (Lipsky 1980). A further means of involving citizens in public management is citizen participation, which is the focus of this chapter.

Development and state of political participation from an international perspective

The notion of citizen engagement has a long tradition (Schmitz 1983: 33) in the 'old' democracies: it has previously been the subject of works by Aristotle, Rousseau, de Tocqueville and others (Kohout 2002: 37). For example, nearly 300 years ago, Rousseau claimed that everyone should have equal political participation rights, which would lead to a state in which decisions are made in the public interest (Rousseau 2011). By the end of the 1960s, the term 'political participation' gained in popularity, and demands for more participation opportunities for citizens were made and partially implemented, particularly in contested policy fields in the social and environmental spheres (Bora 2005: 28).

The repertoire of the forms of participation has expanded in the academic community over time. In the 1940s and 1950s, election research mainly focused on voting and participation in election campaigns. By the end of the 1960s, research addressed aspects such as fundraising, group activities, and contacting civil servants and political decision-makers, extending in the 1970s to unconventional participation forms, such as political protests (van Deth 2003: 171 et seqq.; Kersting et al. 2008: 24). At about the same time, student and peace movements had taken root in a variety of countries (Gabriel and Völkl 2008: 273). At the beginning of the 1990s, scholars acknowledged that certain forms of social engagement and membership in organizations may also be considered forms of citizen engagement (van Deth 2003: 174 et seqq.).

With the emphasis on customers and citizens in the (New) Public Management discussion in recent decades, new trends have also emerged in citizen engagement. Since the 1990s, information and communication technology (ICT) has gained significance in this respect. ICT can enable citizen engagement by creating flows of information from government to citizen as well as from citizen to government (Bailur and Gigler 2014). ICT can help reduce the distance between government and citizens, cutting across time and space with the potential to increase the number of participants. Web 2.0 has opened up additional possibilities for new forms of participation (such as internet-based citizen surveys) and by enabling the formation of communities such as Facebook and web-based forums, which facilitate reciprocity and discursivity, although most governments have not yet realized the full potential of these developments (Sheedy 2008).

Although employing ICT for surveys is already quite widespread, a few governments have begun to use ICT techniques to encourage citizen participation. In addition to informing the public, ICT tools allow public reporting, for example, whereby citizens can report crimes, such as graffiti, littering or damage to public property, by pinpointing the incident on an online map provided by (local) government. Thus, using the ICT tool "Züri wie neu" (Zurich like new), which is provided by the city of Zurich, citizens can report damage to the infrastructure of the city of Zurich by describing the damage and locating the incident on a map by simply entering the appropriate address. The city government then repairs the damage and replies using the same ICT tool, which is publicly visible online.

Internet voting for a binding political election was first used in the US in 2000. Subsequently, additional countries have run trials and pilots for e-voting, including Canada, Estonia, France and Switzerland. Electronic voting at the poll site (i.e. non-remote) is more widespread and is employed in Belgium, the Netherlands, the US, Brazil and India (Esteve, Goldsmith, and Turner 2012). In recent years, however, e-government, e-democracy and e-voting have become the subject of debate. Although there is potential for efficiency gains and higher participation rates, the consequences of failure or misuse may be severe (La Porte, Demchak, and Jong 2002; Moynihan 2004).

Citizen engagement has been used in development projects, such as World Bank Group projects (World Bank Group 2014). Key factors for citizen engagement include the country context including the history of civic participation, willingness and capacity. For example, in East and South Asia, citizen participation has long been applied in development projects. Political transitions in certain regions of the Middle East and North Africa have also provided opportunities for citizens to become more involved. Government ownership is important in terms of sustaining citizen involvement in processes beyond the duration of the development project. Furthermore, clear goals are a success factor in citizen involvement processes. Including women and vulnerable groups is important to ensure stakeholder representation. In 'new' democracies, however, concerns have been raised regarding citizen participation, and it has been argued that merely establishing democratic institutions is not sufficient because people must trust these institutions to engage in the political process, or democracy will 'end up being no more than an empty shell' (Krishna 2002: 437).

The citizen engagement process

The process of citizen engagement may be divided into three main phases: preparation, process design and implementation (Sheedy 2008, see Figure 15.2). The first phase, i.e. the preparation phase, establishes whether citizen engagement is the right strategy for the envisaged policy process. If so, the goals are determined and the requirements such as resources, capacity and timing are assessed. In the second phase, the process is designed and planned. The roles and responsibilities in the process must be considered, such as that of the facilitator, who is a key success factor in the process. The issue then must be framed in such a way that the public at large is able to participate, such as by using accessible language that welcomes participation. For example, people are recruited to participate in an event, whether through an open or selective invitation. As for logistics, the time and place must be fixed.

The appropriate technique reflecting the policy issue and goals must be selected, also considering ICT tools. Necessary background information should be provided to the citizens in advance. Analysis and evaluation of citizen involvement and its outcomes (contributions and decisions) is a crucial part of the process, as well as of the feedback loop, i.e. reporting to the participants and decision-makers. Thus, these elements should be planned ahead. The third phase is implementing the designed citizen involvement process (Sheedy 2008).

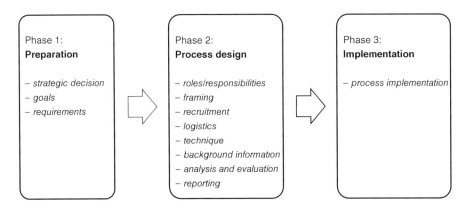

Figure 15.2 The process of citizen engagement

Opportunities and risks of citizen engagement

Involving citizens in the democratic decision-making process is a much-discussed issue in many countries (OECD 2001). Citizen engagement is frequently intended to produce better decisions and more efficient outcomes for society (Irvin and Stansbury 2004; Thomas 1995). However, is it worth the effort? This question is discussed here on the basis of a review of the literature regarding the opportunities and risks of citizen participation (Steiner and Kaiser 2012).

Strengthening the input legitimacy of a political system is one main argument in favor of citizen engagement (Scharpf 1999; Haus and Heinelt 2005: 35). Political decisions are legitimate when they correspond to the will of the citizens because decisions made by a democratic sovereign, i.e. the people, are often widely accepted. The public is typically involved to gain approval, which is a prerequisite for successful implementation (Thomas 1995: 113). Benefits also arise from incorporating multiple perspectives (Denhardt and Baker 2007). By regularly contacting decision-makers and expressing their viewpoint, active citizens can personally try to convince the key actors. Political persuasion thus works in both directions (Irvin and Stansbury 2004).

Citizen participation may also help break gridlocks in the political process, particularly when political discourse has ground to a halt. By means of workshops, consultations and initiatives, citizens' opinions can help council members (politicians) compromise and find solutions (Irvin and Stansbury 2004). Furthermore, some authors argue that citizen participation can reduce litigation costs (Randolph and Bauer 1999).

Interactions between the state and its citizens (in their role as customers) can enhance customer and citizen satisfaction. For example, feedback from a citizen survey regarding the perceived administrative strengths and weaknesses of the state are important for public administration performance. Transparency about citizens' preferences influences priority setting and the allocation of state resources (Schedler and Proeller 2011: 290).

Last but not least, educational benefits should be considered. Informed and involved citizens are more capable of understanding complex situations and generating holistic solutions. Thus, the quality of political decisions and ultimately the societal benefit are enhanced. Political authorities also benefit from knowing the positions of the citizens when implementing their policies (Irvin and Stansbury 2004).

If citizen participation is such a good idea, 'why do we not see it occur more frequently?' (Moynihan 2003). Despite the above-mentioned benefits, citizen engagement also has its risks and disadvantages, which must be considered when enhancing citizen participation.

Involving citizens in the decision-making process is costly as the result mainly of transaction costs, such as information, coordination and participation costs (Kersting et al. 2008: 15). Although these costs are frequently not assessed, it is assumed that they are higher for a political decision in which citizens are involved or a popular vote is undertaken than for a decision made only in parliament and government (Irvin and Stansbury 2004: 58).

A further challenge to citizen participation is the question of representativeness. The modern understanding of democracy requires inclusive citizenship (Dahl 2005), but the pool of active participants is sometimes arbitrary and not representative (Dahl 1989: 228). As a rule, participants are not paid for their time and work. It can thus be assumed that participants are mainly citizens who are strongly affected by the decision or those living comfortably enough to have free time. Empirical studies confirm that there are inequalities on committees insofar as representation is concerned. Thus, it has been observed that 'participants speak with the accent of highly educated middle-aged male urban-dwellers' (Teorell et al. 2007). Highly complex topics may lead to less participation by lower strata of the population, which again leads to legitimacy deficits (see, for example, Linder 2005: 290). An analysis of participation in local assemblies in Switzerland yields similar results: participants do not accurately reflect the pool of eligible voters (Ladner and Fiechter 2012).

The question of indifferent or disinterested citizens is controversial. Some authors assume that citizens would participate more if they had the opportunity to do so. However, others contend that citizens often refuse to engage in the political decision-making and implementation process. Thus, it has been suggested that citizens should only be involved in the political process when there is a certain level of public interest in the topic.

There is potential tension between empowering citizens and the goals of administrators, e.g. bureaucratic norms (Kweit and Kweit 1980), who are frequently not overly enthusiastic about such participation. The administrative decision-making process is prolonged by including more people, and administrators often argue that inclusion thus conflicts with efficiency (Berry, Portney, and Thomson 1989).

Citizen engagement is time-consuming. Allowing 60 participants in a workshop or assembly to have their say for five minutes each requires a five-hour event. Conversely, at a municipal assembly only a few will actively participate with a request to speak, whereas the majority will listen, follow the argument and eventually vote (Dahl 1989: 227).

Defining the appropriate time to involve citizens is an additional challenge. At which phase of the policy cycle – i.e. at agenda setting, policy formulation, political decision, policy implementation or policy evaluation – is it appropriate to involve citizens (see, for example, Fischer et al. 2007)? Although the interest and personal engagement of citizens increase during ongoing political processes, the possibilities of participating become fewer, a phenomenon known as the so-called participation paradox (Reinert 2003: 37 et seq.). Programs that involve citizens earlier in the process tend to be considered fairer by participants (Mazmanian and Nienaber 1979). In practice, however, efforts to involve citizens often occur too late (Kersting et al. 2008) and have been criticized 'for being largely symbolic in nature' (Berry, Portney, and Thomson 1989: 208).

Conclusions

Citizen participation is often expected to lead to better decisions and more efficient outcomes. Repeatedly, demands have been made for more citizen participation. The normative postulate of 'more is better', however, is questionable. In addition to the advantages of political participation in strengthening input legitimacy, this chapter has also shown its limitations, which derive primarily from its high costs and limited representativeness. Such participation may not even produce 'better' outcomes than decisions made by politicians and administrators (Deleon 2007). Furthermore, it does not directly solve problems like poverty, crime and so forth. Thus, citizen engagement should not be understood as a panacea.

Challenges to citizen participation include low levels of representativeness, high costs, inadequate timing in the policy cycle, burdens to the legislative process, and the non-binding character of many forms of participation, to name just a few (Steiner and Kaiser 2012). Thus, the political system is required to provide the right conditions for citizens to be adequately involved: by paying attention to equal inclusion of all strata of the population, by finding solutions to reduce costs (such as through new technologies), by differentiating in which phase of the policy cycle it is useful to involve citizens, and by creating the legislative prerequisites for different forms of citizen participation.

What of the future global development of democracy and citizen engagement? In closing, we set forth some theses. Fundamental changes in the social contract between the rulers and the ruled had already occurred in the West by the time that democratic systems were established.

While there is increasing acceptance in states such as China and Saudi Arabia that rulers are accountable to the people and must earn their legitimacy, it will nonetheless take time before these states become truly democratic (Mahbubani 2013). With increasing global interconnectedness and possible convergence between countries (Mahbubani 2013), it can be argued that a global civil society might arise and that the ties between the citizens of the world may be strengthened thereby (Linklater 2014), which will likely also have important consequences on the extent and form of citizen engagement at the transnational level.

References

Andersen, Uwe, and Wichard, Woyke. *Handwörterbuch des politischen Systems der Bundesrepublik Deutschland.* Fifth edition. Opladen: Leske+Budrich, 2003.

Aristotle. *Politics.* London: Penguin Classics, 1987.

Arnstein, Sherry R. "A Ladder of Citizen Participation." *Journal of the American Institute of Planners* 35:4 (1969): 216–224.

Arrow, Kenneth J. *Social Choice and Individual Values.* New Haven, CT: Yale University Press, 1951.

Bailur, Savita and Gigler, Björn-Sören. "Introduction: The Potential for Empowerment through ICTs." In *Closing the Feedback Loop. Can Technology Bridge the Accountability Gap?,* edited by Björn-Sören Gigler and Savita Bailur, 1–14. Washington, DC: World Bank, 2014.

Berry, Jeffrey M., Portney, Kent E., and Thomson, Ken. "Empowering and Involving Citizens." In *Handbook of Public Administration,* edited by James L. Perry, 208–221. San Francisco: Jossey-Bass, 1989.

Bertelsmann Stiftung (ed.). *Politische Partizipation in Deutschland. Ergebnisse einer repräsentativen Umfrage.* Bielefeld: Bertelsmann Stiftung, 2004.

Bora, Alfons. "Einleitung 1: 'Partizipation' als politische Inklusionsformel." In *Inklusion und Partizipation – Politische Kommunikation im historischen Wandel,* edited by Christoph Gusy and Heinz-Gerhard Haupt, 15–34. Frankfurt/Main: Campus Verlag, 2005.

Bovaird, Tony. "Beyond Engagement and Participation: User and Community Coproduction of Public Services." *Public Administration Review* 67:5 (2007): 846–860.

Bradbury, Mark and Kellough, J. Edward. "Representative Bureaucracy: Assessing the Evidence on Active Representation." *American Review of Public Administration* 41:2 (2011): 157–167.

Brady, Henry E. "Political Participation." In *Measures of Political Attitudes,* edited by John P. Robinson, Phillip R. Shaver and Lawrence S. Wrightsman, 737–801. San Diego: Academic Press, 1999.

Callahan, Kathe. "Citizen Participation: Models and Methods." *International Journal of Public Administration* 30:11 (2007): 1179–1196.

Cleveland, F. A. *The Budget and Responsible Government.* New York: Macmillan, 1920.

Cohen, Carl. *Democracy.* Athens, GA: University of Georgia Press, 1971.

Dahl, Robert A. "What Political Institutions Does Large-Scale Democracy Require?" *Political Science Quarterly* 120:2 (2005): 187–197.

Dahl, Robert A. *Democracy and its Critics.* New Haven, CT: Yale University Press, 1989.

Deleon, Linda. "Public Management, Democracy, and Politics." In *The Oxford Handbook of Public Management,* edited by Ewan Ferlie, Laurence E. Lynn Jr, and Christopher Pollitt, 103–130. Oxford: Oxford University Press, 2007.

Denhardt, Robert B. *Theories of Public Organizations.* Second edition. Belmont, CA: Wadsworth, 1993.

Denhardt, Robert B. and Baker, David L. "Five Great Issues in Organization Theory." In *Handbook of Public Administration,* edited by Jack Rabin, W. Bartley Hildreth, and Gerald J. Miller, third edition, 121–148. London, New York: Taylor & Francis, 2007.

Dunn, John. *Western Political Theory in the Face of the Future.* Cambridge: Cambridge University Press, 1979.

Esteve, Jordi B., Goldsmith, Ben, and Turner, John. *International Experience with E-Voting – Norwegian E-Vote Project,* Washington: International Foundation for Electoral Systems, 2012.

Fischer, Frank, Miller, Gerald, and Sidney, Mara S. *Handbook of Public Policy Analysis. Theory, Politics, and Methods.* Boca Raton/London/New York: CRC Press, 2007.

Gabriel, Oscar W., and Völkl, Kerstin. "Politische und soziale Partizipation." In *Die EU-Staaten im Vergleich. Strukturen, Prozesse, Politikinhalte* edited by Gabriel, Oscar W. and Sabine Kropp, third edition, 268–298. Wiesbaden: VS Verlag für Sozialwissenschaften, 2008.

Haus, Michael and Heinelt, Hubert. "Neue Formen des Regierens auf der lokalen Ebene." In *Partizipation und Führung in der lokalen Politik* edited by Michael Haus, Hubert Heinelt, Björn Egner and Christine König, 15–76. Baden-Baden: Nomos, 2005.

International Association for Public Participation (IAP2). www.iap2.org, 2015.

Irvin, Renée A. and Stansbury, John. "Citizen Participation in Decision-making: Is it Worth the Effort?" *Public Administration Review* 64:1 (2004): 55–65.

Kagan, Donald. *Pericles of Athens and the Birth of Democracy*. New York: The Free Press, 1991.

Kersting, Norbert. *Politische Beteiligung. Einführung in dialogorientierte Instrumente politscher und gesellschaftlicher Partizipation*. Wiesbaden: VS Verlag für Sozialwissenschaften, 2008.

Kersting, Norbert, Schmitter, Philippe C., and Trechsel, Alexander H. "Die Zukunft der Demokratie." In *Politische Beteiligung. Einführung in dialogorientierte Instrumente politischer und gesellschaftlicher Partizipation*, edited by Norbert Kersting, 40–62. Wiesbaden: VS Verlag für Sozialwissenschaften, 2008.

Kohout, Franz. *Vom Wert der Partizipation. Eine Analyse partizipativ angelegter Entscheidungsfindung in der Umweltpolitik*. Münster/Hamburg/London: LIT Verlag Münster, 2002.

Krishna, Anirudh. "Enhancing Political Participation in Democracies: What is the Role of Social Capital?" *Comparative Political Studies* 35:4 (2002): 437–460.

Kweit, Robert W. and Kweit, Mary Grisez. "Bureaucratic Decision-Making: Impediments to Citizen Participation." *Polity* 12:4 (1980): 647–666.

Ladner, Andreas and Fiechter, Julien. "The Influence of Direct Democracy on Political Interest, Electoral Turnout and Other Forms of Citizens' Participation in Swiss Municipalities." *Local Government Studies* 38:4 (2012): 437–459.

La Porte, Todd M., Demchak, Chris C., and de Jong, Martin. "Democracy and Bureaucracy in the Age of the Web: Empirical Findings and Theoretical Speculations." *Administration & Society* 34:4 (2002): 411–446.

Levitan, D. M. "Political Ends and Administration Means." *Public Administration Review* 3 (1943): 353–359.

Linder, Wolf. *Schweizerische Demokratie. Institutionen, Prozesse, Perspektiven*. Second edition. Bern: Haupt, 2005.

Linklater, Andrew. "Globalization and the Transformation of Political Community." In *The Globalization of World Politics: An Introduction to International Relations* edited by Baylis, John, Smith, Steve, and Owens, Patricia, sixth edition. Oxford: University Press, 2014.

Lipsky, M. *Street-Level Bureaucracy*. New York: Russell Sage Foundation, 1980.

Lowndes, Vivien, Pratchett, Lawrence, and Stoker, Gerry. "Local Political Participation. The Impact of Rules-in-use." *Public Administration* 84:3 (2006): 539–561.

Mahbubani, Kishore. *The Great Convergence: Asia, The West, and the Logic of One World*. New York: PublicAffairs, 2013.

Mazmanian, Daniel A. and Nienaber, Jeanne. *Can Organizations Change? Environmental Protection, Citizen Participation, and the Corps of Engineers*. Washington, DC: Brookings Institution, 1979.

Moynihan, Donald P. "Normative and Instrumental Perspectives on Public Participation." *American Review of Public Administration* 33:2 (2003): 164–188.

Moynihan, Donald P. "Building Secure Elections: E-Voting, Security, and Systems Theory." *Public Administration Review* 64:5 (2004): 515–528.

Newman, J. *Modernising Governance: New Labour, Policy and Society*. London: Sage, 2001.

Organisation for Economic Co-Operation and Development (OECD). *Citizens as Partners: OECD Handbook on Information, Consultation and Public Participation in Policy-Making*. Paris: OECD, 2001.

Parry, Geraint, Moyser, George, and Day, Neil. *Political Participation and Democracy in Britain*. Cambridge: Cambridge University Press, 1992.

Pateman, Carole. *Participation and Democratic Theory*. London: Cambridge University Press, 1970.

Perry, James L. *Handbook of Public Administration*. San Francisco: Jossey-Bass, 1989.

Peters, B. Guy. *The Future of Governing: Four Emerging Models*. Lawrence: University of Kansas Press, 1996.

Randolph, John and Bauer, Michael. "Improving environmental decision-making through collaborative methods." *Policy Studies Review* 16:3–4 (1999): 168–191.

Reinert, Adrian. "Bürger(innen)beteiligung als Teil der lokalen Demokratie. " In *Praxis Bürgerbeteiligung – Ein Methodenhandbuch* edited by Astrid Ley and Ludwig Weitz, Bonn: Stiftung Mitarbeit, 2003.

Rouban, L. "Politicization of the Civil Service." In *The SAGE Handbook of Public Administration*, edited by B. Guy Peters and Jon Pierre, second edition. Los Angeles: SAGE, 340–351. London: Sage, 2012.

Rousseau, Jean-Jacques. *Vom Gesellschaftsvertrag oder Grundsätze des Staatsrechts*, revised edition. Stuttgart: Reclam, 2011.

Sartori, Giovanni. *Demokratietheorie*. Darmstadt: Wissenschaftliche Buchgesellschaft, 1992.

Scharpf, Fritz W. *Regieren in Europa*. Frankfurt a. M.: Campus, 1999.

Schedler, Kuno, and Proeller, Isabella. *New Public Management*, fifth edition. Bern: Haupt, 2011.

Schmitter, Philippe C., and Karl, Terry Lynn. "What Democracy Is … and Is Not." *Journal of Democracy* 2:3 (1991): 75–88.

Schmitz, Matthias. "Partizipation. Überlegungen zu einer historischen Rekonstruktion des Begriffs." In *Bürgerbeteiligung und kommunale Demokratie* edited by Oscar W. Gabriel, 9–56. München: Minerva Publikation, 1983.

Schumpeter, J. *Capitalism, Socialism and Democracy*. London: George Allen and Unwin, 1943.

Shapiro, Ian. *The State of Democratic Theory*. Princeton: Princeton University Press, 2003.

Sheedy, Amanda. *Handbook on Citizens Engagement: Beyond Consultation*. Canadian Policy Research Networks, 2008.

Soh, Emily Y., and Yuen, Belinda. "Government-aided participation in planning Singapore." *Cities* 23:1 (2006): 30–43.

Steiner, Reto, and Kaiser, Claire. "Herausforderungen der Bürgerbeteiligung." In *Zukunftsfähige Verwaltung? Herausforderungen und Lösungsstrategien in Deutschland, Österreich und der Schweiz*, edited by Eckhardt Schröter, Patrick von Maravic, and Jörg Röber, 187–205. Opladen/Berlin/Toronto: Verlag Barbara Budrich, 2012.

Teorell, Jan, Sum, Paul, and Tobiason, Mette. "Participation and Political Equality. An Assessment of Large-Scale Democracy." In *Citizenship and Involvement in European Democracies. A Comparative Analysis* edited by Jan W. Van Deth, José R. Montero, and Anders Westholm, 384–414. New York/London: Routledge, 2007.

Thomas, John Clayton. *Public Participation in Public Decisions*. San Franscisco, CA: Jossey-Bass, 1995.

United Nations Development Programme (UNDP). *Human Development Report 2002. Deepening Democracy in a Fragmented World*. New York, Oxford: Oxford University Press, 2002.

Van Deth, Jan W. "Vergleichende politische Partizipationsforschung." In *Vergleichende Politikwissenschaft. Ein einführendes Studienhandbuch*, edited by Dirk Berg-Schlosser and Ferdinand Müller-Rommel, 167–187. Forth edition. Opladen: VS Verlag für Sozialwissenschaften, 2003.

Van Deth, Jan W., Montero, José R., and Westholm, Anders. *Citizenship and Involvement in European Democracies. A Comparative Analysis*. New York/London: Routledge, 2007.

Verba, Sidney and Nie, Normann H. *Participation in America: Political Democracy and Social Equality*. New York/Chicago/London: University of Chicago Press, 1987.

World Bank Group. *Strategic Framework for Mainstreaming Citizen Engagement in World Bank Group Operations*. Washington, DC: World Bank, 2014.

16

THE PUBLIC POLICY CONTEXT FOR RISK GOVERNANCE AND SOCIAL INNOVATION

Sarah-Sophie Flemig and Stephen Osborne

Introduction

Innovation is an imperative of public policy. In a time of resource-constrained governments, the innovation of public services has become a sine qua non of keeping up with society's needs. Yet little attention has been given to its flipside: taking risks. More generally, risk, and how to manage it, has become a central theme of the social sciences: see, for instance, Taylor-Gooby and Zinn's (2006) edited collection of social science writing on risk. Firmly grounded in the actuarial sciences and engineering, social science scholars have acknowledged the importance of how risk is perceived, constructed and managed. This ranges from classical financial risk management to the fields of public health, disaster studies, sociology, social policy, political science and the health and safety studies (Taylor-Gooby and Zinn 2006). In this chapter, we will narrow our focus to the relationship between risk and social innovation in a public policy context.

Innovation and risk taking are inextricably linked. Public policy is no exception in this regard. As Hartley (2013) aptly states, "[i]nnovation, by definition, is uncertain in both process and outcome". Tidd and Bessant (2009) estimate that about 45 per cent of innovation projects in the private sector fail while over 50 per cent exceed their initial budget and/or timeline. Numbers in the public sector are likely to be similar but empirical evidence is rare. Yet, it remains a common notion that the public sector is inherently risk averse[1] (Patterson et al. 2009; Jayasuriya 2004), while governments demand increasingly more risky innovation (e.g. DIUS 2008). In the light of current economic rigors and media scrutiny of any form of public policy (Patterson et al. 2009), an aversion to risk does not seem surprising.

Despite this, even those who claim to acknowledge the connection between risk and social innovation have little to say about how to balance risk and innovation. London-based think tank National Endowment for Science, Technology and the Arts (NESTA, for instance, dedicates a single line to the question of risk in public service innovation, acknowledging that it is – indeed – "important" (NESTA 2013).

This chapter on the nexus of risk and social innovation in public policy critically reviews the literature on the current state of knowledge. In the subsequent sections, we introduce two key propositions based on a differentiated treatment of risk: we distinguish between the effects of risk and uncertainty and highlight the role of reputational risk for public policy innovation. Based on these propositions, we suggest a holistic model of risk management and social innovation in public policy contexts.

Defining risk and social innovation

Featuring widely across the academic literature – as well as common parlance – both "risk" and "innovation" are terms with many meanings. This is itself problematic and leads to a lack of definitional clarity. For sociologists, risk is studied as a social construct (e.g. Green 1997; Green 1999; Zinn 2008a; Zinn 2008b), while financial management scholars mainly focus on actuarial risks defined in monetary terms (e.g. Andreeva et al. 2014).

Our focus is a public policy context for both scholars and practitioners. For this purpose, we adopt Brown and Osborne's (2013) preferred definition of innovation as "the intentional introduction and application within a role, group or organization of ideas, processes, products or procedures, new to the relevant unit of adoption, designed to significantly benefit the individual, the group organization or wider society" (West and Farr 1990: 3). As such, innovation is not synonymous with any change process. Rather, it is "a distinctive category of discontinuous change that offers special challenges to policymakers and service managers alike" (Brown and Osborne 2013: 188).

Such innovation in public policy can furthermore be categorized into evolutionary innovation, expansionary innovation, and total innovation (Brown and Osborne 2013: 198). Evolutionary innovation denotes new skills or capacities that are used to address an existing need; expansionary innovation describes new needs that are being addressed by existing policies, skills or capacities. Finally, total innovation stands for a new need being addressed by new skills or capacities (Brown and Osborne 2013: 199).

On the risk management side, Brown and Osborne differentiate between three different approaches: technocratic risk management, decisionistic risk management, and risk governance. While the technocratic risk approach uses traditional risk management tools (e.g. top-down financial/actuarial risk management, health and safety measures, etc.) and focuses on the minimization of all risk, decisionistic risk management adopts a more differentiated view of risk. It incorporates dialogue and seeks to balance expected benefits with the consequences of potential materialised risk. Finally, transparent risk governance encompasses a dialogue across stakeholder groups to identify a socially optimally (and mandated) level of risk for any given social innovation.

Brown and Osborne stipulate that technocratic risk management provides a framework for evolutionary innovation, while decisionistic risk management can accommodate evolutionary and expansionary innovation. Transparent risk governance, on the other hand, provides the most comprehensive framework that also allows for total innovation.

Furthermore, Brown and Osborne suggest that risk can be conceptualized on three different levels (the "locus of risk"): consequential risk at the level of the individual, organizational risk on the level of the organization and its staff, and behavioral risk at the level of the wider community and environment. This matches Renn's (2008) differentiation between three approaches to risk: technocratic risk management, decisionistic risk management, and transparent risk governance.

Technocratic risk management is based on the minimization of risk through expert decision-making. Risk, in this view, can be defined objectively and minimized through scientific evidence (Brown and Osborne 2013: 197). However, Renn (2008) points out the shortcomings of technocratic risk management, which are based in the bounded rationality of all human decision-making and the fact that acceptable risk is more often socially constructed than it is objectively defined.

Decisionistic risk management extends technocratic risk management by including the possibility of discourse about the evaluation of identifiable risks into the process. While risk is now vetted in both positive and negative terms, the decision-making authority in Renn's decisionistic risk management is still limited to politicians, excluding a vast number of other stakeholders. This leads to a limited point of view from which to analyze risk (Brown and Osborne 2013: 195).

Finally, Renn's third approach, transparent risk governance, "is the core of a genuine engagement with the nature, perceptions and contested benefits of risk in complex situations" (p. 198). This approach is inclusive of all key stakeholders and transparent in its decision-making, a process that is aided by new Information and Communication Technologies that help to connect stakeholders in public services. Brown and Osborne suggest that this description fits most closely with the risk environment of modern public policy and propose, therefore, that "risk governance, rather than risk minimization or management, is the appropriate framework for understanding and negotiating risk in innovation in public services" (2013: 198). This also fits into the theme of "network-oriented governance relationships" explored by Ramesh and Howlett in Chapter 28 in this handbook.

Current scholarship on risk and social innovation

In this section, we briefly provide an overview of the literature on risk and social innovation. There are five main works relevant to the public policy context, corroborating Brown and Osborne's (2013) findings. These are Lodge (2009), Bhatta (2003), Hood (2002), Vincent (1996), and Harman (1994). Whereas Harman discusses the negative impact of risk management on public sector accountability, Vincent argues that the public eye is closely focused on public sector activities, leading to increased risk management as a means of avoiding blame from other officials and the wider public. Along similar lines, Hood introduces the imagery of risk management as a "blame game". In his account, risk management is about avoiding blame and/ or attributing it to other parties. Lodge, finally, suggests that different "variations in instruments" are necessary to offer effective risk management in the public sector (2009: 399). He also identifies the obsession with regulation to insulate public policies from risk and advocates a more complex system of risk appraisal that moves beyond Hood's observed "blame game".

Bhatta (2003) also acknowledges the gap in empirical knowledge regarding the relationship between risk and innovation in public policy. In particular, he notes that there is a qualitative difference between the public and private sector as far as risk is concerned: the existence of "wicked problems" and the fact that decisions, even when made under conditions of uncertainty, need to live up to the standards of democratic scrutiny rather than being unilateral "executive decisions" (p. 2).[2] "Wicked problems" (Churchman 1967) denote problems that are either very difficult or impossible to solve due to a host of factors, such as competing moral values, interdependencies, lack of information, etc. Public services are particularly prone to such wicked problems because allocation choices do not just result in monetary differences but are attached to public goods such as health or defence. Moreover, media scrutiny has increased rapidly over the last 50 years, and public service organizations have had to battle numerous scandals of mismanagement and service failure.

This means that success – unlike in the private sector – cannot be judged "on average": even if the majority of a public organization's service decisions turn out to be beneficial and successful, there is still little tolerance for any sort of even occasional failure. This leads to "playing safe" behavior and "incremental pluralistic policy formation that enables the policies to move forward but only marginally at a time" (Bhatta 2003: 6). Bhatta concludes that, if innovation in the sense set out in this paper is truly to happen, we must learn more about the factors that influence public service managers' risk appetite. He suggests different institutional, contextual and political variables that could be explored in this context (p. 9).

So what distinguishes risk and social innovation in the context of public policy from other social sciences? The aforementioned literature suggests two main factors: reputation and accountability. As Hood illustrates, public accountability among different policy-makers increases the importance of reputation, trying to minimize blame and maximize praise. In addition to more traditional forms of risk, such as financial/actuarial risks and health and safety risks, there is thus a strong *reputational risk* element in public policy-making that we will focus on in the following section.

Reputational risk, public accountability and social innovation

Because of the importance of reputational risk and public accountability, innovation in the public policy context requires a framework of risk management that goes beyond the traditional models. In this section, we explore the underlying assumptions that shape such a framework. Does the public policy context differ from, for example, innovation in the private sector? If so, how? Most importantly, how can we address reputational risk?

First, there is an assumption that risk aversion dominates the public sector (Borins 2014). However, there is more to the story. Bozeman and Kingsley (1998), for instance, challenge this assumption. Their study finds "very little evidence of the *incidence* of risk aversion or that the incidence is greater in the public than in the private sector" (p. 116). Instead, they identify three factors as indicative of the risk approach taken by *any* organization: (1) the more trust employees feel they have from their superiors, the more calculated risks they are willing to take; (2) clarity of goals also leads to a more open risk approach; and (3) the more formalism and red tape that exists, the more risk averse an organization's culture is. Thus, factors such as size and management style seem to be more indicative of an organization's risk management approach than the differentiation between public and private sectors. Hartley (2013) confirms this by comparing public and private features of innovation, indicating that an organization's size and maturity, in particular, may account for differences in innovation behavior.

Second, the literature links reputational risk and the need for accountability in public policy innovation to transparency. Hartley (2013) points out that the public sector can learn from the private sector as regards decision-making processes. For instance, she suggests that public sector organizations adapt traditional management tools such as constructive challenge meetings or competitor analysis (p. 53). However, Hartley notes that accountability differs markedly from the private to the public sector. The democratic values on which public policies are based demand a high degree of transparency at all stages of innovation, meaning that public policy is made in "the full glare of media publicity" (p. 54).

This ties in with Hood's model of the blame game, which dominates the public policy literature on risk and its possible nexus to innovation. As described beforehand, the blame game affects risk management at all stages of the policy process. Because public scrutiny and the potential cost of being associated with a failure are high, there is an incentive for those with decision-making powers (on an individual and organizational level) to shift risks to other stakeholders within their policy network.

Hood and Rothstein (2000) further elaborate that reputational risk is associated with risks to third parties and to the service providers themselves (p. 1). Therefore, they criticize the one-size-fits-all approach that has been adopted across the public sector. As in the private sector, Hood and Rothstein argue that public policy-makers need to adapt their risk management strategies to specific types of risk at different points of the policy process, such as, for example, agenda setting, policy creation and policy implementation, in order to reach similar levels of innovation and efficiency. In their view, this can be achieved through a systemic approach to risk management, based on open and extensive deliberation and communication across and not just within policy domains, similar to Brown and Osborne's transparent risk governance.

Feller's (1981) concept of "public-sector innovation as 'conspicuous production'" aligns with both Hartley's and Hood's findings. He argues that the qualitative context of public policy requires policy-makers to use innovation as a proxy measure of actual performance. Innovation thus becomes "conspicuous production", with blame or praise attributed to failing or successful innovators. Given the negative cost associated with failure, individual public policy-makers therefore often require an additional incentive to innovate such as reward schemes or innovation prizes (Borins 2014).

Two propositions

Based on the insights from the previous sections, we now introduce two propositions that will help us formulate a specific public policy framework for risk and social innovation. This model will be discussed in the final section.

> Proposition 1: Risk management approaches should differentiation between risk and uncertainty and their potential effects on innovation.

There is a difference between the effects of risk in the classical sense, i.e. potential risks that are known *a priori,* and uncertainty, i.e. unquantifiable risk that can only be recognized a posteriori.[3] As mentioned in the previous section, these two types of risk are likely to have different, and probably even conflicting, influences on social innovation. Therefore, we propose that they require different risk management approaches when it comes to spurring innovation in public policy. The underlying reasoning is as follows: known risks can be assumed to drive innovation in so far as they provide the opportunity to find new ways of harnessing these known risks: for example, new waste management techniques in environmental sustainability, new medication in mental health treatment, etc. Thus, known risks most likely spur expansionary innovation.

At the same time, these known risks may also be barriers to innovation, namely through regulatory and contracting specifications that they invite. Statutory bodies initially bear responsibility for all service risks, which they then selectively transfer to service providers if necessary. Quantifiable risks are often addressed through extensive regulation and other attempts to control and minimize risk. In service contracts, this is likely to lead to a decreased potential for innovation, as it may be in breach of contract despite bringing a net benefit for all parties involved.

Uncertainty, on the other hand, can spur innovation by way of sudden shocks. Since uncertainty is unquantifiable and cannot be known ex ante, the innovation it can potentially spur is likely to be of a spontaneous nature and not planned. At the same time, as findings from the private sector suggest, environments and organizations that are prone to high levels of uncertainty will be perceived as riskier overall and there may be a decreased willingness for innovation or, in fact, any change that deviates from the status quo (Bozeman and Kingsley 1998; Mack 1971). In this case, the approaches described by Palermo (2014) and Andreeva et al. (2014) on informal and more extensive communication networks across the entire organization provide strategies for PSOs to manage uncertainty. Uncertainty can thus only be managed through an organizational culture open to constant change. Innovation spurred by uncertainty is therefore likely to be total, encompassing new skills and new needs to be addressed. This follows the reasoning of Peters (1989), who suggested that organizations will need to proactively manage chaos (similarly defined as uncertainty) and channel its driver for constant innovation in order to succeed.

> Proposition 2: Risk management needs to consciously differentiate between "hard" and "soft" approaches to risk management in order to spur social innovation in public policy.

The main risk management tool in public policy described in the aforementioned literature is regulation at a high level (Hood 2002). Risk management thus follows a top-down direction. We suggest that tools such as regulation and rules can be summarized as "hard" risk management. It encompasses technocratic and rule/regulation-driven risk management set at a higher policy level. Standards of behavior are set and guide actions at the implementing organizations. This provides a higher level of standardization in how risks are managed, but also leaves little to no room for personal decisions and risk evaluations at implementation level.

In contrast, "soft" risk management tools refer to Renn's (2008) risk governance approaches, based on the communication strategies and the adaptation of organizational culture also recommended by other authors (Andreeva et al. 2014; Hood 2002; Hood and Rothstein 2000; Bozeman and Kingsley 1998). Here, risk management decisions are delegated to the lowest possible level, sometimes even line managers of frontline staff, with regular communication on an individual and team basis. An example is social care, where assessments regarding the suitability of service users for home care are conducted by frontline social workers. Guidelines are set at a decentralized level, although they may follow a broader national policy standard, which is monitored by a regulator or auditor. The goal of soft risk management tools is to create a pervasive culture of risk governance, in which individuals have a joint responsibility for finding the appropriate measure to address any particular risk. This can result in autonomous evaluations that are tailored to individual scenarios. This creates an opportunity to formulate and adopt social innovation. However, the necessary dilution of direct responsibility can also mean that individuals may play the "blame game" at a lower level. Table 16.1 summarizes this proposition.

Table 16.1 Hard and soft risk management approaches

Type of Risk Management	Technocratic Risk Management	Decisionistic Risk Management	Risk Governance
Hard	Actuarial Risk Minimization	Regulation/Rules	–
Soft	–	Delegation of Risk Management across Organizations	Communication and Deliberation

Conclusion: a public policy framework for risk and social innovation

Policy-makers never face only one type of risk in isolation. Rather, they must address risk and uncertainty constantly and simultaneously. For instance, there may be known risks for service users in care homes, such as their frailty and specific patient history. At the same time, there may be uncertainty about future funding for a new service, such as the cooperation between a care home with a primary school through a befriending initiative.

The holistic framework we propose in Table 16.2 points to the most appropriate risk management approaches given a known risk or an uncertain situation. It also provides an insight on the kind of innovation that is most likely to succeed, given the particular combination of risk type and risk management approach.

Hard risk management tools are best suited to manage known risks and provide the possibility for evolutionary innovation. Given their managerial focus, these risk management tools are more suited for top-down innovation as their structural framework is too rigid for grassroots innovation. This is not necessarily negative: the regulation of the medical and healthcare professions, for instance, requires governmentally set guidelines for quality standards (e.g. Flemig 2015). Innovation in these fields consequently follows the same top-down mechanisms. When applied to uncertainty, however, hard risk management tools are likely to stifle social innovation. Since uncertainty cannot be specified a priori, hard risk management approaches are, as Mack (1971) argued, likely to deter policy-makers from adopting innovative alternatives in favor of traditional options, such as top-down regulations.

For known risks, this may mean that risk management at lower levels of the organization, i.e. the frontline staff and their immediate managers, may be more appropriate, as long as a minimal framework of standards is set. Both innovation and risk management are bottom-up in this case: with the power to address risk more fully at this grassroots stage, frontline staff can react more directly to new service user needs. Thus, soft risk management approaches are likely to result in expansionary innovation in the case of known risks. However, as Andreeva et al. (2014) caution, this diffusion of responsibility may also backfire and lead to a "blame game" as defined by Hood (2002) when it comes to public accountability for the implementation of a policy.

Finally, soft risk management approaches are suggested to manage uncertainty, leading to an organizational culture that "thrives on chaos" (Peters 1989) and invites total innovation. This is dependent on a successful system of communication and joint decision-making across the implementing organization (Palermo 2014).

Thus, efficient risk governance in public policy that encourages social innovation is multifaceted and highly complex. It requires regulatory foresight and a shift in both policy and organizational culture: risk should no longer be seen from a strict actuarial, technocratic point of view that seeks to minimize it at all cost. Rather, risk should be actively considered as variable in social innovation. This requires further structural considerations: In Chapter 28,

Table 16.2 A public policy framework for risk and social innovation

Type of Risk/ Risk Management Approach	Risk	Uncertainty
Hard risk management	Evolutionary Innovation (top-down risk management)	Stagnation (minimization approach)
Soft risk management	Expansionary Innovation (bottom-up management, incentives)	Total Innovation ("Thriving on Chaos")

Ramesh and Howlett, for instance, suggest that different types of non-hierarchical governance structures have specific capacity requirements, while Bovaird and Quirk (Chapter 23) discuss resilience as tolerance for failure and a move away from risk avoidance. Individual incentives should be adjusted accordingly to foster a climate of innovation among policy-makers and implementing staff. Frequent and extensive inter- and intra-organizational communication and a diversification of responsibility emerge as the best tools in addressing public policy risks, in particular when it comes to reputational risks.

Notes

1   The UK National Audit Office reports that six in ten public sector managers feared the risk of missing an opportunity to improve service delivery because of a general tendency for risk minimization (National Audit Office 2000: 5).
2   While this is a de facto possibility even in democratic systems, there is always a potential loss of reputation and, at worst, votes that looms as a consequence, even if a decision should prove beneficial overall.
3   For a thorough treatment of risk and uncertainty, see Mack (1971).

References

Andreeva, G., J. Ansell, T, Harrison. 2014. "Governance and Accountability of Public Risk." *Financial Accountability and Management* 30 (3): 342–361.
Bhatta. G. 2003. "Don't Just Do Something, Stand There!" *The Innovation Journal: The Public Sector Innovation Journal* 8 (2): Article 3. www.innovation.cc/scholarly-style/8_2_3_bhatta_innovate-risk.pdf.
Borins, S. 2014. *The Persistence of Innovation in Government.* Washington, DC: Brookings Institution.
Bozeman, B. and G. Kingsley. 1998. "Risk Culture in Public and Private Organizations." *Public Administration Review* 58 (2): 109–118.
Brown, L. and S. P. Osborne. 2013. "Risk and Innovation." *Public Management Review* 15 (2): 186–208.
Churchman, C.W. 1967. "Wicked Problems." *Management Science* 14 (4): B141–B142.
Department for Innovation, Universities and Skills [DIUS]. 2008. *Innovation Nation.* London: HMSO.
Feller, I. 1981. "Public-Sector Innovation as 'Conspicuous Production'." *Policy Analysis* 7 (1): 1–20.
Flemig, S. S. 2015. "A Game of Responsibility? The Regulation of Health and Social Care Professionals." *Public Money and Management* 35 (2): 169–170.
Green, J. 1999. "From Accidents to Risk: Public Health and Preventable Injury." *Health, Risk and Society* 1 (1): 25–39.
Green, J. 1997. "Risk and the Construction of Social Identity: Children's Talk about Accidents." *Sociology of Health & Illness* 19 (4): 457–479.
Harman, E. 1994. "Accountability and Challenges for Australian Governments." *Australian Journal of Political Science* 29 (1): 1–17.
Hartley, J. 2013. "Public and Private Features of Innovation." In *Handbook of Innovation in Public Services,* edited by Osborne, S. P. and L. Brown. Edward Elgar.
Hood, C. 2002. "The Risk Game and the Blame Game." *Government and Opposition* 37 (1): 15–37.
Hood, C. and H. Rothstein. 2000. *Business Risk Management in Government: Pitfalls and Possibilities.* London: National Audit Office.
Jayasuriya, K. 2004. "The New Regulatory State and Relational Capital." *Policy and Politics* 32 (4): 487–501.
Lodge, M. 2009. "The Public Management of Risk: The Case for Deliberating among Worldviews." *Review of Policy Research* 26 (4): 395–408.
Mack, R. P. 1971. *Planning on Uncertainty: Decision Making in Business and Government Administration.* Chichester: Wiley Interscience.
National Audit Office (NAO). 2000. *Supporting Innovation: Managing Risk in Government Departments.* London: Stationary Office.
National Endowment for Science, Technology and the Arts (NESTA), Young Foundation. 2013. *Social Innovation.* London: NESTA.

Palermo, T. 2014. "Accountability and Expertise in Public Sector Risk Management: A Case Study." *Financial Accountability and Management* 30 (3): 322–341.

Patterson, E., M. Kerrin, G. Gatto-Roissard, and P. Coan. 2009. *Everyday Innovation: How to Enhance Innovative Working in Employees and Organizations*. London: Nesta.

Peters, T. J. 1989. *Thriving on Chaos: Handbook for a Management Revolution*. London: Pan.

Renn, O. 2008. *Risk Governance: Coping with Uncertainty in a Complex World*. London: Earthscan.

Taylor-Gooby, P. and J. O. Zinn. 2006. *Risk in Social Science*. Oxford University Press.

Tidd, J. and J. Bessant. 2009. *Managing Innovation*. 4th ed. Chichester: Wiley.

Vincent, J. 1996. "Managing Risk in Public Services: A Review of the International Literature." *International Journal of Public Sector Management* 7 (3): 57–64.

West, M. A. and J. L. Farr. 1990. *Innovation and Creativity at Work: Psychological and Organizational Strategies*. Chichester: Wiley.

Zinn, J. O. 2008a. *Social Theories of Risk and Uncertainty*. Oxford: Blackwell Publishing.

Zinn, J. O. 2008b. "Heading into the Unknown: Everyday Strategies for Managing Risk and Uncertainty." *Health, Risk & Society* 10 (5): 439–450.

17

GOVERNANCE CHANGE ACROSS POLICY SECTORS AND NATIONS

Jenny M. Lewis

Introduction

Governance refers to state–society interactions. The state steers society through control of critical resources and by coordinating interests, rather than through having authority which is based on legal powers (Pierre and Peters 2000; Rhodes 1997; Kooiman 1993). As Treib et al. (2007) argue, governance is seen differently, depending on whether the main concern is one of politics (state actors share power with private actors in networks), polity (a system of rules that shape the actions of social actors), or policy (steering instruments). It is an encompassing term which implies 'every mode of political steering involving public and private actors' (Héritier 2002: 185).

This chapter examines governance change using a comparative approach. Understanding this requires a framework that is capable of producing an analysis of major shifts that can be empirically tracked over time, in different policy sectors and nations. This is a task that requires a concerted effort to avoid generating either a meta-level analysis where the results are too abstract, or an analysis that is swamped by too much detail. A starting point for achieving the desired balance of parsimony and richness is that such an analysis should rest on a comparison of a single or a small number of policy sectors, and one or a small number of nations. Here, a single policy sector is examined for two nations.

Classifying governance change is discussed first, and then a comparative framework for analysis is proposed, which consists of three dimensions. An empirical test of the framework in relation to health policy in Australia and the Netherlands is then provided.

Classifying governance

The encompassing definition of governance noted above signals that its crucial concerns will include institutional properties, actor constellations and policy instruments. What previous typologies and attempts at classification might be useful in describing governance change? The idea of governance change is widely discussed but conceptually ambiguous and often lacking in empirical analysis.

Some recent attempts to create typologies along a number of dimensions are good starting points. Treib et al. (2007) advocated a two step approach to classifying modes of governance.

The first step is to distinguish between a number of polar opposites on each of three dimensions – institutional, political and regulatory. The second step is to combine a limited number of these dimensions to generate a classification. Tollefson et al. (2012) argued that dichotomising the dimensions as per Treib et al. (2007), understates the significance of hybridity within governance structures. Howlett et al. (2009) argued that the inclusion of a hierarchical-plurilateral axis is crucial (tightly controlled state-centric hierarchies or more informal, flexible plurilateral arrangements), and that each of Treib et al's (2007) three dimensions are important. They used a framework that examines where the locus of power/capacity lies on each dimension, and note that they are interrelated: 'institutional structures affect configurations of political power which in turn constrain the choices of types of regulatory tools used in specific circumstances' (Howlett et al. 2009: 386).

Tollefson et al. (2012) proposed a template for understanding governance dynamics, which maps the monocentric-polycentric continuum on one axis and then contrasts this with the level of formality of institutions, the balance of power between state and societal actors (political), and the nature and form of instruments used (regulation). Monocentric governance refers to state-centric, hierarchically organised, legally prescribed and mutually exclusive jurisdictional mandates, while polycentric refers to more decentralised, multi-level, multi-actor modes of governing. Finally, a multi-country, multi-sectoral examination of governance changes utilised the monocentric and polycentric ideal types and the three dimensions outlined above, to assess governance change (Capano et al. 2012). These authors found a remarkable convergence in terms of polycentric governance, but also uncovered substantial divergence due to the political dimension.

A governance change framework

These studies provide some starting points for a comparative examination of governance change. First, it seems that the shift from monocentric to polycentric arrangements is widespread across both countries and policy sectors, and so perhaps is not very interesting in itself. Second, and related to the first point, the political dimension (the balance of power between state and non-state actors) produces analytical purchase on governance arrangements in a comparative sense. Third, it makes sense to view the institutional context as a significant structural constraint, and other dimensions as nested within this, as others have done (see: Tollefson et al. 2012; Howlett et al. 2009). Finally, it is clear from previous attempts to classify governance change that the initial starting points of each country (and not just institutional starting points) matter a great deal. In other words, path dependence is expected to play a part in the story of governance change.

Clearly, policy instruments are central to a consideration of change. They are often regarded as solid entities, like regulation or output-based funding. Christopher Hood's (1983) classic work on the tools of government argues that governments use different mixes and combinations of a relatively small number of generic administrative tools (nodality, authority, treasure and organisation), used in an endless set of permutations. New governing circumstances spark a search for new tools or the application of old tools in different contexts. A sociological approach to policy instruments opens this out. An instrument is a device that is both technical and social, and it shapes social relations between the state and society (Lascoumes and Le Galés 2007). Instruments confront actors with structures of opportunity, which influence how they behave, frame issues and privilege some actors. The effect of this conceptual move is to broaden the view of instruments from concrete tools (e.g. regulation and contracts) to devices that orient relations between state and society. Instruments are then both procedural and symbolic in their impacts.

A further move is to include the realm of ideation, which is often ignored in the literature on governance change. In analysing change across nations in regard to a particular policy sector, examining whether its foundational ideas have been challenged is important for characterising a sector. Each policy sector has a core set of ideas that underpin it, which affect policy development along with the institutional structures within which policymaking occurs and the interest groups that have influence. Hence, paying close attention to the role of ideas helps explain policy change (Béland 2010) and, likewise, governance change.

To assess governance change, this chapter proposes a framework with three interrelated dimensions:

1   Institutions – historical and sociological institutional features of a state's set of governing arrangements.
2   Politics – relations of power between state and non-state actors and how states negotiate and communicate with important actors.
3   Ideation – the dominant ideas underpinning a policy sector which draws boundaries around what is discussed and who has legitimacy.

Health policy

The health policy sector is distinguished from others by its salience with the public (because matters of life and death are involved), its large (and increasing) share of public budgets, and the presence of large and powerful professions. It has tended to develop from fragmented and unstructured beginnings, into densely populated, self-organising systems (Lewis 2005). Governments have increasingly tried to steer the sector as they have become more involved in financing health care, and as those costs have escalated. A major driver of reform in many wealthy nations has been concern about the rising costs of health systems, associated with apparently unlimited demand and ageing populations.

In relation to the three dimensions of the governance change framework, this chapter concentrates on one aspect of each of institutions, politics and ideation as follows: National health insurance is a defining characteristic of any state's health policy (institutions) and is described first. The relationship between the state and the medical profession (politics) is considered second, and models of health and illness (ideation), third. Each of these dimensions are intertwined.

Institutions

Historical institutionalism emphasises the importance of crucial decisions which then become enduring features of the rules of governing in different countries and in particular policy sectors. These then establish the context in which subsequent decisions are made – in other words, they create path dependence. Particular courses of action once begun can be almost impossible to reverse (Pierson 1997). Since policymaking occurs within a set of institutions with particular characteristics, and within a context of previous policy decisions, all new policy is (to some extent) bounded by the legacy of these institutional histories. In regard to health policy, institutional analyses have been convincingly used to explain how different nations have ended up with disparate health care systems (e.g. Immergut 1992), or whether they have introduced national health insurance (Steinmo and Watts 1995; Rosenau 1994).

Australia, as a federation of states and territories, has more dispersed and contested authority than the unitary national system of the Netherlands. It also has a Westminster parliamentary system with two dominant parties, which is quite different to the multi-party coalition governments of the Netherlands, which must work together in order to achieve their objectives. This difference is important in each state's version of national health insurance and how reforms to these have unfolded.

In addition to considering the structure of national government in regard to policy making authority, a classification of welfare state types (Esping–Anderson 1990) is useful for highlighting the difference between Australia (a 'liberal' welfare state, with means-tested assistance and modest transfers to low income citizens) and the Netherlands (a corporatist welfare state type, where the granting of social rights was hardly ever a contested issue). Based on this, the health care system in the Netherlands could be expected to have a greater emphasis on social solidarity.

The period during which national health insurance was introduced also affects the scope and structuring of the resultant system. The Netherlands has had large friendly societies operating since the late 19th century on a voluntary basis, and mandatory insurance for lower income earners since 1941 (Okma 1997). The system in the Netherlands has its origins in the Second World War, well in advance of the idea that the welfare state was facing a fiscal crisis. The failure to establish a National Health Service (NHS) in Australia along the lines of the British service in the postwar period, meant that the universal scheme finally introduced in 1983 was established in the face of growing concern about public budgets (Lewis 2014).

In 2005, with little political debate or public opposition, a new form of health insurance was introduced in the Netherlands. A series of reforms to increase competition between insurers and providers was suggested by the Dekker commission in the 1980s (Okma 1997). These were partially implemented during the 1980s and 1990s, but the system only changed dramatically in 2006. All residents now have to take out basic health insurance with an insurer of their choice and insurers have to accept any applicant. The Dutch health policy discourse has shifted from one that constructs health care as a public good, to one that sees it as a market good (Okma and de Roo 2009). However, while the changes are market inspired, the country has not moved away from its social solidarity principle, with tight regulation, oversight of competition and safeguards for care standards, continuing to ensure equity (Jakubowski et al. 2013; Rosenau and Lako 2008). As one report observed: "The role of the national government has changed from directly steering the system to safeguarding the proper functioning of the health markets" (Schäfer et al. 2010: xix).

This reform also illustrates that in the Netherlands, while changes in political coalitions occur, these do not appear to have much impact on the overall direction of reform. An analysis of Dutch health care reforms from 1987 to 2007 by Okma and de Roo (2009) concluded that, although the governing coalition changed seven times over this period, incoming coalitions either carried on with implementing their predecessors' plans, or at least rarely undid the reforms already undertaken. This includes the survival of the 2006 universal health insurance, after the electoral comeback of the Labor Party in 2007.

In contrast, the Australian system lends itself to policy reversals. The initial universal health insurance scheme, Medibank, had barely been introduced when the Labor Government was dismissed in 1975, and it was effectively abolished by the new conservative government. Just as the population had returned to voluntary health insurance, another Labor Government was elected in 1983, and Medicare – the new universal health insurance scheme – was introduced. Here we can see the contrast between what Klein (1997) describes as two different types of incrementalism – a series of adjustments that result in substantial change in one direction (Dutch), compared to a series of adjustments in different directions that amount to reversals (Australian).

Reforms aligned with changes in national government have continued in Australia, although these have more recently been smaller moves. A deliberate attempt to grow the private sector's involvement occurred during the years of the Howard (conservative) Government from 1996 to 2006, through a raft of changes directed at encouraging private insurance through rebates for all people taking it out (regardless of income). The Rudd (Labor) Government that followed in 2007 introduced an income test on the private health insurance rebate. The main reason for having this insurance (all citizens are still covered by Medicare) is to 'jump the queue' and gain quicker access to non-emergency health care.

A striking difference found in relation to institutions is the different type of incrementalism in the two cases. In addition, while the impetus for reforming health systems in both cases has been cost containment and some adherence to the idea that greater private sector involvement and competition is needed, the implementation of change in the Dutch case continues to reflect the solidarity principle, regardless of the government in power. The Australian approach remains more individualistic and more likely to include policy reversals.

Politics

The state–profession relationship represents the political bargain struck between the state and the medical profession in any country (Giaimo 1995). What better focal point could there be for examining the political dimension of governance change? Kuhlmann and Allsop (2007) introduced a concept of governance which includes national configurations of state–profession relationships and places self-regulation in the context of other forms of governance. Within the health policy process, professional self-regulation is a source of blockage, but this self-regulatory capacity of the medical profession may also act as a buffer, indirectly serving the interests of government by acting as an intermediary institution. In health, policymaking is shaped by the self-governing capacity of the medical profession, which in turn is related to how state institutions such as health insurance are structured.

Professions can be seen as actors in the configuration of institutions that provide the foundations for the policy process, or as interest groups that exert pressure on governments and policy making, or as groups with important expertise and knowledge (Lewis 2005). One important consideration is whether the corporate structure of the professions is more internal or external to the state. In Australia the medical profession has functioned as an external pressure group, as in other Anglo nations, where professions are mainly self-regulating, with powerful professional bodies that formulate and enact their own rules. In many European countries the profession has been much more integrated with the state, particularly in continental Europe (Erichsen 1995; Freidson 1994). In the Netherlands there is a long history of a limited number of associations being granted the legitimacy necessary to be able to pursue their collective self-interests through negotiations with the state (corporatism). In Australia, professions largely developed externally to the state and then functioned as pressure groups, rather than beginning as internal to the state apparatus.

In all countries, governments are tightly coupled to professions. A profession that operates internally with the state has authority by dint of this relationship. A profession that operates externally may have less authority but greater autonomy in health service delivery (Erichsen 1995). It is the *authority* of the corporate elite of a profession, rather than the *autonomy* of individual practitioners, that is of interest here. This refers to the structure of state–profession relationships, how professions talk to government and what level of representation they have in policy making (Lewis 2002).

Over the last four decades, many health policy reforms which have sought to restrict or stop the growth in expenditure on publicly funded services have presented direct or indirect challenges to the ideal of professional control and autonomy by recasting the work of professionals and redefining 'profession'. Freidson (1994) argued that while professions have been through important changes in industrialised nations, professional elites continue to exercise considerable technical, administrative and cultural authority. Larkin (1995) argued that the medicine–state alliance is being displaced by managers as the custodians of cost control and performance measurement. How has this played out in the two nations of interest here?

An analysis of changes in Australia and the Netherlands during the 1990s indicated that, in Australia, new organisations were established which fragmented the profession to some extent (Lewis 2002). A number of challenges to the Australian medical profession have come from governments' insurers and health service delivery organisations in the search for ways to contain costs, but these do not represent a general loss of authority by the profession (Lewis 2014).

In the Netherlands, the state reconfigured its corporatist relationships during the 1990s in order to reduce the number and size of the bodies involved in policymaking and to eliminate stakeholder representation (Okma 1997). This reduced the ability of provider (including professional) interests to intervene at multiple points – as is illustrated by the relatively easy passing of the 2006 Health Insurance Law (Okma and de Roo 2009). However, the Dutch consensual style of policymaking (the Polder Model) has not disappeared and the state–medicine relationship in the Netherlands remains strong. Even after major changes in neo-corporatist structures, the Dutch health insurers, as well as the hospital association and the medical association remain heavily involved (Okma and de Roo 2009).

The manipulation of structures of interest representation by the state, to a greater degree in the Dutch case than in Australia, is clear from this description. This reflects both the more integrated state–profession relationship and broader corporatist structures in the Netherlands, and the more separated position of the profession in Australia.

Ideation

Ideation is used here to refer to a policy paradigm as an overarching set of ideas that specifies how problems are perceived, which goals might be attained and what techniques can be used to reach them (Hall 1989). Individuals with conflicting policy positions still share understandings and a larger reality about the sector they are interested in (Baumgartner and Jones 1993; Schön and Rein 1994). Ideas are important in policy change in three ways (see: Béland 2010). They help define the social and economic issues and problems of the day. They are also important as assumptions (paradigms) that guide the development and selection of policy choices. Finally, they are an important framing device that helps actors legitimise policy decisions.

Struggles over health policy clearly involve ideas about health which support particular actors and shape the range of possible policy options. There is an obvious link between the power of the medical profession and how health is conceived (Lewis 1999). What are the fundamental assumptions about health? The dominant paradigm is biomedicine, which sees the human body as a machine that sometimes breaks down and needs to be fixed. Molecular biology is its scientific basis, leaving no room for the social, psychological and behavioural dimensions of illness (Engel 1977). A generalised enactment of its values, meanings and practices ensures that particular modes of service delivery, patterns of resource allocation and associated relationships of power are recreated and placed beyond challenge (Degeling and Anderson 1992).

A threat to biomedicine as the dominant idea is posed by the social determinants of health approach. This focuses on addressing the social, economic and cultural conditions that produce ill health, and it has been emerging since the 1970s. This casts health as a product of society rather than of individual attributes and behaviours. The World Health Organization (WHO) began calling for a reorientation towards disease prevention and health promotion strategies in the 1970s. A long period of inaction followed until the late 1990s and early 2000s (WHO 2005). Policy in some nations began to emphasise that the multiple influences on health status from the social and environmental context are crucial, with inequities in society contributing significantly to unequal health outcomes (Marmot 1999).

In Australia, there is mostly a reliance on the restoration of health or curative care. Apart from the introduction of community health programmes in Australian in the 1970s, there has been relatively little that suggests a national-level agenda to move away from traditional, biomedical concerns, towards more inclusive and societal based approaches to health policy (Lewis 2014). The national (conservative) government did not embrace a social determinants approach during its time in power from 1996 to 2007, but the following (Labor) Government began to make some tentative steps in this direction. A national preventative health agency was established in 2011 as a partnership of Federal Government, state governments and the private sector (Lewis 2014). But it focused on strengthening individual responsibility for prevention, and critics argued that it did not move towards a collective and community approach to disease prevention (Jakubowski et al. 2013). A stronger sign of a social determinants approach to health was the application of the WHO's framework to the Australian context of 'closing the gap' – an initiative to improve the situation of Indigenous Australians. The current conservative national government, elected in 2013, abolished the national prevention agency and the partnership agreement (Lewis 2014).

In the Netherlands there is scant evidence of discussions about health promotion and the social determinants. While an effective Dutch health plan would include health promotion and at least secondary and tertiary prevention, private health insurers have made little progress in active purchasing, which has been focused on acute hospital services (Stoelwinder 2008). This is likely related to preventive health care being mainly provided by public health services. In addition, disease prevention, health promotion and health protection fall under the municipalities (Schäfer et al. 2010).

In summary, the challenges to biomedicine over the last four decades from the social determinants of health have been muted in both Australia and the Netherlands. There have been some visible attempts at the national level in the Australian case, particularly in relation to Indigenous Australians. The lack of visibility of this in the Dutch case likely reflects that it does not sit easily within a context where social solidarity is still the norm, plus it seems to fall outside national policy in the Netherlands.

Conclusion

The comparative framework for analysing governance changes presented here includes three dimensions, which can be used to assess governance change in comparing across nations – institutions, politics and ideation. Each of these dimensions has been explored using empirical information. This analysis of governance change in health in Australia and the Netherlands over the last four decades demonstrated some interesting and varied shifts in the two nations, both of which have been responding to largely similar narratives about the need to contain health care costs. The changes and different national characteristics are summarised in Table 17.1.

This demonstrates how existing institutions, different political systems and societal traditions strongly shape governance change. Two different versions of incrementalism are neatly illustrated by the case of insurance changes, with the Dutch moving steadily in one direction while Australia oscillates one way and then the other. Changes to the state–profession relationship are stronger in the Dutch than the Australian case, reflecting the more integrated role of the professions. Australia has (sporadically and to a small extent) embraced the need for

Table 17.1 Governance change in two nations

Dimension	Australia	The Netherlands
Institutions (national health insurance)	Multiple changes in different directions *Individualism*	Multiple changes in same direction *Solidarity*
Politics (state-profession relationship)	Little change in professional authority *External to state*	Some reduction in professional authority *Internal to state*
Ideation (foundational model of health)	Small attempts to shift to social determinants *Biomedical*	Little discussion of social determinants *Biomedical*

a social determinants approach to health, while the Netherlands has paid little attention to this, at least at the national level.

Extending this to an analysis of another two federal nations – Canada and Germany – highlights some interesting differences between national federal arrangements, and also some similarities between the two European and the two Anglophone ex-colonial nations: First, the institutional story of health system reform is similar in the Dutch and German cases, with major system reform being achieved in the face of growing concerns about the rising costs of health care, while in Australia more minimal change has occurred and in Canada, there have been no major reforms for decades. Canada's competitive federalism model is more akin to Australia's than to Germany's cooperative federalism, but the federal government lacks a constitutionally recognised role in health care. The story is similar in relation to the political dimension, with the Dutch and German governments effectively using their strong corporatist traditions to rebalance their relations with the medical profession, while little has changed on this front in Australia and Canada. Finally, while there has been discussion about the social determinants of health in both Australia and Canada, particularly in relation to the original indigenous habitants of these two nations, this has been much more muted in the Netherlands and Germany, where the idea of solidarity remains strong and perhaps obviates the need for a greater focus on social equity that is core to a discussion of social determinants.

This suggests one further point about examining governance change around the world. The pressure to reform a particular policy sector is likely to be influenced by transnational discourses, such as the one facing health about the need to contain the costs of health care. But even where national governments respond with reforms that rest on similar market-inspired reforms, the ability to make changes and the choices made, will always reflect prevailing institutional, political and ideational arrangements in any nation. It remains for future studies to examine whether these three dimensions constitute a useful framework for assessing governance change in other policy sectors, and across more nations and regions.

References

Baumgartner, F., and B. Jones. 1993. *Agendas and Instability in American Politics.* Chicago: University of Chicago Press.

Béland, D. 2010. "Policy change and health care research." *Journal of Health Politics, Policy and Law* 35 (4): 615–641.

Capano, G., J. Rayner, and A. R. Zito. 2012. "Governance from the bottom up: Complexity and divergence in comparative perspective." *Public Administration* 90 (1): 56–73.

Erichsen, V. 1995. "State traditions and medical professionalization in Scandinavia." In *Health Professions and the State in Europe*, edited by T. Johnson, G. Larkin, and M. Saks, 187–199. London: Routledge.

Esping-Anderson, G. 1990. *The Three Worlds of Welfare Capitalism*. Cambridge: Polity.

Engel, G. 1977. "The need for a new medical model: a challenge for biomedicine." *Science* 196: 129–136.

Degeling, P., and J. Anderson. 1992. "Organisational and administrative dimensions." In *Health Policy: Development, Implementation, and Evaluation in Australia*, edited by H. Gardner, 51–72. Melbourne: Churchill Livingstone.

Freidson, E. 1994. *Professionalism Reborn. Theory, Prophecy and Policy*. Cambridge: Polity.

Giaimo, S. 1995. "Recasting the political bargain with the medical profession." *Governance* 8: 354–379.

Hall, P. 1989. *The Political Power of Economic Ideas: Keynesianism across Nations*. Princeton NJ: Princeton University Press.

Héritier, A. 2002. "New modes of governance in Europe: Policy-making without legislating?" In *Common Goods. Reinventing European and International Governance* edited by A. Héritier, 185–206. Lanham: Rowman and Littlefield.

Hood, C. 1983. *The Tools of Government*. London: Macmillan.

Howlett, M., J. Rayner, and C. Tollefson. 2009. "From government to governance in forest planning? Lessons from the case of the British Columbia Great Bear rainforest initiative." *Forest Policy and Economics* 11: 383–391.

Immergut, E. 1992. *Health Politics: Interests and institutions in Western Europe*. Cambridge: Cambridge University Press.

Jakubowski, E., R. B. Saltman, and A. Duran. 2013. "Country governance profiles." In *The Changing National Role in Health System Governance: A Case-Based Study of 11 European Countries and Australia*, edited by E. Jakubowski, and R. B. Saltman, 9–70. Copenhagen: WHO European Observatory on health systems and policies.

Klein, Rudolph. 1997. *The New Politics of the NHS*. London: Longman.

Kooiman, J. 1993. *Modern Governance: New Government–Society Interactions*. London: Sage.

Kuhlmann, E. and J. Allsop. 2007. "Professional self-regulation in a changing architecture of governance: Comparing health policy in the UK and Germany." *Policy and Politics* 36 (2): 173–189.

Larkin, G. 1995. "State control and the health professions in the United Kingdom: historical perspectives." In *Health Professions and the State in Europe*, edited by T. Johnson, G. Larkin, and M. Saks, 45–54. London: Routledge.

Lascoumes, P. and P. Le Galés. 2007. "Understanding public policy through its instruments." *Governance* 20 (1): 1–14.

Lewis, J. M. 2014. "Health policy in Australia: change and continuity" In *Social Policy in Australia: Understanding for Action*, 3rd edition, edited by A. McLelland, and P. Smyth, 190–203. Melbourne: Oxford University Press.

Lewis, J. M. 2005. *Health Policy and Politics: Networks, Ideas and Power*. Melbourne: IP Communications.

Lewis, J. M. 2002. "Policy and profession: elite perspectives on redefining general practice in Australia and England." *Journal of Health Services Research and Policy* 7 (Suppl. 1): S1: 8–13.

Lewis, J. M. 1999. "The durability of ideas in health policy making." In *Public Policy and Political Ideas*, edited by D. Braun and A. Busch, 152–167. Cheltenham: Edward Elgar.

Marmot, M. 1999. "Acting on the evidence to reduce inequalities in health." *Health Affairs* 18 (3): 42–44.

Okma, K. 1997. *Studies on Dutch Health Politics, Policy and Law*. Medical Faculty. Utrecht: Utrecht University.

Okma, K. and A de Roo. 2009. "The Netherlands: From polder model to modern management." In *Comparative Studies and the Politics of Modern Medical Care*, edited by T. Marmor, R. Freeman, and K. Okma, 120–152. New Haven and London: Yale University Press.

Pierre, J. and B. Guy Peters. 2000. *Governance, Politics and the State*. London: Macmillan.

Pierson, P. 1997. *Path Dependence, Increasing Returns and the Study of Politics*. Cambridge, MA: Harvard University Centre for European Studies.

Rosenau, P. V. 1994. "Impact of political structures and informal political processes on health policy: Comparison of the United States and Canada." *Policy Studies Review* 13: 293–314.

Rosenau, P. V. and C. J. Lako. 2008. "An experiment with regulated competition and individual mandates for universal health care: The new Dutch health insurance system." *Journal of Health Politics, Policy and Law* 33 (6): 1031–1055.

Rhodes, R. 1997. *Understanding Governance: Policy Networks, Governance, Reflexivity and Accountability*. Milton Keynes: Open University Press.

Schäfer, W., M. Kroneman, W. Boerma, M. van den Berg, G. Westert, W. Devillé, and E. van Ginneken. 2010. "The Netherlands: Health System Review." *Health Systems in Transition* 12 (1). Copenhagen: European Observatory on Health Systems and Policies.

Schön, D. and M. Rein. 1994. *Frame Reflection: Toward the Resolution of Intractable Policy Controversies*. New York: Basic Books.

Steinmo, S. and J. Watts. 1995. "It's the institutions, stupid! Why comprehensive national health insurance always fails in America." *Journal of Health Politics, Policy and Law* 20: 329–372.

Stoelwinder, J. 2008. *Medicare Choice? Insights from the Netherlands Health Insurance Reforms*. Melbourne: Australian Centre for Health Research.

Tollefson, C., A. R. Zito, and F. Gale. 2012. "Symposium overview: Conceptualizing new governance arrangements." *Public Administration* 90 (1): 3–18.

Treib, O., H. Bähr, and G. Falkner. 2007. "Modes of governance: Toward a conceptual clarification." *Journal of European Public Policy* 14 (1): 1–20.

World Health Organization. 2005. *Action on the Social Determinants of Health: Learning from Previous Experiences*. Geneva: WHO.

18

DEVOLUTION AND FEDERALISM

Owen E. Hughes

Introduction

The traditional bureaucratic model of public administration and management assumes that government is strong, able to exert its authority, and to have its edicts implemented without question. Even if there may not have a been a direct supposition of a unitary model of government in the traditional model – as usually typified by the United Kingdom – this was implicit, in that other systems were seen as inferior.

However, the reality of governance is, that for much of the world, there are levels of government and devolution, from agreements on power sharing to explicit federal systems. Coordination, negotiation and compromise across levels are more common than the model of a single government, holding all the power that can simply carry out its wishes. Nation-states that are formally federations include: the United States, Germany, Canada, Switzerland, Australia, Argentina, Brazil and Mexico. In addition, Russia, India and China provide some function sharing and power sharing between national, state, provincial and even city governments. With states once regarded as exemplars of centralism, such as Spain and Italy, offering sub-national governments at least some role (Cepiku, Jesuit, and Roberge, 2013), it becomes more difficult to list nation-states that are actually unitary, particularly those with large populations or areas. Even the UK agreed in 1997 to power sharing with parliaments in Scotland and Wales and promised even greater devolution before the Scottish independence referendum in 2014.

If the reality of governance in much of the world involves federalism and devolution, perhaps the model of public management needs to take this reality into account. Theories where government is all-powerful are unlikely to be realistic where government is divided across levels. Once it is realized that there is no single best way of organizing and managing (Alford and Hughes, 2008), theories based on negotiation, compromise and adjustment may work rather better. Divided power, overlapping roles, the inability to assign accountability for shared programs and implementation problems may well occur with the devolution of authority, but these realities can be considered part of the price for having government closer to the people.

Much of the day-to-day work of public managers is negotiation with their counterparts in other levels of government. The field of intergovernmental relations more often becomes management by diplomacy, management by personality, leadership and, fundamentally, management and leadership without authority (Heifetz, 1999). Federalism is perhaps surprisingly strong and persistent. The reality of government in many parts of the world is one of internal division and negotiation rather than neat systems of hierarchy and accountability.

The federal principle

Despite a history claimed to go back to biblical times (Davis, 1978), exactly what constitutes a federation is contested. Riker defines federalism as "a political organisation in which the activities of government are divided between regional governments and a central government in such a way that each kind of government has some activities on which it makes final decisions" (1975, p. 101). To Riker "a constitution is federal if (1) two levels of government rule the same land and people (2) each level has at least one area of action in which it is autonomous, and (3) there is some guarantee (even though merely a statement in the constitution) of the autonomy of each government in its own sphere" (1964, p. 11).

These three points provide a good working definition of a formal federal state, but there is also a range of power sharing arrangements without some of these features. For instance, as the UK has no written constitution, power sharing with Scotland and Wales could be changed by an act of the parliament. It is not, then, a federal state in the formal sense. Italy and Spain have limited power sharing but this is not constitutionally protected. Neither do Russia and China. However, the key point is not the precise definition, but rather the management task of working across jurisdictions.

Formal federations, most notably the longstanding ones, arise when a group of previously independent states or colonies desires to be united for some purposes but stay separate for others. They desire, that is, to be united but not unitary. The usual motives for federating are to permit further expansion, both territorial and economic, and to achieve greater military security (Riker, 1964; Wheare, 1963).

A fundamental question in the whole theory of federalism is just how much independence or power regional governments can lose to the centre before a federal state becomes a unitary state in all but name. As a federation develops, there is an inevitable change in relative power, with the centre usually gaining in power at the expense of the periphery. This development can be interpreted by some as a sign that federalism is really a transitional system, an inherently second best or inefficient polity that is evolving somehow towards a more efficient system. Questions of efficiency from centralization are of limited relevance, given that the prospect of changing a long-lasting federal system to a unitary one is highly unlikely.

There does, though, need to be some means of preserving a degree of independence for regional governments. In practice, they cannot be separate or independent, but there are different views about what kind of independence, and how much, should be given to the states before one can have a distinctively federal system. These differences are reflected in the three main approaches to conceptualizing the nature of federalism: federal systems may be classified as *coordinate*, *cooperative* or *organic*.

Coordinate federalism most emphasizes the idea of governmental separateness. In carrying out its functions, each tier in the federation is independent of the other and the two tiers of jurisdiction are coordinate — equal in rank or status — so that neither is legally superior. In Wheare's classic definition of the "federal principle", federalism itself means "the method of dividing powers so that the general and regional governments are each, within a sphere, co-ordinate and independent of the other" (1963, p. 10). This represents the "highest" or purist stage of federalism: where powers and responsibilities between the central government and the regional governments are so precise and well known that each level goes about its business without conflict.

Bryce, an even earlier theorist, saw federalism as being "like a great factory wherein two sets of machinery are at work, their revolving wheels apparently intermixed, their bands crossing one another, yet each doing its own work without touching or hampering the other" (1914, p. 432). But while this is an appealing picture, it does not convey a wholly realistic impression of the balance of power within any federation.

Coordinate federalism makes theoretical demands that have never been met by any system. It presupposes a substantial amount of independence as suggested by the phrase "coordinate and independent". The major problem with this is the practicality of the attempt to make the two spheres of jurisdiction independent. In practice it is impossible to draw up any constitution so precisely that powers are specified clearly and unambiguously. Through events and constitutional change over time, a strictly legalistic approach can be overtaken by reality.

Cooperative federalism permits a good deal of shared activity. Rather than being highly legalistic, this type is more political. Regional governments still need some autonomy, some bargaining power, or "cooperation" could be a euphemism for "coercion". The two levels must compromise to carry out functions jointly which, constitutionally, might belong to one level or the other. Rather than a precise division of powers, cooperative federalism incorporates and rests on a series of accommodations between the levels of government. In addition, cooperation does not necessarily mean peaceful negotiation and harmony, only that the different levels can reach agreements. Intergovernmental disputes can be seen as part of a continual, ongoing game of bargaining analogous to international diplomacy. But rather than being dysfunctional or inefficient, conflict is quite normal and even functional for the political system. Either level could prove stronger than the other without undermining the reality of federalism.

Organic federalism is where the centre is dominant. It has substantial control over financial resources and can decide the major policy questions. Regions can still have some autonomy, but more coercion from the centre is involved than in the other models. The regions may become mere administrative arms of the dominant centre. What is sometimes called "asymmetric federalism" would also fit within this category (Cepiku, Jesuit, and Roberge, 2013).

Sometimes, those who speak gloomily about the decline of federalism are presuming that real federalism is coordinate federalism. But coordinate federalism is an ideal type. Whether or not a particular system is really federal has as much or more to do with how the system functions as a political entity than with the formal legal details of how power is shared.

Federalism is a complex system of government which seems to invite conflict and in which lines of accountability are messy rather than neat and ordered. Not surprisingly, federalism is criticized strongly by those who would prefer, apparently, a more rational and efficient system.

Centralization and decentralization

Within public management and public administration, issues around centralization and decentralization are "hardy perennials" (Pollitt 2005); at one point the one appears to be in favor, at another time the other. Despite the apparent success of federalism's reach across countries, it has always attracted criticism.

Arguments over federalism could be seen as reflecting two differing conceptions of democracy. Those who support federalism identify more with a type of consensus democracy. Those against federalist arrangements favour a form of majoritarian democracy and a greater concentration of powers in the hands of a single, elected government (Lijphart 1984). Those who sympathize with the British system of parliamentary sovereignty have frequently been critical of the lack of uniformity and the costs and delays in legislation and administration that accompany federalism. At the turn of the twentieth century, the British jurist Dicey expressed considerable reservations about federalism. Dicey (1959) accused it of producing conservatism and excessive legalism. Federalism, he said, means weak government; he clearly found it difficult to understand why any sensible nation would prefer to adopt a federal system ahead of British-style institutions.

Negative reactions should be seen as reflecting two underlying influences. First, there is a bias against federalism deriving from British notions of responsibility and the tradition of parliamentary sovereignty. Secondly, there may be a view that achieving a more rational society requires a strong and centralized government. Critics stress its tendency to divide and blur lines of responsibility. It is sometimes difficult to get the various governments to agree on necessary legislation.

Writers on the Left have also seen federalism as an obstacle to achieving social reform. In the early 1980s, Wilenski argued, referring to Australia, "any form of federal structure is conservative in nature. Federal arrangements, as compared to those in a unitary state, invariably limit the powers of the elected central government." He added that in a whole range of fields "only central government can effect the changes in society that thorough-going reform would require" (1983, pp. 84–85). While of a particular time and place, this comment points to some suspicion on the Left that federalism restricts the positive power of government.

On the other hand, those who support federalism stress the need to keep government as close as possible to the people and allow regional communities who feel themselves to be separate and distinct from others a substantial measure of self-government. It is, of course, arguable as to how substantial the regional, geographic and cultural differences really are in some countries, but those who see them as real also see federalism as a highly significant device for limiting and dividing the power of the central government. Otherwise, it might pose more of a threat to the interests of citizens in parts far distant from the formal capital.

In the UK, for example, successive governments have tried to do something about regional disparities in economic and social prospects between the London region of the southeast and other areas such as the northeast. Government in the UK means mostly London government, although local governments provide a limited range of services, which are often restricted by Whitehall rules anyway. Even if distances are not far when compared to, say, Canada, it could be argued that for most UK citizens government is indeed a long way away. The economic divide may not be directly attributable to centralized government but its existence may well contribute to local disillusionment with the centre and even with government itself.

The problem with centralists who criticize federalism because of its particular flaws is that they assume that the nation-state could and should be re-made on a completely different basis, and that a new charter of association or constitution could be devised and implemented. This is extremely doubtful, precisely because many people see federalism as an important part of their conception of what a free society should entail.

Centralists tend to undervalue the importance of the link between federalism, limited government and a certain conception of the free or just society. They do not allow sufficiently for the import of federalism within the conception of liberal or constitutional democracy held especially by those on the political Right. The latter, at least those who are within the liberal democratic tradition, tend to favour limited and dispersed powers of government rather than centralization and a form of consensual rather than a majoritarian form of democracy. Elazar argues, for example:

> Federalism in its most limited form is usually defined as having to do with the distribution and sharing of power, but even in that limited form there is an implicit commitment to a

conception of justice that holds, among other things, that a distribution of powers is necessary and desirable. On the other hand, federalism in its broadest sense is presented as a form of justice – emphasising liberty and citizen participation in governance – but one which is inevitably linked to political reality because it must still be concerned with the distribution of powers.

(Elazar 1987, p. 84)

The very problems which federalism tends to create, such as its opaqueness, are seen by its supporters to be an advantage for promoting individual freedom and resisting bureaucratic encroachments or statism.

Certainly there is no axiomatic link between federalism and limited government or with democracy itself. Conservative parties have traditionally supported a federalist ideology whereby the checks and balances of the federal system would constitute a safeguard against socialist centralization. They believe that individual liberty would thus be preserved, and the interests of regions be better served, by strong state-level governments in closer touch with local needs.

Service delivery

Even if there is acceptance of the principle of devolution of powers between levels of government, there is still substantial debate over what kinds of activities each level of government should look after. The governing constitution sets out powers at varying levels of detail. In Australia and the US, the powers of the central government are nominated in the Constitution and the states have the residual powers or what is left. In Canada, the federal government was given some specific powers, as were the provinces, which also gained residual powers. Most constitutions provide the central government with those powers that most would agree to be necessary for a national government: foreign policy, defence, currency and the like. Lower-level governments generally deal with land use and some environmental matters. Other functions are mixed, such as health care and education, but there is no set list.

There have been attempts to formalize the appropriateness of level of administration and to set principles for allocating functions to different levels (Oates, 1972). Generally, the central government should have responsibility "for the macroeconomic stabilization function and for income redistribution in the form of assistance to the poor" (Oates, 1999). The first of these is obvious, in that action by a sub-national government to stabilize the economy is unlikely to be effective. On the second point, if welfare payments are devolved to lower levels of government, there may be migration effects as potential welfare recipients relocate to a jurisdiction that pays higher amounts (Borjas, 1999). Perhaps, then, social welfare transfer payments should be a national government responsibility rather than that of local or state levels. On the other hand, having Ottawa, Berlin or Canberra responsible for the collection of garbage at household levels in other cities of their federation is unlikely to be as efficient or effective as having it dealt with locally.

One argument in favour of federalism which has enjoyed a recent resurgence is the general notion that good government means having smaller government closer to the people. Federalism can better accommodate variations in public sector tastes. It means that the public sector can provide different kinds of goods and services to suit different states. Delegating the control of local programs to local state-level communities can mean a more precise delivery of programs and better administration, which in turn reduces overall costs.

In 1992, as part of the Maastricht Treaty, the European Union prompted rethinking of the old Catholic social principle of subsidiarity, which then was applied to levels of government within the EU. The subsidiarity principle extends the principle of devolution: governmental services should be devolved to the lowest possible level dependent on the kind of service in question – foreign policy to the EU itself and national governments, garbage collection to local authorities. However, it is difficult in practice to divide issues so neatly. Even garbage collection can affect wider areas, such as states or nations; environmental issues cross national boundaries. Perhaps subsidiarity was brought into the EU as a substitute for a federalism that some European states were not willing to contemplate. And while the principle may be good in reducing the complaint about Brussels' centralization, in practice subsidiarity does not appear to have resolved the allocation of powers within the EU.

There does not appear to be any robust framework for the division of powers and allocation of public roles between different levels of government. The original framing document may provide only a guide with the actuality depending more on political compromise than on formal processes.

Public management within a federation

For serving public managers, the most pressing issues involve being able to get a result, and in ways that serve their political masters. Within a federation this means making agreements that prevail with multiple political players. If it is agreed that the strict separatism of coordinate federalism is unrealistic, there are still practical issues to be dealt with in order to achieve goals. As Agranoff and McGuire argue (2001, p. 671):

> as policy responsibilities between the national and sub-national governments have evolved and devolved, governing authority has overlapped across levels to a point where all actors are involved simultaneously to varying degrees. Attention must be given to operations in such a system.

Managing where all actors are involved is clearly challenging. Coordinate federalism at least has the advantage of being clear about who has accountability for particular policies or their implementation: it is simply the level of government with the constitutional power over that issue. If, on the other hand, and as is more realistic, there is endemic overlap and a lack of clarity, public managers need to be able to negotiate and work with other governments but without any formal authority. Principles increasingly characterizing managing within federal systems include a "shared commitment to goals and projects, independent but cooperative jurisdictions and organizations, voluntary linkages involving extensive participation and crisscrossing relationships, multiple leaders and people working at different levels within and between organizations" (Agranoff and McGuire, 2001, p. 279). These are neither neat nor directive.

Public management inside a federation is innately complex. Managers operate within constraints, notably legal and financial, along with those imposed by political arrangements involving governments at various levels, often of different ideological persuasion.

Managing within legal constraints

Even if strict demarcation between levels, as set out by coordinate federalism, is not possible, public managers still need to carry out their work within some formal or legal constraints. If one level of government has an explicit mandate or power expressed in the constitution, this fact needs to be respected even if another level intrudes. There will always be arguments about the legal division of powers between levels and subsequently over what governments can and cannot do. For one level of government to take legal action against another level over jurisdiction is quite common. However, taking legal action to establish constitutional power is more often a last resort rather than a first option. If through political process and negotiation an outcome can be found that satisfies all parties, the precise legal power becomes much less relevant.

Managing the financial arrangement

The ability to spend and to tax is fundamental to all governments. It follows that much of the practice of intergovernmental relations within a federation inevitably involves arguments over finance. All federal systems have problems with deriving financial arrangements satisfactory to both levels of government (Oates, 1972). Revenue for each level is ultimately derived from the same set of taxpayers, while outlays from the different levels of government go to the same citizens in the end. Ideally, there should be a match between functions and revenue, but this rarely happens in a federation. Even if a fair balance was struck at the beginning, there is no certainty that revenues for each level will grow in precise proportion to changes in their functions.

In consequence, there are two key financial issues in all federations. The first is vertical balance where each level of government has enough revenue resources to meet its spending commitments. Vertical imbalance refers to the disparity between the taxing and spending responsibilities of each level of government. If there is great disparity, one level of government may be able to exert a degree of control over the affairs of the other. It is also desirable that each level be directly responsible to its own electors for raising taxes to finance its own proposed expenditures. For example, the Australian federation is characterized by marked vertical fiscal imbalance, in that the national government has more and better taxation assets than the states, and large-scale transfers occur from the central government to the state. Such transfers can have more or less onerous conditions placed on them. Additionally, having one level of government provide the funding for another level to spend is a recipe for blurring responsibility.

The second is horizontal balance or imbalance. Horizontal imbalance arises from the difference in economic circumstances between the regions in a federation. Any federal system has some horizontal disparity in economic conditions in the sub-national areas, and this affects the ability of the regions to provide comparable public goods and services. A revenue-sharing or grants scheme is usually set in place by the central government to reduce inequalities. There are substantial transfers of income from wealthy provinces or states to poorer ones in the federal systems of Australia, Canada and Germany. For example, the relatively less developed maritime provinces in Canada are assisted by the Canadian government to a greater extent than the wealthier provinces.

Public managers at each level constantly work within the financial constraints. Arguments over resources are intense, as funding is obviously needed for any program to work.

Managing within the political constraints

Federalism is, fundamentally, a political arrangement involving continual negotiations over the division and exercise of political power. The politics of intergovernmental relations are just as important as legal power and finance in determining the reality of the federal system. Making sense of federalism means seeing how these three aspects affect each other.

It has been argued that public management reforms cut across the democratic values of federalism (Radin, 2012). Maybe there are tensions here, but perhaps too there is simply a greater realization that getting results rests with public managers from the different levels of government being involved in constant negotiation and bargaining. More recent public management theories of networks, coproduction and governance accommodate the ambiguity of the federal system quite well. Indeed, the traditional bureaucratic model fits the coordinate view of federalism in its clear hierarchy and clear accountability. Both are simply unrealistic.

Public management skills

In working across jurisdictions, public managers are often required to operate in circumstances in which they do not have real authority. They are then in the difficult position of having to get results from players for whom they are not personally responsible, in the sense of being able to direct or to make authoritative rulings. In turn, this means finding new organizational cultures and, for many public managers, a need to acquire a completely different set of skills.

The skills required become more akin to those of diplomacy than to the recourse to authority that might have been more common during a more bureaucratic era. Public management skills become those of personality, deal making, operating through networks and coalition building but with the invoking of actual authority rare. Collaborative managers need to "know how to bargain and how to negotiate" (O'Leary and Bingham, 2009, p. 266). Public managers need to learn to make deals, be entrepreneurs of a kind and work together (Bardach, 1998). The skills involved are essentially about personality and the exercise of soft power (Nye, 2008). As Agranoff and McGuire argue (2001, p. 679):

> Managers who deal with the federal system have entered the information age through expanded contacts and networks. While bureaucracy was the hallmark of the industrial age, inter-organizational teamwork and networks are the hallmark of the information age. Managing across organizations meets the need to deal with greater complexity, scope, speed, flexibility, and adaptability.

The skills required are very different from those of traditional public servants.

Governments still have authority and power to coerce citizens. However, most of the time and on most issues they do not need to do so. Furthermore, the outcomes in policy and delivery when raw power is used are likely to be sub-optimal. It would now be almost inconceivable for government to pass legislation without extensive consultation with stakeholders, including other levels of government.

Conclusion

Public management aims to deliver services and public goods to citizens in the most efficient way possible consistent with the democratic values of a government. The financial and administrative details of federalism may need some improvement, but reforms presume the need to take federalism seriously, and not to proceed as if it should evolve into a different form of government. It is simply unhelpful to continue arguing about federalism as if some radically different form of government were either available, or had enough support to be implemented. Once a federal state is established, the chances are high that if it survives, it will survive as a federation.

The reality in much of the world, particularly the developed world, is that service delivery occurs in a shared-power environment. Devolution of power in recent years seems to have come – if a single theme can be picked out of disparate movements – from the desire of citizens to have government nearer to where they are. Centralized governments do seem to have lost popularity. The task then remains for public managers from different levels to get together and work on outcomes that are beneficial to citizens on behalf of the federation for which they are working. It is unhelpful to simply say that centralization is better. There are no axiomatic economies of scale in service delivery to be found from centralization; if having sub-national governments can help allay feelings that government is a long way away, perhaps that is no bad thing. Federalism endures.

References

Agranoff, R. and M. McGuire. 2001. "American federalism and the search for models of management." *Public Administration Review* 61 (6): 671–681.

Alford, J. and O. E. Hughes. 2008. "Public value pragmatism as the next phase of public management." *American Review of Public Administration* 38: 130–148.

Bardach, E. 1998. *Getting Agencies to Work Together: The Theory and Practice of Managerial Craftsmanship.* Washington, DC: Brookings Institution Press.

Borjas, G. 1999. "Immigration and welfare magnets." *Journal of Labor Economics* 17 (4): 607–637.

Bryce, J. 1914. *American Commonwealth*, Vol. 1, London: Macmillan.

Cepiku, D., D. K. Jesuit, and I. Roberge. 2013. *Making Multilevel Public Management Work: Stories of Success and Failure from Europe and North America.* Boca Raton: CRC Press.

Davis, S. R. 1978. *The Federal Principle: A Journey Through Time in Quest of Meaning.* Berkeley and Los Angeles: University of California Press.

Dicey, A.V. 1959. *An Introduction to the Law of the Constitution.* 3rd ed. London: Macmillan.

Elazar, D. 1987. *Exploring Federalism*, Tuscaloosa: University of Alabama Press.

Heifetz, R. A. 1999. *Leadership without Easy Answers.* Cambridge, MA: Belknap.

Lijphart, A. 1984. *Democracies.* New Haven and London: Yale University Press.

Nye, J. S. 2008. "Public diplomacy and soft power." *Annals of the American Academy of Political and Social Science* 616 (1): 94–109.

Oates, W. E. 1999. "An Essay on Fiscal Federalism." *Journal of Economic Literature* 37: 1120–1149.

Oates, W. E. 1972. *Fiscal Federalism.* New York: Harcourt Brace Jovanovich.

Pollitt, C. 2005. "Decentralization." In *The Oxford Handbook of Public Management*, edited by E. Ferlie, L. E. Lynn, and C. Pollitt. Oxford: Oxford University Press.

Radin, B. 2012. *Federal Management Reform in a World of Contradictions.* Georgetown: Georgetown University Press.

Riker, W. H. 1975. "Federalism." In *Handbook of Political Science, Vol. 5: Governmental Institutions and Processes*, edited by F. I. Greenstein, and N. W. Polsby. Reading, MA: Addison-Wesley.

Riker, W. H. 1964. *Federalism: Origin, Operation, Significance.* Boston: Little, Brown.

Wheare, K. C. O. 1963. *Federal Government.* 5th ed. Oxford: Oxford University Press.

Wilenski, P. 1983. "Six states or two nations?" In *Fractured Federation? Australia in the 1980s*, edited by J. Aldred and J. Wilkes, 79–86. Sydney: Allen & Unwin.

19

EMERGENCY AND CRISIS MANAGEMENT

The Soma mine accident case, Turkey

Fatih Demiroz and Naim Kapucu

Introduction

On May 13, 2014 Turkey was shaken by a disaster that claimed hundreds of lives in Soma district of Manisa province (528km southwest of Istanbul). An accident in a coalmine in the Eynez region of Soma trapped hundreds of miners 1,300 feet below the surface. The incident was breaking news not only in Turkey, but also across the world. Four days after the accident, the Minister of Energy Taner Yildiz officially announced 301 miners were killed.

The accident was the deadliest mine and work accident in the history of Turkey. Despite the fact that all disasters urge public sensitivity and have political implications, the Soma mine accident was disputed mainly because of pre- and post-disaster management practices. Public scrutiny focused specifically on the government practices that had allegedly paved the road to disaster and the mismanagement of the incident. The elected government was criticized due to its licensing and regulation of mines, contract management in public–private partnerships (PPP) with the mining industry, crisis leadership and communication in the aftermath of the incident. Although contracting-out services, PPPs, and collaborative public management are widely used governmental tools (or tools of the government); poor execution can create undesirable outcomes. The purpose of this chapter is to explore the management of the Soma mine disaster using a collaborative public management framework. Application of collaborative public management in the context of disasters is discussed as collaborative emergency management (Demiroz and Kapucu 2015; Kapucu, Arslan, and Demiroz 2010). The first term will be used for understanding overall cross-sector partnerships in Turkey, whereas the second term will be applied to discussing the management of the mine disaster.

The chapter aims to answer the following questions: What role does collaborative public management play in the success or failure of policies related to the Soma accident? What role did leadership play in collaborative governance in the context of the Soma accident? This research is valuable since the disaster reflects the nature of policy formulation and implementation in partnership with the private sector when accountability and transparency is lacking. In addition, the leadership of top elected officials and ministers, first responders and experts in the mining industry is integral to the successful management of a disaster. In essence, leaders' attitudes in the aftermath of the disaster hold a mirror to citizen–government relationships in the context of citizens' grievances.

The chapter is organized as follows. First, the theoretical framework of the chapter is laid out. This section explains collaborative public management, how it is used in service delivery in general and for disaster management specifically (i.e. collaborative emergency management). Additionally, Turkey's governmental and disaster management systems are briefly explained. Second, a detailed account of the Soma mine accident is presented with some information about the mining industry in Turkey, management of the Soma mine, government–mining industry relations (i.e. PPPs), and management of the disaster. The final section will discuss implications of the accident and provide conclusions.

Collaborative public management

Public management is a broad concept that can be defined in various ways (Lynn 2007). Hill and Lynn (2009) use public administration and public management *interchangeably* and develop a three-dimensional approach (structure, culture, and craft) in their analysis of public management. Hughes (2012) has a different perspective and views on public management as a transition from the traditional (hierarchical) public administration (which is established based on Max Weber's bureaucratic theory, Woodrow Wilson's politics–administration dichotomy, and Fredrick Taylor's scientific management) towards a managerial approach, as a result of reform movements that started in 1980s. Traditional public administration is about following the procedures to the letter, whereas public management is about taking responsibility and achieving results. Public management practices include various government tools for solving complex policy problems (Salamon 2002). Collaborative public management can be considered as one of the service delivery tools under Hughes' conceptualization of public management.

In simple terms, collaborative public management is defined as delivering services to the public through the collaboration of public, private, and nonprofit sectors. The evolving nature of governance inevitably brings change in the delivery of services (particularly after 1980s) (Hughes 2012). As the traditional bureaucratic government entities recede, private companies and nonprofit organizations replace government in the production of goods and delivery of certain services. The relationships between public, private, and nonprofit organizations encapsulate different characteristics depending on specific policy issues. For example, government can form a PPP for relatively simple policy questions, such as building a bridge or to contract out maintenance of high-tech military systems. However, complex social problems, such as catastrophic disasters, healthcare delivery, or refugee inflow from a neighboring state, require a different type of cross-sector relationship (Kapucu 2009). Policy makers seek to utilize community resources via inter-organizational and cross-sector networks for managing complex issues.

Disaster management is a complex and multidimensional policy problem and benefits from various types of governance forms. There are four fundamental phases of a disaster, which are preparedness, mitigation, response, and recovery (see Table 19.1). Public management solely for disaster response is a limited approach, although response is the most visible phase to the public. Management of all the phases of disasters generates much better results, although this approach requires greater resources. The next step after managing all the phases of disasters is to build disaster-resilient communities. Disaster resiliency can be defined as efforts to link a network of adaptive capacities in a community (Norris et al. 2008). These adaptive capacities are economic development, social capital, information and communication, and community competence. Thus, building disaster-resilient communities (i.e. linking these adaptive capacities) requires a *whole community* approach. The *whole community* approach means bringing together

Table 19.1 Four phases of emergency management

Disaster Management Phase	Definition
Preparedness	State of readiness to respond to a disaster
Mitigation	Sustained action to reduce or eliminate risk to people and property from hazards. (e.g. insurance, land-use planning, enforcing building codes)
Response	Actions taken to save lives and property in the immediate aftermath of a disaster (e.g. fire suppression, search and rescue, evacuation)
Recovery	Actions needed to help individuals and communities return to normal

Source: Haddow, Bullock, and Coppola, 2011

government agencies, private businesses, nonprofit organizations, and individual citizens to reduce vulnerabilities and build adaptive capacities. The role of the government in this approach is to: (1) carry out preparedness, mitigation, response, and recovery efforts with the resources at their disposal and different tools of government; and (2) facilitate, maintain, and manage partnership networks for building adaptive capacities in communities (see Chapter 23 by Bovaird and Quirk in this handbook).

First, there are a variety of government tools that can be instrumental in managing each phase of disaster management. For example, a government can contract out recovery of a disaster-stricken area (principle–agent relationship), form PPPs for implementing a local mitigation strategy, or develop a collaborative network (equal partners) for responding to disasters.

Collaborative networks are widely used in disaster response, particularly in the United States. Bardach (1998: 8) defines collaboration as "any joint activity by two or more agencies that is intended to increase public value by their working together rather than separately". Relationships in collaborative networks function based on trust and commitment in a nonhierarchical (i.e. horizontal) structure (Mandell and Keast 2007). Governance of collaborative networks is complicated due to their political, configurational, and loosely coupled nature (Lynn et al. 2000). Policy mandates, laws, statutes, and administrative and institutional rules either constrain or enable provision of goods and services for the public interest (Kapucu 2015).

During disasters public, nonprofit, and private players are expected to share resources and collaborate extensively to ensure that the crisis is managed well. However, as Kapucu (2008: 256) states, "organizing a cooperative effort … is almost as difficult as the problems that the initiative is created to address". Lack of coordination between different players is the most obvious failure of disaster management networks. A key strategy to overcome this is to create interoperable systems and standardize communication protocols. In addition, collaborative emergency management is effective when there are pre-existing relationships and trust (i.e. social capital) between public, non-profit, and private organizations, strong relationships with the media, and elected officials with strong leadership skills (Kapucu 2005, 2008, 2015).

Second, government agencies serve as leading *agencies* (players) or facilitators of community partnership networks for building community adaptive capacities. Economic development policies for diversification of local and regional economies (Godschalk 2003; Rose 2004, 2005), building robust, redundant, and readily available infrastructure (e.g. information communication technologies, alternative roads, etc.), developing continuity of business plans, and fostering community-level social capital are some critical tasks that government agencies of all levels are expected to perform for building disaster-resilient communities.

Both tasks (managing four phases of disasters and facilitating, managing, and maintaining community networks) overlap with each other to a certain extent. Managing four phases of disasters requires community resources and collaboration with community partners. Moreover, developing and managing community networks creates results that are vital inputs to four phases of disaster management. Both tasks rely heavily on collaborative governance networks, and a key issue of interest in collaborative governance is how governance succeeds when involved stakeholders hold conflicting, diverse ideas and views about policy objectives. This leads us to exploring the literature on good governance practices.

Bovaird and Quirk in this volume (Chapter 23) suggest that transformation in public management practices creates risks *for* government and risks *from* government. One particular risk from government that we would like to highlight in this chapter is lack of good governance, poor quality of government, and the failure of leadership for using appropriate government tools for achieving the aforementioned two tasks.

A government's transparency, accountability, rule of law, and administrative competency are indicators of a good governance and quality of government (Kapucu 2010). In his book on comparative governance reforms, Kapucu (2010) presents a framework of four pillars of good governance, which cover accountability, transparency, rule of law, and citizen participation. He also considers a strong civil society to be the foundation of the four pillars of good governance. In case of disasters, issues such as corruption, lack of transparency, and insufficient leadership can create two critical outcomes that possess risk for people. First, these conditions can undermine government's regulatory capacity. If government loses its technical or managerial capacity to regulate risky businesses (e.g. mines, water treatment facilities), or if corruption creates an environment in which business owners can easily evade costly safety precautions, risks increase dramatically for those who are influenced by these industries.

A recent example is the lead poisoning scandal in Flint, Michigan, US. In 2014, the City of Flint decided to switch from the City of Detroit's high-quality water to a newly established pipeline system in order to reduce the water bills. City officials decided to use water from the Flint River until new pipes were established. The State Department of Environmental Quality made a decision not to add chemicals to the water to avoid corrosion of the pipes, which in turn caused lead to leach from the pipes into the water. Later, public officials did not take any precautions, despite the fact that they found out that the water from the Flint River was not safe to use (New York Times 2016; Milbank 2016). Poisonous water leads to irreparable damage to children's health, as well as other health costs for the residents of the city. A second outcome is that poor quality of government undermines the capacity of the government to handle incidents. Consequently, the need for involvement of nongovernmental actors (i.e. private and nonprofit organizations) becomes apparent. Regardless of the government capacity, political leadership is imperative in effectively managing disasters. Leaders are expected to make accurate decisions under stress, play the honest broker role among equal partners handling a disaster, and facilitate collaboration between partners from different backgrounds (Ansell and Gash 2008; Vangen and Huxham 2003). Lack of capacity to carry out these operations impedes the success of disaster management.

Leadership and collaborative governance in managing disasters

Crisis leadership can take the shape of sympathizing and empathizing with victims, facilitating and leading response and recovery, coordinating between different response entities, providing correct and reliable information in disasters, and conducting timely communication with citizens (Kapucu and Ozerdem 2013). The concepts of crisis and leadership create an important relationship requiring a more thourough study.

The common way to study leadership in the context of disaster situations is to focus on the presidential and political leadership of individuals or emergency managers. During disasters, the public generally look for leaders to make responsible and intelligent decisions to mitigate risks and threats. Uncertain and confused feelings during crises encourage the public to look towards a strong, transformational leader and alter their leadership expectations (Bligh et al. 2004). Boin and 't Hart (2003) studied President Bush's and Mayor Rudolph Giuliani's post 9/11 leadership. Their study shows Bush and Giuliani's approval ratings and personal reputations improved tremendously after their response and proposed plans to the disaster. According to Boin and 't Hart (2003: 544), "successful performance in times of collective stress turns leaders into statesmen. But when the crisis fails to dissipate and 'normality' does not return, leaders are obvious scapegoats." Thus, poor disaster management perpetuates a move to find leaders to blame and, as critics suggest, advocates reform by leaders post-crisis. These are interpreted as common tools or strategies to circumvent public criticism and blame.

A leader's communication with media and public is critical for success in disaster management. Timely, accurate, and constantly flowing information from public officials prevents circulation of inaccurate information, agitation of victims and their families, and loss of trust of public authority. It also builds trust between government and citizens. A successful communication in a crisis has four main components. First, a public leader (be it an elected official or the head of a government agency) should tell the public the truth. If the leaders fail to do this, incorrect information would invade all the news sources and cause significant disruption in the society. Additionally, not telling the truth compromises public trust in government in future press releases. Second, a complete message should be given. The entire truth must be spoken and no information should be hidden if its accuracy is confirmed. Third, the message must be given immediately, as other sources of information will fill the gap if public leaders fail to provide timely information to the public. Finally, leaders must work hard to fix the problem and communicate their efforts to the public in appropriate ways.

Soma mine accident

Coal mining is a critical industry for the Turkish economy. Coal is used for heating millions of households and produced 26.3 per cent of the country's electricity in 2013 (TKI 2014). Moreover, the Ministry of Energy and Natural Resources has distributed over 17 million tons of coal to low-income families within the last ten years. The distribution of free coal to families raised public disagreement, especially from the political opposition. Oppositional parties accused the government of distributing free coal and food to low-income families to secure their votes. Further, government critics claimed that the government was signing contracts with certain business groups, excluding those deemed to dissent from it politically (Taraf 2013).

Coal production

Publicly owned corporations and the private sector are the leaders of coal production in Turkey. Turkiye Komur Isletmeleri (TKI) and Elektrik Uretim A.S. (EUAS) are the two state-owned corporations (state economic enterprises) controlling the majority of coal production. TKI's share in coal production was reduced from 85 per cent to 38 per cent in the last 20 years, mostly as a result of privatization or transferring operations to EUAS. In addition, in 2014, EUAS accounted for 42 per cent of total coal production (TKI 2014). Both organizations produced coal either in their own right or through contractors. The accident occurred in a mine owned by TKI in the Soma district of Manisa province. The private contractor Soma Komur A.S. has operated the mine since 2010.

The mine had initially been contracted to Ciner Holding in 2006 and classified in the high-risk category because of methane gas and fire potential. As a result, the first contractor gave up production and Soma Komur A.S. took over the mine in 2009 (TMMOB 2014). The first contractor produced 50,000 tons of coal in 2006, 270,000 tons in 2007, 230,000 tons in 2008, and 300,000 tons in 2009. After Some Komur A.S. took over operations, annual production increased dramatically to 2.6 million tons in 2010 (TMMOB 2014). According to the agreement between TKI and Soma Komur A.S., TKI was obliged to buy all the coal produced by Soma Komur A.S. The incentive led to overproduction and work overload in the mine (TMMOB 2014). In an interview published in the *Hürriyet Daily News* paper in 2012, the owner of Soma Komur A.S. reported that they reduced the cost of coal per ton from $140 to $23.8 (Hurriyet 2012).

The management of the contract between Soma Komur A.S., TKI, and the Ministry of Energy and Natural Resources was problematic. TKI was ready to buy all the coal produced without any restrictions on the quality and quantity. It is stated in the Court of Accounts (Sayistay) report that the company delivered coal deemed below the designated standard to TKI and paid for the shipment regardless of the quality (CNN Turk 2014; Sayistay 2014). In addition, the reports about the accident demonstrate that most of the cost reduction from $140 to $23.8 was achieved at the expense of employee safety. The report prepared by Bogazici University (BUSAG 2014) identified numerous safety problems in the mine which put the lives of miners in danger, such as lack of proper air circulation, increasing the number of miners to work in each shift above the mine's capacity, lack of proper equipment to monitor methane (CH_4), carbon monoxide (CO), and carbon dioxide (CO_2), lack of early warning systems against dangerous gases, lack of proper guidelines for mine evacuation in case of an emergency, and lack of safety rooms for miners' refuge in an emergency situation. Nevertheless, Soma Komur A.S. passed all the government inspections before the accident. The last inspection in the mine was made four months before the accident (T24 2014a). Nine months before the accident, on July 9, 2013, the Minister of Energy and Natural Resources Taner Yildiz visited the mine and praised the safety and technology used there (Internethaber 2014).

The accident

In the early afternoon of May 13, 2014, the mine accident started to make headlines. The accident was initially announced as the explosion of a power distribution unit in the mine as a result of which 17 miners had been affected. Subsequently, conflicting announcements about the cause of the accident and number of miners impacted continued to be made throughout the day. According to the report prepared by Bogazici Univerity's Soma Solidarity Team's report (BUSD 2014), the accident happened because of a wall collapsing in the mine. One of the walls in the mine gallery failed, exposing tunnels to self-burning coal and its gases caused a fire to spread in the tunnels in which the miners were working. On the day of the accident, no one knew exactly how many miners were present because the incident happened during a shift change. Moreover, there was no system in place to track miners in the tunnels. Several hours after the accident, Minister Taner Yildiz announced 205 miners lost their lives with more to be discovered. According to official records published long after the accident, there were 787 miners underground when the event happened. Four days after the accident, Minister Yildiz announced that 301 workers had lost their lives. According to the investigative expert's report, the autopsies of the deceased miners showed that 70–85 percent of the miners lost their lives as a result of carboxyhemoglobin (COHb) poisoning (Soma Bilirkisi Raporu 2014).

Political leadership in response

The response to the accident can be analyzed in two ways: (1) the response of professional search and rescue teams and emergency response agencies, and (2) the response of elected officials (i.e. leadership). AFAD is the primary government agency responsible for responding to disasters; however, they mostly held support roles during the incident. Miners and private rescue teams carried out search-and-rescue operations underground. AFAD teams and other volunteers assisted the main operators. Nasuh Mahruki, director of AKUT, a volunteer search and rescue organization, reported the rescue operations should not be deemed unsuccessful due to the death of 301 miners because when the rescue teams arrived on the scene there were very few things they could do to save lives (HaberTurk 2014). Most of the deaths occurred in the first few minutes of the accident. On the other hand, the length of the rescue operations drew significant media attention and upset the families of victims as well as the broader public.

The political leadership portrayed a completely different view of the Soma disaster to what was needed. Minister Taner Yildiz went to the mine area and tried to oversee the rescue operations. Prime Minister Erdogan visited Soma and made a press release stating that accidents are part of the process of mining and gave examples of 19th- and 20th-century mine accidents in other countries (T24 2014b). This led to significant public outrage. Erdogan faced major protests when he visited the town and walked through the streets. Accompanied by his security guards, Erdogan found refuge in a grocery store, where, according to cellphone footage, he beat a citizen. Prime minister's aide Yusuf Yerkel was photographed kicking a miner who fell when apprehended by law enforcement forces (T24 2014c). In the following days, police suppressed protests by using rubber bullets, pepper gas, and water cannons (T24 2014e). As the work conditions in the mine and details of the accident were revealed by the media, the Ministry of Employment and Social Security and the Ministry of Energy and Natural Resources blamed each other for the death toll (T24 2014d).

Lessons learned

Building resilient communities involves combined efforts from government agencies at all levels: the private sector, nonprofit organizations, and individuals. Poor quality of government and lack of governmental capacity are a source of risk. In the case of the Soma disaster, several government practices (or lack of them) undermined the capacity of the community as well as its resiliency, increasing the risks to miners and the townspeople. First, the local town economy lacked any diversity and relied heavily on mining. The Soma region is very fertile and particularly suited to olive farming, but poor agricultural policies discouraged people from agricultural production, and mining became the primary source of employment in the region. Second, the government failed to inspect and regulate the mining industry. The Minister of Energy and Natural Resources visited the mine nine months before the accident and praised its safety and technology. This situation incentivized private contractors to press for efficiency at the expense of safety, which increased the risks for miners.

Response to disasters depends a great deal on the onset of the incident. Interviews with search and rescue teams show that the majority of the miners were killed immediately after the accident, causing rescue efforts to focus on finding the bodies of dead miners. Additionally, the resources and skills required during a mine accident are quite different from those relating to earthquakes or other common disasters in Turkey. In the case of the Soma mine, much had to be done before the accident happened. The private contractor operating the mine did not take actions pertaining to prevention, mitigation, and preparedness. The government also failed to ensure the safety of the mine via faulty inspections, poor contact management, and letting the contractor over-produce at the expense of employee safety.

Leadership and governance are two concepts very central to disaster management. The case study in this chapter is an example of leadership failure in managing pre- and post-disaster conditions. Politicians' understanding of leadership was limited to representing government authority and normalizing the accident rather than conducting a speedy and effective response and showing sympathy to victims' families. The government officials' post-accident communication was far from satisfactory. The Minister of Energy and Natural Resources' first press release came hours after the accident. In the mean time, conflicting information about the scope of the accident and the death toll was in circulation. As the minister was supervising the search and rescue operations, his praises of the technology and safety of the mine nine months earlier were being aired on the evening news. The contrast between the messages from his visit to mine in July 2013 and the scene of the disaster gained significant attention and harmed the credibility of the Minister as well as the government.

The Prime Minister's visit to Soma and the press release comparing the accident in Soma with 19th- and 20th-century mine accidents in other countries was counterproductive. His words further distressed the shaken townspeople, causing protest to erupt. The miners' families were suffering from the working conditions in the mine and did not have an alternative industry in which to find employment. The government's pseudo-inspections of the mine and the contractor's aggressive push to lower production costs deteriorated the mining conditions, significant increasing pressure on the workers. The government's poor contract management with Soma Komur A.S. fueled more controversies, as they concentrated on the provision of free coal for low-income families.

Conclusion

Disaster management is a collaborative effort and governments must involve public organizations at all levels, private actors, and nonprofit organizations in each phase of disaster management. The relationship between governmental and nongovernmental actors may be different in each phase. Resources needed for recovery are different than the requirements of mitigation, response, and preparedness. Government may rely on private contractors for recovery purposes, while also utilizing collaborative ties with equal partners from private and nonprofit sectors. Managing contracts with private vendors and ensuring the safety of employees in certain industries through regulations and inspections are an integral part of the government's responsibilities in managing disasters (i.e. their prevention and mitigation).

The tragic accident in Soma has numerous implications for disaster management professionals, as well as policy makers. The government's inability to enforce safety regulations in the mines was the primary reason behind the accident and the scope of the disaster. First, the government failed to inspect the mine appropriately and ensure that miners were working in safe conditions. Second, the contract with the private company was not managed effectively, leading to excessive production and work overload. This eventually undermined the working conditions in the mine.

After the accident, political leadership failed. The public was not informed in a timely and accurate fashion. The relationship between the government and the coal industry undermined leaders' credibility. Finally, the Prime Minister's aggressive display in Soma led to greater disruption in the town. The victims' families found none of the sympathy they expected and were further distressed by the government's attitude to protests.

As reflected in our discussion, government responsibilities in relation to managing disasters vary to a significant extent. The government is not only expected to carry out traditional response roles, but must also prevent disasters and mitigate their impact through effective enforcement of policies such as land use, building codes, safety regulations and inspections. Moreover, during disasters leadership needs to be multi-dimensional and reflect the government's ability to keep the disaster under control, to effectively disseminate information, and to express sympathy for victims and families.

References

Ansell, C. and A. Gash. 2008. "Collaborative Governance in Theory and Practice." *Journal of Public Administration Research and Theory* 18 (4): 543–571.

Bardach, E. 1998. *Getting Agencies to Work Together.* Washington, DC: Brookings Institution Press.

Bligh, M.C., J. C. Kohles, J. R. Meindl. "Charisma under Crisis: Presidential Leadership, Rhetoric, and Media Responses before and after the September 11th Terrorist Attacks." *The Leadership Quarterly* 15: 211–239.

Bogazici Universitesi Soma Arastirma Grubu (BUSAG). 2014. "Geliyorum Diyen Facia." Accessed April 8, 2015.

www.busomarastirmagrubu.boun.edu.tr/sites/default/files/calismaraporu.pdf.

Bogazici Universitesi Soma Dayanismasi (BUSD). 2014. "Soma iş cinayeti/kazasi gözlem, aktarim ve teknik inceleme raporu Kasim." Accessed April 5, 2015. www.bogazicisomadayanismasi.boun.edu.tr/sites/default/files/Bogazici%20Soma%20Dayanismasi%20Soma%20Raporu_Kasim%202014.pdf.

Boin, R.A. and P. 't Hart. 2003. "Public Leadership in Times of Crisis: Mission Impossible." *Public Administration Review* 63 (5): 544–553.

CNN Turk. 2014. "Soma A.S. devlete komur diye tas satmis." Accessed April 1, 2015. www.cnnturk.com/video/turkiye/soma-a-s-devlete-komur-diye-tas-satmis.

Demiroz, F. and N. Kapucu. 2015. "Cross-sector partnerships in managing disasters: Experiences from the United States." In D*isaster Management and Private Sector,* edited by T. Izumi and R. Shaw, 169–186. New York: Springer.

Godschalk, D. 2003. "Urban Hazard Mitigation: Creating Resilient Cities." *Natural Hazards Review* 4, 136–143.

HaberTurk. 2014. "AFAD Başkanı ve AKUT Başkanı Soma'daki çalışmaları değerlendirdi." Accessed April 6, 2015. www.haberturk.com/gundem/haber/949480-afad-baskani-ve-akut-baskani-somadaki-calismalari-degerlendirdi.

Hill, C. and L. E. Lynn. 2009. *Public Management: A Three Dimentional Approach.* Washington DC: CQ Press.

Hughes. O. 2012. *Public Management and Administration.* New York: Palgrave Macmillan.

Hurriyet. 2012. "TTK 10 milyar lira alacak." Accessed April 5, 2015.

www.hurriyet.com.tr/yazarlar/21586913.asp.

Internethaber. 2014. "9 ay once ayni madende bunlari soylemisti." Accessed April 1, 2015. www.internethaber.com/9-ay-once-ayni-madende-bunlari-soylemisti672211h.htm.

Kapucu, N. 2015. "Leadership and Collaborative Governance in Managing Emergencies and Crises." In *Risk Governance: The Articulation of Hazard, Politics, and Ecology,* edited by U. F. Paleo, 211–235. New York: Springer.

Kapucu, N. 2010. *Governance Reforms: Comparative Perspectives.* Ankara: International Strategic Research Organization (ISRO).

Kapucu, N. 2009. "Public Administration and Cross-sector Governance in Response to and Recovery from Disasters."*Administration and Society* 41(7): 910–914.

Kapucu, N. 2008. "Collaborative Emergency Management: Better Community Organizing, Better Public Preparedness and Response." *Disasters* 32 (2): 239–262.

Kapucu, N. 2005. "Interorganizational Coordination in Dynamic Context: Networks in Emergency Response Management." *Connections* 26 (2): 33–48.

Kapucu, N., T. Arslan, F. Demiroz. 2010. "Collaborative Emergency Management and National Emergency Management Network." *Disaster Prevention and Management* 19 (4): 452–468.

Kapucu, N. and A. Ozerdem. 2013. *Managing Emergencies and Crises.* Boston: Jones & Bartlett Publishers.

Lynn. L. E. 2007. "Public Management: A Concise History of the Field." In *Oxford Handbook of Public Management*, edited by E. Ferlie, L.E. Lynn, and C. Pollit, 27–50. New York: Oxford University Press.

Lynn, L. E., C. J. Heinrich, and C. J. Hill. 2000. "Studying Governance and Public Management: Challenges and Prospects." *Journal of Public Administration Research and Theory* 10 (2): 233–261.

Mandell, M. and R. L. Keast. "Evaluating network arrangements: toward revised performance measures." *Public Performance & Management Review* 30 (4): 574–597.

Milbank, D. 2016. "The Flint Disaster is Rick Snyder's Fault." Accessed January 29, 2016. www.washingtonpost.com/opinions/the-flint-disaster-is-rick-snyders-fault/2016/01/25/9c77e036-c3b1-11e5-a4aa-f25866ba0dc6_story.html.

New York Times. 2016. "Michigan's Failure to Protect Flint." Accessed January 29, 2016. www.nytimes.com/2016/01/15/opinion/michigans-failure-to-protect-flint.html?smid=tw-nytopinion&smtyp=cur&_r=0.

Norris, F. H., S. P. Stevens, B. Pfefferbaum, K. F. Wyche, and R. F. Pfefferbaum. 2008. "Community Resilience as a Metaphor, Theory, Set of Capacities and Strategy for Disaster Readiness." *American Journal of Community Psychology* 41(1–2): 127–150.

Rose, A. 2005. "Analyzing Terrorist Threats to the Econmoy: A Computable General Equlibrium Approach." In *Economic Impacts of Terrorist Attacks*, edited by P. Gordon, J. Moore, and H. Richardson, 196–217. Cheltenham: Edward Elgar.

Rose, A. 2004. "Defining and Measuring Economic Resilience to Disasters." *Disaster Prevention and Management*, 13, 307–314.

Salamon, L. M. 2002. *The Tools of Government: A Guide to New Governance.* New York: Oxford University Press.

Sayistay. 2014. "Turkiye Komur Isletmeleri Kurumu 2013 Denetim Raporu." Accessed April 5, 2015. www.sayistay.gov.tr/rapor/kit/2013/6-TK%C4%B0%202013.pdf.

Soma Bilirkisi Raporu. 2014. "Soma Komur Isletilen A.S. Tarafindan Isletilen Manisa Ili, Soma Ilcesi, Eynez Koyundeki Komur Madeninde 13.5.2014 Tarihinde Meydana Gelen Maden Kazasi ile Ilgili Bilirkisi Raporu, Eylul 2014." Accessed April 5, 2015. www.madenmuhendisleri.org/?Syf=18&Hbr=721377&/Soma-Maden-Kazas%C4%B1-Bilirki%C5%9Fi-Raporu-Manisa-Barosu-web-sayfas%C4%B1nda-yay%C4%B1nland%C4%B1.T%C3%BCm-meslekta%C5%9Flar%C4%B1m%C4%B1n-okumalar%C4%B1-gerekir.

T24. 2014a. "Patlamanın gerçekleştiği maden en son ocak ayında denetlenmiş." Accessed April 5, 2015. http://t24.com.tr/haber/o-maden-ocagi-ocak-ayinda-denetlenmis,258315.

T24. 2014b. "Başbakan Soma'da: Literatürde iş kazası var, bunlar olağan şeyler." Accessed April 5, 2015. http://t24.com.tr/haber/basbakan-somada-olu-sayisi-232,258370.

T24. 2014c. "Yusuf Yerkel gorevinden alindi." Accessed April 6, 2015. http://t24.com.tr/haber/yusuf-yerkel-gorevden-alindi,259251.

T24. 2014d. "Taner Yildiz Soma'nin sorumlulugunu Calisma Bakanligina Atti." Accessed April 5, 2015. http://t24.com.tr/haber/taner-yildiz-somanin-sorumlulugunu-calisma-bakanligina-atti,265487.

T24. 2014e. "Somada ki eyleme TOMA'li, biber gazli, plastic mermili mudahele." Accessed April 5. 2015. http://t24.com.tr/haber/somadaki-eyleme-tomali-biber-gazli-plastik-mermili-mudahale,258566.

Taraf. 2013. "CHP ve MHP'yi fisledik." Accessed April 6, 2015. http://arsiv.taraf.com.tr/haber-chp-ve-mhp-yi-fisledik-136458/.

Tukiye Komur Isletmeleri (TKI). 2014. "Komur Sektor Raporu 2013." Accessed April 1, 2015. www.enerji.gov.tr/File/?path=ROOT%2F1%2FDocuments%2FSekt%C3%B6r+Raporu%2FK%C3%B6m%C3%BCr+Sekt%C3%B6r+Raporu+-+Linyit+2013.pdf .

Turkiye Muhendis ve Mimar Odalari Birligi (TMMOB). 2013. "Soma Maden Kazasi Raporu." Accessed April 5, 2015. www.tmmob.org.tr/sites/default/files/somaraporu.pdf.

Vangen, S. and C. Huxham. "Enacting leadership for collaborative advantage: Dilemmas of ideology and pragmatism in the activities of partnership managers." *British Journal of Management* 14: 61–76.</ref>

20

REGULATORY REFORM AND THE BETTER REGULATION AGENDA

Traveling from center to periphery

Alketa Peci

Introduction

This chapter discusses the processes and outcomes of regulatory reforms and the recent "better regulation" agenda in the developing context of Latin America. Two complementary forces shaped the apparently mimetic processes and outcomes of the regulatory reforms in the region: (1) pressure from the developed center to the developing periphery, fuelled by the actions of international organizations such as the World Bank and Organisation for Economic Cooperation and Development (OECD), as were the previous market-oriented reforms during the late 1980s (Dubash and Morgan 2012; Jacobs 2005; Kirkpatrick et al. 2004, 2003), and (2) the simultaneous role of important domestic factors that also influenced the processes and outcomes of such "center to periphery" diffusion of regulatory reforms.

Considering the political and institutional heterogeneity of the Latin American region, we will focus on specific countries which share a willingness to become an important part of the globalized agenda, by actively participating in international agreements beyond Latin American region, such as Brazil, Mexico, Peru and Chile (some examples are Trans-Pacific Partnerships, BRICS, OECD membership), rather than those focusing on a local or regional political agenda, as in Bolivia, Venezuela or Ecuador. The "Latin American" version of the "Regulatory State" (Levi-Faur and Jordana 2006; Majone 1997) is being expanded through independent or semi-autonomous regulatory (or executive arm's length) agencies in different economic and social sectors, whose actual independence from the Executive varies from one sector to another. Although the "independence" of such regulatory agencies is contested, they constitute a central institutional innovation of important sectoral reforms.

Two cross-border aspects are particularly relevant for comprehending the diffusion of regulatory reforms in Latin America: the context of economic liberalization and regulatory reforms and the role of international organizations such as the OECD or World Bank. Many of the region's countries have been deeply involved in structural economic changes related to privatization and liberalization since the late 1980s. The regulatory reforms in the region have embraced many different sectors and gone beyond privatization to involve large-scale economic and political changes addressing the problems of the import-substitution State-centered "developmental" model. In fact, since the early 1990s, most Latin American countries involved in the introduction of new regulatory regimes have aimed to transform the manner in which the market operates by moving away from state protection and central control of the economy (Levi-Faur and Jordana 2006; Murillo 2002). The regimes have transformed the very nature of the state, weakening the direct protection, intervention and control of economic and social sectors while strengthening the state's regulatory role.

The immediate outcomes of such reforms embrace the creation of independent (or semi-autonomous) regulatory agencies (IRAs) or the adoption of other regulatory instruments, such as contracts, to move towards a market-oriented economy, although the depth and nature of such reforms varies from one country to another (Guasch and Spiller 1997). More recently, several Latin American countries are embracing a better regulation agenda, following other international trends and OECD recommendations.

However, the Latin American countries are not merely copying international fads, and important domestic factors influence the outcomes of the regulatory policies diffusion in the region. The main objective of this chapter is to discuss the role of such domestic factors by focusing on two key processes of regulatory reforms: (1) the adoption of independent or semi-autonomous regulatory agencies, and (2) the adoption of a better regulation agenda.

The creation of independent or semi-autonomous regulatory agencies, and their impressive growth in the 1990s, has been the most astonishing outcome of regulatory reform (Gilardi et al. 2006). According to a study by Jordana and Levi-Faur (2005), in 19 Latin American countries and 12 economic and social sectors, the number of new regulatory entities has grown from 43 (mostly financial regulatory institutions) before 1979 to an overall number of 138 by 2002. Agencies were created in sectors such as: utilities, including telecommunication, electricity, gas, water, etc.; competition; social, including environment, pharmaceuticals, food safety, health insurance; and finance, including central banking, securities and exchange; among others. We will discuss how the regulatory agencies' independence and autonomy is traduced in the Latin American context, focusing on Brazil.

The most recent trend in several Latin American countries, such as Brazil, Mexico and Chile, has been the adoption of a "better regulation" agenda through the introduction of administrative instruments and procedures, such as Regulatory Impact Assessments (RIAs), the Standard Cost Model, etc. (Jordana and Levi-Faur 2005; Kirkpatrick et al. 2004; Levi-Faur 2003). However, the formal diffusion of better regulation instruments has not converged in terms of actual practices because of domestic political forces or the low availability of institutional and organizational capacities (Peci and Sobral 2011; Kirkpatrick and Parker 2007). We will discuss these countries' heterogeneous trajectories and demonstrate how local bureaucracies are changing the dominant perspective on RIA from an instrument of political control to an instrument used for their own benefit.

In other words, the Latin American version of the "regulatory state" (Levi-Faur and Jordana 2006; Majone 1997) influences the manner in which such instruments are adopted, interpreted and implemented by domestic political actors. Latin American countries are adopting/adapting regulatory labels to their political, institutional and legal contexts. Our analysis will privilege the pivotal role of bureaucracy in the region, aiming to show that the apparent homogenizing outcomes of the regulatory reforms might not overshadow the diversity of the institutional-building processes that are taking place in the different countries of the region.

Independent regulatory agencies: an institutional innovation?

Our first analysis will focus on the diffusion of the independent regulatory agency (IRA) in the Brazilian context, highlighting the historical role of the bureaucracy as a key political actor.

Brazil was an earlier adapter of bureaucratic reform in the 1930s, and the consolidation of a strong techno-bureaucracy was explicitly supported by an ambitious, import-substitution state-centered "developmental" project. One of its unintended consequences was the expansion of numerous state-owned companies into different sectors and levels of the government (the "bras"-model of companies such as Telebras, Eletrobras, Petrobras, among many others) with their respective techno-bureaucracies, although this expansion was also marked by huge regional and inter-governmental disparities (Bresser-Pereira and Diniz 2009; Bresser-Pereira 1981).

The great surge of regulatory reforms and privatizations of public services in the 1990s was propelled by many economic, social and political factors, generally denominated as the "state crises". The reforms substantially modified the institutional design of several economic and social sectors, privatizing a good part of the "bras" and other state-owned companies. As a consequence, the economy shifted from a predominantly state-centered, highly centralized ownership and control model to a market-centered one (Abranches 1988).

Regulatory reform invaded the political agenda and was strongly associated with the privatization and liberalization reforms of the 1990s. Since 1996, more than 50 new IRAs, which were created as independent or semi-autonomous agencies, have been adopted at all three levels of the government and across different sectors. Agencies were established not only in privatized utility sectors, such as electricity, telecommunications, oil, gas, and transportation but also in non-infrastructure sectors and at other subnational levels.

Because of its relation to economic and liberalization reform, regulation was defined in terms of economic incentives and tools, as opposed to the broader image of regulation as encompassing the normative powers of the state translated into a body of rules that constrain the behavior of citizens or firms. The focus on regulation as efficiency-seeking "economic regulation" pervaded the Brazilian governmental and regulatory culture and continues to influence the perceptions of public officials regarding regulation today (Peci and Sobral 2011).

As non-economic sectors adopted regulatory agencies, the concept of a regulatory state conquered the Brazilian political agenda, and the agencies' independence became very attractive to other public sector organizations. New RIAs were expanded in other sectors such as water, transportation, health, food, and drugs. RIAs also proliferated at the state and municipal levels, reaching their current number of 50 (Peci 2007; Martins 2004).

Despite their different regulatory purposes, these agencies are characterized by a high degree of organizational isomorphism. They are executive bodies dependent on their respective ministries or state/municipal secretaries responsible for developing regulatory policies. The agencies are more similar to European executive arm's-length institutions instead of independent regulators (Faria 2004; Faria and Ribeiro 2002; Melo 2002). Table 20.1 presents a list of federal regulatory agencies, highlighting the characteristics of the regulated sector, their regulatory purposes, and the sectors where IRAs mainly operate.

As a consequence of such overreaching regulatory reform, Brazil can be considered an interesting case of a "Regulatory State" (Levi-Faur and Jordana 2006; Majone 1997) and is in a privileged position to understand how regulatory agencies are adopted, interpreted and implemented by domestic political actors. Although Brazil has experienced a boom of IRAs, the process of agencification was particularly curious, as some agencies were never implemented, some were extinguished and others have grown – in number of employees and budget, for example – and responsibility beyond their regulatory purposes. Exceptions are far from isolated cases. Brazil has probably the only IRA for the support, funding and regulation of the video, phonographic and cinematographic sector, but not the audiovisual sector as a whole, which is most common worldwide. At the state level, it is very common to find agencies that were formally created but never got off the ground, and it is even possible to find a multi-sectoral

Table 20.1 Federal regulatory agencies

	Type of Regulated Sector	*Type of Regulation*	*Sector*
ANA National Water Agency	Private and public	Social and environmental	Hydric resources
ANAC National Civil Aviation Agency	Private and public	Economic	Civil aviation, airports infrastructure
ANATEL National Agency of Telecommunications	Public and private	Economic	Telecommunications
ANCINE National Cinema Agency	Public and private	Social (funding)	Video, phonographic and cinematographic sector
ANEEL National Agency of Electrical Energy	Public and private	Economic	Generation, transmission and distribution of electrical energy
ANP National Agency of Oil and Gas	Public and private	Economic	Oil, gas, and biofuels
ANS National Health Agency	Private	Economic and social	Private health insurance
ANTAQ National Agency of Water Transportation	Public and private	Economic	Water transportation and ports
ANTT National Agency of Transportation	Public and private	Economic	Railways, highways, and railroad infrastructure
ANVISA National Health Surveillance Agency	Public and private	Social	Sanitary surveillance of products, services, ports, airports and borders

Source: Elaborated by the author

IRA that regulates lottery activity or public–nonprofit partnerships. In sum, Brazilian IRAs are an excellent case of policy "innovation and reinvention" (Glick and Hays 1991).

Independence – what does it mean in the Brazilian context?

Theoretically, the legitimacy of delegation to autonomous IRAs, granting more autonomy to Brazilian regulators was justified based on (1) reduction of the cost of decision-making, and (2) insurance of credible commitments (Majone 2001). The presence of an independent IRA, then, can be attributed to the necessity of high levels of technical information when expected political benefits are low (Epstein and O'Halloran 1999) or simply when it politicians tend to avoid responsibility for negative consequences (Fiorina 1982). The arguments about credible commitments, political uncertainty, blame shifting and bureaucratic influence can also be found in the extant literature examining Brazilian IRAs (Prado 2012; Melo 2002; Mueller and Pereira 2002). It seems natural that this type of explanation has predominated, as the first IRAs were set up concomitant to the widespread privatization process that marked the opening of the infrastructure sector to private capital.

However, the diffusion of IRAs can also be seen as part of a broader agencification process, which has been characterized as an international fad in the field of public administration. Although the agency form and its global dissemination is a highly popular phenomenon, what each local context understands as an agency and the observed differences in their degree of autonomy and control indicate divergences – particularly because the agencies have unique trajectories given their countries and sectors (Verhoest and Laegreid 2010; Verschuere and Barbieri 2009; Yesilkagit and Christensen 2009; Levi-Faur 2006; Nakano 2004; Pollitt et al. 2001). As a result, agencies not only differ in their shapes and trajectories but also in the rhetoric that upholds them (Smullen 2010) in a process of "divergent convergence" (Tenbucken and Schneider 2004).

Formally, Brazilian IRA's autonomy is traduced in a more flexible organizational model based on traditional mechanisms, such as: (1) the creation as a "special autarchy" – a traditional form of indirect public administration; (2) independent and non-coincident terms for regulators; (3) independent funding; and (4) less formal internal and external controls.

Although IRAs are presented rhetorically as a more autonomous organizational model, there are strong indicators that this "autonomy" is more an ideal-type model than a genuine institutional innovation. In most of the IRAs, the independent and non-coincident terms for regulators are commonly "paralyzed;" "independent" funding is usually channeled to other governmental purposes, and IRAs suffer under the weight of internal and external controls that do not differentiate them from other traditional public administration entities. In practice, agencies have variable degrees of autonomy, indicating more independence in sectors like telecommunications that were previously characterized by a strong professional bureaucracy (Prado 2012).

However, over the years, the strengthening of the regulatory agencies' technical skills through public competition entries and their growing specialized knowledge, combined with certain undefined ministerial roles and responsibilities, concentrated the formulation and implementation process of public policies in regulatory bodies. The roles of the respective ministries and central government political leaders, which were traditionally pivotal in policy-formulating processes in Brazil, were weakened. Indeed, as Bianculli (2013) explains, the consolidation of IRAs entailed the establishment of a new arena for the definition of public policies. Although Brazilian IRAs are not highly independent because executive power still largely controls funding and political appointments, their bureaucracy is becoming a relevant force in the policy process. Consequently, IRAs have strengthened their political role, and there have been many attempts by discontented political leaders to influence agencies' decision-making processes over recent years, thus threatening their autonomy (Peci 2007; Faria 2004; Martins 2004; Faria and Ribeiro 2002).

Despite an apparently adverse context, Brazilian regulators have been able to claim expertise to secure independence from political interference, particularly at the federal level, highlighting the role of the bureaucracy of regulatory agencies – regulocrats – as pivotal political actors. In fact, the main outcomes of Brazilian regulatory reform have been the growing legitimacy of IRAs as a more flexible management model and the strengthening of such "regulocracy" (the stable technocrats and professionals of such arm's-length bureaucracies), which spans a wide range of sectors beyond infrastructure (Gilardi, Jordana, and Levi-Faur 2007; Peci 2007).

Consequently, regulocrats are continuously strengthening their political role, which marks the diffusion of regulatory policies in the Brazilian context.

What is the typical professional profile and career path of a Brazilian regulocrat? In recent research we analyzed the bibliographical profiles of 10 federal agencies and 157 federal regulators, as well as 27 state-level agencies and 233 state regulators, and compared our data with Eckert's (1981) and Spiller's (1990) studies about United States' (US) federal regulators. Table 20.2 highlights some important differences and similarities between Brazilian and US federal and state regulators.

Our research reveals that, differently from the US where lawyers are the majority of regulators, Brazilian regulocrats are predominantly engineers or sector-related graduates. Similarly to the US, Brazilians regulators demonstrate expansive prior experience in the regulated sector. This highlights technical expertise as the most important source of an IRA's autonomy legitimation (Schrefler 2010; Majone 1996). As noted, important historical factors influence the current profile of Brazilian federal regulocrats. In Brazil, most of the currently regulated sectors used to be state owned before the privatization reforms of the 1990s, and most of the current Brazilian regulators originated from former state-owned and currently regulated companies.

However, there are strong similarities in the post-agency destination of Brazilian Federal and US regulators. Although for different reasons, both countries' regulators had pre-agency experience in the public sector, they have similar patterns of post-agency behaviors: 45 per cent

Table 20.2 Brazilian vs. US regulators

Characteristics of Regulators	Federal Regulators (Brazil)	State-Level Regulators (Brazil)	Federal Regulators (USA)
	42.6% Engineers	33% Engineers	7% Engineers
Field of graduate specialization	31.2% (Applied Social Sciences, such as Economics, Law or Management)	52% (Applied Social Sciences, such as Economics, Law or Management)	71% (Lawyers)
	14% (Health-related field)		
Previous experience in the regulated sector (public or private)	82.2%	67.38%	Not measured
Previous experience in the public sector	79.8%	62%	74.4%
Previous experience in the regulated private sector	16%	Not measured	15.5%
Post-agency job in the regulated private sector	49%	13%	45%
Post-agency job in the public sector	41.5%	72%	17%
Post-agency job in another regulatory agency	8.9%	7.2%	Not measured

Source: Elaborated by the author

and 49 per cent, respectively, took private sector jobs in the regulated industries. In Brazilian infrastructure agencies such as electricity, telecommunication or petroleum, these numbers reach 80 per cent, indicating that almost all federal regulators are apparently being headhunted from private companies. However, these post-agency jobs can also be seen as a consequence of the learning and expertise accumulated during a regulator's term.

In fact, when we compare the data with state-level regulators, we perceive different dynamics, particularly related to lower levels of post-agency jobs in the regulated sectors and the dominance of the public sector jobs. Most of the state-level agencies are multi-sectoral, inhibiting sector learning and expertise accumulation. Only 21 out of 157 regulators shifted to regulated industry-related jobs, and all of them did so after demonstrating expertise in the sector. Most of the regulators return to public-sector or political careers (being elected), indicating competing capture dynamics from the public-sector bureaucracy or politics in Brazilian states. Bureaucratic capture is a particularly compelling interpretation in the Brazilian context, especially considering the emerging trend of post-agency-related jobs inside regulatory agencies in both federal and state-level IRAs.

Such competing capture dynamics, as well as the pivotal political role of the bureaucracy, are central in comprehending how regulatory independence is actually traduced in the Brazilian context.

The adoption of a better regulation agenda: regulatory impact assessments in LA

The overly sectoral focus of the regulatory reform, which sustained IRA creation in LA countries, eclipsed a "whole-of-government" approach (Christensen and Lægreid 2006) and revealed pervasive institutional weaknesses (Minogue and Cariño 2006). Consequently, the current agenda has focused on strengthening the capacity for high-quality regulation and modernizing the institutional framework by defending the former approach (Christensen and Lægreid 2006).

The process of Regulatory Impact Assessments (RIAs) implementation is part of such efforts in countries such as Mexico, Chile and Brazil, revealing, again, the role of the OECD as an important "mechanism of external validation" (Minogue and Cariño 2006).

However, domestic factors have yielded great variability in RIAs across these countries. Brazil is developing RIA programs based on an incremental strategy fuelled by regulocrats and coordinated by the Presidential Program PRO-REG (Program for the Strengthening of the Institutional Capacity for Regulatory Management). In Brazil, RIAs are primarily focusing on independent regulatory agencies, whereas other countries, like Uruguay, are focusing on alternative local or regional policy priorities and RIAs are not yet part of the formal agenda.

In Mexico, the oldest Latin American member of the OECD, the diffusion of RIAs did not focus on a specific sector. It was supported by the creation of the regulatory oversight body COFEMER (*Comisión Federal de Mejora Regulatoria*) in 2000, in an attempt to overcome the overly sectoral focus of regulatory reform (Levi-Faur and Jordana 2006). The commission is a trans-sectoral oversight body that oversees a large number of legal dispositions, such as decrees, regulations, presidential pacts, departmental resolutions, and norms, among other legal instruments. Before issuing any official regulation, all centralized and decentralized entities of the Public Administration must submit their proposals to COFEMER for approval (Carballo 2012). As a small, functionally autonomous agency, its objective is to promote transparency in the elaboration and application of new regulations to obtain greater benefits and lower costs for society.

The creation of COFEMER, following RIA diffusion, was unique in Latin America. It is an attempt to introduce wiser regulation in the country in parallel with the development of specialized regulatory institutions in sectors such as telecommunications, energy, food safety, and health (Levi-Faur and Jordana 2006). In an OECD report about the institutional capacity for regulatory reform, Mexico achieved a superior classification to the UK, the Netherlands, Germany and Canada (Carballo 2012).

The adoption of a better regulation agenda has produced positive outcomes for Mexico, such as the clarification of procedures for new regulations and quality controls, the introduction of a consultation process, and the introduction of stricter criteria for new proposed regulations (Levi-Faur and Jordana 2006: 46). As in other countries, certain failures in Mexico are attributed to the poor quality of available information, which hampers the reliable quantitative analyses of regulatory proposals (Kirkpatrick et al. 2003).

The role of a strong and professional bureaucracy, not found in the majority of the regions' countries, associated with the influence of external pressures (particularly from the OECD, where Mexico holds a permanent member position) has helped to overcome a fragmented and sector-based regulatory reform. As a consequence, Mexico can be considered a pioneer in advancing a better regulation agenda.

However, the centralizing Mexican experience is unique in the region. Chile, which is also an OECD member, is an interesting case of ad hoc RIA diffusion without the existence of an oversight body or any institutional coordination mechanism related to regulatory governance. In fact, Chile has insulated itself from similar external pressures to adopt regulatory reforms (Levi-Faur and Jordana 2006) or a better regulation agenda, mainly because it did not experience the negative consequences of a fragmented and sector-channeled regulatory reform. Consequently, there is a high variability of RIA requirements and procedures in Chile. Such an ad hoc diffusion of RIAs may be due to alternative institutional arrangements that assure quality regulations and are related with the institutional strength, coherence, and inter-agency cooperation that exist within the Chilean bureaucratic landscape, as well as the liberal and market-oriented ideological consensus of the Chilean state (Minogue and Cariño 2006). These domestic factors may diminish the contribution that instruments like RIAs may play in improving the overall quality of regulatory governance.

The Brazilian RIA experience demonstrates the interplay of international pressures with domestic factors and is illustrative of the uniqueness of the processes and outcomes of such a center to periphery diffusion. Triggered by a 2008 OECD recommendation, RIAs have been progressively adopted by independent regulatory agencies (IRAs) at the federal level on a voluntary basis and without the supervision of an oversight body.

In fact, IRAs were introduced as a presidential initiative by the *Casa Civil da Presidência da República's* (Office of the President) chief advisers and its Program to Strengthen the Institutional Capacity for Regulatory Management (PRO-REG). They never assumed a mandatory or compulsory nature, indicating the more flexible nature of the Brazilian "coalition presidentialism" (Abranches 1988). RIAs seemed to be a promising tool for politically controlling the bureaucracy (Radaelli and Francesco 2007; Radaelli 2005), and we previously demonstrated that they were actually perceived as such by regulatory bureaucrats (Peci and Sobral 2011). However, in a short period of time, initial resistance was overcome, and the latter became the RIAs' main supporters.

Agencies that did not fit the traditional model of regulatory institutions were pioneers in RIA adoption. Such non-utility IRAs, for which regulatory competence or sector are not clearly defined, embraced RIAs as a new form to legitimate their position in the regulatory arena. The first RIA pilot project was adopted by Anvisa (National Health Surveillance Agency), a federal multi-sectoral agency that was not covered by the OECD report (2008a). Anvisa established a strong relationship with PRO-REG and played a leading role in the RIA diffusion process by serving as a benchmark for other regulatory agencies. It gradually gained the support of Anvisa's directors and a wider audience of regulocrats by demonstrating the contribution of RIAs in improving the quality of regulatory decisions.

In the context of scarce conditions for actual regulatory independence, RIAs rapidly became an instrument of bureaucratic (regulocratic) legitimation. The Anvisa case and the immediate adoption of RIAs by non-utilities agencies, such as Ancine (National Cinema Agency), demonstrate the symbolic nature of the instrument's utilization to gain legitimacy vis-à-vis other policy actors – in the Brazilian case, typical utility IRAs (Schrefler 2010). Other agencies, including ANP (National Petroleum Agency), Aneel (National Regulatory Electricity Agency), ANS (National Health Agency), Antaq (National Water Transportation Agency), Anac (National Aviation Agency), and ANA (National Water Agency), followed gradually. In Brazil's vertically-oriented federalism, new initiatives generally originate at the federal level and disseminate to the subnational levels of the government, and so RIAs have been adopted in several Brazilian states.

The Brazilian case of RIA diffusion is interesting because it demonstrates how the initial vision of RIA as an instrument for political control of bureaucracies was rapidly substituted with a positive assessment, shielding IRA regulocrats from exogenous political pressures. Again, the growing political role of the regulocracy is key to comprehending the displacement of the traditional vision of RIAs as instruments of political control. Such a regulocracy, with its technical-rational orientation, has provided fertile ground for RIA adoption. There is still some resistance, particularly from the high-level administration of traditional utilities' IRAs. Although they support RIA as an instrument for improving regulatory decision-making, they are resistant to the idea of creating a regulatory oversight body to supervise RIAs' quality, as in Mexico. This resistance has to be seen in the context in which most Brazilian IRAs still struggle to ensure and strengthen their independence, an institutional feature that is relatively new to the Brazilian executive branch.

Conclusions

This chapter discussed the processes and outcomes of regulatory reforms and the more recent "better regulation" agenda in developing contexts, as seen in the specific Latin American countries Brazil, Mexico and Chile.

As in other developing contexts, most of the regulatory reforms embraced by the LA countries might be observed from a center to a periphery (or, better, north–south) perspective. Here, the role and the pressure of international organizations such as the World Bank and the OECD are pivotal in understanding the earlier adoption of several regulatory reforms after the market-oriented processes of the late 1980s (Dubash and Morgan 2012; Jacobs 2005; Kirkpatrick et al. 2004, 2003). These international organizations have been crucial in introducing several institutional regulatory innovations, particularly in selected LA countries that share a willingness to become an important part of the globalized agenda, participating in several international forums (such as the OECD, BRICS, Trans-Pacific Partnership) rather than focusing on a local or regional political agenda.

However, the connotation of the Latin America region as developing may hinder or excessively homogenize regulatory diffusion processes, thereby reducing the outcomes of such processes to a lack or insufficiency of institutional or organizational capacities to adopt more advanced regulatory reforms (Kirkpatrick et al. 2004). This has been the main focus of best practices recommended by international organizations. Instead, the divergent processes and outcomes of regulatory reforms indicate the need to comprehend how local actors understand and rely on instruments such as RIA or adapt the principles of IRAs' autonomy to their own interests.

The processes of regulatory diffusion are complex and present heterogeneous outcomes because of the interplay of important international and domestic factors. To demystify the dominant vision of weak institutional capacities, we privilege the analysis of bureaucracy as a key political actor in the institution-building processes of regulatory reforms in countries such as Brazil and Mexico. The growing bureaucracy of recent independent regulatory institutions (IRAs), although still distant from actual autonomy, is strengthening its role and building new sources of legitimation in expertise and professionalization or adopting, in innovative and unexpected ways, instruments such as Regulatory Impact Assessments (RIAs).

The Latin American version of the "Regulatory State" (Levi-Faur and Jordana 2006; Majone 1997) is characterized by a complex triad of regulatory capture, where the market, bureaucracy and politics compete in menacing the recent and unfamiliar concept of regulatory autonomy. As opposed to the US experience, where there are clearer indicators of a market capture, Brazilian regulators are pressured from other constituencies, particularly bureaucracy.

When we analyze the most recent diffusion of a better regulation agenda, the role of bureaucracy is still prominent. In fact, the rational ideal-type model of impact assessment reflected in RIAs (Radaelli 2005) is echoed in strong bureaucratic constituencies, which are also characterized by a rational-legal authority dimension. The three countries that have championed RIA adoption in the region are characterized by strong professional bureaucracies, although the latter permeate their institutional landscapes in different ways. In such contexts, the malleability of RIAs beyond their technical dimension is evident. The Brazilian case demonstrates that the regulocrats are using RIAs to shield themselves from political pressure and gain legitimacy relative to other policy actors, thereby overcoming the initial perception of RIAs as instruments of political control. Mexico constituted a centralized organizational model to challenge overly sector-oriented regulatory reforms, whereas Chile, with its state exceptionality, avoided the negative consequences of a fragmented reform and opted for an ad hoc RIA diffusion.

A closer look at the regulatory diffusion processes in developing contexts reveals a complex interplay of international and domestic political factors and demonstrates the malleability of apparently homogeneous institutional models such as IRAs, or "neutral" regulatory instruments such as RIAs, beyond their technical dimensions.

References

Abranches, S. H. H. 1988. "Presidencialismo de Coalizão: O Dilema Institucional Brasileiro." *Revista Brasileira de Ciências Sociais* 31 (1): 5–34.

Bianculli, A. C. 2013. "The Brazilian Association of Regulatory Agencies: Integrating levels, Consolidating Identities in the Regulatory State in the South." *Regulation & Governance* 7 (4): 547–559.

Bresser-Pereira, L. C. 1981. *A sociedade estatal e a tecnoburocracia.* São Paulo: Editora Brasiliense.

Bresser-Pereira, L. C. and Diniz, E. 2009. "Empresariado Industrial, Democracia e Poder Político." *Novos Estudos CEBRAP (Impresso)* 84: 82–99.

Carballo, A. 2012. *I Seminario Latino-Americano sobre Experiencies Exitosas em Regulación: Experiencia Mexicana.* In *Experiencias Exitosas em Regulação na America Latina e Caribe,* edited by Proença, J. D., and Paulo, C. B. Brasilia: Presidencia da Republica.

Christensen, Tom and Lægreid, P. 2006. "Agencification and Regulatory Reforms." Paper prepared for the SCANCOR/SOG workshop on Automization of the State: From Integrated Administrative Models to Single Purpose Organizations. Stanford University, April 1–2, 2005.

COFEMER (Comisión Federal de Mejora Regulatoria). 2013. Antecedentes. www.cofemer.gob.mx/ (accessed 15 March 2014).

Dubash, N. K. and Morgan, B. 2012. "Understanding the rise of the regulatory state of the South." *Regulation & Governance* 6 (3): 261–281.

Eckert, R. D. 1981. "The Life Cycle of Regulatory Commissioners." *Journal of Law and Economics* 24: 113–120.

Epstein, D. and O'Halloran, S. 1999 *Delegating Powers: A Transaction Cost Politics Approach to Policy-Making under Separate Powers*. Cambridge: Cambridge University Press.

Faria, P. L. C. 2004. "Desempenho, Transparência e Regulação: O Mito das Incompatibilidades Congênitas." Paper persented at the IX Congreso Internacional del CLAD sobre la Reforma del Estado y de la Administración Pública, Madrid, España, November, 2–5.

Faria, P. L. C. and Ribeiro, S. 2002. "Regulação e os Novos Modelos de Gestão no Brasil." *Revista do Serviço Público* 53 (3): 79–93.

Fiorina, M. P. 1982. "Legislative Choice of Regulatory Forms: Legal Process or Administrative Process?" *Public Choice* 39 (1): 33–66.

Gilardi, F, Jordana, J., and Levi-Faur, D. 2007. "Regulation in the Age of Globalization: The Diffusion of Regulatory Agencies across Europe and Latin America." In *Privatization and Market Development: Global Movements in Public Policy Ideas*, edited by Hodge. G. A., 127–147. Edward Elgar, Cheltenham: Edward Elgar Publishing.

Glick, Henry R. and Hays, S. P. 1991. "Innovation and Reinvention in State Policymaking: Theory and the Evolution of Living Will Laws." *Journal of Politics* 53 (3): 835–850.

Guasch, J. L. and Spiller, P. 1997. *Managing the Regulatory Process: Design, Concepts, Issues and The Latin America and Caribbean Story*. Directions in Development Series. Washington, DC: World Bank.

Jacobs, C. 2005. "The Role of Regulatory Impact Assessment in Democratization: Selected Cases from the Transition States of Central and Eastern Europe." Working Paper 101. Center on Regulation and Competition: University of Manchester.

Jordana, J. and Levi-Faur, D. 2006. "Toward a Latin American Regulatory State: The Diffusion of Autonomous Regulatory Agencies Across Countries and Sectors." *International Journal of Public Administration* 29 (4–6): 335–356.

Jordana, J. and Levi-Faur, D. 2005. "The diffusion of regulatory capitalism in Latin America: Sectoral and national channels in the making of a new order." *The Annals of the American Academy of Political and Social Science* 598 (1): 102–124.

Kirkpatrick, C. and Parker, D. 2007. *Regulatory Impact Assessment: Toward Better Regulation?* Cheltenham: Edward Elgar Publishing.

Kirkpatrick, C., Parker, D., and Zhang, Y. F. 2004 "Regulatory Impact Assessment in Developing and Transition Economies: A Survey of Current Practice." *Public Money & Management* 24 (5): 291–296.

Levi-Faur, D. 2011. "Regulation & Regulatory Governance." In *Handbook on the Politics of Regulation*, edited by Levy-Faur, D., 1–25. Cheltenham: Edward Elgar Publishing.

Levi-Faur, D. 2003. "The Politics of Liberalisation: Privatization and Regulation For-Competition in Europe's and Latin America's Telecoms and Electricity Industries." *European Journal of Political Research* 42 (5): 705–740.

Levi-Faur D. and Jordana, J. 2006. "Strengthening Regulatory Agencies: Institutional Designs for Autonomy, Accountability and Professionalism." In *Estudio Especializado para la Primera Conerencia Internacional sobre Corrupcion y Transparencia: Debatiendo las fronteras entre Estado, Mercado y Sociedad*. Ciudad de Mexico.

Majone, G. 2001. "Two Logics of Delegation: Agency and Fiduciary Relations in EU Governance." *European Union Politics* 2 (1): 103–122.

Majone, J. 1997. "From the Positive to the Regulatory State: Causes and Consequences of Change in the Mode of Governance." *Journal of Public Policy* 17 (2): 139–167.

Martins, H. F. 2004. *Reforma do Estado na era FHC: diversidade ou fragmentação da agenda de políticas de gestão pública*. Rio de Janeiro: Tese de Doutorado – Ebape/FGV.

Melo, M. A. 2002. "As Agências Reguladoras: Gênese, Desenho Institucional e Governança." In *O Estado Numa Era de Reformas: Os Anos FHC*, edited by Abrucio, F. L., and Loureiro, M. R., 247–306. Brasília: Ministério do Planejamento, Orçamento e Gestão. Secretaria de Gestão (MP, SEGES).

Minogue, M. 2005. "Apples and Oranges: Problems in the Analysis of Comparative Regulatory Governance." *Quarterly Review of Economics and Finance* 45 (2–3): 195–214.

Minogue, M., and Carinõ, L. 2006. "Introduction: Regulatory Governance in Developing Countries." In *Regulatory Governance in Developing Countries*, edited by Minogue, M., and Carinõ, L. Cheltenham: Edward Elgar Publishing.

Mueller, B. P. and Pereira, C. 2002. "Credibility and the Design of Regulatory Agencies in Brazil." *Brazilian Journal of Political Economy* 22 (3): 65–88.

Murillo, M. V. 2002. "Political Bias in Policy Convergence: Privatisation Choices in Latin America." *World Politics* 54 (4): 462–193.

227

Nakano, K. 2004. "Cross-National Transfer of Policy Ideas: Agencification in Britain and Japan." *Governance* 17 (2): 169–188.

OECD. 2008. *Brasil: Fortalecendo a Governança Regulatória. Relatório Sobre Reforma Regulatória.* Brasília: OECD.

Peci, A. 2007. "Reforma Regulatória Brasileira dos Anos 90 à Luz do Modelo de Kleber Nascimento." *Revista de Administração Contemporânea* 11 (1): 11–30.

Peci, A. and Sobral, F. 2011. "Regulatory Impact Assessment: How Political and Organizational Forces Influence its Diffusion in a Developing Country." *Regulation & Governance* 5 (2): **204–220.**

Pollitt, C., Bathgate, K., Caulfield, J., Smullen, A., and Talbot, C. 2001. "Agency Fever? Analysis of an International Fashion." *Journal of Comparative Policy Analysis: Research and Practice* 3 (3): 271–90.

Prado, M. M. 2012. "Implementing independent regulatory agencies in Brazil: The contrasting experiences in the electricity and telecommunications sectors." *Regulation & Governance* 6 (3): 300–326.

Radaelli, C. M. 2010. "Regulating Rule-Making via Impact Assessment." *Governance* 23 (1): 89–107.

Radaelli, C. M. 2005. "Diffusion without Convergence: How Political Context Shapes the Adoption of Regulatory Impact Assessment." *Journal of European Public Policy* 12 (5): 924–843.

Radaelli, C. M., and Francesco. F. D. 2007. "Regulatory Impact Assessment, Political Control and the Regulatory State." Paper presented at the 4th General Conference of the European Consortium for Political Research, Pisa, Italy, September, 6–8.

Schrefler, L. 2010. "The Usage of Scientific Knowledge by Independent Regulatory Agencies." *Governance* 23 (2): 309–330.

Smullen, A. 2010. "Translating Agency Reform through Durable Rhetorical Styles: Comparing Official Agency Talk across Consensus and Adversarial Contexts." *Public Administration* 88 (4): 943–959.

Spiller, P. T. 1990. "Politicians, Interest Groups and Regulators: A Multiple-Principals Agency Theory of Regulation or 'Let them be bribed'." *Journal of Law and Economics* 1: 65–101.

Tenbucken, M., and Schneider, V. 2004. "Divergent Convergence: Structures and Functions of National Regulatory Agencies in the Telecommunications Sector." In *The Politics of Regulation*, edited by J. Jordana and D. Levi-Faur. Cheltenham: Edward Elgar Publishing.

Verhoest, K. and Laegreid, P. 2010. Organizing Public Sector Agencies: Challenges and Reflections. In *Governance of Public Sector Organizations: Proliferation, Autonomy and Performance*, edited by Laegreid, P. and Verhoest, K., 275–297. Basingstoke: Palgrave Macmillan.

Verschuere, B. and Barbieri, D. 2009. "Investigating the 'NPM- ness' of Agencies in Italy and Flanders." *Public Management Review* 11 (3): 345–373.

Yesilkagit, K. and Christensen, J. G. 2010. "Institutional Design and Formal Autonomy: Political versus Historical and Cultural Explanations." *Journal of Public Administration Research and Theory* 20(1): 53–74.

21

GLOBAL HEALTH

Eduardo Missoni

Introduction

After World War II, international public policies understood as "international actions that serve broadly agreed public ends" (Severino and Ray 2009) largely coincided with North–South relations and the international development cooperation system. With the acceleration of the globalization process, the rapidly changing geo-political scenario, and the ever-expanding range of transnational challenges confronting the international community, the situation changed substantially over the last two decades, dramatically increasing the scale and complexity of public policies. These changes can be described as a triple revolution of objectives, players and instruments. Indeed, development goals and targets are being reset "post-2015" to respond to the new challenges. Public policies are increasingly subject to transnational actors and new power balances that override the traditional domain of international relations and policy-making, and may undermine the mandate of existing multilateral institutions, while a "bustling creativity of development finance is precipitating a change of era" (Severino and Ray 2009). Indeed, the global health domain offers a good example of such changes and challenges.

The interdependency among national health systems and the interconnectedness between health and the multifaceted aspects of development have dramatically increased. Thus, a wide range of health determinants is of worldwide relevance. In the global health system alone, medical technologies are developed and traded globally by transnational companies, medical knowledge is shared by a global community of professionals and patients, and, finally, the health care workforce and, increasingly, cross-border services have increased the fluidity of national borders.

Since the late 1990s, the role of health in global development policies became more relevant; three out of the eight Millennium Development Goals (MDGs) set forth in the year 2000 by the United Nations Millennium Declaration, are related to health targets (MDG 4: Reduce child mortality, MDG 5: Improve maternal health, MDG 6: Combat HIV/AIDS, Malaria and other diseases). This shift in attention to health also resulted in an unprecedented growth at a global level of financial resources destined for the development of the health sector (IHME 2014).

The mushrooming of new private actors and a vast array of global alliances and public–private partnerships, together with the growing role of emerging countries, brought about considerable changes in global health governance, posing new challenges to international institutions with the mandate of international coordination, particularly to the World Health Organization (WHO).

"Health policy is about process and power"; thus it becomes extremely important to understand "who influences" whom in policy-making (Walt 1994). A number of factors exogenous to national governments and political systems influence national health policy formulation and implementation. Indeed, in an interdependent world, "governments are increasingly affected by international policy procedures"; thus, identifying who is and how they are driving decision-making at global level is of vital importance (Walt 1994). Over the years, a multitude of different actors, each accountable to different constituencies and with different agendas, influenced the global health agenda beyond the programme of the World Health Assembly (WHA).

Meanwhile, many policies directly or indirectly influencing health and health systems were increasingly defined in other international and global arenas. The current global changes (and challenges) include the cross-border displacement of populations, goods and services, monetary resources, ideas and information as well as global environmental degradation and climate change. All of these dimensions have a strong influence on the living and health conditions of people globally. Thus, the need to go beyond global health governance, to embrace global governance *for* health – i.e. to privilege health as a priority goal in decision-making processes outside the traditional domain of health authorities – is increasingly being recognized (Ottersen et al. 2014).

In the following sections, a brief historical review of the evolution of global health policies highlights some of the "processes and powers" that have been shaping global health governance. Subsequently, a brief analysis of main actors will attempt to map influences and identify main global governance issues at stake.

The evolution of global health policies

In 1946, the member states of the newly formed United Nations gathered in New York to draft and sign the constitution for the WHO, which entered into force in 1948. "The attainment by all peoples of the highest possible level of health" was the objective of the new organization, while its mandate was to "act as the directing and co-ordinating authority on international health work". Health was recognized as a fundamental human right and defined as "a state of complete physical, mental and social well-being and not merely the absence of disease or infirmity", implicitly recognizing that the promotion of good health is not the sole responsibility of health authorities, but requires a much wider and inter-sectorial approach (WHO 2005).

In 1977, the World Health Assembly, the organization's representative body, adopted the goal of "Health for all by the year 2000", and the following year, with the Alma-Ata Declaration, Primary Health Care (PHC) was identified as the best strategy toward that objective. The Alma-Ata Declaration promoted an approach based on equity and community participation, focusing on prevention and appropriate technology, with an integrated inter-sectorial approach to development. The approach would have immediately had substantial societal and structural implications; thus, a number of governments and agencies quickly pushed to reduce the spirit of Alma-Ata to a practical set of technical interventions, giving birth to "selective Primary Health Care": low-cost interventions, pragmatic and limited in scope (Brown et al. 2006). This reductionist, centralist approach would soon become dominant with the advent and prevalence of neoliberal policies.

Attention was drawn away from health and focused on the control of single diseases. Under the strong influence of international organizations and bilateral agencies, this soon resulted in the reorganization of health systems into "vertical programs", prompting a multiplication of costs and a waste of resources, not to mention the complete detachment of these programs from development actions being implemented in other sectors (education, agriculture, industry, social infrastructure, etc.).

In those years, under the inspired leadership of its Director General Hafdan Mahler, WHO openly challenged the commercial practices of transnational pharmaceutical and food industries (Global Health Watch 2005). The International Code of Marketing of Breast-Milk Substitutes – adopted by the 34th World Health Assembly – and the Essential Drugs Program were fiercely opposed by the government of the United States of America, under the influence of powerful food and pharmaceutical lobbies, which claimed those initiatives to interfere with global trade and marketing practices.

As a consequence, the US led the World Health Assembly to freeze WHO's regular budget and later (1985) withheld their assessed contribution to WHO. The financial challenge that WHO had to face initiated a significant change in the way global health priorities were defined. A crucial shift took place from predominant reliance on the regular budget, drawn from member states' assessed contributions, to greatly increased dependence on extra-budgetary funding, defined as "voluntary" contributions from member states and external contributors who pledged according to their own priorities for programs with a variable degree of independence from WHO's institutional decision-making structure. By the beginning of the 1990s extra-budgetary funds represented 54 per cent of WHO's total budget, and that percentage would progressively grow over the years to nearly 80 per cent in the current decade.

Toward the end of the 1980s, as an integral part of neoliberal macroeconomic structural adjustment programs (SAPs), the World Bank pushed developing countries to adopt a single-recipe Health Sector Reform, encouraging privatization of health services, fostering the introduction of private insurance schemes, and enforcing user fees for health services. Structural adjustment policies imposed on poor countries were among the main determinants in the worsening of people's living conditions and in the collapse of countries' health systems. In the 1990s, the World Bank started to directly orient the global debate on health.

During this decade, the international health scene was progressively changing. WHO's role was further weakened by an increasing number of players in the global health arena. In addition to the World Bank and other UN organizations, regional development banks and funds, multinational pharmaceutical companies, actors from the private and corporate sectors, and a growing number of non-governmental organizations (NGOs) from the non-profit-making sector were all claiming a role in the health sector. Among the new actors appearing on the global health scene in that period was the Bill and Melinda Gates Foundation, which would soon become the single most important non-institutional player on the global field.

In the changing scenario, Global Public–Private Partnerships (GPPPs) emerged as a new approach to improve the delivery of health services for a number of health problems. Many GPPPs were created during the late 1990s to focus on specific diseases.

Claiming a lack of public resources, wherein the reality was instead one of reduced public commitment and of progressive privatization of international aid, the rhetoric of partnership became the dominant topic in the global debate. The creation of joint public–private ventures was presented as a "requirement" to bring health to the centre of poverty reduction and development strategies (WHO 2001). No evidence was provided for that requirement.

The number of health-related GPPPs increased rapidly, soon surpassing 90 in the first years of the new millennium, thus duplicating interventions and further fragmenting global action for health, with heavy consequences in terms of health governance, both at national and global levels (Missoni 2004). Initiated by the Gates Foundation, the Global Alliance on Vaccines and

Immunizations (GAVI), launched in the year 2000, became the reference model for that approach, and inspired the Group of Eight (G8) to launch the Global Fund to fight against HIV/AIDS, Tuberculosis and Malaria (GFATM) the following year. Multilateralism, represented by the United Nations, has been progressively depleted while the G8 has grown in importance under the leadership of a few wealthy countries.

Despite advocating for a systemic approach to health and "Healthy Public Policies" (orienting public policies in other sectors toward health objectives), a concept established in the Ottawa Charter (WHO 1986), in practice, under Gro Harlem Brundtland's direction, WHO openly supported GPPPs and their "vertical" approach toward specific diseases and health issues. No attention was paid to possible consequences in terms of overall global health governance, fragmentation and WHO's own organizational policy. Indeed, partnerships and other interactions with the corporate sector also represented an important shift in organizational policy (Deacon et al. 2003).

The influence of private foundations (e.g. Gates) and public–private partnerships (e.g. GFATM, GAVI) continued to grow throughout the decade, undoubtedly representing the most significant trend in the global health scene. Although in some cases they may have facilitated access at a national level to drugs and services for the treatment of specific diseases (Buse and Harmer 2007), the fragmentation produced by the increasing number of "vertical" initiatives in the wider context of development aid, their arguable sustainability, and the waste of resources due to duplication and lack of alignment to national health plans, gave rise to increasing doubts about effectiveness and appropriateness of that approach among very diverse observers (Conway et al. 2007; Garrett 2007; Hsiao and Heller 2007; IDA 2007) and raised new questions about global health governance and the role of WHO (Bartsch 2007; Nishtar 2004).

Despite an increase in participants and an increased interest in the global health arena, the political space for a comprehensive approach to health and a systemic approach was getting progressively narrower.

The systemic approach to health was revamped by the almost contemporaneous publication of the Report of the Commission on Social Determinants of Health (CSDH) and, on the 30th anniversary of the Declaration of Alma-Ata, the WHO's 2008 Annual Report, which refocused on Primary Health Care. The latter critically assessed the way that health care is organized, financed, and delivered in rich and poor countries around the world, challenged by hospital-centrism, fragmentation deriving from multiplication of programs and projects, and the pervasive commercialization of health care driving health systems away from their intended directions (WHO 2008). The CSDH concluded its Report by redefining the overarching significance of health as possibly the most comprehensive indicator for development (CSDH 2008).

The recognition of the relevance of health determinants (social, economic, political and environmental) and their strong relationship with processes of production and consumption, with societal structure, and with decisions made outside the traditional domain of health authorities, prompted the need for a global governance that would take health goals and the priorities of public health into every arena (e.g. agriculture, commerce, industry, education, environment) in which public policies are developed and negotiated (Frenk and Moon 2013).

In the wider debate also traditional *inter*-national decision-making and governing mechanisms between and among nation states was challenged, and it was suggested that a wider range of public and private *trans*-national stakeholders should be involved in a multi-stakeholder, multi-level approach (Kirton and Cooper 2009).

In this changing global scenario, the WHO faced increasing challenges in playing its original leading role derived from its constitutional mandate and proposals were made for new governance frameworks, including a Framework Convention on Global Health which would redesign current global governance mechanisms into an international binding agreement (Gostin et al. 2013).

The current scenario: players and interests at stake

In a first attempt to define and shape the architecture of Global Health Governance, Dodgson and his collaborators represented it graphically in progressive circles, according to distance from central "leadership and authority" (Dodgson et al. 2002). Although already recognizing the emergence of new actors (i.e. the Gates Foundation), in the central circle they only put WHO, the World Bank and the USA. After just over a decade, the scenario is totally different and rather unstable. A short analysis of main players will allow us to better understand the balance of powers and to re-draw the map (Figure 21.1).

The World Health Organization (WHO)

Due to its mandate, the WHO formally remains the international health authority at the centre of the map. The resolutions of the World Health Assembly are not binding, but are still regarded as a reference for international action, so much so that on more than one occasion when a decision was perceived as contrary to individual interests, single member states and/or external actors acted to derail the decision-making process.

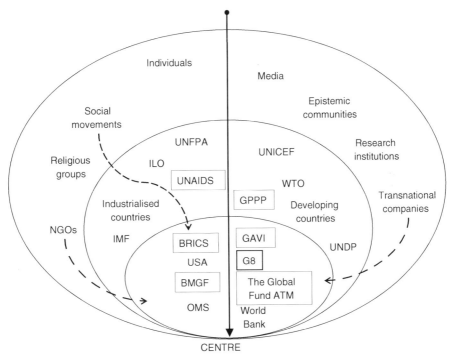

Figure 21.1 Global health governance
Source: Dodgson et al. 2002; modified
Note: Arrows show increased centrality of actors. Actors in boxes were not present in the original map.

With the regular budget frozen since the early 1980s, the prevalence in the overall budget of donors' earmarked voluntary funds remains the most visible obstacle to WHO autonomy. In 2014 extra-budgetary funds represented 76 per cent of total funding. Of these, the highest portion – approximately 18 per cent – came from a single private donor: the Gates Foundation, which ranked second only to the United States of America (which also provides assessed contributions) as a contributor to WHO's total budget (WHO 2014).

Although facing dynamics for which it was not designed, WHO still has the normative and regulatory instruments, seldom used until today, to affirm and defend the right to health. Experience has shown that forming strong alliances may be key in confronting the most difficult challenges. For example, in the case of the Framework Convention on Tobacco Control (FCTC), allying with wide civil society movements, WHO was able to promote and attain a binding international agreement, despite the harsh opposition of the United States and of the powerful tobacco lobbies (Collin and Lee 2009).

Accused of lack of transparency or ineffectiveness in complex situations (such as the swine flu and the Ebola pandemics), and with a tendency to bow to the will or large economic powers, the Organization underwent a serious credibility crisis (Prah Ruger 2014). However, one should not underestimate the role of the member states themselves, and especially major contributors, in undermining WHO credibility and sustainability, by deviating their financial support toward an entropic plethora of new actors, which in many cases they themselves created and finance as in the case of the GFATM (Lidén 2014).

It was the debate about "The Future of Financing for WHO" presented at the 64th WHA in 2011 that actually introduced a broader reform process. While the results are still uncertain, the reform contained a far-reaching agenda that hoped to reshape the way in which the organization operates, is governed, makes decisions and is financed, and probably its overall role in the global public health arena.

Some consider that politics should be maintained out of WHO and would prefer to see its role reduced to that of a purely technical body, and eventually a provider of technical assistance for new initiatives, alliances and other groupings. However, this would further weaken the highly fragmented global health architecture and its current coordination mechanisms; instead, a healthier political functioning should be pursued (Lee 2009).

In this context a highly sensitive issue is how to give voice to multiple stakeholders, but particularly how to differentiate between very different interests. It may be dangerous to group very different entities such as NGOs advocating for health as a human right, businesses lobbying for their commercial trade-off, and influential Global Philanthropies sometimes pursuing individual objectives and sets of values all under the same umbrella category of "non-state actors" (Richter 2014).

The World Bank

In 2007, the World Bank launched its new Health, Nutrition and Population Strategy re-focusing on long-term, country-driven and country-led support. Based on its comparative advantages, the World Bank proposed itself as the lead global agency for health system strengthening, health financing and economics (Hafner and Schiffman 2013). This raised immediate concern when considering the World Bank's previous role in pushing structural adjustment programs and health sector reforms, and its continued promotion of pro-private market-oriented policies that underpin many of the current problems in poor countries (McCoy 2007).

In 2009, the World Bank joined the GFATM and the GAVI in the establishment of a "Health Systems Financing Platform". Again, doubts were raised about the credibility of such a platform, and the will of the World Bank (beyond mere rhetoric) to follow principles of aid effectiveness including ownership and alignment, especially in the absence of formal agreements for a real collaboration at country level (Brown et al. 2013).

In 2012 the appointment to the Presidency of the World Bank of Jim Kim, a medical doctor, anthropologist and global health expert, was seen as a sign of change; a potentially unique opportunity for the World Bank to exercise its authority to assist countries in agenda setting and generating political will for collective action on health (Prah Ruger 2013). Certainly, the World Bank remains a major channel of Official Development Aid (ODA) (IHME 2014) and a fundamental actor in the macroeconomic scenario.

Other UN system entities

Several other organizations and bodies belonging to the UN system directly or indirectly include health in their mandate and often develop joint programs with WHO. The role of UNAIDS, born to ensure coordination of HIV/AIDS control activities among UN agencies, grew with the relevance of the pandemic; however, it was later somewhat dwarfed by the UN Secretariat and main donors' choice to establish the GFATM.

The United Nations Fund for Population Activities (UNFPA) is widely involved in reproductive health initiatives, and UNICEF integrates children and youth health into the wider context of its mission for the promotion of children's rights.

Although acting in a different sector, the mandate of a number of the UN's specialized agencies is linked to health determinants. This is the case for example of the Food and Agriculture Organization (FAO), through food policies, or the International Labour Organization (ILO) which engages in social protection.

World Trade Organization and trade agreements

The health consequences of trade policies and agreements have been too often neglected. Thus, the World Trade Organization (WTO), with a mission of promoting free trade and tasked with the management of multilateral trade agreements, also plays a role in determining health policies. Binding provisions such as the Trade Related Intellectual Property Rights (TRIPS) agreement or the General Agreement on Trade in Services (GATS) have significant impacts on health when applied in certain cases. Other agreements make specific reference to international health standards, for example those of the *Codex Alimentarius*, jointly developed by WHO/FAO, which evaluates technical barriers that may interfere with free trade. The Agreement on Technical Barriers to Trade (TBT) and the Sanitary and Phytosanitary measures (SPS) are also valid examples of the ways in which trade agreements directly impact health. The rigid regulation of these international agreements (*hard law*), may serve an important function in the free circulation of goods and services, but may simultaneously have catastrophic impacts on health and access to health services.

In the last decade the multilateral trade system has been challenged by the increasing tendency of major economic powers to privilege bilateral and regional trade agreements. Lack of transparency in their negotiations and power asymmetry among stakeholders increase the chances that public interest and hazards to health are not taken into consideration. The weakening of legislation is ultimately detrimental to the protection of the environment, agriculture, the food chain, and, subsequently, citizens and consumers (Cattaneo 2015)

Bilaterals and their groupings

Dodgson and co-authors (2002) did not put any bilateral donor but the USA, at the centre of their "Global Health Governance Map". Other wealthy OECD countries instead influence global health through their participation in WHO and other multilateral contexts, including the governance of GPPPs. The G8 influence on the global health agenda as a collective body received an important push in 2000 under the Japanese presidency and has since increased considerably in importance with the launch of the GFATM the following year. However, the modification of international geopolitical and economic balances may soon modify that supremacy.

China, already the second world economy is also playing a growing role on the global health stage. Together the BRICS (Brazil, Russia, India, China, South Africa) are progressively engaging in a common global health strategy (Acharya et al. 2014), including in WHO (Gautier et al. 2014). In contrast, 2014 was the first time that the G20 directly addressed a health issue in a separate statement, and this was specifically due to the ravaging Ebola epidemic (Kirton 2014). The rise of new power blocs, such as the BRICS, might eventually change the balance in negotiations. However, it has been argued that these emerging economies do not alter the dominant development paradigm; instead they aim at rapid growth at any cost, regardless of negative socio-environmental and health impacts, thus making them part of the problem instead of the solution (Ferreira et al. 2013). In addition, major differences between BRICS countries and marked inequalities within each of them, represent an additional hardship.

Transnational private actors

Private actors first need to be differentiated between profit and non-profit, and the latter must be further subdivided into the so called Global Philanthropies, such as foundations and a multiplicity of other non-profit distributing associative entities. Direct or indirect influence of transnational companies (TNCs) on decision-making processes that influence global health should not be underestimated. TNCs exercise pressure, and not always in the most transparent ways, to favour the widening of their markets and to limit public regulation as much as possible. Individually, or through their associations, TNCs have progressively extended their influence on the development of health policies at an international level, both by lobbying national governments to support their positions and through direct interaction with the relevant international organizations. Historical examples include the previously mentioned resistance toward the WHO/UNICEF code on baby food, the WHO essential drugs programme, and the FCTC.

TNCs also engage in health and social development as part of their "corporate social responsibility" (CSR) which is increasingly becoming part of business as usual to respond to accountability issues, ensure strategic positioning, influence the socio-political milieu, and promote TNCs' own commercial interests. Massive donations, largely to United Nations programs or the initiatives of corporate foundations, are usually motivated by marketing purposes rather than the philanthropy and legacy that normally motivate family foundation decisions (Buse and Lee 2005).

Foundations established by wealthy individuals or their families (e.g. the Rockefeller Foundation, Wellcome Trust, Ford Foundation, UN Foundation, Aga Khan Foundation) have often played an important role in financing health activities and influencing policies transnationally, directly or through WHO and other international institutions (Birn 2014).

With the emergence of the Gates Foundation in the late 1990s the volume of financial contribution passed from millions of US dollars to billions. With a capital of about 40 billion dollars invested in the stock exchange and yearly grants for about 2 billion dollars in global health (US$1.98 billion in 2011) the Gates Foundation is the largest individual financial contributor to global health behind the US, whose contributions are equivalent to 7 per cent of the total amount of development assistance in health (IHME 2014). As mentioned above, it is the second largest contributor to WHO's total budget, substantially contributes to several GPPPs, and sits on various boards including of the GFATM and the GAVI. Besides considerations about the heavy influence of the Gates Foundation on global policies, in recent years the contradiction between its health mission and the fact that grant money is generated from investments in industries whose processes and products may have very negative impacts on health, such as Coca Cola, Exxon, and Monsanto, has been highlighted. Similarly palpable conflicts of interests exist between the Foundation and bio-medical industry (Birn 2014; Ricciuti 2014).

Finally, the scenario for other transnationally acting non-profits is highly diversified and complex. The sector includes subjects that differ greatly in nature, cause and membership. The distinction is often made between Public interest International NGOs (PINGOs), such as Médecins sans Frontières, Oxfam or Medicus Mundi International, and Business interest International NGOs (BINGOs), such as the International Federation of Pharmaceutical Manifacturers & Associations (IFPMA). Civil society organizations (CSOs) also connect in transnational networks, which play an important role in advocacy and monitoring for governments and international institutions, giving voice to small CSOs. The Peoples' Health Movement (PHM), for example, develops a systematic monitoring of WHO governance through its "WHO Watch" and publishes a Global Health Watch report every two years (PHM 2014).

Global Health policies are certainly also influenced by academia and the debate in the epistemic community. The *Lancet*, one of the most authoritative medical journals, has become an opinion leader in global health, hosting several series and mobilizing task forces on specific transnational issues. The 2014 Manifesto calling for a new approach to "planetary public health" is a good example (Horton et al. 2014).

Transnational hybrid organizations and initiatives

Over the past decades, the interactions between international institutions and NGOs have considerably increased and progressively extended to other transnational private actors such as Global Philanthropy and the corporate sector. These interactions have spurred global initiatives and action networks, establishing new forms of transnational public–private hybrids and substantially contributing to the fragmentation and complexity of global governance. Varying from relatively informal alliances to highly structured organizations, most of these multi-stakeholder initiatives share a vertical, technological and quick-fix approach to single issues, and lose sight of the complex, structural causes at the origin of a problem. Without a constitutive international agreement (as is the case for international institutions), most initiatives follow two organizational alternatives. A number of GPPPs are hosted by international institutions. Although they have various degrees of autonomy, these hosted partnerships are not separate entities legally and tend to present a burden for the host institution, and sometimes a cause of conflicting relations. Examples are UNITAID, Stop TB and, initially, the GAVI alliance.

The alternative to being hosted is establishing the GPPP itself as an autonomous private organization (although with public and private representation in governing bodies) incorporated according to the national law of the host country; both the GFATM and GAVI are private Swiss foundations. Nevertheless, thanks to the creative and flexible use of legal instruments both were able to obtain the privileges of international institutions from the Swiss government (Missoni 2014).

The Global Alliance on Vaccines and Immunizations (GAVI) was launched in 2000 with an initial contribution of US$750 million from the Gates Foundation. Today its yearly grant is above US$1 billion (IHME 2014). GAVI represented the most advanced prototype for GPPPs. Hosted by UNICEF until 2009, it is currently a Swiss foundation and is recognized as a public charity in the United States. Its mission is the distribution of new or underutilized vaccines to children in developing countries. In addition to the Gates Foundation, international institutions such as WHO, the World Bank and UNICEF as well as a dozen of other subjects including governments, international NGOs and representatives of the pharmaceutical industry sit on the board with full voting rights.

GAVI also became the channel for innovative financing mechanisms for the development and distribution of medical products such as the International Financing Facility for Immunizations (IFFIm) and the Advance Market Commitment (AMC). IFFIm issues bonds, which are guaranteed by the long-term commitment of participating governments. Sold on the financial market, they generate consistent amounts of capital to be spent in advance for GAVI's activities. With the AMC, participating governments pledge availability of funds that will assure bio-medical manufacturers a stable, long-term market for products, which otherwise would have no adequate market, thus incentivizing related research and development (Le Gargasson and Salomé 2010)

GAVI was the model for the GFATM, which today occupies a central position on the global health stage, financing initiatives for the control of the three diseases with over US$3 billion annually (IHME 2014). It was incorporated from the beginning as a Swiss private foundation, but it operated as a trust fund managed by the World Bank and with an administrative services agreement with WHO, who acted as its Secretariat until 2009, when the agreement was terminated. Despite the declared purpose of attracting private funds, the GFATM still relies on governments' contributions for more than 95 per cent of its funds. Nevertheless, the private sector is represented on the board with full voting rights and the WHO is a non-voting member. Although it has been observed that the GFATM contributed to reducing the price of antiretroviral drugs and bed nets in low- and middle-income countries, its activities at the global level (monitoring, surveillance, data collection, etc.) often overlap with those of the WHO (Blanchet et al. 2014), whose authority and mandate may be undermined by GPPPs such as the GFATM and the GAVI.

A nascent experiment in the late 1980s, GPPPs are now part of mainstream development discourse and a dominant model for cooperation in a complex world. The efficiency and the effectiveness of the model remain, however, controversial.

Conclusions

An increasing number of international institutions and transnational organizations have contributed over the last two decades to deeply modify the global health governance map. However, we have barely mentioned the complexity of actors and interactions impacting the vast array of social, economic, environmental and political determinants of health, which should be considered in the attempt to draw a more comprehensive map of governance *for* health.

Global health is increasingly determined by economic and trade policies developed under the powerful influence of TNCs, thus weakening the firewalls necessary for effective regulation and normative actions at both global and national levels. The UN, and specifically WHO, seems to have lost sight of its mission and purpose, and fails to advocate on issues that challenge the profit motives and market logic of companies.

It is precisely in the field of governance *for* health that a new normative and ethical framework will have to be built to face today's unprecedented health challenges and inequities.

Notwithstanding the many health actors with global scope, WHO remains the only multilateral institution with the political legitimacy and dedicated mandate to promote and protect health. However, there is no doubt that it needs to be empowered in that leading role, supported by the necessary resources, trust, and possibly by new international legal frameworks, as well as a redefined scope of global governance with the sole interest of public health and peoples' right to "the attainment of the highest possible level of health".

References

Acharya, S., S. L. Barber, D. Lopez-Acuña, N. Menabde, L. Migliorini, J. Molina, B. Schwartlander, and P. Zurn. 2014. "BRICS and global health." *Bulletin of the World Health Organization* 92 (6): 386–386A.

Bartsch, S. 2007. "Accountability of global public–private partnerships in health." *Sixth Pan-European Conference on International Relations*. University of Turin, Italy, (14 September), 24.

Birn, A. E. 2014. "Philanthrocapitalism, past and present: the Rockefeller Foundation, the Gates Foundation, and the setting(s) of the international/global health agenda." *Hypothesis* 12 (1).

Blanchet, N., T. Milan, R. Atun, D. Jamison, F. Knaul, and R. Hecht. 2014. "Global Collective Action in Health: the WDR+20 Landscape of Core and Supportive Functions." WIDER Working Paper 2014/011, *World Institute for Development Economics Research*, January.

Brown, T. M., M. Cueto, and E. Fee. 2006. "The World Health Organization and the transition from international to global public health." *American Journal of Public Health* 96 (1): 62–72.

Brown, S. S., K. Sen, and K. Decoster. 2013. "The health systems funding platform and World Bank legacy: the gap between rhetoric and reality." *Globalization and Health* 9: 1–7.

Buse, K. and A. M. Harmer. 2007. "Seven habits of highly effective global public–private health partnerships: Practice and potential." *Social Science & Medicine* 64: 259–271.

Buse, K., and K. Lee. 2005. "Business and global health governance." Geneva: WHO.

Cattaneo, A. 2015. "Bilateral free trade agreements and health." *Sistema Salute*.

Collin, J. and K. Lee. 2009. "Globalization and the politics of health governance: the framework convention on tobacco control." In *Innovation in Global Health Governance: Critical Cases*, edited by Cooper A. F. and J. J. Kirton, 219–241. Farnham: Ashgate.

Conway, M. D., S. Gupta, and S. Prakash. 2006. "Building better partnerships for global health." *McKinsey Quarterly* 1–8.

CSDH. 2008. "Closing the gap in a generation." Geneva: WHO, Commission on Social Determinants of Health, Geneva.

Deacon, B, E. Ollila, M. Koivusalo, and P. Stubbs. 2003. "Global social governance. themes and prospects." Ministry of Foreign Affairs of Finland, Hakapaino Oy, Helsinki.

Dodgson, R., L. Lee, and N. Drager. 2002. "Global health governance: a conceptual review." (Discussion paper no. 1), Centre on Global Change & Health, London School of Hygiene & Tropical Medicine, London, February.

Ferreira, J. R., C. Hoirisch, and P. M. Buss. 2013. "Global Governance for Health." *Face à face*, October 21. http://faceaface.revues.org/801.

Frenk, J. and S. Moon. 2013. "Governance Challenges in Global Health." *New England Journal of Medicine* 368: 936–942.

Garrett, L. 2007. "The Challenge of Global Health." *Foreign Affairs* 86 (1): 14–38

Gautier, L., A. Harmer, F. Tediosi, and E. Missoni. 2014. "Reforming the World Health Organization: what influence do the BRICS wield?" *Contemporary Politics* 20 (2): 163–181.

Global Health Watch. 2005. "Global Health Watch 2005–2006. An alternative world health report." London: Zed Books Ltd.

Gostin, L. O., E. A. Friedman, K. Buse, A. Waris, M. Mulumba, et al.. 2013. "Towards a framework convention on global health." *Bulletin of the World Health Organization* 91 (10): 790–793.

Hafner, T. and J. Shiffman. 2013. "The Emergence of Global Attention to Health Systems Strengthening." *Health Policy and Planning* 28 (1): 41–50.

Horton, R., R. Beaglehole, R. Bonita, J. Raeburn, M. McKee, and S. Wall. 2014. "From public to planetary health: a manifesto." *Lancet* 383(9920): 847.

Hsiao, W. and P. S. Heller. 2007. "What should macroeconomists know about health care policy?" IMF, Working Paper, WP/07/13, January.

IDA. 2007. "Aid architecture: an overview of the main trends in official development assistance flows." Washington, DC: IDA.

IHME. 2014. "Financing global health 2103: transition in an age of austerity." Institute for Health Metrics and Evaluation, University of Washington.

Kirton, J. 2014. "The G20 Discovers global health at Brisbane." G20 Research Group, G20 Information Center, University of Toronto, November 15. www.g20.utoronto.ca/analysis/141115-kirton-ebola.html.

Kirton J. J. and A. F. Cooper. 2009. "Innovation in global health governance." In: *Innovation in Global Health Governance: Critical Cases* edited by Cooper, A.F. and J. J. Kirton, 309–331. Farnham: Ashgate.

Le Gargasson, J. B. and B. Salomé. 2010. "The role of innovative financing mechanisms for health." *World Health Report* (2010). Background paper 12. Geneva: WHO.

Lee, K. 2009. "The World Health Organization (WHO)." Routledge Global Institutions. New York: CUNY Graduate Center & UK: University of Manchester.

Lidén, J. 2014. "The World Health Organization and global health governance: Post-1990." *Public Health* 128 (2): 141–147.

McCoy, D. 2007. "The World Bank's new health strategy: reason for alarm?" *Lancet* 369 (9572): 1499–1501.

Missoni, E. 2014. "Transnational hybrid organizations, global public–private partnerships and networks." In *Management of International Institutions and NGOs. Frameworks, practices and challenges*, edited by Missoni, E. and D. Alesani, 77–102. London: Routledge.

Missoni, E. 2013. "C'è bisogno di una riforma. Ma di che riforma? L'OMS di fronte alla sfida di una ricollocazione strategica." In *OMS e diritto alla salute: quale future*, edited by Cattaneo, A. and N. Dentico, 195–204. Osservatorio Italiano sulla Salute Globale.

Missoni, E. 2004. "Le partnership globali pubblico-privato." [The Global Public-Private Partnerships] In *Osservatorio Italiano sulla Salute Globale, Rapporto 2004 salute e globalizzazione*, 210–216. Milano: Feltrinelli.

Nishtar, S. 2004. "Public–private 'partnerships' in health – a global call to action." *Health Research Policy and Systems* 2(1), 5. http://doi.org/10.1186/1478–4505–2–5.

Ottersen, O. P., J. Dasgupta, C. Blouin, et al., 2014. "The Lancet–University of Oslo Commission on Global Governance for Health." *Lancet* 383 (9917): 630–667.

PHM. 2014. "About the people's health movement." Accessed 20 January 2015. www.phmovement.org/en/about.

Prah Ruger, J. 2014. "International institutional legitimacy and the World Health Organization." *Journal of Epidemiology & Community Health* 68 (8): 1–4.

Prah Ruger, J. 2013. "The World Bank and global health: time for a renewed focus on health policy." *Journal of Epidemiology & Community Health* 68 (1): 1–2.

Ricciuti, E. 2014. "Case study: the Bill and Melinda Gates Foundation." In *Management of International Institutions and NGOs: Frameworks, Practices and Challenges*, edited by Missoni, E. and D. Alesani, 71–75. London: Routledge.

Richter, J. 2014. "Time to turn the tide: WHO's engagement with non-state actors and the politics of stakeholder governance and conflicts of interest." *BMJ* 348: g3351–g3351.

Severino, J. M. and O. Ray. 2009. "The end of ODA: death and rebirth of a global public policy." CGD Working Paper 167. Washington, DC: Center for Global Development.

Walt, G. 1994. *Health Policy: An Introduction to Process and Power*. London: Zed Books.

WHO. 2014. *Financial Report and Audited Financial Statements for the Year Ended 31 December 2013*. Geneva: WHO.

WHO. 2007. "WHO welcomes new World Bank strategy on health, nutrition and population." Geneva: WHO Media Centre.

WHO. 2005. *Constitution of the World Health Organization*. 5th ed. Basic Documents. Geneva: WHO, pp. 1–22.

WHO. 1986. *The Ottawa Charter for Health Promotion*. First International Conference on Health Promotion, Ottawa, 21 November 1986. www.who.int/healthpromotion/conferences/previous/ottawa/en/.

World Bank. 2007. "Healthy development: The world bank strategy for health, nutrition, and population results." Washington, DC: World Bank.

22

GLOBAL CULTURAL POLICIES AND THEIR MANAGEMENT

The case of Italian UNESCO World Heritage Sites

Marianna Elmi and Alessandro Hinna

Introduction

In the late 1990s, the academic debate on Public Administration Management began to question the validity or completeness of the paradigms of Public Administration (Beetham 1987) and New Public Management (Hood 1991). There was a need to find theories capable of moving beyond the sterile dichotomy of "administration versus management" (Osborne 2006), in favor of theories able to include (and exclude) issues related to the governance of policy processes (Klijn and Koppenjan 2000) or, more generally, to the governance of the public realm (Stoker 2006). According to these perspectives, policy processes are increasingly taking place on horizontal, vertical and network levels (OECD 2009). In these contexts, management develops differently compared to traditional hierarchical practices (O'Toole and Laurence 1997; Klijn and Koppenjan 2000). While, on the one hand, most of the literature agrees that public sector management is an issue of coordination and integration among different levels and actors, on the other hand, the way in which these processes happen in practice and the reasons for their success or failure require a deeper analysis (see Chapter 13 in this volume).

This chapter investigates – through a theoretical framework based on a multilevel approach – the process of elaboration and implementation of the specific cultural policy of the UNESCO World Heritage Convention. This policy, over three decades old, maintains a key role in the definition of cultural heritage policies worldwide, while developing according to the social and economic dynamics of each territory. The main aims of the Convention are the worldwide preservation and promotion of cultural heritage of "outstanding universal value" (UNESCO 1972). The main instrument for achieving this goal is the World Heritage List (WHL), which includes all World Heritage Sites containing "properties forming part of the cultural heritage and natural heritage [...] having *outstanding universal value*" (UNESCO 1972: 6). The Convention defines cultural heritage as composed of "monuments, group of buildings and sites", including cultural landscapes (ICOMOS 2005; UNESCO 1972). Through the List, World Heritage policies are implemented at different territorial scales – global, national and local (site) – and administrative levels, constituting an example of multilevel public policy (Hooghe and Marks 2001). Single UNESCO World Heritage Sites allow analysis of public policy in a multilevel context and the impact that this context has on the choices of local public administrations. This analysis can then be generalized to multiple national contexts.

The chapter also finds the most relevant fostering elements and obstacles to implementing World Heritage policy. The explanation for success or failure is sought in the extent to which the key actors are able to share resources in a context of mutual dependence, to cooperate towards a common aim and to develop coordinating structures and strategies (Klijn et al. 2010; McGuire 2002).

Global cultural heritage policies as a multilevel governance phenomenon

Cultural policies in Europe and elsewhere are now at the center of the debate on the social development of nations and single territories (European Commission 2014; Dümcke and Gnedovsky 2013). These policies are considered to be the motor of an endogenous development model, in which the exploitation of cultural heritage is assessed not only in terms of its artistic value, but also for its expected benefits to:

- the level of quality of life and therefore the degree to which a territory can attract talent (Florida 2002);
- the capacity of the territory to produce innovative goods and services through the use of methods and advanced technologies (Porter 1998);
- the knowledge and expansion of individual freedoms useful for achieving individual and socially relevant objectives (Sen 1999);
- individual employment and/or enterprise opportunities in the productive sectors directly or indirectly linked to the process of "promotion" of cultural heritage (Throsby 2001).

At the same time, as in other public policy areas related to the "commons" (Ostrom 1990), the increasingly complex processes of formulating and implementing cultural policy in a context of austerity have highlighted the limits of traditional hierarchical and centralized approaches. In contrast with a centralized model of direct provision, in which the central state formulates, implements and directly finances cultural policy, there are advantages related to decentralization and contracting out, such as cost reduction and more effective and empowered local actors (Matarasso and Landry 1999: 47–50).

Decentralization opens spaces for "the development of diverse forms of policy intervention by sub-national actors" (Gray 2009: 580), where cultural policies are implemented across different policy domains. These types of processes can be referred to as *multi-level governance* processes characterized by a multiplicity of actors, heterogeneous territorial scales, a vast number of jurisdictions and the allocation of "complex or resource-intensive competences to [different] levels of government" (OECD 2009: 2; Hooghe and Marks 2001). Although the multilevel approach to cultural policy can be interpreted as a natural consequence of decentralization, its concrete implementation still presents some challenges, such as the dependence on central governments to provide resources and the potential lack of administrative capacity of sub-levels to carry out planned activities. Other major gaps are the lack of information exchange and coordination between the horizontal, vertical and networked levels (Charbit and Michalun 2009).

The issue of coordination for addressing these gaps is therefore very relevant. The need for cooperation between actors (see Cepiku, Chapter 13 in this volume) and to establish coordinating bodies able to address "capacity and information gaps" (OECD 2009: 6) has been pointed out before. Recent literature has highlighted how *public networks*, defined as "groups of three or more legally autonomous organizations that work together in order to achieve not only their own goals but also a collective goal" (Kenis and Provan 2009: 231) can, due to the flexibility of their design, mobilize different actors in multilevel contexts to create coordinating structures (Hooghe and Marks 2001). The network approach has been particularly successful in analyzing structures for both policy formulation and implementation through the provision of public services. In the cultural sector, network theory analyzed cultural policy implementation processes, including multiple actors like museums or festival networks (Barreca et al. 2013; Hinna et al. 2009).

The implementation of UNESCO World Heritage policy can be interpreted as a multilevel process implemented through network-like structures, based on the following relevant dimensions:

- The presence of *multiple organizations, non-hierarchically related and located at heterogeneous territorial scales* (OECD 2009; Hooghe and Marks 2001). The typology of actors encompasses private, public and non-profit organizations. These operate in a context of *mutual dependence,* where neither policy responsibilities nor outcomes can be clearly separated (OECD 2009: 2).
- The *collaborative* nature of actors' interaction, due to the *presence of a common aim* and the *need to share resources.* The degree to which this aim is constructed through game-like interactions varies (Klijn and Koppenjan 2000). Although the presence of a common problem implies the need for collaboration in order to solve it, this does not mean that interactions between the actors are always non-conflictual.
- The *establishment of a coordinating body* and the related *adoption of coordination strategies,* which appear particularly relevant in multilevel settings (Charbit and Michalun 2009). In this context, public management is characterized by strategies and behaviors that differ from those in hierarchical settings. Rather, these strategies and behaviors refer to the "activation" of the involved partners and their resources (Klijn et al. 2010; Klijn and Koppenjan 2000), to the facilitation of interactions among partners and to mediation and arbitration among them (Kickert and Koppenjan 1997). Such strategies can benefit cultural heritage management (Elmi et al. 2014).

Given the scarcity of empirical research in this field, we have adopted an explorative case study approach applied to the World Heritage Policy in the Italian context (Yin 1994). We analyze policy implementation according to specific characteristics of the multilevel process: the multiplicity of organizations involved, the collaborative nature and presence of a common aim, the sharing of resources and the presence of a specific coordination body in which management strategies are adopted.

Following a triangulation strategy for data collection, we base our case study on the analysis of official documentation at global, national and local levels, and interviews of public managers at the UNESCO Office – the coordinating body responsible for the implementation of UNESCO policy at a national level – and in local management bodies responsible for Italian World Heritage Sites.

The selected case is particularly suited to reflection on and analysis of cultural heritage policy: since its ratification of the World Heritage Convention, the country – holding the highest number of World Heritage Sites worldwide (50, 46 of them cultural) in 2014 – has been widely represented in the World Heritage List. The results deriving from the specific case can also help in the interpretation of the World Heritage policy worldwide.

The UNESCO World Heritage Sites: challenges and management requirements

The World Heritage Convention includes 192 State Parties (UNESCO 2014a) and represents a transnational legal instrument for the definition of cultural and natural heritage of universal value and for the identification of the actions, bodies and mechanisms to be adopted to protect heritage worldwide.

The "Heritage of Outstanding Universal Value" (OUV) included in the World Heritage List can be defined as a "global common good" (Frey and Steiner 2011: 562), regulated by the global World Heritage policy. This policy is unique in its global formulation while the identification and management of each World Heritage Site takes place at national and local levels (Figure 22.1). The implementation of World Heritage policy can therefore be defined through multilevel processes, which refer "to negotiated, non-hierarchical exchanges between institutions at the transnational, regional and local levels and to a vertical 'layering' of governance processes at these different levels" (Peters and Pierre 2001: 31, cited in Cepiku et al. 2013).

The declination of the multilevel World Heritage policy at local levels varies according to the states where it is implemented and according to the characteristics of the sites on the list. These characteristics are related, in turn, to the administrative and geographical contexts and the variety of stakeholders involved (UNESCO 2014b). Each process of enlisting a site at national level and each sub-process of management can thus be regarded as unique; this makes the concrete implementation of the policy a "wicked" problem (Rittel and Webber 1973), lacking a single standardized solution. Solving this issue requires the contribution of a series of organizations and institutions that share resources, tasks and responsibilities. To this end, the World Heritage Committee explicitly encourages "States Parties [...] to prepare their Tentative Lists with the participation of a wide variety of stakeholders, including site managers, local and regional governments, local communities, NGOs and other interested parties and partners" (UNESCO 2013: 18). This applies also to the management of single sites, where conservation and promotion have to be equally emphasized and where the impact of the site on the broader communities plays a key role.

The inclusion of a site in the World Heritage List is seen as a powerful tool to increase tourism (Van der Aa 2005); nevertheless, a parallel lack of adequate management measures can create negative impacts and represent a threat to the integrity of the sites (Hoi An Centre for Monuments Management and Preservation 2008). This is why, since 2002, applicant sites have to present a management plan for the preservation and promotion of the sites during the application process for the List (UNESCO 2013). Moreover, states have to periodically report on the status of conservation of all national sites. Sites facing a concrete threat to their outstanding value can be included in the List of World Heritage in danger (UNESCO 2014c) and if no initiative is undertaken for preserving their integrity can be excluded from the List altogether.

The implementation of the World Heritage Convention at national level: the case of Italian UNESCO World Heritage Sites

As a state party to the Convention, Italy is responsible for implementing it at the national level by identifying potential World Heritage Sites, coordinating all existing national sites and periodically monitoring their conservation status.

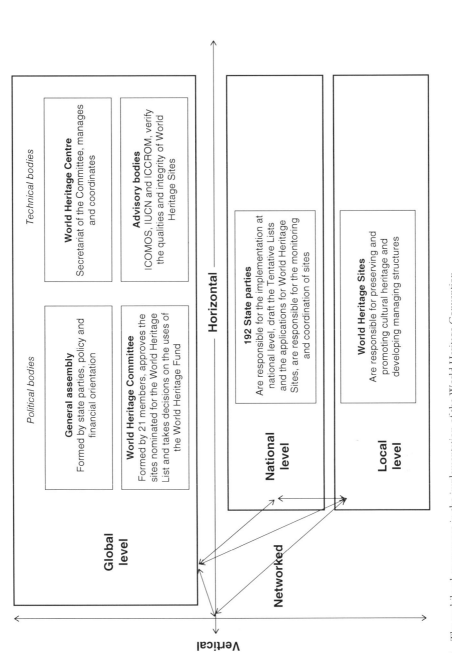

Figure 22.1 The multilevel governance in the implementation of the World Heritage Convention

Source: own elaboration, based on UNESCO (2014d) and Ministero per i beni e le attività culturali 2010

Multiplicity of actors and territorial levels

Despite the fact that national cultural policies are defined mostly by the Italian Ministry of Culture, the Ministry itself cannot be considered the only actor responsible for the national implementation of the World Heritage Convention (Figure 22.2). Rather, several key actors are responsible (Ministero per i Beni e le Attività Culturali, 2010):

- The Office for UNESCO World Heritage at the Italian Ministry of Culture, which coordinates the implementation of the World Heritage Convention at a national level through activities such as drafting the national Tentative List (namely, the list of potential World Heritage sites in the country), supporting individual sites in the nomination and management processes, drafting the periodical reports to be submitted for the monitoring of the sites' conservation and supporting the Permanent Interministerial Working Group.
- The Permanent Interministerial Working Group, which coordinates different actors involved nationally, not only in the protection of cultural heritage but also natural and immaterial heritage (natural heritage is handled separately by the Italian Ministry for the Environment, Land and Sea).
- The UNESCO National Commission, established in order to promote the broader implementation of the main UNESCO priorities, not just heritage.
- The association of Italian UNESCO World Heritage Cities, established in order to promote common projects in all Italian World Heritage Sites. The Association is mainly a political instrument, with members at different territorial levels: provinces, regions, municipalities, protected areas.
- The individual Italian World Heritage Sites, responsible for drafting the application dossier and preserving and promoting a Site's OUV.

In its technical functions, the Office for UNESCO World Heritage interacts with actors at all levels of UNESCO policy (see Figures 22.1 and 22.2). At the international level, it works with the World Heritage Committee, advisory bodies, the World Heritage Centre and other state parties (when applying for transnational World Heritage Sites). Nationally, the Office interacts with the UNESCO National Commission and the Permanent Interministerial Working Group. Sub-nationally, the Office interacts with the individual cultural World Heritage Sites and their Association. The UNESCO Office is therefore the core of the network of actors implementing UNESCO policy and coordinates the multilevel process.

Mutual dependency, resource scarcity and sharing

While the UNESCO Office at the Ministry of Culture operates on the basis of a budget mainly employed for internal organizational activities and aims, the Italian Sites rely on public financing allocated through National Law 77/2006. This financing has several limitations: first of all, it has a limited scope of activity, since it was specifically introduced to finance the development of management plans for the sites after these were made compulsory in 2002. Second, it is characterized by a scarcity of available budgetary funds. This limits the concrete application of this financial instrument to actions such as studies, information initiatives and the development of management plans. The result is, according to the words of one interviewee, "a lack of specific funding for [all other activities concerning] the management of UNESCO World Heritage Sites". This scarcity of financial resources has an impact on the development of common initiatives, since the single organizations involved tend to allocate the available funds

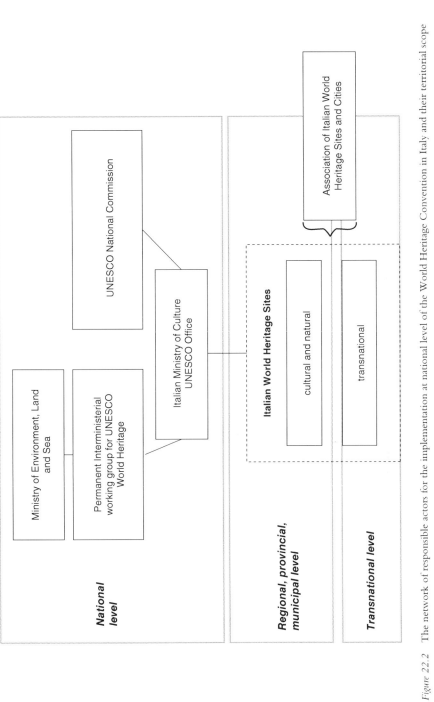

Figure 22.2 The network of responsible actors for the implementation at national level of the World Heritage Convention in Italy and their territorial scope

for their internal day-to-day management. In order to compensate for the lack of finances, the UNESCO Office has started sharing other types of resources, mainly the skills of the staff employed, through initiatives such as translating World Heritage policy documents into Italian and developing guidelines for drafting management plans for the Sites. However, for those responsible for individual sites, this solution is not completely effective. According to one site manager, "the documents and guidelines provided are clear in purpose, but not simple in application, requiring specialist skills that site managers do not have". This lack of specialist skills causes the development of "standardized" management plans, resulting from an uncritical application of policies and guidelines provided by the World Heritage Policy documents or by the Italian UNESCO Office. As a result, management plans lose their effectiveness, also in the short term.

Multiple conflicting aims

The presence of a common aim is important to stimulate cooperation between actors at all levels. Nevertheless, the implementation of Italian national-level World Heritage policy lacks a common aim because of the divergence of interests among the actors involved, which is partly due to the multilevel nature of the process. While the aim of the ministerial actors is, according to one interviewee, "to interact with the local bodies and […] to respond to UNESCO requests", local actors mainly aim to get a site included in the World Heritage List, enhancing its visibility and promoting positive economic and social impacts for local communities. They see inclusion as a tool to gain political prominence and obtain a positive image.

This divergence of interests is also caused by some choices of the Italian government through the "Italian Code for Cultural and Landscape Heritage", which delegates heritage promotion policies to local authorities, while assigning the protection and conservation of heritage to the central government. This results in a high interest from local actors in the inclusion process and to a rather low engagement in subsequent management activities. Moreover, this divergence does not promote cooperation between technical and political actors. As one interviewee in the UNESCO Office pointed out, "it is not that we do not dialogue with politicians, but our priority is to speak with the experts nominated by politicians; therefore there is the impression, sometimes, that the involved parties do not speak". The local level tends to focus more on the "organizational [internal]" and the "community" aims, while the ministerial level actors strive to find a balance between "organizational, network and community" aims (Provan and Milward 2001). This is exacerbated by the fact that the local implementation level is subjected to a constant and very rapid change of the responsible political and administrative actors, each of them bringing in new aims and different levels of commitment in the process. As a consequence, the UNESCO Office has to devote significant efforts to making "an endless work of explaining the objectives of the Convention, what the Convention is, what are the parameters and the criteria to which the Convention refers".

The UNESCO Office as coordinating body: factors influencing effectiveness

Because of its structural "centrality" in the network of actors (Rowley 1997) and its institutional role, the UNESCO Office acts as the coordinating body for the national implementation network of the World Heritage Policy. As such, it employs what can be interpreted as network management strategies in a multilevel setting. The first of these strategies is the spreading of information, which is recognized by members of the Office as *the* key task ("it is indeed our role to interact with local subjects in order to inform and raise awareness"). This role is relevant because of the UNESCO Office's intermediate position between global policy and its local implementation ("every time there is a request from the World Heritage center, our office *deciphers* it; it passes it on by meeting the local subjects and [...] exposing it to them in a much more understandable form"). This type of strategy can be referred to as "exploring content" (Klijn et al. 2010): by spreading information, the UNESCO Office aims to build consensus on common aims and, thus to promote cooperative behavior among network partners.

Another action of the UNESCO Office for "exploring content" is the implementation of common projects for all Italian sites. The three main recent projects of this type concern revising the cartography of Italian Sites, the retrospective inventory of the OUV – initiated by the World Heritage Committee in order to harmonize the formulations of OUV in all sites worldwide – and reporting on the state of conservation. While the first project is an independent initiative of the UNESCO Office, the latter two are part of its institutional tasks. The UNESCO Office aims at using these common projects as strategies for "facilitating interaction" and "activation" (Kickert and Koppenjan 1997), building consensus among the sites and promoting their active involvement at several levels. The issue of the activation of the individual sites is especially relevant. Nearly three quarters of the Italian sites (UNESCO 2014b) were included in the World Heritage List before 2002; thus before UNESCO made the need to draft the sites' management plans during the nomination process compulsory. The introduction of this requirement has increased the complexity of the application process, resulting in enhanced motivation of the sites applying for the nomination after 2002.

However, due to the previous absence of compulsory formal requirements, several sites included before 2002 (according to one interviewee, "from 20–30%") have not kept up with management activities and can be therefore considered "silent" (according to an estimation by Badia (2011) in 2011, 69% of Italian Sites did not have a management plan). The strategy of activating specific projects carried out by the UNESCO Office partly had the effect of reactivating some "silent" sites, by re-involving them in common activities and putting them in contact with other actors.

Conclusions

This chapter has analyzed the processes of implementation of World Heritage Policy at national and local levels. The analysis of the Italian case study has shown how a wide variety of non-hierarchically related actors at different levels are responsible for implementing the World Heritage Convention. This suggests that the World Heritage policy in Italy is implemented in a multilevel setting through network-like structures, with the UNESCO Office as the coordinating body. The case study has shown how this formal arrangement often does not correspond to concrete, fully activated and coordinated processes. This is especially visible in a lack of cooperation between actors at different levels and in the presence of "silent" sites, despite the initiatives aimed at their activation. The main causes are multifold and should be addressed in order to make the network of actors implementing the World Heritage policy more effective.

First, the strategies of the UNESCO Office alone are not sufficient to ensure a complete activation of the individual sites. In the analyzed case, the presence of a formal requirement to compulsorily draft a management plan in the application process, introduced at the global level, had a noticeable effect at the local level of implementation, causing an increase in activity of "silent" sites. In this case, the introduction of a mechanism at the highest layer of the multilevel process has, in part, positively influenced all the other layers. The lack of specific financing for the management of the individual sites and for the development of common initiatives also limits the spectrum of activities that can be carried out and the skills that can be used by the sites. This is consistent with previous theoretical contributions, which include the identification of skills, knowledge and resources as one of the conditions for the activation of partners (Agranoff and McGuire 1999).

Second, the case study has highlighted how the conflicting aims of national and local implementation levels result in the lack of a single vision for the Italian Sites as a whole. In particular, the UNESCO Office reinforces the work of the World Heritage Sites as a network of actors at different levels and is therefore aware of its role as coordinating body. This, however, is not enough. In line with the literature (Kenis and Provan 2009), the case highlights the importance exogenous factors can have on the actual operation of the network and, in particular, on its potential for cooperation. The Italian case shows that decentralization from the national to the local level of competencies for the valorization of cultural heritage – defined by law – increases the need to coordinate the different subjects involved. Moreover, decentralization also implies, in the analyzed case, the need to integrate preservation and valorization plans with broader relevant policies and planning instruments at local and regional levels.

The case has also shown that some exogenous causes of potential failure are crucial if coordinating managers lack the capacity to intervene (McGuire and Agranoff 2007). Strategies of conflict management are essentially missed, despite the potential divergence of interests among the network actors. Among the actions taken by the UNESCO Office, we do not find tentative collaborative discussions or, at the very least, effective negotiation processes. These processes did not happen even in the formulation of guidelines for the management of sites, since these were independently drafted by the UNESCO office. On the contrary, such processes, if carried out, could create common meanings, added knowledge and collective cognitive capabilities (Innes and Booher 1999; Lipnack and Stamps 1994), helping to improve the degree of cooperation among the actors involved.

Despite the focus on the Italian specificities, the results of the case analysis can be useful for understanding the factors that foster or hinder multilevel implementation of the UNESCO World Heritage policy – and of cultural policy – worldwide.

In particular, the case of Italian World Heritage sites has shown how the introduction of initiatives at a global level can have positive effects on the activation of partners at all levels; nevertheless, when the different levels interact according to different policy focuses, this can also result in local initiatives that do not fully fit with global policy. Specifically, in the case analyzed, this issue has strongly influenced the implementation of the World Heritage policy, the potential for cooperation inside the network and, ultimately, even the choice of possible leverage by managers in the coordinating body.

Finally, a conclusion particularly relevant for other countries concerns the need, in multilevel settings, to activate each partner in order to establish and reach common policy goals. The presence of a coordinating body adopting strategies that are different from the ones employed in hierarchical settings plays a key role in this activation. Although no unique success model can be drawn from the analysis of a single case, the results suggest that the presence of formal coordinating structures is not enough to guarantee partners' activation; it can rather be reached by combining informal strategies for fostering collaboration with the definition of formal requirements to be fulfilled by all partners.

References

Agranoff, R. and McGuire, M. 1999. "Managing in Network Settings." *Review of Policy Research* 16 (1): 18–41.

Badia, F. 2011. "Contents and Aims of Management Plans for World Heritage Sites." *Journal of Cultural Management and Policy* 1(1): 40–49.

Barreca, M., Catalfo, P., Fiorani, G., and Meneguzzo, M. 2013. "Cultural Creative Networks as Drivers for Entrepreneurship and Innovation: Puglia Sounds." Paper presented at the AIDEA Conference, Lecce, September, 19–20.

Beetham, D. 1987. *Bureaucracy*. Milton Keynes: Open University Press.

Cepiku, D., Jesuit, D. K., and Roberge, I. 2013. *Making Multilevel Public Management Work. Success Stories from Success and Failure from Europe and North America*. London: Taylor & Francis.

Charbit, C. and Michalun, M. V. 2009. "Mind the Gaps: Managing Mutual Dependence in Relation among Levels of Government." OECD Working Papers on Public Governance, no. 14. Paris: OECD Publishing.

Dümcke, C. and Gnedovsky, M. 2013. "The Social and Economic Value of Cultural Heritage: literature review." East European Expert Network on Culture Paper Series. Retrieved at www.eenc.info/wp-content/uploads/2013/08/CD%C3%BCmcke-MGnedovsky-Cultural-Heritage-Literature-Review-July-2013.pdf (accessed April 20, 2015).

Elmi, M., Cepiku, D., and Giordano, F. 2014. "Network Performance Determinants: A Comparative Analysis of UNESCO World Heritage Sites." Paper presented at the EURAM Conference, Valencia, June, 4–7.

European Commission. 2014. *Towards an Integrated Approach to Cultural Heritage for Europe*. Communication from the Commission to the European Parliament, the Council, the European Economic and Social Committee and the Committee of Regions.

Florida, R. L. 2002. *The Rise of Creative Class*. New York. Basic Books.

Frey, B. S. and Steiner. L. 2011. "World Heritage List: Does It Make Sense?" *International Journal of Cultural Policy* 17 (5): 555–573.

Gray, Clive. 2009. "Managing cultural policy: pitfalls and prospects." *Public Administration* 87 (3): 574–585.

Hinna, A., Minuti, M., and Ferrari R. 2009. "From Cultural Site Management to Networking Management: A Case Study Analysis." In *Culture meets Economy. Culture and Creativity as Location Factors – Looking beyond Metropolitan Areas*, edited by Abfalter, D, Pechlaner, H., and Lange, S. Innsbruck: Innsbruck University Press.

Hoi An Centre for Monuments Managements and Preservation. 2008. *IMPACT: The Effects of Tourism on Culture and the Environment in Asia and the Pacific: Cultural Tourism and Heritage Management in the World Heritage Site of the Ancient Town of Hoi An, Viet Nam*. Bangkok: UNESCO.

Hood, C. 1991. "A Public Management for all Seasons?" *Public Administration* 69 (1): 3–19.

Hooghe, L. and Marks, G. 2001. "Types of Multi-Level Governance." *European Integration online Papers* 5 (11). http://eiop.or.at/eiop/texte/2001–011a.htm (accessed April 20, 2015).

ICOMOS. 2005. *Definition of Cultural Heritage: Reference to Documents in History*. Revised version. http://cif.icomos.org/pdf_docs/Documents%20on%20line/Heritage%20definitions.pdf (accessed April 5, 2015).

Innes, J. E. and Booher, D. E. 1999. "Consensus Building and Complex Adaptive Systems: A Framework for Evaluating Collaborative Planning." *Journal of the American Planning Association* 65 (4): 412–423.

Kenis, P. and Provan, K. G. 2009. "Towards an Exogenous Theory of Public Network Performance." *Public Administration* 87 (3): 440–456.

Kickert, W. J. M. and Koppenjan, J. 1997. "Public Management and Network Management: An Overview." In *Managing Complex Networks. Strategies for the Public Sector*, edited by Kickert, W. J. M., Klijn, E. H., and Koppenjan, J. London: Sage.

Klijn, E. H. and Koppenjan, F. 2000. "Public Management and Policy Networks." *Public Management* 2 (2): 135–158.

Klijn, E. H., Steijn, B., and Edelenbos, J. 2010. "The Impact of Network Management on Outcomes in Governance Networks." *Public Administration* 88 (4): 1063–1082.

Lipnack, J. and Stamps, J. 1994. *The Age of the Network*. New York: Wiley.

Matarasso, François and Landry, C. 1999. *Balancing Act: Twenty-One Strategic Dilemmas in Cultural Policy*. Cultural Policies Research and Development Unit, Policy Note No. 4. Strasbourg: Council of Europe Publishing.

McGuire, M. 2002. "Managing Networks: Propositions on What Managers Do and Why They Do It." *Public Administration Review* 62 (5): 599–609.

McGuire, M. and Agranoff, R. 2007. "Answering the Big Questions, Asking the Bigger Questions: Expanding the Public Network Management Empirical Research Agenda." Paper presented at the 9th Public Management Research Conference, Tucson, October, 25–27.

Ministero per i Beni e le attività culturali. 2010. *Organismi di riferimento della Convenzione sul Patrimonio Mondiale.*

OECD. 2009. *Bridging the Gaps between Levels of Government.* OECD Policy Brief. http://78.41.128.130/dataoecd/43/8/43901550.pdf (accessed May 15, 2015).

Osborne, S. P. 2006. "The New Public Governance?" *Public Management Review* 8 (3): 377–387.

Ostrom, E. 1990. *Governing the Commons: The Evolution of Institutions for Collective Action.* Cambridge: Cambridge University Press.

O'Toole, Laurence J. 1997. "Treating Networks Seriously: Practical and Research-Based Agendas in Public Administration." *Public Administration Review* 35 (3): 361–371.

Peters, B. G. and Pierre, J. 2001. "Multi-Level Governance: A Faustian Bargain?" Paper presented at Conference on Multi-Level Governance, University of Sheffield, July.

Porter, M. E. 1998. "Clusters and the New Economic Competition." *Harvard Business Review*, 77–90.

Provan, K. G. and Milward, H. B. 2001. "Do Networks Really Work? A Framework for Evaluating Public-Sector Organizational Networks." *Public Administration Review* 61 (4): 414–423.

Rittel, H. W. and Webber. M. M. 1973. "Dilemmas in a General Theory of Planning." *Policy Sciences* 4 (2): 155–169.

Rowley, T. 1997. "Moving beyond Dyadic Ties: A Network Theory of Stakeholder Influences." *Academy of Management Review* 22 (4): 897–910.

Sen, Amartya. 1999. *Development as Freedom.* Oxford: Oxford University Press.

Stoker, G. 2006. "Public Value Management a New Narrative for Networked Governance?" *American Review of Public Administration* 36 (1): 41–57.

Throsby, D. 2001 *Economics and Culture.* Cambridge: Cambridge University Press.

UNESCO. 2014a. *State Parties Ratification Status.* http://whc.unesco.org/en/statesparties/ (accessed June 10, 2016).

UNESCO. 2014b. The World Heritage List. http://whc.unesco.org/en/list (accessed June 10, 2016).

UNESCO. 2014c. World Heritage in Danger. http://whc.unesco.org/en/danger/ (accessed June 10, 2016).

UNESCO. 2014d. World Heritage List Nominations. http://whc.unesco.org/en/nominations/. (accessed January10, 2015).

UNESCO 2013. Operational Guidelines for the Implementation of the World Heritage Convention. Paris: UNESCO.

UNESCO. 2003. Convention for the Safeguarding of the Intangible Cultural Heritage. Paris: UNESCO.

UNESCO. 1972. The World Heritage Convention. Paris: UNESCO.

Van der Aa, Bart J. M. 2005. Preserving the Heritage of Humanity? Obtaining World Heritage Status and the Impacts of Listing. Netherlands Organization for Scientific Research: Amsterdam.

Yin, R. K. 1994. *Case Study Research: Design and Methods.* Thousand Oaks, CA: Sage.

PART III

Forging a resilient public administration

Introduction

The former two sections of the handbook make clear that the public sphere is still relevant in an age of globalization, when the nation-state can no longer be taken for granted as the natural frame for social and political debate, and global governance institutions often seem inadequate. The third section of the handbook asks: can public management play a role in forging a resilient public administration? Public management is the most rapidly developing field of public administration since the New Public Management (NPM) of several decades ago. Recent reforms implemented worldwide show that public management:

- is highly context dependent;
- has its own specificities vis-à-vis management of profit firms;
- is about outcomes and processes and not only outputs;
- is not politically neutral (or when this happens it becomes irrelevant);
- can make a difference in achieving global goals, in addressing challenges such as terrorism, climate change, mass migration, and in promoting sustainable social and economic development.

Some universities, including the University of Rome Tor Vergata (Italy) and the Rockefeller College of Public Affairs and Policy at the University at Albany (USA), now offer courses on global public management, acknowledging the wider relevance of public management for public policy effectiveness. In research, evidence is however limited to case studies and more is needed to understand cause-related mechanisms between certain public management practices and outcomes.

This section focuses on some key areas that are critical for achieving the transformation of public management from a set of uncritically imported tools and techniques from the private sector to an approach that can contribute to protecting and enhancing the public interest. The chapters that follow analyze: risk management, leadership, strategic management and long-term thinking, performance management, program evaluation, public budgeting, policy capacity, motivation, public procurement and e-government.

In Chapter 23, "Resilience in public administration: moving from risk avoidance to assuring public policy outcomes", Tony Bovaird and Barry Quirk from the United Kingdom argue that traditional approaches to risk management in public administration have tended to focus on likely future negative events, leading naturally to an emphasis on risk avoidance and losing sight of the trade-off whereby risk reduction for the agency normally also entails outcome reduction for service users and communities. They propose the adoption of integrated resilience strategies based on risk enablement, so that a better balance between risk and outcomes can contribute directly to more cost-effective public services and more desirable outcomes.

In Chapter 24, "The changing roles of politicians and public servants", Robert Shepherd, Christopher Stoney and Lori Turnbull from Canada address a key issue in public sector leadership: the relationship between politicians and public servants. Reviewing the increased emphasis in the literature on the politicization of public services in Western democracies, the authors discuss the changing relationship between ministers and public servants and consider the implications in terms of a declining state of trust and confidence between elected leaders, who are expected to be partisan, and public servants, whose role in a modern and professional public service is based on principles of merit, a non-partisan conceptualization of public good and a longer-term view of public policy aims. They conclude by observing a steady decline in the value placed by political masters on a traditional merit-based and professional public service, and a corresponding change in the role and importance of the public sector, particularly in relation to political staff.

Chapter 25, entitled "Strategic management and public governance in the public sector", by Paul Joyce from the United Kingdom, proposes a definition of strategic management that puts the emphasis on achieving long-term goals based on thorough analysis and assessment of the situation, options and resources. The chapter looks at strategic management consequences in a public sector context and considers strategic management and reforms to modernize civil service policy-making and systems of public governance. The concept of the strategic state is introduced and it is suggested that governments must take strategy and long-term thinking more seriously so as to increase the effectiveness of services.

The following two chapters are dedicated to performance management in the public sector, which can occur at four different levels: the global level refers to rankings and measures produced by international institutions to assess the aggregate performance levels of different countries' public sectors; the level of public sector policies is connected to the main component of public sector reform agendas since the late 1980s; the organizational level is represented by performance management activities that are part of strategic planning and managing efforts; finally, at the individual or team level, performance management can operate by integrating human resources management through instruments such as performance-related pay.

Although there should be cause–effect links between these different levels, empirical research on these links offers mixed results.

Chapter 26, "Performance management in public administration", by Denita Cepiku from Italy, focuses on performance management at the organizational level: such systems comprise a bundle of activities quantifying performance: defining a measurement object, formulating indicators, collecting, analyzing, and reporting data. The chapter illustrates the multi-dimensional concept of performance in the public sector and the characteristics of effective systems and processes that govern it. The performances of public and for-profit organizations are compared and key issues regarding the future of performance management systems in public administrations are illustrated with practical examples. Conditions ensuring – what is considered the Achilles' heel – the meaningful use of performance information by public managers, politicians, citizens, civil society organizations and the media are highlighted.

Managing performance is a complex and expensive activity, which is carried out assuming that organizations have a greater probability of achieving their objectives. However, the author notices that there is insufficient empirical evidence to back up this claim and, as with any investment, it makes sense to ask if performance management leads to better results.

She concludes by arguing that the future of performance management will depend on the extent to which it will be able to adapt to address emerging trends, including: critiques of its use for performance improvement, the recent explosion in the availability of data, and the shift of public management from competition to collaboration.

Joshua L. Osowski and Sanjay K. Pandey from the United States utilize Chapter 27, entitled "Public policies promoting performance management: Australia and the United States", to review public policies promoting performance management within national governments, including legislative as well as executive measures. They choose to compare Australia and the United States because of the relatively long and sustained use of performance management at the national level, despite changes in ideology and governmental leadership over the years.

Similarities between these two countries tend to suggest that there is a rather orderly progression that takes place as national level governments grapple with (1) initiating, then (2) incorporating, and (3) improving the performance management process.

The analysis of performance policy and practices commonalities along these three stages contain lessons that Australia and the United States learned during several decades of experience and can be useful in other national contexts as well. In particular, leadership commitment and creating a formal requirement are key in the first stage. Subsequently, the use of inclusion in goal setting and decentralized decision making, linking performance to consequences and making performance reports available to the public become relevant. Finally, it is important to have sustained effort to improve performance methods by analyzing and learning from past performance policies and practices.

The next chapter, "The role of policy capacity in policy success and failure", by M. Ramesh from Singapore and Michael Howlett from Canada, analyses the nature of the competencies and capabilities that governments must possess in order to be able to develop and implement effective policies and deliver successful programs. The authors argue that there are different modes of governance that can be identified around the world, such as network governance, market governance and government governance. In recent decades there has been a transition – as analysed in other chapters in this handbook – from government service delivery and regulation to more market-based types of governance regimes. This has been accompanied by a shift from hierarchical and market forms of governance to more network-oriented governance relationships. However, as the authors explain, a new form of governance requires the relevant policy capacity to be high in order to reach its policy-making potential.

Chapter 29, "The program evaluation function: uncertain governance and effects", is dedicated to the program evaluation function. In his analysis, Robert Shepherd from Canada positions internal program evaluation functions in the context of public management reform efforts, shifting governmental expectations, and the role of rationalistic evidence in policy decision making. He argues that although change is commonplace in public sector operations, some sub-functions of government have the unique responsibility to ensure that decision makers not only have the information they need to make critical decisions, but must also serve to support public good objectives of speaking the truth about the effectiveness of government policies and programs. Speaking truth has always been difficult for the evaluation function given that evaluation is not a politically neutral enterprise; nonetheless, there is no consensus on how to cope with the political dimension of assessments. Increasingly, governments rely on many forms of evidence, and evaluation is not as privileged as it once was. With the increasing influence of think-tanks, lobbyists, and political staff, evaluation that is dependent on rationalistic methods supposedly removed from politics has declined in prominence.

In Chapter 30, "Motivation in the public sector", Adrian Ritz and Oliver Neumann from Switzerland and Wouter Vandenabeele from the Netherlands uncover another critical aspect: human resources motivation in the public sector. They observe how the provision of public services is heavily dependent on the knowledge, skills, attitudes and motives of public employees. Unsurprisingly people are the main asset of most public organizations and their actions are significant drivers of organizational outcomes. The authors argue that motivation becomes a crucial factor in both the provision of public service and the quality of public sector work.

The authors sketch out some of the most important general theories of motivation and draw a distinction between public sector motivation, which is based on self-interest, and public service motivation, which is additionally rooted in the desire to serve the public interest and to comply with specific institutional rules. After summarizing how the stream of research on public service motivation has developed over time, they develop a conceptual model to provide an overview of the antecedents and outcomes of public service motivation that have been investigated to date.

Chapter 31, "Public budgeting from a managerial perspective", authored by Riccardo Mussari from Italy, reviews the public budgeting function from a managerial and political perspective. The approaches used to explain and justify budget formulation, including classical rationality, with its variant bounded rationality, and disjointed incrementalism are compared; the functions and principles of budgeting introduced; and budget formats described. The main functions of a public budget are: political; steering and programming; authorization; and cyclical economic policy, with specific regard to the federal/national government. As Mussari makes clear, the budget is not simply a financial forecast but a document that, starting from a strategy defined upstream, guides the actions of those called upon to use financial and non-financial (human, material, immaterial) resources to achieve expected results. From this perspective, the budget is a managerial tool and budgeting is mainly approached as a technical problem.

Giulia Di Pierro from England and Gustavo Piga from Italy use Chapter 32, entitled "The road ahead for public procurement in Europe: is there life after the directives?" to focus on the purchase of goods, services and works by governments, public authorities and the public sector. The authors make clear the several reasons that make public procurement an increasingly critical function for governments worldwide. It represents a significant share of GDP in both developed and developing countries and influences directly not only the economy, but also broader government objectives such as job creation, industrial policy, the environment and innovation. The authors analyze the recent modernization of several procurement regulations that occurred in response to new market dynamics. With a focus on Europe, they show how reforms of public procurement could leverage the socio-economic development of the region.

This handbook concludes with Chapter 33, "Korean e-government in a social media environment: prospects and challenges", which reviews the role of e-government in enhancing transparency, participation, accountability and trust in government. M. Jae Moon, from South Korea, focuses on that country during the past several decades as a case study. With continued advancement of information and communication technologies, e-government has evolved from simple automation of administrative works and back-office applications to provision of customized online services and crowdsourcing through which individual citizens often become co-producers of public services. The author identifies the key success factors of the Korean e-government experience in the strong commitment by the central government, which strategically promoted the national informatization and e-government projects with the support of top policy-makers, capable institutions, and financial resources. E-government continues to evolve in a social media environment, which offers both challenges and prospects while the crowdsourcing and e-government 3.0 paradigm are being gradually adopted.

The Korean government has been a forerunner in e-government both in back-office and front-office (Korean Immigration Service System) applications of ICTs. However, the Korean government faces a new set of e-government challenges in the social media environment, where more openness, interaction, participation, information sharing and collaboration are demanded by citizens. The author notes that the government needs to be cautious when it attempts to correct biased, incorrect and cyber-cascaded information in social media. Unless trust in government is well secured, government actions could be perceived to be unnecessary interventions and an overreaction to social media communications. Both quantity and quality of citizen participation and social and information connectivity based on social media and other web 2.0 technologies will further shape future e-government and make government more open, connected, participatory and collaborative.

23

RESILIENCE IN PUBLIC ADMINISTRATION

Moving from risk avoidance to assuring public policy outcomes

Tony Bovaird and Barry Quirk

Introduction: why resilience?

Traditional approaches to risk management in public administration have tended to focus on likely future negative events, resulting in complex "blame avoidance strategies" through which public agencies attempt to minimise damage to themselves and deflect blame for failure. This leads naturally to an emphasis on risk avoidance, so that these negative events are rarer. However, this comes with a cost – it loses sight of the trade-off whereby risk reduction normally also entails outcome reduction. A radically different approach is to accept the inevitability of some failures and to seek to embed resilience in the way in which the overall service system works, and in each of its components. In this way, the negative consequences of failure can be minimised. More importantly, the transformative potential of a responsible risk culture, based on proportionate rather than over-cautious responses to risk, can be realised.

In this chapter, we explore the interrelationship between risk and resilience, the elements of the resilience chain linking citizens and service users to the overall service system, and ways in which the "resilience" chain can be managed to achieve a desirable balance between system outcomes and outcomes for individual citizens.

Risk for government – and from government

Risk is how we measure today the adverse impact or losses we think may happen in the future (Knight 1921). Economists have traditionally defined risk as those elements of uncertainty to which probability estimates can be attached, typically only a subset of the overall influences on uncertainty. However, risk assessment and management specialists in the "risk industry" nowadays normally use "risk" to cover all the factors which contribute to uncertainty, whether or not they can be captured by probability estimates.

This definition is consistent with some "risks" turning out to be advantageous in their effects. However, in practice there tends to be an asymmetry in how negative and positive risks are regarded (Peters and Slovic 2000). The public expects government to take action in relation to any negative social, economic and environmental risks identified, even when it is not clear what has caused the problems or whether proposed interventions might reduce the risk.

Consequently, in a world of open government and high transparency, the risk of future failure looms as a spectre over public action and the potentially positive effects of some actions with uncertain outcomes are overlooked or underestimated.

Moreover, "just as there is a risk to government so, from a citizen's perspective, there is also a risk from government" (Quirk 2011: 160). In the current climate of public spending cuts throughout OECD countries, there are now major risks to citizens (particularly the most vulnerable) when services upon which they depend face major cuts. At this time public agencies need increasingly to look outward, helping their public to cope with the changing character and intensity of economic and environmental risks, and helping their communities to develop resilience to social and economic changes. Paradoxically, however, just at such times public agencies tend to look inward, getting their budgets under control and reducing the risk that they will be held responsible for the decreasing outcomes which occur. Sight is lost of the trade-off which means that risk reduction normally also entails outcome reduction.

Focusing on the UK public sector, this chapter argues that public policies need to focus more on risks to the outcomes experienced by service users and communities (and less on the internal risks to the agency); to place more emphasis on embedding resilience within the behaviours and resources of users, communities, providers and service systems. This approach develops the taxonomy suggested by Flemig and Osborne (Chapter 16 in this handbook) which distinguishes consequential risk at the level of the individual, organisational risk on the level of the organisation and its staff, and behavioral risk at the level of the wider community and environment. We then explore how public sector organisations can adopt integrated resilience strategies based on risk enablement, so that a better balance between risk and outcomes can contribute directly to more cost-effective public services and more desirable outcomes.

Relationship of risk to public services failure

Citizens potentially face multiple sources of hazards and harms from their general environments. At the most dramatic, "macro" level, potentially affecting large populations, hazards range from hurricanes, floods and public health risks through to terrorism. At first sight, it might seem that public policymakers have already become highly attuned to managing such adverse risks. Emergency preparedness planning, disaster recovery and business continuity work have mushroomed at every level of government. However, the extent to which these risks have actually been reduced by public intervention is still in dispute.

The UK White Paper on Open Public Services (HM Government 2011) proposed "continuity regimes", as an integral part of public agency modernisation programmes but offered few details of what this might mean in practice, focusing instead on key principles. Remarkably, these principles focused more on protecting potentially failing providers from too early intervention by service commissioners and on monitoring signals of financial failure, rather than signals of outcome failure.

While many of the major dangers external to the public services system listed above threaten much greater damage than the more micro-level risks to everyday quality of life posed by most internal failures of public services, these latter are generally clear and present, while macro-level risks often appear remote and unlikely. Consequently, these micro-level risks have driven a major redesign of UK personal social services in the past two decades. Children's services in the public sector have put a much higher emphasis than ever before on "safeguarding", i.e. protecting children from maltreatment, preventing impairment of their health or development, and ensuring children grow up in safe circumstances (NHS Commissioning Board 2013; Martin et al. 2010; Bonnerjea 2009). This has partly been driven by a genuine concern for the wellbeing of children – but it has partly also arisen from concern about the reputation damage to politicians and public agencies from the major media publicity given to a series of gruesome and highly publicised cases of neglect and abuse; and partly by concern on the part of public agencies to reduce their legal liability in case "looked after" children and adults come to significant harm.

Again, as with the more dramatic macro risks, the extent to which these risks have been reduced by public intervention is still unclear. Indeed, a recent review (Moran 2009: 25) concluded that "research is lacking in the evidence required to guide practitioners in the development and delivery of interventions to prevent or reduce neglect and its impact", that many current interventions are "promising" but no more and "intervening in neglect is likely to be costly, requiring intensive, long-term, multi-faceted work by a highly skilled workforce". It appears that the new emphasis on and policies for children's safeguarding, with the intrusive and costly bureaucratic mechanisms they entail, may be having limited effect on outcomes, although they may be serving to protect public service organisations, their managers and staff from blame. This seems a low-value way to organise public sector responses to risk.

Why has this situation arisen? Smith et al. (2011: 3) suggest that we have become captured by "process" and the allure of "risk tools, frameworks, registers, matrices, spreadsheets, guidance and software … elegant risk registers, local risk champions and 'traffic-light' dashboards" – what Ellis (2013: 8) calls the "ratcheting up of managerial technicist practices". In practice, these approaches have not been developed with the primary purpose of reducing risk. They respond rather to demands for accountability in respect of budgetary control and/or service failure, based on an audit approach that internalises risk and institutionalises its management. They therefore partly reflect the "blame-avoidance" and self-preservation strategies of public institutions (Hood 2011) rather than a thorough framework for reducing public risk and improving resilience. Moreover, they may even be counter-productive in giving decision makers an illusion of control over risk – decision makers may well believe that they are monitoring and responding to the major risks they face, although in fact the real risks are largely unknown and the degree of control available to policymakers is very low. Rather than opening up options, this internally oriented approach often closes them down, undervaluing pragmatism and common sense, encouraging low-risk appetites and risk-averse behaviour, and undermining proper responses to the opportunities facing public agencies and the citizens they serve.

Understanding risk in different knowledge domains

The theoretical underpinnings of current risk assessment and management approaches are largely to blame for their relatively weak role in tackling the uncertainties facing public policy. To see why, we employ the Cynefin framework proposed by Snowden and Boone (2007) to classify the kind of information available about an organisation's environment into four domains of knowledge (see Figure 23.1).

Simple domain: Here the relationship between cause and effect is widely believed to be obvious, with solid evidence for predicting policy outcomes – in this domain, we are dealing with "knowns" and we can expect to apply best practice. This is the domain for which current risk assessment and management tools are most appropriate.

Complicated domain: Here the problem is generally understood but cause-and-effect relationships behind the problem, although "knowable" in principle, need application of expert knowledge to predict how policy outcomes are likely to be affected by specific interventions. In this domain, we can expect to apply good practice. The tools of risk assessment and management are appropriate but difficult to apply because the set of "knowns" that can be modelled is quite limited.

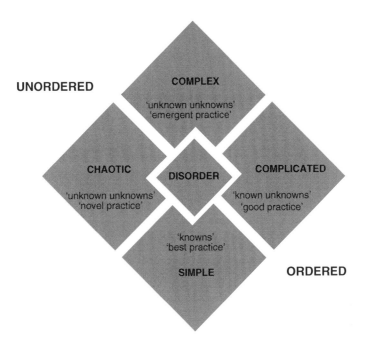

Figure 23.1 The Cynefin framework: domains of knowledge in decision making
Source: Adapted from Snowden and Boone (2007)

Complex domain: Here, because of the strong interconnectedness of the phenomena being managed, the relationship between cause and effect can only be perceived in retrospect. The best we can do is to sense emergent practice. Techniques such as agent-based modelling, assuming that actors are adaptive rather than "fully rational", and simulating how their multiple interactions create complex social patterns allow a range of scenarios to be explored (Bryson et al. 2005). This analysis can inform policymakers only at a broad level of decision but not give detailed predictions. Risk assessment and management are necessarily very different in this domain. Since we are dealing with variables which are only predictable to a very limited extent, the role of risk management here is to warn against the temptation to look for "facts", rather than allowing patterns to emerge. Risk management also has to signal how the interdependence of the organisation and its environment can create the conditions for "emergent" threats that are traceable to no specific element within the system (Buchanan 2004) – a particularly hard task. This emergent property of collectively generated risk suggests that over-confident policy prescriptions should be avoided, that experimentation is likely to be fundamental, and that a range of policy approaches is likely to be superior to "putting all your eggs in one basket".

Chaotic domain: Here there is no discernible relationship between cause and effect at systems level, so nothing can be predicted in relation to policy outcomes – the best we can do is to explore novel practice. In this domain we can place the arrival of "black swans" – unpredicted (and unpredictable) negative events with such dramatic consequences that they threaten the very existence of the organisation (Taleb 2007). The role of the risk manager here is simply to monitor and point out the level of turbulence, so that the organisation does not fall for off-the-peg solutions which were appropriate to more ordered knowledge domains. Anyone offering to do a risk assessment in these circumstances is revealing that they are disqualified to comment.

(Even more threatening, of course, is the "disorder" domain in Figure 23.1, where we do not even know which knowledge domain we are in).

So, how can we tell in which knowledge domain we are currently operating? In practice different parts of organisations are likely to be working in different knowledge domains, so that most of the knowledge domains in Figure 23.1 may be appropriate in different circumstances. Many public services may operate at least partly in the simple knowledge domain (e.g. technical services such as transport or waste collection and disposal). However, this seems unlikely to be true for social policy, which is more likely to be operating in the "complicated" or "complex" knowledge domains (or even, at times, in chaotic conditions). Duit and Galaz (2008) present evidence which they suggest justifies the need for policymakers to consider the implications of complex adaptive systems (CAS), because nonlinear behaviour can spark off political crises in governance systems, e.g. through disasters triggered by passing critical biophysical/technical thresholds; or through significant changes in interconnected social or economic systems – especially if they occur in already vulnerable systems. There has also been significant interest in modelling health and social services systems as CAS (e.g. Health Foundation 2010; Tsasis et al. 2010; Plsek and Greenhalgh 2001).

In summary, risk assessment and management approaches have to differentiate between different knowledge domains and therefore between different parts of public service organisation which are working in different domains. Where applications of risk assessment and management stray from the domain in which their approach could be relevant into domains where their assumptions are irrelevant, their subsequent conclusions are, literally, nonsensical.

Strategies for managing risk

We can distinguish a range of quite distinct strategies towards risk in public services:

- activity portfolio management: choosing a portfolio of activities with lower risk attached;
- risk reduction in the environment: either ensuring key risks are less likely or influencing their character so that particularly damaging features of those risks are reduced;
- building resilience into the service system, including the activities of providers and the behaviours of service users, their support networks and their communities;
- risk enablement: encouraging decision makers in the service system to choose activities with appropriate levels of risk, rather than always aiming at risk minimisation.

These strategies are not, of course, mutually exclusive. The first two are essentially preventative, the third is about mitigation of risks and the fourth is about learning to live appropriately with the levels of risk that the organisation faces. As such, all could be pursued simultaneously. The third and fourth strategies have a mutually reinforcing characteristic, in that the more successful is the resilience strategy, the more confidently can a public service organisation pursue a risk enablement strategy. In the rest of this chapter, we focus on the strategies of *building resilience into the service system*, in conjunction with the strategy of *risk enablement*.

The concept of resilience

However cleverly public policy tries to prevent identified risks eventuating, the service system has to be able to cope with some things going wrong. For this, it needs resilience. There is no universally agreed definition of resilience but the recent social sciences literature has stressed the idea of resilience as "adaptive ability" (Simmie and Martin 2010: 28). This goes beyond the traditional definitions of resilience – "engineering resilience" (where the level of resilience is measured by the speed of return to the pre-existing equilibrium) and "ecological resilience" (where the level of resilience is measured by the size of shock or disturbance that can be absorbed before the system changes structure or function, shaped by a different set of processes).

For the purposes of this chapter, we adopt the definition of resilience from Edson (2012), as adaptation that supports successful achievement of goals and objectives, as well as learning for future planning and preparation. This definition accepts the Simmie and Martin requirement that the concept of resilience should incorporate learning and adapting and, in addition, gives some clear pointers as to how it can be made operational.

Whose resilience?

A key political question in relation to the concept of resilience is *whose* resilience is being assured? We need to distinguish between the resilience of individuals and communities to the risks which eventuate (both those arising from the external environment and those which arise from agency decisions and actions) and the resilience of public agencies and their individual stakeholders – policymakers (politicians and top managers), senior managers, frontline staff, etc. The current balance of public policy in relation to the resilience of these different stakeholders is questionable, often appearing to give more weight to the risks and resilience of public service organisations than to those of the citizens and clients they serve. Mitchell and Glendinning (2007: 71) talk of "continuous risk assessment but actually very little time to sit down and work directly with clients in thinking and planning ways to address the risks users have identified in their own lives".

In practice, there is a conflict of interest between stakeholders in the choice between risk avoidance and resilience strategies. Service users are likely to feel that their outcomes are most likely to be protected and enhanced by a focus on strategies of resilience and risk enablement, which offer the potential for minimising the damage done by the risks they face, while, where appropriate, trading off potential benefits against potential risks. Yet the choice of strategies is typically dominated by internal stakeholders, who are naturally keen to avoid those elements of risk that affect themselves – particularly financial risks (e.g. where redress has to be paid) or "reputational" risks to the agency (e.g. from court cases or "scandals" highlighted in the media), and personal risks to top agency managers (e.g. through scapegoating by political leaders) or to staff (e.g. by losing their professional registration). For example, Ellis (2013: 10) summarises previous research as suggesting that UK frontline social workers, managing (under pressure of severely limited resources) the reputational and financial risks of giving personal budgets to their clients, are more likely to act defensively to avoid risk, rather than seek proactively and creatively to promote choice and control – and may even behave in actively obstructive ways (such as not informing their riskiest clients of the choices available to them).

This highlights the importance of a mature approach to accountability, rather than an immature blame culture, if approaches to risk and resilience are to be improved. This is only likely to be achieved if the power imbalance in public agencies is directly addressed, so that users and communities become directly involved in the strategic decisions around risk, in an explicit strategy of co-production of outcomes (Loeffler 2015). Only then will the risks to users and communities be foregrounded and their views on those risks enter directly into the decision-making calculus of the public agency. As Quirk (2011: 158) says, in relation to public risks, "Government's first role is to help people reckon and reduce risks for themselves." Moreover, co-production allows users and communities to participate in decisions about the trade-off between perceived risks and the potential payoffs which they might experience, something that may be particularly important to many service users, as highlighted in a recent Department of Health report:

> there was a very clear message from people that they wanted to be able to choose what they thought was right for them. Many reported they were offered "safety" often at the expense of other qualities of life, such as dignity, autonomy, independence, family life and self-determination – and many older people and people with learning disabilities said this was a very high price to pay.

(DH 2009: 16)

Embedding resilience within the service system: the "resilience chain"

The current systems-based literatures around urban, environmental and economic resilience tend to ignore that these systems comprise socially constructed organisations and social networks of people, which means that systems are shaped by the characteristics of constituent agents. Consequently, a truly resilient system of public services, fashioned to achieve publicly desired outcomes, also requires attention to the resilience of the agents within the system, specifically citizens (both individually as service users and collectively as communities) and organisations (both service providers and commissioners). Taken together, these form the "resilience chain".

User resilience: Clearly people who use services may already be partially resilient, if they have private resources to buy alternative services when public services fail. However, public organisations need resilience mechanisms to go further, so that they offer protection to a high proportion of citizens, especially the most vulnerable users of services. The most direct mechanism for improving resilience of users is likely to be a co-production approach. This includes the role of citizens in co-deciding risk levels in the policy process, but can go much wider. Service users know things that many professionals don't ("users as thinking people"), can make a service more effective by the extent to which they go along with its requirements ("users as critical success factors") and have energy and skills which they may be prepared to devote to ensuring higher outcomes from services, both for themselves and others ("users as resource-banks and asset-holders") (Bovaird and Loeffler 2012). When these assets and potential contributions are identified and harnessed, users are more able to take on some of the functions that professionals play, if those professionals become unavailable or can only play a more limited role. In this way, user co-production through co-commissioning, co-design, co-delivery and co-assessment of services can build up the capacity of service users to cope with less input from public services and to adapt to different configurations of services – or their sudden absence. Similarly, it makes sense to build upon the capacity of users' direct support network – their family, friends, neighbours and the volunteers who help them.

Community resilience: Communities, like users, know and understand things that go beyond the knowledge bases of professionals ("It takes a village to raise a child"), can exert social pressure to alter anti-social behaviour ("Notice: The following people are not welcome in this pub because of misbehaviour in local pubs during the past year") and can mobilise effort and skills to help achieve publicly desired outcomes ("Emergencies and disasters bring out the best in folk"). Identifying community assets and potential contributions and mobilising them in community co-production means that communities are more able to cope when public services fail to deliver as expected (Wilding 2011) – they must "plan for not having a plan" (Norris et al. 2008: 127). This is a role long played by community capacity building, which has been topical sporadically since the 1960s, although not widely funded from mainstream public budgets. As Demiroz and Kapucu (Chapter 19 in this handbook) suggest, policy makers can access community resources via inter-organisational and cross-sector networks for managing complex issues.

Service provider resilience: Service providers have an interest in ensuring resilience in the face of potential service failure – as, of course, do service commissioners. As well as encouraging user and community resilience, providers can build resilience into their services through their own internal mechanisms. These start with flagging up potential failure sufficiently early for appropriate avoidance action to be taken, e.g. performance management frameworks and feedback channels from users and staff. Moreover, it is important that providers have functional quality assurance systems (e.g. ISO 9001: 2015) to ensure that service delivery does not fail, together with recovery mechanisms (such as membership of provider networks, so that alternative provision can be arranged quickly in emergencies). Service commissioners need to insist that potential service contractors show they have credible mechanisms such as these in place. The UK Cabinet Office (2013) defines business continuity management (BCM) as "a process that helps manage risks to the smooth running of an organisation or delivery of a service, ensuring continuity of critical functions in the event of a disruption, and effective recovery afterwards". However, this government guidance does not identify the need for BCM in organisations to encourage both user and community resilience as part of an integrated resilience policy.

Service system resilience: Service commissioners can build resilience into the overall service system both by ensuring that mechanisms for resilience of service users, communities and service providers have been put in place but also by implementing system-wide mechanisms, such as:

- System entry barriers: restricting potential bidders to those who can prove financial stability, successful track record and high staff qualifications ("vigilant gatekeeping").
- Structural solutions: several suppliers, retainer arrangements with alternative suppliers, residual in-house capability, emergency budgets ("system redundancy").
- Complexity solutions: accepting some promising "black box" approaches, which have a plausible narrative, with quasi-grants and rigorous evaluation ("meta-planning").
- Process solutions: compulsory insurance bonds, several different supply methodologies or "pathways to outcomes" ("built-in flexibility").

The overall "resilience chain" depends on each link in the chain of user-community-organisation-system being sound and strongly connected to the next link. In the words of Coaffee (2011: 335): "the governance of resilience ... is progressively 'responsibilizing' and increasingly putting the onus of preventing and preparing for disruptive challenges onto an array of institutions, professions, communities and individuals, rather than the state—the traditional provider of citizens' security and emergency planning needs".

It is clear that public agencies too often have given more emphasis to embedding resilience into the formal service provision process rather than ensuring that all the links in this resilience chain are effective. For example, the Cabinet Office (2011) guidance on resilience of critical infrastructure and essential services emphasises information sharing amongst organisational stakeholders about their infrastructure but not joint planning for building citizen or community resilience in the event of major crises. While understandable, given the potential for damage to agencies and their staff when service provision fails, this narrow approach to resilience, with its under-emphasis on ensuring the resilience of service users and communities, is logically indefensible.

Moreover, refusing service users the right to make their own service decisions (e.g. through control over personal care budgets), on the grounds of the potential risks involved, ignores the "inherent risks" of conventional services, determined by professional staff, that "do not always meet people's needs and sometimes are abusive and neglectful" (Manthorpe and Samsi 2013, 898). However, we should not underestimate the magnitude of a cultural change towards co-production of risk and resilience decisions. Public agencies in the past have often refused to accept that people should have the right to influence decisions concerning their welfare and have even actively connived at the disenfranchisement of citizens in risk and resilience policy decisions (Bovaird and Quirk 2013). Of course, there is also a danger that the scales can be tipped in the other direction – if citizens are given a greater role in decisions about the risks they can take and the resilience strategies they adopt, public agencies could seek wholly to "privatise" the risk by offloading all of it onto service users, carers and their support networks (Stevens et al. 2011; Ferguson 2007). Here, too, a co-production approach is important to ensure that citizens have the power to resist such "risk-dumping" (Bovaird and Quirk 2013).

Of course, relying on resilience to cope with risks of service failure brings its own risks. Resilience can never be assumed to be fully reliable. When novel threats appear, they may be distinctively different and render some resilience mechanisms useless. Indeed, as resilience is about adaptation, the potential for embedding it in the service system will differ markedly, depending on the knowledge domain in which we are operating – it will be easiest in the Simple domain and increasingly difficult as we move from Complicated through Complex to Chaotic domains. Resilience, as with all features of the service system, emerges as well as being planned. The emergence of resilience cannot be predicted but it can be facilitated by appropriate approaches, particularly design-based experimentation.

The design approach: experimentation as antidote to service failure

We have argued that there needs to be radical change in public policy to reorient resilience approaches and risk strategies towards a focus on achieving the outcomes most desired by service users and their communities, taking on board the emotional as well the "rational" elements of risk. This needs to build encouragement of user and community resilience into the risk policies of public agencies. The implications of such a radical policy shift will be substantial, so far relatively unexplored and therefore only partially understood. In a period of such radical change, experimentation is essential. By their very nature, not all experiments are successful. The key design principle of experimental approaches to policy learning is: "fail early, fail fast, fail cheap … and learn how to correct quickly". In the words of Samuel Beckett (1984):

> Ever tried. Ever failed.
> No matter. Try Again.
> Fail again. Fail better.

Experimentation is hard in the public sector. The very thought of failure is often anathema, even if it is intellectually understood as part of the path to learning. Each time failure occurs it is liable to be highlighted – by opponents and the media – as a "scandal" or as evidence of incompetence. Hindsight shows us the mistakes, errors, omissions and commissions of the past – these can then be ascribed to failures of foresight. One example of this can be found in the serious case reviews of deaths of children and adults. These case reviews attempt to draw general conclusions from individual cases of the most serious and tragic circumstances. And while it is essential to investigate and learn from operational failings, too often these reviews draw the same narrow conclusions. They tend to list the number of "missed opportunities to intervene" that (with the benefit of hindsight) could have prevented the incident or at least led to a less serious outcome. This search for operational errors is right and understandable. But the method used is a form of analysis using a backward-looking narrative as though it were a predetermined plot from a novel or a film. The real lessons ought instead to involve the separation of human error from process or systemic failure and the search for ways in which each of these in turn can be reduced (not eliminated), with an understanding of what the cost will be, both in terms of resources used up and potential outcomes no longer available under the new, more constricting system.

Experimentation means that there will be multiple approaches to policy and to service delivery, only some of which will prove cost effective. Naturally, multiple approaches to policy and service delivery can easily be parodied, by opponents or the media, as an admission of ignorance or dithering. However, ensuring resilience in all the links of the resilience chain allows a strategy of risk enablement to be adopted, in which experimentation, which is fundamental in the Complex and Chaotic knowledge domains (and may even be valuable in the Complicated domain), can be protected and encouraged.

Towards a strategy of risk enablement within the context of a resilience chain

We are not suggesting that public organisations or staff should launch into accepting radically higher levels of risk – what we are proposing is more likely to result in a different portfolio of risk, enabled by having an appropriate resilience chain in place. Indeed, this analysis mainly suggests that we own up to the current facts – namely, that service users are already facing quite high levels of risk to their desired outcomes, that they are already putting in place some (imperfect) resilience mechanisms at the individual and community levels, and that the interventions of the public sector are generally only achieving limited risk reduction. The key is that the appropriate risk reduction and resilience strategies should be negotiated with users and communities, not just imposed by agency leaders (based on organisation-based interests).

This "risk enablement strategy" builds on innovative risk enablement practices already being used in adult safeguarding in social care. It involves taking a balanced and proportionate approach to risk, finding ways to enable individuals, communities and organisations to achieve what is important to them, while considering preventative and resilience mechanisms which keep individuals and the community safe from harm in a way that makes sense for them (Neill et al. 2008: 7). It requires public agencies to foster a culture of positive risk taking, where these risks are inherent in policies that nevertheless, on balance, are likely to improve outcomes for citizens. Kaplan and Mikes (2012) suggest that this focus on the "positive risk- negative risk" trade-off be done by anchoring risk discussions within strategic planning, which already brings together organisational goals and objectives and points to positive action rather than constraints, thus aligning the risk conversation with a "can do" culture, rather than a "must not do" culture.

Social construction of resilience approaches

Clearly, decisions on risk and resilience are not simply based on technical assessment of options. Government strategies around risk and resilience have to recognise the importance of views that citizens hold for emotional reasons. For example, public resilience initiatives to save loss of life in some contexts are likely to be much more acceptable than in others (Tengs et al. 1995), as the value placed by the public on the possibility of saving a human life varies hugely between public programmes – some save more than they cost, while others cost over $2bn per life saved.

Consequently, the social construction of risk and resilience (as shaped by the media) is a key driver of public policy. Indeed, Beck (1992: 49) argues that modern welfare society, based on an underlying public concern with equality, is being replaced by the "risk society", where the public's overriding value is safety, which is "peculiarly negative and defensive".

Unpacking the processes behind the social construction of resilience, research shows that recent personal experience strongly influences how people evaluate risky options and therefore their commitment to achieving greater resilience – low-probability events generate less concern than their probability warrants on average, but more concern than they deserve after those rare instances when they do occur (Weber 2006: 103).

However, effective risk communication can influence the social construction of risk and resilience (Chenok 2013), so that agencies can analyse the risks as seen by their constituents, the public can increase its preparedness and, if the risks become realities, the public discourse is built around a sound response to an expected problem, rather than focusing on reactions to an unanticipated event.

The resilience chain is damaged when either citizens exhibit an emotional rejection of "scientific" evidence or organisations refuse to take full account of the evidence. The legitimacy of policy decisions is further undermined where states and localities are clearly ill-equipped to make the political judgments required or, even more damagingly, where "expert" assessments of risk and the results of intervention policies exhibit disagreement rather than scientific consensus, thus undermining their own credibility.

Public decision making may be made even more difficult by the ideological responses of many citizens – and indeed many of their representatives and even some top managers – to "reject science" altogether, i.e. refuse to accept propositions which are supported by strong evidence bases conforming to conventional scientific criteria. Public reluctance to support scientific advice on the risks of specific interventions rules out resilience options which are strongly supported by the evidence and privilege some resilience interventions which seem unlikely to succeed.

The public's emotional response to risk is even more problematic with issues which are sudden, highly dangerous and dramatic (e.g. unexpectedly frequent hurricanes on the Eastern USA seaboard or outbreaks of mass shootings in public places in the USA, UK and Sweden). Here, public reaction is often emotionally highly charged and demands new interventions to protect against future occurrences. Where the risk of further occurrences appears low, most systematic interventions are likely to be disproportionately expensive, compared to likely benefits.

Conclusions

Resilience strategies have typically been based on the traditional approach to risk management, which is founded in audit and has privileged financial control by pricing future uncertainties in a measurable way. It fosters managerial compliance strategies that attempt to reduce or avoid repeated or systemic operational errors as well as measure foreseeable hazards and harms. These approaches are useful up to a point. However, they have also resulted in constrictive "blame avoidance strategies", where a public agency attempts to minimise damage to itself and to deflect blame for failure, rather than systematically preparing to deal with anticipated risks in a way which will maximise expected outcomes.

A radically new approach to risk and resilience is urgently needed, enabling a responsible risk culture, proportionate responses to risk and the building of robust resilience chains. Risk assessment and resilience management have to be tailored to the knowledge domains within which they operate. In a world where there is major uncertainty, not only about the consequences of known risks but also about how amenable they will be to public sector interventions, many of the probability-based instruments of current risk assessment and resilience management are simply irrelevant.

A systematic approach to the resilience chain requires a transformation from risk avoidance strategies towards risk enablement strategies, focusing on citizen outcomes as well as organisational outcomes, a culture of taking collective responsibility for improving publicly desired outcomes, transparency about risks actually existing and likely to be tackled by proposed interventions, user and community co-production of agreed interventions to deal with risk, and a wide-ranging set of measures to increase resilience across the resilience chain, at user, community, organisational and service system levels.

However, this new approach must itself be seen as tentative and unproven. The uncertainty in complex and chaotic knowledge domains requires us to be humble about how much we can know, how much we can change and how cost-effective public interventions are likely to be. Indeed, for all the excitement in the UK over the new approaches to risk enablement and resilience, there has still been little investigation into their effectiveness.

Consequently, this new approach requires both experimentation and research. Until better evidence is available, we need to own up to how little we really know about the risks we face in relation to the outcomes that matter to citizens, the unknowns which can undermine even the best thought-out services and the likely effectiveness of resilience mechanisms that can protect us from future harms. Such humility is a prerequisite to learning. Refusing to acknowledge the limitations to our knowledge is perhaps the biggest threat of all to building appropriate and proportionate resilience systems.

Acknowledgements

This chapter has been developed from the short paper by Bovaird and Quirk (2013) published online by the Institute of Local Government Studies, University of Birmingham.

References

Beck, U. 1992. *The risk society: toward a new modernity*. London: Sage.

Beckett, S. 1984. *Worstword Ho!* New York: Grove Publishers.

Bovaird, T., and E. Loeffler. 2012. "From engagement to co-production: the contribution of users and communities to outcomes and public value." *Voluntas* 23 (4): 1119–1138.

Bovaird, T. and B. Quirk. 2013. "Reducing public risk and improving public resilience: an agenda for risk enablement strategies." In *Making sense of the future: do we need a new model of public services?*, edited by C. Staite. Birmingham: INLOGOV.

Bryson, J. M., F. S. Berry, and K. Yang. 2010. "The state of public strategic management research: a selective literature review and set of future directions." *American Review of Public Administration* 40 (5): 495–521.

Buchanan, M. 2004. "Power laws and the new science of complexity management." *Strategy and Business* 34: 2–10.

Cabinet Office. 2013. "Resilience in society: infrastructure, communities and businesses." Accessed on 21 November 2013. www.gov.uk/resilience-in-society-infrastructure-communities-and-businesses.

Cabinet Office. 2011. *Keeping the country running: natural hazards & infrastructure – a guide to improving resilience of critical infrastructure & essential services*. London.

Chenok, D. 2013. "Taking on the risk of government." Accessed on 23 February 2015. www.govexec.com/excellence/promising-practices/2013/11/taking-risks government/73679/.

Coaffee, J. 2013. "Toward next-generation urban resilience in planning practice: from securitization to integrated place making." *Planning Practice & Research* 28 (3): 323–339.

Department of Health (DH). 2009. *Safeguarding adults: a consultation on the review of the No Secrets guidance*. London: Department of Health.

Duit, A. and V. Galaz. 2008. "Governance and complexity-emerging issues for governance theory." *Governance* 21 (3): 311–335.

Edson, M. 2012. "A complex adaptive systems view of resilience in a project team." *Systems Research and Behavioral Science* 29 (5): 499–516.

Ellis, K. 2013. "Professional discretion and adult social work: exploring its nature and scope on the front line of personalisation." *British Journal of Social Work* 1–18. doi:10.1093/bjsw/bct076.

Ferguson, I. 2007. "Increasing user choice or privatizing risk? The antinomies of personalisation." *British Journal of Social Work* 37 (3): 387–403.

Health Foundation. 2010. *Evidence scan: complex adaptive systems.* London: Health Foundation.

Hood, C. 2010. *The blame game: spin, bureaucracy and self-preservation in government.* Princeton, NJ: Princeton University Press.

HM Government. 2011. *Open public services.* London: Stationery Office.

Kaplan, R. and A. Mikes. 2012. "Managing risks: a new framework." *Harvard Business Review* 90 (6): 48–60.

Knight, F. H. 1921. *Risk, uncertainty, and profit.* Boston, MA: Riverside Press.

Loeffler, E. (2015), "Co-production of public services with users and communities." In Bovaird, T. and Loeffler, E. (eds), *Public management and governance.* 3rd edition. London: Routledge.

Manthorpe, J. and K. Samsi. 2013. "'Inherently risky?': personal budgets for people with dementia and the risks of financial abuse: findings from an interview-based study with adult safeguarding coordinators." *British Journal of Social Work* 43(5): 889–903. doi: 10.1093/bjsw/bcs023.

Martin, K., J. Jeffes, and S. MacLeod. 2010. *Safeguarding children: literature review.* Slough: NFER.

Mitchell, W. and C. Glendinning. 2007. *A review of the research evidence surrounding risk perceptions, risk management strategies and their consequences in adult social care for different groups of service users.* York: SPRU, University of York.

Moran, P. 2009. *Neglect: research evidence to inform practice.* London: Action for Children.

Neill, M., J. Allen, N. Woodhead, S. Reid, L. Irwin, and H. Sanderson. 2008. *A positive approach to risk requires person-centred thinking.* London: TLAP.

NHS Commissioning Board. 2013. *Safeguarding vulnerable people in the reformed NHS: accountability and assurance framework.* www.england.nhs.uk/wp-content/uploads/2013/03/safeguarding-vulnerable-people.pdf. Accessed 06/06/2016.

Norris, F. H., S. P. Stevens, B. Pfefferbaum, K. F. Wyche, and R. L. Pfefferbaum. 2008). "Community resilience as a metaphor, theory, set of capacities, and strategy for disaster readiness." *American Journal of Community Psychology* 41(1–2): 127–150.

Peters, E. and P. Slovic. 2000. "The springs of action: affective and analytical information processing in choice." *Personality and Social Psychology Bulletin* 26: 1465–1475.

Plsek, P. E. and T. Greenhalgh. 2001. "The challenge of complexity in health care." *BMJ* 323: 625–628.

Quirk, B. 2011. *Re-imagining government: public leadership and management in challenging times.* Basingstoke: Palgrave Macmillan.

Simmie, J. and R. Martin. 2010. "Economic resilience of regions: toward an evolutionary approach." *Cambridge Journal of Regions, Economy and Society* (3): 27–43.

Smith, M., S. Rocks, and S. Pollard. 2011. *Uncertainty, risk and decision making in local government.* London: LARCI and Cranfield University.

Snowden, D. J. and M. Boone. 2007. "A leader's framework for decision making." *Harvard Business Review.* November: 69–76.

Taleb, N. N. 2007. *The black swan: the impact of the highly improbable.* London: Random House.

Tengs T. O., M. E. Adams, J. S. Pliskin, D. G. Safran, J. E. Siegel, et al. 1995. "Five-hundred life-saving interventions and their cost-effectiveness." *Risk Analysis* 15 (3): 369–390.

Tsasis, P., J. M. Evans, and S. Owen. 2012. "Reframing the challenges to integrated care: a complex-adaptive systems perspective." *International Journal of Integrated Care* 12 (5).

Weber, E. U. 2006. "Experience-based and description-based perceptions of long-term risk: why global warming does not scare us (yet)." *Climatic Change* 77: 103–120.

Wilding, N. 2011. *Exploring community resilience.* Dunfermline: Fiery Spirits.

24

THE CHANGING ROLES OF POLITICIANS AND PUBLIC SERVANTS

Robert P. Shepherd, Christopher Stoney and Lori Turnbull

Introduction

It is increasingly argued in the literature that public services in Western democracies have become more responsive and even politicized in recent decades (Savoie 2008, 2010; Sausman and Locke 2004; Peters and Pierre 2004; Norman 2003; Dwivedi and Gow 1999). Public servants, it is claimed, must now as a matter of their regular responsibilities to superiors and political masters pay greater attention to the political implications of their work than ever before. Likewise, politicians are exerting more pressure on public bureaucracies to support partisan and political preferences through the creation of external policy advisory committees, use of external consultants and task forces, independent advisors and lobbyists (Savoie 2010: 158–160). From this perspective, public services are regarded as obstacles to the preferences of political parties attempting to effect change, in essence miring progress in red tape or the long view. Although some scholars attribute these changes to New Public Management, and getting government out of the way of economic progress, this argument does not explain fully the purported shifts in human resource processes, regulatory systems, internal management and control structures, and oversight and accountability systems, to name a few aspects of public administration.

The ongoing debate about the appropriate role of the public service in navigating shifts in merit-based or neutral competence responsibilities versus responsive competencies necessitates that scholars and practitioners alike consider implications for traditional notions of the politics/administrative dichotomy, public service leadership, and the nature of institutional oversight. As uncertain and malleable as the relationship between public servants and political masters may be, however, protagonists on both sides of the debate seem to accept that lines can be crossed. Nevertheless, exactly where the line should be drawn remains a contentious and politically charged question that also produces widely differing assessments of the longer-term implications, benefits and dangers of responsiveness for the Westminster system of parliamentary democracy. Although some would have us believe it is of little significance, others, including the Supreme Court of Canada, have confirmed that the convention of political neutrality is central to the principle of responsible government (Rasmussen and Julliet 2008: 125).

In this chapter, we will discuss the changing relationship between ministers and public servants and consider the implication of these shifts for leadership within the public service. There is a declining state of trust and confidence between elected leaders, who are expected to be partisan, and public servants, whose role in a modern and professional public service is based on principles of merit, a non-partisan conceptualization of public good, and a longer-term view of public policy aims. The chapter highlights the resulting tensions between these two branches of the state and examines the broader implications of continued centralization of power within the executive branch and particularly the Prime Minister's Office (PMO). We also examine the effects of these shifts in power on the role of MPs and consider the implications for parliamentary democracy. We conclude that there has been a decline in the value placed by political masters on a traditional merit-based and professional public service in favour of greater responsiveness to political directives. Although our comments draw mainly on the experience of the Canadian Westminster system of government, we believe our assessment can be extended to other jurisdictions.

Changing nature of the politics/administrative dichotomy

Traditionally, academics and students of public management have understood and been taught the value of an impartial, objective, and politically neutral public service. According to Westminster government, public servants must maintain "appropriate" distance and independence from their political masters at all times. This is to preserve their ability to offer sound policy advice to any government that holds office, regardless of its partisan banner. As Kernaghan and Langford (2014) note, "Political neutrality is a constitutional convention whereby public servants should avoid activities that are likely to impair, or seem to impair, their political impartiality or the political impartiality of the public service" (p. 91). This convention has been a central feature of the constitution since Confederation and has featured in numerous legal cases, codes and laws ever since. Political neutrality and anonymity are central tenets of individual ministerial responsibility as an organizing function of responsible government.

To provide neutral and competent policy advice, often cited as the capacity to "speak truth to power," is thought to be a fundamental role of the public service (Page 2012: 1–26; Canada Privy Council Office 1996). This is clearly a fine line to tread, as Kernaghan and Langford (2014) acknowledge. On the one hand, in exercising their discretion to make decisions, public servants must "strive to reflect or anticipate the wishes of political superiors" (Kernaghan and Langford 2014: 68). However, in making recommendations public servants should set forth a range of alternatives rather than a single or favoured option and, presumably, be prepared to disagree with a minister's preferred choice of action. The agency enjoyed by public servants enables and, to some extent, necessitates the development of their own sense of the public good, which may of course differ from their minister's interpretation of public good. The key area of disagreement may well be the degree to which partisan interests are included in calculations of public good and the importance attached to short- versus long-term outcomes.

Today, governments are accused of ignoring the fundamental importance of public service neutrality. Rather than keeping their distance, governments are said to be encouraging and, in some cases, even *demanding* recognition of political preferences, even from its most senior public servants. The tension between the neutral competence model and the political responsiveness model is long documented and not at all exclusive to Canada. Writing in 1956 and from an American perspective, Herbert Kaufman observed that historically, public service institutions in the US had been organized in accordance with three different and sometimes conflicting principles: representativeness, neutral competence, and executive leadership (Kaufman 1956, 1057).

Kaufman acknowledged that despite its democratic credentials, the representative model carries with it some negative implications. For example, elected officials are understandably sensitive to political realities and considerations. However, an emphasis on short-term political goals does not always make for the best policy outcomes, as it can undermine the pursuit of long-term policy objectives, and even compromise the public good. The neutral competence paradigm accepts this reality and places value on an independent, non-partisan public service that can tender impartial, long-term and competent advice. Unfortunately, an empowered public service can become fragmented, unfocused and unresponsive. Bureaucrats dispersed in each department can acquire tunnel vision by focusing on their own goals and fostering relationships with agents in their specific mandates. In such a situation, it is difficult for governments to develop broad, horizontal yet integrated policies and programmes. When there are too many heads, there is a need for centralization. The executive leadership model, premised on the Hamiltonian ideal type, values a single, central authority to combat fragmentation and to coordinate the entire public service in accordance with the government's policy goals (Kaufman 1956: 1057–1063). In the American context, the President's Office is the obvious national and central institution. In the Westminster context, executive power is firmly concentrated in the hands of the prime minister federally, and in the hands of premiers provincially (Savoie 1999).

Kaufman explains how each of the three systems can be seen as a reaction to the weaknesses of the other systems, part of the so-called checks and balances. Each offers an answer or counterweight to the other systems' shortcomings. He demonstrates how each of the three different models gained popularity at different times in history for different reasons, which suggests that external political imperatives can affect normative assumptions about the role of the public service best seen perhaps as simultaneous cycles with any one in priority at any given time. When applied to the present day, and to the ongoing debate about the purpose and independence of the Westminster public service, Kaufman's observations challenge us to question whether the neutral competence model, which values policy expertise and objectivity above all else, is still prominent or in decline. Moreover, is it possible, in the Westminster context, to conceive of an argument in favour of a public service politically responsive to partisan preferences? Could political responsiveness in the bureaucracy add value? Are there times when there is a public good argument for political responsiveness in the public service?

A rational manifestation of political self-interest would be to ensure that state institutions work in favour of, or become more responsive to, those who hold power. Consequently, for Peters and Pierre, this could lead to the rise of politicization of the public service referred to as "the substitution of political criteria for merit-based criteria in the selection, retention, promotion, rewards, and disciplining of members of the public service" (Peters and Pierre 2004: 2). Although this definition refers to a particular form of politicization, the key operative concept in our view is the "substitution of political criteria for merit-based criteria," wherever that may apply. In Western democracies, it is contended that the intent of politicization more broadly is to advance political control over bureaucratic and other functions of government and create the conditions whereby partisan considerations and advantage can be maximized.

Role of the public service and leadership

Westminster constitutions (both written and unwritten) invest the executive powers of government in the Crown. Such powers are exercised on the advice of ministers who are held to account by the elected representatives of the citizenry. The public service acts as agents of the executive branch and carries out the programmes and services decided upon by the Crown on the advice of its ministers, who are members of the Privy Council of Canada. The way in which such executive powers are exercised is dependent on the preferences of ministers. The point is that the role of public services can be regarded as independent, professional, and non-partisan, or it can be considered at the other extreme to be responsive to the political and/or partisan interests of the government of the day. There is room between these possibilities for other relational forms and the appropriate role is to a large extent a matter for interpretation and debate. As indicated previously, however, there appears to be a shift toward responsive public services in Westminster countries, which has implications for how bureaucratic leaders exercise their responsibilities.

As in other countries the extent, causes, implications and appropriateness of responsive government have become topics of significant debate in recent years. In addition to the scholarly and pioneering work of Savoie (2010, 2008), Aucoin (2012, 2008, 2006), Kernaghan and Langford (2014), and Bakvis and Jarvis (2012), a recent report by Heintzman (2014) has further intensified and polarized views on the topic in Canada, for example, and other Westminster countries alike. Like the Tait Report (1996) in Canada almost two decades earlier, Heintzman (2014), and Kernaghan and Langford (2014: 253) stress the importance of the values of neutrality and merit. They call for a new moral contract or charter of public service between the bureaucracy and the government-of-the-day. Although clear rules governing these relationships are always important, they believe that the need for an ethical charter is more critical today for a public service that has been "neglected," "devalued" and has seen its neutrality "abused."

Likewise, Bourgault and Dunn (2014) recently completed a major comparative study of federal and provincial deputy ministers in Canada, and argue that their traditional responsibilities of guardians, gurus, managers and leaders change over time, each one waxing and waning as priorities and preferences of government decision-makers shift. They maintain that each of these traditional responsibilities or archetypes carries certain importance, but the current emphasis appears to be on leadership that pays attention to "corporate issues, emphasizes corporate human resources planning, engages in succession planning, monitors employee engagement, and generally is sensitive to the issue of government as 'employer of choice'" (2014: 436). In this regard, leadership is taking the corporate management view, thereby protecting their institutions, and therefore, struggling to balance leadership with that corporate management. For them, deputy ministers must manage their four archetypical roles, and balance accordingly between them especially under times of stress.

These views are fiercely contested by other academics and former public servants, including Ruth Hubbard (a former Canadian deputy minister) and Gilles Paquet who, in responding to Heintzman (also a former deputy minister), maintain that the current Canadian government is no different from any other she has served, and that being able to "integrate the wishes of the elected government with the best advice about how to translate them constructively into legal and implementable actions is the essential part of the job" (Hubbard and Paquet 2014). Hubbard argues that assuring the competencies of public servants is a more pressing issue than a renewed moral or ethical charter, and that responsiveness and collaboration between the political and administrative branches is both healthy and desirable. The challenge, of course, is that developing competencies can be time-bound, whereas charting a moral contract takes the long view.

Despite the disagreement over roles, there appears to be some common ground on the effects of responsive leadership. Hubbard and Paquet conclude that there have been some troubling effects of responsiveness with respect to the roles and relationships between public servants and ministers in today's changing power dynamics. For them, senior public servants have essentially been reduced to implementers of policy directions rather than a full participant in the thinking behind such larger policy decisions. They argue that:

[M]any in the senior executive ranks are in denial when it comes to the pathologies of their life world. These Panglossian defenders of the present Canadian federal public administration are not friends of the federal public service, but their worst enemies. Their denials of flagrant problems can only lead to further deterioration, and perhaps ultimately to the fading away of an institution that has served Canadians well, but is, at present, in distress.

(Hubbard and Paquet 2014: 115)

In the process of aggregating their conversations with several senior federal public servants, they noted unflattering qualities that defined the distress noted, including

decline of open critical thinking, lack of gumption, willful blindness in the face of mental prisons and neuroses, incapacity and/or unwillingness to take the initiative, impatience with contextual issues, and focus on operational details, cognitive dissonance, the presence of latent fear, moral vacancy, crippling epistemologies, risk aversion and fear of experimentation, failure to understand systems, reluctance to admit that experts must learn, [and] disinterest in the face of new perspectives difficult to understand.

(Hubbard and Paquet 2014: 118)

This is clearly an indictment of the state of leadership in the senior ranks of the federal public service, attributed in large part to conservative governments in Canada, Australia and elsewhere with a history of mistrust of their public services.

Savoie (2013) in his latest book, *Whatever Happened to the Music Teacher?*, echoes Hubbard and Paquet's view, making the argument that several recent Canadian federal public service reforms are based on the faulty belief that "[g]overnment bureaucracy was the villain, and weak management practices were the problem" (p. 129). For him, the true villain is what he refers to as the naïve assumptions of politicians, lobbyists, consultants, and government advisors that private sector management is the repair to all inefficiencies and ineffective programmes (i.e., new public management), coupled with the weakness and timidity of senior public servants in particular to come forward and question decisions. For Savoie and others, these public servants lack the courage, imagination or critical thinking to defend their merit-based profession against the rise of new public governance (Peters 2010: 36–51). They despair that senior public servant judgement has failed to withstand such weak political assertions, which will ultimately mean an erosion of public service expertise in areas such as policy planning, programming and oversight (Savoie 2013: 240; Peters 2010: 36–51).

According to Gill, building leadership brand is essential to the survival of organizations in dynamic times, which is "the collective leadership capacity of an organization and the sum total of leadership behaviour across all organizational functions and all hierarchical levels" (Gill 2011: 377). Leadership brand is a distinctive form of leadership that engages stakeholders, especially employees, and requires a leadership strategy around matters of vision, purpose, values, strategy, empowerment, and engagement. Ultimately, organizations should be recognizable for the manner in which these are practised: its leadership brand.

This view of leadership is much closer to the view that the role of the public service does not exist merely to serve the government of the day but to mediate and accommodate various power interests and policy horizons through an open and informed process of engagement. It is also specifically this type of role that Savoie fears will be lost through a return to a pre-merit system that favours consultants, party insiders, or hired guns and potentially distances citizens from the policy-making conversation (Savoie 2010: 162).

Whether proponents believe that responsive or neutral competence is the appropriate model, there appears to be some agreement that public service competencies are shifting, that the role of public services must change accordingly, and that required leadership is sorely lacking in the public service. To be responsive and loyal public servants is not a sufficient response to changing dynamics between public servants and ministers. There is a strong case for "gumption," "taking the initiative," and seeing the long view that ministers appear reluctant to acknowledge or promote. Acknowledging there is a problem with leadership may be the first step toward a debate on the appropriate role of public services, and in this context the Canadian "Blueprint 2020" initiative reflects growing recognition of the challenges that lie ahead.

Role of parliament and oversight

As power continues to be vested in the executive, this model is shifting to one in which disempowered members of parliament work to support the leader, understanding that their own political survival is largely dependent on that of the political leadership. This reduces both the visionary and the scrutiny aspects of parliament. For the public service, this means that power is further concentrated in the executive branch.

Westminster systems of parliamentary government are prone to concentrated power, perhaps in large part because the formal system of checks and balances present in the American congressional system, for instance, is absent in the Westminster context. The checks on power are less formal and, therefore, more easily ignored or silenced. Under the Canadian interpretation of the Westminster system, power is even more concentrated than is the case for Australia, New Zealand, and the United Kingdom. A number of factors contribute to this: although the theory of responsible government states that the government must maintain the confidence of the majority of members in the House of Commons in order to govern legitimately, the reality is that it is the government that holds the balance of power, not the other way around. MPs virtually always vote according to the party line and espouse the party platform in committees; there is little evidence of independence, autonomy or a willingness to depart from the party's position to act as a true delegate for one's constituency. Floor crossings occur on occasion, but only so that an MP can join another political party that is equally disciplined in its approach. Party leaders maintain MPs' loyalty through a carrot-and-stick approach. Leaders, especially the prime minister, can offer MPs their preferred positions in committees, cabinet or shadow cabinet in exchange for their continued support. Or, they can withhold these rewards from those MPs who have too much of an independent streak (Aucoin, Jarvis, and Turnbull 2011: 12–17).

The prime minister also has a variety of tools with which to maintain a grasp on power. They select all chairs of all committees that are chaired by a government MP. They determine the agenda of the House of Commons, and in many jurisdictions schedule opposition days, during which the opposition parties are able to take control instead. The prime minister, as well as all party leaders, commonly has the power to approve candidates to run under the party's banner. This issue has been the subject of many proposals for reform, including in Canada a scheme to remove party leaders' power to approve (read: veto) candidates for the party who have been nominated by local constituency associations.

This results in political parties that are made up of MPs who will toe the party line in exchange for the promise of promotion. Further, because the primary duty of the MP is to support the party's platform rather than to represent constituents, and the resources that MPs have to scrutinize pale in comparison with those on the government side, the function of MPs is understood to be more tactical than principled. As Robert Asselin notes, MPs on committees "often lack the technical knowledge and expertise to effectively challenge senior officials who come to testify before them" (Asselin 2014: 11). Both MPs' offices and committees themselves are understaffed, which renders MPs unable to perform the important scrutiny function with effectiveness. So, instead, MPs often engage in low politics by hurling insults at one another, in the legislature and through negative advertising. This further entrenches the concentration of power by ensuring that government bills enjoy trouble-free passage through the parliamentary process.

The locus of power in the parliamentary system is the Prime Minister's Office (PMO), which consists of a group of political advisers who are appointed by the prime minister on the basis of their qualifications as analysts, strategists, writers, and communicators. Although the public service has never had a monopoly on good advice, it is increasingly the case that the prime minister and cabinet are more dependent on advice coming from their own political staffers or advisors (Yong and Hazel 2014). The public service is often seen as too large, slow, bureaucratic, and set in its own ways to respond to today's fast-paced environment, in which the 24/7 news cycle demands immediate responses to the issues that arise, even those that are complex, multifaceted and thus require a longer term focus.

Public servants under this perspective are regarded as being in the way of progress leading to recent innovations to curtail existing public service oversight, or quicken the pace of public service decision-making at the expense of evidence collection and appropriate analysis. Tactics such as the use of omnibus bills to pass budgets are designed to clear away unwanted public service or parliamentary oversight into areas such as transportation safety, environmental assessment, and economic development. When public services raise concerns around these issues, public programmes and public servants are regarded as standing in the way of the government agenda. If parliament does not have the tools to check the power of governments through effective and professional public services, then parliament itself is weakened. Again, the exercise of public service leadership becomes even more important.

Notwithstanding such concerns, a bill was introduced into Canada's parliament in February 2014 that calls upon public servants working in positions associated with parliament to declare their political colours with the stated objective of ensuring fairness in the rulings of these agents. No other federal departments are expected to make such declarations, and it has been argued in the media that the bill is entirely vindictive as some agents of parliament have done their jobs and taken the federal government to task on questionable decisions and transactions. Not seen in Canada in recent years, these agents have appeared before parliamentary committees vigorously fighting the bill on a number of grounds, including the fact that such behaviour is already addressed in foundational legislation governing the public service, and that no evidence has been given by the Conservative government that supports claims of biased or partisan rulings by such agents. The fact that such bills are being introduced into parliament suggests a preference on the part of political leaders: public servants, including those responsible for exercising effective parliamentary oversight, are expected to provide loyal and unquestioned service to the government or risk being maligned as politically biased, and thereby discredited and undermined in the process.

Conclusion

Overall, we conclude there is evidence of a decline in the value placed by political masters on a traditional merit-based and professional public service, and a corresponding change in the role and importance of the public sector, particularly in relation to political staff. Although this trend has been postulated for several decades, concerns about the pace of change have intensified. This has produced a notable theme in the public administration literature, and it is one of concern about expediency over evidence, politics over management, loyalty over reasoned argument, and political priorities over process and outcomes. None of this is new, of course, but what has taken decades to create in terms of merit-based bureaucracy is beginning to show signs of tension and strain as the Westminster system attempts to adapt to the changing balance of power between political and bureaucratic agents and institutions.

Political trust in the public service is seen to be in decline at least since the 1970s. Several examples can be seen over time that attempt to provide or extend political advantage for the party in power. For example, centralizing tactics are and remain a common feature of contemporary governing. What has changed, however, is that some politicians openly display a transparent and unhealthy disdain for the public service, the evidence and policy rationale they provide, and the due process that is intended to safeguard the public good. In the process public servants complain of being marginalised, while government scientists complain of being muzzled when attempting to share research findings with the media and the public. Simultaneously, public service anonymity is no longer assured with ministers increasingly willing to shift responsibility from themselves onto unelected bureaucrats, managers and watchdogs when politically expedient to do so. While this trend has attracted the attention of scholars and other commentators, its nuanced and technical nature has evoked little if any reaction on the part of citizens suggesting that it will continue unabated for the foreseeable future.

Although governments and leaders come and go and the administrative–political divide will continue to evolve, it is the institutionalization of these trends that will have longer-term importance for our systems of government. We are beginning to see legislation that overtly undermines merit, a professional public service, and due process in the name of efficiency, the economy, or greater economization of resources. As with public servants, the power and influence of MPs has steadily declined as a result of the centralization of executive power over several decades. As a result, their role has changed from one that includes scrutiny and oversight of the executive to one primarily concerned with championing the party leader, attacking opponents, and spinning the message.

In outlining trends in the roles of politicians and public servants, the chapter has illustrated that they are two parts of the same phenomenon arising out of the shifting balance of power within our political system. For example, politicization is primarily about control and influence by the political centre over the various branches of the state. As a consequence, we should not be surprised to see the diminishing of important checks and balances within our political systems. Although arguments can and will be made in favour of the concentration of state power, the chapter has endeavoured to demonstrate that it is not without consequences for diluting institutional safeguards that are in place precisely to ensure the functioning of a healthy democracy.

References

Aucoin, P. 2012. "New Political Governance in Westminster Systems: Impartial Public Administration and Management Performance at Risk." *Governance: An International Journal of Policy, Administration, and Institution* 25 (2): 177–199.

Aucoin, P. 2008. "New Public Management and the Quality of Government: Coping with the New Political Governance in Canada." Paper delivered at the Conference on Public Management and the Quality of Government, University of Gothenburg, Sweden, 13–15 November.

Aucoin, P. 2006. "The Staffing and Evaluation of Canadian Deputy Ministers in Comparative Westminster Perspective: A Proposal for Reform." *Research Studies* 1: 297–336.

Aucoin, P., M. Jarvis, and L. Turnbull. 2011. *Democratizing the Constitution: Reforming Responsible Government.* Toronto: Emond-Montgomery.

Bakvis, H. and M. D. Jarvis. 2012. *From New Public Management to New Political Governance.* Montreal and Kingston: McGill-Queen's University Press.

Bourgault, J. 2011. "Minority Government and Senior Government Officials: The Case of the Canadian Federal Government." *Commonwealth & Comparative Politics* 49 (4): 510–527.

Bourgault, J. and C. Dunn. 2014. *Deputy Ministers in Canada: Comparative and Jurisdictional Perspectives.* Toronto: University of Toronto Press.

Canada Privy Council Office. 2015. "Open and Accountable Government." Available at: http://pm.gc. ca/eng/news/2015/11/27/open-and-accountable-government. Accessed June 18, 2016.

Dwivedi, O. P. and J. I. Gow. 1999. *From Bureaucracy to Public Management: The Administrative Culture of the Government of Canada.* Toronto: University of Toronto Press.

Gill, R. 2011. *Theory and Practice of Leadership.* London: Sage.

Heintzman, R. 2014. "Renewal of the Federal Public Service: Toward a Charter of Public Service." A paper prepared for Canada 2020. www.canada2020.ca.

Hubbard, R. 2014. "The Real Problem with the Public Service." *Ottawa Citizen*, June 17.

Hubbard, R. and G. Paquet. 2014. *Probing the Bureaucratic Mind: About Canadian Federal Executives.* Ottawa: Invenire.

Kaufman, H. 1956. "Emerging Conflicts in the Doctrines of Public Administration." *American Political Science Review* 50: 1057–1073.

Kernaghan, K. and J. W. Langford. 2014. *The Responsible Public Servant.* 2nd ed. Montreal: Institute for Research on Public Policy.

Norman, R. 2003. *Obedient Servants? Management Freedoms & Accountabilities in the New Zealand Public Sector.* Wellington, NZ: Victoria University Press.

Page, E. C. 2012. *Policy Without Politicians: Bureaucratic Influence in Comparative Perspective.* Oxford, UK: Oxford University Press.

Peters, B. G. 2010. "Meta-Governance and Public Management." In *The New Public Governance: Emerging Perspectives on the Theory and Practice of Public Governance,* edited by S. P. Osborne, 36–51. New York: Routledge.

Peters, B. G. 2004. "Politicization in the United States." In *Politicization of the Civil Service in Comparative Perspective: The Quest for Control,* edited by J. H. Meyer-Sahling, 125–138. New York: Routledge.

Peters, B. G. and J. Pierre. 2004. *Politicization of the Civil Service in Comparative Perspective: The Quest for Control.* New York: Routledge.

Rasmussen, K. and L. Juillet. 2008. *Defending a Contested Ideal: Merit and the Public Service Commission, 1908–2008.* Ottawa: University of Ottawa Press.

Sausman, C. and R. Locke. 2004. "The British Civil Service: Examining the Question of Politicisation." In *Politicization of the Civil Service in Comparative Perspective: The Quest for Control,* edited by B. Guy Peters and Jon Pierre, 101–124. London: Routledge.

Savoie, D. J. 2010. *Power: Where Is It?* Montreal and Kingston: McGill-Queen's University Press.

Savoie, D. J. 2008. *Court Government and the Collapse of Accountability in Canada and the United Kingdom.* Toronto: University of Toronto Press.

Savoie, D. J. 1999. *Governing from the Centre: The Concentration of Power in Canadian Politics.* Toronto: University of Toronto Press.

Tait Report. 1996. "Canada, Deputy Ministers' Task Force on Public Service Values and Ethics." *A Strong Foundation: Report of the Task Force on Public Service Values and Ethics.* Ottawa: Canadian Centre for Management Development, 1996; reprinted in 2000.

Yung, B. and R. Hazel. 2014. *Special Advisors: Who They Are, What They Do, and Why They Matter.* London: Hart Publishing.

25

STRATEGIC MANAGEMENT AND PUBLIC GOVERNANCE IN THE PUBLIC SECTOR

Paul Joyce

Introduction

Strategic management can be defined as management action oriented to achieving long-term goals based on thorough analysis and assessment of situation, options, and resources (Joyce 2015). It is often assumed, wrongly or rightly, that strategic management is a management innovation that was developed originally in the private sector and was subsequently adopted in the public sector.

In private sector management literature the use of the name strategic planning was commonplace in the 1970s but during the 1970s and 1980s there was an increasing switch to the use of the name strategic management. Arguably, this reflected a growing appreciation of the difficulties of forecasting the future and the challenges of implementing strategic plans. In effect, the adoption of the name strategic management seemed to imply acknowledging that formulating a plan might be difficult but the challenges of implementation (and learning during implementation) deserved a lot of respect. Strategic management could therefore be defined as a process that involved both strategic planning and the implementation of strategic plans, with the latter potentially defined as involving strategic learning. Making a distinction between strategic planning and strategic management might have made sense in the evolving experience of businesses in the private sector context, but it has never seemed so important to insist on a distinction between strategic planning and strategic management in the public sector. Perhaps public sector practitioners (politicians and managers) always appreciated that strategic planning was much more than the use of analytical techniques and drawing up plans, that the future could be surprising, and getting things done was bound to be hard?

Research into strategic management can study the experiences of individuals. For example, there have been surveys of individual public sector managers to assess the benefits, nature and spread of strategic planning in the public sector. "Strategy as practice" research, which has attracted some attention in recent years, also focuses on individuals. It has been defined as concerned with the performance of the individual practitioner (Whittington 1996). This can be applied to public sector organizations. For example, Jarzabkowski (2005, 2003) used strategy as practice to investigate the variations in strategic management system in three UK universities and spent some time in her analysis looking at the discussions of strategy in major committees.

Arguably the most common studies have been ones looking at the application of strategic management to public sector organizations. Some used case studies to build theoretical frameworks (e.g. Moore 1995; Heymann 1987; Wechsler and Backoff 1987). Some have been studies of strategic planning at national and sub-national levels of government (e.g. Corvo et al. 2014; Berry and Wechsler 1995). Some have been concerned with testing models of strategic choice developed for private sector businesses (e.g. Hodgkinson 2012; Boyne and Walker 2010). Finally, it can be noted that some research studies have tried to explain variations in the impact of strategic plans (Poister and Streib 2005).

As well as studies of individuals and organizations, it is possible to research strategic management as a process or an element of public governance systems (Joyce and Drumaux 2014; Joyce 2008). Studies that fit here include ones that have examined matters of democratic concern such as the respective strategic management roles of elected politicians and appointed officials (e.g. Lumijarvi and Leponiemi 2014; Niiranen and Joensuu 2014) and public participation in the formulation of strategic plans (e.g. Cristofoli, Macciò, and Meneguzzo 2014). Studies of government organizations working with public and private partner organizations, or using networks for policy making and service delivery, can also be seen as part of this branch of study of strategic management in the public sector. While the amount of research on the role of politicians and the public in strategic planning is still modest, it seems likely that there may be much more research into strategic management within public governance systems in the future. See Figure 25.1.

This chapter has the aim of looking at strategic management in a public sector context. It considers its benefits and the causes of its effectiveness. It examines strategic management in relation to modernizing civil service policy-making and systems of public governance. It outlines the concept of the strategic state and its importance.

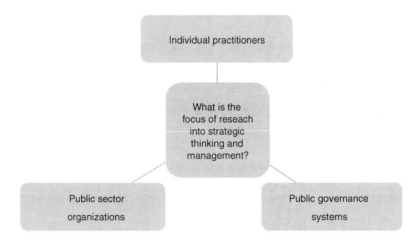

Figure 25.1   Research into strategic thinking and management – concerned with individual practitioners, organizations or public governance systems?

Strategic planning

There were examples of strategic planning in the public sector in the 1960s and 1970s, although strategic planning practices were known by other names at the time. In the US, strategic plans became common in public sector organizations at the sub-national level in the 1980s (Berry and Wechsler 1995). The trend to using strategic planning at the national or federal level was evident from the 1990s onwards in a wide variety of countries. Some countries passed laws on strategic planning by government (e.g. the US in 1993 and 2010, Turkey in 2003, and the Russian Federation in 2014). Some countries used strategic planning concepts to evolve their system of five-year plans for national development (e.g. China and Saudi Arabia).

The essence of strategic thinking and strategic decision making is often represented through diagrams known as "decision flow diagrams", which have been very popular in the public sector literature on strategic management (see Nutt and Backoff 1992; Bryson 1988). A simple one is shown in Figure 25.2.

Decision flow diagrams are very useful, even simple ones such as that shown in Figure 25.2. They help politicians, civil servants and public managers to learn how to do strategic management. They provide an overview of what is involved and how information searching, analysis and decisions can be sequenced. For experienced practitioners the diagrams can be aide-memoires and can serve to stimulate experimentation with changes in ways of making strategic decisions.

But such diagrams are not theoretical models of public sector strategic planning; nor are they simple representations of the reality of strategic planning in the public sector. The diagrams should not be seen as implying that competently applying the prescribed sequence of steps will lead to almost certain success in making major strategic changes. In reality, both strategy formulation and strategy implementation are often very difficult to accomplish skilfully. Both can be hard work and demanding. Rumelt (2011) has stressed that bad strategy is not the result of miscalculations but the "active avoidance of the hard work of crafting a good strategy" (Rumelt 2011: 58).

Figure 25.2   Decision flow diagram for public sector strategic planning and implementation

Consequences and benefits of strategic planning

Studies in the 1990s suggested that individual public sector managers found strategic planning very beneficial (Flynn and Talbot 1996; Berry and Wechsler 1995). Reported benefits included: clarity about an organisation's future direction, help with planning a path to future success, help with preparing a vision for staff, making better resource and budget decisions, increasing cost effectiveness, finding new opportunities and new ideas, and improving policy making. The last mentioned benefit is interesting since it relates strategic planning to a key aspect of the work of civil servants, namely policy making.

Strategic planning is also found to help organizations be successful in achieving their goals. Poister and Streib's (2005) study of local government in the United States found that most respondents to their survey were satisfied with the results being achieved by strategic planning and that more than two-fifths of strategic goals were being delivered. Some of the lessons of their findings for increasing the impact of strategic planning can be summarized as follows:

1   Involve citizens and other stakeholders in developing strategic plans.
2   Report performance measures to the public regularly.
3   Make feasibility assessments of options before deciding on strategic actions.
4   Use new money in the budget to resource strategic plans.
5   Set annual objectives for managers using the strategic plan.
6   Use annual performance reviews of managers to look at their contribution to the delivery of strategic plans.
7   Evaluate strategic effectiveness by tracking performance data over time.

In terms of public governance systems, it has been suggested that the most successful governments are ones that have been more strategic (Mulgan 2009). We come back to this point later in the chapter.

Strategic policy making

Sir Michael Bichard, a successful UK civil servant, told a House of Commons Select Committee in 2007 that his career as a public servant was based on a belief in the political process and democracy and that he saw his role as a public servant as one of giving the best advice he could to enable decision making and policy formulation. This can be contrasted with an analysis that implies the elected politicians may be formally in charge of policy making but are faced by civil servants who are more expert, and in fact it is the bureaucrats who are ruling society, not politicians (Weber 1970). This analysis suggests that it is the civil servants who are actually the policymakers, and not the politicians.

There is much confusion nowadays about the relationship between the concepts of policy and strategy, and there is a multiplicity of possibilities about how they relate to one another. If we look at documents bearing the name "policy" or the name "strategy", they may be seen as interchangeable labels.

The policy making process may be outlined as follows. The process begins with the politicians clarifying priorities and planning legislative programmes. Then civil servants in government ministries draft policy proposals, prepare legislation, consult within government, etc. This is followed by a government decision on the policy and (in some cases) a parliamentary stage in which law is debated and voted on; and then, finally, there is a phase of policy implementation with monitoring and evaluation to check that the policy is being delivered and is worthwhile.

By comparison, a strategic planning process for a government could have the steps shown in Figure 25.2. A comparison of these two processes would suggest that the policy process, as depicted here, is much clearer about who does what and also clearer that policy making may involve preparing legislation (although not always). The strategic planning process, however, seems to pay more attention to direction setting, the future, and analytical techniques than the policy-making model.

It is often reported that the reality of policy making (and strategic planning) is not identical to any of the usual formal models of the processes. Moreover, if we look at attempts to modernize policy making and modernize how the civil service works, very different issues are brought to the surface from those that might be inferred from formal models. In fact, an OECD report on policy making suggested a number of weaknesses in government policy making (OECD 2007). One weakness is inadequate analysis leading to wrongly drafted legislation. Another is failure to consult stakeholders. A third is a failure by civil servants to evaluate the success of policies. As a result of poor policy making, policy implementation is difficult, intended beneficiaries of policies are unhappy, and legislation requires early amendment. Poor policy making also tarnishes the reputation of civil servants.

There have been efforts in the UK to reform policy making so that it is more strategic. As long ago as 1999, a UK government white paper on modernizing government identified a number of desirable changes to policy making. Modernized policy was to be strategic, outcome focused, joined up, inclusive, flexible, innovative, and robust. In the same year a civil service team in the UK Cabinet Office in Whitehall diagnosed a number of shortcomings in the policy development work of civil servants (Strategic Policy-Making Team, Cabinet Office 1999). Policy making was criticized for not being long term and for a lack of learning. Policy makers were said to be insufficiently forward looking and outward looking. Just over a decade later another report on civil service policy making in the UK suggested that there had been improvements in the practice of policy making (Hallsworth et al. 2011). Policy making had become more outward looking, evidence-based, inclusive and forward looking. But weaknesses persisted, in relation to evaluation, review and learning, being joined up, being innovative, being flexible, and being creative.

In fact, strategic management at its best does seem designed to address many of the weaknesses identified in the policy making of the past and the weaknesses that remain; for example, strategic management can encourage more integrated organizational activities (joined up), more entrepreneurial action (looking for new ideas and opportunities and moving resources), and should include monitoring and evaluation. Attempts to make policy making more strategic, that is, to move it toward strategic policy making, will inevitably face resistance to change either for reasons of vested interests, or reasons of habit and inertia. Reflecting on the UK experience of reforming policy making, the most challenging areas in which to make progress are those of, first, creating more integration between ministries and, second, carrying out evaluation and learning.

Characterizing a public sector context

While there have been thoughtful speculations on the differences between private and public sector contexts (Nutt and Backoff 1992), there has probably been insufficient attention given to characterizing the nature of the public context in order to understand variations in strategic management and its effects. In this section of the chapter some possible approaches to addressing this matter are suggested, but it is not claimed that what is offered here should be seen as the definitive way forward or conclusive.

It has been common to see the public sector as a bureaucratic context. Weber's ideas (1970) are a frequent point of departure for understanding a bureaucratic context. He suggested that bureaucratic organization was to be found in large private corporations as well as in the state. Why did it develop in the public sector? Argyriades (2001) suggested that the bureaucratic model represented an early response to the emerging problems of complexity and scale in government, the quest for cost effective service delivery and also for objectivity, legality and integrity.

Against this view of the public sector as bureaucratic can be posed the reinventing government literature. This suggests that the public sector context is changing: the reform of governments can be seen as creating the possibility of post-bureaucratic forms of state administration involving a shift of emphasis from government self-sufficiency in policy making and implementation to the state providing a steering (strategic management) function for society (Osborne and Gaebler 1992). However, this reinventing government perspective is weak on the political and democratic aspects of the public sector context.

It is possible to see the rise of a strategic function in government, based on the development of a strategic management function within government, as being consistent with bureaucracy. The argument in this case can draw attention to Weber's idea that bureaucracy offered a system of decision making by bureaucrats based on "reasons". Bureaucracy might be seen as a decision making culture in which officials were able to explain the decisions they made as in accordance with norms or rules. But Weber also said that reasons might be provided by officials through a decision making process that involved the weighing of means and ends. If we define strategic management as action based on goals, analysis of the situation, identification of choices for action, resource analysis and a long-term orientation, then it is seems clear that it is compatible with Weber's definition of bureaucracy as a system of making decisions that could be accounted for rationally in terms of weighing means and ends.

Turning to the political dimension of a public sector context, a possible starting point is Aristotle (1981), who identified three different types of public governance system and described in each case a dysfunctional development of that type. Kingships could deteriorate into a tyranny suited to the interests of one person (the king). Aristocracies could deteriorate into oligarchies that were run in the interests of the rich minority (a plutocracy). And the third type, a polity, could degenerate into a democracy that only looked after the interests of the poor who were the majority.

Weber offered a way of viewing the politics of bureaucratic public administration. A crucial part of his analysis of the administration of the state bureaucracy, with clear echoes of Aristotle's ideas, was that there were at least two rival groupings that might be served by the bureaucrats: the propertied classes (the bourgeois) and the "propertyless masses". Describing the reality as a crypto-plutocracy, Weber suggested that the bureaucrats might actually be serving the interests of the propertied classes, whereas the propertyless masses wanted the state to compensate them for their relatively disadvantaged economic and social life-opportunities.

Weber problematized the idea that the public could directly take part in public governance. He stressed that democracy was based on electing representatives to rule society. As is well known, nowadays in many countries with political institutions based on representative democracy and competing political parties, there are concerns about long run trends such as declining public trust in politicians, public cynicism and complaints that governments are out of touch with the public. It is possible that this coincides with a trend toward a less deferential electorate leading to politics that are more "populist" in character. This gives rise to the following possible framing of the options facing political systems: do politicians have to work harder to court public opinion, or can representative democratic institutions be (re)invested with more legitimacy through public and stakeholder participation in government decision making? See Figure 25.3 for a representation of the possible contexts formed by politics and bureaucracy in countries with institutions based on representative democracy, and of a hypothesis about what types of strategic management system might flourish depending on the context.

There have been examples of technocratic strategic management by governments, when experts and politicians have together sought to take a long-term view in the interests of society, without much interaction by politicians or experts with the public (Alberts 1998). The question being posed in Figure 25.3 is: can strategic management be harmonized with increased democratization? This can be split into two subsidiary issues: can strategic management in government empower politicians and can public opinion become more important?

Tentative answers can be suggested here. Politicians can be empowered by strategic management. This is suggested by at least one case study of the experience of a corporate planning system (an earlier form of strategic planning) at Greenwich Council (in London). According to Cartwright (1975), the corporate planning system at the Council had strengthened political leadership, giving elected politicians more and not less control over the Council. He identified the following factors as important: elected politicians had a better understanding of Council activity, were better informed of relevant facts, and were better able to monitor progress.

There is evidence from research into strategic planning by Italian cities that participatory strategic planning is more likely if there is a higher level of civic culture (as measured by newspaper circulation numbers, numbers of voters, level of blood donation, and membership of sports associations) (Cristofoli et al. 2014). It would be rash to conclude that civic culture determines the potential for public participation. However, the study could point to the possibility that public opinion might count for more when governments used participatory strategic planning methods providing there was a favourable culture in the local community or providing such a culture could be stimulated and fostered. This needs testing by future research on this important topic.

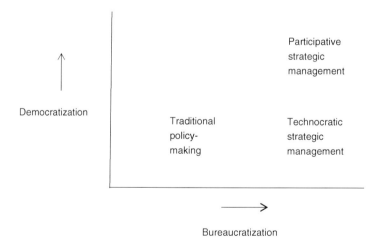

Figure 25.3 The public sector context

The strategic state

There are numerous examples of long-term thinking in government. More than 50 years ago, British Prime Minister Harold Macmillan commissioned a study to provide a basis for policy-making that involved a ten-year horizon (looking forward to the year 1970). More recently, Finland has been cited as a good example of public governance based on a long-term orientation (Anckar et al. 2011). Its government had prepared a long-term report on the future for Finland's parliament, it had a Parliamentary Committee for the Future, and its strategic planning was an important element of its decision-making. Saudi Arabia set out an intention in its Eighth Development Plan to deliver a long-term vision through four successive five-year plans ending in 2024 (Saudi Ministry of Economy and Planning 2005).

The existence of electoral cycles and changes of government might be expected to disrupt long-term visions or strategic goals. An OECD report put the issue this way (OECD 2012: 15): "Achieving linkages between umbrella strategy documents and government political agendas can be difficult." In the case of the US, by 2004 it looked as though the election of a new President was compromising the system of strategic planning by federal agencies (introduced by legislation enacted in 1993). An attempt to reconcile the federal agencies' planning cycle and the presidential electoral cycle was made through legal changes brought in by President Obama in 2010. This was to be achieved by establishing a new strategic planning cycle that would always follow the start of a new presidential term of office. Despite the challenges of linking strategic planning and electoral cycles, there are examples of governments formulating long-term plans for public services reforms extending well beyond the lifetime of a parliament (e.g. the UK government in 2000, just one year before the general election in 2001, published ten-year plans for health and transport systems).

In recent years, concerns about the lack of coherence in decision making and a lack of more integrated working across the boundaries of government ministries have been repeatedly articulated. And most recently, there have been expressions of the need to develop strategic plans and reforms that are more responsive to citizens, and based on more participation by citizens, social partners, and stakeholders during the formulation stage.

The OECD has done more than anybody to clarify the meaning of "strategic state" capabilities (see, for example, OECD 2013). Based on the public governance reviews carried out by the OECD, the chief features of a public governance system informed by a strategic-state concept are:

- the formulation by politicians of a long-term vision and the setting of long-term priorities for national development;
- effective two-way communication between politicians and their top officials about strategic visions and plans;
- the "centre of government" providing the required coordination of the civil service to deliver government strategies that deliver the government's long-term vision of national development and its priorities;
- budgetary and performance measurement systems deployed to make the national government's strategies effective;
- cooperative and coherent working between all levels of government (national, sub-national and supra-national if appropriate); and
- participation by the public and external stakeholders in the formulation of strategies and reforms.

The Europe 2020 strategy, agreed in 2010, provided an example of this new-style public governance in action, and it was specifically intended that citizens would be involved in the formulation of reform plans to deliver the top priorities set out in the strategy (European Commission 2014).

Are strategic states more effective than other types of state? Obviously, research is urgently needed to see if there is a strong correlation between government effectiveness and strategic-state capabilities. In the absence of systematic research, the opinion of Mulgan (2009) may be noted that the top countries in terms of government effectiveness have tended to be ones that have taken strategy seriously. He mentioned, for example, Denmark, Finland, Iceland, the Netherlands, Norway and Switzerland.

In Table 25.1 there is a selective list of countries showing their "government effectiveness" score (which was published by the World Bank). This is being used here as an indicator of strategic-state capabilities. The table also shows two national performance indicators: GDP per capita and confidence in national government. One country really worth singling out in this table is Sweden. According to Doz and Kosonen (2014), an important reform of Swedish government took place in 1997, when a "single unified government" model was brought in. The reform was focused on the integration and coordination of central government, with implications for the role and importance of the prime minister, the Prime Minister's Office, individual ministers and agencies. In the years that followed there was a sustained fall in central government debt and GDP per capita rose impressively over a number of years. One possible interpretation is that the reform increased the strategic capacity of the Swedish Government. In consequence, it got a grip on central government finances and was more able to steer national economic performance toward more economic growth.

Table 25.1 World Bank "government effectiveness" and performance indicators (2011 and 2012): various countries

Country	An indicator for strategic-state capabilities and two national performance indicators		
	Government effectiveness (percentile rank) 2011	*GDP per capita (000s; constant 2005 US$)* 2012	*Confidence in National Government (%; Gallup)* 2012
Finland	100	40	62
Denmark	99	48	55
Sweden	99	45	65
Germany	93	39	45
UK	92	40	48
US	90	45	35
Chile	86	9	33
Czech Republic	78	15	18
Poland	72	11	31
Italy	66	30	30
Turkey	65	8	56
Greece	62	19	14

Sources: (1) World Bank data on government effectiveness and GDP per capita obtained from: http://databank.worldbank.org/data/home.aspx. (2) Gallup data taken from OECD (2014) *Society at a Glance 2014*, OECD Publishing

Table 25.1 shows that there was a tendency for the public to have confidence in their national government when it is a country that was credited with a high level of government effectiveness. This could be spurious with confidence in government being really an effect of increasing economic well-being: we can note that countries in which GDP per capita is higher also tend to be countries with a high score on government effectiveness. Turkey is an interesting case in terms of public confidence in national government. Even though it had a relatively low score on government effectiveness and a relatively low GDP per capita, it still scored high on confidence in government. Turkey's public administration, it might be noted, had been working hard since 2003 to introduce strategic planning as part of its reforms of public financial management. Turkey had also been enjoying stable national government and a good economic record over most of the period since 2003. Perhaps we can infer from the Turkish experience (at least in the period 2003 to 2012) that governments attempting seriously to work as a strategic state appear competent and credible to their publics.

Conclusion

Strategic management in government can be successful providing it is properly integrated into management systems and effectively deployed and supported. Recent systematic research into the causes of effective strategic planning has revealed important lessons for the public sector. These included lessons about how to monitor and evaluate strategic plans and about the benefits of involving the public in the development of strategic plans. It should be noted that surveys have shown that many practitioners in the public sector have found strategic planning to be useful.

This chapter has argued that more research on strategic management is needed that pays attention to the effects of the public sector context. The specificities of the public sector were illustrated using a discussion of the concepts of democratization and bureaucratization. It might be tempting to locate the rise of strategic management in the public sector with the onset of a post-bureaucratic era. But, referring back to the ideas of Max Weber, it is also possible to make a case that the introduction of strategic management coincides with an evolution in the character of bureaucracy in public administration. This chapter has also raised the question of the possibility of strategic management being developed in such a way as to increase democratic culture. Some research findings on the effects of strategic planning on the power of elected politicians and the way in which civic culture may assist the development of participatory strategic planning were noted. These findings point to the possibility that strategic management could be used to reinforce democracy.

The implications of attempts to make policy making strategic, that is, to move it toward strategic policy making, were considered. It was accepted that such attempts could encounter resistance. The UK experience suggested the most challenging areas for modernization of policy making, for introducing strategic policy making, appear to be those of, first, creating more integration between ministries and, second, carrying out evaluation and learning.

The concept of the strategic state was outlined. This is a concept that has been developed primarily through reviews of public governance in various OECD countries, but the chapter noted a suggestion that government taking strategy and long-term thinking more seriously could increase government effectiveness (Mulgan 2009).

While the strategic state concept has been developed to the point where it is a robust tool for studies of the state and public governance, in a global perspective it would be useful to know how it relates to the widely used World Bank governance indicator of government effectiveness. The stability in the meaning of the governance indicator is very attractive when we are looking for ways to understand other developments, but this very stability in its meaning becomes highly problematic when it is considered that in the last 20 years there has been a surge in support for an effective state that can help and enable the business community to spearhead a return to higher rates of sustainable growth. Is this type of effective state captured by the government effectiveness indicator?

Becoming clear about how strategic-state capabilities relate to the World Bank governance indicator for government effectiveness would help with widening our understanding of the contrasting experiences of groups of countries. Take, for example, the group of countries that formed an important part of the OECD membership – countries such as the United States, Canada, Australia, the UK, Sweden and other Northern European states. They are all characterized as countries at the top end of the range of government effectiveness, and that is where they have remained for a number of years. They appear to fit the "model pattern" prescribed by the government effectiveness indicator. They appear to be at the top end of the evolutionary scale of government effectiveness. It is this same group of countries that appear to be stalled in terms of global competition. Then there is another group of countries, including Argentina, Brazil, Ghana, and South Africa, where the growth rates have been slightly better but government effectiveness has been tumbling. How can this be? Surely good governance, including government effectiveness, ought to be an important factor in economic growth performance. Their experience over the last decade or so contradicts this expectation (at least based on government effectiveness).

A third group of countries seem to have found the best path in terms of international comparisons. Their growth rates have been excellent and they have all achieved sharp increases in government effectiveness. These are the countries of China, India, the Russian Federation, Saudi Arabia and Turkey. Delving into some of their recent experiments with more strategic government suggests that they may have become quite serious about strategic planning as a core element in their governance systems. This is even true of India, which after 65 years of five-year plans, decided in 2015 that it had had enough of central planning and is now set on introducing strategic planning. The government of India has set up a new planning institution, which is named NITI Aayog. This new institution replaced the Planning Commission and was given the responsibility to "provide the strategic policy vision for the government" and to "provide a critical directional and strategic input into the governance process" (Government of India 2016).

None of this provides conclusive evidence that "strategy" is the addition to public governance that will galvanize societies into action and propel them into a new phase of inclusiveness and effectiveness. But there is sufficient evidence to say we need to know more about how extensive and established is the strategic state and what are its consequences.

References

Alberts, G. 1998. *Jaren van Berekening*. Amsterdam: Amsterdam University Press, quoted by De Vries, Michiel S. 2010. *The Importance of Neglect in Policy Making*. Basingstoke: Palgrave Macmillan.

Anckar, D., K. Kuitto, C. Oberst, and D. Jahn. 2011. *Sustainable Governance Indicators 2011: Finland Report*. Gutersloh: Bertelsmann Stiftung.

Argyriades, D. 2001. "Bureaucracy and Debureaucratization." In *Handbook of Comparative and Development Public Administration*, edited by Farazmand, A., 901–917. New York: Marcel Dekker.

Aristotle. 1981. *The Politics*. London: Penguin Books.

Berry, F. S. and B. Wechsler. 1995. "State Agencies' Experience with Strategic Planning: Findings from a National Survey." *Public Administration Review* 55 (2): 159–168.

Boyne, G. A. and R. M. Walker. 2010. "Strategic Management and Public Service Performance: The Way Ahead." *Public Administration Review* 70 (s1): S185–192.

Bryson, J. M. 1988. *Strategic Planning for Public and Nonprofit Organizations*. San Francisco: Jossey-Bass Publishers.

Cartwright, J. 1975. "Corporate Planning in Local Government: Implications for the Elected Member." *Long-Range Planning* 8 (2): 46–50.

Corvo, L., A. B. A. Bonomi Savignon, D. Cepiku, and M. Meneguzzo. 2014. "Implementation of Performance Management Reforms in Italian Central Government." In *Developments in Strategic and Public Management: Studies in the US and Europe*, edited by Joyce, P., J. M. Bryson, and M. Holzer. Basingstoke, UK: Palgrave Macmillan.

Cristofoli, D., L. Maccio, and M. Meneguzzo. 2014. "When Civic Culture Meets Strategy: Exploring Predictors of Citizen Engagement in Participatory Strategic Plans in Italy." In *Strategic Management in Public Organizations European Practices and Perspectives*, edited by Joyce, P. and A. Drumaux, 133–147. New York: Routledge.

Doz, Y. and M. Kosonen. 2014. *Governments for the Future: Building the Strategic and Agile State*. Erweko, Helsinki: Sitra.

European Commission. 2014. *Europe 2020*. Accessed 3 May 2014.

http://ec.europa.eu/news/economy/100303_en.htm.

Flynn, N. and C. Talbot. 1996. "Strategy and strategists in UK local government." *Journal of Management Development* 15 (2): 24–38.

Government of India. 2016. "Government constitutes National Institution for Transforming India (NITI) Aayog." [online]. Accessed January 31, 2016. http://pmindia.gov.in/en/news_updates/government-constitutes-national-institution-for-transforming-india-niti-aayog/?tag_term=niti-aayog&comment=disable.

Hallsworth, M., S. Parker, and J. Rutter. 2011. *Policy Making in the Real World: Evidence and Analysis*. London: Institute for Government.

Heymann, P. B. (1987) *The Politics of Public Management*. London: Yale University Press.

Hodgkinson, I. R. 2012. "Are Generic Strategies 'Fit for Purpose' in a Public Service Context?" *Public Policy and Administration* 28 (1): 90–111.

Jarzabkowski, P. 2005. *Strategy as Practice: An Activity-Based Approach*. London: Sage Publications.

Jarzabkowski, P. 2003. "Strategic Practices: An Activity Theory Perspective on Continuity and Change." *Journal of Management Studies* 40 (1): 23–55.

Joyce, P. 2015. *Strategic Management in the Public Sector*. London: Routledge.

Joyce, P. 2008. "The Strategic and Enabling State: A Case Study in the UK, 1997–2007." *The International Journal of Leadership in Public Services* 4 (3): 24–36.

Joyce, P. and A. Drumaux. 2014. "Conclusion: The Development of the Strategic State in Europe." In *Strategic Management in Public Organizations: European Practices and Perspectives*, edited by Joyce, P. and A. Drumaux, 310–327. New York: Routledge.

Lumijarvi, I. and U. Ulriika Leponiemi. 2014. "Strategic Management in Finnish Municipalities." In *Strategic Management in Public Organizations: European Practices and Perspectives*, edited by Joyce, P. and A. Drumaux, 41–56. New York: Routledge.

Moore, M. 1995. *Creating Public Value: Strategic Management in Government*. London: Harvard University Press.

Mulgan, G. 2009. *The Art of Public Strategy: Mobilizing Power and Knowledge for the Common Good*. Oxford: Oxford University Press.

Niiranen, V. and M. Joensuu. 2014. "Political Leaders and Public Administrators in Finland: Key Values and Stumbling Blocks in Decision Making and Interaction." In *Strategic Management in Public Organizations: European Practices and Perspectives*, edited by Joyce, P. and A. Drumaux, 95–114. New York: Routledge.

Nutt, P. C. and R. W. Backoff. 1992. *Strategic Management of Public and Third Sector Organizations*. San Francisco: Jossey-Bass Publishers.

OECD. 2013. *Poland: Implementing Strategic-State Capability*. *OECD Public Governance Reviews*. Paris: OECD Publishing.

OECD. 2012. *Slovenia: Toward a Strategic and Efficient State*. Paris: OECD Publishing.

OECD. 2007. "The Role of Ministries in the Policy System: Policy Development, Monitoring and Evaluation." Sigma Paper No. 39. Paris: OECD.

Osborne, D. and T. Gaebler. 1992. *Reinventing Government: How the Entrepreneurial Spirit Is Transforming the Public Sector*. Reading, MA: Addison Wesley.

Poister, T. H. and G. Streib. 2005. "Elements of Strategic Planning and Management in Municipal Government: Status after Two Decades." *Public Administration Review* 65 (1): 45–56.

Rumelt, R. 2011. *Good Strategy Bad Strategy: The Difference and Why It Matters.* London: Profile Books.

Saudi Ministry of Economy and Planning. 2014. "The Eighth Development Plan, 2005–2009." Accessed 30 June 2014. www.planiplois.iiep.unesco.org.

Strategic Policy Making Team, Cabinet Office. 1999. *Professional Policy Making for the 21st Century.* London: Cabinet Office.

Weber, M. 1970. "Bureaucracy." In *From Max Weber*, edited by Gerth, H. H. and C. Wright Mills, 196–244. London and Boston: Routledge & Kegan Paul Ltd.

Wechsler, B. and R. W. Backoff. 1987. "The dynamics of strategy in public organizations." *Journal of the American Planning Association* 53 (1): 34–43.

Whittington, R. 1996. "Strategy as Practice." *Long Range Planning* 29 (5): 731–735.

26

PERFORMANCE MANAGEMENT IN PUBLIC ADMINISTRATION

Denita Cepiku

Performance management in public administrations: trends and specificities

The move towards performance management in the public sector is not new, although it has intensified during the past three decades, increasing formalized planning, control and reporting across all the OECD countries (Bouckaert and Halligan 2008: 29). The first wave was the scientific management movement in the 1900s–1940s, introducing planning, programming and budgeting systems (PPBS) and management by objectives (MBO). The New Public Management (NPM) theory arose during the1980s to 2000, along with the Public Governance approach starting in the mid-1990s in the Scandinavian countries (Van Dooren, Bouckaert, and Halligan 2010). The evolution of performance management practices mirrors modernization trends: its focus shifted from rules and input regulation (Weberianism), to outputs and efficiency (NPM) to outcomes and effectiveness (Public Governance) (Imperial, 2005: 395).

Different literature streams have contributed to the development of performance management theory, including public administration, public management, strategic planning and management controls, evidence-based policy, and evaluation (Van Helden, Johnsen, and Vakkuri 2012). Such multidisciplinary attention may be one reason why the concept of performance is characterized by a degree of ambiguity. "It must be viewed as a set of information about achievements of varying significance to different stakeholders" (Bovaird 1996: 147). Performance is both about results and about intentional behaviours that lead to those results. Such behaviours "can be individual or organizational" while the outputs can refer to outputs, outcomes and public values (Van Dooren, Bouckaert, and Halligan 2010: 2, 16).

Performance management includes measurement, i.e. the construction and measurement of decision-relevant performance indicators, and monitoring, but also reporting to relevant administrative and political bodies and, most importantly, the meaningful use of this information (Van Helden, Johnsen and Vakkuri 2012).

During the NPM period, performance management was introduced as part of reforms aimed at making public management more similar to private management, and therefore more efficient in the intentions of the promoters of the NPM. Thus, it has been accused of neglecting the specificities of public administrations such as their increased goal ambiguity, fewer economic incentives, higher levels of bureaucracy, greater number of stakeholders and higher relevance of public values (Hvidman and Andersen 2014: 38; Lee, Rainey, and Chun 2009; Rainey 1989; Perry and Rainey 1988; Bozeman 1987; Rainey, Backoff, and Levine 1976). On the one hand, public administrations are characterized by low managerial autonomy in defining strategic objectives and managing resources; on the other, public managers have more flexibility than private ones to choose relevant performance measures, notwithstanding the compulsory nature of such procedures in many countries (Behn 2003: 599).

The literature now acknowledges the relevance of the differences between for-profit firms and public administrations regarding performance management. Most importantly, outcomes matter more than output for the latter. For instance, sales represent a prompt and objective indicator for the success of a firm; presumably, in low inflation contexts, high sales will lead to high profits and good dividends for the shareholders. With a public administration, even one providing services such as a hospital, school or university, output measures alone – for example, the number of surgical interventions or graduate students – although useful, are difficult to interpret according to either metric. The impact of output on the areas of need, like the quality of life after discharge from the hospital or employment opportunities after graduation, is the most meaningful performance indicator. However, it is difficult to measure as it refers to a social rather than an economic impact. It takes time to manifest and depends on the context as well as on the activities of the specific public administration being measured.

This fundamental specificity leads to differences in performance management systems. One direct consequence is the recommendation, found in the literature, for performance management systems in the public sector to be multidimensional rather than balanced towards one specific performance dimension, such as inputs, processes, outputs or outcomes.

Levels of performance management

There are at least four perspectives through which public sector performance can be assessed (see Figure 26.1). First, performance can be viewed at a global level. International institutions produce rankings and measures to assess the aggregate performance levels of different countries' public sectors.[1] Fukuyama (2013) classifies the available empirical measures of public administration quality into four approaches:

1 Procedural measures, such as the Weberian criteria of bureaucratic modernity. These include the impartiality of bureaucrats, a hierarchical organization and well-defined spheres of competence, recruitment and promotion on the basis of merit and technical qualifications, and separation between ownership and management.
2 Capacity measures, which include both resources (e.g. tax extraction measures) and the level of education and professionalization of government officials.
3 Output and outcome measures such as literacy, primary and secondary education test scores, or various measures of health.
4 Measures of bureaucratic autonomy, referring to principal–agent theory: that is, how the political principal issues mandates to the bureaucrats acting as its agent.

The main weaknesses of these measures include being based extensively on expert surveys and being characterized by normative policy preferences that colour the final results. Moreover, output is not considered a valid measure of a state's performance quality, due to difficulties in divorcing output and outcome measures from procedural and normative measures and exogenous factors (Fukuyama 2013: 351–356).

A second level of assessment is public sector policies. Performance management has been at the centre of public sector reform agendas since the late 1980s. Reforms have made it compulsory in public administrations and often link resource allocations to performance achievements (Bouckaert and Halligan 2008). Public sector reforms were driven by the belief that requiring agencies to define and measure strategic goals and achievements would reduce the performance deficit (Moynihan and Pandey 2010: 849; Poister 2010; Moore 1995). Although deriving from global trends like NPM and Public Governance, the actual implementation of performance management reforms has been affected by national administrative traditions and cultures, resulting in differences between common law and administrative law jurisdictions and between more and less developed countries (Tillema et al. 2010; Alawattage, Hopper, and Wickramasinghe 2007). Some policy sectors have been more affected than others. For instance, centrally defined performance indicators directly influence financial resource allocations in healthcare and higher education in several countries.

At this level, performance management systems have been classified into four ideal types, according to institutional coverage and the learning and development process (Bouckaert and Halligan 2008: 69):

- performance administration;
- management of performance of specific functions;
- performance management;
- performance governance.

The third level is organizational, represented by performance management activities that are part of strategic planning and managing efforts. They comprise a bundle of activities quantifying

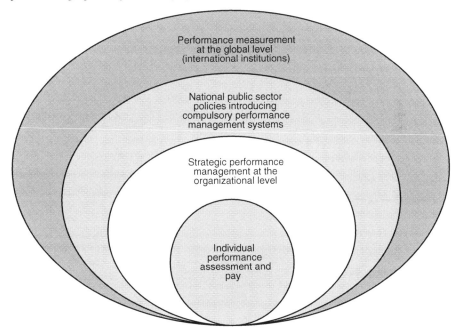

Figure 26.1 Levels of performance management

performance: defining a measurement object, formulating indicators, collecting, analysing and reporting data (Van Dooren, Bouckaert, and Halligan 2010: 25). This chapter focuses on this level.

Finally, performance management can operate at the individual or team level, integrating human resources management through instruments such as performance-related pay.

In theory, there should be cause–effect links between these different levels, leading to higher levels of performance of public services and policies, with the ultimate beneficiaries being citizens. International institutions' rankings are supposed to put pressure on national governments to introduce reforms promoting performance management. These reforms should lead to higher levels of performance orientation in planning and managing resources in organizations and to higher individual performances by public employees. The final result should be better public services and more effective policies. The effects also work the other way around. National-level policies such as spending reviews and budgeting are often dependent on well-functioning performance measurement and reporting systems at the organizational level.

Empirical research on these links offers mixed results, highlighting both the positive and negative effects of performance policies. Although the cause–effect link between performance management and improvement may be problematic to prove, studies show that the former is a crucial determinant of the latter.

Managing performance at the organizational level

Performance can be planned, measured, assessed and acted upon. When such actions occur in an integrated and systemic way, it is usually referred to as performance management. Performance measurement is focused on: how to measure what the administration is doing; detecting the most significant performance deficits and formulating a strategy for mitigating them; and motivating everyone in the organization to pursue the strategy (Behn 2013). Performance measurement without management and leadership is useless. "Despite the universal appeal of the seductive cliché, the data never speak for themselves. When the data speak, they do so only through some framework, some theory, some causal model, some logical construct, some perception of the world and how it works" (Behn 2009).

Performance management at the organizational level is a pillar supporting national government effectiveness and a condition for the non-arbitrary evaluation of individual-level performance. It is a process supporting strategic management and managerial controls, as illustrated in Figure 26.2. It "generates information through strategic planning and performance measurement routines and […] connects this information to decision venues, where, ideally, the information influences a range of possible decisions" (Moynihan 2008: 5). In other words, to be effective, performance measurement systems should not operate on their own but support and strengthen other management and decision-making processes, such as planning, budgeting, human resources management, grants and contract management, among others (Poister, Aristigueta, and Hall 2015).

In April 2011, the *New York Times Magazine* dedicated its cover to Ramón González, principal of public middle school 223 in South Bronx, whose office overlooks one of the largest, most dangerous housing projects in New York. The M.S. 223 case study (Box 26.1) is very useful to illustrate:

- the links between public sector reforms that emphasize outputs and competition, and performance management at the organizational level, which focuses on outcomes, public value and collaboration;

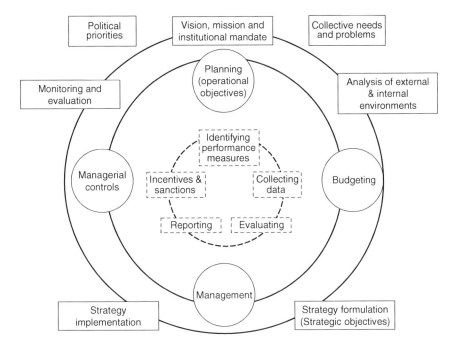

Figure 26.2 Performance management as part of the strategic management and managerial control cycles

- the nature and activities of performance leadership, which go beyond performance measurement;
- the impact of a specific organizational mission and vision on performance measures – or, in other words, the specificities of performance management in public vis-à-vis private organizations.

Box 26.1 Performance management in a public middle school in the Bronx

About 70 per cent of M.S. 223 students are Hispanic, and the remainder are black, either African-American or recent immigrants from West African countries like Senegal. Roughly 11 per cent are English-language learners and about 17 per cent have learning disabilities. Many live in impoverished conditions and about 15 per cent live in shelters.

In 2010, after seven years under González's management, 60 per cent of the students tested at or above grade level in math and 30 per cent did the same in English, making 223 one of the top middle schools in the South Bronx and, according to the progress report from the Department of Education, the 10th-best middle school in the entire city.

But 223's success remains mixed. Studies dating back to the 1960s have suggested that children's experiences inside the classroom are responsible for as little as 20 per cent of their overall educational development. No less important is how they spend their evenings, weekends, and vacations.

González is trying to reverse this trend by bringing parents into their children's lives at 223 in any way he can, whether it's through sporting events, plays, recitals or classroom celebrations.

And yet even as school reform made it possible for González to succeed, as the movement rolls inexorably forward, it also seems in many ways set up to make him fail.

The grading system imposed by the NYC Department of Education, which has bestowed three consecutive As on González, is based in part on how well 223 does on state tests. But the school's relative success on these tests and other measures also disqualifies it from additional state resources earmarked for failing schools. The ever-growing number of charter schools, often privately subsidized and rarely bound by union rules, skims off the neighborhood's more ambitious, motivated families. And every year, as failing schools are shut down, a steady stream of children with poor intellectual habits and little family support continues to arrive at 223. González wouldn't want it any other way – he takes pride in his school's duty to educate all comers – but the endless flow of underperforming students drags down test scores, demoralizes teachers and makes the already daunting challenge of transforming 223 into a successful school, not just a relatively successful one, that much more difficult. González, who prefers to think of himself as a community activist, has an anachronistic vision for 223 vis-à-vis policies of education reform, which is based on school freedom of choice by low-income families and competition between public and charter schools. This idea of school reform is against the very idea of the neighborhood school with deep roots in a community, which is precisely what González is trying to revive and reinvent. "You know what you have to do to come to school here?" González told the *NYT Magazine* journalist. "Walk through that door" (Mahler 2011).

Source: extracted and adapted from Mahler 2011.

Further information: www.ms223.org/results.html

The Achilles' heel: performance information use

Obviously, performance management benefits depend, first and foremost, on the extent to which public managers and other decision makers and stakeholders make use of performance information. The literature on public sector performance management has only recently moved from the analysis of measurement instruments and indicators to question the actual use of information these tools generate, considering this to be "the most pressing challenge for scholarship on performance management" (Kroll 2015; Moynihan and Pandey 2010: 849).

Potential users of the performance information being produced include politicians (Askim 2009), audit institutions, citizens and civil society organizations (Pollitt 2006), and public managers (Kroll 2013; Moynihan and Pandey 2010), among others.

Public managers can use performance information in different ways: managerial, political or merely bureaucratic. This use can be purposeful, aimed at improving management and allocation decisions, or passive, satisfying the procedural requirements of law (Moynihan and Lavertu 2012: 1; Radin 2006). The main factors influencing the use of performance information by public managers are summarized in Table 26.1. These are grouped under three categories: supply side (characteristics of performance information systems); demand side (features of public managers as users of information); context (both internal and external) (Moynihan and Pandey 2010: 850).

Table 26.1 Drivers and effects of performance use: the literature in a nutshell

Area	Drivers and effects of performance use	Main bibliographic references
Design of performance management system	Aims pursued with the introduction of a performance management system (political intentions and managerial aims).	Behn (2003)
	Involvement of employees and other stakeholders in building the system and in measuring and reporting performance information.	de Lancer and Holzer (2001) Ho (2006) Melkers and Willoughby (2005) Yang and Hi (2007) Moynihan and Pandey (2010)
	Paying attention to implementation: training, dialogue and learning forums.	Wholey (2002) Yang and Hi (2007) Askim, Johnsen and Christophersen (2008) Moynihan and Lavertu (2012)
	Adaptability (of timing and formats of delivery of performance information). Fit for use and fit for purpose. Different purposes require different measures.	Bouckaert and Halligan (2008) Van Dooren, Bouckaert and Halligan (2010)
	Contents: accessibility, relevance to users, trustworthiness, quality, reliability and validity.	Heinrich (1999) Behn (2003) Ammons and Rivenbark (2008) Van Dooren, Bouckaert and Halligan (2010) Kroll (2013)
	Resources (time, people, money) available for performance measurement.	Mintzberg (1975) Weiss and Bucuvalas (1980) de Lancer and Holzer (2001) Askim, Johnsen and Christophersen (2008)
	Integration of performance management into the management systems of the organization. Incorporation in documents and procedures and in the culture and memory of the organization.	Bouckaert and Halligan (2008) Ammons and Rivenbark (2008) Van Dooren, Bouckaert and Halligan (2010) Hammerschmid, Van de Walle and Stimac (2013)
Features of users	Performance information needs.	Ammons and Rivenbark (2008)
	Adequacy of competencies and time for analysing and using performance information (including task experience).	Bourdeaux and Chikoto (2008) Moynihan and Pandey (2010)
	Expectations over the usefulness and benefits that derive from performance information use.	Moynihan and Pandey (2010)

Table 26.1   continued

Area	Drivers and effects of performance use	Main bibliographic references
Context elements	(Perceived) leadership commitment.	de Lancer and Holzer (2001) Moynihan and Ingraham (2004) Moynihan and Pandey (2004, 2010) Yang and Hi (2007) Moynihan and Lavertu (2012)
	Political-administrative relations. Administrative stability.	Ho (2006)
	External (law and administrative regulations) and internal requirements needing the use of performance information.	Taylor (2009)
	Organizational culture (openness to innovation and risk-taking). Efforts in accommodating and motivating performance culture as supra structure.	de Lancer and Holzer (2001) Broadnax and Conway (2001) Hofstede (2005) Bouckaert and Halligan (2008) Van Dooren, Bouckaert and Halligan (2010) Moynihan and Pandey (2010)
	Public service motivation.	Moynihan and Pandey (2010)
	Decision flexibility and level of discretion enjoyed.	Moynihan and Pandey (2010) Moynihan and Lavertu (2012)
	Influence from professional and citizens' associations. Media coverage.	Ho (2006)
Performance information use and effectiveness of use	Categories of uses of performance information. Dysfunctional use and unintended consequences. Gaming.	Hatry, Blair, Fisk, Greiner, Hall and Schaenman (1992) Hatry (1999) Wholey and Newcomer (1997) de Lancer and Holzer (2001) Miller, Hildreth and Rabin (2001) Behn (2003) Christensen and Lægreid (2004) Melkers and Willoughby (2005) Bevan and Hood (2006) Bouckaert and Halligan (2008) Moynihan and Pandey (2010) Van Dooren, Bouckaert and Halligan (2010) Hammerschmid, Van de Walle and Stimac (2013)
	Effectiveness (or effects) of use.	Ho (2006) Yang and Hi (2007) Bourdeaux and Chikoto (2008) Van Dooren, Bouckaert and Halligan (2010) Poister, Pasha and Edwards (2013)

Categories of performance information managerial uses range from the 44 listed in Van Dooren (2006) to the three found in Van Dooren, Bouckaert, and Halligan (2010), who distinguish between learning, steering and control, and accountability. de Lancer and Holzer (2001) distinguish between measuring efficiency, output and outcome for strategic planning, resource allocation, programme management, monitoring and evaluation, and reporting to internal management, elected officials, citizens or the media. Miller, Hildreth, and Rabin (2001) view performance measurement as helping managers make decisions about the budget cycle, human resources management, evaluation and contracting. Melkers and Willoughby (2005) list the following possible uses:

- reporting to elected officials, management and staff, citizens, citizen groups, or media;
- assessing programme results;
- budgeting, including resource allocation or discussions about resource changes;
- planning, such as for programmes, planning, annual business planning, oversight activities like programmatic changes, and strategic planning;
- managing operations (e.g. services or contractors);
- establishing or changing policies and evaluations to determine the underlying reasons for results;
- personnel decisions including staffing levels and evaluations;
- establishing contracts for services;
- benchmarking, or comparison of programme results with other entities;
- holding local jurisdictions accountable for state-funded or state-regulated programmes; determining which programmes, local jurisdictions, or contractors to target for audits;
- special studies and technical assistance.

Bouckaert and Halligan (2008: 28) consider the following uses of performance information: designing policies, making decisions, allocating resources, competencies and responsibilities, controlling and redirecting implementation, self-evaluating and assessing behaviour and results, confirming reporting and accountability mechanisms. They distinguish between internal use by agencies and individuals, budget decisions and processes, and reporting (p. 144). Behn (2003) envisages eight potential uses: evaluating activities under review; control; budgeting; motivating staff, contractors, citizens and other stakeholders; promoting the agency externally; celebrating achievements in order to strengthen organizational culture; learning; and improving performances. These are shown in Figure 26.3.

The benefits of performance management systems

Managing performance is a complex, time-consuming and expensive activity for every organization. It is carried out assuming that organizations have a greater probability of achieving their objectives "if they use performance measures to monitor their progress along these lines and then take follow-up actions as necessary" (Poister, Aristigueta, and Hall 2015: 24). However, there is insufficient empirical evidence to back up this claim and, as with any investment, it makes sense to ask if performance management leads to better results.

The benefits of performance management – also called the effectiveness of performance information use – are closely linked to its goals. Van Dooren, Bouckaert, and Halligan (2010) identify: learning and innovation, the improvement of steering and control, and better accountability. Bourdeaux and Chikoto (2008) propose the following categories: improving the effectiveness of agency programmes, reducing duplicated services, reducing/eliminating

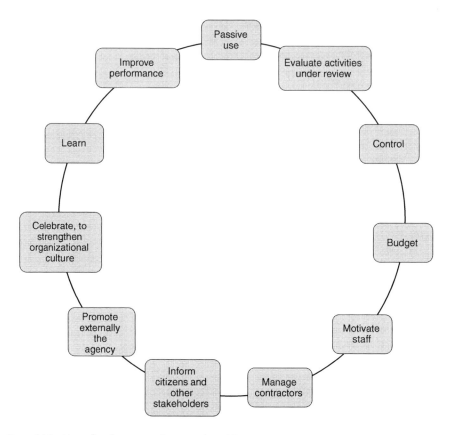

Figure 26.3 Uses of performance information by public managers

ineffective services/programmes, changing strategies to achieve desired results, improving programmes/service quality, and increasing awareness of factors that affect performance results. To these, the three effects on communication proposed by Melkers and Willoughby (2005) can be added: the improvement of communication internal to the agency, with other agencies, and with citizens.

Hvidman and Andersen (2014) have conducted empirical research on how performance management influences performance outcomes by comparing Danish public and private schools. They showed that the effectiveness of performance management in private schools is not transferred to public schools, although the latter use performance management much more than private schools. Poister, Pasha and Hamilton (2013) examined the impact of performance management practices on organizational effectiveness in 88 small and medium-sized local transit agencies in the United States, showing that an extensive use of performance management practices does in fact contribute to increased effectiveness.

The shortcomings of performance management systems

The dysfunctional effects of performance management systems have been widely illustrated, albeit mainly anecdotally, by the literature developed after the first wave of NPM reforms and refer to the perverse and unexpected effects of performance measures that create opportunistic or blame-avoidance behaviour: for example, Hood (2002) distinguishes between agency, presentational and policy strategies. Other negative consequences refer to tunnel vision, sub-optimization, myopia, convergence, ossification, gaming, and misrepresentation (Vakkuri and Meklin 2006; Smith 1995).

It is interesting to notice that several private firms are abandoning traditional performance management systems – the same systems that recent public sector reforms have forced public administrations to adopt. Excellent examples include Microsoft, Adobe and Deloitte (Box 26.2). This shift in the private sector is occurring following studies highlighting the negative unintended consequences of performance management or at best ineffectiveness. According to a recent survey of private sector managers, today's widespread ranking and ratings-based performance management is "damaging employee engagement, alienating high performers, and costing managers valuable time" (Barry, Garr, and Liakopoulos 2014: 45). Only 8 per cent of companies report that their performance management process drives high levels of value, while 58 per cent say it is not an effective use of time. Therefore, organizations are scrapping the annual evaluation cycle and replacing it with continuous employee development. In the case of Adobe, a company of 11,000 employees, the traditional performance management system was deemed inconsistent with the company's culture of teamwork and collaboration. The new system brought about a 30 per cent reduction in voluntary turnover.

Box 26.2 The simplification and improvement of the performance management system at Deloitte

The radical transformation of the performance management system at Deloitte was decided after finding out that creating the ratings consumed close to two million hours a year. The new system aimed at pursuing three objectives: (1) recognize performance; (2) be able to see it clearly; (3) be able, not only to measure and reward performance, but also enable leaders to improve it.

The new system is based on four simple questions that, at the end of every project, team leaders were asked about each team member:

1. Given what I know of this person's performance, and if it were my money, I would award this person the highest possible compensation increase and bonus (measures overall performance and unique value to the organization on a five-point scale from "strongly agree" to "strongly disagree").
2. Given what I know of this person's performance, I would always want him or her on my team [measures ability to work well with others on the same five-point scale].
3. This person is at risk for low performance (identifies problems that might harm the customer or the team on a yes-or-no basis).
4. This person is ready for promotion today (measures potential on a yes-or-no basis). Some key features are meant to make the system work better than traditional performance management systems based on cascading objectives and backward-looking assessments. First, raters are asked to assess their own actions, rather than the qualities or behaviours of the ratee. Second, the questions refer to extreme performance levels and to single, easily understood concepts such as pay, teamwork, poor performance, and promotion.

Other authors have emphasized how the benefits promised by the performance management movement have not materialized (Grundy 2015; Brodkin 2011). These include: (1) the enhancement of transparency and accountability; (2) unequivocal information about organizational activity; and (3) the enhancement of staff efficiency and performance. Performance management at the organizational level may run up against equity, due process or service quality concerns, actually worsening the problems of transparency and accountability that it intends to resolve. Information produced by performance management systems can be ambiguous, especially when referring to outcomes, as it is often the result of influences besides organizational activity. Finally, organizational efficiency increase may erode staff morale by increasing job insecurity due to missing performance targets, and adding undue administrative burdens of reporting requirements.

Big, small, open data and the impact on performance management

A recent and relevant factor is the sheer volume of data, which public administrations can use in new ways that often reach beyond the conventional definition of performance measurement. Local governments, in particular, are using this information to understand and work within their fiscal constraints and meet citizens' needs. Examples include the following (Goldsmith 2015; Peters 2015):

- In Boston, Uber is sharing a massive and anonymous volume of data about rides to help the city plan for better transportation. Boston's Chief Information Officer uses how long it takes to get between different neighbourhoods and to make decisions on growth, development, and changes to the transportation system, such as how the city might redesign roads or plan for new housing.
- Boston also uses a mobile app, called Street Bump, to help detect potholes using the accelerometers built into mobile phones.
- The New York City Fire Department collects information from various city departments about building characteristics, such as construction material, fireproofing, height, the date of construction, and the last inspection date to prioritize buildings for inspections.
- Detroit collects information about response times, medical emergencies, and calls for assistance and other matters from the Fire Department, computer-aided dispatch, 911 dispatch, and a geographic information system (GIS) through FireView Dashboard, a real-time tracking system. Budget cuts have forced the department to temporarily shut down some fire stations on a rolling basis to save on overtime costs, but the city had little information about how the brownouts would affect response times. Now City officials use the information to allocate resources for the Fire Department, estimate response times, and plan community outreach.

Small data as well as big data can be valuable for public management. The *Economist* (2015a) highlighted the improved treatments and outcomes deriving from health data that do not come from big databases on genomics, population health and treatment but from modest amounts of information from an individual patient. Relatively small groups of patients with chronic conditions account for a disproportionate share of health costs, so being able to monitor and receive data from patients in real time holds the promise of significant financial benefits for hospitals and health funders. Many personal monitoring devices now transmit data via the patient's smartphone.

The use of such data by public administrations is changing the way performance management occurs. Decision makers find cross-agency and cross-sector data more useful than the traditional statistics produced by single departments. Such data are also available in real time and are future-oriented, allowing public managers to be more responsive and efficient and to anticipate outcomes. Finally, such data are increasingly becoming open, which means that citizens and advocacy groups may use them as well.

Conclusion

The future of performance management will depend on the extent to which it will be able to adapt to address emerging trends, including: critiques of its use for performance improvement, the recent explosion in the availability of data, and the shift of public management from competition to collaboration.

The many negative effects of performance management are not a reason to abandon performance management systems; rather, they suggest that performance should be governed rather than simply measured. Indeed, often research that concludes performance management is ineffective is just reporting the simple collection of data which "might (or might not) be related to performance – to some public purpose that the organization might (or might not) be trying to achieve" (Behn 2014). As Mintzberg (2015) points out: "Measuring as a replacement for managing has done enormous damage."

The last global financial and economic crisis, which has passed in some countries and is still taking place in others, has multiple effects on performance management. It strengthens the pressure on public managers to maintain the same levels of performance with decreasing resources, thus increasing their need to rely on data to guide cutback decisions. Meanwhile, fewer resources are dedicated to implementing and developing performance management systems. A different type of performance management is needed, as policy makers need a tool that helps them centralize and control expenditures, rather than decentralize.[2]

An example of how data can help decision-makers in times of crisis is the case of cities' response to homelessness (Economist 2015b). Housing subsidies and services are often doled out on a first-come, first-served basis, regardless of need. With waiting times measured in years, and little co-ordination between agencies, the homeless who are best served tend to be the easiest to treat. The Housing First project provides homeless people in the most perilous circumstances with homes up front, and then delivers the support these people need – such as drug rehabilitation or job training – to help them stay there, rather than using expensive services such as jails and emergency rooms. But such savings are possible only if cities can identify and prioritize those who need the most help. A new web-based tool designed by Community Solutions and Palantir Technologies, called Homelink, helps cities to collect data about individual homeless clients, such as income, medical history and substance-abuse problems, and then assign a severity score. The results are gathered in a centralized database for each city, which participating agencies can access and update. An algorithm then matches homeless people with the services available, targeting the neediest clients with the most immediate help.

As public sectors across the world are abandoning competition-based management in favour of collaborative arrangements, such as networks and co-production, performance management systems need to respond to the need of evaluating and managing collaborative performance.

Notes

1   The most renowned include: 1) World Bank's Governance Indicators, which purport to assess state capacity through six composite indexes: voice and accountability, government effectiveness, regulatory quality, political stability and absence of violence, rule of law, and control of corruption, since 1996: www.govindicators.org/ 2) World Bank's Doing Business ranking, since 2003: www.doingbusiness. org/ 3) OECD's more recent Government at a Glance project, a dashboard of key indicators of public sector performance. since 2009: www.oecd.org/gov/govataglance.htm.
2   For instance, a comparison of the 2012 and 2007 OECD surveys of budget practices shows less reliance on performance information in budget negotiations between central agencies and line ministries (Schick 2013).

References

Alawattage, C., Hopper T., & Wickramasinghe D., Management accounting in less developed countries, *Journal of Accounting & Organizational Change*, 3, 3 (2007), Special Issue.

Barry, L., Garr, S., & Liakopoulos, A., Performance management is broken: replace "rank and yank" with coaching and development. *Global Human Capital Trends 2014: Engaging the 21st-Century Workforce* (London: Deloitte Development LLC: 2014): 45–52.

Behn, R.D., *What Performance Management Is and Is Not*, 12, 1 (Bob Behn's Public Management Report: 2014). Retrieved from www.hks.harvard.edu/thebehnreport.

Behn, R.D., *Measurement, Management, and Leadership*, 11, 3 (Bob Behn's Public Management Report: 2013). Retrieved from www.hks.harvard.edu/thebehnreport/All%20Issues/BehnReport November2013.pdf.

Behn, R.D., *The Data Don't Speak for Themselves*, 6, 7 (Bob Behn's Public Management Report: 2009). Retrieved from www.hks.harvard.edu/thebehnreport.

Behn, R.D., Why Measure Performance? Different Purposes Require Different Measures. *Public Administration Review*, 63, 5 (2003): 588–606.

Bouckaert, G., & Halligan, J., *Managing Performance: International Comparisons* (London: Routledge: 2008).

Bourdeaux, C., & Chikoto, G., Legislative influences on performance management reform. *Public Administration Review*, 68, 2 (2008): 253–265.

Bovaird, T., The political economy of performance measurement. In A. Halchmi & G. Bouckaert (eds), *Organizational Performance and Measurement in the Public Sector: Toward Service, Effort and Accomplishment Reporting.* (Westport, CT: Quorum Books: 1996): 145–165.

Bozeman, B., *All Organizations Are Public: Bridging Public and Private Organizational Theories* (San Francisco: Jossey-Bass: 1987).

Brodkin, E., Policy work: street-level organizations under new managerialism. *Journal of Public Administration Research and Theory*, 21, 1 (2011): 253–277.

de Lancer, J.P., & Holzer, M., Promoting the utilization of performance measures in public organizations: an empirical study of factors affecting adoption and implementation. *Public Administration Review*, 61, 6 (2001): 693–708.

Economist, The. Bedside manners: small data from patients at home will mean big cost savings. May 30, 2015a. www.economist.com/news/business/21652327-small-data-patients-home-will-mean-big-cost-savings-bedside-manners.

Economist, The. Data and homelessness: just like Airbnb. January 6, 2015b. www.economist.com/blogs/democracyinamerica/2015/01/data-and-homelessness.

Fukuyama, F., What is governance? *Governance*, 26, 3 (2013): 347–368.

Goldsmith, S., *Moving Cities Beyond Performance Measurement* (Pew Charitable Trusts: February 4, 2015). Retrieved from www.pewtrusts.org/en/research-and-analysis/analysis/2015/02/04/moving-cities-beyond-performance-measurement.

Grundy, J., Performance measurement in Canadian employment service delivery: 1996–2000. *Canadian Public Administration*, 58, 1 (2015): 161–182.

Hood, C., The risk game and the blame game. *Government and Opposition*, 31, 1 (2002): 15–37.

Imperial, M.T., "Collaboration and performance measurement: lessons from three watershed governance efforts." In J. M. Kamensky & A. Morales (eds), *Managing for Results* (Lanham, MD: Rowman & Littlefield Publishers, Inc. 2005): 379–424.

Kroll, A., Drivers of performance information use: systematic literature review and directions for future research. *Public Performance & Management Review*, 38, 3 (2015): 459–486.

Kroll, A., Explaining the use of performance information by public managers: a planned-behavior approach, *American Review of Public Administration* (2013), DOI: 10.1177/0275074013486180.

Hvidman, U., & Andersen, S.C., Impact of performance management in public and private organizations. *Journal of Public Administration Research and Theory*, 24, 1 (2014): 35–58.

Lee, J.W., Rainey, H.G., Chun, Y.H., Of politics and purpose: political salience and goal ambiguity of US federal agencies. *Public Administration*, 87, 3 (2009): 457–484.

Mahler, J., The Fragile Success of School Reform in the Bronx. *New York Times Magazine*. April 6, 2011. www.nytimes.com/2011/04/10/magazine/mag-10School-t.html?_r=0.

Melkers, J., & Willoughby, K., Models of performance-measurement use in local governments: understanding budgeting, communication, and lasting effects. *Public Administration Review*, 65, 2 (2005): 180–190.

Miller, G., Hildreth, B., & Rabin, J., *Performance Based Budgeting* (Boulder, CO: Westview: 2001).

Mintzberg, H., *The epidemic of managing without soul.* www.mintzberg.org/blog/managing-without-soul. May 21, 2015.

Mintzberg, H., The manager's job: folklore and fact. *Harvard Business Review*, 53, 4 (1975): 49–61.

Moore, M. H., *Creating public value: strategic management in government* (Cambridge, MA: Harvard University Press: 1995).

Moynihan, D.P., *The dynamics of performance management: Constructing information and reform* (Gerogetown: Georgetown University Press: 2008).

Moynihan, D., & Lavertu, S., Does involvement in performance management routines encourage performance information use? Evaluating GPRA and PART. *Public Administration Review*, 72, 4 (2012): 592–602.

Moynihan, D.P., & Pandey, S.K., The big question for performance management: why do managers use performance information? *Journal of Public Administration Research and Theory*, 20, 4 (2010): 849–866.

Moynihan, D.P., & Pandey, S.K., Creating desirable organizational characteristics: How organizations create a focus on results and managerial authority. Paper presented at the eighth International Research Symposium on Public Management, Budapest, Hungary, 2004.

Perry, J.L., & Rainey H.G., The public–private distinction in organization theory: A critique and research strategy. *Academy of Management Review* 13.2 (1988): 182–201.

Peters, A., Boston is using Uber data to plan better urban transportation (Co.Exist: January 16, 2015). www.fastcoexist.com/3040964/boston-is-using-uber-data-to-plan-better-urban-transportation.

Poister, T.H., The future of strategic planning in the public sector: Linking strategic management and performance. *Public Administration Review* 70.s1 (2010): s246–s254.

Poister, T.H., Aristigueta, M.P., & Hall, J.L., *Managing and Measuring Performance in Public and Nonprofit Organizations: An Integrated Approach* (San Francisco: Jossey-Bass, 2nd ed.: 2015).

Poister, T.H, Pasha, O.Q., and Hamilton Edwards, L., Does performance management lead to better outcomes? Evidence from the U.S. public transit industry, *Public Administration Review*, 73, 4 (2013): 625–636, DOI: 10.1111/puar.12076.

Pollitt, C., Performance Information for democracy: the missing link? *Evaluation*, 12, 1 (2006): 38–55.

Radin, B., *Challenging the Performance Movement: Accountability, Complexity, and Democratic Values* (Washington, DC: Georgetown University Press: 2006).

Rainey, H.G., Public management: recent research on the political context and managerial roles, structures, and behaviors. *Journal of Management* 15.2 (1989): 229–250.

Rainey, H.G., Backoff, R.W., & Levine, C.H., Comparing public and private organizations. *Public Administration Review* (1976): 233–244.

Schick, A., *The Metamorphoses of Performance Budgeting,* Annual OECD Meeting of Senior Budget Officials, Paris, 3–4 June 2013.

Smith, P., On the unintended consequences of publishing performance data in the public sector. *International Journal of Public Administration*, 18, 2–3 (1995): 277–310.

Taylor, J., Strengthening the link between performance measurement and decision making. *Public Administration*, 87, 4 (2009): 853–871.

Tillema, S., Putu, N., Mimba, S.H., & Van Helden, G.J., Understanding the changing role of public sector performance measurement in less developed countries. *Public Administration and Development*, 30 (2010): 203–214. DOI: 10.1002/pad.561.

Vakkuri, J. & Meklin P., Ambiguity in performance measurement: a theoretical approach to organisational uses of performance measurement. *Financial Accountability & Management*, 22, 3 (2006): 235–250.

Van de Walle, S., & Bouckaert, G., Comparing measures of citizen trust and user satisfaction as indicators of good governance: difficulties in linking trust and satisfaction indicators. *International Review of Administrative Sciences*, 69, 3 (2003): 329–344.

Van Dooren, W., *Performance Measurement in the Flemish Public Sector: A Supply and Demand Approach.* Leuven, Belgium: Doctoral Dissertation (Katholieke Universiteit, Faculty of Social Science: 2006).

Van Dooren, W., Bouckaert, G., & Halligan, J., *Performance Management in the Public Sector* (Routledge 2010).

Van Helden, J.G., Johnsen, Å., & Vakkuri, J., The life-cycle approach to performance management: implications for public management and evaluation. *Evaluation* 18, 2 (2012): 159–175.

27

PUBLIC POLICIES PROMOTING PERFORMANCE MANAGEMENT

Australia and the United States

Joshua L. Osowski and Sanjay K. Pandey

Introduction

Drawing upon Frederick Mosher's characterization of trends and values dominating public administration in different historical time periods, Moynihan and Pandey (2005) pronounced the beginning of the era of performance management a decade ago. As other reform movements and practices have waned, performance management has become an enduring part of a new global "good government" movement (Pandey et al. 2014; Pandey 2015). In this chapter, our focus is on public policies promoting implementation of performance management at the level of federal/national government. In focusing on public policy initiatives promoting performance management at the federal/national level, we include policy initiatives emanating from the legislative as well as executive branches of national/federal government.

In order to provide continuity and context to our review of national policies promoting performance management, we chose the United States and Australia. Both of these countries have a long and sustained record of promoting performance management policy at the national level, despite changes in ideology and governmental leadership over the years. These two countries also operate under different styles of governance, Australia uses a Westminster-style parliamentary system and the United States uses a presidential one. In Figure 27.1 below, we summarize key historical events that promoted performance management in Australia and the US.

By no means do we seek to advance a claim that the first policies shown in Figure 27.1 represent the very first and definitive national-level performance management policy actions in the two countries. We recognize that the US Federal government has seen the use of different performance management measures over the past 60 years (Hatry 2013). These individual measures do not, however, equate to a systemic and institutional commitment to performance management.

In the sections that follow we will more closely examine the performance policies just described, and look for the lessons we can draw from them. In order to differentiate periods of time, the policies will be grouped together by who was the Prime Minister or President when they were enacted. We will begin with Australia and then examine the United States. This will be followed by a comparative assessment, from which lessons are drawn, that will be useful for other national-level governments. It is important to note that in the Australian context, evaluation is at the core of performance management and therefore we include it in discussion of Australian

Figure 27.1 Timeline of Australian and US national performance management policy

performance management efforts. We do not, however, treat program evaluation in the US in a similar manner because it is a large-scale enterprise quite distinct from performance management.

Australian performance policy during the Hawke government

Between the two countries, Australia was a first mover. When Bob Hawke became Prime Minister of Australia in 1983, Australia was experiencing a poor economy and tight constraints on their budget (Mackay 2011). In order to deal with this, many changes were made in the way the government operated and among these changes, the government actively sought out evidence-based decision making (Mackay 2011). The first of these initiatives was the 1983 Financial Management Improvement Program (FMIP) whose focus was on results (Hawke 2007). The initial reforms of FMIP did not have requirements for mandatory performance evaluation, so in 1987, it became policy that budgetary spending proposals should include performance measures and procedures for evaluation; however, it was soon realized there were too many inconsistencies in the way evaluations were being conducted and that more rigorous procedures were needed (Mackay 2011). To remedy these issues, in 1988, a formal evaluation strategy was approved that required: (1) all programs to be evaluated on a regular basis (every three to five years) and this information to be used in governmental decision making; (2) managers were to be involved with the evaluation process and use it to improve their performance; and (3) transparency was to be increased by publishing evaluation reports (Mackay 2011). The final results of this evaluation system were quite impressive, and accordingly it has been described as "a model of evidence-based decision making and performance-based budgeting" (Mackay 2011: 41).

Schick (2002) notes that few countries have tried using evaluation as the primary source of performance measurement, but of those that have, Australia stands out because it decentralized decision making and required departments to help determine the performance criteria by which they would be evaluated. This inclusion of upper-level career public servants helped make Australia's evaluation system a success (Schick 2002; Campbell 2001; Keating and Holmes 1990) and evaluation "is a crucial element of the system of managing for results and has a key role in linking program implementation and policy development" (Keating and Holmes 1990: 174). In order to further improve the evaluation process, in 1991 the Department of Finance created a new unit whose focus was to train, give support and provide advice to departments that needed assistance (Mackay 1998).

This evaluation process had its detractors who felt the process was too burdensome and did not allow managers the discretion they needed to be innovative and improve performance. In the next section we will turn to the Howard government, who had just this type of philosophy and examine their attempts at reform.

Australian performance policy during the Howard government

When the Howard government took control in 2007, the economy was booming and the government had budget surpluses, and with less of a need to control spending coupled with a shift in ideology, the emphasis on performance management began to diminish (Mackay 2011). Evaluations began to be seen as a cumbersome process that prevented managers from using their discretion to find innovative solutions to government's problems and by 2008 the evaluation process was abolished and replaced with performance indicators whose focus was on outputs and outcomes (Mackay 2011).

Although a focus on outputs and outcomes is better than just measuring inputs, Campbell (2001) suggests that all three are important and that policy makers must find the right balance of inputs, outputs and outcomes. Another weakness with wholly relying on performance indicators is that though they "can be used to highlight examples of good or bad performance, a major limitation is that they fail to explain the reasons for this performance" (Mackay 2011: 43). In addition to favoring outputs and outcomes, which contained less information, the Howard government also relied on a smaller pool of information when making decisions, and Mackay (2011) states that except for the input from a few trusted advisors, decisions were often made with little regard to discussion and input from others.

The Howard government was responsible for ending two of Hawke's most successful performance management strategies – evaluations and decentralized decision making – and replaced them with initiatives that were arguably inferior (Mackay 2011). Although leaders will often denigrate previous reforms in order to differentiate their efforts as something new and improved, Campbell (2001) urges "that governments in similar situations must do a better job of reassessing the rationales for reforms, taking stock of where previous initiatives have actually taken a system and then specifying the theoretical justifications for continued reforms" (280–281). In the next period of Australian performance policy, we will see a government that recognized the decline in Australia's performance management and was determined to learn from the mistakes made in the past (Mackay 2011).

Australian performance policy during the Rudd government

Prime Minister Rudd was elected in late 2007 and set out to reverse the course of weakened performance management left by the Howard government by reinstating a style of governance that used evidence to determine policy (Mackay 2011). They wasted no time and immediately began reviewing performance management practices (Mackay 2011) and in 2008 they launched Operation Sunlight, whose objective was to increase transparency and improve upon Howard's outcome model by "tightening the outcomes and outputs framework" (Tanner 2008: 2). In 2010 they continued to improve upon the performance management reforms with a policy entitled, "Ahead of the Game", that required agency and department performance to be reviewed every three to five years (Moran 2010). It should be noted that a "review" during this time was not the same as an "evaluation" during the Hawke government. The review was less cumbersome than the evaluation process, but more comprehensive and robust than the performance measures the Howard government relied on (Mackay 2011). In some ways the review was a hybrid between the two, thus demonstrating how the Rudd government was assessing past reforms for their strengths and weaknesses, and then using this information to create better performance policy. In addition to improving performance policy, the Rudd Government wanted more levels of government to use performance management. So in 2008, it began requiring states to submit performance reports for the federal funding they received (Mackay, 2011). These performance reports required states to reach benchmarks based on output and outcome measures. However, Mackay (2011) notes that one weakness with this policy was there were no budgetary consequences if agencies did not meet the goals.

As we have seen, Australia has had some ups and downs in their history with performance management, but even attempts that are unsuccessful can provide insight for future reforms. In the next section we will examine another country, the United States, which has its own unique history with performance management, and from which additional insights can be drawn.

US performance policy during the Clinton administration

Bill Clinton became President in 1993 and there were two important performance management policies that occurred during his administration. The first was the 1993 executive branch initiative titled the National Performance Review (NPR). The NPR's major goals included the downsizing of government, reducing administrative costs and reforming administrative systems (Thompson 2000). This initiative made it clear that the President believed performance management was imperative to governmental success. Without this type of strong leadership, performance management policies cannot take root and succeed (Moynihan and Pandey 2010: 862). Other countries and jurisdictions from around the world that lack strong political leadership and support have not been able to implement a meaningful and lasting performance management agenda (Evans 2005; Behn 2004; Root et al. 2001; Xavier 1998). The second major performance policy during the Clinton presidency occurred later in 1993 when congress passed the Government Performance and Results Act (GPRA). This act required federal agencies to begin: (1) developing strategic plans; (2) creating annual performance plans complete with measurable goals; and (3) providing an annual performance report with actual performance compared to the goals it had set (Heinrich 2002: 713). Though GPRA was successful in getting agencies to begin reporting performance data (Joyce 2011), there is doubt whether this performance data guided decision making in any meaningful way (Moynihan and Lavertu 2012; Joyce 2011). However, what is important is that these initiatives began a process of data gathering that others would build upon. In the next section we examine how George W. Bush would further the cause for performance management.

US performance policy during the G.W. Bush administration

George W. Bush became President in 2001, and despite a change in party and ideology, performance management continued to play a prominent role. President Bush used his leadership to proclaim a need for improved performance management by announcing his 2001 President's Management Agenda (PMA) in his first year of office. According to the PMA document produced by the White House, the agenda was guided by three main principles: (1) a need for citizen-centered approach as opposed to a bureaucracy-centered one; (2) it should be results-oriented; and (3) promote a market-based approach that encourages innovation through competition (Bush 2001). The following year the President announced a new Program Assessment Rating Tool (PART) that rated the effectiveness of government programs and used the information to guide budgetary decision making. In this aspect PART was different than its predecessors because it linked a program's performance to actual budgetary consequences, thus strongly motivating agencies to use performance management. Though critics have argued that PART scores were not used as extensively as they could have been (Gilmour and Lewis 2006) there is still agreement that it was an improvement on GPRA. According to Breul and Kamensky (2008) PART was an improvement on GRPA because "PART renders a *judgment* about whether programs are effective" and it "enables decision makers to attach budgetary and management *consequences* to those programs that cannot demonstrate their effectiveness" (1018, italics in original). PART also differed from GPRA in another key aspect: it was more transparent and it posted the assessment scores of over 1,000 governmental programs on its website, ExpectMore.gov (Kamensky 2011). This transparency gave citizens and interest groups almost unprecedented access to information about government decision making, which we will see in the next section the Obama administration continue and further strengthen.

US performance policy during the Obama administration

Unlike his predecessors, President Obama did not start out with a formally written mandate to reform performance management, as had Clinton with NPR or Bush with PMA. However, just because the declaration was not made does not mean that improvements to performance management were not being made, resulting in some describing Obama's strategy as a "stealth revolution" (Kettl 2009: 40). The Obama administration has used a variety of inclusionary methods to promote their performance agenda (Joyce 2011; Kettl 2009). Inclusion has been encouraged by having agencies involved with determining the details of their performance goals (Joyce 2011). Another inclusionary practice, which helped government work outside of normal routines has been through Obama's expanded use of "czars" (Kettl 2009). These czars were given a responsibility to not only work across agency lines but to work beyond bureaucratic lines, in what Kettl (2009) describes as "post-bureaucratic, with players across many federal agencies, multiple levels of government, public-private-nonprofit sectors, and international boundaries" (41). The Obama administration was also committed to increasing transparency, as evidenced by the vast amount of performance information that was posted on the American Recovery Act Website as well as the creation of performance.gov (Kamensky 2011). Kamensky (2011) suggests that increased transparency combined with citizen involvement can lead to useful "mash-ups" (145), and these mash-ups could be "apps" that connect citizens to governmental information or services. Another important policy reform was the GPRA Modernization act of 2010 that resulted in: (1) increased performance reporting frequency; (2) a reduction in the overall number of goals; and (3) setting a small number of high-priority and cross-agency goals (Moynihan and Lavertu 2012; Kamensky 2011). Though each of these changes in and of themselves are not monumental, they are incrementally substantial improvements from "more than 15 years of experience – documented through numerous GAO reports" (Kamensky 2011: 141).

Comparative assessment: drawing lessons for other national-level governments

Whereas the performance management policies of Australia and the United States have significant differences, there are similarities in implementation of policies to promote performance management at the federal/national level as well. These similarities also tend to suggest that there is a rather orderly progression that takes place as national level governments grapple with (1) initiating, then (2) incorporating, and (3) improving the performance management process. These performance policy and practices commonalities can be summarized as follows:

1   Initiating
   - The need for leadership to promote performance management.
   - Creating a requirement to begin performance reporting.
2   Incorporating
   - Tying performance levels to consequences.
   - Use of inclusion in goal setting and decentralized decision making.
   - Increasing transparency by making performance reports available to the public.
3   Improving
   - Analyzing and learning from past performance policies and practices.
   - A sustained effort to improve performance methods.

These three stages contain lessons that Australia and the US learned during their now several decades experience with performance policy and practice, and since these experiences can be useful in other national contexts as well, we review each in more detail.

Initiating: Before a nation can implement performance management, it must begin by initiating it. This takes place in several ways: first, a prominent governmental leader must actively promote performance management and second, a policy requiring government administrators to begin reporting performance measures must be enacted. Both Australia and the US initiated performance management with the use of strong leadership. In the US this first took place in 1993 when President Clinton announced his executive initiative for a National Performance Review. Similarly, the Hawke government used its leadership to promote a strategy to improve governmental performance with its 1983 Financial Management Improvement Program (Hawke 2007). No governmental reform can occur without leaders being committed to push an agenda forward, and reforms for performance management are no different. This commitment is not easy because performance management has costs associated with it, and these costs cause dilemmas for a government (Bouckaert and Peters 2002). In order to overcome these dilemmas, it takes strong commitment from leadership (Moynihan and Pandey 2010; de Waal 2007; Root et al. 2001).

In addition to strong leadership to initiate performance management, there also needs to be a mandate to begin collecting and reporting performance measures. In Australia, the FMIP served this purpose when it stated that budget spending proposals should include performance measures and procedures for evaluation (Mackay 2011). In the United States GPRA, updated in 2010 with the GPRA modernization act, fulfilled this role by requiring agencies to create performance plans and reports (Heinrich 2002). Both of these policies are credited for increasing the use of data gathering, which is an important first step in performance management. However, GPRA and FMIP in the long run both failed to procure effective performance measures (Joyce 2011; Hawke 2007). Despite these failures, what is important for performance management is that it was initiated, and modifications to policy and practice would continue in the incorporating stage. Indeed, success of performance management is assured in the "trenches" with imaginative leaders at the organizational level making small but consequential decisions that are feasible given administrative and political constraints (see Harris 2015 for an in-depth first-person account).

Incorporating: After performance management has been initiated, the next stage requires that a government fully incorporate performance management into its very fabric, this means that decisions, evaluations and the dialogue about government all use performance as an essential criteria (Moynihan and Lavertu 2012). In Australia and the US, performance management was incorporated by first, creating policy that connected budgetary consequences to levels of performance, second, increased administrative buy-in through techniques of inclusion in goal setting and decentralized decision making, and third, by increasing transparency of performance reports to the public. Although FMIP and GPRA initiated performance management in their respective countries, these policies had weak requirements for usage and little penalty for noncompliance, and performance management was not widely used (Mackay 2011; Gilmour and Lewis 2006). Realizing this weakness, both countries tied real consequences to performance levels in order to increase the use of performance management. Only one year after the FMIP was introduced, the Howard government approved the formal evaluation strategy, which required all programs to be evaluated and this information was used in governmental decision making (Mackay 2011). The US saw similar additional requirements when President Bush implemented PART. This Program Assessment Rating Tool goal was to link a program's performance to actual budgetary consequences (Breul and Kamensky 2008). Both programs used a carrot and stick strategy in order to change behavior and it did lead to an increase in reporting, however, there were still issues with the quality of the reports (Joyce 2011; Mackay 2011).

In order to further increase performance usage and improve the quality of its reports, both Australia and the US realized that in addition to a carrot and stick approach, positive motivational techniques need to be used. This included the use of inclusionary practices in goal setting and decentralized decision making. Hawke's formal evaluation strategy required departments to help determine the performance criteria by which they would be evaluated. This turned out to be very successful because when upper level career public servants are involved and help shape the criteria by which they will be judged, it increased buy-in and commitment to the performance management agenda (Schick 2002; Campbell 2001; Keating and Holmes 1990). President Obama similarly involved government agencies to determine the details of their performance goals (Joyce 2011). The quality of evaluations was also significantly improved in Australia in 1991 because the Hawke government allocated significant resources in training and support for workers (Mackay 1998). Though no equivalent performance training program was found in the US, it is noted here because of the positive impact it had in Australian performance management. The US has also used a unique technique to improve inclusion with its use of "czars" during the Obama administration. These "czars" were tasked to dismantle governmental "silos" by working on issues from a broad performance perspective rather than looking at them from an agency perspective. Prior to this, multiple agencies independently worked on similar priorities, but it was now the "czars'" task to promote inclusion by working not only across agency lines but also beyond bureaucratic ones to include those outside of government (Kettl 2009). These inclusionary practices are more than just a nice ideal, they are also practical, and others have found that top-down reforms often struggle (Moynihan 2012) but programs where details are worked out by rank and file employees tend to be more successful (Thompson 1999). As such, when policy-makers write policy, they should be sure to include mechanisms that mandate inclusion and decentralized decision making.

Another way to incorporate performance management into government is through the use of transparency and publishing performance reports. Australia during the Rudd government took transparency to new levels with its aptly named policy called Operation Sunlight. The amount of performance information available to the public also dramatically increased with the Obama administration's launching of performance.gov (Kamensky 2011). Transparency not only helps agencies to be held accountable but it also increases citizen participation. One way that government can encourage citizen participation is by being transparent and allowing citizens to scrutinize the measures (Heinrich 2007). Citizens and stakeholders can keep politicians and administrators on track when their commitment to performance begins to waiver. It has also been found that citizen support is necessary in order to successfully implement performance management policy (Moynihan and Pandey 2010).

Improving: Although over the years both Australia and the United States have made changes to their methods of performance management, they have remained steadfast in their commitment and now have several decades of experiences from which to draw lessons. Two important lessons include that governments learn from their past successes and failures and second, they have a long term commitment to improve performance methods. With regard to learning from past experience, Prime Minister Rudd examined the strengths and weaknesses of past performance practices, before creating their performance reviews, which was a hybrid of Hawke's evaluations and Rudd's performance measures (Mackay 2011). In the US the GPRA Modernization Act of 2010 was the culmination of lessons learned from over 15 years of experience (Kamensky 2011). Even after a country has had a successful performance management program, continued success is not guaranteed, as evidenced by the Howard's government reversal of evaluations and inclusionary decision making (Mackay 2011). It takes sustained commitment to continually improve performance (de Waal 2007). The length of time that this commitment will be needed should not be underestimated. Schacter (2000) notes the strong influence of history in today's successes, arguing that precursors to performance management go as far back as 100 years ago. Along with commitment, politicians and policy makers must have realistic expectations and understand that progress is going to be incremental and require continual improvement. Though progress may at times seem slow "viewed through the lens of history, these reforms can be seen as part of a general upward trend in attention to performance concerns … each reform taught us things, developed capacity, and made it more likely future reforms would be implemented" (Joyce 2011, 358).

Conclusion

Policies promoting performance management within national governments have been with us for many decades and the numbers continue to increase. This chapter has focused on Australia and the United States because of the relatively long and sustained use of performance management at the national level there. There are common points in the Australian and American experiences that can be useful in other national contexts as well. Both countries used techniques such as performance leadership, tying performance to consequences, inclusion, transparency and continual improvement in order to promote performance management policy and practice. Although these policies and practices at the national level have promise and potential, it is necessary to note that success in performance management depends on long-term commitment. For the sake of completeness, we must also note that national/federal government performance is a complex phenomenon and is dependent on the performance of a variety of other actors such as sub-national governments and the performance of contracted private for-profit as well as nonprofit organizations (Pandey 2010; Brown, Potoski, and Van Slyke 2007).

References

Behn, R. D. 2004. *Performance leadership: 11 better practices that can ratchet up performance*. Washington, DC: IBM Center for the Business of Government.

Bouckaert, G. and B. Guy Peters. 2002. "Performance measurement and management: The Achilles' heel in administrative modernization." *Public Performance & Management Review* 25(4): 359–62.

Breul, J. D. and J. M. Kamensky. 2008. "Federal government reform: lessons from Clinton's 'reinventing government' and Bush's 'management agenda' initiatives." *Public Administration Review* 68 (6): 1009–26.

Brown, T. L., M. Potoski, and D. M. Van Slyke. 2007. "Trust and contract completeness in the public sector." *Local Government Studies* 33 (4): 607–23.

Bush, G. W. 2001. *The President's Management Agenda, Fiscal Year 2002.* Washington, DC: Executive Office of the President.

Campbell, C. 2001. "Juggling inputs, outputs, and outcomes in the search for policy competence: recent experience in Australia." *Governance* 14 (2): 253–82.

de Waal, André A. 2007. "Is performance management applicable in developing countries? The case of a Tanzanian college." *International Journal of Emerging Markets* 2 (1): 69–73.

Evans, G. 2005. "Exporting governance: Lithuania adapts a Canadian policy management model." *Canadian Public Administration* 48 (1): 4–14.

Gilmour, J. B. and D. E. Lewis. 2006. "Does performance budgeting work? An examination of the Office of Management and Budget's PART scores." *Public Administration Review* 66 (5): 742–52.

Harris, S.D. 2015. "Managing for social change: improving Labor Department performance in a partisan era." *West Virginia Law Review* 17: 101–57.

Hatry, H. P. 2013. "Sorting the relationships among performance measurement, program evaluation, and performance management." *New Directions for Evaluation* 2013 (137): 19–32.

Hawke, L. 2007. "Performance budgeting in Australia." *OECD Journal on Budgeting* 7 (3): 133.

Heinrich, C. J. 2007. "Evidence-based policy and performance management challenges and prospects in two parallel movements." *American Review of Public Administration* 37 (3): 255–77.

Heinrich, C. J. 2002. "Outcomes-based performance management in the public sector: implications for government accountability and effectiveness." *Public Administration Review* 62 (6): 712–25.

Joyce, P. G. 2011. "The Obama administration and PBB: building on the legacy of federal performance-informed budgeting?" *Public Administration Review* 71 (3): 356–67.

Kamensky, J. M. 2011. "The Obama performance approach." *Public Performance & Management Review* 35 (1): 133–48.

Keating, M. and M. Holmes. 1990. "Australia's budgetary and financial management reforms." *Governance* 3 (2): 168–85.

Kettl, D. F. 2009. "Obama's stealth revolution: quietly reshaping the way government works." *Public Manager* 38 (4): 39.

Mackay, K. 2011. "The performance framework of the Australian government, 1987 to 2011." *OECD Journal on Budgeting* 11 (3): 1–8.

Mackay, K. 1998. *The Development of Australia's Evaluation System.* World Bank, Operations Evaluation Department.

Moran, T. 2010 *Ahead of the Game: Blueprint for the Reform of Australian Government Administration.* Canberra: Australian Public Service Commission.

Moynihan, D. P. and S. Lavertu. 2012. "Does involvement in performance management routines encourage performance information use? Evaluating GPRA and PART." *Public Administration Review* 72 (4): 592–02.

Moynihan, D. P. and S. K. Pandey. 2010. "The big question for performance management: why do managers use performance information?" *Journal of Public Administration Research and Theory* 20 (4): 849–66.

Moynihan, D. P. and S. K. Pandey. 2005. "Testing how management matters in an era of government by performance management." *Journal of Public Administration Research and Theory* 15 (3): 421–39.

Pandey, S. K. 2015. "Performance information use: making progress but a long way to go." *Public Performance & Management Review* 39(1): 1–6.

Pandey, S. K. 2010. "Cutback management and the paradox of publicness." *Public Administration Review* 70 (4): 564–71.

Pandey, S. K., Y. Dwivedi, M. Shareef, and V. Kumar. 2014. "Introduction: markets and Public Administration". In *Public Administration Reformation: Market Demand from Public Organizations*, edited by Dwivedi, Y. K., M. A. Shareef, S. K. Pandey, and V. Kumar. Routledge/Taylor and Francis.

Root, H. L., G. Hodgson, and G. Vaughan-Jones. 2001. "Public administration reform in Sri Lanka." *International Journal of Public Administration* 24 (12): 1357–378.

Schacter, M. 2000. *Public sector reform in developing countries: Issues, lessons and future directions.* Institute on Governance.

Schick, A. 2002. "Does budgeting have a future?" *OECD Journal on Budgeting* 2 (2): 7–8.

Tanner, L. 2008. *Operation Sunlight: Enhancing Budget Transparency.* Canberra: Australian Government.

Thompson, J. R. 2000. "Reinvention as reform: assessing the National Performance Review." *Public Administration Review* 60 (6): 508–21.

Thompson, J. R. 1999. "Devising administrative reform that works: The example of the reinvention lab program." *Public Administration Review* 59 (4): 283–92.

Xavier, J. A. 1998. "Budget reform in Malaysia and Australia compared." *Public Budgeting & Finance* 18 (1): 99–118.

28

THE ROLE OF POLICY CAPACITY IN POLICY SUCCESS AND FAILURE

M. Ramesh and Michael Howlett

Introduction: policy capacity as a prerequisite of good governance

Efforts at policy reform have been omnipresent in many developed and developing countries over the past several decades. Many of these efforts have featured waves of management reforms and administrative re-structuring, privatizations, de-regulation, re-regulation and the like (Ramesh and Howlett 2006). These types of reforms can be characterized as efforts to shift governance styles between different modes of governing (Treib et al. 2007). Initially, for example, the sentiment behind many reform efforts and coalitions in the 1980s and 1990s favoured transitions from government service delivery and regulation to more market-based types of governance regimes. Similarly in more recent years the tilt has shifted towards transitions from hierarchical and market forms of governance to more network-oriented governance relationships (Lange et al. 2013; Weber, Driessen, and Runharr 2011; Lowndes and Skelcher 1998).

Even more recent efforts at reform in many countries and sectors have sought to correct for or reverse excesses in this earlier era of "de-governmentalization", often introducing hybrid elements into existing governance modes (Ramesh and Fritzen 2009; Ramesh and Howlett 2006). Many policy sectors in many countries - from health to education and elsewhere - are now "hybrids" of "metagovernance" styles (Meuleman 2010). That is, they feature elements of either or both hierarchical approaches – regulation, bureaucratic oversight and service delivery – as well as both market- and network-based hierarchical and non-hierarchical approaches such as markets, voluntary organizations, and, increasingly, co-production (Pestoff 2012, 2006; Brandsen and Pestoff 2006, Pestoff et al. 2006).

Not all of these reforms have been successful (Ling 2002). Many proponents, for example, claim "collaborative governance" combines the best of both government- and market-based arrangements by bringing together key public and private actors in a constructive and inexpensive way (Rhodes 1997). This claim is an article of faith which has little direct evidence supporting it (see Adger and Jordan 2009; Howlett Rayner, and Tollefson 2009, Hysing 2009; Kjær 2004; Van Kersbergen and Van Waarden 2004). That is, it is entirely possible that network governance combines and indeed compounds the ill effects of both governments and markets rather than improves upon them, and this is a subject area requiring further empirical examination (Tunzelmann 2010).

Whether and how well such different modes of governance perform, we argue, is based in large part on their capacity requirements or pre-conditions (Howlett 2009; Howlett and Ramesh 2015). That is, each form of governance requires a high level of state and actor capacity in order to function effectively (Bullock et al. 2001). Whether such capacity exists and how it is mobilized is a significant but little understood factor affecting the effectiveness and efficiency of any single governance mode (Canadian Government 1996).

In order to shed light on this issue, in this chapter we briefly revisit the concept of governance, derive a model of governance types from it and discuss their policy capacity prerequisites. As the analysis will show, each mode of governance requires a specific type of capacity if it is to be high functioning and match its theoretical optimal potential.

Governance modes in theory and practice: ideal types, hybrid forms, and their performance

Governing is what governments do: controlling the allocation of resources among social actors; providing a set of rules and operating a set of institutions setting out "who gets what, where, when, and how" in society; and managing the symbolic resources that are the basis of legitimacy (Lasswell 1958).

In its broadest sense, "governance" is a term used to describe the mode of government coordination exercised by state actors in their efforts to solve familiar problems of collective action inherent to government and governing (Klijn and Koppenjan 2000; Kooiman 2000, 1993; Majone 1997; Rhodes 1997; de Bruijn and ten Heuvelhof 1995). That is, "governance" is about establishing, promoting and supporting a specific type of relationship between governmental and non-governmental actors in the governing process. In modern capitalist societies this means managing relationships with businesses and civil society organizations also involved in the creation of public value and the delivery of goods and services to citizens (Hall and Soskice 2001).

Governance thus involves the establishment of a basic set of relationships between governments and their citizens. Although early models such as Pierre (2000), for example, distinguished between two only modes – state-centric "old governance" and society-centric "new governance" – and many economists similarly compared and contrasted only two types of "market" and "hierarchical" relationships (Williamson 1975), even with just these three basic sets of actors and relationships governance arrangements can take many shapes (Treib et al. 2007). Other significant modes have been proposed by others such as Peters (1996), Considine and Lewis (1999), Newmann (2001), Kooiman (2003) and Cashore (2002) including types such as community-based "network" governance and pure "private" governance with little if no state involvement and which operate on "network" as opposed to hierarchical or market-based relationships.

As Steurer (2013) suggested, the three basic governance actors can be portrayed as interacting within a set of inter-related spheres of activity generating at least four ideal governance types (see Figure 28.1).

Beyond these "ideal types", however, other studies also identified a range of intermediate or "hybrid" governance modes or styles existing between the two ends of the state-society or state-market spectrums put forward by Pierre and Williamson (Rhodes 2007; Bevir and Rhodes 2003).

Such distinctions proved useful in distinguishing between the principal modes of state-centric governance. However different combinations of government, civil society and businesses exist since different sets of actors can have different "strengths" within each relationship. When variations on the strength of each actor in a governance relationship are included, this stretches to at least a dozen types (see Figure 28.2).

Figure 28.1 Logic of ideal types of governance
Source: Modified from Steurer 2013

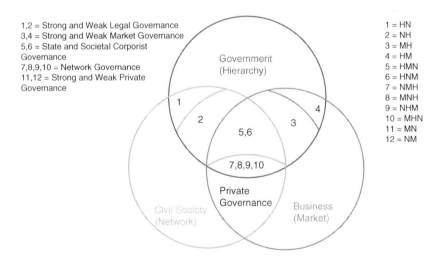

Figure 28.2 Nuanced model of modes of governance including variation by actor strength

This added complexity might appear at first glance to make it difficult to assess the nature of success and failure in each mode and this initial insight is largely correct. However, some simplifications can be made. First, as Cashore (2002) noted, pure non-governmental governance arrangements such as those found in certification and private standard setting schemes are not in the public realm and need not always concern governments and those studying governmental or "public" policy making (see also Cutler et al. 1999). Second, as Capano (2011) argued, in most cases of bilateral or trilateral governance arrangements the presence of hierarchy is overpowering and nuances pertaining to, for example, market and network leadership in bilateral legal and market regimes are less significant than in trilateral arrangements, where governments may be dominated by the presence of both market and network actors. That is, network and corporatist forms of governance modes exist as hybrids which are based on different mixes of coordination principles (hierarchy, market and network) (Meuleman 2010).

Even the more extreme horizontal or plurilateral arrangements governance modes, however, need to be "steered" or led towards constructive, positive coordination. That is, the hierarchical government role in any governance arrangement may vary considerably, and change, but remains a core determinant and element of governance, rather than something existing in opposition to or outside of it. Government has the inescapable task of defining what governance is, or can be, and may choose to allow a higher degree of freedom to other policy actors with regard to the goals to be pursued and the means to be employed (Capano 2011). The policy capacity of a government is hence a key indicator and requisite of governance and administrative success.

Governance modes and their requisites: defining actor capabilities and competences

"Policy Capacity" in this sense describes the preconditions a government requires in order to make sound policy choices and implement them effectively in achieving its potential to steer a governance mode. This is a broader definition than the widely used one offered by Painter and Pierre (2006) who focus their attention on capacity for policy formulation rather than both formulation and implementation in their definition of the term as: "the ability to marshal the necessary resources to make intelligent collective choices, in particular to set strategic directions, for the allocation of scarce resources to public ends". Theirs is an unduly restrictive definition, as policy capacity is not only about the ability to formulate and make policy choices but also to implement them and evaluate their performance (Wu et al. 2015).

At heart, policy capacity is a function of the interaction of three levels of competences or skills which affect the ability of governments in their relationships with other governance actors: analytical ones which allow policy alternatives to be effectively generated and investigated; managerial ones which allow state resources to be effectively brought to bear on policy issues; and political ones which allow policy makers and managers the room to manoeuvre and support required to develop and implement their ideas, programs and plans (Rotberg 2014; Fukuyama 2013; Gleeson et al. 2011; Wu et al. 2010; Gleeson et al. 2009; Tiernan and Wanna 2006; Wu et al. 2015).

These skills or competences are crucial to policy and governance success. However, they also rely on their availability and the availability of adequate resources to allow them to be mobilized. Resources or capabilities must exist at the individual level to allow individual policy workers (Colebatch et al. 2011; Colebatch 2006) and managers (Howlett and Walker 2012) to participate in and contribute to designing, deploying, and evaluating policies. It includes not only their ability to analyze but also to learn and adapt to changes as necessary. Resources must also be available at the level of the organization. These are aspects of the structure and make-up of policy-relevant organizations that affect their members' ability to perform policy functions come. Organizational features that unduly circumscribe individual decision capabilities or morale among policy workers, for example, can undermine an agency's ability to acquit its functions. The organizational conditions most relevant to policy capacity include those related to information, management, and political support (Gleeson et al. 2011; Tiernan and Wanna 2006). Finally, system level capabilities include the level of support and trust a public agency enjoys from its political masters and from the society at large (Blind 2006). Such factors are a critical determinant of organizational capabilities and thus of public managers' capability to perform their policy functions. Political support for both from both above and below are vital

Table 28.1 Dimensions and levels of policy capacity

Resource Level Skill Dimension	Individual Capabilities	Organizational Capabilities	System Capabilities
Analytical Competences	*Policy Analytical Capacity* Knowledge of policy substance and analytical techniques and communication skills	*Organizational Information Capacities* Storing and Disseminating Information on client need; service utilization; Budgeting, Human Resource management. E-services	*Knowledge System Capacity* Presence of high quality educational and training institutions and opportunities for knowledge generation, mobilization and use
Managerial Competences	*Managerial Expertise Capacity* strategic management, leadership, communication, negotiation and conflict resolution, financial management and budgeting	*Administrative Resource Capacity* Funding, staffing, levels of Intra- and inter-agency communication, consultation, and coordination	*Accountability and Responsibility System Capacity* Presence of rule of law and transparent adjudicative and career systems
Political Competences	*Political Acumen Capacity* Understanding of the needs and positions of different stakeholders; judgment of political feasibility; Communication skills	*Organizational Political Capacity* Effective Civil Service bargain. Politicians' support for the agency programmes and projects. Levels of Inter-organisational trust and communication	*Political-Economic System Capacity* Presence of Public Legitimacy and Trust; Adequate fiscal system to fund programs and projects; Access to information

Source: Modeled after Wu et al 2010 and Tiernan and Wanna 2006

because agencies and managers must be considered legitimate in order to access resources from their authorizing institutions and constituencies on a continuing basis, and such resources must also be available for award in the first place (Painter and Pierre 2005; Wu et al. 2015).

The nine basic types of capacity which affect a government's policy role are set out in Table 28.1 above.

The specifics of each of the types are discussed in the section which follows.

Nine specific components of competence and capabilities integral to policy capacity

First, dealing with analytical competences, governments must have the individuals with the ability to acquire and use and internal external knowledge (Ouimet et al. 2010; Cohen and Levinthal 1990) as well as (1) *policy analytical capacity*, which refers to the ability to access and apply technical and scientific knowledge and analytical techniques (Howlett 2009a; Riddell 1998). What governments do, indeed can do, and the likelihood of their success depend critically on their policy analytical skills in diagnosing problems and developing appropriate strategies for addressing them. Evidence-based policy making, for example, requires that agencies have the necessary absorptive capacity at the individual level, which refers to their ability to absorb and process information or evidence in recognizing, formulating, deciding upon, implementing, and evaluating policy. Governments often do not use evidence even when it is available, more due to lack of skills than intention (Grimshaw et al. 2012; Howlett 2009; UK Cabinet Office 1999). The lack of internal capacity in this area cannot be easily offset by appointing external consultants because it requires considerable technical skills even to develop terms of reference for consultants, assess their output, and put them into practice (Howlett and Migone 2013).

Governments must also have the (2) *organizational information capacity* to allow an effective information and policy analysis system, which plays a critical role in effective formulation, implementation, and evaluation of public policies to operate (Craft et al. 2013; Tiernan 2011). Analytical skills are especially important in the context of the present emphasis on evidence-based policy, which requires not only the ability to analyze data but also its availability in a timely and systematic manner (Davies et al. 2000). An effective information system can play a pivotal role in enhancing overall governance and policy capacity if properly designed and implemented. An effective information system for policy development allows finding and sharing information more quickly and provides for re-use of existing information without duplication of efforts. There is often a vast amount of information on policy experiences stored across countless sites in an organization, which can offer insights into the range of policy options available and their real-life consequences. Collating the information and making it accessible to other policy makers brings great benefits to governments at small cost (Kwaterski 2010).

A good system can also accelerate innovation, as users connect and collaborate more easily and frequently, and it can connect governments to people by facilitating popular input into the policy process and the delivery of public services (Moon et al. 2014; Akeroyd 2009). Internally, information technology offers vast potential for improving integration and coordination within the public sector while enhancing the use of other analytical skills (Ambali 2010). Another vital function for which ICT has tremendous potential is maintaining institutional memory within an organization and promoting policy learning. Policy learning and policy emulation are a vital part of the policy making and policy managers need broad understanding of the policy practices and their performance in other countries, agencies, and sectors (May 1999; Huber 1991). Increased emphasis on accountability, transparency, and participatory government has similarly accentuated the importance of information technology and the state of the knowledge system present in a jurisdiction or society (Oh 1997).

At a higher level, the nature of the knowledge system in society or (3) *knowledge system capacity* is also a significant element of overall policy and governance capacity. This refers to the general state of educational and scientific facilities in a society, the availability, speed, and ease of access generally to high-quality information. Although many aspects of this type of capacity may be difficult to change or beyond the scope of individual government organizations and individual actors, they rely upon it implicitly and explicitly in order to perform their own analytical tasks effectively.

Managerial competence is also a high priority if policy capacity is to be enhanced or exercised effectively. At the level of individual managers, (4) *managerial expertise capacity* or their ability to perform key managerial functions such as planning, staffing, budgeting, and directing – is a vital determinant of the government's overall policy capacity (Howlett and Walker 2011; Hicklin and Godwin 2009). In a survey conducted by the National Association of Schools of Public Affairs and Administration (Zhang, Lee, and Yang 2012), city and county managers reported the following as the most important individual competencies and management skills needed in local government):

- communication skills;
- leadership;
- teamwork;
- budgeting and financial management.
- decision-making and problem solving;
- ethics and integrity.

Communication skills in particular must be available in abundance. Internally, organizations must communicate their goals, operational plans, and operating procedures to their employees and, no less importantly, must give the latter a say in shaping them (Kuipers et al. 2013; Matland 1995). Leadership appears high on the ranked list of skills for public managers not only in the above survey but also in similar surveys in Manitoba (2001) and New Zealand (State Services Commission 1999). Research shows that leadership is especially critical if groups are to assume new challenges and devise new strategies for meeting them. Contemporary conceptions of leadership see it less as related to charisma and more about coordinating group dynamics. As a UK Cabinet Office (2001) report observed:

> Research suggests that creating the appropriate climate within a team can account for approximately 30% of the variation in its performance and that the leader has a critical influence on this climate. About 70% of organisational climate is influenced by the styles (or consistent patterns of behaviour) a leader deploys in relating to others within the team.

Groups exist in all organizations at all levels and they function best when there is a commonly defined purpose and roles and expectations are broadly shared by members.

Developments in information technology have facilitated internal communication and augmented some aspects of managerial capacity but also pose new challenges, as mentioned in the preceding section. Modern managers also need a modicum of expertise in budgeting, accounting, and human resource management in order to perform effectively. These are skills that can be imparted by organizations and acquired by managers. There are established training programs of varying quality to train managers in principles of public sector accounting and skills in comprehending the balance sheet, cash flow statement, accrual accounting, and managerial cost accounting.

As was the case with analytical competences, managerial capacity extends beyond individual skill sets, however, to the organizational and system-levels. At the organizational level, managers need (5) *administrative resource capacity* in order to function effectively (Craft et al. 2013; Edwards 2009). This is a well-known aspect of capacity and comprises the funding and staffing levels within which managers work as well as the nature of intra- and inter-agency communication, consultation, and coordination (Peters 2001). At the system level, how well managers perform also depends on (6) *accountability and responsibility system capacity*, that is, how well they are trained and recruited, having career systems which promote competence and the presence of clear rules of law and engagement characteristic of Weberian administrative systems (Howlett 2004).

Necessary skills and competences go beyond the analytical and managerial to the level of political competences. In the public sector beyond leadership and negotiation skills, conflict resolution, and financial and human resources management, a key skill required of policy actors is political knowledge and experience or (7) *policy acumen capacity* (Wu et al. 2011). This is a combination of what Head (2008) calls "political knowledge" and what Tenbensel (2008) termed "practical wisdom". Policy acumen allows policy managers to develop quick judgment on the desirability and feasibility of different policies: what will be considered feasible or acceptable by managers, politicians, stakeholders or the public, what will not, and why. A keen nose for politics not only within but also the broader environment is essential for policy actors to be able to play an effective role in the policy process. Identifying the key actors and understanding their essential interests and ideologies as well as the relationships among them are essential traits of successful public managers. So is an understanding of the political trade-offs necessary for an agreement among contending actors and interests. Understanding of the key stakeholders, their key interests, and their strategies and resources is a key component of the political acumen capacity on the part of individual policy actors.

At the organizational level factors such as the existence of a good working relationship or "public service bargain" between ministers and the public service are central to (8) *organizational political capacity* and effective governance (Salmonsen and Knudsen 2011). In principle, ministers are usually in charge of policy and the bureaucracy in charge of administration, although there is often no such clear distinction between the two roles in practice. Ministers need to remember that their function is to set directions and priorities and should not be involved in day-to-day operation. Involvement in their agencies' routine operational matters is viewed as meddling, which undermines public service's morale. At the same time, all must work within an accountability system in place to ensure that the decisions are carried out and performance is rewarded or punished appropriately. Another vital function of the minister is to publicly defend the bureaucracy against possible criticisms when it is merely carrying out the government's policies. In the real world of public policy, the line between making and implementing policy is thin and porous as both are involved in different capacities in the entire policy process. Yet a defined operational space for each needs to be delineated and accepted.

Communication with stakeholders and the general public is essential for policy and governance effectiveness because it enhances awareness, understanding, and support for government policies. Skillful communication can increase support for government's policy objectives and make the task of governance easier and more effective (CommGAP 2009).To succeed, governments need to define the issue and draw the public into focusing on it and actively contributing to its resolution (Post, Salmon, and Raile 2008). Crucially, two-way communication allows citizens to monitor the states' activities, to enter into dialogue with the state on issues that matter to them, and to influence political outcomes. Strategies and tools for two-way communication with the public include "public interest lobbying, facilitating networks among like-minded political elites, building coalitions, and measuring and informing public opinion" (Haider, Mcloughlin, and Scott 2011).

At the system level, a significant aspect of policy capacity is (9) *political-economic capacity*. This extends beyond the wealth and resources a jurisdiction has to the presence of legitimacy and trust in government on the part of stakeholders and the public. Two-way communication with citizens is a complex web of "interlocking structures, processes, and practices" (World Bank 2011). For meaningful two-way communication to occur, governments need to create a public space where citizens can discuss and debate issues that matter to them with the aim of influencing policy makers. Public discussion and debate in the policy process helps to increase public awareness of the issues and provides a sense of ownership of reform. This requires an active civil society, an independent media, and freedom of speech and assembly (Haider, Mcloughlin, and Scott 2011). Freedom of information or right to information is increasingly viewed as an essential precondition for citizens to participate in the policy process.

Critical capacity deficits as the Achilles heel of governance

In recent years, as pointed out above, the default reform often adopted in practice by government seeking to improve upon hierarchical governance is to turn to a market or network mode of governance. In contrast to networks, the adoption of market governance arrangements, in at least their simplest form, is relatively easy because all the government has to do is reduce its involvement in the provision of goods and services in question with the expectation that the market would fill the void. In all likelihood, however, the resulting market will be both inefficient and inequitable due to the deep market failures that characterize many sectors and activities and prevent markets from functioning efficiently or effectively (Weimer and Vining 2009).

That is, in order to function effectively markets require tough but sensible regulations that are diligently implemented, conditions that are difficult to meet for most governments due to lack of analytical, managerial, and/or political competences or capabilities. Without adequate capacity to regulate the sector, governments may turn to subsidizing users and particularly providers. While such subsidies can improve access and may be politically expedient, they are vulnerable to explosion in costs that will undermine the long-term viability of the regulatory system (Howlett and Ramesh 2015).

In such circumstances, hierarchical governance need not be as dysfunctional as stylized descriptions by proponents of market and network governance may suggest and, in fact, may be superior to the alternatives (Hill and Lynn 2005; Peters 2004). A health care system characterized by government provision and financing supplemented by capped payment, for example, is an effective means of delivering health care at affordable cost (Li et al. 2007). There are of course inherent limitations to command and control, the adverse effects of which may be contained through offsetting measures in some instances. Thus, market competition in standardized services or when consumer preferences are diverse may improve efficiency without compromising access. Similarly, network governance may perform well when dealing with sensitive issues such as aspects of health or education when trust and understanding is paramount (Pestoff et al. 2012). In other instances civil society may not be well enough constructed or resourced to be able to create beneficial network forms of governance (Tunzelmann 2010).

In general, governments would like to enjoy high levels of capability and competence in all aspects of capacity in order to enjoy high capacity to perform their policy functions. Shortcomings in one or a few of the dimensions may be offsets by strengths along other dimensions but no government can expect to be capable if lagging along the key dimensions linked to a governance mode (Tiernan and Wanna 2006). That is, shortfalls in critical capacity areas are especially important to specific modes of governance. Menahem and Stein (2013), for example, have outlined some of the critical capacity issues in the case of network governance relations, identifying the capacity pre-conditions for high-, medium- and low-performing network governance relationships (see Table 28.2).

Networks, for example, will fail when governments encounter capability problems at the organizational level such as a lack of societal leadership, poor associational structures and weak state steering capacities which make adoption of network governance modes problematic. As Keast, Mandell, and Brown (2006) note, at the level of competences, networks also raise severe managerial challenges: "Networks often lack the accountability mechanisms available to the state, they are difficult to steer or control, they are difficult to get agreements on outcomes and actions to be taken, and they can be difficult to understand and determine who is in charge." A recurrent problem faced by efforts to utilize network governance is that the routines, trust, and reciprocity that characterize successful network management (cf. Klijn and Koppenjan 2012) take a long time to emerge. Such relationships cannot simply be established by fiat as in the case

Table 28.2 Capacity links to network governance requirements

	Low-capacity governance networks (LCGN)	Medium-capacity governance networks (MCGN	High-capacity governance networks (HCGN)
Steering the composition of networks: Public actors' ability to select partners	Limited	Medium	High
Steering of goals, objectives, and scope: Public actors' ability to determine goals and scope of network	Challenged	May be compromised	Retained
Professional steering ability: Public actors' ability to retain professional considerations in decision-making	Non-public actors' preferences dominate decision-making regarding service provision	Public actors negotiate with non-public actors over professional considerations in service provision	Public actors' professional considerations have primacy in decision-making regarding service provision
Quality and quantity of resources generated by the network	Low	Medium	High
Overall capacity of the network to generate and activate resources	Low	Medium	High

Source: Menahem and Stein 2013

with hierarchy or emerge spontaneously in response to forces of demand and supply, as in markets. Networks are thus hard to establish where none exist already and a very critical capacity issue for them is "managerial expertise capacity".

Legal systems of governance similarly also require high level of managerial skills in order to avoid diminishing returns with compliance or growing non-compliance with government rules and regulations (May 2005). Thus for example, while there have been advances in identifying the key traits of effective manager, little is known about how to train managers to be effective leaders and this is especially crucial in hierarchical modes of government featuring direct government direction and control. Shortfalls in system-level capabilities are also crucial in this mode of governance. Recruiting and retaining leaders is somewhat difficult for the public sector for a variety of reasons (UK Cabinet Office 2001). The cumbersome accountability mechanisms in place in the public sector promote risk aversion, whereas risk taking is an essential trait of leaders. The culture of blame for failures is another factor that stymies leadership in the public sector (Hood 2010). The unclear division of responsibilities between elected and appointed officials also makes it difficult for the latter to exercise leadership. These barriers need to be comprehended and addressed if leadership is to improve and this element of policy capacity enhanced. Thus for legal modes of governance a critical capacity issue is accountability and responsibility system capacity (Aucoin 1997).

For corporatist regimes, the importance of efficient administrative structures and processes and the vital importance of coordination therein, cannot be overstated. Inspired by conceptions of chain of command in the military, corporatist regimes stress hierarchy, discipline, due process, and clear lines of accountability. Unlike markets where prices seamlessly perform coordination functions, this must be actively promoted in corporatist forms of government and combined with political skills in understanding stakeholder needs and positions (Lehmbruch and Schmitter 1982; Berger 1981). At the level of capabilities, corporatist modes of governance require a great deal of coherence and coordination to function effectively due to horizontal divisions and numerous hierarchical layers found in their bureaucratic structures (Wilensky and Turner 1987; Lehmbruch and Schmitter 1982). Hence for such this mode of governance "organizational political capacity" is critical and a sine qua non of its successful performance.

As for market governance, as already mentioned above, technical knowledge is a critical competence required for its administration. Analytical skills at the level of individual analysts and policy workers are key here and the "policy analytical capacity" of government needs to be especially high to deal with complex quantitative economic and financial issues involved in regulating and steering the sector and preventing crises (Rayner et al. 2013). As early as 1999, the UK Cabinet Office (1999) recommended the appointment of "policy researchers" in government agencies, the establishment of a "Centre for Evidence-Based Policy", and the promotion of "knowledge networks" to gather, analyze, and disseminate policy evidence. It further recommended enhanced training in public policy analysis for both political and bureaucratic officials. However, there is a shortage of people with the required analytical skills in public policy and administration who may be appointed. The recent proliferation of Master's programs in public policy and public administration is a welcome trend, but it will be a long time before these graduates will be sufficiently significant in number to make a noticeable difference to the analytical capacity of governments.

Re-visiting the four dominant governance modes set out in Figure 28.2 with the nine components of capacity set out in Table 28.1, the "critical" capacity element in each mode is set out in Table 28.3.

If critical capacity deficits are not taken into account then any short-term gain enjoyed by pandering to contemporary political preferences are likely to be offset later when the consequences of governance failures and poor institutional design become apparent (Hood 2010; Weaver 1986; Howlett and Ramesh 2015).

Table 28.3 Critical competences and capabilities of governance modes

Mode	Critical Competence Level	Critical Capability Level	Critical Capacity Element
Legal	Managerial	System	Accountability and Responsibility System Capacity
Market	Analytical	Individual	Policy Analytical Capacity
Corporatist	Political	Organizational	Organizational Political Resource Capacity
Network	Managerial	Organizational	Managerial Expertise Capacity

Conclusion: policy capacity deficits and governance performance

Practical experience and ideological predilections have shaped the substance of much of the debate on governance, ranging from preferences for democracy, popular participation and consensus to concerns about budget deficits and public sector inefficiencies in hierarchy-based systems that have often driven preferences for the use of network and market forms of governance. These conditions have fostered a strong preference for shifts towards non-legal governance modes in many countries in recent years, with countries in the Anglo-American tradition usually preferring market forms of governance while others with more corporatist traditions often display a penchant for corporatist and networks hybrids (Meuleman 2009).

Lost in the pursuit of these alternatives, however, is the understanding of whether or not a preferred governance mode can actually address a particular sector's problems. Instead of analyzing and understanding the specifics of the sector in question, the protagonists often simply extrapolate from idealized conceptions of how non-hierarchical modes of governance might work in practice and then apply them across sectors regardless of the contexts in which they are being applied and the capacity prerequisites of the mode of governance in question. Each of these gaps highlights the need for adequate capacity in these critical areas if a governance system is to achieve its potential (Wu et al. 2015). Specific governance modes are prone to specific types of failure caused by specific capacity shortages in critical areas required for that mode to function and this prerequisite of successful governance must be bolstered (Howlett and Ramesh 2015) if not already present in a given policy context.

References

Adger, W. N. and A. J. Jordan. 2009 *Governing Sustainability*. Cambridge: Cambridge University Press.

Akeroyd, J. 2009. "Information Architecture and E-government". *INFuture*, 687–701. http://infoz.ffzg.hr/INFuture/2009/papers/INFuture2009.pdf. Accessed June 6, 2016.

Ambali, A. R. 2010. "E-government in Public Sector: Policy Implications and Recommendations for Policy-makers." *Research Journal of International Studies*, 17: 133–45. www.eurojournals.com/RJIS_17_10.pdf.

Aucoin, P. 1997. "The Design of Public Organizations for the 21st Century: Why Bureaucracy Will Survive in Public Management." *Canadian Public Administration* 40 (2): 290–306.

Berger, S. 1981. *Organizing Interests in Western Europe: Pluralism, Corporatism and the Transformation of Politics*. Cambridge: Cambridge University Press.

Bevir, M. R. and R. A. W. Rhodes. 2003. *Interpreting British Government*. London: Routledge.

Blind, P. K. 2006. *Building Trust In Government In The Twenty-First Century: Review of Literature and Emerging Issues*. Vienna: UNDESA.

Brandsen, T. and V. Pestoff. 2006. "Co-Production, the Third Sector and the Delivery of Public Services." *Public Management Review* 8 (4): 493–501.

Bullock, H., J. Mountford, and R. Stanley. 2001. *Better Policy-Making*. London: Centre for Management and Policy Studies, Cabinet Office, United Kingdom.

Canadian Government. 1996. "Strengthening Our Policy Capacity." Report of the Task Force on Strengthening the Policy Capacity of the Federal Government.

Capano, G. 2011. "Government Continues to Do its Job. A Comparative Study of Governance Shifts in the Higher Education Sector." *Public Administration* 89 (4): 1622–1642.

Cashore, B. 2002. "Legitimacy and the Privatization of Environmental Governance: How Non-State Market-Driven (NSMD) Governance Systems Gain Rule-Making Authority." *Governance* 15 (4): 503–529.

Cohen, W. M. and D. A. Levinthal. 1990. "Absorptive Capacity: A New Perspective on Learning and Innovation." *Administrative Sciences Quarterly* 35 (1): 128–152.

Colebatch, H. K. 2006. "What Work Makes Policy?" *Policy Sciences* 39 (4): 309–321.

Colebatch, H. K., R. Hoppe, and M. Noordegraaf. 2011. *Working for Policy*. Amsterdam: Amsterdam University Press.

CommGAP. 2009. "Communication for Good Governance." Communication for Governance and Accountability Program. Washington, DC: World Bank. www.gsdrc.org/go/display&type=Document&id=3718. Accessed June 6, 2016.

Considine, M. and J. Lewis. 1999. "Governance at Ground Level: The Frontline Bureaucrat in the Age of Markets and Networks." *Public Administration Review* 59 (6): 467–480.

Craft, J., M. Howlett, M. Crawford, and K. McNutt. 2013. "Assessing Policy Capacity for Climate Change Adaptation: Governance Arrangements, Resource Deployments, and Analytical Skills in Canadian Infrastructure Policy Making." *Review of Policy Research* 30 (1): 42–65.

Cutler, A. C., V. Haufler, and T. Porter. 1999. "The Contours and Significance of Private Authority in International Affairs." In *Private Authority and International Affairs*, edited by Cutler, A. C., V. Haufler, and T. Porter, 333–376. Albany: State University of New York.

Davies, H. T., S. M. Nutley, and P. C. Smith. 2000. *What Works? Evidence-Based Policy and Practice in Public Services*. Bristol: Policy Press.

De Bruijn, J. A. and F. Ernst. 1995. "Policy Networks and Governance." In *Institutional Design*, 161–79. Amsterdam: Springer.

Edwards, L. 2009. "Testing the Discourse of Declining Policy Capacity: Rail Policy and the Department of Transport." *Australian Journal of Public Administration* 68 (3): 288–302.

Fukuyama, F. 2013. "What Is Governance?" *Governance* 26 (3): 347–368.

Gleeson, D., D. Legge, and D. O'Neill. 2009. "Evaluating Health Policy Capacity: Learning from International and Australian Experience." *Australia and New Zealand Health Policy* 6 (1): 3.

Gleeson, D., D. Legge, D. O'Neill, and M. Pfeffer. 2011. "Negotiating Tensions in Developing Organizational Policy Capacity: Comparative Lessons to Be Drawn." *Journal of Comparative Policy Analysis: Research and Practice* 13 (3): 237–263.

Grimshaw, J. M., M. P. Eccles, J. N. Lavis, S. J. Hill, and J. E. Squires. 2012. "Knowledge Translation of Research Findings." *Implementation Science* 7 (1): 50.

Haider, H., C. Mcloughlin, and Z. Scott. 2011. *Communication and Governance*. Washington, DC: World Bank.

Hall, P. A. and D. Soskice. 2001. *Varieties of Capitalism: The Institutional Foundations of Comparative Advantage*. Oxford: Oxford University Press.

Head, B. 2008. "Three Lenses of Evidence-Based Policy." *Australian Journal of Public Administration* 67 (1): 1–1.

Hicklin, A., and E. Godwin. 2009. "Agents of Change: The Role of Policy Managers in Public Policy." *Policy Studies Journal* 37 (1): 1320.

Hill, C. J. and Lynn, L. E., 2005. "Is Hierarchical Governance in Decline? Evidence from Empirical Research." *Journal of Public Administration Research and Theory* 15 (2): 173–195.

Hood, C. 2010. *The Blame Game: Spin, Bureaucracy, and Self-Preservation in Government*. Princeton, NJ: Princeton University Press.

Hood, C. 2002. "Control, Bargains and Cheating: The Politics of Public Service Reform." *Journal of Public Administration Research and Theory* 12 (3): 309–332.

Howlett, M. 2009. "Government Communication as a Policy Tool: A Framework for Analysis." *Canadian Political Science Review* 3 (2): 23–27.

Howlett, M. 2004. "Administrative Styles and the Limits of Administrative Reform: A Neo-Institutional Analysis of Administrative Culture." *Canadian Public Administration* 46 (4): 471–494.

Howlett, M. and A. Migone. 2013. "Policy Advice through the Market: The Role of External Consultants in Contemporary Policy Advisory Systems." *Policy & Society* 32 (3): 241–254.

Howlett, Michael and M. Ramesh. "Achilles' Heels of Governance: Critical Capacity Deficits and Their Role in Governance Failures." *Regulation & Governance*, June 1, 2015. doi:10.1111/rego.12091.

Howlett, M., J. Rayner, and C. Tollefson. 2009. "From Government to Governance in Forest Planning? Lesson from the Case of the British Columbia Great Bear Rain Forest Initiative." *Forest Policy and Economics* 11 (5): 383–391.

Howlett, M. and R. M. Walker. 2012. "Public Managers in the Policy Process: More Evidence on the Missing Variable?" *Policy Studies Journal* 40 (2): 211–233.

Huber, G. P. 1991. "Organization Learning: The Contributing Processes and the Literatures." *Organization Science* 2 (1): 88–115.

Hysing, E. 2009. "From Government to Governance? A Comparison of Environmental Governing in Swedish Forestry and Transport." *Governance* 22 (4): 547–572.

Keast, R., M. Mandell, and K. Brown. 2006. "Mixing State, Market and Network Governance Modes: The Role of Government in 'Crowded' Policy Domains." *International Journal of Organization Theory and Behavior* 9 (1): 27–30.

Kjær, A. M. 2004. *Governance*. Cambridge: Polity Press.

Klijn, E. H. and J. Koppenjan. 2012. "Governance Network Theory: Past, Present and Future." *Policy & Politics* 40 (4): 587–06.

Klijn, E. H. and J. Koppenjan. 2000. "Public Management and Policy Networks: Foundations of a Network Approach to Governance." *Public Management* 2 (2): 135–158.

Kooiman, J. 2000. "Societal Governance: Levels, Models, and Orders of Social-Political Interaction." In *Debating Governance*, edited by Pierre, J., 138–66. Oxford: Oxford University Press.

Kooiman, J. 1993. "Governance and Governability: Using Complexity, Dynamics and Diversity." In *Modern Governance*, edited by Kooiman, J., 35–50. London: Sage.

Kuipers, B. S., M. Higgs, W. Kickert, L. Tummers, J. Grandia, and J. Van der Voet. 2014. "The Management of Change in Public Organisations: A Literature Review." *Public Administration* 92 (1): 1–20.

Kwaterski, J. 2010. "Opportunities for Rationalizing the Capacity Development Knowledge Architecture." World Bank Institute and Learning Network for Capacity Development.

Lange, P., P. P. Driessen, A. Sauer, B. Bornemann, and P. Burger. 2013. "Governing towards Sustainability: Conceptualizing Modes of Governance." *Journal of Environmental Policy & Planning* 13 (3): 403–425.

Lasswell, H. 1958. *Politics: Who Gets What, When, How*. New York: Meridian.

Lehmbruch, G. and P. Schmitter. 1982. *Patterns of Corporatist Policy-Making*. London: Sage.

Li, C., X. Yu, J. R. Butler, V. Yiengprugsawan, and M. Yu. 2011. "Moving towards Universal Health Insurance in China: Performance, Issues and Lessons from Thailand." *Social Science & Medicine* 73 (3): 359–366.

Ling, T. 2002. "Delivering Joined Up Government in the UK: Dimensions, Issues and Problems." *Public Administration* 80 (4): 615–642.

Lowndes, V. and C. Skelcher. 1998. "The Dynamics of Multi-Organizational Partnerships: An Analysis of Changing Modes of Governance." *Public Administration* 76 (2): 313–333.

Majone, G. 1997. "From the Positive to the Regulatory State: Causes and Consequences of Changes in the Mode of Governance." *Journal of Public Policy* 17 (2): 139–167.

Manitoba Office of the Provincial Auditor. 2001. *A Review of the Policy Development Capacity within Government Departments*. Manitoba: Office of the Provincial Auditor.

Matland, R. E. 1995. "Synthesizing the Implementation Literature: The Ambiguity-Conflict Model of Policy Implementation." *Journal of Public Administration Research and Theory* 5 (2): 145–174.

May, P. J. 2005. "Regulation and Compliance Motivations: Examining Different Approaches." *Public Administration Review* 65 (1): 31–44.

May, P. J. 1999. "Fostering Policy Learning: A Challenge for Public Administration." *International Review of Public Administration* 4 (1): 21–31.

Menahem, G. and R. Stein. 2013. "High-Capacity and Low-Capacity Governance Networks in Welfare Services Delivery: A Typology and Empirical Examination of the Case of Israeli Municipalities." *Public Administration* 91 (1): 211–231.

Meuleman, L. 2010. *Public Management and the Metagovernance of Hierarchies, Networks and Markets: The Feasibility of Designing and Managing Governance Style Combinations*. Physica-Verlag HD.

Meuleman, L. 2009. "Metagoverning Governance Styles: Increasing the Metagovernors' Toolbox." Paper presented at the panel "Metagoverning Interactive Governance and Policymaking", ECPR General Conference, Potsdam, September 10–12.

Moon, M., J. Lee, and C. Y. Roh. 2014. "The Evolution of Internal IT Applications and E-Government Studies in Public Administration Research Themes and Methods." *Administration & Society* 46 (1): 3–36.

Newmann, J. 2001. *Modernising Governance: New Labour Policy and Society* London/Newbury Park, CA: Sage.

Oh, C. H. 1997. "Explaining the Impact of Policy Information on Policy-Making." *Knowledge and Policy* 10 (3): 22–55.

Ouimet, M., P. O. Bédard, J. Turgeon, J. N. Lavis, F. Gélineau, F. Gagnon, and C. Dallaire. 2010. "Correlates of Consulting Research Evidence among Policy Analysts in Government Ministries: A Cross-Sectional Survey." *Evidence & Policy: A Journal of Research, Debate and Practice* 6 (4): 433–460.

Painter, M. and J. Pierre. 2005. *Challenges to State Policy Capacity: Global Trends and Comparative Perspectives*. London: Palgrave Macmillan.

Pestoff, V. 2006. "Citizens and Co-Production of Welfare Services." *Public Management Review* 8 (4): 503–519.

Pestoff, V., T. Brandsen, and B. Verschuere. 2012. *New Public Governance, the Third Sector and Co-Production.* New York: Routledge.

Pestoff, V., S. P. Osborne, and T. Brandsen. 2006. "Patterns of Co-Production in Public Services." *Public Management Review* 8 (4): 591–595.

Peters, B. G. 2004. "The Search for Coordination and Coherence in Public Policy: Return to the Center?" Unpublished paper. Department of Political Science, University of Pittsburgh.

Peters, B. G. 2001. *The Politics of Bureaucracy.* London; New York: Routledge.

Peters, B. G. 1996. *Governing: Four Emerging Models* Lawrence, KS: University Press of Kansas.

Pierre, J. (ed.). 2000. *Debating Governance: Authority, Steering and Democracy.* Oxford: Oxford University Press.

Post, L. A., T. Salmon, and A. Raile. 2008. "Using Public Will to Secure Political Will." In *Governance Reform Under Real World Conditions,* edited by Odugbemi, S. and T. Jacobson, chapter 7. Washington DC: Communication for Governance and Accountability Program, World Bank. www.gsdrc.org/go/display&type=Document&id=3710. Accessed June 6, 2016.

Ramesh, M. and S. Fritzen. 2009. *Transforming Asian Governance: Rethinking Assumptions, Challenging Practices.* London: Routledge.

Ramesh, M. and M. Howlett. 2006. *Deregulation and Its Discontents: Rewriting the Rules in Asia.* Aldershot: Edward Elgar.

Rayner, J., K. McNutt, and A. Wellstead. 2013. "Dispersed Capacity and Weak Coordination: The Challenge of Climate Change Adaptation in Canada's Forest Policy Sector." *Review of Policy Research* 30 (1): 66–90.

Rhodes, R. A. W. 2007. "Understanding Governance: Ten Years On." *Organization Studies* 28 (8): 1243–1264.

Rhodes, R. A. W. 1997. *Understanding Governance: Policy Networks, Governance, Reflexivity and Accountability.* Buckingham: Open University Press.

Riddell, N. 1998. *Policy Research Capacity in the Federal Government.* Ottawa: Policy Research Initiative.

Rotberg, R. I. 2014. "Good Governance Means Performance and Results." *Governance* 27 (3): 511–518.

Salomonsen, H. H. and T. Knudsen. 2011. "Changes in Public Service Bargains: Ministers and Civil Servants in Denmark." *Public Administration* 89 (3): 1015–1035.

State Services Commission. 1999. "High Fliers: Developing High Performing Policy Units." Occasional Paper No. 22. Wellington: State Services Commission.

Steurer, R. 2013. "Disentangling Governance: A Synoptic View of Regulation by Government, Business and Civil Society." *Policy Sciences* 46 (4): 387–410.

Tenbensel, T. 2008. "The Role of Evidence in Policy: How the Mix Matters." Paper presented at the International Research Society for Public Management, Queensland University of Technology, Brisbane, Australia, March 26–28.

Tiernan, A. 2011. "Advising Australian Federal Governments: Assessing the Evolving Capacity and Role of the Australian Public Service." *Australian Journal of Public Administration* 70 (4): 335–346.

Tiernan, A. and J. Wanna. 2006. "Competence, Capacity, Capability: Towards Conceptual Clarity in the Discourse of Declining Policy Skills." Paper presented at the Govnet International Conference, Australian National University. Canberra: ANU.

Tollefson, C., A. R. Zito, and F. Gale. 2012. "Symposium Overview: Conceptualizing New Governance Arrangements." *Public Administration* 90 (1): 3–8.

Treib, O., H. Bahr, and G. Falkner. 2007. "Modes of governance: Towards a conceptual clarification." *Journal of European Public Policy* 14 (1): 1–20.

Tunzelmann, N. 2010. "Technology and Technology Policy in the Postwar UK: Market Failure or Network Failure?" *Revue d'économie industrielle* 129–30: 237–258.

UK Cabinet Office. 2001. *Strengthening Leadership in the Public Sector.* London: Performance and Innovation Unit, Cabinet Office. www.nursingleadership.org.uk/publications/piu-leadership.pdf. Accessed June 6, 2016.

UK Cabinet Office. 1999. *Professional Policy Making for the Twenty-First Century.* London: Strategic Policy Making Team, Cabinet Office.

Van Kersbergen, K. and F. Van Waarden. 2004. "Governance as a Bridge between Disciplines: Cross-Disciplinary Inspiration Regarding Shifts in Governance and Problems of Governability, Accountability and Legitimacy." *European Journal of Political Research* 43 (2): 143–171.

Weaver, R. K. 1986. "The Politics of Blame Avoidance." *Journal of Public Policy* 6 (4): 371–398.

Weber, M., P. P. J. Driessen, and H. A. C. Runhaar. 2011. "Environmental Noise Policy in the Netherlands: Drivers of and Barriers to Shifts from Government to Governance." *Journal of Environmental Policy and Planning* 13: 119–137.

Weimer, D. L. and A. Vining. 2011. *Policy Analysis: Concepts and Practice.* 5th ed. Upper Saddle River NJ: Pearson Prentice Hall.

Wilensky, H. L. and L. Turner. 1987. *Democratic Corporatism and Policy Linkages: The Interdependence of Industrial, Labor-Market, Incomes, and Social Policies in Eight Countries.* Berkeley, CA: Institute of International Studies.

Williamson, O. E. 1996. *The Mechanisms of Governance.* Oxford: Oxford University Press.

Williamson, O. E. 1975. *Markets and Hierarchies.* New York: Free Press.

World Bank. 2011. "The Contribution of Government Communication Capacity to Achieving Good Governance Outcomes." Brief for Policymakers: Communication for Governance & Accountability Program. Washington, DC: World Bank.

Wu, X. and M. Ramesh. 2014. "Market Imperfections, Government Imperfections, and Policy Mixes: Policy Innovations in Singapore." *Policy Sciences* 47 (3): 1–6.

Wu, X, M. Ramesh, M. Howlett, and S. Fritzen. 2010. *The Public Policy Primer: Managing Public Policy.* London: Routledge.

Wu, X., M. Ramesh, and M. Howlett. "Policy Capacity: A Conceptual Framework for Understanding Policy Competences and Capabilities." *Policy and Society*, Special Issue on The Dynamics of Policy Capacity, 34 (3–4): 165–171. doi:10.1016/j.polsoc.2015.09.001.

Zhang, Y., R. Lee, and K. Yang. 2012. "Knowledge and Skills for Policy-Making: Stories from Local Public Managers in Florida." *Journal of Public Affairs Education* 18 (1): 183–208.

29

THE PROGRAM EVALUATION FUNCTION

Uncertain governance and effects

Robert P. Shepherd

True genius resides in the capacity for evaluation of uncertain, hazardous, and conflicting information.

Winston Churchill[1]

Introduction

To suggest that western bureaucracies are experiencing tectonic shifts in the way they operate would be trite. As this handbook demonstrates, continuous change in epistemological terms is occurring on several fronts with respect to the expectations of public sector performance, responsibilities and characteristics of leadership, ethical management, and what constitutes appropriate and effective oversight of policies, programs, systems and processes. Most importantly, however, questions abound regarding the role of government in light of such changes. The entire ontological framework of the Westminster system is being questioned even by those working within it, as significant proportions of public servants have "mentally opted out" (Hubbard and Paquet 2015: 3). Indeed, citizens are losing confidence in their governments to resolve the complex problems they face, and have also mentally checked out of exercising their franchise to vote, or participate in the governing process.

The Westminster system of bureaucracy itself has come under much attack for failing to keep its promises of flexibility, resilience, and innovation in light of persistent global policy challenges, and shifting citizen expectations for participation. As New Zealand's Fulton Report on civil service reform assessed in the 1960s, "The Home Civil Service today is still fundamentally the product of the nineteenth century philosophy of the Northcote-Trevelyan Report. The tasks it faces are those of the second half of the twentieth century. This is what we have found; it is what we seek to remedy" (New Zealand Committee on the Civil Service 1968: 9). In Canada, civil service reform has been a familiar story with more than 20 reforms since 1867, few of which have led to satisfying change in its ability to wrestle with complex problems, confront its own inefficiencies in management, and engage the potential of its human resources to repair systemic coordinative issues and mediocre performance (Hubbard and Paquet 2015; Savoie 2013; Rhodes, Wanna, and Weller 2009; Dwivedi and Gow 1999).

Situated within this larger reform effort has been the sometimes schizophrenic responsibilities and ineffectual results associated with governmental program evaluation functions. Savoie comes to the damning conclusion in a recent book that "evaluations were very costly and that contributions to the government's policy making and decision making was negligible" (Savoie 2013: 149). Although such a conclusion could be considered severe, it nonetheless raises important questions about the role program evaluation plays in informing policy and decision-making as these relate to budget-making and controlling expenditures, and whether the expectations placed on that function are actually appropriate and realistic.

The chapter begins with the conventional rationales for program evaluation as a function and the promises it has made, followed by a discussion on whether the function is positioned to speak truth, given recent shifts in the role of evidence in policy making. Subsequently, the chapter explores the complexity of contemporary objects of evaluation (evaluands), and whether evaluation is able through methods to understand that complexity. It then gives a comparative review of where the function is situated typically in the Westminster public management as this constrains or facilitates speaking truth to power (Wildavsky 1987). Finally, the chapter concludes with some insights on the potential of the function to inform better policies and programs. Although this potential varies according to country contexts and conditions, there are some common themes that provide a way forward for this beleaguered function.

Program evaluation traditions: the debate

There are two broad traditions regarding the approach to evaluation: the rationalistic and the argumentative. The rationalistic tradition maintains that neutral advice and objective assessment will insulate the evaluation function from political pressures. Under this perspective, evaluation research is applied social research (Alkin 2004: 127). As an input to decision-making, it consists of the application of various social research methods to provide objective, credible and reliable information to support decisions regarding the design of programs, and assessing the effectiveness and efficiency of those programs. This view is consistent with Rossi and Freeman's proposition that "evaluation is the systematic collection and analysis of evidence on the outcomes of programs to make judgments about their relevance, performance and alternative ways to deliver them or to achieve the same results" (World Bank 2014; Rossi 2004: 4). This perspective of evaluation is also consistent with several country understandings as stated in centralized policies, including that of Canada's "Evaluation Policy" (Canada Treasury Board Secretariat 2009). At the root of each of these definitions is the idea that evaluation serves to understand whether policies and programs are actually delivering the effects expected to solve a defined public problem.

Conversely, the argumentative tradition suggests that evaluation is a contributor to public debate, which incorporates competing interests, and explicitly accounts for politics in the ex post assessment of policy performance (Shillabeer, Buss, and Rousseau 2011: 3–16; Mabry 2002). DeLeon (1998) refers to this approach as "consensus through deliberation," which is rooted in the deliberative democracy literature (Bohman and Rehg 1997).

Contemporary policy and program evaluation approaches emanate from positivism, and reside in the rationalistic tradition. Evaluators contend, not incorrectly, that contributions and judgments about policies and programs must be rooted in empirical evidence (Scriven 1997). For Berk and Rossi (1999: 3), evaluation research is "essentially about providing the most accurate information practically possible in an even-handed manner." According to Chelimsky (1987), positivism assumes that policies have clearly defined and measurable goals and objectives, expected results, and sound information upon which to draw rational judgments of effect. With the increasing complexity of public problems, such assumptions rarely hold as decision-makers wrestle with limited resources, capacity, skills shortages, and poor coordination. In addition, governments are also realizing that they are often unable to resolve these problems alone, which means that partners or other contracted agents are being leveraged for their expertise or services. Non-profit groups, for example, are contracted to work with governmental partners, who may have different visions or approaches to resolving particular problems than do governments or other non-profit agents. As the complexity of social issues increases, so too do the arrangements to address them. Rationalistic approaches to understanding effectiveness, for example, are not straightforward, especially as attribution to specific interventions may not always be possible, nor will they always be aligned with policy objectives (Forss, Marra, and Schwartz 2011).

This raises the value of the argumentative tradition, which asserts that positivist approaches are distorted in their view of separating empirical facts from argumentation based on social virtues. Policy examples, such as climate change, despite the appearance of issues with repairs to be found in science, are actually value-laden and are inherently prone to bias given the multiplicity of perspectives, information, and political will that can be brought to bear on them. In this respect, the post-positivist would maintain that climate change is not merely a set of physical objects to be measured, but the interpretation of the scientists that matters (Fischer 1995; Guba and Lincoln 1989). This tradition is rooted in realistic evaluation, whereby facts are considered dependent on underlying assumptions that give meaning to the reality as we collectively understand it. The advantage of this tradition is that it helps decision-makers to understand ethical and epistemological differences in disagreements, rather than prioritizing facts provided by the rational tradition. The promise of the argumentative tradition is that assessments inform consensus building based on beliefs, rather than on detached and contestable prioritization of facts and figures. In this respect, this tradition places evaluation at the front end of the policy analysis, whereas the rationalistic tradition pays attention to the outcomes, or end, of the assessment narrative.

In essence, governmental evaluation functions have tended to rely almost exclusively on rationalistic and (post-)positivist approaches in the contestable belief that analysis is factual and impartial. As the line between policy and intervention becomes increasingly blurred, the greater is the need to find alternative ways of understanding the complexity of public problems (Forss, Marra, and Schwartz 2011). Whether the issue is climate change, health of Indigenous communities, or encouraging technological innovation, more fulsome assessments are required that take into account context and conditions, and the felt reality of all direct participants (Mertens 2012). Alkin (2012) maintains that the field of evaluation is attempting to bridge the two traditions, especially with respect to realistic and transformative approaches (Mertens 2012). The transformative approach, for example, maintains that evaluation must engage and advocate for public discussion, and live the reality of individuals and groups directly affected by public policy decisions, whether implicit or explicit.

Program evaluation and speaking truth

Speaking truth has always been difficult for the evaluation function given that evaluation is not a politically neutral enterprise. For example, when Canada's Auditor General, Sheila Fraser, pronounced on a particular program in 2004 and concluded that "Parliament was not informed of the [program's] true objectives," there was a "weak control environment," and a "lack of transparency in decision-making" (Canada Office of the Auditor General 2004: ch. 3), it caused a firestorm that cast the government under then Prime Minister Paul Martin into an election. That this was an Auditor General giving this report gave it credibility unparalleled anywhere else in government. And, increasingly as public services become ever more politicized, there is pressure to turn to agents of parliament to conduct such assessments. Even then, the most upright and impartial of actors may find themselves in the middle of controversy (Pawson and Tilley 1997; Stone 1997). In Westminster systems, loyal and impartial service is a cornerstone convention. Telling ministers that their ideas are bad or questionable is not regarded as prudent. To be safe then, the bureaucracy focuses on evaluating the interventions rather than the ideas underlying them, on the premise that governments decide, bureaucracies execute.

One of the several benchmarks of ideal governmental evaluation functions is the extent to which these inform ex post analyses of policies and programs. Although there is an enormous normative literature on ex ante policy analysis conducted by evaluation functions, this will not be addressed in this short chapter as the philosophical debates are voluminous (Alkin 2012; Dunn 2004). Although speaking truth to power is the ideal objective behind any form of policy analysis (Wildavsky 1987), the fact is that like any internal governmental function, evaluation responds to political and bureaucratic imperatives. Ideally, both policy and program evaluation would serve to inform choices around interventions in public problems, provide valuable learning and feedback from past activities, and suggest ways to improve (Funnell and Rogers 2011: 3–13). However, evaluation is subject to many influences that can either enhance its effect, or reduce it to narrow examinations of process and outputs (Shepherd 2012).

The ideal structure of a formal evaluation process is agreed in the evaluation literature: the evaluating organization may initiate investigations independent of intervention with agreed scope and depth of inquiry (i.e., policies, initiatives, programs, outputs, outcomes); it draws on centrally derived or implicit evaluation criteria; it uses an array of tools to assess data; it comes to findings based on evidence, and makes recommendations for the future; and it reports according to accepted standards of practice. There are several recipes prescribed on evaluation systems based on these accepted elements, but the aim is the same: to contribute meaningfully to decisions (McDavid, Huse, and Hawthorn 2013; Funnell and Rogers 2011; Dunn 2004; Weiss 1998; Vedung 1997). The internal evaluation function is highlighted here as the largest contributor to most formal governmental evaluation assessment systems. However, this contribution is indeed shifting, especially at the level of policy analysis, given reduced efficacy of governmental program evaluations (Shepherd 2012).

There is no consensus on how to cope with the political dimension of assessments. This idea is combined with the idea that governments rely on many forms of evidence, and evaluation is not as privileged as it once was (if it ever was). With the increasing influence of think-tanks, lobbyists, and political staff, evaluation that is dependent on rationalistic methods supposedly removed from politics has declined in prominence (Shillabeer, Buss, and Rousseau 2011). This observation is not new, as policy and program evaluation has seen this decline since at least the mid-1980s, leading some to conclude that the field is experiencing a prolonged identity crisis. Given the lack of consensus in the field about its contribution (Savoie 2013: 149; Aucoin 2005), political actors have defined the scope of assessment in the absence of field advice: to examine value for money, rather than support budget making.

Situating the program evaluation function in government operations

Institutions, and the way they operate matters. Where functions such as program evaluation reside in the public administration, these frame to a large extent what responsibilities they will carry out and how they will carry them out. Many Westminster countries have created centralized policies or functions that guide their conduct, whether implicit or explicit. These policies and their forms vary based on country preferences regarding governance and methods, institutions, approaches, and the degree to which they are held in priority or relevance by decision-makers. The extent to which these policies and forms can be translated into the regular public management have been debated in an attempt to find common insights into how to make these evaluation policies and their resultant frames more effective (Mayne 2006; Pollitt and Bouckaert 2004; Furubo, Rist, and Sandahl 2002).

Centralized (as opposed to dispersed) evaluation functions are created for three, generally but not necessarily, overlapping reasons: to supply political and/or management decision-makers with the information they need to make better budgetary or policy decisions on their programs; to demonstrate fiscal prudence, efficiency and accountability (Good 2008); and to provide decision-makers with information as to whether the right programs are in place to address the problems effectively. In many countries, attempts have been made at different times to find a balance among these. However, as is often the case, one or more of these rationales generally predominates at any given time or is held in higher priority than the others, often leading to some confusion about the ongoing role and value of evaluation in the overall public management (Aucoin 2005). In Canada, Australia and New Zealand, for example, fiscal austerity has tended to drive the nature of evaluation information sought in the last few decades that supports political concerns for financial accountability, and the need to reduce expenditures (Savoie 2013: 150–153).

With respect to physical location of evaluation functions, most Westminster countries have tended to locate these in the executive branch. Some countries have clear lines that distinguish evaluation from audit, while others have tended to regard the functions as similar, or seen the line as unimportant. Always used as a point of comparison, the United States houses its evaluation function mainly within the Government Accountability Office (GAO), which is part of the legislative branch, although there are other institutions that conduct evaluation research. The scope and approaches used by the US function have been debated for decades, especially around the appropriate limits of its reach, the types of studies it can initiate, and the skills it can bring to bear on the function. Unlike many Westminster countries, the GAO has shown a willingness to conduct policy evaluation (Derlien 1999: 148–150). As a part of the legislative branch, the GAO has been asked by legislators to understand the effects of interventions so as to support decision-making on budgets. In an ideal sense, all program evaluation functions aspire to informing sound policy decisions, and the US is considered a role model in this respect.

The location of the program evaluation function in Westminster countries is varied. In the United Kingdom, Canada, Australia, and New Zealand, program evaluation is housed mainly in the executive branch, associated often with Treasury or finance departments, whose mandates relate mainly to expenditures control. The creation of the Program Analysis Review (PAR) in the United Kingdom in 1970, which was coordinated by the Central Policy Review Staff (CPRS) and the Treasury, was an attempt to coordinate program evaluation efforts across all departments with the aim of coming to holistic understandings on the effects of cross-departmental policies, but failed by the mid-1980s as departments exercised ministerial control over studies. It was not until the Thatcher government that evaluation was reactivated with an emphasis on value for money (Derlien 1999). Most recently, efforts aimed at policy evaluation have tended to reside with the National Audit Office, something increasingly common to other external audit functions, with variations on the extent to which such offices can examine programmatic outcomes. Departments continue to produce evaluation studies as a regular part of overall departmental management with some prescriptive guidance from the Comptroller General.

In Australia, formal and centralized evaluation has been evident since the 1950s, mainly with respect to education programs. However, the function did not become a major priority until the Coombs Report, *Report of the Royal Commission on Australian Government Administration*

(Australian RCAGA 1976) and Braume Report, *Through a Glass Darkly* (Australian Senate Standing Committee on Social Welfare 1979). The Coombs Report aimed to introduce organizational diagnosis, and benchmarking (performance measurement) as a way to understand departmental performance. The Braume Report recommended a whole-of-government approach to evaluation for the purpose of "reviewing the efficiency, effectiveness and appropriateness of any program or group of programs" (SSCSW 1979a: 5). Despite efforts at the federal and state levels, however, and Australia's national government investments in evaluation capacity in the 1970s, it did not become mandatory as a whole-of-government approach to accountability until the 1980s, and even then was evident only in a handful of policy areas (Sharp 2004: 9).

Australia has been shown to be a leader since 1984, incorporating performance measurement into its program evaluations as a tool of management improvement. Even this innovation has proved problematic. According to a recent examination of performance measurement in departments, they "continue to find it challenging to develop and implement performance indicators, in particular effectiveness indicators that provide quantitative and measurable information, allowing for an informed and comprehensive assessment and reporting of achievements against stated objectives" (Australian Audit Office 2011: 12). Performance measurement has proved to be less of a panacea than hoped, and Australia's experience in this respect is not unlike that of other countries that have moved in this direction, including the UK and Canada.

The Canadian experience is also not unique. Canada's system, the second oldest evaluation function next to the US, was centralized in 1977 under the direction of the Treasury Board Secretariat, and framed under a new Results Policy, introduced in July 2016. This replaces the previous Evaluation Policy 2009, which maintained a separate evaluation function. Program evaluation is now subsumed under a larger results framework to "improve the achievement of results across government" (s.3.1.1). Evaluations are also used to support resource allocation decisions based on performance (s.3.2.3). The argument is that departments will better understand success by linking programs to centralized policy priorities. This approach appears to build on the Australian and British experience.

The efficacy of evaluation in Westminster countries to inform sound policy, or even program decisions as a benchmark of effectiveness has been less than stellar (Shepherd 2012; Canada Office of the Auditor General 2009; Mulgan 2008; UK Committee of Public Accounts 2001). Resident within the executive branch, internal evaluation functions are concerned with management and accountability, and questions of austerity, limiting the scope of programs, and reducing government. Although this has not always been the case, much of its history as an internal function can be characterized in this way. Indeed, in Canada several decades of Auditor General's reports on the effectiveness of the evaluation function have cited concerns for lack of effectiveness information on programs. The repair for legislators has been to turn to agents of parliament for greater attention to program effects, thereby blurring the lines between audit and evaluation. Although there remains a role for internal program evaluation, it is highly bounded by political imperatives to tell good news stories, and not to embarrass the government. And, with increasing concern for financial accountability, finding reports that provide rigorous conclusions on the effect of programs has been increasingly challenging.

The way forward: a different model?

Any discussion on the future of internal or accountability-focused evaluation functions is wrought with epistemological differences in perspective, and competing value and worth claims about the internal evaluation function as a governmental enterprise. This is indeed highly contestable territory, as the entire evaluation function (dependent admittedly on rationalistic approaches) is struggling to rediscover its place in the public sphere. The field continues with great rigour to debate the merits of objectivity in evaluative analysis, validity and reliability of data, flavour-of-the-month analytic and data-gathering approaches, and establishing attribution and contribution of interventions. These debates are attempts at insulating the field and the rationalistic tradition from epistemological relativism, and understanding the increasing primacy of political involvement in the assessment process no doubt related to current movements toward new political governance.

One could argue that such debates are to miss the point, as political and other forces and their desire for realistic analysis are not going away anytime soon, as shown in other contributions to this volume. Such an argument could suggest that the merits of the argumentative approach are worthy of consideration, and one would be advised to look in this direction at least for part of the way forward for improving the relevance of evaluation within the public sector. Given the growing number, complexity and globalization of many public problems today, it makes intuitive sense that rationalistic approaches to policy making are not enough. In fact, it is reasonable to suggest that our knowledge about social outcomes, including public policy making, is increasingly based (if this was not always the case) on social constructions, which assumes limited information and understanding of those constructions. Such constructivist understandings necessarily move assessments into depending on multiple evidentiary sources, including argumentative or deliberative approaches. Of course, this is the ideal state of evaluation research. It assumes that governmental actors would welcome such approaches, and would be willing and committed to policy debates. Unfortunately, as shown in other contributions here, secrecy is actually increasing in many public sectors, and there is a movement toward politicizing public services in such a way as to restrict further any information that would act as an obstacle to re-election or government messaging.

The way forward, therefore, for policy analysts and evaluators is not straightforward. However, as Majone (1989: 182) explains:

> It is not the task of analysts to resolve fundamental disagreements about evaluative criteria and standards of accountability; only the political process can do that. However, analysts can contribute to societal learning by refining the standards of appraisal and by encouraging a more sophisticated understanding of public policies than is possible from a single perspective.

Majone goes on to argue that the role of policy analysts and evaluators is to create a dialogue among "advocates of different criteria" (Majone 1989: 183). This perspective aligns well with that of Mertens and Wilson (2012), who suggest that only by engaging in dialogue among competing interests can evaluation be relevant and useful. In effect, they promote the idea of advocacy of policy ideas rather than relying on traditional notions of objective analysis. In their view, this *one can lead a horse to water, but cannot force it to drink* approach to evaluation use is no longer effective, nor even widely assumed to be true any longer (Shillabeer, Buss, and Rousseau 2011).

The problem with rationalistic evaluation is that it is premised on the simple view that governments should be held to account for their promises. We know from decades of evaluation work that this view is rife with faulty assumptions, including that governments even want to be held to account, despite their rhetoric to the contrary (Shillabeer, Buss, and Rousseau 2011). This is not to suggest that the rationalistic approach be discarded, but that it qualify discussions on effectiveness with organizational learning considerations (Pawson and Tilley 1997). This is not a new idea: in addition to holding governments to account and understanding effect, the evaluator is asked to consider the organization's ability and capacity to adapt to changes in its internal and external environments over time, and to assess its ability to control costs of the intervention being evaluated (Bovens, 't Hart and Kuipers 2006: 330). This learning approach to evaluation would examine all three criteria, and make an assessment about the relative merit of each in program implementation. Bovens et al. (2006: 330) suggest, as one possible avenue forward, combining this rational logic with the argumentative approach that understands how policy and other decision-makers are involved, represented and assessed in the political arena through an understanding of "symbols, emotions, political ideology, and power relationships." For them, it is not the social consequences of policy that matter, "but the political construction of these consequences, which might be driven by institutional logics and political considerations of wholly different kinds."

In Canada, an inquiry was called in 2000 to examine the events surrounding the contamination of water at a plant in Walkerton, a town of approximately 5,000 people in central Ontario. The inquiry looked into an outbreak of *E. coli* that resulted in the deaths of seven people. The inquiry, led by the Honourable Dennis R. O'Connor, did not simply want to understand the series of events that resulted in the deaths, but the systemic policy and implementation problems as well. He examined the role of various governmental institutions, both operational and regulatory, and followed the evidence on the effects of systemic failures in other jurisdictions in the province. He sought out experts, ministry and local operations officials, municipal councils, health authorities, and citizens to figure out not simply who to blame, but how to recognize and address the contributing factors that led to the outbreak. He actually sought out political and bureaucratic perspectives to understand the decisions, contexts and conditions that framed the tragedy. In the end, the report did find culpability, but it also made and insisted on changes to Ontario's safe water legislation (Ontario Walkerton Inquiry 2002). Such assessments take time, but the objective of the study was to identify different perspectives, and generate a common understanding of the problems through dialogue. Unfortunately, this is but one of very few examples of such an approach in the Canadian context.

Concluding thoughts

The field of governmental evaluation has not fully resolved conceptual challenges in the field, thereby clinging to limited insights provided by studies buttressing expenditure control decisions and management decisions around implementation. Little question is given in internal evaluation to the ideas that support programs, leaving some to doubt the relative worth of the function (Savoie 2013; Mulgan 2003: 87–90). As shown, the dependence on rationalistic methods has lost its sheen once enjoyed (maybe) in the 1960s and 1970s. Again, these arguments are not new: legislators are unconcerned by bureaucratic efficiency, and auditors and evaluators are reticent to question government policy.

Another challenge for internal evaluation, and public services more broadly is a reluctance on the part of politicians to trust that bureaucrats will come to reasonable expenditure budgets. In Australia, UK and Canada, evaluations have been tasked alongside audits to address matters of value for money to rectify this problem. Again, this is not a new development as it has been suggested many times in various forms with limited success that bureaucrats will be able to come to reasoned ideas about controlling spending. It is no wonder that politicians believe they have little choice but to implement wide-sweeping operating reviews in order to curb spending. Internal evaluators are reluctant to suggest cutting or trimming programs, even inefficient or irrelevant ones. It may make better sense for evaluation to support budgetary decisions that recommend calibrating or re-allocating of resources, rather than to review expenses alone. The fact is that even as a management tool, internal evaluation has failed to live up to expectations.

The repair appears to be more reflexive approaches to evaluation. These are sensitive to testing assumptions in policy and program theories of change and action, contexts and conditions of interventions, and depend on open systems of debate. As shown elsewhere in this volume, these are high ideals indeed, but they nonetheless set the stage for useful evaluation that enables public sector reform efforts. Debates abound in many Westminster countries as to evaluation approaches, criteria, scope, and institutional arrangements, and these are important as it defines the realities of many public sector evaluators. Discussions about instituting independent and impartial evaluators general or other similar models, while meritorious, neglect ongoing epistemological deficiencies in the field. Human beings are social creatures, and as such, are rooted in contexts. We want to understand causality as established in these methods, but we also want to know that the findings from research are relevant and useful to informing better policy choices, and their resultant interventions.

The promise of evaluation to understand policy and program effects remains intact especially as more and more jurisdictions regard it as a useful decision tool. The challenge for the field is to re-stake its ground as the voice for holistic assessment of public interventions and the ideas that inform these. This means that it must embrace both rationalistic and argumentative approaches, especially as public decisions and the information that surrounds such decisions is removed increasingly from the view of citizens. Perhaps there is a place for evaluators to become advocates and promoters of change, rather than remain insulated in scientific objectivity.

Note

1   Churchill, Winston. BrainyQuote.com. Xplore Inc, 2015. Available at: www.brainyquote.com/quotes/quotes/w/winstonchu144998.html.

References

Alkin, M. 2004. *Evaluation Roots: Tracing Theorists? Views and Influences*. Thousand Oaks, CA: Sage Publications.

Alkin, M. 2012. *Evaluation Roots: A Wider Perspective of Theorists? Views and Influence*. 2nd ed. Thousand Oaks, CA: Sage Publications.

Aucoin, P. 2005. "Decision-Making in Government: The Role of Program Evaluation." Discussion Paper for Treasury Board Secretariat. Ottawa: Supply and Services.

Australian National Audit Office. 2011. *Development and Implementation of Key Performance Indicators to Support the Outcomes and Program Framework*. Canberra: National Audit Office.

Australian Senate Standing Committee on Social Welfare. 1979a. *Through a Glass Darkly: Evaluation in Australian Health and Welfare Services*, Volume 1. The Report. Canberra, Australian Government Publishing Service.

Australian Senate Standing Committee on Social Welfare. 1979b. *Through a Glass Darkly: Evaluation in Australian Health and Welfare Services*, Volume 2. Papers. Canberra, Australian Government Publishing Service.

Berk, R.A. and Rossi, P.H. 1999. *Thinking about Program Evaluation*. Thousand Oaks, CA: Sage.

Bohman, J. and R. William, eds. 1997. *Deliberative Democracy: Essays on Reason and Politics*. Cambridge, MA: MIT Press.

Bovens, M.,'t Hart, P., and Kuipers. S. 2006. "The Politics of Policy Evaluation." In *The Oxford Handbook of Public Policy*, edited by Michael, M., Martin, R., and Goodin, R.E, 310–335. London: Oxford.

Canada Office of the Auditor General. 2009. "Report of the Auditor General of Canada 2009." Chap. 1 in *Evaluating the Effectiveness of Programs*. Ottawa: Supply and Services.

Canada Office of the Auditor General. 2004. "November Report of the Auditor General of Canada 2004." Chap. 3 in *The Sponsorship Program*. Ottawa: Supply and Services.

Canada. Treasury Board Secretariat. 2016. "Policy on Results." Ottawa: TBS.

Chelimsky, E. 1987. "The Politics of Program Evaluation." *Society* 25: 24–32.

DeLeon, P. 1998. "Introduction: The Evidentiary Base for Policy Analysis: Empiricist Versus Post-Positivist Positions." *Policy Studies Journal* 26: 109–113.

Derlien, H.U. 1999. "Genesis and Structure of Evaluation Efforts in Comparative Perspective." In *Program Evaluation and the Management of Government: Patterns & Prospects across Eight Nations*, edited by Ray, R. London: Transaction Publishers.

Dunn, W. 2004. *Public Policy Analysis: An Introduction*. 3rd ed. Upper Saddle River, NJ: Prentice-Hall.

Dwivedi, O.P. and Gow, JI. 1999. *From Bureaucracy to Public Management: The* Administrative *Culture of the Government of Canada*. Toronto: Broadview.

Fischer, F. 1995. *Evaluating Public Policy*. Chicago: Nelson Hall.

Forss, K., Marra, M., and Schwartz, R. 2011. *Evaluating the Complex: Attribution, Contribution, and Beyond*. 18 vols. London: Transaction Publishers.

Funnell, S. and Rogers, P. 2011. *Purposeful Program Theory: Effective Use of Theories of Change and Logic Models*. San Francisco, CA: Jossey-Bass.

Furubo, J.E., Rist, R., and R. Sandahl, eds. 2002. *International Atlas of Evaluation*. New Brunswick, NJ: Transaction Press.

Good, D. 2008. *The Politics of Public Money: Spenders, Guardians, Priority Setters, and Financial Watchdogs Inside the Canadian Government*. Toronto: University of Toronto Press.

Guba, E.G. and Lincoln, V.S. 1989. *Fourth Generation Evaluation*. Newbury Park, CA: Sage.

Hubbard, R., and Paquet, G. 2015. "The Canadian Federal Public Service: Tinkering Can No Longer Suffice." *Optimum Online* 45 (3).

Mabry, L. 2002. "Postmodern Evaluation – Or not?" *American Journal of Evaluation* 23 (2): 141–157.

Majone, G. 1989. *Evidence, Argument and Persuasion in the Policy Process*. New Haven: CT: Yale University Press.

Mayne, J. 2006. "Audit and Evaluation in Public Management: Challenges, Reforms, and Different Roles." *Canadian Journal of Program Evaluation* 21 (1): 11–45.

McDavid, J.C., Huse, I. and Hawthorn, L. 2013. *Program Evaluation and Performance Measurement: An Introduction to Practice*. 2nd Edition. Thousand Oaks, CA: Sage.

Mertens, D. and Wilson, A. 2012. *Program Evaluation Theory and Practice: A Comprehensive Guide*. New York: Guilford Press.

Mulgan, R. 2008. "The Accountability Priorities of Australian Parliamentarians." *Australian Journal of Public Administration* 67 (4): 457–469.

Mulgan, R. 2003. *Holding Power to Account*. New York: Palgrave Macmillan.New Zealand. 1968. Committee on the Civil Service (Fulton). *Final Report*, Cnnd. 3638. London: HMSO.

Ontario Walkerton Inquiry. 2002. *Report of the Walkerton Inquiry: The Events of May 2000 and Related Issues*. Toronto: Ontario Ministry of the Attorney General, Part One.

Pawson, R. and Tilley, N. 1997. *Realistic Evaluation*. London: Sage.

Pollitt, C. and Bourckaert, G. 2004. *Public Management Reform: A Comparative Analysis*. 2nd Edition. New York: Oxford.

Royal Commission on Australian Government Administration (RCAGA). 1977. *Report*. Canberra: Acting Commonwealth Government Printer.

Rhodes, R.A.W., Wanna, J., and Weller, P. 2009. *Comparing Westminster*. New York: Oxford.

Rossi, P.H., Lipsey, M., and Freeman, H. 2004. *Evaluation: A Systematic Approach*. 7th ed. Thousand Oaks, CA: Sage Publications.

Savoie, D. 2013. *Whatever Happened to the Music Teacher?: How Government Decides and Why*. Montreal and Kingston: McGill-Queen's University Press.

Scriven, M. 1997. "Truth and Objectivity in Evaluation." In *Evaluation for the 21st Century: A Handbook*, edited by Chelimsky, E. and Shadish, W.R., 477–500. Thousand Oaks, CA: Sage.

Sharp, C. 2004. "Development of Program Evaluation in Australasia and the Australasian Evaluation Society: The Early Decades." *Evaluation Journal of Australasia* 3 (2): 6–16.

Shepherd, R. 2012. "In Search of a Balanced Evaluation Function: Getting to Relevance." *Canadian Journal of Program Evaluation* 26 (2): 1–45.

Shillabeer, A., Buss, T., and Rousseau, D. 2011. *Evidence-Based Public Management: Practices, Issues and Prospects*. London: M.E. Sharpe.

Stone, D. 1997. *Policy Paradox: The Art of Political Decision-Making*. New York: Norton.

United Kingdom Committee of Public Accounts. 2001. "Holding to Account." Report of the Review by Lord Sharman of Redlynch. Office of the Treasury.

Vedung, E. 1997. *Public Policy and Program Evaluation*. New Brunswick, NJ: Transaction.

Weiss, C.H. 1998. *Evaluation: Methods for Studying Programs and Policies*. Upper Saddle River, NJ: Prentice-Hall.

Wildavsky, A. 1987. *Speaking Truth to Power: The Art and Craft of Policy Analysis*. New Brunswick, NJ: Transaction Publishers.

World Bank. 2014. "What is Monitoring and Evaluation?" Available at: http://ieg.worldbankgroup.org/what-monitoring-and-evaluation. Accessed June 6, 2016.

30

MOTIVATION IN THE PUBLIC SECTOR

Adrian Ritz, Oliver Neumann and Wouter Vandenabeele

Introduction

The provision of public services is heavily dependent on human resources. First and foremost, this consists of the knowledge, skills, attitudes and motives of public employees. Public organizations are more than mere production units; they are highly specialized groupings of expertise and services. Given this observation, it is unsurprising that people are the main asset of most public organizations and that the actions of those people are significant drivers of organizational outcomes. In this context, motivation becomes a crucial factor in both the provision of public service and the quality of public sector work.

There are several reasons why employee motivation is a pivotal concept in the field of Public Administration and Public Policy. First, in the future, demographic change will result in a dwindling labor supply and significantly increased competition among employers. These changes will affect public organizations in a dramatic way, due to the fact that in the labor market, as opposed to in the service sector, public administration faces direct competition from private sector employers. Therefore, public personnel policies need to strengthen the management of motivation as a decisive means of attracting, retaining, and rewarding employees. Second, more than ever before, public organizations are under pressure to enhance their performance, whereby employee motivation has been identified as one of the key variables in advancing both the performance of individuals and the performance of the organization as a whole. Thus, the main challenge facing human resources managers and line managers in the public sector is creating working conditions that give due consideration to the human factor, allowing for the enhancement of individuals' motivation in order to influence organizational performance.

Third, whereas society as a whole and policy-makers in particular put efficiency goals to the fore, performance in the public sphere goes beyond the simple level of efficiency. The creation of societal outcomes, formulation of public policies, guaranteeing citizens' rights, or adherence to the rule of law are some examples of the complex set of goals and principles that guide public task fulfillment. Institutional and societal values are, therefore, the main foundation of both motivation in the public sector and of the associated performance outcomes. Fourth, accountability within the public sector has been extended during the period of New Public

Management by complementing the input perspective with an output orientation (Ritz and Sager 2010). Here, the motivation to act appropriately for the benefit of society and various stakeholders can compensate for more complex, diminished or distorted accountability processes. Thus, the motivation of individuals is essential in keeping a balance between outcome and process values, such as equity and quality, regardless of whether or not these aspects are monitored (Vandenabeele and Van Loon 2015).

Against the backdrop of the arguments outlined above relating to the relevance of motivation of public employees, this chapter will be structured as follows: In the next section, the role of motivating employees in public sector organizations will be presented from a classical motivation theory perspective. This allows us, in the next step, to illustrate how research on motivation in the public sector has developed its own peculiarities and concepts. The research stream on public service motivation in particular has produced an original concept, stimulating new research within and beyond the boundaries of the discipline. Furthermore, it is one of the few scholarly developments in the field of Public Administration. Therefore, the third and fourth sections of this chapter focus mainly on public service motivation. In doing so, we adopt an institutional perspective on motivation, drawing a distinction between public sector motivation and public service motivation. Finally, we develop a conceptual model to provide an overview of the antecedents and outcomes of public service motivation that have been investigated to date.

Classic foundations of employee motivation in the public sector

Motivation describes processes by which certain motives are activated and transferred into actions. From this results a state of goal-oriented behavior that is characterized by direction, intensity, and persistence. The motivation to pursue a goal depends on situational incentives, personal preferences, and their interdependency. Motivation at the workplace is a central driver of success for any organization, regardless of sector, which is why numerous attempts have been made in various disciplines to theoretically explain the emergence, persistence, and decline of individual motivation levels. Motivation acts as a predictor of individuals' behaviors and performance, all of which in turn contribute to organizational performance. More specifically, motivation determines the direction, intensity, and the power of endurance of behaviors (Heckhausen 1989).

However, motivation alone is not sufficient to explain performance. Acting as a catalyst, volition stimulates individuals to transfer motivations into behavior. In other words, motivation needs to be accompanied by the will to act in accordance with that motivation in order to produce behavioral outcomes. Such volition is based on concentrated attention, management of emotions, self-efficacy, goal-oriented self-discipline, and seeing the meaning in a task. The latter is of crucial significance in the public sector. The will to act in accordance with the motivation to attain an outcome depends greatly on a deeper understanding of why public institutions exist and what role they play in society. For instance, at the interface between politics and administration, public managers often face situations in which the motivation to engage in policy formulation needs to be accompanied by high levels of volition in a rather difficult and politically infused environment.

Advocating a somewhat different notion of the interplay between motivation and behavior, McClelland (1985) pointed out that behavior may be understood as a function of motivation, ability, and situational factors such as resources and interpersonal support. Either way, individuals' behaviors and performance are crucially dependent on the existence of some form of motivation, which is why we will proceed to review some general theories of work motivation before turning to the specifics of motivation in public sector settings. The general theories mainly include, first, process-based theories, and second, content-based theories, as will be discussed below.

Process-based theories

Regarding the process-based theories, *expectancy theory*, as developed by Vroom (1964), attempts to explain why individuals rationally choose to perform or not to perform specific behaviors based on the expectancy of either pleasure or pain resulting as a consequence of this decision. More specifically, the theory is that individuals are motivated if they believe that effort and performance are positively associated, that performance will enable them to attain rewards which satisfy a given need, and that the desire to satisfy said need is so pronounced that the effort is deemed appropriate. This theory is based on three concepts: valence, expectancy, and instrumentality – sometimes referred to as the VIE model. Valence describes the personal emotions and value-attributions regarding extrinsic (pay, benefits, promotions, etc.) and intrinsic (enjoyment, satisfaction) rewards. Instrumentality pertains to an individual's prospects of actually receiving the desired reward upon task completion. Expectancy refers to the beliefs of what one is capable of doing and could also be described as self-confidence. These three factors taken together lead to motivation, which, in turn, is associated with other desired work-related concepts such as job satisfaction and tenure. From a public sector perspective, the VIE model leads us to the question of how instrumental an individual's effort is in regard to satisfying his needs. Today, extrinsic rewards such as performance-related pay, promotion, and life-long tenure are the subject of considerable dispute in public organizations (Perry et al. 2009). Thus, the valence of intrinsic public service motives and their role within the VIE process is becoming increasingly important.

Another process-based approach is adopted by *goal-setting theory* (Locke and Latham 1991). Goal-setting theory, as a motivation theory, suggests that goals are immediate regulators of human behavior (Latham and Locke 2007). The main claim of this theory is that people differ in their levels of motivation and the outcomes thereof, in the same way that they also differ regarding the goals they pursue. Accordingly, goals to be set out by management should be considered carefully. Nowadays, management by objectives exemplifies goal-setting theory in most public organizations in Western countries, although the five relevant principles of goal setting according to Locke and Latham are not always met in practice. Those five principles of goal setting, designed to improve success at the workplace through better motivated employees, are as follows: First, goals need to be precise, avoiding vagueness and ambiguity so that individuals know exactly what it is they should be trying to achieve. Second, goals need to be challenging so they are able to arouse an individual's interest. Third, stimulating the commitment to work towards a goal is vital and can best be achieved by letting the individual participate in the process of formulating the goal. Fourth, acknowledging feedback is crucial to ensure that expectations can be clarified and that goals can be adapted should difficulties arise.

Lastly, task complexity needs to be taken into account in order for goals not to be overly ambitious, meaning they cannot be achieved within the given time frame. Jung and Ritz (2014) point out that goal-setting theory has been researched in a variety of public sector settings, clearly suggesting that government organizations tend to have multiple, often competing, contradictory, and ambiguous goals (e.g. Allison 1983; Downs 1967; Moynihan 2008). Quite frequently, this is due to lack of profit indicators (Rainey 2010), conflicts among values (e.g. preservation and development of natural resources) (Wildavsky 1979), political intervention, or competing demands by multiple interest groups (Rainey 2010). Thus, such goal characteristics in the public sector may be a source of difficulties, both as regards motivating employees and in terms of measuring performance (Chun and Rainey 2006; Jung 2011).

Equity theory, as postulated by Adams (1965), is a third process-based theory which focuses on the interpersonal fairness aspect of reward allocations. It assumes that employees strive for equity regarding the efforts they exert for an employer and the rewards they receive in return, and that this equity assessment is based on comparisons with other individuals either within or outside the same organization. This theory postulates that people view equity or fairness as an important commodity which, when present, contributes to their motivation to work. If there is a perceived imbalance in equity from the individual's perspective, there are four strategies to reinstate equity. First, inputs or efforts may be reduced. Second, individuals may press for outcomes or rewards to be increased. Third, one may overrate or underrate one's own or others' efforts to psychologically justify imbalances, and fourth, individuals may choose to quit. Equity-theory calls for procedural and distributive justice in the realms of motivation management (Osterloh et al. 2001). Fundamental public sector principles such as equal treatment, uniformity in the application of law and policies, and the requirement to justify decisions illustrate the institutional values, which are extremely relevant from a motivational perspective in order to enhance employee performance. Equity theory has significant practical implications. For instance, criticism of inflexible public pay structures (e.g. executive salaries below market average, lack of room for maneuver concerning bonuses) should not simply be refused on the basis of institutional arguments, but should also be tested by sound empirical comparisons of reference groups and pay systems within and outside the public organization.

To summarize, while emphasizing specific elements within the development of motivation, process-based theories elucidate the relevance of the institutional environment for enhancing employee outcomes. The magnitude of certain needs and the instrumentality of one's effort in the process leading from motivation to behavior are strongly influenced by the public-sector-specific incentive regime and the links between individual effort and performance, which are rudimentary at best. One major reason for this is the type of goal characteristics typical in public sector organizations, which make it difficult to measure performance. Thus, output-oriented efficiency is only one of multiple rationales in initiating effort within such an institutional environment. Institutional values such as equal treatment, uniformity in the application of law and policies, and the required justification of decisions or democratic and constitutional principles are equally important motivational drivers.

Content-based theories

Moving on to the content-based theories, an early but consistently prominent approach is Maslow's *hierarchy of needs* (1943), which distinguishes between five basic needs that are ranked based on their importance for human survival. In this theory, the emergence of motivation to pursue a need which is less crucial for survival, placed near the top of the hierarchy, is unlikely unless all of the more basic needs classified below have been met. Instead, motivation is predominantly focused on the lowest-ranking need that is still unfulfilled. *ERG theory* (Alderfer 1969) utilizes a needs categorization similar to Maslow's approach, the basic category being "existence needs" such as hunger, thirst, safety, and sex; the second category being relatedness needs such as social involvement, family, and social recognition; and the third category being growth needs, such as the desire for self-fulfillment, the need to be creative and to work on meaningful tasks. In either one of these hierarchy-based theories, individuals' motivation is directed at moving up in the hierarchy to achieve satisfaction, while the motivation to fulfill an unmet need becomes stronger as time passes (e.g. hunger gradually increases). Public organizations in highly developed societies find themselves increasingly confronted with personnel aspiring for higher order needs and, thus, need to use their opportunities to emphasize social involvement, social recognition, autonomy, and meaningful tasks when motivating employees. From an organizational viewpoint, public management reforms implementing performance contracts and lump sum budgeting may help to create such opportunities. A central result of these reforms is increased autonomy at the workplace, provided changes are designed to truly enhance room for maneuver within a public office.

There is another group of content-based theories that was crucially influenced by Herzberg's (1968) two-factor theory, or *motivation-hygiene theory*. In this approach, a distinction is drawn between motivators (such as challenging work, responsibility, and success), and hygiene factors (such as salary, status, relations to managers and colleagues, and security). Whereas the existence of motivators is theorized to cause job satisfaction, as opposed to non-job-satisfaction, hygiene factors are believed to reduce job dissatisfaction, leading to non-job-dissatisfaction. Thus, job satisfaction and job dissatisfaction are treated as two independent concepts, resulting in four ideal-type states of work motivation depending on the low-to-high values of either one of the two dimensions. Herzberg's dichotomy is largely in line with the popular extrinsic–intrinsic motivation framework. Here, extrinsic motivation is described as the prospect of satisfying one's needs indirectly either through material rewards (e.g. monetary such as salary and bonuses, or non-monetary such as a public transportation pass) or immaterial rewards (e.g. social status and prestige, opportunities for personal development, workplace location) in exchange for work efforts. In contrast, intrinsic motivation is characterized as pertaining to valuing an activity per se which means that needs are satisfied directly (Osterloh et al. 2001). Intrinsic motivation is sometimes further sub-divided into a hedonic facet that emphasizes enjoyment and pleasure (e.g. satisfaction drawn from the flow of an activity, working on a challenging task) as the basis of motivation, and an eudaemonic component that focuses on the role of meaning and purpose (e.g. help clients, coworkers, society) in motivating humans (Grant 2008a; Houston 2011).

One of the most salient theories based on the extrinsic–intrinsic motivation framework is *self-determination theory* (SDT) as postulated by Deci and Ryan (2002), who put the basic human needs of autonomy, competence, and relatedness at the frontline of their approach. In fact, SDT is a set of six associated theories, the most popular of which, Organismic Integration Theory, focuses on the autonomy aspect and distinguishes between amotivation, four types of extrinsic motivation, and intrinsic motivation. These types of motivation can be ranked according to the degree to which a behavior is self-determined, as manifested in six types of regulation. Activities that are entirely non-self-determined, for instance, are theorized to lead to a lack of motivation to behave in situations in which no regulation is present, as described by the term amotivation. The least self-determined type of extrinsic motivation, characterized by external regulation, is typical in situations in which tasks grant very little autonomy and where people attempt to attain contingent external rewards or avoid punishment through their work on said tasks.

Moving up the hierarchy of self-determination, introjected regulation is the next type of extrinsic motivation. Here, people partially internalize the previously external regulation, anticipating and avoiding the shame or guilt associated with the failure to comply with contingent consequences. The following state of extrinsic motivation is characterized by identified regulation, which is when the individual starts to recognize and accept a behavior's underlying value and internalizes it more, an example being identifying that exercising regularly contributes to good health and acting accordingly to maintain one's well-being. The most self-determined type of extrinsic motivation is based on integrated regulation, meaning that beyond the identification of the importance of a behavior, people will fully accept that behavior and integrate it into their personal values and identity. Finally, intrinsic motivation is characterized by entirely intrinsic regulation and behaviors are fully self-determined as they are in line with the individual's values. This means that the activity is pursued since it is deemed interesting and free from external pressures, rendering it fully volitional and often making intrinsic motivation the most desirable and powerful form of motivation. However, intrinsic motivation is difficult to achieve and it is not uncommon that individuals at the workplace have to move through various types of extrinsic motivation before becoming intrinsically motivated. In the following, we will explain why SDT is of great relevance in regard to motivation of public employees.

Against the backdrop of motivation-hygiene theory and self-determination theory, the eudaemonic component which focuses on the role of meaning and purpose exemplifies why public sector work tasks have the potential to promote employees' identification with underlying values of work (e.g. incorruptibility) and to integrate them with their personal values. Such values at the individual, organizational, or societal level are called public values (Jorgensen and Bozeman 2007). They have been defined as "the ideals, coined as principles, to be followed when producing a public service or regulating citizens' behavior, thus providing direction to the behavior of public servants" (Andersen et al. 2013: 294). Therefore, we argue that it is key when seeking to understand motivation in the public sector to also consider public-value-focused approaches of explaining motivation, since a large portion of jobs and tasks in public sector settings are concerned with providing support and help to citizens. Spitzmueller and Van Dyne (2013), for instance, distinguish between two types of helping behavior: proactive helping in which individuals are motivated by self-interest and seek out opportunities to help others, in order to meet their own personal needs; and reactive helping, where individuals behave altruistically and help others in response to their (others') observed need, which primarily benefits others (see also Spector 2013). The concept of *prosocial motivation*, often defined as the desire to exert effort to benefit others (Batson 1987), is geared more towards reactive helping behaviors and, consequently, is understood to be more altruistic in nature.

The concept of *public service motivation* (PSM), which also pertains more to the notion of reactive helping behavior (Koehler and Rainey 2008), is of particular relevance in public sector settings (Ritz et al. 2016). Both prosocial motivation and public service motivation are often subsumed under types of intrinsic motivation, and, more specifically, of the eudaemonic component thereof (Houston 2011; Grant 2008a). However, as discussed above, SDT postulates that extrinsic motivation may exhibit intrinsic qualities as autonomy increases (Koehler and Rainey 2008). According to SDT, public service motivation reflects a highly self-determined type of extrinsic motivation, which is based on integrated regulation, since the reference object of public service motives is external. For instance, certain public service motives are directed towards society and those individuals who profit from public service delivery. Thus, people motivated by public service fully accept the institutional public values and integrate these with their personal values and identity.

Specific types of motivation in the public sector

Motivation in the public sector is strongly linked to the institutional setting, as has been discussed above. From a theoretical viewpoint, institutional theory may provide further insights into the origins of employee motivation in the public sector. Values, norms, and rules – as the defining parts of institutions – infuse social structures with values and promote stability and persistence over time (Peters 2000; Selznick 1984). Viewed as organizations, institutions are shaped in response to their external environment and transcend to the individual level of an employee's identity, influencing his/her values and motives, which, in turn, define a range of permissible and prohibited behavior (Ritz and Brewer 2013; Perry 2000; Scott 1987). Thus, employee motivation in the public sector is a function of the degree to which an organization shares the individual's values or provides opportunities for the employee to satisfy these values (Christensen and Wright 2009). In addition, it is not the sector that is the decisive element in the development of motivation. Instead, employees' values are influenced by the organization's degree of "publicness". This characteristic defines organizations not only in the public sector, but also in the private and non-profit sectors (Bozeman 1987). However, in the following we simply distinguish between two major types of employee motivation in the public sector: public sector motivation and public service motivation. In doing so, we disentangle the various roles public sector organizations play both in public servants' motivation and in their internalization of different types of values (Christensen and Wright 2009; Brewer and Selden 1998).

Public sector motivation

The first motivation concept with a key focus on public organizations is public sector motivation. According to institutional theory, public sector motivation implies a "logic of consequentiality" involving institutional rules and interpretations to be treated as alternatives in a rational choice problem (March and Olsen 1989). Rational choice theory characterizes administrators as generally rational individuals (constrained by certain informational and cognitive boundaries) who have a fixed set of preferences and who seek to maximize their utility (Brennan and Buchanan 1985). The assumption of rationality implies that an individual will choose the alternative that yields the greatest value for him and that is likely to occur (Neumann and Ritz 2015; Gordon 1972).

As far as the attractiveness of public sector employment is concerned, there are several institutional values and extrinsic incentives that allow for individual utility maximization. Public organizations, for instance, offer relatively high job security and protection against dismissal, good career perspectives, relatively high salaries in low- and mid-level ranks, stable salaries overall, as well as a robust salary development scale, all of which can be attractive to certain individuals motivated by such benefits (Buelens and Van den Broeck 2007; French and Emerson 2014; Karl and Sutton 1998; Lewis and Frank 2002; Perry and Hondeghem 2008). Furthermore, pension schemes for public employees generally guarantee security and independence, and the attractiveness of a civil service career is that it practically guarantees a certain standard of living in retirement (OECD 2013).

It should also be noted that public organizations often offer more favorable working hours and vacation schemes. Thus, we define public sector motivation as the desire to behave in accordance with motives grounded in an individual's self-interest and directed at extrinsic incentives typically found in the public sector. This includes, for instance, job security, guaranteed salary and career development, and further privileges. That said, we may also conclude that certain incentives motivate individuals regardless of their employers' sector (French and Emerson 2014). In this line of reasoning, the relationship between employee and employer reflects a form of psychological contract based on an exchange of loyalty and duty in return for salary and privileges. Such a relationship is different from an exchange of effort and performance in return for skill development and employability. Public sector motivation is based more on the former type of psychological contract, in which the attainment of output and outcome goals is of secondary interest to an employee. First and foremost, an employee performs certain actions based on the experience of individual needs being satisfied. Shirking behavior is a typical consequence if public organizations are unable to satisfy employees' needs in regard to the incentives described above, since organizational outcomes are not to the fore for the individual (Francois 2000). Thus, public sector motivation is closely linked to the specific work context and working conditions within government organizations. Nevertheless, such working conditions also exist in the private sector, although they are far more common in the public sector (Wright 2001).

Public service motivation

The second type of motivation, public service motivation, has been part of the scientific discourse in public administration literature for more than 25 years (Ritz et al. 2016), and is the first theory to specifically address the topic of employee motivation in the public sector, although it also applies to public service-related jobs in other sectors (Brewer and Selden 1998). Public service motivation fits very well into a "logic of appropriateness" as distinguished by institutional theory (March and Olsen 1989): employees act not only (but also) out of self-interest; instead, their actions are driven by rules of appropriate and exemplary behavior inherent to the institution. Such rules "are followed because they are seen as natural, rightful, expected, and legitimate. Actors seek to fulfill the obligations encapsulated in a role, an identity, a membership in a political community or group, and the ethos, practices and expectations of its institutions. Embedded in a social collectivity, they do what they see as appropriate for themselves in a specific type of situation" (March and Olsen 2009: 2). Viewing public service motivation within this context responds to a call for more contextualized and less individual-level-based types of motivations, distinguishing it from certain classical, and – above all – process-based types of employee motivation (Perry 2000).

Initially, the concept of public service motivation was defined as "an individual's predisposition to respond to motives grounded primarily or uniquely in public institutions and organizations" (Perry and Wise 1990), while more recent definitions, such as the one put forward by Perry and Hondeghem (2008), have adopted a broader perspective, describing it as a type of motivation which generally refers to "motives and action in the public domain that are intended to do good for others and shape the well-being of society" (Perry and Hondeghem 2008: 3). We simply define Public Service Motivation as the desire to behave in accordance with motives that are grounded in the public interest in order to serve society. The concept is deeply rooted in history (Vandenebeele and Van Loon 2015). The idea that public officials should be concerned with the public interest, leaving aside individual interests, can be traced as far back as to Aristotle and Plato. Throughout history, the idea regularly surfaces in various guises – in the works of philosophers such as Thomas of Aquinas, Rousseau, and John Rawls, for instance – and it became a consistent feature in the majority of dominant western public service systems (Horton 2008). Nevertheless, it was not until Rainey (1982) first mentioned public service motivation and Perry and Wise (1990) first formalized the definition and theory thereof, that this became a concept in its own right. Numerous concepts related to public service motivation such as altruism, prosocial motivation and public service ethos have been part of public administration and adjacent disciplines for a long time. However, we do not understand public service motivation as a purely altruistic concept. Instead, it reflects a mix of motives composed of enjoyment-based intrinsic motivation, extrinsic motivation, and prosocial intrinsic motivation (Neumann and Ritz 2015). Furthermore, all these motives can be understood as parts of an individual's set of preferences and rationality (Akerlof and Kranton 2010).

Thus, research on public service motivation based the concept on a full range of behavioral motives, taking into account the fact that individuals' motives are mixed (Bolino 1999; Brewer et al. 2000). Perry and Wise (1990) included rational, norm-based, and affective motives in their definition. Kim and Vandenabeele (2010) distinguish between instrumental motives, value-based motives, and identification with beneficiaries as the main drivers of public service motivation. These different types of motives are reflected in the research on measurement of public service motivation. The first measurement scale developed by Perry (1996) comprised four dimensions. These were: attraction to public policy making, commitment to the public interest, compassion, and self-sacrifice. An international team of 16 researchers further developed the so-called Perry scale into a four dimensional measure, designating its dimensions: attraction to public service, commitment to public values, compassion, and self-sacrifice (Kim et al. 2013). Other researchers added their own measurement dimensions, such as democratic governance (Vandenabeele 2008; see also Giauque et al. 2011) or shortened the original scale to create an abridged measurement instrument (Coursey and Pandey 2007).

Research on public service motivation has increased enormously and an increasingly global research community has responded to Perry and Wise's (1990) call for the advancement of theory and measurement on public service motivation. While most of the empirical research on PSM has been conducted in Europe and North America, research in Asia has gained significant momentum in recent years and some first publications have appeared in Oceania, Africa, and South America (Ritz et al. 2016). For this reason, we will first provide an overview of the main lines of empirical research on the topic in the following section.

A model of antecedents and outcomes of public service motivation

Since PSM is an important facet in enhancing public sector organizations' success, the question of how such motivation emerges and whether this emergence can, in fact, be facilitated from the outside at all are of key interest. Similarly, it is crucial to understand how exactly PSM contributes to which desirable (or adverse) individual and organizational outcomes. Unsurprisingly, extensive research efforts have been devoted to theorizing and empirically testing both potential antecedents and outcomes of the concept (Ritz et al. 2016).

Figure 30.1 depicts a conceptual model that schematically illustrates the theorized groups of antecedents and outcomes of PSM, many of which have been subject to more or less thorough empirical testing. It is important to note in regard to this model that in many cases, it is still subject to debate whether certain concepts are actually antecedents, correlates, or outcomes of PSM. This is due to the fact that research efforts on causality are still scarce in this field (two notable exceptions are Bellé 2013; Moynihan, 2013). Moreover, the model shown focuses on illustrating the breadth of the variable relationships surrounding PSM, neglecting the fact that many of the associations might be mediated or moderated (or both) by other variables, meaning that, in reality, relationships may be substantially more complex. There are several other models in PSM literature which focus more on the complexity of a smaller number of variable relationships, theorizing and testing moderations and mediations. Wright (2001), for instance, suggested a mediation-model of public sector work motivation including motives, work context, job attitudes, job characteristics, and work motivation, whereas Perry (2000) developed a process model of PSM including various socio-historical context variables, motivational context variables, individual characteristics, and certain behavioral variables. In addition, the relationships differ depending on which dimension of the public service motivation construct is associated with the antecedents and outcomes. For instance, empirical research showed that the dimension of compassion has stronger associations with females when compared to the other dimensions (Camilleri 2007; DeHart-Davis et al. 2006).

As for the antecedents, the scientific discourse has centered around seven broad categories. These include personal and socio-demographic attributes (which are included in many studies as control variables); organizational characteristics; socialization, political preference and

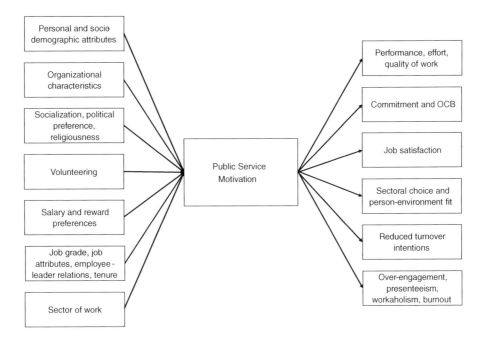

Figure 30.1 Conceptual model illustrating groups of antecedents and outcomes of public service motivation

religiousness; volunteering; salary and reward preferences; job grade or management level, job attributes, employee relations with the leader and tenure; and sector of work (Ritz et al. 2016; Vandenabeele 2011; Perry et al. 2008; Camilleri 2007; Perry 1997). We would like now to briefly discuss a few examples of empirical research regarding three of these categories. First, with respect to socialization, Perry (1997) demonstrated that both parental and religious socialization were significant predictors of elevated levels of PSM, using a sample of diverse public-sector employees and MPA students. He argues that parental socialization is relevant in the process of developing altruistic motivations such as compassion and self-sacrifice, whereas religious socialization is particularly important in the US when it comes to learning how got get involved in the community. Second, with respect to volunteering, Anderfuhren-Biget (2012) demonstrated, based on a large dataset from the multicultural country of Switzerland, that engaging in benevolent activities and donating to charitable organizations are associated with the PSM-dimension self-sacrifice across cultural borders. Third, in regard to job attributes, Grant (2008b) demonstrated that the motivation of public service employees can be increased by enabling them to see the prosocial impact associated with their job.

Regarding the outcomes of PSM, six major groups can be identified. These are: performance, work effort and quality of work; commitment and organizational citizenship behaviors; job satisfaction; sectoral choice and person–environment fit; reduced turnover intentions; and, finally, a group of potentially harmful outcomes such as over-engagement, presenteeism, workaholism, and burnout, which can be seen as the "dark side" of PSM (Ritz et al. 2016; Bellé and Cantarelli 2012; Taylor 2007). Again, we will discuss examples of empirical research regarding three of the most frequently researched outcome categories. First, regarding performance, Bellé (2013) showed in a field experiment involving 138 nurses in Italy that transformational leadership positively interacts with PSM to increase employee performance as measured in the number of surgical kits assembled in a shift. Second, regarding job satisfaction and using a public servant sample from Korea, Kim (2012) demonstrated that PSM is associated with satisfaction both directly, and indirectly through mediation by means of person–organization fit, which was measured using three value congruence items. Third, as regards sectoral choice, Christensen and Wright (2011) found that individuals featuring high levels of public service motivation prefer jobs emphasizing service to others regardless of organization type, meaning that no clear link was established between PSM and organization or sector choice.

Conclusion

This chapter addresses the longstanding and important issue of employee motivation in the public sector from a theoretical perspective, while also integrating empirical findings from Public Administration research. In today's context of politico-administrative institutions, the task of motivating employees is becoming increasingly vital. Financial resources are scarce, competition in the labor market is increasing, while an aging society and workforce demand successful retention strategies, and complex accountability regimes characterize the modernized and managerialized government organization.

Motivation has the potential to make a difference regarding outcomes both on the individual and on the organizational level. Insights from classical process-based motivation, such as expectancy theory, goal-setting theory, and equity theory, stress three specific characteristics of the public sector for motivating employees. First, the instrumentality of one's own effort towards receiving the desired reward upon task completion is not always clear-cut. Second, goal setting within a context that has multiple, often competing, contradictory, and ambiguous goals is a great challenge. Lastly, the important role of values and principles that call for procedural and distributive fairness concerning reward allocation shows that equity perception in public sector workplaces is strongly supported by the institutional context and the organizational culture.

Several content-based theories of motivation emphasize the eudaemonic facet of motivation, which focuses on the role of meaning and purpose in motivating humans. In the societal context of government organizations, public values have the potential to infuse organizations' and individuals' value structures, leading to forms of prosocial motivation focusing on providing support to the public interest and helping citizens. Public service motivation, in contrast to public sector motivation, explains why employees act upon a mix of motives in which prosocial, public-value-focused motives are at the fore as their environment and identity demands them to – the so-called logic of appropriateness. Research on public service motivation has developed into one of the few original streams of research in Public Administration. Theoretical development, supplemented by a great variety of empirical research, has also increased considerably. This is particularly true where the core components of such motivation are concerned; these relate to the attraction to public service and policy making, the commitment to public values, and affective components such as compassion and self-sacrifice. Public service motivation is not an entirely new concept and can be found in various historical texts and eras. Thus far, empirical research has generated a broad range of insights on the antecedents and outcomes of public service motivation. This is of particular relevance to Public Administration research since, for the first time, it marks the existence of a fully-fledged concept of motivation based on institutional theory and related to individuals' needs, values and behavior, as well as to the wider context of public organizations and society.

References

Adams, J. S. 1965. "Inequity in social exchange." In *Advances in experimental social psychology*, Vol. 2, edited by Berkowitz, L., 267–299. New York: Academic Press.

Akerlof, G. and R. Kranton. 2010. *Identity Economics*. Princeton, NJ: Princeton University Press.

Alderfer, C. 1969. "An Empirical Test of a New Theory of Human Needs." *Organizational Behavior and Human Performance* 4 (2): 142–175.

Allison, G. T. 1983. "Public and private management: Are they fundamentally alike in all unimportant respects?" In *Public Management*, edited by Perry, J. L. and K. L. Kraemer, 72–92. Palo Alto: Mayfield.

Anderfuhren-Biget, S. 2012. "Profiles of Public Service-Motivated Civil Servants: Evidence from a Multicultural Country." *International Journal of Public Administration* 35 (1): 5–18.

Andersen, L. B., T. B. Jorgensen, A. M. Kjeldsen, L. H. Pedersen, and K. Vrangbaek. 2013. "Public values and public service motivation: conceptual and empirical relationships." *American Review of Public Administration* 43 (3): 292–311.

Batson, D. C. 1987. "Prosocial motivation: Is it ever truly altruistic?" In *Advances in Experimental Social Psychology*, Vol. 20, edited by Berkowitz, L., 65–122. New York: Academic Press.

Bellé, N. 2013. "Leading to make a difference: a field experiment on the performance effects of transformational leadership, perceived social impact, and public service motivation." *Journal of Public Administration Research and Theory* 24 (1): 109–136.

Bellé, N. and P. Cantarelli. 2012. "Public service motivation: the state of the Art." In *Reforming the Public Sector. How to achieve better Transparency, Service, and Leadership*, edited by Tria. G. and G. Valotti, 96–125. Washington, DC: Brookings Institution Press.

Bolino, M. C. 1999. "Citizenship and impression management: Good soldiers or good actors?" *Academy of Management Review* 24: 82–98.

Bozeman, B. 1987. *All Organizations are Public: Bridging Public and Private Organization Theory*. San Francisco: Jossey-Bass.

Brennan, G. and J. M. Buchanan. 1985. *The Reason of Rules. Constitutional Political Economy*. Cambridge: Cambridge University Press.

Brewer, G. and S. Selden. 1998. "Whistle blowers in the federal civil service: new evidence of the public service ethic." *Journal of Public Administration Research and Theory* 8 (3): 413–440.

Brewer, G., S. C. Selden, and R. L. Facer II. 2000. "Individual conceptions of public service motivation." *Public Administration Review* 60 (3): 254–264.

Buelens, M. and H. Van den Broeck. 2007. "An analysis of differences in work motivation between public and private sector organizations." *Public Administration Review* 67 (1): 65–74.

Camilleri, E. 2007. "Antecedents affecting public service motivation." *Personnel Review* 36 (3): 356–377.

Christensen, R. K. and B. E. Wright. 2011. "The effects of public service motivation on job choice decisions: disentangling the contributions of person–organization fit and person–job fit." *Journal of Public Administration Research and Theory* 21 (4): 723–743.

Christensen, R. K. and B. E. Wright. 2009. "The effects of public service motivation on job choice decisions: exploring the contributions of person–organization fit and person–job fit." Paper presented at the 10th Public Management Research Conference in Columbus, OH.

Chun, Y. H. and H. G. Rainey. 2006. "Consequences of goal ambiguity in public organizations." In *Public Service Performance: Perspectives on Measurement and Management*, edited by Boyne, G. A., K. J. Meier, J. Laurence, J. O'Toole, and R. M. Walker, 92–112. New York: Cambridge University Press.

Coursey, D. H. and S. K. Pandey. 2007. "Public service motivation measurement: testing an abridged version of Perry's proposed scale." *Administration & Society* 39 (5): 547–568.

Deci, E. L. and R. Ryan. 2002. *Handbook of Self-Determination Research*. Rochester: University of Rochester's Press.

DeHart-Davis, L., J. Marlowe, and S. K. Pandey. 2006. "Gender dimensions of public service motivation." *Public Administration Review* 66 (6): 873–887.

Downs, A. 1967. *Inside Bureaucracy*. Boston: Little, Brown.

Francois, P. 2000. "'Public service motivation' as an argument for government provision." *Journal of Public Economics* 78 (3): 275–299.

French, P. E. and M. C. Emerson. 2014. "Assessing the variations in reward preference for local government employees in terms of position, public service motivation, and public sector motivation." *Public Performance & Management Review* 37 (4) 552–576.

Giauque, D., A. Ritz, F. Varone, S. Anderfuhren-Biget, and C. Waldner. 2011. "Putting public service motivation into context: a balance between universalism and particularism." *International Review of Administrative Sciences* 77 (2): 227–253.

Gordon, S. B. 1972. "A Theory of political ambition: career choices and the role of structural incentives." *American Political Science Review* 66 (1): 144–159.

Grant, A. M. 2008a. "Does intrinsic motivation fuel the prosocial fire? Motivational synergy in predicting persistence, performance, and productivity." *Journal of Applied Psychology* 93 (1): 48–58.

Grant, A. M. 2008b. "Employees without a cause: The motivational effects of prosocial impact in public service." *International Public Management Journal* 11 (1): 48–66.

Heckhausen, H. 1989. *Motivation und Handeln.* Berlin: Springer.

Herzberg, F. 1968. "One more time: how do you motivate employees?" *Harvard Business Review* 46 (1): 53–62.

Horton, S. 2008. "History and persistence of an idea and an ideal." In *Motivation in Public Management: The Call of Public Service*, edited by Perry, J. L. and A. Hondeghem, 17–32. New York et al. Oxford: Oxford University Press.

Houston, D. J. 2011. "Implications of occupational locus and focus for public service motivation: attitudes toward work motives across nations." *Public Administration Review* 71 (5): 761–771.

Jorgensen, T. B. and B. Bozeman. 2007. "Public values: an inventory." *Administration & Society* 39 (3): 354–381.

Jung, C. S. 2011. "Organizational goal ambiguity and performance: conceptualization, measurement, and relationships." *International Public Management Journal* 14 (2): 193–217.

Jung, C. S. and A. Ritz. 2014. "Goal management, management reform, and affective organizational commitment in the public sector." *International Public Management Journal* 17 (4): 463–492.

Karl, K. A. and C. L. Sutton. 1998. "Job values in today's workforce: a comparison of public and private sector employees." *Public Personnel Management* 27 (4): 515–527.

Kim, S. 2012. "Does person–organization fit matter in the public-sector? Testing the mediating effect of person–organization fit in the relationship between public service motivation and work attitudes." *Public Administration Review* 72 (6): 830–840.

Kim, S. and W. Vandenabeele. 2010. "A Strategy for Building Public Service Motivation Research Internationally." *Public Administration Review* 70 (5): 701–709.

Kim, S., W. Vandenabeele, B. E. Wright, L. B. Andersen, F. P. Cerase, et al. 2013. "Investigating the meaning and structure of public service motivation across populations." *Journal of Public Administration Research and Theory* 23 (1): 79–102.

Koehler, M. and H. G. Rainey. 2008. "Interdisciplinary foundations of public service motivation." In *Motivation in Public Management: The Call of Public Service*, edited by Perry, J. L. and A. Hondeghem, 33–55. New York/Oxford: Oxford University Press.

Latham, G. P. and E. A. Locke. 2007. "New developments in and directions for goal-setting research." *European Psychologist* 12 (4): 290–300.

Lewis, G. B. and S. A. Frank. 2002. "Who wants to work for the government?" *Public Administration Review* 62 (4): 395–404.

Locke, E. A. and G. P. Latham. 1991. "Self-regulation through goal setting." *Organizational Behavior and Human Decision Processes* 50 (2): 212–247.

March, J. G. and J. P. Olsen. 2009. "The logic of appropriateness." Arena working papers 04/09. Olso: Arena Center for European Studies University of Oslo.

March, J. G. and J. P. Olsen. 1989. *Rediscovering Institutions: The Organizational Basis of Politics.* New York: Free Press.

Maslow, A. H. 1943. "A theory of human motivation." *Psychological Review* 50 (4): 370–396.

McClelland, D. C. 1985. "How motives, skills, and values determine what people do." *American Psychologist* 40 (7): 812–825.

Moynihan, D. P. 2013. "Does public service motivation lead to budget maximization? evidence from an experiment." *International Public Management Journal* 16 (2): 179–196.

Moynihan, D. P. 2008. *The Dynamics of Performance Management: Constructing Information and Reform.* Washington, DC: Georgetown University Press.

Neumann, O. and A. Ritz. 2015. "Public service motivation and rational choice modeling." *Public Money and Management* 35 (5): 365–370.

OECD. 2013. *Pensions at a Glance 2013: OECD and G20 Indicators.* Paris: OECD Publishing.

Osterloh, M., B. S. Frey, and J. Frost. 2001. "Managing motivation, organization and governance." *Journal of Management and Governance* 5 (3–4): 231–239.

Perry, J. L. 2000. "Bringing Society in: toward a theory of public-service motivation." *Journal of Public Administration Research and Theory* 10 (2): 471–488.

Perry, J. L. 1997. "Antecedents of public service motivation." *Journal of Public Administration Research and Theory* 7 (2):181–197.

Perry, J. L. 1996. "Measuring public service motivation: an assessment of construct reliability and validity." *Journal of Public Administration Research and Theory* 6 (1): 5–22.

Perry, J. L., J. L. Brudney, D. H. Coursey, and L. Littlepage. 2008. "What drives morally committed citizens? A study of the antecedents of public service motivation." *Public Administration Review* 68 (3): 445–458.

Perry, J. L., T. A. Engbers, and S. Y. Jun. 2009. "Back to the future? Performance-related pay, empirical research, and the perils of persistence." *Public Administration Review* 69 (1): 39–51.

Perry, J. L. and A. Hondeghem. 2008. "Editors' Introduction." In *Motivation in Public Management: The Call of Public Service*, edited by Perry. J. L., and A. Hondeghem, 1–14. New York et al.: Oxford University Press.

Perry, J. L. and L. R. Wise. 1990. "The motivational bases of public service." *Public Administration Review* 50 (3): 367–373.

Peters, B. G. 2000. *Institutional Theory in Political Science: The New Institutionalism*. London: Continuum.

Rainey, H. G. 2010. "Goal ambiguity and the study of American bureaucracy." In *The Oxford Handbook of American Bureaucracy*, edited by Durant, R. F., 231–251. New York: Oxford University Press.

Rainey, H. G. 1982. "Reward Preferences among Public and Private Managers: In Search of the Service Ethic." *American Review of Public Administration* 16 (4): 288–302.

Ritz, A. and G. A. Brewer. 2013. "Does culture affect public service motivation? Evidence of sub-national differences in Switzerland." *International Public Management Journal* 16 (2): 224–251.

Ritz, A., G. A. Brewer, and O. Neumann. 2016. "Public service motivation – a systematic literature review and outlook." *Public Administration Review* 76 (3): 414–426.

Ritz, A. and F. Sager. 2010. "Outcome-based public management and the balance of powers in the context of direct democracy." *Public Administration* 88 (1): 120–135.

Scott, W. R. 1987. "The adolescence of institutional theory." *Administrative Science Quarterly* 32 (4): 493–511.

Selznick, P. 1984. *Leadership in Administration: A Sociological Interpretation*. Berkeley, CA: University of California Press.

Spector, P. E. 2013. "Introduction: the dark and light sides of organizational citizenship behavior." *Journal of Organizational Behavior* 34 (4): 540–541.

Spitzmueller, M. and L. Van Dyne. 2013. "Proactive and reactive helping: Contrasting the positive consequences of different forms of helping." *Journal of Organizational Behavior* 34 (4): 560–580.

Taylor, J. 2007. "The impact of public service motives on work outcomes in Australia: a comparative multi-dimensional analysis." *Public Administration* 85 (4): 931–959.

Vandenabeele, W. 2011. "Who wants to deliver public service? Do institutional antecedents of public service motivation provide an answer?" *Review of Public Personnel Administration* 31 (1): 87–107.

Vandenabeele, W. 2008. "Development of a public service motivation measurement scale: corroborating and extending Perry's measurement instrument." *International Public Management Journal* 11 (1): 143–167.

Vandenabeele, W. and N. Van Loon. 2015. "Motivating employees using public service." In *Handbook of Public Administration*, 3rd edition, edited by Perry, J. L. and R. K. Christensen, 353–365. San Francisco: Jossey-Bass.

Vroom, V. H. 1964. *Work and Motivation*. New York: Wiley.

Wildavsky, A. 1979. *Speaking Truth to Power*. Boston: Little, Brown.

Wright, B. E. 2001. "Public-sector work motivation: a review of the current literature and a revised conceptual model." *Journal of Public Administration Research and Theory* 11 (4): 559–586.

31

PUBLIC BUDGETING FROM A MANAGERIAL PERSPECTIVE

Riccardo Mussari

Introduction

Nowadays, there is a recognized right to have a budget in all democracies. Citizens have the right to know in advance the amount of taxes they will be required to pay, and for what purposes and objectives that money will be spent. The literature on budgeting is immense even though, while several European countries have a long public accounting and budgeting tradition (Mussari, Ruggiero, and Monfardini 2010), in the US, "budgeting as we know it is a twentieth-century phenomenon. Indeed, until about 1910, the president, governors and mayors did not prepare formal budget documents" (Downs and Larkey 1986: 146).

Several disciplines study budgets and the budgeting process using diverse but complementary research methods and approaches: public policy, political science, economics, public management, public accounting and public finance (Caiden 1978). Such a complex and much-debated issue cannot be confined to a single chapter. Thus, we have limited our analysis to a few topics: the budget as a political and managerial document; approaches used to explain and justify budget formulation, including classical rationality, with its variant bounded rationality, and disjointed incrementalism; the functions and principles of budgeting; and budget formats. The perspective used in the presentation and discussion of these topics is consistent with public financial management theories and practices, though reference will also be made to public policy literature. While we will focus mainly on the political and managerial perspectives of budgeting, it is worth mentioning that the public budget also has a macro-economic dimension, constituting a tool for the redistribution of income and the stimulation of growth and development through the promotion of economic stability and equity.

The budget as a managerial and political document

The budget is a two-faceted financial plan composed of the sources of funds and their uses. The financial resources to be used in a future period in order to implement a specific plan of action are quantified on one side while the other side identifies the sources from which the resources will have to be drawn. The period covered by the financial forecast may be short (one year), medium (up to three years) or long (over three years). The word budget traditionally refers to a short-term forecast or annual budget. When the time horizon of the budget is longer, we have a medium-term or long-term budget. The budget is always related to the future; hence it is a planning tool. Its contents, regardless of any choices made concerning its organization and presentation, refer to events that have not yet occurred or, at least, whose financial effects are not yet fully manifested, even when they are dependent on decisions made in the past. For example, consider the case of predicting the future payment of a loan instalment. The loan agreement was signed in the past, but that decision determines a future payment that must be forecast and covered in the budget.

Yet the budget is also a control tool. Its financial data will be used in order to achieve future targets. Consequently, the budget can also be interpreted as the basic information necessary to check whether, and to what extent, what was intended is effectively achieved. It is a yardstick against which to measure actual performance. The type of control that the budget makes possible to exercise depends on the approaches, methods and techniques followed when defining its content and format. Control of the budget could essentially cover only the resources spent (control of input) and/or performance (volumes, efficiency, effectiveness, outcomes) achieved following the use of the forecast resources. At the very least, the budget is indispensable in exercising control over government finances, in order to ensure that public money has been spent according to the will of the legislature (micro-control), and over fiscal risk (Petrie 2013), which is "the possibility of short-to medium-term deviations in fiscal variables compared with what is anticipated in the government budget" (Budina and Murray 2013: 176).

The budget is not simply a financial forecast but a document that, starting from a strategy defined upstream, guides the actions of those called upon to use financial and non-financial (human, material, immaterial) resources to achieve expected results. From this perspective, the budget is a managerial tool and budgeting is mainly approached as a technical problem.

In this chapter we will only refer to the public budget, prepared by any level of government: federal/central, state/regional and local. Deciding how much public money to spend and on what, where to draw it from and in what proportion are tasks that belong exclusively to elected representatives. A public budget is the output of political decisions taken within the context of a system of rules that govern the budgeting process at different levels of government (Lienert 2013a, 2013b). In countries with parliamentary systems, the budget is proposed by the executive and approved by the parliament. The budget is therefore a political document, in the sense that political bodies are responsible for the distribution of funds between competing and legitimate interests. Indeed, there is always a political side to the budget, since one "cannot take politics out of budgeting" (Donohue 1982: 62). Furthermore, the majority of financial resources quantified in the budget directly or indirectly derive from taxes levied as well as from fees and charges. Money drawn *directly* from the tax levy is used to fund the implementation of programmes and the provision/distribution of public services. Resources are used *indirectly* to repay the debts incurred to cover deficits momentarily generated by differences between income and expenditure.

Budget and decision-making theories

Dealing with budgets inevitably entails addressing how decisions are taken, as the budget is the output, or the last stage, of a decision-making process, and every decision is an act of choice (Simon 1965). To try to explain how budget decisions are made we could use normative models or descriptive models. If we use the first, we intend to explain how we can reach a decision using systems of formal rules (logical and mathematical models) that, in theory, should lead to optimal and rational choices. On the contrary, if we prefer to explain how individuals and groups make their decisions in practice, we use descriptive models. For the purposes of this chapter, we shall briefly recall the classical rational model, with its variant of bounded rationality, and disjointed incrementalism.

The rational model is a prescriptive one. It draws its support from economics, management and statistics. The rational decision maker (*homo economicus*):

- is consciously rational, and her or his behavior is rationally oriented to the achievement of goals chosen consciously;
- is always able to identify all possible alternatives;
- knows all the likely consequences of each possible alternative;
- evaluates all the alternatives and their consequences, even in the medium and long-term, and ranks them according to the result of the relationship between the costs and benefits of each alternative;
- chooses the best alternative (optimizing calculation) that shows the best ratio between benefits and costs;
- always chooses the same option, under equal conditions;
- is able to run through the behavior that led to her or his decision again, to explain and justify the decision taken.

The key element of the rational model is that the analysis must be both systematic and comprehensive, i.e. it must consider all the alternatives and factors relevant to the decision. This model is known as rational because the process by which the decision is arrived at is rational; not because its objectives are rational. In the rational perspective, the means are evaluated and chosen according to the ends, which are selected prior to and independently of the means. This implies not only that there is certainty about the values to which the ends are always related, but also that these values are sufficiently stable over time. The most significant attempt to introduce rational decision making into the budgeting process was the Planning–Programming–Budgeting System (PPBS). Created by analysts at the RAND Corporation in the 1950s, PPBS was first applied experimentally by Robert S. McNamara, Secretary of Defense, in the US Department of Defense. The basic ideas behind the experiment were, on the one hand, the need for explicit criteria to assess national defence needs in a long-term, five-year perspective and, on the other hand, the need to evaluate the costs and benefits of each alternative in order to justify and support budget decisions (Downs and Larkey 1986: 153–154). The key role of analysts in budgetary decisions was one of the main features of PPBS. In 1965, President Johnson ordered all federal agencies to introduce PPBS, only to revoke the order three years later. The following quotation explains why the introduction of rationality into public budget processes was a huge failure:

> No one knows how to do program budgeting … many know what program budgeting should be like in general, but no one knows what it should be in any particular case.
>
> *(Wildavsky 1969: 193).*

Other important attempts to introduce rational budgeting processes in the US were Management by Objectives, introduced in many federal agencies during the Nixon administration in 1973 and withdrawn in 1975, and zero–based budgeting (ZBB). ZBB was developed by Peter Pyhrr for Texas Instruments (USA) in 1969, with the specific aim of controlling rising overhead costs. It was first tried in Georgia under Jimmy Carter's governorship and then employed by US federal agencies under the Carter Administration from 1977. Neither attempt produced the expected changes.

A significant variant of the classical rational model is that of bounded rationality, proposed by Herbert A. Simon (Simon 1945). In an extreme synthesis, while he considered human behavior as intentionally rational, i.e. oriented towards a goal achieved by selecting possible alternative means:

- not all the goals and preferences are clear;
- knowledge of the alternatives and their consequences is always limited because gathering information is costly and not all possible alternatives can be considered;
- the ability to process information is also limited;
- it is not possible to order all the alternatives perfectly in rank;
- choice is a sequential process based on what is satisfactory, not optimal. The decision maker does not choose the best solution among all the possible alternatives but, within the limits of her or his computational capacity, analyzes the options until she or he finds one that meets her or his goals and aspirations.

Charles E. Lindblom (1959) seriously questions the rational model in his famous article, "The science of muddling through". He proposes an alternative model, disjointed incrementalism, clearly explaining why the classical model of rational decision making is inapplicable in practice and therefore not suitable to predict the actual behavior of individuals and groups. Indeed, identifying all possible alternatives, assessing them in terms of costs and benefits, and comparing them is not practically feasible, above all when many of the related decisions are taken by political bodies. Policy makers need consent and operate in an environment highly conditioned by the legitimate interests of different stakeholders. This specificity significantly limits the number of possible alternatives. In other words, the political decision maker is not wholly free to choose among all possible options. Moreover, even with the help of modern information technology, it is impossible to collect and process all the information that the rational model requires. It is also not realistic to choose first the ends, which are always conditioned by the decision maker's value system and then the means. In practice, choices are often performed simultaneously or in a reverse order to what is assumed: first you analyze the possible means, then you identify the ends that, given the available means, you will be able to achieve. In this way, the means become the ends or significantly determine them.

According to Lindblom, it is not only inevitable but also desirable that many public choices are based on a limited number of alternatives. Public decision making does not start from the specific objectives to be achieved through public policy but from existing policies, which have the advantage of being the output of a previous agreement. The decision concerns only incremental changes and marginal adjustments in relation to the existing policy, and develops through successive and limited comparisons within a reduced number of alternatives. Consequently, the analysis conducted will never be exhaustive and the relationship between means and ends is both continuous and reciprocal. As the object of the decision changes throughout the analysis, adjustments concern not only the solution to the problem but also its definition, meaning that the problems to be dealt with are constantly redefined according to the resources available to resolve them. Not surprisingly, theories are relatively influential in decision-making, tending to focus primarily on the short-term and most significant consequences that could arise from a certain decision, not on all possible consequences.

The most well-known scholar who empirically supported Lindblom's theory when applied to public budgeting was Aaron Wildavsky: "[t]he beginning of wisdom about an agency budget is that it is almost never actively reviewed as a whole every year ... Instead, it is based on last year's budget with special attention given to a narrow range of increases or decreases" (Wildavsky

1964: 15). Several scholars have criticized incrementalism (cf. Dror 1964; and Etzioni 1967). According to Dror (1964), it is conservative and does not incentivize innovation, reinforcing the interest groups and social forces that have always been more powerful, while potentially leaving out interests with little or no political representation. In fact, incrementalism works better when the results of public policies in place are sufficiently satisfactory and the social problems to be dealt with quite stable.

Budget functions and principles

The main functions of a public budget are: political; steering and programming; authorization; and cyclical economic policy, with specific regard to the federal/national government (Mussari 2003).

The *political function* derives from the fact that budget preparation and approval constitute the point at which different social interests are mediated by elected representatives and social aims are selected, as well as the ways of pursuing them. Budget approval by the parliament concretizes a traditional foundation of democracy, since it quantifies the resources that the parliament allows the government to take from citizens and allocate to specific public aims.

The *steering and programming function* consists in predetermining (quantifying and assigning to departments/agencies) the means (financial resources) needed to reach the objectives set. Although the emphasis is on the control of resources, in the budget forecast financial figures (appropriations) can be associated with information about expected operating results (outputs) and performance (efficiency, effectiveness, impact, outcomes). Information about the purposes of expenditure is also obtainable through budget classification by functions/objectives. The most known examples of standards for economic classification are those of the Classification of Functions of Government (COFOG), developed by the OECD.

The *authorization function* is the most typical feature of government budgets. Constraints regard not only the overall amounts of revenues and expenditures, which are related more to the political or economic policy functions, but also the specific purposes of each appropriation. In other words, appropriations approved by the parliament are binding for the managers of the departments/agencies in charge of spending them. Appropriations in the budget constitute limits to commitments and, in a more general sense, to assessments.

The *economic policy function* is due to the great weight and influence of government activities in the national economy; moreover, some interventions, such as transfers, investments in infrastructure, incentives to industry and social welfare, are clearly intended to have an effect on the economic cycle. Lastly, managing the huge flows of money connected with public expenditures and revenues is an important tool of monetary policy. This function is clearly connected to macrobudgeting.

Annual budgets and multi-year budgets have to be prepared and managed respecting the following principles: annuality; unity; specificity; universality; integrity; financial balance; publicity; truthfulness; and clarity (Di Rienzo, 2013: 139; Mussari 2003).

Annuality (only for the annual budget)

The annual budget refers to the financial year, which in the majority of countries coincides with the calendar year. For this reason, after December 31 of each year assessments of revenues and commitments cannot be carried out regarding the accounts of the year that has elapsed. At the end of the calendar year, the annual forecast expires and can no longer be used as a legitimate basis for ascertaining financial flows in revenues and using them in expenditures. Naturally, this implies that the annual budget must be proposed by the executive and approved by the parliament every year, and that the law must regulate possible delays in the approval of the new budget in order to avoid blocking public spending.

Unity

The whole amount of revenues indiscriminately finances the whole amount of expenditures. It is not possible to correlate a single revenue to a single expenditure. In other words, the budget refers to an aggregate amount of financial resources that can be comprehensively correlated to the aggregate amount of expenditures: every Euro that comes in indistinctly serves to finance every Euro that goes out. This principle is not threatened by the obligation to cover new or higher expenditures with new or higher revenues or fewer expenditures of a different kind.

Specificity

The term means an adequate classification of the revenues and expenditures in the budget in homogeneous and sufficiently analytical aggregates. This makes the budget clearer to read and, above all, renders control more effective, so that the legislative power functions over that of the executive through the budget. On the one hand, rigorous respect for the principle of specificity means avoiding an excessively summarized presentation of the items in the budget, particularly expenditures, so that the parliament can exercise effective prior control over the executive. On the other hand, it means seeking not to over-parcel the items in the budget, which would make the forecast incomprehensible and improperly rigid. The budgeting and accounting reforms of the late 1990s seem to have responded to this last need, having promoted changes to the classical line-item budget format by introducing performance budgeting.

Universality

All government revenues and expenditures must be listed in the budget. The financial management must be unique in the same way that the budget is unique, meaning that the use of off-budget funds and separate accounts is prohibited. The law should precisely regulate possible exceptions to this principle, i.e. contingent liabilities.

Integrity

All revenues must be listed in the budget, inclusive of the expenditures for collection to be charged to the collecting institution and of other possible connected expenditures. Likewise, all expenditures must be listed in their entirety without any reduction for the related revenues. The offsetting of budget items is prohibited. In this way, greater clarity regarding the budget values is ensured and the possibility of concealing the exact amount of particular operations is reduced.

Financial balance

Financial balance consists in perfect equality between the total revenues to be assessed and the total expenditures to be made. This means that the budget must be balanced at the time of its approval but also when it is changed during the financial year. When a comparison is made between all the revenues and all the expenditures, the overall balance can be achieved due to the inclusion of financial inflows coming from long-term loans. In other words, balancing does not automatically imply the neutrality of public finances. Yet in several countries the law regulates the possibility of taking out loans.

The golden rule and the EU

Recourse to the "golden rule", allowing government to take up debt only to finance public investments as a fiscal policy tool, has been the subject of lively debate, concerning both its application and its interpretation (Fabbrini 2013). As an emergency response to the 2009 sovereign debt crisis, European Union Member States signed the Treaty on Stability, Coordination and Governance in the Economic and Monetary Union (the so-called "fiscal compact"). This Treaty addresses the weaknesses of the previous Stability Growth Pact, which entered into force in 1999, in the field of fiscal policy. Article 3(1)(a) of the fiscal compact states that "the budgetary position of the general government of a Contracting Party shall be balanced or in surplus". Article 3(1)(c) allows for exceptions and states "the Contracting Parties may temporarily deviate [from their respective medium-term objective] … only in exceptional circumstances". These circumstances are defined in article 3(3)(b) as "an unusual event outside of the control of the Contracting Party concerned which has a major impact on the financial position of the general government or … periods of severe economic downturn". To ensure that Member States consider this provision as strictly binding, each contracting party is required to incorporate it in their domestic system through the highest source of law. The motivation is that the financial stability of the whole Monetary Union can be preserved by enhancing fiscal discipline in each Member State. Nonetheless, such a stringent fiscal policy could turn out to stifle public spending, thus limiting public investment that, in the past, was used in many European countries to deal with unemployment.

Publicity

The budget must be public and accessible to anyone interested in its contents. This means that budgets and annexes must be open to public scrutiny. The publication of all budget information on government websites is now the most effective way of applying this principle.

Truthfulness

The revenues and expenditures listed in the budget must be realistically achievable. The overestimation and/or underestimation of revenues and expenditures are prohibited: only predictable revenues and authorized expenditures can be listed in the budget. Budget forecasts should be as realistic as possible, in order to reduce discrepancies between forecast and actual data and guarantee the right to effective information for the parliament and citizens.

Clarity

This requirement is connected with those of specialization, publicity and truthfulness. Clarity means that the budget must be easy and comprehensible for citizens to read, while respecting budgeting and accounting rules and language.

Main budget formats

The financial information contained in a budget can be organized and presented according to different formats. The choice between them cannot be regarded as a simply technical matter. Formats "not only establish the rules by which the budgeting game is played (the decision rules), but they also create the standards by which success is measured (rules of evidence)" (Morgan 2002: 71). The most well-known budget formats are line-item/object/expenditure code budgets and performance budgets.

Line-item budget

The line-item budget is the simplest way of organizing and presenting budget information. It does not require the government to have trained specialists or analysts. Paraphrasing Wildavsky, it could be said that anyone can prepare a line-item budget! Its structure is based on objects of expenditure organized into three main classes: current, capital, and loan reimbursement. Current expenditures are devoted to the purchase of nondurable goods and services, i.e. costs to be sustained for the normal functioning of administration, such as staff, supplies, interest on loans, telephone charges, travel expenses, etc. Capital expenditures are sustained for the purchase of durable goods such as roads, bridges, rail networks, weapons, buildings, equipment, vehicles, etc.

The main classes of expenditure are broken down into categories and, in turn, each category can be divided into subcategories, and then into more detailed items. The greater the detail provided, the lower is management's discretion in the process of spending public money. Since line-item budgeting was introduced as a mechanism to increase control over public spending, i.e. control on the input, detailed and binding appropriations are normally used. Consequently, piecemeal appropriations make the budget very stiff and require frequent changes in appropriation. Other defects of this format are easily discerned from the description above. The line-item budget favours an incremental approach, since the amount of each detailed appropriation constitutes the basis for the formulation of the budget, without any need to link the budget requirements to performance or to any detailed quantitative or qualitative analysis. Managerial success often lies in simply spending all the money available, since this is the best way to increase the probability of obtaining the largest possible amount of monetary resources in the next budget negotiation. The line-item budget limits managerial accountability to financial compliance. The achievement of performance, and above all, efficiency, is not only independent of the quantity of resources that will become available, but can be counterproductive for public managers. Hypothetically, efficient behavior and consequent savings in expenditure end up generating negative side effects because, by reducing a budget base, an efficient manager is very likely to have reduced resources in future budget negotiations.

Performance budget

The first Hoover Commission in the USA called for the adoption of performance-based budgeting in 1949. However, performance management and measurement became more relevant to governments and other public sector organizations with the so-called New Public Management (NPM) movement (Hood 1995, 1991). This approach, which favours the quantification and measurement of economic performance (economy, efficiency and effectiveness) and shifts the focus of public administration from procedures to results, gives budgets and accounting systems a central role to play (Mussari 2013). Consequently, for many countries pursuing public administration reform, the use of financial and non-financial performance information has become a key element in budget reforms (Jones and Mussari 2004; Rubin 1996). Several countries have substituted traditional line-item budgets with forms of budgeting aimed at establishing a link between forecast expenses/expenditures and results to be achieved in terms of outputs and/or outcomes.

A performance budget (PB) is a form of budgeting that relates funds allocated to measurable results, in order to inform budget decisions and to "instil greater transparency and accountability throughout the budget process" (OECD 2011: 13). Depending on the degree of linkage between appropriations and performance information, three variants of PB can be distinguished (OECD 2007): presentational, performance-informed and formula-based. In practice, however, the general idea of PB has been implemented in very different ways over the last few decades, depending on the type and level of detail of the data, its role in different stages of the budget cycle, and its integration into general performance management (cf. Schick 2014). Here, we consider performance budgeting as the whole process aimed at linking resources employed (inputs) to measurable results (outputs/outcomes) in order to improve the efficiency, effectiveness and transparency of both goals and results. Thus, the ultimate purpose of PB is to satisfy both managerial and political needs. The former should be met by increasing internal accountability, making each organizational unit responsible for the resources allocated, activities defined and results planned, while the latter should focus more on external accountability, providing information to the public regarding performance objectives and results.

The level of aggregation of performance information included in the budget differs (Mussari et al. 2014; Robinson 2013): sometimes budgets are quite detailed, such as those of local government in Germany (Reichard 2014) and focus on single products or services, while in other countries, such as Italy, the budgets are relatively aggregated and concentrate on missions and programmes. The PB usually provides data and facts regarding different kinds of performance information: inputs, outputs, efficiency, effectiveness, quality, impacts and outcomes. Input figures (e.g. data concerning existing capacities, etc.) and physical output figures (e.g. the quantity of services provided) are most popular, since it is easier to link these performance targets to appropriations. Quality information is less frequently displayed, while information about impacts and outcomes, which usually comes from policy evaluations, remains quite rare.

The main advantages of PB are the increased pressure on departments to take targets seriously and greater consistency between targets defined and resources assigned (Robinson 2013: 51). Gaming and negative side effects are always possible consequences when performance information is calculated and used to distribute financial resources. Above all, the causal relationship between the quantity of money to be spent for a specific programme or service and the impact of improving the social problem being dealt with is very difficult to determine in the ex ante phase. Programme monitoring and management control systems become indispensable tools to support PB during implementation.

Outcome-based budgeting – Michigan

The US State of Michigan's Outcome-Based Budget was an approach to performance budgeting guided by Governor Jennifer M. Granholm in 2003 to develop "a better government" in response to the state's difficult financial position. (Cf. http://osbm2.osbm.state.nc.us/ncosbm/budget/view_rbb_background.shtm.) The first step in its implementation was the formation of planning groups focusing on six priority areas: Economy, Education, Environment, Health and Human services, Hometown Security, and Better Government. The Governor gained useful information from citizens regarding the budget. These important inputs were used as the basis for budget decisions. All agency budgets were then divided into activities, and each of them was assigned to the appropriate goal. Within work groups, activities were ranked to determine which of them could be funded within the budget cap assigned, so work group members were encouraged to look at current performance measures and focus on activities to improve results for the public.

Results-based budgeting – North Carolina

The State of North Carolina introduced results-based budgeting for fiscal year (FY) 2007–9 with the aim of encouraging more efficient and effective government. In the initial phase, every agency developed a mission statement, goal statements, fund purpose statements, service statements, service analyzes and performance measures (Cf. www.michigan.gov/documents/A13-16_115963_7.pdf.) RBB elements permitted more informed decisions and made stakeholders more conscious of the purpose behind each agency and the resources dedicated to each service. Furthermore, it became possible to assess programme effectiveness thanks to the newly introduced performance measures. The focus was placed on the alignment between goals, strategies and budgets, in order to strengthen monitoring and accountability.

For the purpose of clarity, it should be mentioned that we consider programme budgeting as a form of performance budgeting. Examples of programme budgeting systems can be found in France and Italy (Mussari 2013; Robinson 2013). This form of PB cannot be labelled as a formula funding performance budgeting, since the appropriations are not specifically quantified by applying an algebraic formula based on the costs and quantities of the output. Yet the programmes should undoubtedly be prioritized in terms of cost/benefit analysis and expected performance targets – above all, effectiveness – should be associated with each programme in the planning documents, which are prepared upstream of the budget.

Italian Programme budget

The Italian programme budget is a relevant example. In 2009, the central government budget reform law introduced programme budgeting. For expenses, funds are allocated to programmes, which are conceived as aggregates of expenditures aimed at the achievement of objectives defined within the scope of missions. The latter represent the main functions and the strategic objectives to be pursued through government expenditure. The achievement of each programme is attributed to a unique administrative unit, each of which is named according to the COFOG. If a programme is attributed to more than one unit, the relative percentage must be reported. The graph below, referring to the fiscal year 2014, shows how funds devoted to a specific mission – "social rights, social policies and family" – were allocated among its component programmes, and thus among the Ministries engaged in the achievement of that mission. (Cf. www.rgs.mef.gov.it/_Documenti/VERSIONE-I/e-GOVERNME1/Contabilit/Pubblicazioni/BudgetdelloStatoaLB2016-2018/Budget_a_LB_2016-2018.pdf.)

The histogram also shows the distribution of the total funds allocated to the mission (€86,070,048,289) among the Ministries involved. The Ministry of Economy and Finance (MEF) was involved in the accomplishment of six out of eight programmes on this mission, while the remainder was within the scope of the Ministry of Labor and Welfare. Thus, the Italian budgeting format boosts the prioritization of expenditure, identifying certain priorities within each mission and distributing funds only on that basis. Each unit is responsible for accomplishing its own programmes without over-spending the limits provided.

ZBB can also be considered a kind of performance budget. Each decision unit coincides with a formal organizational unit or with a programme, as long as only one person is responsible

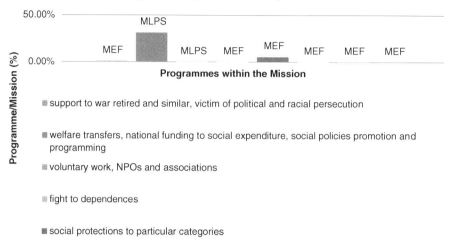

MISSION: social rights, social policies and family

support to war retired and similar, victim of political and racial persecution

welfare transfers, national funding to social expenditure, social policies promotion and programming

voluntary work, NPOs and associations

fight to dependences

social protections to particular categories

Figure 31.1 Mission: social rights, social policies and family
Source: our elaboration based on the Italian State budget – 2014–16, Allen et al. 2013

for the performance of the unit. According to Pyhrr (1973), each unit has to propose alternative ways of performing the same functions (decision packages) with consequent cuts or increases in funding. Then, the decision packages have to be evaluated in terms of their impact on the performance of the unit and consequently ranked. When ranking is complete, a detailed operating budget can be prepared for the decision packages approved. "One of the basic advantages of ZBB is that an organization can identify a reduced budget level, which still allows it to achieve the most important objective for which is responsible" (Morgan 2002: 127). However, ZBB does not mean that every organizational unit or programme must always start from zero at the beginning of budget negotiation. In practice, there are always expenditures that cannot be cut, which is the consequence of previously signed and unchangeable contracts.

Conclusions

All theoretical propositions, especially the descriptive ones, and consequent practices end up being influenced by the peculiarities of the economic, social and political scenarios in which they are proposed and implemented. Budget theories and practices cannot be an exception.

Incrementalism dominated the post–World War II period and was perfectly consistent with "budgeting for growth" (Schick 1990) in a period characterized by economic expansion and increasing tax revenues. Incrementalism was a successful microbudgeting theory, being short-term oriented and focused on portions of the administration (agencies, departments) rather than the government as a whole.

"Macrobudgeting – high-level decisions on spending, revenue and deficit totals and relative budget shares, often made from the top down – became increasingly prevalent because of the historically large, chronic deficits … [while] … Monetary union among European Union members and the accession criteria for prospective members required strict deficit control" (LeLoup 2002: 18). Although "the shift toward macrobudgeting in response to chronic deficits… did not witness the emergence of a single theory to replace incrementalism" (p. 19), the processes of reform have shown a general tendency towards results-based budgeting. Of course, "results" can have different meanings according to the theoretical perspective chosen to interpret public budgeting. From a microbudgeting perspective, different models of PB have been adopted in many countries, with the aim of motivating and inspiring public managers to perform more effectively and efficiently on the basis of the NPM doctrine. At the same time, from a macrobudgeting perspective, in many countries the focus is on fiscal discipline and on maintaining their financial position, with a growing need to find "fiscal space" to finance public investment without increasing public debt (Marcel 2014).

References

Budina N. and Murray P. (2013). Managing and Controlling Fiscal Risks, in Cangiano M., Curristine T., and Lazare M., *Public Financial Management and Its Emerging Architecture*. International Monetary Fund, Washington, DC, pp.175–204.

Caiden, N. (178). Patterns of Budgeting. *Public Administration Review*, Vol. 38, n. 6, pp. 539–544.

Di Rienzo, P. (2013). Assessing and Comparing the Quality of Public Financial Management Systems: Theory, History and Evidence, in Allen R., Hemming R.R., and Potter B.H. (eds), *International Handbook of Public Financial Management*. Palgrave Macmillan, Basingstoke, pp. 137–163.

Donohue, L. (1982). You Can't Take Politics Out of Budgeting. *Public Budgeting and Finance*, Vol. 2, No. 2, pp. 62–72.

Downs, G.W. and Larkey, P.D. (1986). *The Search for Government Efficiency: From Hubris to Helplessness*. Temple University Press, Philadelphia.

Dror, Y. (1964). Muddling Through "Science" or Inertia? *Public Administration Review*, Vol. 24, No. 3, pp. 153–157.

Etzioni, A. (1967). Mixed-Scanning: A "Third" Approach to Decision-Making. *Public Administration Review*, Vol. 27, No. 5, pp. 385–392.

Fabbrini, F. (2013). The Fiscal Compact, the "Golden Rule," and the Paradox of European Federalism. *Tilburg Law School Legal Studies Research Paper Series No. 013/2013*.

Hood C. (1995). The "New Public Management" in the 1980s: Variations on a Theme. *Accounting Organizations and Society*, Vol. 20, No. 2–3, pp. 93–109.

Hood, C. (1991). A Public Management for All Seasons? *Public Administration*, Vol. 69, No. 1, pp. 3–19.

Jones, L.R. and Mussari, R. (2004). Management Control Reform in the Public Sector: Contrasting the USA and Italy, in Jones, L.R., Schedler, K., Mussari, R. (eds), *Strategies for Public Management Reform*. Elsevier, London, pp. 205–226.

LeLoup, L. (2002). Budget Theory for a New Century, Khan A. and Hildreth (eds), *Budget Theories in the Public Sector*. Quorum Books, Westport, pp. 1–21.

Lienert, I. (2013a). The Legal Framework for Public Finances and Budget Systems, in Allen R., Hemming R.R. and Potter B.H. (eds), *International Handbook of Public Financial Management*. Palgrave Macmillan, Basingstoke, pp. 63–83.

Lienert, I. (2013b). Role of the Legislature in the Budget Process, in Allen, R., Hemming, R. and Potter, B.H. (eds), *International Handbook of Public Financial Management*. Palgrave Macmillan, Basingstoke, pp. 116–136.

Lindblom, C.E. (1959). The Science of "Muddling Through". *Public Administration Review*, Vol. 19, No. 2, pp. 79–88.

Marcel, M. (2014). Budgeting for Fiscal Space and Government Performance beyond the Great Recession. *OECD Journal on Budgeting*, Vol. 13, No. 2, pp. 1–39.

Morgan, D. (2002). *Handbook on Public Budgeting*. State of Oregon Edition.

Mussari, R. (2013). La comptabilité publique, instrument et enjeu des rapports entre pouvoir central et collectivités locales: le cas du processus d'harmonisation en Italie. *Revue Politiques et Management Publique*, Vol. 30, no. 3, pp. 395–410.

Mussari, R. (2003). Governmental Accounting and Budgeting in Italy, National Government, in Lüder, K. and Jones, R. (eds), *Reforming Governmental Accounting and Budgeting in Europe*. Fachverlag Moderne Wirtschaft, Frankfurt am Main, pp. 414–474.

Mussari, R., Ruggiero, P., Monfardini, P. (2010). Retorica e pratica della contabilità finanziaria: i bilanci negli stati pre-unitari e del Regno d'Italia in "Contabilità e bilanci per l'amministrazione economica

– Stato e Istituzioni di interesse pubblico in Italia dal XVI al XX secolo". *Atti del X Convegno nazionale della Società Italiana di Storia della Ragioneria*. Rirea, Roma, pp. 637–676.

Mussari R., Tranfaglia, A.E., Reichard, C., Bjørnå, H., Nakrošis, V., and Bankauskaité-Grigaliūnienė, S. (2014). Design, trajectories of reform and implementation of Performance budgeting in local governments – A comparative study of Germany, Italy, Lithuania and Norway, paper presented at *2014 EGPA Annual Conference*, 10–12 September 2014, Speyer (Germany).

OECD (2011). Introduction to 2011 OECD Performance Budgeting Survey. Paper presented at the *7th Annual Meeting on Performance & Results*. OECD Conference Centre, Paris. 9–10 November 2011.

OECD (2007). *Performance Budgeting in OECD Countries*. OECD, Paris.

Petrie, M. (2013) Managing Fiscal Risk, in Allen R., Hemming R. and Potter B.H. (eds), *International Handbook of Public Financial Management*. Palgrave Macmillan, Basingstoke, pp. 590–618.

Pyhrr, P. (1973). *Zero-Base Budgeting: A Practical Management Tool for Evaluating Expenses*. John Wiley and Sons, New York.

Reichard, C. (2014). Leistungsinformationen im neuen Kommunalhaushalt – welche Rolle spielen diese Daten in der Praxis? *Verwaltung & Management* Vol. 20, No. 3, pp. 125–129.

Robinson, M. (2013). Performance Budgeting, in Allen, R., Hemming, R. and Potter, B.H. (eds), *International Handbook of Public Financial Management*. Palgrave Macmillan, Basingstoke, pp. 237–258.

Rubin, I.S. (1996). Strategies for the New Budgeting, in Perry J.L. (ed.). *Handbook of Public Administration*, second edition. Jossey-Bass, San Francisco,

Schick, A. (2014). The Metamorphoses of Performance Budgeting. *OECD Journal on Budgeting*, Vol. 13, No. 2, pp. 1–31.

Schick, A. (1990). *The Capacity to Budget*. Urban Institute Press, Washington, DC.

Simon, Herbert A. (1965). Administrative Decision Making. *Public Administration Review*, Vol. 25, No. 1, pp. 31–37.

Simon, Herbert A. (1945). *The Administrative Behaviour*. Free Press, Macmillan, London.

Wildavsky, A. (1964). *The Politics of the Budgetary Process*. Little, Brown & Company, Boston, 1964.

Wildavsky, A. (1969). Rescuing Policy Analysis from PPBS, *Public Administration Review*, Vol. 29, No. 2, pp. 189–202.

32

THE ROAD AHEAD FOR PUBLIC PROCUREMENT IN EUROPE

Is there life after the directives?

Giulia Di Pierro and Gustavo Piga

Introduction[1]

Public procurement consists in the purchase of goods, services and works by governments, public authorities and the public sector. Public procurement represents a significant fraction of the total economy of a country, ranging in size between 15–20 per cent of the Gross Domestic Product (GDP). An efficient and effective public procurement process is therefore a key priority for policy makers worldwide, whose main objective is to deliver the greatest value for taxpayers' money and make a real contribution to sustainable development. This can be achieved not only focusing on short-term objectives, often convenient for political purposes, but also, on long-term objectives. By purchasing a very large volume of goods and services, public authorities have the bargaining power to encourage the achievement of broader government objectives, i.e. increasing employment, SME and regional development, social inclusion and cohesion, innovation and sustainability.

These goals assume even more importance during periods of economic downturn and recessions, when there is a general increase of unemployment, a decrease of investment, a deadlock of private sector activity, and rising poverty and social inequality. The recent financial crisis led a vast majority of countries around the world into severe budgetary constraints and economic difficulties. In that scenario, the optimal management of public procurement is a matter of primary importance for governments and represents a powerful, market-based instrument for the socio-economic growth of both developed and developing countries. As Sykes (2003) stated, "increasingly governments around the world see public procurement as a vehicle for changing behavior and leveraging policy outcomes".

A study conducted by the United Nations demonstrated that a reform in public procurement could potentially yield up to 5–10 per cent efficiency benefits. Recently, numerous public procurement legislative acts, regulatory frameworks and regulations were revised to better adapt to new evolving market dynamics and to act as a lever for economic recovery and social development. Outcomes include an updated UNCITRAL Model Law on Public Procurement by the United Nations (2011), a revised Agreement on Government Procurement by the World Trade Organization (entered into force in April 2014) and three new Directives by the European Union (published in March 2014 and entered into force in April 2016).

This case study focuses on the innovative aspects of new European Directives on public procurement, highlighting some of the main provisions that could significantly influence European development in the medium- and long-term. Key topics discussed include: SME involvement, simplification of procedures and how to cut "red tape", green public procurement, social inclusion, corruption and other anti-competitive behaviors, and innovation. For each topic, the authors point out if and how the new Directives succeeded in achieving the main objectives communicated by the European Commission in its Impact Assessment (Table 32.1).

The main aim of the chapter is to demonstrate how critical public procurement is to achieving government objectives, especially in times of economic downturn, and how much the new EU Directives reflect this. The authors provide a critical analysis of the new provisions, outlining emerging trade-offs, major future challenges and opportunities for further improvement.

Table 32.1 Objectives of the European Directives

General objectives
Promote EU-wide and cross-border competition for contracts
Deliver best value for money whilst achieving the best possible procurement outcomes for society
Aid the fight against corruption
Specific objectives
Improve the cost-efficiency of EU public procurement rules and procedures
Take full advantage of all opportunities to deliver the best possible outcomes for society
Create European rather than national markets for procurement
Operational objectives
Ensure that the rules capture the appropriate actors and subject-matter of procurement
Provide clarity and legal certainty with respect to said scope and coverage
Streamline and simplify procurement procedures to (1) reduce operational costs (2) ensure proportionality and (3) provide for more legal certainty
Improve the flexibility of procedures to better respond to purchasing needs of authorities
Help public procurers to use public procurement to support other policy objectives (e.g. environmental, social, initiatives related to the innovative economy) in a legally compliant and fair manner
Simplify the rules and introduce instruments to increase the transparency of EU public procurement rules and open-up the markets to greater cross-border competition
Ensure that the rules facilitate participation by MSMEs
Ensure consistent application, controls and monitoring of public procurement policy and outcomes across Member States
Reduce errors and problems with compliance with EU public procurement rules

Source: European Commission – Impact Assessment (2011)

Private vs public procurement

Both private and public procurement consist in the purchase of goods, services or works for a particular group of stakeholders with the goal of maximizing the value for money and the efficiency of the transaction. However, although sharing the main objective, public authorities and private companies follow different procurement procedures and are subject to different regulation.

Why do public authorities conduct their procurement activities differently from private organizations? There are many possible reasons.

Firstly, the source of funding of public procurement is different, as public procurement involves citizens' money, thus public money. This implies additional scrutiny beyond that of a private company (McCue et al. 2007), in order to ensure not only that the money is spent in a responsible and optimal way, minimizing the waste of public resources, but also to guarantee the respect of the principles of transparency, competition, equal treatment and non-discrimination. For instance, it is of utmost importance that all the public procurement process is carried out under maximum level of transparency so that every supplier willing to participate to a public tender can have access to the same set of information and have equal opportunity to compete; or it is crucial that the selection and award criteria are chosen in a way that is not discriminatory for any potential supplier. To this end, public authorities must comply with a stricter set of regulations and organizational procedures than the private sector (Murray 1999).

A second major difference between public and private procurement regards the size of the demand for goods, services or works. In the public sector, the procurement demand is greater than in the private sector, considering that, as previously mentioned, public procurement generally accounts for 15–20 per cent of a country's GDP. The demand is also much more heterogeneous in the public sector, as public authorities do not buy only for their own organization, but mainly for the citizens they are expected to serve. Many different stakeholders are indeed involved in public purchasing activity, whose interests may not always be in line with each other, creating challenging situations for public authorities that need to balance them.

A third reason consists in the role that public procurement has in society. Public entities are expected to show exemplary behavior in their procurement activities, efficiently using public funds and, at the same time, complying with ethical, social and environmental standards (Telgen et al. 2007).

Public procurement in Europe

The recent financial and economic crisis led the majority of European countries into situations of decreased GDP and tight budget constraints (Figure 32.1).

The optimal management of public resources is therefore a matter of primary importance for European public policy-makers, especially if we consider that public procurement accounts for around 15–17 per cent of the EU's GDP. Currently, Europe has its public procurement budget managed by more than 250,000 Contracting Authorities (hereinafter CAs) that annually conduct around two million procedures for the award of public contracts. The result is a highly heterogeneous and complex system. For this reason, the main purpose of the EU public procurement legislation is to harmonize the various procurement regulations in order to ensure that all European companies can participate in cross-border tenders without any legal or administrative barriers. The general principles of public procurement regulations are equal treatment of all the economic operators, transparency, non-discrimination and open competition.

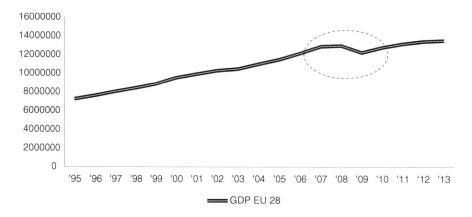

Figure 32.1   GDP EU 28 in million euro
Source: Eurostat 2014

European public procurement is currently governed by secondary provisions, as Directives and Regulations, to which all the European CAs must adhere when awarding public contracts. In particular, the core provisions of EU public procurement are expressed in the following three Directives:

- *Directive 2014/24/EU* on public procurement (repealing the Directive 2004/18/EC).
- *Directive 2014/25/EU* on procurement by entities operating in the water, energy, transport and postal services sectors (repealing the Directive 2004/17/EC).
- *Directive 2014/23/EU* on the award of concession contract.

These Directives regulate only procurement procedures for high-value contracts, i.e. contracts whose value is above the thresholds set by the European Commission and updated every two years. All public contracts below these thresholds are outside the Directives' scope. On January 1, 2016 the European Commission published the new thresholds for the procedures for the award of contracts valid until December 31, 2017.

The development of these three new Directives on public procurement was a result of a long and complex process of consultations and debates among interested parties, started in January 2011 and completed in March 2014. This new package does not entail a change of the paradigm in force since 2004, but it introduces major changes (Meideros 2014). At this moment, the main challenge faced by each Member State is to accomplish a balanced and effective application of these Directives through the timely implementation in national legislation and the change of the existing institutional and organizational systems as well as of the most relevant public procurement policies (Tavares 2014). Although a timely implementation is desirable, policy makers must avoid the dangerous phenomenon of "gold plating", intended as a direct adoption of the new Directives' provisions in the national legislation without harmonizing them to the specific situation of the country. What follows is an overview of the most innovative aspects of these EU Directives.

Sustainable public procurement

One key objective of every public procurement policy is to make a real contribution to sustainable development. There are several definitions of the concept of sustainable development and the most commonly used is "a development that meets the need of the present without compromising the ability of future generations to meet their own needs" (World Commission on Environment and Development 1987). Sustainability involves three specific interlinked dimensions that every organization should consider in its operations: economic efficiency, social performance and environmental performance. As Norman and MacDonald (2003) suggested in their triple bottom line approach, an organization can be successful in the long term only if it considers the interests of all the stakeholders and measures its success not only "by the traditional financial bottom line, but also by its social, ethical and environmental performance".

Whenever governments or public authorities carry out their purchasing activities, taking into account these three main pillars of sustainability, they are engaged in the so-called "sustainable public procurement". As of now, there is a common tendency of public administrations to focus mostly on the economic dimension, trying to maximize the efficiency and effectiveness of the procurement, while reducing costs and minimizing the waste of public resources. Although the latter is extremely important, an appropriate balance of all the three aspects (economic, social and environmental) is crucial in order to achieve sustainable public procurement in the long term.

During the last decade, the European Union has paid increasing attention to the role played by governments in promoting sustainable public procurement both through the regulatory framework and through a system of incentives given to public authorities. Coherent with this aim, in 2010 the EU published the strategy "Europe 2020", whose main priorities are:

- *Smart growth*: developing an economy based on knowledge and innovation.
- *Sustainable growth*: promoting a low-carbon, resource-efficient and competitive economy.
- *Inclusive growth*: fostering a high employment economy, equal opportunities (particularly for small and medium enterprises) and social cohesion.

The 2014 European Directives on public procurement show a clear trend toward the instrumental use of public contracts to achieve the broader government objectives mentioned above (Medeiros 2014).

Micro, small and medium enterprises

Representing 99.8 per cent of all enterprises, micro, small and medium enterprises (hereinafter MSMEs) are considered the backbone of the European economy as well as key drivers for European growth, competitiveness and social integration. MSMEs employ approximately 67.4 per cent of Europeans (Eurostat 2012), and contribute to innovation (Anschoff et al. 2009), entrepreneurship (Reed et al. 2004) and job creation (Morand 2003). Due to their importance, European policy makers commit themselves to fostering a favorable business environment for MSMEs by removing major factors that hamper their participation in public procurement.

Many barriers discourage or prevent MSMEs from being awarded public contracts, including:

- large size of contracts;
- difficulties in obtaining information about tender opportunities and lack of clarity in tender requirements;

- cost of participation and preparation of proposals (tender securities, onerous pre-qualification documentation, registration fees, large number of documents and certificates required);
- insufficient time to prepare and submit an offer;
- high administrative burden, including disproportionate financial requirements, long-term payments or delays in payment to suppliers.

The new Directives introduced important provisions to help MSMEs to reach a level playing field and to deal with some of these barriers.

The large size of public contracts is one of the major obstacles faced by MSMEs, due to their capacity constraints and due to the broad technical capabilities and financial resources required by CAs in the selection phase. To this end, the new Directives introduced a provision that gives Member States the potential to require public authorities to divide a public contract into lots, providing a detailed justification if that is not possible. The provision allows potential suppliers to submit an offer for one, several or all the lots, encouraging the participation of large firms that could lack adequate incentives to compete if the contract was too small. On the other hand, it allows CAs to award contracts combining several or all lots, whenever more than one lot can be awarded to the same tender. This practice, commonly known as combinatorial auction, is a very flexible and powerful tool that allows SMEs to be competitive in a market while still exploiting relevant economies of scale (Spagnolo 2014).

This new provision achieves two of the objectives of the EU Directives, as listed in Table 32.1:

- to promote EU-wide and cross-border competition for contracts, as the division of contracts into lots has the positive effect of increasing competition, especially when the number of expected bidders is high;
- to ensure that the rules facilitate participation by MSMEs.

Considering that in 2012 single-contract tenders accounted for 71 per cent of all Contract Award Notices published in the EU, the introduction of an obligation to divide into lots could be an important step forward. However, some potential concerns need to be pointed out. First, there is the risk that by splitting a contract into several lots, the possibility of anti-competitive behaviors or collusive agreements among participants is greater, due to the temptation to "share the pie". A useful rule to prevent this situation could be to offer a number of lots that is lower than the expected number of bidders, and to create asymmetric lots when the potential bidders have symmetric technical capabilities (Grimm et al. 2006). Another consideration regards the obligation for public authorities to always divide a contract into several lots and to provide a justification whenever this is not possible. The main problem is that there is no reference to past practices and no benchmark for the size of the lots (Spagnolo 2014). This means, for instance, that a public administration that used to split a contract in five lots every year and now aggregates the demand, awarding a contract for two bigger lots every two years, does not need to justify this choice because it divides the contract into lots, even though this lowers competition and SME participation. Moreover, it is not clear to what extent this justification can be appealed and how detailed it should be; i.e. if it is sufficient to state that unbundling the contract is not economically convenient or if specific documentation should be submitted to support the justification. Potential future improvements of this provision could be the possibility of reserving the award of some contracts or lots exclusively to MSMEs, much like US "set-asides". Nowadays, this practice is considered a violation of the principles of equal treatment, fair competition or non-discrimination and, therefore, not permitted in the EU, even though discrimination occurs when similar situations are treated differently, which is not the case with MSMEs.

MSMEs often face difficulties bidding on public contracts due to the lack of time to prepare bids, excessive bureaucracy, onerous documentation and certificates required. The new Directives simplify the application phase through several provisions. On the one hand, CAs are allowed to verify the existence of ground for exclusions and the respect of selection criteria only after evaluating bids, thus giving more time for enterprises to gather all the documentation and certificates required. On the other hand, the administrative burden is reduced thanks to the adoption of the European Single Procurement Document (ESPD), an updated self-declaration of the bidder used as preliminary evidence in lieu of certificates issued by public authorities or third parties. The ESPD was officially adopted by the European Commission in January 2016. Through the ESPD, economic operators can self-declare that they meet the necessary requirements, and then only the winning firm will need to submit the supporting documentation.

The short time given for proposal preparation is a critical barrier for MSMEs, due to their limited organizational and technical capabilities. Contrary to large firms, MSMEs often do not have tender-writing specialists or personnel dedicated full-time to the preparation of the offer. In addition to the everyday workload, employees must write a proposal and prepare all the required documentation, and therefore the time needed is much greater for MSMEs than for large firms. Unfortunately, the new Directives seem to move in the opposite direction from the objective to "ensure that the rules facilitate participation by MSMEs", as they reduce the time given both to present a participation request (from 37 to 30 days) and to submit a bid (from 40 to 30 days) in a particular procurement procedure.

Another relevant barrier to MSMEs' participation is disproportionate financial requirements in the selection phase. The new Directives try to address this issue by lowering the volume of required yearly turnover to participate in a public tender. The latter cannot exceed two times the estimated contract value, except for duly justified cases.

Finally, evidence shows that the majority of firms' bankruptcies (96 per cent) are due to a string of late payments. MSMEs are usually more vulnerable than large companies to this problem, especially considering that they are often subcontractors and this could increase the dilemma of late payments even more. The new Directives introduce the possibility for subcontractors choosing to be paid directly by the contracting authority, but it is not yet clear whether this provision will help to reduce the risk of delayed or no payments, or will simply create additional delays.

Social inclusion

The new Directives strengthen the protection of people with disabilities or disadvantages in order to promote social and professional integration. The major intervention has been the increase in the range of people allowed to participate in so-called "reserved contracts". This practice consists in allowing CAs to restrict the participation in bidding on public contracts only to certain economic actors in order to foster their social inclusion.

The 2014 Directives allow the reservation of public contracts not only to sheltered workshops or sheltered employment programs, as per the previous Directive, but also to social businesses working for the inclusion of "disadvantaged people", i.e. the unemployed, members of disadvantaged minorities or otherwise socially marginalized groups. Moreover, it requires a lower share of disabled or disadvantaged people in a company in order to benefit from these reserved procurement procedures: from 50 per cent to 30 per cent of the workforce. The opportunity to reserve public contracts to unemployed people reinforces the role of public procurement as a tool for addressing unemployment (McCrudden 2004), which is a major dilemma today. In fact, according to a report published by Eurostat in June 2014, unemployed people in the EU amount to approximately 25.005 million, of whom 5.129 million are young people under 25 years old. The youth unemployment rate is generally higher than unemployment rates for all ages, but the recent economic crisis made the situation much worse, as the unemployment rate reached a peak of 23.6 per cent in 2013 compared to 15.1 per cent in 2008 (Figure 32.2). As a result, fostering a high-employment economy is a crucial goal for Europe and public procurement plays an important role in achieving that.

This modernization represents an important step forward for the protection of economic agents who might not be able to secure a public contract under normal conditions of competition. However, a further consideration is needed with regard to the above mentioned reduction in the percentage of disadvantaged employees required under the new Directive in order to be qualified for the reserved contract. In fact, although this has been a positive change for social inclusion, as it enlarges the pool of companies allowed to participate, this reduction has one relevant risk: the creation of fake workshops or social enterprises whose real aim is not to protect disadvantaged people, but only to take advantage of these reserved contracts. If that happened, the purpose of reserved procurement procedures would be totally changed. This could be prevented through the establishment of specific tools that help CAs verify the share of employees, such as the introduction in the reserved contract of the requirement to register social businesses in dedicated lists at the regional, national or international level.

This new provision fully achieves the following two objectives of the EU Directives:

- to take full advantage of all opportunities to deliver the best possible outcomes for society, as reserving contracts for disabled or disadvantaged people helps to fulfill broader social outcome for the society;

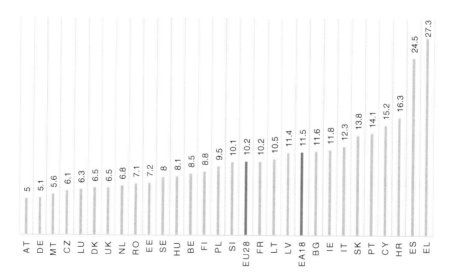

Figure 32.2 Unemployment rates, seasonally adjusted, June 2014
Source: Eurostat (2014)

- to help public procurers support other policy objectives (e.g. environmental, social, initiatives related to the innovative economy) in a legally compliant and fair manner.

Green public procurement

Green Public Procurement (hereinafter GPP) consists in the purchase by public administrations of goods, services and works with a reduced environmental impact toward a more sustainable development and the economic growth of the country. Indeed, the latter can be achieved not only through fiscal reforms or macro-economic policies that may yield more immediate and tangible benefits, but also through the continuous improvement of environmental performances and better management of the available natural resources that are increasingly scarce.

Nowadays, GPP is a voluntary instrument and has not been widely adopted among EU countries (Figure 32.3).

This may be due to the many potential barriers arising when implementing GPP not addressed at the national and/or international level yet. These include:

- low awareness of the potential benefits that adopting GPP could yield in the long term;
- the common perception among economic operators that buying green is more expensive;
- lack of (or few) obligations in the national and international regulatory framework;
- lack of the necessary political support or incentives for the implementation of GPP;
- lack of training for public administration or CAs on how to implement GPP.

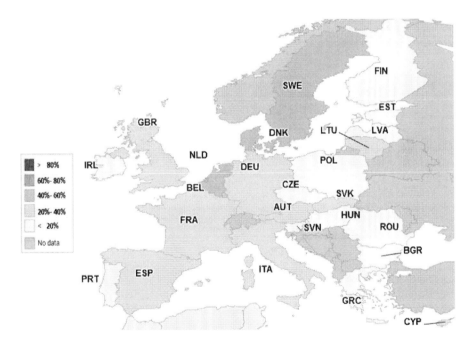

Figure 32.3 Uptake of GPP in the EU 27 (Luxembourg and Malta excluded due to unavailability of data)

Source: Analysis report of the European project "Buying Smart"

The EU regulatory framework regarding GPP has been widely developed in the 2014 Directives on public procurement, which turned out to be particularly environmentally intensive. There is now the possibility for CAs to include requirements concerning the environmental characteristics of a product or service in the technical specification. This can be done only in compliance with the mandatory national technical rules and in relation to the "subject matter" of the public contract to be awarded. CAs can also ask for specific labels to prove that the good, service or work procured corresponds to the required environmental characteristics. An additional provision of the new Directives allows CAs to require specific certificates to prove the compliance of the supplier with certain environmental management systems or standards such as the Eco-Management and Audit Scheme (EMAS). In all the situations mentioned, it is important that CAs assure the respect of the EU general principles of non-discrimination, transparency, open competition and equal treatment. To this end, they shall always accept any equivalent labels or environmental management standards or other means of proof or evidences that meet the environmental requirements set by the CAs (European Commission 2014).

One of the most innovative provisions on GPP of the new Directives is the so-called Life-Cycle Costing approach (LCC), where the lowest *cost* criterion supersedes the lowest *price* ones. The first one is a wider concept that includes the evaluation not only of the purchasing price of a product, but also many costs involved during its life cycle. Some of these costs may be defined as internal cost, such as acquisition, production, transportation, use, maintenance, recycling and disposal costs. Others can be referred to as external costs and are mainly related to the environmental impact, as emissions of pollutants or greenhouse gases.

The new provisions on GPP fully achieve the following two objectives of the EU Directives:

- take full advantage of all opportunities to deliver the best possible outcomes for society;
- help public procurers to use public procurement to support other policy objectives (e.g. environmental, social, initiatives related to the innovative economy) in a legally compliant and fair manner.

Corruption and anti-competitive behavior

Considering the high cost to society, the fight against corruption and other anti-competitive behaviors (i.e. collusion or abuse of dominant position) is a key priority for EU governments. A corrupt environment causes not only significant losses in investment, the deadlock of private sector development and economic growth, but also increases infant mortality, poverty and inequality (Kauffmann et al. 2006).

The 2014 Directives gives particular attention to this issue by:

- enhancing the transparency of procedures through appropriate monitoring systems, advertisement policies, and specific reports of public procurement procedures;
- introducing a dedicated provision to identify, prevent and address conflicts of interest situations;
- strengthening the grounds for exclusion, including illicit conduct (corruption of public officials and collusive agreements with other economic operators aimed at distorting competition).

This new scenario significantly increases the discretion of CAs, as they need to verify the existence of these grounds for exclusion. This discretion can potentially lead to abuse of their position, altering the original objective of the provision. Therefore, each Member State must intervene through appropriate regulation in order to avoid a similar situation and minimize the risk of abuse.

These new provisions allow the achievement of the following objectives of the EU Directives:

- to aid the fight against corruption;
- to simplify the rules and introduce instruments to increase the transparency of EU public procurement rules and open up markets to greater cross-border competition.

Innovation

Public procurement is a multi-objective policy and innovation is an important secondary goal. In fact, innovation in public procurement allows society to obtain better products to carry out government functions and to exploit government market power to foster innovation when market forces may not effectively stimulate it.

Innovation can be promoted in different ways according to the specific needs of a public authority:

- by allowing variants during the execution of the contract;
- through the functional description of technical specifications;
- through pre-commercial procurement;
- via innovation partnerships.

The focus of this analysis is on the last two options only: pre-commercial procurement and innovation partnerships. These procedures share the main goal: the provision of a good or service that does not already exist in the market and that private firms are reluctant to develop due to an uncertain or low economic return on the investment. However, they significantly differ in terms of structure, time perspective and regulatory coverage. Pre-commercial procurement (PCP) can be defined as

> an approach to procuring Research and Development (R&D) services other than those where the benefits accrue exclusively to the contracting authority for its use in the conduct of its own affairs, on condition that the service provided is wholly remunerated by the contracting authority and that it does not constitute State aid.
>
> *(EC-COM 799 2007)*

Therefore, the main goal of PCP is to steer the development of solutions for concrete public sector needs, whilst comparing and validating alternative approaches from various vendors. This procedure has not been widely used by European CAs so far, mainly due to difficulties of implementing a separate procurement procedure for the purchase of innovative products or services, the reluctance of public authorities to engage in a similar practice, and issues related to conflict of interest and unfair competition.

The 2014 EU Directives introduced a new procedure that may help to overcome the problems related to PCP: the "innovation partnerships". This procedure consists in establishing a long-term relationship with some qualified suppliers for the development and subsequent procurement of an innovative good or service that is not available in the market.

Every economic agent can participate in an innovation partnership, submitting all the information required for a preliminary qualitative selection. This procedure is divided into

Table 32.2 Possible formats of innovation partnership

Competitive procedure with negotiation to set up partnership with one or more operators		
Partner A	*Partner B*	*Partner C*
Phase I R&D activities	*Phase I R&D activities*	*Phase I R&D activities*
Intermediate target and payment for R&D phase.	Intermediate target and payment for R&D phase.	Intermediate target and payment for prototype.
	Phase II prototyping. Intermediate target and payment for prototype.	Phase II prototyping. Intermediate target and payment for prototype.
		Purchase of resulting supplies, services or works.

several subsequent stages, starting from the qualification phase, when the CA chooses a minimum of three suppliers as a partner, to the development of an innovative product, to the final production and purchase on a large scale. The procedure used to select suppliers must include competitive negotiations.

During the partnership, intermediate targets are determined and partners are remunerated as soon as these objectives are achieved. The structure of partnership and, in particular, the duration and value of the various phases must reflect the degree of innovation of the proposed solution and the sequence of activities of research and innovation required for its development. The estimated value of the supplies or services must therefore be proportionate to the investment required for their development. Table 32.2 shows a possible format for innovative partnership, where three different suppliers are involved.

The innovation partnership represents a valuable opportunity for European public authorities to foster investment in R&D for complex and future products or services. Through a proper application of this procedure, the following objective can be fully achieved:

- to help public procurers support other policy objectives (e.g. environmental, social, initiatives related to the innovation economy) in a legally compliant and fair manner.

The main issue of this procedure is how to share intellectual property rights, especially after the end of the partnership. For this reason, contracts should be drawn up in full, including all the most relevant information regarding property rights, the duration of the partnership, financial remuneration of involved parties and early termination.

Conclusion

Public procurement is a powerful market-based instrument for the achievement of countries' sustainable development. This chapter discussed how the European Union has recently modernized its public procurement legislation to leverage economic growth, social inclusion and improved environmental performances. In particular, the European case study shows how it is possible to foster SMEs' participation in public tenders through a balanced division into lots of a public contract, timely payments and adequate financial requirements in the qualification phase; how it is possible to promote social inclusion by reserving contracts for disadvantaged people; how the environmental impact of public procurement can be significantly reduced through the adoption of specific practices or tools, as the life-cycle approach; how the general principle of fair competition and equal treatment can be respected and anti-competitive behaviors discouraged through an increased level of transparency, stronger grounds for exclusion at the selection stage; and, finally, how companies could be encouraged to engage in innovative activities through a set of incentives and specific procedures, as innovation partnerships.

The success of this modernization strictly depends on the timeliness of its implementation by EU countries in their national legislation and on the willingness of policy makers to invest in capacity-building activities in order to guarantee correct understanding and adoption of all the new provisions. Although the new Directives focus extensively on some major issues in public procurement, especially regarding its sustainability, many trade-offs and challenges have not yet been fully addressed. This creates opportunity for further improvements and developments, both in the short run, through the implementation process of each Member State, and in the long run, through a continuous modernization and update of the regulatory framework in response to the evolving market dynamics.

Note

1   The information and views set out in this chapter are those of the authors and do not reflect the official opinion of the European Bank for Reconstruction and Development.

References

Ashhoff, B. and Sofka W. 2009. "Innovation on demand: can public procurement drive market success of innovations?" *Research Policy* 38(8): 1235–1247.

Grimm, V., Pacini, R., Spagnolo, G., Dimitri, N., and Zanza, M. 2006. "Division into lots and competition in procurement," in *Handbook of Procurement*, edited by Nicola Dimitri, Gustavo Piga, and Giancarlo Spagnolo, 168–169. Cambridge: Cambridge University Press.

European Commission. 2014. "Public Procurement Factsheet No 7: Green Public Procurement. Public Procurement Reform." European Commission.

European Commission. 2010. "EUROPE 2020. A strategy for a smart, sustainable and inclusive growth." Communication 2020.

European Commission. 2007. "Pre-commercial procurement: driving innovation to ensure sustainable high-quality public services in Europe." COM 799 final. Eurostat. 2014. *Europe in Figures. European Yearbook 2014*. Brussels: EU.

Eurostat. 2014. "Unemployment statistics." http://ec.europa.eu/eurostat/statistics-explained/index.php/Unemployment_statistic.

Eurostat. 2012. "Structural business statistics." Available from http://ec.europa.eu/eurostat. 7.

Kaufmann, D., Kraay, A., and Mastruzzi, M. 2006. *Measuring Corruption: Myths and Realities*. Geneva: World Bank.

McCrudden, C. 2004. "Using public procurement to achieve social outcomes." *Natural Resources Forum* 28 (4): 257–267.

McCue, C., Buffington, K.W., and Howell, A. 2007. "The fraud/red tape dilemma in public. A study of US state and local government," in *Public Procurement International Cases and Commentary*, edited by Louise Knight, Christine Harland, Jan Telgen, Khi V. Thai, Guy Callender and Katy McKen, 247–248. Abingdon: Routledge.

Meideros, R. 2014. "The new Directive 2014/24/EU on public procurement: a first overview." Paper presented at the 2nd European Conference on e-Public Procurement, Portugal.

Morand, P.H. 2013. "SMEs and public procurement policy." *Review of Economic Design* 8 (3): 301–308.

Murray, J.G. 1999. "Local government demands more." *European Journal of Purchasing and Supply Management* 5 (1): 33–42.

Norman, W. and MacDonald, C. 2003. "Getting to the bottom of 'triple bottom line.'" *Business Ethics Quarterly*.

Reed, T., Luna, P., and Pike, W. 2004. "Balancing socioeconomic and public procurement reform goals: effective metrics for measuring small business participation in public procurement," in *Challenges in Public Procurement: An International Perspective*, edited by Araujo, A. et al., 81–100. Florida: Florida Academic Press.

Spagnolo, G. 2014. "Lots." Paper presented at the 2nd Interdisciplinary Symposium on Public Procurement, Hungary.

Sykes, M. 2007. "Procurement: a strategic weapon for change," in *Public Procurement International Cases and Commentary*, edited by Louise Knight, Christine Harland, Jan Telgen, Khi V. Thai, Guy Callender and Katy McKen, 343–344. Abingdon: Routledge.

Tavares, L. V. 2014. "The new Directive 2014/24/EU on Public Procurement: policy issues and next steps," *Proceedings of the 2nd European Conference on e-Public Procurement*, Lisbon, PT, May 27.

Telgen, J., Harland, C., and Knight, L. 2007. "Public procurement in perspective," in *Public Procurement International Cases and Commentary*, edited by Louise Knight, Christine Harland, Jan Telgen, Khi V. Thai, Guy Callender and Katy McKen, 16–22. Abingdon: Routledge.

World Commission on Environment and Development. 1987. "Our common future: the World Commission on Environment and Development." Oxford: Oxford University Press.

33

KOREAN E-GOVERNMENT IN A SOCIAL MEDIA ENVIRONMENT

Prospects and challenges

M. Jae Moon

Introduction

E-government has been one of the most compelling and fast-growing areas in public administration in the last two decades. New information and communication technologies (ICTs), such as Internet and mobile communication technologies, have been widely introduced to improve the quality of internal administrative operations as well as public service delivery. With the continued advancement of ICTs and the evolution of e-government, many scholars have attempted to define the locus and focus of e-government studies in the discipline of public administration. In fact, increasing number of e-government studies began to appear in both general public administration journals and specialist journals after the Internet was developed and applied in the public sector.

With the advent of the Internet, the concept of e-government began to emerge and continued to improve the efficiency of internal administration as well as external online services for citizens. Recently, e-government has evolved thanks to the advancement and diffusion of social media, which enables ordinary citizens to share more information among themselves and interact actively with governments. The nature and scope of e-government has recently shifted to e-governance with the continued development of web 2.0 technologies (i.e. social media, tagging, mash-up, and RSS). Thanks to these technologies, e-governance or e-government 2.0 tends to emphasize information sharing, openness, connectivity, and interactivity. Web 2.0 technologies also offer citizens more opportunities to be part of the coproduction of public services because they not only enable participation in policy decision-making processes but also the co-production of public services.

Recently, Korea has been recognized as an exemplary country which has actively promoted e-government by establishing information infrastructure and introducing front- and back-office applications for ICTs in the public sector, based on strategically-planned roadmaps for national informatization and e-government. Korea developed its National Informatization Initiative in 1994 and actively pursued the effective establishment of information infrastructure, administrative informatization as well as the provision of e-government services. Korea ranked at the first place in the 2010, 2012, and 2014 UN e-Government Surveys, and the Korean government is actively searching for new ways to apply web 2.0 technologies. As social media spreads in

Korea, the government has begun to recognize its impact as an important communication channel.

This chapter first briefly reviews the current status of e-government studies in the discipline of public administration. Then we survey the background of the establishment of ICT infrastructure and Korean e-government. Examining the scope and nature of web 2.0 technologies, the chapter will also study the evolution of Korean e-government and its development in the social media environment. The strengths and weaknesses, as well as prospects and challenges of Korean e-government will be discussed. Some policy recommendations will also be offered.

The evolution of e-government and e-government studies

ICT has the potential to improve the quality of government (QoG) and empower citizens. It helps make governments more efficient, effective, transparent, and accountable by reengineering administrative processes, improving public service delivery, and promoting citizen engagement and participation in policy-making processes. In addition, to reap the economic benefits of ICT, many countries have actively introduced ICT to transform the public sector in both front- and back-office operations. By digitizing administrative procedures and providing public information and services to citizens via the Internet, E-government makes governments not only more efficient and effective but also more accountable and transparent.

E-government has evolved through a number of stages, from emerging stage, interaction stage, transaction stage, and transformation stage, or seamless integration stage (United Nations 2010; Moon 2002). Many countries are offering more online government services to citizens and businesses, including developing economies. The emerging stage refers to one-way communication based on the presence of a government website. E-government is limited, functioning simply as an e-brochure that provides public information to citizens, government officials and businesses. In the interaction stage, governments are equipped to interact and communicate with citizens and other social actors. In the transaction stage, governments provide citizens and businesses with various online services such as e-tax, e-procurement, e-licensing, and other systems. The last stage is the seamless integration or transformation stage, where many related online services and databases are integrated vertically and horizontally.

For example, the Korean government established the Social Welfare Integrated Management Network System to improve the efficiency and quality of social security administration, by integrating 16 social welfare service institutions and 17 other public agencies. This system allows the government to prevent duplicate benefit payments, fraud, and incorrect payments, as well as to effectively manage eligibility and benefit history information by integrating 31 different kinds of public data, including residency, land, finance, tax, and welfare.

Anderson (2009) provides empirical evidence of a positive association between e-government development and reducing corruption. It has also been found that citizens' use of e-government helps restore and improve trust in government, as the provision of information improves citizens' perceptions of the efficiency, transparency, and effectiveness of government and enhances their sense of participation and empowerment (Tolbert and Mossberger 2006; Welch et al. 2005).

Arguably, the origin of e-government studies traces back to various studies on the impact of computers on public organizations, when mainframe or personal computers were introduced to the public sector. The primary focus was to improve time and cost efficiencies in producing, processing and storing public data such as censuses, budget and payroll data. More recent and narrowly defined e-government studies began to be conducted after the Internet was developed

Table 33.1 Three competing approaches of IT/e-government articles

	Managerial Approach	*Political Approach*	*Legal Approach*	*Total*
Phase III (1996–2010)	83(15) (61.5%)	47(18) (34.8%)	5(5) (3.7%)	135(38)/116
Phase II (1980–1995)	84(7) (81.5%)	15(7) (14.6%)	4(2) (3.9%)	103(16)/95
Phase I (1965–1979)	23(1) (79.3%)	4(1) (13.8%)	2 (6.9%)	29(2)/28
Total (%)	190(23) (71.7%)	66(26) (24.7%)	11(7) (4.1%)	267(56)/239

Source: Modified from Moon et al. (2014)

Note: The articles examined here are the ones published in six selected public administration journals including *Public Administration Review, Administration and Society, Journal of Public Administration Research and Theory, Public Performance and Management Review, American Review of Public Administration*, and *Public Administration Quarterly*. The total number of articles relevant to IT applications and e-government studies is 239 (seven articles on IT curriculum and two review and prospect papers are not included). In the last column, 56 is the number of themes counted twice because 28 articles have two themes (e.g. managerial and political). Thus, the number of themes (267) is equal to the total number of articles (239) plus the number of articles with two themes (28).

and applied to public organizations, particularly for online public service delivery and interaction with citizens (Moon et al. 2014). Defining and examining the status of e-government studies published in six journals between 1965 and 2010, Moon et al. (2014) differentiated between conventional IT applications and e-government studies then categorized them into three different areas of research based on the different public administration approaches proposed by Rosenbloom (1983): managerial, political, and legal.

The study showed that the number of IT applications and e-government studies increased from 28 in Phase I (1965–1979) to 101 in Phase II (1980–1995) and 119 in Phase III (1996–2010). The proportion of IT applications and e-government studies to the total number of published articles in the selected journals also grew from 1.8 per cent in Phase I to 3.6 per cent in Phase II. The growth is noteworthy given the fact that specialized e-government journals began to become major outlets for e-government studies in the mid-1990s. As Table 33.1 (above) summarizes, the study also found that the majority of IT application and e-government studies (about 80 per cent) in earlier phases largely took a managerial approach to the impact of ICT applications on the efficiency and effectiveness of public organizations. However, an increasing number of studies have begun to take a political approach and pay attention to responsiveness, participation, representativeness and accountability.

Background sketch of evolution of Korea e-government

The development of Korean e-government[1] traces back to the late 1970s when the government introduced the First National Computerization Project (1978–1982). The Second National Computerization Project (1983–1986) computerized conventional administrative works in government agencies. The two National Computerization Projects later evolved into the National Computer Network Projects, which began in 1987. Promoting computer networks among central agencies and between local and central governments, the First National Computer Network Project identified major public records (i.e., residence, real estate, employment, vehicle registration, custom services, and economic statistics management) and laid the groundwork for the establishment of a nation-wide computer network system for their management. The Second National Computer Network Project (1992–1996) enhanced the utility of the administrative computer system to increase administrative efficiency and public service quality. In the meantime, in 1994 the government established the Ministry of Information and Communication and launched the Korea Information Infrastructure (KII) Plan. In 1996, the government developed the Master Plan for National Informatization Promotion, which aimed to achieve world-class informatization by 2010. The government implemented various projects (i.e., Cyber Korea 21, e-Korea Vision 2006, Broadband IT Korea Vision 2007, and u-Korea), and the plan was followed by the Master Plan for National Informatization Promotion in 2008, which continues to the present day.

Despite this long history, the current status of Korean e-government arguably originated from the vision proposed by the Kim Dae Jung administration in 1998. It proposed a national e-government plan of 18 specific projects in six major areas. The six major areas include the realization of public-oriented government services, business process reengineering for administrative efficiency, the promotion of information sharing among agencies, upgrading government information infrastructure, the enhancement of public officials' ICT skills, and improving legal and institutional arrangements.

In 2001, the Korean government launched the Special Presidential Committee for E-government to plan, promote, and effectively implement e-government projects, including: G2C (Government to Citizens), G2B (Government to Business), G2G (Government to Government) and information infrastructure projects. The Committee highlighted 11 major presidential projects and monitored their progress closely: (1) a single portal for e-government; (2) an integrated information system for four social insurance systems; (3) an integrated e-procurement system; (4) an online tax system; (5) a financial information management system; (6) a local government information system; (7) an education management information; (8) a public personnel information system; (9) an online report and digital document management system; (10) a digital signature system; and (11) an integrated management information system. The 11 core projects were further developed into 31 specific projects belonging to one of four targeted areas including: business process reengineering, public service delivery, information resource management, and legal changes. These continued to advance in the Roh Mu-Hyun administration.

Main drivers in Korean e-government

There is a consensus that strong leadership, inter-agency collaboration, IT governance, and IT infrastructure advance Korean e-government. The Korean government pursued e-government projects through a centralized governance structure, in which the Special Presidential E-Government Committee worked with other related public agencies. Historically, Korean e-Government governance was led by committees in public institutions that coordinates related public agencies. Table 33.2 summarizes the leading organizations that drove e-government projects at different stages.

Currently, e-government governance includes various public organizations, including the Presidential Council for Information Society (PCIS), the Ministry of Government and Home Affairs (MOGAHA), and the National Informatization Agency (NIA). The PCIS (later changed to the Information and Communication Strategy Council chaired by the Prime Minister) reviews and provides the overall direction of Korean e-government while MOGAHA is the leading cabinet-level agency that makes related policy decisions. NIA is a government-affiliated research and policy institution under the supervision of the Ministry of Science, ICT, and the Future, which manages technical support and e-government projects. Different public agencies

Table 33.2 The stages of e-government development

Stage	Beginning Year	Main Actors	Outputs
Computerization Stage	1978	Computerization Promotion Committee	Computerization
Infrastructure Preparation Stage	1987	Information Network Coordination Committee	Establishment of 5 Information Infra Networks
Infrastructure Founding Stage	1995	Informatization Promotion Committee	Super Information Highway
E-government Initiation	2001	Special Presidential Committee for E-government	11 Major E-government Projects
Implementation Stage	2003	E-government Sub Committee	31 major E-government Projects
Maturation Stage	2009	Presidential Council for Information Society	Coordination and Management of Informatization

Source: Modified from Internal Report, MOPAS (2012.2)

and local governments are also supposed to appoint a Chief Information Officer (CIO) in charge of e-government projects.

The budget has increased to develop new e-government systems as well as maintain existing systems. The budget increased from 23 billion Won in 2003 to 288 billion Won in 2007 (MOPAS 2012). This is more than a 12-fold growth in five years. However, the growth rate began to decrease after 2008 because governments began to slow down the development of new e-government systems, in order to focus on maintaining existing ones.

In the early stages, the government made investments in national information network construction. Between 1993 and 2004, the Ministry of Information and Telecommunication used the Informatization Promotion Fund for 11 major e-government projects. It was established under the 1995 Framework Act of National Informatization to support the foundation of ICT industry, ICT infrastructure, e-government, etc. The fund succeeded the National Informatization Support Fund (1993–1995), which was established based on the Act of ICT Research and Development of 1992. The Promotion Fund was established with contributions from the government (about 40 per cent), private telecommunication companies (45 per cent) and other miscellaneous sources (14 per cent), and it became an important financial resource for various initiatives, including e-government projects. The Fund was used to implement the Master Plan for Informatization Promotion (1996), Cyber Korea 21 (1999–2002), and u-Korea (2006–2010). The National Informatization Promotion Fund along with annually appropriated budget also made great contributions to the establishment of initial infrastructure, the ICT business environment and R&D. However, unlike the latter, the government was able to use the fund more flexibly and strategically. For example, the government spent USD 5.33 billion between 1994 and 2003 for ICT R&D (38 per cent), informatization promotion (20 per cent), ICT human resource development (18 per cent), broadband infrastructure and promotion (15.1 per cent), infrastructure for ICT industry (7 per cent) and standardization (3 per cent) (Suh and Chen 2007). The fund was renamed the Information and Communication Fund in 2004 and continued to play critical roles in the initial establishment of Korean informatization and e-government projects in the 1990s and 2000s.

The current status of Korean e-government

With its strong governance and leadership along with strategic plans and allocation of financial resources, Korea has rapidly advanced its e-government development. The country was ranked first in the 2010, 2012, and 2014 United Nations E-government Surveys, as shown in Table 33.3.

Many Korean e-government services have been internationally recognized for their quality. They include KISS (Korean Immigration Service System), KONEPs (Korean National E-procurement System), HTS (Home Tax Systems), uTradeHub (Korea's National Paperless Trade Platform), KIPOnet (Korean Patent Online System), and UNIPASS (Online Custom Service).

Under the Park Geun Hye administration, the Korean government recently took the Korean 3.0 Initiative,[2] which pursues transparent government, enabled government, and service-oriented government based on openness, information sharing, communication, and collaboration. The government implements the initiative as an extension of e-government in a sense that many of the Government 3.0 projects are ICT-based. The government is aggressive in opening public data to citizens and businesses not only to satisfy the right to know but also to promote public data-based enterprises. The government also tries to lower the walls among different agencies and units by promoting collaborative and information sharing systems in the public sector. The government actively searches find various solutions to provide more online public services and promote online citizen participation in policy-making processes. In addition, the government attempts to find ICT-based solutions to various public problems by using new technologies including cloud computing technologies, Internet of Things (IoT), social media, and big data.

Advancement of Web 2.0 technologies and social media

This section summarizes and reviews the major characteristics of web 2.0 technologies. Since the term web 2.0 was first coined by Tim O'Reilly in 2005, web 2.0 technologies have begun to be widely used by many students and practitioners. Web 2.0 technologies include various ICT technologies such as mash-up, tagging, and RSS (Really Simple Syndication). Mash-up refers to technology used to collect relevant information for particular purposes while RSS technology helps to simultaneously update relevant information for subscribers. These

Table 33.3 2014 UN e-government survey results

Rank	2014	2012	2010
1	Korea	Korea	Korea
2	Australia	Netherlands	USA
3	Singapore	UK	Canada
4	France	Denmark	UK
5	Netherlands	USA	Netherlands
6	Japan	France	Norway
7	USA	Sweden	Denmark
8	UK	Norway	Australia
9	New Zealand	Finland	Spain
10	Finland	Singapore	France

Source: UN E-Government Survey 2010, 2012, and 2014

technologies promote collective intelligence, participation, information sharing, long-tail customization, the role of prosumers (combination of producers and consumers), collaboration, openness, and user convenience.

A study (2010) conducted by the Pew Research Center indicates that 66 per cent of Internet users visit social networking sites. Interestingly, women are more social media users than men while (as expected) the younger generation is more active in using social media. This raises the important question of how social media affects the participation of different socio-economic groups.

The emergence and development of web 2.0 technologies enable governments to take advantage of collective intelligence, information sharing, openness and participation, and personalized e-government services (Lee 2007). Di Maio (2009) suggested that e-government continues to socialize and commoditize government services, processes, and data. Di Maio also believes that web 2.0 technologies and social media will make e-government more citizen-driven, employee-centric, continuously evolving, transformational, and interactive.

In an era of web 2.0 technologies and social media, e-government puts more emphasis on the quality of citizen participation, responsiveness, interactivity, and engagement. This suggests that its key feature is providing citizens with opportunities to create their own content and communicate with government officials and other citizens. Hypothetically, this is easily pursued but it is often not facilitated or promoted by government agencies, thanks to conventional bureaucratic culture. For example, a high school student developed a free bus schedule mobile phone application for the Seoul and surrounding region in 2009. Rather than appreciating and promoting self-initiated content creation, the regional government initially blocked the service; however, the government later reevaluated the application and even encouraged further citizen participation in designing applications.

Responding to the great emergence of social media, the Korean government also began to actively utilize it for citizen communication. The government recognized the importance of social media communication and online public relations, particularly since the rapid diffusion of smartphones after 2009. The first action was taken in 2011, when the Presidential Office (*Cheongwadae*) introduced a special presidential secretary in charge of online PR and new media applications. The Presidential office even appointed a Chief Online Communicator. A new unit called 'Online Public Relations' was established in the Ministry of Culture, Sports and Tourism. To respond to the demand for social media communication, the government established an official application where citizens can connect various social media including Facebook, Twitter, YouTube, Blog, and Me2Day with various government agencies. The Korean government also set its budget for new media applications from about US$20,000 in 2008 to US$200,000 in 2011. The size of the budget is not large; however, it has increased 10 times over the last three years. Park (2012) reported that the performance of SNS applications in government agencies remains very poor, despite the substantial increase in their budget. The utilization of SNS by government agencies is minimal and simply links each agency portal site to public announcements and other related social media. Actual communications with citizens in social media (i.e., tweets, and retweets) is rare. Agencies have poor content that does not draw citizen attention, they lack personnel (18 out of 42 public agencies have less than one member of staff in charge of social media) and several agencies have fewer than 10 tweets in their feeds.

It is interesting to examine recent statistics by the Pew Research Center (2010) on government social media users, defined as those people who use any government social media channels as summarized in Table 33.4. The report indicates that 31 per cent of Internet users are government social media users (counted as those who use at least one of these six activities:

Table 33.4 Government social media users in the US

Government Social Media Users	%
1 Watching a video on a government website	15
2 Receive email alerts from a government agency or official	15
3 Read blog of government agency or official	13
4 Follow a government agency on a social networking site	5
5 Receive text messages from a government agency or official	4
6 Follow a government agency or official on Twitter	2
Total	31%

Source: Pew Research Center (2010)

(9% of social networking site profile owners: 7% of total tweets)

(1) watching a video on a government website; (2) receiving email alerts from a government agency or official; (3) following a government agency on a social networking site; (4) reading the blog of a government agency or official; (5) receiving text messages from a government agency or official; or (6) following a government agency or official on Twitter.

The proportion of those who follow government agency tweets or social media services is limited. Only five per cent of Internet users follow government social networking sites and only two per cent follow government-related Twitter feeds.

Though comparable information is not available for Korea, the proportion of government social media users does not seem to be high. The followers of government social networking sites and Twitter feeds might be as few as mentioned above.

The connectivity of social media with key politicians and opinion leaders seems to be much more active and its impact is greater than with government agencies. This is particularly true when so many politicians actively engage in social media during elections. For example, during the 2011 Seoul mayoral election, the social media connectivity and activities of candidate Park Won-soon was more active and intense than that of rival Na Kyung-won. A report by Twitmix (Chung 2012) suggests a relationship between social media communications and the election results by pointing out the numbers of tweets for Park and Na was 45,962 (54.07 per cent) and 39,034 (45.92 per cent), and the earned votes were 53.4 per cent and 46.2 per cent, respectively. The causal linkage between Twitter communications and earned votes is at best hypothetical; however, the point is still worth further examination in both volume and tone (negative versus positive) of social media communication content.

The impact of social media communication is maximized when a particular issue does not remain local. The Seoul mayoral election received national attention and became a nationally salient issue. Because of the boundless nature of social media, social media might be more powerful in a presidential election than in a general contest, where public attention is distracted by 254 election districts, though the contest between the ruling and opposition parties remains a national issue. This suggests that the impact of social media communication is closely associated with the salience and boundaries of a particular issue.

With the advent of the social media era, governments tend to emphasize openness and transparency because of more available communication channels and the public information demands of citizens. As stressed by the Obama administration, the Open Government Initiative highlights the significance of transparency, online public information revisions, citizen participation in policy-making processes, and collaboration with other agencies.

In addition to enhancing transparency by disclosing public information, citizen participation is also important to the Open Government Initiative. The Obama administration has begun an experimental crowdsourcing initiative, "Challenge.gov", in which various departments ask for citizens' help with policy problems. This is an attempt to move problem solving from traditional insourcing (problems solved by government itself) and outsourcing (problems solved by contracted entities) to crowdsourcing (problems solved by the public). Though the experiment itself is not entirely effective at this point, it shows the direction and possibility of crowdsourcing. It can open opportunities for citizens to offer any solution (including the creation of new smartphone applications) by using available public and private information.

Recently the UK government reduced and eliminated red tape using a crowdsourcing approach called "Red Tape Challenge", which was launched in 2014 as a Cabinet Office initiative. The initiative's website invites any citizen to openly discussion burdensome regulations. The opinions, comments, and debates on specific rules and regulations are reviewed by related agencies and used as important material for reform. The guiding principle is that the regulations questioned by citizens will be removed or improved unless they are justified by the relevant agencies. A recent report suggests that 3,095 regulations have been removed or improved, while 1,376 regulations have benefited businesses.[3]

Currently, the Korean government has not adopted a crowdsourcing approach like "Challenge. Gov" or "Red Tape Challenge". However, there is an active search for citizen participation in policy-making processes and ideas. The number of policy proposals by citizens and public officials has increased, particularly since the mid-2000s. The proposals are often made via an official online proposal website, epeople.go.kr, and are managed by 303 government organizations, including the administrative units of central and local governments as well as public institutions. According to the MOPAS Statistics Yearbook (2012), the number of policy proposals made by citizens increased from 316 in 2001 to 154,168 in 2010. More than 3,209 proposals were actually adopted by the government. The policy proposals by public officials also increased from 22,577 in 2001 to 99,112 in 2010. Though the quantitative growth of policy proposals is quite dramatic, the current system is not a full-fledged crowdsourcing approach. The qualitative improvement in policy proposals and government responses to the proposals is also far from satisfactory. The Korean government needs to continue to introduce more sophisticated crowdsourcing approaches and make its e-government more participatory, collaborative, and open.

Conclusions

The Korean government has been a forerunner in e-government both in back-office and front-office (Korean Immigration Service System) applications of ICT. However, the Korean government faces a new set of e-government challenges in the social media environment, where more openness, interaction, participation, information sharing, and collaboration are demanded. The Korean government recently launched "Government 3.0", similar to Obama's Open Government Initiative. While Korea drove e-government successfully in the web 1.0 environment with strong leadership, effective e-government governance, infrastructure, and a technologically savvy population, the success of e-government in the social media and web-friendly 2.0 environment remains in question. E-government 1.0 can be obtained more easily than e-government 2.0 or 3.0, partially because the former can be achieved by establishment of hardware systems. The success of e-government 2.0 and 3.0 relies on software instead of hardware, as well as the quality of communication rather than the quantity of communication.

We have found that the government's utilization of social media communication is currently limited; in addition, the quality of information and communication in social media is problematic. Public trust in government (public information and government performance) is closely associated with the quality of citizen participation and open government. Whether the success of Korean e-government 1.0 can be extended to 2.0 depends on the degree and quality of social and information connectivity in social media.

To advance to e-government 2.0 in the social media environment, as Ko (2011) has pointed out, the government needs to meet the rising demand of citizens for social media interactivity by conducting empathetic communication with citizens and providing continuous information that is trustworthy and useful. The government also needs to make additional efforts to promote more participatory, trust-based and information-sharing interactions in social media. The government needs to be cautious when it attempts to correct biased, incorrect, and cyber-cascaded information in social media. Unless trust in government is well secured, government actions could be perceived to be unnecessary interventions and an overreaction to social media communications. Both quantity and quality of citizen participation and social and information connectivity based on social media and other web 2.0 technologies will further shape future e-government and make government more open, connected, participatory, and collaborative.

Notes

1   Chung (2015) summarized a brief history of Korean e-government in his recently updated book. This section is written based on the information obtained from Chung's book entitled *The Theory of Electronic Government* written in Korean.
2   For more details, see the information found in website for the Government 3.0 Initiative.
3   For more details, see the information found in the website for Red Tape Challenge (www. redtapechallenge.cabinetoffice.gov.uk/about/).

References

Anderson, Thomas Barnebeck. 2009. E-Government as an Anti-Corruption Strategy. *Information Economics and Policy*, 21, 201–210.
Chung, Chungsik. 2015. *The Theory of Electronic Government* (4th edition). SeoulKyungjeKyugyoung. (in Korean)
Chung, Hyungsoo. 2012. The Impact of Twitters Statistics for Seoul Mayoral Candidates. Moneytoday. October27,2012.www.mt.co.kr/view/mtview.php?type=1&no=2011102708150213212&outlink=1.
Di Maio, Andrea (2009) Government 2.): A Gartner Definition. http://blogs.gartner.com/andrea_dimaio/2009/11/13/government–2–0-a-gartner-definition/.
Ko, Yongsam. 2011. Media Paradigm Shift and New Direction for Government's Use of Social Media Communication. December 23, 2011.
Lee, Haejung (2007) The Evolution of Future Ubiquitous Government, Government 3.0. Ubiquitous Society Research Series. No. 29. National Informatization Society Agency.
Ministry of Public Administration and Security (MOPAS). 2012. MOPAS Statistics Yearbook 2011. MOPAS.
Ministry of Public Administration and Security (MOPAS). 2012. Internal Report on Korean E-government (Feb. 2012). MOPAS.
Moon, M. Jae. (2002). The evolution of e-government among municipalities: Rhetoric or reality? *Public Administrative Review*, 62, 424–433.
Moon, M. Jae, Jooho Lee, and Chul-Young Roh. 2014. The Evolution of Internal IT Applications and e-Government Studies in Public Administration: Research Themes and Methods. *Administration & Society*, 46 (1), 3–36.
National Informatization Agency (NIA). 2012. *Yearbook of Information Society Statistics*. Degu: NIA.
Park, Seunghyon. SNS Communications of Korean Government. DongA Daily Newspaper. April 3, 2012.

Pew Research Center. 2010. *How Americans Interact with Government Online.* HHPew Internet and American Life Project.

Rosenbloom, David. (1983). Public administrative theory and the separation of power. *Public Administration Review,* 43, 219–226.

Suh, J., and D. H.C. Chen. 2007. *Korea as a Knowledge Economy.* Washington, DC: World Bank Institute.

Tolbert, Caroline and Karen Mossberger. 2006. The effects of e-government on trust and confidence in government. *Public Administration Review,* 66 (3), 354–369.

United Nations. 2014. *United Nations E-Government Survey 2014.* New York: United Nations.

United Nations. 2012. *United Nations E-Government Survey 2012.* New York: United Nations.

United Nations. 2010. *United Nations E-Government Survey 2010.* New York: United Nations.

Welch, Eric, Charles Hinnant, and M. Jae Moon. 2005. Linking Citizen Satisfaction with E-government with Trust in Government. *Journal of Public Administration Research and Theory,* 15 (1), 37–58.

Websites

E-people, www.epeople.go.kr
Challenge.gov, www.challenge.gov
Red Tape Challenge, www.redtapechallenge.cabinetoffice.gov.uk/about/

GLOSSARY

Administrative change: It is at times argued that, in the perspective of Historical Institutionalism, change may occur only through rupture mode: the collapse of an equilibrium, which is then replaced by another equilibrium, which in turn will tend to last over relatively long time spans. This is only part of the picture: a third option between stability and perpetuation, on one hand, and breakdown of the system and replacement by another one, on the other, can be identified. Mechanisms whereby gradual transformation – incremental change with transformative results – may occur include: layering; conversion; displacement; drift; exhaustion [also in this glossary: Historical institutionalism].

Administrative tradition: It may be defined as a historically based set of values, structures and relationships with other institutions that defines the nature of appropriate public administration within society. Four basic dimensions are used to characterize a tradition: the conception of the state and its fundamental relation to society; the relationship of the bureaucracy with political institutions; the relative importance attached to law versus management; the nature of accountability in the public sector.

Collaborative governance: Refers to replacing traditional modes of government with networks, partnerships and cross-sector collaborations. It is a hybrid mode of decision making and service provision in which a public agency deliberately and directly engages non-state entities in a formal, consensual and collective decision-making process to manage programs, and to address problems that cannot be easily or at all solved by single organizations. Typical examples are collaborative service delivery networks for complex issues such as disaster response and public–private partnerships [also in this glossary: Governance; Network; Wicked problem].

Collaborative emergency management: Refers to application of collaborative governance tools in managing disasters. Since managing disasters requires collaboration between stakeholders from all sectors, collaborative emergency management is the most widely used governance concept.

Community resilience: The capability of communities to adapt to shocks to the welfare of their members (such as breakdown of relationships between community members or radical performance deterioration of critical local services) in such a way as to allow continued achievement of their priority outcomes and objectives and to learn how to plan and prepare for future shocks [also in this glossary: Resilience; Service resilience; User resilience].

398

Co-production: Founded on the idea that not only the consumption but also the production of public services can require the participation of those who consume them. It is about government agencies involving members of the public "in the execution of public policy as well as its formulation" (Whitaker 1980: 241).

Corruption: Refers to the misuse of public office for private gain. Comprehensively, it also encompasses public officials' behaviour deviating from the public interest, legal rules or moral norms. It is used to mean different things in different contexts. Corruption has been blamed for the failures of national development and economic growth. It is also viewed as one of the main obstacles that countries face in attempting to consolidate democratic institutions and make public policies optimal.

Decentered policy-making: A policy process characterized by complexity, fragmentation, interdependencies, ungovernability, and the rejection of a clear public/private dichotomy.

Decision flow diagrams: suggest a way of making and implementing strategic plans. They help politicians, civil servants and public managers that would like to learn how to do strategic management. They provide an overview of what is involved and how information searching, analysis and decisions can be sequenced. For experienced practitioners the diagrams can be aide memoires or can serve to stimulate experimentation with changes in ways of making strategic decisions [also in this glossary: Strategic management; Strategic-state capabilities].

Democracy: The understanding of democracy differs based on a country's specific history and circumstances. Key institutions of democratic governance defined in the literature include having elected officials, free and fair elections, freedom of expression for citizens, access to alternative information, associational autonomy and inclusive citizenship. A distinction is made between indirect and direct democracy. In an indirect democracy – or representative democracy – the people themselves do not rule but instead elect representatives who rule. Direct democracy may be understood in terms of people's rights, the exercise of such rights or single-item referenda put to a popular vote.

Devolution: Delegation of power to a lower level of government, especially from central government to local or regional administration [also in this glossary: Federalism].

Directive: A legislative act of the European Union that requires Member States to achieve a particular result without dictating the means of achieving that result. Although obligatory to implement, Directives normally leave Member States with a certain margin of discretion as to the exact rules to be adopted.

Disaster management: Disasters are incidents that cause disruptions in the society. Disaster management is the combination of efforts, policies and procedures that aim at managing pre (i.e. mitigation and preparedness) and post (response and recovery) disaster in order to prevent or minimize impacts of disasters [also in this glossary: Collaborative emergency management].

Dodd–Frank Act: The Dodd–Frank Wall Street Reform and Consumer Protection Act is the reform adopted in the United States after the 2007–2008 global financial crisis. Among other challenges, the Act tackled "too big to fail" and other policy issues that emerged during the crisis.

E-government: Refers to both back-office applications and front-office applications of information and communication technologies (ICTs) in such areas as G2C (government to citizens), G2B (government to business) and G2G (government to government), which enables 7-24-365 provision of government information and services beyond space and time constraints.

Epidemiological transition: Changes in leading causes of death in a given population. The main epidemiological transition that the world is currently experiencing is a shift from acute and infectious diseases, including HIV/AIDS, pneumonia and influenza, to chronic and non-communicable diseases characteristic of old age, such as cerebral-vascular disease, cancers, and ischemic heart disease.

Federalism: A system of government in which power is divided between a national (federal) government and regional governments with the powers of each level set out in a written document [also in this glossary: Devolution].

Finance: Finance facilitates the distribution of limited resources within the economy and it provides the means by which capital through investment can support economic activity. The safety, soundness and effectiveness of the financial services sector are, thus, essential to ensure prosperity. Governments regulate, among other reasons, to prevent or contain a market breakdown.

Global aging: A worldwide demographic shift characterized by an increase in the size of older people as a share of the total population of the world. This shift is caused partly by the trend that people around the word have come to live longer and in better health than previous generations.

Global care drain: A global trend in which a growing number of younger workers in search of economic opportunity is drawn from developing countries, such as the Philippines, to developed countries of the world, such as the United States, as health care workers, including long-term care workers for the elderly.

Global governance for health: Refers to global governance processes outside the global health system that regard health as a political challenge tied to fairness and justice rather than biological variance, not merely as a technical outcome. Global governance for health deals with health equity as a cross-sectoral political concern, since the health sector cannot address these challenges alone, and aims at promoting and defending the goal and the priority of public health every where public policies are negotiated and elaborated, beyond the domain of the global health system alone.

Global health: An emerging area for interdisciplinary studies, research and practice that considers the effects of globalization on health – understood in the comprehensive meaning of a complete state of physical, mental and social well-being – and the achievement of equity in health for all people worldwide, emphasizing transnational health issues, determinants and solutions, and their interactions with national and local systems.

Global health governance: refers to the governance of the global health system –defined as the actors and institutions with the primary purpose of health, through the use of formal and informal institutions, rules, and processes by states, intergovernmental institutions, and non-state actors to deal with challenges to health that require cross-border collective action to address effectively.

Governance: The act of steering state and society interactions. Governance is what a governing body does and how rules are decided upon and implemented. It is a broader term than "government", referring to the public, private and not-for-profit sectors and the interdependence between these.

Gross Domestic Product: A measure of a country's overall economic output. It is the market value of all final goods and services made within the borders of a country in a year.

Historical institutionalism: A theory for explaining the influence of context as the consolidation of past choices and events on present choices and events, in political systems and beyond. Both a logic of appropriateness (a logic whereby decisions mainly lie in matching the specific circumstances with general patterns of what is deemed to be "appropriate" behaviour, and institutions shape what is appropriate) and a logic of consequences (institutions shape the convenience structure of decision-makers) may be employed to explain causality in historical institutionalism.

Ideation: The fundamental conception of a policy sector, a policy paradigm. It underpins where the boundaries of a policy sector are set – what is included and what is not, and in what terms problems and solutions can be discussed.

Inputs: A measure of the resources that an organization uses to make an output. These resources could include time, staff or finances (e.g. the amount of money spent on teachers to educate second graders). Inputs are often simple to measure, so many performance management programs focus on these types of measures. However, programs that rely solely on inputs are considered inferior to those which include outputs and outcomes [also in this glossary: Performance].

Institutions: The set of elements that establish rules to limit the options available to actors, establishing both constraints and opportunities. They are the "hardware" that underpins the "software" of policy-making, shaping how that process occurs and its limits.

Inter-governmental relations: How different levels of government interact with each other, how the management task is carried out across jurisdictions [also in this glossary: Devolution; Federalism].

Macro- and micro-prudential supervision: Macro-prudential supervision refers to government policy that addresses the overall state of the financial services sector. Micro-prudential supervision refers to government policy to ensure that firms are solvent. The current policy trend favors macro-prudential supervision.

Macrobudgeting: The economic policy function of the budget. It is due to the great weight and influence of government as a whole on the national economy. Macrobudgeting decisions are aimed at generating an effect on the economic cycle as a consequence of total spending and taxing budget policies of a government. Macrobudgeting decisions are inherently political, top-down long-term oriented and related to macro-objectives of the public expenditure (missions). Macrobudgeting – high-level decisions on spending, revenue and deficit totals and relative budget shares – becomes critical when strict deficit control is required.

Microbudgeting: Concerns bottom-up decisions related to the distribution of the financial resources among different competing agencies/programs. Microbudgeting decisions are inherently short-term oriented and focused on portions of the administration (agencies, departments) rather than the government or the economy as a whole. Microbudgeting was predominant during historical periods characterized by increasing public expenditure and it was consistent with incrementalism. A microbudgeting approach is a way to explain how governments make public policies during periods of growth or stability. Yet microbudgeting decisions can be also taken within a predefined macrobudgeting framework and orientation: programs to be cut or taxes to be raised without changing the political decisions concerning total deficit or fiscal pressure.

Modernized policy-making: This type of policy-making is strategic, outcome focused, joined up, inclusive, flexible, innovative and robust.

Motivation: Processes by which certain motives are activated and transferred into actions. From this results a state of goal-oriented behavior that is characterized by direction, intensity and persistence. The motivation to pursue a goal depends on situational incentives, personal preferences and their interdependency [also in this glossary: Public sector motivation; Public service motivation].

Municipal austerity: This term refers to the reduction in the amount of money local governments have available to spend on the services they provide within their local jurisdictions. Municipalities are subject to ongoing cuts in their grants from higher levels of government (regional and national) and face increasing restrictions on their ability to borrow money and to raise their local tax rates. Hence, they face reduced budgets and so have to subject their services to austerity-induced cuts, with the result that their citizens experience reduction in the availability of municipal services.

Network: Enduring patterns of social relations among multiple and interdependent organizations, tied by some form of structural interdependence in which one unit is not the subordinate of others by virtue of its formal position. Pooled authority systems that are based more on expertise than on position and take shape around policy problems and programs [also in this glossary: Governance; Collaborative governance].

New Public Governance: The collection of ideas to supplement new public management and traditional public administration. It focuses on the rise and importance of collaborative networks, inter-organizational governance and processes, citizen satisfaction, citizen as customer, and other ideas related to networked governance and citizens at the centre of governmental activity [also in this glossary: Governance; Collaborative governance].

New Public Management: A diverse group of ideas and initiatives, originating in the late 1980s and early 1990s, that were inspired by private sector values. These ideas were increasingly popular in governments who sought to lower costs, provide better service, contain deficits and incorporate new technologies. The precepts were embedded in earlier postwar reports and reforms but were not as influential or integrated as in the newer NPM literature.

Omnibus bill: A bill designed to include many subjects, rather than single focus subjects, to ensure what is arguably an efficient passage.

Outcomes: A measure of a program's effect on producing a desired outcome (e.g. examining the amount a specific program reduces recidivism amongst released inmates over a certain period of time). Outcomes should focus on the core values or mission of an organization. Performance management programs that use outcomes in addition to inputs and outputs are considered superior to those that do not [also in this glossary: Performance].

Outputs: A measure of the goods or services that are made from an organization's inputs and resources (e.g. the amount in miles paved with asphalt in a given time period). Outputs are often somewhat simple to measure, so many performance management programs focus on measuring outputs along with inputs. However, programs that rely solely on outputs and inputs, though better than those that only measure inputs, are considered inferior to those that include outcomes [also in this glossary: Performance].

Pension privatization: A global trend of reforming existing public old-age pension programs in response to a growing public concern about projected fiscal insolvencies to sustain the conventional programs. This trend features an introduction of market-oriented mechanisms such as funded individual accounts to the conventional model based on non-prefunded, inter-generational contract mechanisms.

Performance: Results achieved by individuals, teams or organizations; can refer to inputs (eg. cost efficiency; motivated and professionalized workforce), processes (eg. transparency, accessibility), outputs (both in terms of quantity and quality) and outcomes (impact of outputs on collective needs), as well as relations among them (efficiency, effectiveness, cost-effectiveness, value for money, etc.).

Performance management: Is the bundle of activities aimed at generating information on performance, through strategic planning and performance measurement routines, and that connects this information to the different decision venues (Van Dooren, Bouckaert, and Halligan 2010: 17; Moynihan 2008: 5).

Performance use: An organizational behavior influenced by the characteristics of performance information systems, by the features of users of information and by the context. It is distinguished between a purposeful use aimed at improving management and allocation decisions, and a passive use, which stands for the use of performance data limited to satisfy the procedural requirements of law (Radin 2006; Moynihan and Lavertu 2012: 1).

Performance budgeting: A form of budgeting aimed at establishing a link between the forecast of expenditures/expenses and results to be achieved (outputs/outcome) as a consequence of the use of those resources. According to the degree of linkage between appropriation and performance information, three variants of performance budget can be distinguished: presentational, performance-informed, and formula based. In practice, the general idea of performance budget has been implemented in very different ways over the last few decades, depending on the type and level of detail of the data, its role in different stages of the budget cycle, and its integration into general performance management.

Performance leadership: Leadership that actively promotes a performance management agenda, which uses evidence about performance to help guide decision making. Though in government performance leadership could be performed by any person who has leadership capability, in this handbook the term is especially used to describe those leaders who have the ability to enact policy that promotes a performance management agenda.

Political neutrality: The convention that prohibits public servants from engaging in activities that impair or seem to impair their impartiality or the impartiality of the public service as a whole (e.g. partisan political activities) [also in this glossary: Politics–administrative dichotomy].

Political participation: Definitions of political participation have certain essential aspects in common. First, they refer to people in their role as citizens and not to politicians or civil servants. Second, participation requires an activity to be performed by the citizen. Third, participation is a rather broad term, involving the entire political system and not just single phases in the decision-making process. As a rule, political participation is voluntary and may occur at different levels in the political system.

Politicization: A trend that extends from new political governance that argues merit-based and neutral criteria for the recruitment and hiring of public servants (for example) is replaced with political responsive and non-merit-based criteria. The definition has been extended in the literature to transcend human resources applications to wider emanations related to non-merit-based governmental communications, procurement and other systems that are informed by political directives rather than statutory or non-politically motivated directives or systems.

Politics–administrative dichotomy: Originally developed to oppose the spoils system, and to promote a more professional business-like public service, this idea holds that administrative areas of government have more in common with business practices (technical implementation) than with political activities (the development of laws, policies, and public values).

Privatization: Material or substantial privatization is the divesture of public enterprises partially or completely owned by the state to private investors. Other forms of privatization are formal and functional privatization.

Public administration: The implementation of decisions made by politicians. This involves the organization of human, financial and other resources to attain the goal(s) established by a public policy.

Public policy: Decisions leading to action (or inaction) chosen by the government to address a problem or interrelated set of problems.

Public procurement: The purchase of goods, services and works by governments, public authorities and, generally, by all the public sector.

Public sector motivation: The desire to behave in accordance with motives grounded in an individual's self-interest and directed at extrinsic incentives typically found in the public sector. This includes, for instance, job security, guaranteed salary and career development, and further privileges [also in this glossary: Motivation].

Public service motivation: The desire to behave in accordance with motives that are grounded in the public interest in order to serve society [also in this glossary: Motivation].

Regulation: Contemporary conceptions view regulation as all sustained and focused attempts to alter the behavior of others according to defined standards or purposes with the intention of producing a broadly identified outcome or outcomes. This notion contrasts with narrower traditional views of regulation as an activity of government including laws and regulations determined through the legislative processes of parliament.

Regulatory capitalism: An era in which regulation grows in scope, importance and impact at the national and global levels; where greater investments in regulation occur by political, economic and social actors; and where regulatory regimes are increasingly diverse, hybrid and complex. Regulatory regimes may see the co-evolution of statist-civil regimes, national and international structures, expanding regimes encompassing private with public, and voluntary regulation co-existing with coercive regimes.

Regulatory tools of government: Six sets of tools exist: economic (making markets or influencing markets via taxing or pricing); transactional (through contract or grant conditions); authorizing tools (registration, licensing or accreditation); informational (product labeling or disclosing ratings; structural (physical design or processes); or traditional legal tools (laws, rules and regulations). Regulation activities may be either positive (encouraging particular behaviours) or negative (discouraging behaviours).

Risk: Anticipated likelihood of failure of complications that will force decision makers to adapt their project management. Risk can affect any variable and actor, from budgetary concerns and time planning to service users and staff. Moreover, risk can also work on a meta-level and affect organizational reputation. A key characteristic of risk is that the resulting outcome has been conceptualized and analysed as for the probability of its occurrence before the start of a given project.

Risk governance: Denotes a system of risk approaches that goes beyond individual risk management tools and thus engages with "the nature, perceptions and contested benefits of risk in complex situations" (Brown and Osborne 2013: 198). Risk governance includes all key stakeholders and promotes transparent decision making based on an open risk discourse and risk deliberation within the public sector organization.

Risks in later life: Challenges that countries face in securing socio-economic resources that are necessary to maintain their citizens' well-being in later life, including economic resources to cure common diseases, financial resources to support retirees, and a workforce for long-term care for the elderly.

Service models: Local public services can be provided to citizens in alternative ways, usually either in direct provision by municipalities themselves or by municipalities enabling their provision by agreeing service supply contracts with other organizations in the public, private and/or voluntary/charity sectors. More radically, municipalities may empower local communities within their jurisdictions to provide services for themselves by devolving to neighborhoods' decisions about services and the finances necessary to support those decisions. Municipalities may adopt a catalytic role within this empowering model. The availability of the required skills and capacities will ultimately determine which model is feasible for each specific service.

Service resilience: The capability of service providers to adapt to shocks to their service delivery process (such as breakdown of the supply chain, loss of key personnel or radical performance deterioration) in such a way as to allow continued achievement of their priority outcomes and objectives and to learn how to plan and prepare for future shocks [also in this glossary: Resilience; Community resilience; User resilience].

Social innovation: Best defined as "the intentional introduction and application within a role, group or organization of ideas, processes, products or procedures, new to the relevant unit of adoption, designed to significantly benefit the individual, the group organization or wider society" (West and Farr 1990: 3).

Social media: Computer-mediated communication platforms that often enable people to share user-generated contents by allowing them to create and share any digitalized data, information, and visual and audio materials in virtual and network environments.

State-owned enterprises (SOEs): Enterprises that are partially or completely owned by the state, often prevalent in utilities and infrastructure industries, such as energy, transport and telecommunication.

Strategic management: Management action oriented to achieving long-term goals based on thorough analysis and assessment of situation, options and use of resources.

Strategic-state capabilities: Governments that have strategic-state capabilities have the ability to: formulate long-term visions and priorities for national development; ensure that government as a whole works in a coherent and integrated way; deploy budgetary systems and performance management to deliver government strategies; work in a cooperative and coherent manner with other levels of government; and engage the public and stakeholders in the formulation and delivery of government strategies.

Sustainable procurement: A procurement operation that takes into account economic, social and environmental aspects, such as: job creation, social inclusion of disadvantaged people, compliance with social and labor rights, equal opportunities for all economic operators, MSMEs development, environment protection and innovation.

Sustainable public finance: The term "public finance" refers to public spending, revenues from taxes and other sources (sales, fees and charges, privatization receipts, etc.), borrowing by public sector organizations and public sector debt. Each of these four categories of public finance must be sustainable. Public spending is only sustainable over a period of time if public sector revenues are sufficient to finance that spending without becoming ever more dependent upon borrowing to cover persistent budget deficits arising from a shortfall in revenues from taxes, sales, fees, charges and other receipts. Ultimately, the public finances are only sustainable if decisions to spend and to raise revenues do not lead to an increase in public sector debt over a prolonged period of time.

Transnational hybrid organizations: Regional or global independent organizations (i.e. with their own statute, legal personality, membership, governance structure and resources) that include states in their membership, represented by governmental institutions and/or international institutions, and at least one private transnational for-profit and/or non-profit, single-country and/or multi-country organization, with all components having representation and voice in the collective decision making.

Trust: Trust refers to a psychological state that one is willing to accept vulnerability based on positive expectation of the intention of another party. Scholars have defined trust by using various concepts such as belief, expectation, attitude and rational assessment. Scholars investigating interpersonal trust commonly emphasize the psychological aspect of trust. One can classify types of trust into three, including calculative trust, relational trust and institutional trust. Calculative trust emerges when a trustor perceives that a trustee performs an action out of benefit motives. Relational trust is based on repeated interactions between trustee and trustor. It is differentiated from calculative trust in that it has emotional elements. Institutional trust is trust in certain institutions. Citizens' trust in government is an example. Institutional trust is differentiated from calculative and relational trust, which are categorized as interpersonal trust where the object of trust is person.

Trustworthiness: Trustworthiness works as an antecedent of trust. Relevant elements of trustworthiness can be synthesized into three core factors: ability, benevolence and integrity. Ability means a trustee's competence in the given role within an organization. Benevolence is the extent to which a trustee is believed to want to do good to the trustor, aside from an egocentric profit motive. Integrity is a broad concept encompassing several factors, such as the consistency of the trustee's past actions, credible communications about the trustee from other parties, belief that the trustee has a strong sense of justice, and the extent to which the trustee's actions are congruent with his or her words.

Uncertainty: Unquantifiable element of decision making, denoting possible states of the world that were not anticipated and accounted for in decision making. These do not necessarily have to be undesirable (e.g. positive externalities). Uncertainty is at best approximated as an error term, but cannot, by definition, be anticipated.

User resilience: The capability of service users to adapt to shocks to the service (such as breakdown or radical performance deterioration) in such a way as to allow continued achievement of their priority outcomes and objectives and to learn how to plan and prepare for future shocks [also in this glossary: Resilience; Community resilience; Service resilience].

Wicked problem: Problems with causes and effects are difficult to identify and continuously evolving that cross multiple policy domains, levels of government and jurisdictions and, consequently, several stakeholders, each bringing in different views, priorities, values, cultural and political backgrounds.

References

Brown, L. and Osborne, S. P. 2013. "Risk and innovation." *Public Management Review* 15 (2): 186–208.

Moynihan, D. P. 2008. *The dynamics of performance management: constructing information and reform.* Washington, DC: Georgetown University Press.

Moynihan, D. and Lavertu, S. 2012. "Does involvement in performance management routines encourage performance information use? Evaluating GPRA and PART." *Public Administration Review* 72 (4): 592–602.

Radin, B. 2006. *Challenging the performance movement: accountability, complexity, and democratic values.* Washington, DC: Georgetown University Press.

Van Dooren, W., Bouckaert, G., and Halligan, J. 2010. *Performance management in the public sector.* Abingdon: Routledge.

West, M. A. and Farr, J. L. 1990. *Innovation and creativity at work: psychological and organizational strategies.* Chichester: Wiley.

Whitaker, G. 1980. "Co-production: citizen participation in service delivery." *Public Administration Review* 40 (3): 240–246.

INDEX OF NAMES

SUBJECT INDEX

413

Made in the USA
Middletown, DE
15 April 2024

53062542R00252